NICKNAMES AND SOBRIQUETS OF U.S. CITIES, STATES, AND COUNTIES THIRD EDITION

JOSEPH NATHAN KANE & GERARD L . ALEXANDER

1979

THE SCARECROW PRESS, INC.
METUCHEN, N.J., & LONDON

Library of Congress Cataloging in Publication Data

Kane, Joseph Nathan, 1899-
  Nicknames and sobriquets of U.S. cities, States,
and counties.

  Second ed. (1970) published under title: Nicknames
and sobriquets of U.S. cities and States.
  Includes indexes.
  1. Names, Geographical--United States. 2.
names--United States. I. Alexander, Gerard L., joint
author. II. Title.
E155.K24 1979   917.3'003   79-20193
ISBN 0-8108-1255-X

CONTENTS

PREFACE

Joseph Nathan Kane in his book "1,000 Facts Worth Knowing" published in 1938, out of print for more than a score of years, devoted a small section to nicknames. Thirteen years later, Gerald L. Alexander compiled "Nicknames of American Cities, Towns and Villages (Past and Present)," which is also out of print.

A mutual friendship and interest of the authors resulted in this larger and more complete list to which explanatory text has been added. The idea was broached to Scarecrow Press and it first appeared as a book in 1965. Five years later 5,000 additional listings were added. Thousands more have since been added. Still unfound must be further nicknames which it is hoped will be collected for a future edition.

INTRODUCTION

Practically all the states, cities, towns, even counties, in the United States, regardless of location, size or age, have nicknames. Some of them are well known, others are seldom used and rarely printed. Very few such nicknames become "official" or are adopted by legislative action. It is usual for a locality to have more than one nickname.

Nicknames have been conferred in numerous ways by chambers of commerce, literary sources, advertising executives, publicity representatives and by rival cities.

Over the years, some cities have acquired so many nicknames that each has lost its importance. These may be completely diversified and bear no relation to each other. New York, for example, is called America's Leading Tourist Resort, the Babylonian Bedlam, the Capital of the World, the City of Skyscrapers, the Coliseum City, the Empire City, the Entertainment Capital of the World, the Front Office of American Business, the Metropolis, the Money Town, the Nation's First City, the Seat of Empire, the World's Fair City, the World's Metropolis, just to mention a few besides the Big Apple (or, more lately, just "the Apple").

In the same vein, the various nicknames a place enjoys may be so similar as to be easily interchanged with little loss. Boston, for example, is known as Beantown, the City of Baked Beans, the City of Bean Eaters, and the Home of Baked Beans, among other names.

The most common form of nicknames is the descriptive one: the Battlefield City, the Border City, the Cockade City, the Crescent City, the Druid City, the Empire City, the Exposition City, the Family City, the Frosty City, the Golden City, the Lookout City, the Prison City, the Stone City.

Industry

Another form of nickname associates the city with its
most prominent industry, frequently but not always in the
form, the So-and-So City.   Examples are the Aircraft Center, the Aluminum City, the Anthracite City, the Atomic
Energy City, the Auto City, the Aviation City, and so on.
Others in this form contain the word(s) Beer, Bituminous,
Brass, Brewing, Camera, Canoe, Car Shop, Cash Register,
Celluloid, Cement, Ceramic, Chair, Chemical, Chemurgic,
Chocolate, Cigar, and Circus.   A few are "the City of ...,"
such as the City of Bicycles, of Black Diamonds, of Reso-
nance, or, another variation, the City Where Industry Profits.

Others in the "the --- City" form are those for the
Clipper City, Clay, Clock, Coal, Coke, Collar, Copper,
Cordage, Cotton, Cream, Crystal, Derrick, Electrical, Elec-
tronic, Emerging Industrial, Financial (Center), Flower, For-
estry, Furniture, Gem, Glass, Granite, Gypsum, Hardware,
Hat, Helicopter Capital of the World, Hoist City, Industrial
City, Insurance, Iron, Kodak, Lock, Lumber, Marble, Mill
(Town), Mineral, Mining (Town), Missile, Motor, Nail, Oil,
Paper, Pearl, Plow, Port, Pottery, Power, Rifle, Rock,
and the Rocket Capital of the Nation.

Others in traditional format are the Rubber City, the
Salt, Sawdust, Ship-Building, Shoe, Shovel, Silk, Silver,
Smelter, Soil Pipe Center of the World, Space City, Spindle, Sponge, Steel, Sweatshop Capital, the Tannery City,
the Telegraphic Hub, the Textile City, Thread, Transportation, Tube, the Typewriter Capital of the World, the Uranium City, the Water City, and the Wool City.

Geography

Geographical attributes often account for the nicknames
of cities.   Examples are Alabama's Only Port City, the Alamo City, the Battlefield City, the Bay, Bayou, Bluff, Border,
Canal, Canyon, Catacomb, and Cavern cities; the City by the
Lake, the City by the Sea, the City on the Gulf, the Cockade
City, the Dixie Gateway, the Falls and Flood cities, the Gem
of the Gold Coast, the Hill, Lookout, and Lake cities, and
the Midwest Metropolis.

Others are the Mile-High City, the Mound, Mountain,
and Natural Gas cities, the Oasis of Nevada, the Panama

Port, the Paradise of New England, the Park, Port, and Railroad cities, the Spanish Town, the Summit City, the Top of the World, and the Trimountain, Windy, and Zenith cities.

Flattery

Many cities and towns borrow the lustre of older or more famous places, nicknaming themselves the other cities' names. Examples of such fancied comparisons with United States cities are the Annapolis of, the Atlantic City of, the Boston of, the Brooklyn of, the Chicago of, the Coney Island of, the Denver of, the Detroit of, the Greenwich Village of, the Hartford of, the Hudson of, the Kansas City of, the Las Vegas of, the Lexington of, the Little Detroit of, the Little Las Vegas of, the Little Louisville of, the Lowell of, the Minneapolis of, the Newport of, the New York of, the Niagara of, the Phoenix of, the Pittsburgh of, the Plymouth of, the Saratoga of, the Spokane of, the Utah Zion of, the West Point of, and the Williamsburg of.

Other cities resort to calling upon foreign places in order to bring credit or description upon themselves. There are such cities as America's Bit o' Ireland, the Alexandria of, the Athens of, Bagdad-by-the-Bay, the Bermuda of the North, the Birmingham of, the Carlsbad of, the Czech Capital, the Dutch City, the Eden of, the Edinburgh of, the Essen of, the Gibraltar of, the Hong Kong of, the Heidelberg of, the Indian Capital of, the Italy of, and the Little Denmark of.

Others are the Little Heidelberg, the Little Holland, the Little Norway, the Little Switzerland, the Little Venice, the Lyons of, the Manchester of, the Naples of, the New Helvetia, the New Jerusalem, the Paris of, the Riviera of America, the St. Moritz of, the South Sea Island of, the Spanish City, the Switzerland of, the Thermopylae of, and the Venice of America.

Local

Nicknames are often specifically limited to locality: Alabama's Only Port City, Alaska's First City, the Annapolis of the Air, Arizona's First Capital, Arkansas' Only Seaport, Bagdad on the Hudson, Benton County's Fastest Growing City, the Broadway of the Desert, the Brooklyn of the South, the

Coastal Town of Charm and Beauty, Colorado's Second City, and Delaware's Summer Capital.

Also there are such places as the Eden of Ohio, the Eskimo Village, Georgia's First Inland Port, the Gibraltar of the South, the Gold Coast of Oregon, the Gretna Green of Maryland, the Hartford of the West, the Heart of the Florida Keys, Idaho's Farm Market, Iowa's Own City, the Jones Beach of New England, the Little Italy, Maine's Fastest Growing Industrial and Recreational Area, the Metropolis of New Mexico, Michigan's Dynamic City, Michigan's Most Famous Summer Resort, the Milwaukee of the East, Montana's Largest and Friendliest City, the Naples of America, the New England Garden Spot, the New Jerusalem, the New Settlement, New York's First Capital, the Newport of the Pacific, North Dakota's Queen City, the Oasis of Nevada, and the Prairie City. Also noted are Rhode Island's Most Historic Town, the Riviera of America, the Roof Garden of Texas, the Saratoga of the West, South Arkansas' Busy Port City, South Carolina's Capital City, South Dakota's City of Opportunity, Tallest Town in Oregon, Tennessee's Beauty Spot, the Tip of Cape Cod, the Trade Center of Southwest Georgia, and the Venice of America.

Botany

Flowers, trees, and shrubs lend their influence to nicknames. Among them are the Azalea Trail City, the Camellia City, the Christmas Tree City, the City of Flowers, the City of Gardens, the City of Oaks, the City of Palms, the City of Roses, the City of Trees, the Dogwood City, the Elm City, the Evergreen City, the Floral City, the Flower Box City, the Flower City, the Forest City, the Garden City (another is called America's Garden Spot), the Holly City, the Iris City, the Lawn City, the Lilac City, the Magnolia City, the Maple City, the Oak City, the Oleander City, the Orchard City, the Palm City, the Palmetto City, the Park City, the Petunia Capital, the Peony Center, the Poinsettia City, the Rose Capital of America, the Rose City, the Sycamore City, the Tulip City, the Valley of the Gardens, and the World's Largest Seed and Nursery Center.

Sports and Recreation

Sports and games often serve as the nucleus for nick-

names.   Examples are the All-Year Sports Center, America's
Sports Mecca, the Birthplace of Professional Football, the
Birthplace of Surfing, the Cradle of the Trotter, the Foot-
ball Capital of the South, the Glider Capital of America, the
Golf Capital, Hockey Capital of the Nation, Home of Base-
ball, the Home of the Athletes, Home of the Packers, the
Midwest Golf Capital, Packer's Town, the Polo Capital, the
Rodeo City, the Ski Capital, the Sportfishing Capital of the
World, the Sportsman's Paradise, the Tennis Capital of the
World, the Winter Sports City, the World's Winter Golf Capi-
tal, and the Yachting Capital of New England.

Nationality and Religion

National, ethnic, and religious identifications have inspired nicknames for some cities. They are: America's
Little Switzerland, the American Munich, the Bermuda of the
North, the Christmas City, the City in the Heart of Pennsylvania Dutch Country, the City of Little Wedding Churches,
the City of the French, the City of the Gauls, the Czech
Bethlehem, the Czech Capital of Nebraska, the Danish Capital of the United States, the Deutsch Athens (also the German
Athens), the Druid City, the Dutch City, Dutchtown, the Gibraltar of America, Holland's Corner, the Hong Kong of the
Hudson, the Italy of America, the Little Denmark, the Mormon City, the Mormon's Mecca, the New Helvetia, the Pioneer Mormon City, the Polish City, the Polish City in Texas,
Quaker City, Quaker Town, the Russian-American Capital,
the Saintly City, the Saint's Rest, the Spanish Town, and the
Switzerland of the Catskills.

Meaningless

Many cities have adopted nicknames so bland and col-
orless that they have lost their original individuality and are
no longer meaningful. Many of the nicknames cited in other
sections of this introduction are in this category. Others are
the Action City, the Air Capital, the Bluff City, the Capital
City, the City Beautiful, the Church City, the City by the Sea,
the City of Beauty, the City of Bridges, the City of Churches,
the City of Destiny, the City of Firsts, the City of Homes,
the City of Hospitality, the City of Opportunity, the City of
Progress, the City on the Move, the City with a Future, the
City with a Heart, the Convention City, the Electric City, the
Exciting City, the First City, the Friendly City, the Gate

City, the Gateway City, the Gem City, the Granite City, the
Historic City, the Hub City, the Industrial City, the International City, the Lake City, the Magic City, the Model City,
the Modern City, the Port City, the Power City, the Progressive City, the Queen City, the Summit City, the Sunshine City, the Twin Cities, the Vacation City, and the
Wonder City.

Hyperbole

Many nicknames are inspired by wishful thinking and
hyperbole. Some of them are America's Only International
Playground, America's Sweetest Town, the Baby of the Colorado Ski Resorts, the Best Known City, the Biggest Little
Town, the Bit of America at Its Best, the Blonde Beauty of
the Lakes, the Brightest Spot in Eastern Oregon, the Center
of the World's Biggest Market, the Charmed Land of Unequalled Beauty, the Choicest Spot in All Florida, the City
Next to the Greatest Spot in the World, the City That Turned
Back Time, the Cleanest Beach in the World, the Cleanest
Big City in the World, the Closest State to Heaven, the Danc-
ingest Town in the U.S., the Farthest Inland Deep Water Port,
the Fastest Growing City, the Finest Beach in the World,
the Friendliest Town, the Greatest Primary Winter Wheat
Market, the Greenest Spot in Arizona's Famous Valley of the
Sun, the Highest Incorporated Town in Eastern America, the
Hottest Town, the Last Outpost of Civilization, the Last Place
on the Map, and the Loveliest Modern City in Mid-America.
Others call themselves the Most Beautiful City, the Most
Colorful Exciting City in the World, the Most Eastern West-
ern Metropolis, the Most Historic City, the Most Scenic City
on the Continent, the Nation's Greatest City, the Nation's
Most Beautiful City, the Nation's Most Hospitable City, the
Number One Host of the Jersey Coast, the Oldest Summer
Resort in America, the Prettiest Little Town This Side of
Heaven, the Proudest Small Town in America, the Richest
Hill on Earth, the Safest Spot in the World, the South's Fast-
est Growing City, the South's Greatest City, the South's Most
Beautiful and Interesting City, the Tourist's Paradise, the
Town Where Summer Is Air Conditioned, the Town with the
Most to Offer Industry, Virginia's Biggest Little City, the
Westernmost Port on America's Fourth Seacoast, the West's
Most Western Town, the Wickedest City in America, the
Winter Playground of America, the World's Largest Mobile
Home Manufacturing City, the World's Liveliest Ghost Town,
and the Youngest of the World's Great Cities.

Slander

Just as a proud local citizenry is eager to accent these encomiums, there are jealous or hostile groups who swing the pendulum in the opposite direction, to foster such slander as: Bad Birmingham, Bitch's Heaven, the Catchall of Suckers, the City with Two Faces, Gangland, Gas House of the Nation, the Great Dismal, Hangtown, the Hole in the Ground, the Jawbone Flats, Mobtown, the Modern Gomorrah, the Mud Hole City, the Murder Capital, the Pig's Eye, Sin City, Sinema City, Sodom, the Suicide Capital of the United States, the Wickedest City, the Witchcraft City.

Picturesque or Fanciful

Other cities prefer a picturesque or fanciful name, such as the Best Known City of Its Size in the World, the Bit of the Old West Transplanted in the Twentieth Century, the Bluff City of the Chattahoochee, the Buckle on the Kansas Wheat Belt, the Bushwacker's Capital, the City Built on Oil Soil and Toil, the City of Streets without Houses, the City That Belongs to the World, the City That Trees Built, the City Where Ambition Meets Opportunity, the City Where Mexico Meets Uncle Sam, the City Where Oil and Water Mix, the City Where Oil Flows, Gas Blows and Glass Glows, the City Where Progress and Pleasures Are Partners, the City Where Summer Winters, the City Where the Breezes Blow, the City Where There Are No Strangers--Just Friends, the City Where Winter Wears a Tan, the City Where Work and Play Are Only Minutes Away, the City Without a Toothache, and the Dimple of the Universe. Others are the Dream City Come True, the Eden of the Closest State to Heaven, the Fruit Bowl of the Nation, the Highest Incorporated Town in Eastern America, the Jacaranda City With the Mile Long Mall, and the Land of Cheese, Trees and Ocean Breeze. There are also the Magic Mascot of the Plains, the Nineteen Suburbs in Search of a Metropolis, the Peerless Princess of the Plains, the Postmark of Distinctive Trade Marks, the Shangri-La of the Western Hemisphere, the Small Town with the Bustling Activity of a Growing City, and the Town of Tumbling Waters.

Food

Often cities have adopted foods as the basis for their nicknames. Some general examples are the Bran Town, the

Cereal Food Center, the Chocolate Town, the Flour City, the Honey Capital, the Maple Center, the Pancake Center, the Pretzel City, the Rice City, and the Scrapple City. Subdivided into various classifications, here are others:

Fruits, Berries, and Nuts: the Apple City, the Berry City, the Blackberry Capital of the World, the Blueberry Capital, the Cherry City, the Citrus Center, the Filbert Center, the Fruit Bowl of the Nation, the Home of the Tangerine, the Land of Hazel Nuts, the Lemon Center, the Orange Capital, the Peach Bowl, the Peach Capital, the Peanut City, the Pear City, the Pecan Capital, the Pumpkin Capital, the Raisin Capital, the Strawberry Capital, the Walnut City, and the Watermelon Capital of the World.

Meat and Dairy: the Bratwurst Capital, the Broiler Capital, the Butter City, the Cheese Capital of the World, the Dairy City, the Holstein Capital, the Lamb and Cattle Capital of the West, the Milk City, the Pheasant Capital, the Pork City, the Poultry Capital of the World, the Swiss Cheese Capital, and the Turkey Capital.

Seafood: the Bass Capital of the World, the Blue Marlin Capital of the World, the Clam Town, the Crawfish Town, the Fish City, the Home of the Famous Silver King Tarpon, the Lake Trout Capital, the Sailfish Capital, the Salmon City, the Salt Water Trout Capital, the Sea Turtle Capital, and the Seafood Capital of the World.

Vegetables and Legumes: America's Carrot Capital, the Artichoke Capital of the World, the Asparagus Capital of the World, Bean Town, the Celery City, the Green Bean Center, the Lettuce Center, the Mushroom City, the Potato Capital, the Soybean Center, the Spinach Capital, the Tomato Capital, and the Vegetable Bowl.

Made-Up Names

Coined names, made-up words and meaningless combinations of letters are sometimes used: Arkopolis, Bostonia, Cornopolis, Crumptown, Dupontia, Gotham, Hogopolis, Jacksonopolis, Kringleville, Mushroomopolis, Newarks, Paincourt, Pigopolis, Porkopolis, Sacto, Soo, Squawkiewood, Touropolis, Tusselburgh.

Humorous

Humorous or facetious names often fasten to a town: Annie's Town, Betsytown, Bumgannon, Lunchburg, Tater Town, Taterville, Unsainted Anthony.

The Straightforward

Towns often acquire nicknames based upon the birth of some outstanding individual (the Birthplace of Calvin Coolidge, the Birthplace of Daniel Webster) etc.; other "birthplaces" are commemorated such as the Birthplace of American Liberty, the Birthplace of Aviation, the Birthplace of California, of Dixie, of Liberty, of Maine, of Oklahoma, of Radio, of Speed, of the Nation, of the Republican Party, and the Birthplace of United States Naval Aviation.

Some cities have acquired their nicknames from some event associated with their history: the Home of the Apple Blossom Festival, the Home of the Boll Weevil Monument, the Home of the Comstock Lode, the Home of the Florida Derby, the Home of the Mining Barons, the Home of the Miss Universe Pageant, the Home of the Pacific Fleet, and the Home of the Snake River Stampede.

The Literary

Historical and literary allusions account for some nicknames. Examples are the Cradle of Liberty, the Cradle of Secession, the Green Felt Jungle, the Mission City, the Modern Phoenix, Paul Bunyan's Capital, and the Rebel Capital.

Joint or Collective

Many cities have jointly adopted the same nickname with neighboring cities and use it individually or collectively: Dual Cities, Fall Cities, Quad Cities, Tri-Cities, Twin Cities.

Abbreviations and Diminutives

Abbreviations and word contractions often serve as

nicknames: Alex City, Ark City, Billtown, Bison City, Chi,
Frisco, Jax, Jeff City, Jimtown, L. A., Philly, Sacto, San
Berdoo.

Peculiarities

Some cities have nicknames somewhat at cross pur-
poses with one another, such as the Sleepy Town and the
World's Greatest Workshop; the Babylonian Bedlam and the
Wonder City; the Crime Capital and the Metropolis of the
West; the Gas House of the Nation and the Nation's Head-
quarters.

In every state, one city bears the nickname "the Capital City" or "the Capitol City." Capital and capitol are
often interchanged, either correctly or incorrectly, so that
it is impossible to state which is correct or which was originally intended.

Another point of dispute might be the use of the arti-
cles a, an and the in the various nicknames. Both are often
used, in some instances neither are used, and in other cases
are interchanged: a City of Homes, the City of Homes,
City of Homes. A similar situation arises with regard to the
use of "of" and "to": the Gateway of the South and the Gateway to the South are both correct. Another variation is the
use of the singular and the plural: City of Diversified Industry, City of Diversified Industries.

When a locality has a particular designation, it is
possible that it may also have an unlimited number of varia-
tions. To illustrate the point, a city might be called the
Celery Capital, the Celery Capital of Michigan, the Celery
Capital of the United States, the Celery Capital of the World,
the Celery City, the Celery City of Michigan, the Celery
City of the United States, the Celery City of the World,
Michigan's Celery City, the United States' Celery City, the
World's Celery City. The ramifications may be extended
indefinitely.

As the nuances are unlimited, a complete list of all
the combinations of one city would be a mighty undertaking
and when multiplied by the large number of places listed in
this book, would make an encyclopedia seem minute by comparison. Furthermore, this overspecialization would decrease
rather than increase the utility of this book. Consequently,

the temptation to strive for bulk has been disregarded, and
no effort has been made to list all the existing possible combinations for the basic nicknames. However, exceptions have
been made in instances where the deviations have become almost as commonplace and acceptable as the original name.

Often a newly published brochure, map or publicity
circular, the handicraft of public relations or promotion people, tries to bring about a new image. This is one of the
major sources of nicknames and, being in print, remains
for posterity.

Occasionally, nicknames are coined by some orator
or political campaigner and find their way into the language.

Nicknames of cities often undergo metamorphoses.
Sometimes the change is proportionate to the exaggerative
powers of the publicity person responsible for it. Again,
many nicknames have completely outlived their usefulness,
or the purpose for which they were originally intended. Town
may become City; the Hub of the Territory may change to the
Hub of the State.

ABOUT THIS BOOK

County nicknames have been added for the first time.

Where a city has more than one nickname, the nicknames have been listed alphabetically without attempting to
grade them in importance or value.

The source or origin of many nicknames is unknown.
In many instances, authorities differ as to the reasons for
their selection and consequently several versions exist. Where
there are several different explanations, they have been listed
without attempting to rate their importance.

When the nickname is descriptive or self-explanatory
such as the Capital City, the City of Beauty, the Friendly
City, or the Progressive City, no attempt has been made to
explain the obvious. Also, when no logical explanation can
be given, it is likewise omitted.

The listing or inclusion of a nickname does not neces-
sarily imply that it is official, in constant use, or is "ap-

proved" by any particular party.   Certain nicknames are appropriate, others seem not to be; some are sheer wishful hyperbole, while some have been named judiciously.   Some are grammatically incorrect, plurals being used for singulars and vice versa.   Apostrophes are often applied in the wrong places, or omitted with possessives.   Hyphens are occasionally used unnecessarily and often omitted when required.

All known nicknames have been recorded impartially as this book constitutes a record, not propaganda.

In addition to the informative material, this book portrays the field to the publicity departments and public relations executives of the various cities, states, and counties, and enables them to revalue their efforts.   It may stimulate them to strive for originality (or adopt oft-repeated platitudes if they desire).   If this compilation serves to encourage the former, it will have well served its purpose.

The authors realize that this book is not the last word on the subject.   There are many places in the United States for which no nicknames are known.   This may be because the place has none, or because its use is so limited it has not escaped local confines, or because it is oral and has not been captured by print.   If any of these sites have been omitted, or if others inherit new nicknames, we would like to hear of them for inclusion in future editions.   Advice from chambers of commerce and local officials will be especially appreciated.

It would be remiss not to thank the librarians, historians, public officials, city, county and state agencies and individuals whose assistance has been of inestimable value in the compilation of this book.   As the authors primarily used the facilities of the New York Public Library, the Library of Congress and the Free Library of Philadelphia, special thanks are due their staffs who obligingly facilitated this work.

We have added close to 2300 new entries in the third edition.   It is possible that there are many more cities to which nicknames apply.   It is a fond hope that we can eventually make this a complete list of all cities, but as new nicknames are constantly being added, it is unlikely that this goal will ever be achieved.

J. N. K.   January 23, 1979 G. L. A.

CITY INDEX

by state; showing all nicknames
for each city

ALABAMA

ALBERTVILLE
The Friendly City

ALEXANDER CITY
Alex City
The City with a Great Civic
Pride and a Sound Busi-
ness Climate
The Industrial and Recrea-
tional Center of East Ala-
bama

ANDALUSIA
The Gem City of Southern
Alabama

ANNISTON
Annie's Town (named for Mrs.
Annie Scott Tyler)
The Brooklyn of the South
The City of Churches
The Magic City
The Model City (town laid out
before plots were sold to
the public)
The Model City of Alabama
The Pearl of the South
The Soil Pipe Center of the
World (manufactures cast
iron soil pipe and plumb-
ers specials)

ATMORE
The City Where Industry
Profits
The City with Room to
Stretch and Grow in

AUBURN
The Loveliest Village of the
Plains
The Village of the Plains

BESSEMER
The Iron City (steel furnaces)

BIRMINGHAM
Bad Birmingham
The City Beautiful
The City of Executives
The City Where the Mighty
Smith Stands (the Vulcan
statue)
The City with a Heart in the
Heart of Dixie
The Emerging Industrial Cen-
ter
The Football Capital of the
South (Legion Field holds
75, 000 people)
The Home of Vulcan (statue)
The Industrial Center of the
Great South (major iron
and steel production center
in the south)
The Industrial Center of the
Southeast
The Industrial City Beautiful
The Industrial City of Dixie
The Industrial City of the
South
The Inland Metropolis
The Magic City

Alabama Cities 2

The Magic City of the South
The Mineral City of the South
The Murder Capital of the
World (1932)
The Pittsburgh of the South
The Youngest of the World's
Great Cities (settled in
1813, Jones Valley)

CITRONELLE
The Oil Capital of Alabama
(more than 200 producing
oil wells in the vicinity)
The Oil City

DECATUR
The City of Achievement
The City of Hospitality
The City Where River, Air,
Rail and Highway Meet
The City with Opportunity
for All
The Four Leaf Clover City
(short circle tours from
this hub encompass the
numerous mountain and
lake attractions)
The Hub of the North Alabama
Resort Areas
The Northern Gateway to Ala-
bama
The Saturday Town
The South's Most Strategic
and Distribution Center
The South's Most Strategic In-
dustrial and Distributional
Center
The Wonder City

DEMOPOLIS
The City of People
The City of the People
(founded in 1817 by Napo-
leonic exiles)
The Peoples' City
The Wine and Olive Colony

DOTHAN
The City of Pines and Flow-
ers
The Home of the National
Peanut Festival
The Perfect Spot to Work,

to Play, to Enjoy Life

ENTERPRISE
The Home of the Boll Weevil
Monument (dedicated 1919)
The Peanut Capital of the
World (peanut oil mills,
peanut butter factory, pea-
nut shelling plants)

EUFAULA
The Bluff City (bluff rises
150 feet on the west bank
of the Chattahoochee River)
The Bluff City of the Chattahoochee
The Natchez of the Chattahoochee

FAIRHOPE
The Eastern Shore of Mobile
Bay (on a bluff above Mo-
bile Bay)
The Home of the Jubilee
(marine life in summer
months comes to the beach
line and the cry of "ju-
bilee" is made when a
catch is made)

FLORENCE
The City of Beautiful
Churches, Homes and
Buildings
The City of Outstanding Edu-
cational Advantages
The Home of Florence State
College (the oldest teach-
er's institution in the
south)
The Tri-Cities (with Sheffield
and Tuscumbia on the Ten-
nessee River)

FOLEY
The Gateway to Alabama's
Gulf Coast
The Heart of the American
Riviera (on the Gulf of
Mexico)
The Town Where Industry's
Contribution to the Com-
munity Is Appreciated

GADSDEN
The Queen City of Alabama
The Queen City of the Coosa
(Coosa River)

GREENVILLE
The Camellia City

GUNTERSVILLE
The Boat Racing Capital of
the South (Dixie Cup
Races)

HUNTSVILLE
The City of Contrasts
The City of Governors
(Thomas Bibb, Gabriel
Moore, Clement Comer
Clay, Reuben Chapman,
John Winston, David P.
Lewis)
The City of Gracious Living
The First Capital of the State
(1819)
The Geographical Center of
the South
The Guided Missile Research
and Space Flight Center
(U. S. Army Missile Com-
mand)
The Hub of the Powerful Ten-
nessee Valley
The Industrial City of North
Alabama
The Rocket Capital of the
Nation (where Redstone
rocket was designed and
placed in orbit)
The Rocket City (The Jupiter
"C" rocket was perfected
here)
Rocket City, U. S. A.
The Space Capital of the Na-
tion
The Space Capital of the
World (George C. Marshall
Space Flight Center)
Space City, U. S. A. (missile
production center of the
free world)
The Watercress Capital of
the World

JASPER
The Home of Hospitality

MOBILE
Alabama's City in Motion
Alabama's Only Port City (on
the west side of the Mo-
bile River)
The Charm Spot of the Deep
South
The City by the Bay
The City for All Seasons
The City of Five Flags
The City of Six Flags
The Gulf City (on the Gulf
of Mexico)
The Picnic City
The Port City (the only sea-
port in Alabama)
The Queen City of the Gulf
The Sportland of the Gulf

MONROEVILLE
The Hub of Southwest Ala-
bama (county seat of Mon-
roe County)

MONTEVALLO
The Heart of Alabama (in the
exact geographical center)

MONTGOMERY
One of America's Most In-
teresting Cities
The Birthplace of Dixie
The Capital City (population
about 145, 000)
The City of Beauty
The City of Opportunity
The Cow Town of the South
The Cradle of the Confed-
eracy (the first capital of
the Confederacy)
The Dixie City
The Thriving Capital City

MUSCLE SHOALS
The Aluminum City (home of
second largest producer of
aluminun in U. S.)
The Niagara of the South (the
Tennessee River drops 134

feet in almost 40 miles)
The Space Age City

OPELIKA
The Industrial and Trading
Center of East Alabama
The Trading Center of East
Alabama

OZARK
The City of Churches
The Helicopter Capital of
the World
The Helicopter City
The Home of Fort Rucker,
the Army Aviation
Center

PHENIX CITY
The City of Progress and
Opportunity
The Hub of the Chatta-
hoochee Valley
The Wickedest City in
America (title of book
by Edwin Strickland)

ROBERTSDALE
The Hub City

SELMA
The Electrical Center of
America
The Queen City of the
Black Belt (black belt
soil of cotton and soy-
bean plantations)

SHEFFIELD
The Iron City on the Ten-
nessee River
The Tri-Cities (with Florence
and Tuscumbia)

SYLACAUGA
The Marble City (marble
quarries)

TALLADEGA
The Bride of the Mountains
(in the foothills of the
Appalachian Mountains)

TRUSSVILLE
The City With Small Town
Hospitality (population
about 3,000)

TUSCALOOSA
The Athens of Alabama (Uni-
versity of Alabama)
The City of Oaks
The Druid City (oak trees and
mistletoe)

TUSCUMBIA
The Home of Helen Keller
("Ivy Green" now a state
shrine)
The Tri-Cities (with Florence
and Sheffield)

ALASKA

ANCHORAGE
The Air Crossroads of the
World (SAS field on
Europe-Orient flight)
The Chicago of the North
The Crossroads of the
World
The Financial Center of
Alaska
The Front Door Entrance to
an Alaska Vacation
The Hub City
The International Polar Air
Cross Roads of the World
The Largest City in the
Largest State (population
about 166,000)
The Miracle City
The Most Air-Minded City in
the World
The Nerve Center of Alaska

BARROW
The City of Exciting Contrasts

CORDOVA
Alaska's Friendly City

5 Alaska Cities

The Friendly City
The Razor Clam Capital of
the World

DOUGLAS
The Ideal Home Community

FAIRBANKS
The Centennial City (1867
Centennial Exposition)
The Friendly Frontier City
The Gateway City for the
Far North
The Gateway to the Arctic
The Golden Heart Metropo-
lis of the Interior
The Golden Heart of Alaska
The Golden Heart of the
North
The Kansas City of Alaska

HAINES
The Strawberry Capital of
Alaska
The Twin City (with Port
Chilkoot)

HOMER
The City Where People
Like to Live (population
about 1,500)
The City where the Trail
Ends and the Sea Begins
The Shangri-la of Alaska

JUNEAU
Alaska's Capital City
(population about 17,000)
Alaska's Scenic Capital
America's Most Scenic
Capital
The Capital City
The Capital City of Alaska
The Capital of an Empire
The Convention City
The Gateway to Glacier
Bay National Monument
The Scenic and Recreation
Center of Alaska
The Scenic City of Night-
less Summer Days

KENAI
The Oil Capital of Alaska
The Village With A Past,
The City With A Future

KETCHIKAN
Alaska's First City
The Canned Salmon Capital
of the World
The First City
The First City in Alaska
The Gateway to Adventure
The Gateway to Adventure
on North America's
Spectacular Marine High-
way
The Gateway to Salt and
Freshwater Fishing,
Hunting, Scenic Beauty
and Fun
The Gateway Port of Alaska
The Gateway to Alaska
The Rain City (precipitation
reaches 156 inches)
The Salmon Capital of Alaska
The Salmon Capital of the
World
The Southern Sea-Air Gate-
way to Alaska
The Totem City (contains
more totem poles than
any other city in the
world)
The World's Salmon Capital

KODIAK
The Home of the World's
Largest Bear
The King Crab Capital of
the World

KOTZEBUE
The Eskimo Village

NOME
The Famed Gold Rush Town

NORTH POLE
The Home of Santa Claus

PETERSBURG
Alaska's Little Norway

The Center of Southeast
  Alaska's Vacationland
The Hospitality Center of
  Alaska
The Little Norway of Alaska
The Shrimp Capital of
  Alaska

POINT BARROW
The Top of the World

PORT CHILKOOT
The Twin City (with Haines)

SELDOVIA
The City of Seclusion

SEWARD
The City of Contrasts
The Gateway to Kenai
  Peninsula (between Cook
  Inlet and Prince William
  Sound)
The Gateway City (on Resur-
  rection Bay)

SITKA
Alaska's Most Scenic His-
  toric Playground
Alaska's Number One Tourist
  City
The City by the Sea in
  Beautiful Southeastern
  Alaska
The City Where Scenic
  Grandeur, History, Legend
  and Bustling Modern
  Economy Are Blended Into
  Everyday Life
The First Capital City
The Historic Gateway
The Paris of the Pacific
The Portal to Romance
  (title of book by Barrett
  Willoughby)
The Russian-American Capital
The Showplace of Southeast
  Alaska

SKAGWAY
The Gateway to the Golden
  Interior
The Gateway to the Yukon

SOLDATNA
The Hub of the Kenai Penin-
  sula
TOK
The Crossroads of Alaska
The Million Dollar Camp

VALDEZ
The Copper City
The Gateway to the Interior
The Photographer's Paradise
The Switzerland of Alaska

WRANGELL
The Center of Scenic South-
  east Alaska
The Gateway to the Stikine
The Hub of Thlingit Totem
  Land
The Lumber Capital of Alaska
The Lumber Export Capital
  of Alaska

ARIZONA

AGUILA
The Lettuce Center of the
  Nation

AJO
The Gateway to Sonoyta,
  Mexico, and the Gulf of
  Lower California

APACHE JUNCTION
The Community Nestled in
  the Shadow of the Super-
  stition Mountains
The Gateway to the Fabulous
  Desert Lake Region
The Gateway to the Salt River
  Chain of Lakes
The Wonderful Community

BISBEE
Arizona's Copper Capital
The Gateway to Fort Huachuca
  (U.S. electronic proving
  ground)

BOWIE
  The City in the Garden of
  the Sun
  The Gateway to Chiricahua
  National Monument
  (Cochise County, S. E.
  Arizona)

CHANDLER
  The City where Summer
  Winters
  The Five Star City in the
  Valley of the Sun
  The Green Spot in Arizona's
  Famous Valley of the Sun

DOUGLAS
  The City where Progress
  and Pleasure Are Part-
  ners
  The Friendly City in the
  Heart of the Old West

FLAGSTAFF
  Friendly Fabulous Flagstaff
  The Business, Finance,
  Industry, Shopping, and
  Transportation Hub
  The Center of Everything
  in Northern Arizona
  The Center of North Ari-
  zona's Scenic Vacation-
  land (on the Coconino
  Plateau)
  The City in the Center of
  the Most Amazing and
  Beautiful Country in the
  World
  The City in the Heart of
  Coconino National Forest
  The City in the Pines (pon-
  derosa pine forests)
  The City of Seven Wonders
  The County Seat of Coco-
  nino County
  The Home of Ten Thousand
  Friendly People (population
  about 31,500)
  The Hub of Arizona's
  Lumber Industry
  Touropolis of America (three
  major tour routes enter
  the city)

FORT HUACHUCA
  The Electronic Center of the
  Southwest

GLENDALE
  The City in the Valley of
  the Sun
  The Land of Perpetual
  Harvest
  The New Car Capital of
  Arizona (factory repre-
  sentatives of all major
  automobile concerns lo-
  cated here)

GLOBE
  The Capital City of the County
  with a Copper Bottom
  (county seat of Gila County
  noted for its copper mines)
  The Gateway to Arizona's
  Scenic and Recreational
  Area

HOLBROOK
  The Gateway to the Petrified
  Forest National Park

JEROME
  The Largest Ghost Town in
  America (1960 population
  243)
  The Most Unique City in
  America
  The West's Largest Ghost
  Town

KAYENTA
  The Gateway to Monument
  Valley (red sandstone
  buttes 1,000 feet high in
  N.E. Arizona and S.E.
  Utah)

KINGMAN
  The Gateway to Hoover Dam
  (726 feet high on Colorado
  River between Clara
  County, Nev., and Mohave
  County, Ariz.)
  The Gateway to "Wanderland"
  in Mohave County, Ari-
  zona

LAKE HAVASU CITY
The London Bridge Town
The Town of Progress

MESA
Arizona's Third Largest
City (population
about 95, 500)
The City in the Heart of
Arizona Vacationland
The City where It's June
in January Along the
Romantic Apache Trail
The Gem City in Arizona's
Valley of the Sun
The Heart of the Romantic
Southwest in the Valley
of the Sun
The Little City of Charm

MIAMI
The Concentrator City

NOGALES
The Gateway to Mexico's
Great West Coast
The Key City to the West
Coast of Mexico

PHOENIX
America's Favorite Sun
and Fun Vacationland
Nature's Greatest Boon to
Arizona
The Air Conditioned Capital
of America (a manu-
facturing city)
The Capital City (population
about 705, 000)
The Capital City of Arizona
(1889)
The City in Arizona's
Valley of the Sun
The City that Has Every-
thing Under the Sun
The City where Summer
Winters
The Gateway to the Valley
of the Sun
The Heart of the Sun Country
The Hub of the Great South-
west

The Liveliest Resort Area
The Metropolis of the Desert
The Miracle City in the
Desert (in the Valley of
the Sun)
The Nation's Warmest,
Driest, Sunniest Spot
The Palm City
The Profit Center of the
Southwest
The Southwest's Sightseeing
Center
The Valley in the Sun (Salt
River Valley)
The Youngest Big City in the
United States (settled 1870)

PORTAL
The Yosemite of Arizona
(Cave Creek Canyon in
Chiricahua Mountains)

PRESCOTT
Arizona's First Capital (first
territorial legislature
1864, also 1877-1889)
The Center of the Nation's
Greatest Concentration of
Varied Natural Attractions
The Center of Yavapai (seat
of Yavapai County)
The City Rich in Western
Tradition
The Cowboy Capital
The First Capital of Arizona
(1864-65)
The Mile High City (altitude
5, 346 feet)
The Mile High City of Health
The Sentinel City in the
Pines (in the Sierra
Madre mountains)

QUARTZSITE
The Hottest Town (average
July temp. 108.7˚)
The Nation's Hottest Town

SALOME
The City where She Danced
(town named for Mrs.
Grace Salome Pratt)

SAN CARLOS
  Hell's Forty Acres (on the
    San Carlos Indian Reser-
    vation)

SCOTTSDALE
  The Fun'n Excitement
    Center
  The West's Most Western
    Community
  The West's Most Western
    Town (new buildings
    simulate frontier struc-
    tures)

SEDONA
  The Most Colorful Country
    in the West

SPRINGERVILLE
  The Gateway to the White
    Mountains of Eastern
    Arizona

SUN CITY
  The Town that Changed
    America's Viewpoint on
    Retirement Living
  The Twin City (with Youngs-
    town, Ariz.)

TEMPE
  The Home of the Fabulous Sun
    Devil Athletic Team and
    Arizona State University
  The Swell Place to Live
  The Valley's College Town
    (Arizona State University)

TOMBSTONE
  The City of Health, History,
    Hospitality
  The City of Sunshine and
    Silver (famous mining
    center)
  The Town Too Tough to
    Die (water flooded the
    mines in 1886, but the
    people did not leave)

TUCSON
  America's First City of
    Sunshine

Arizona's Second Largest
  City
The Ancient and Honorable
  Pueblo
The Bustling Resort City in
  the Desert
The City of Sunshine
The City where There's
  Always Something to Do
  and See Under Sunny Skies
The City where Winter Wears
  a Tan
The City with a Difference
The City with Everything
The Heart of the Old South-
  west
The Heart of the Scenic
  Southwest
The Historic Heart of the
  Southwest
The Home of the University
  of Arizona
The Hub of the Southwest's
  Sun Country
The New Pueblo
The Old Pueblo (oldest city
  in Arizona, first settle-
  ment 1776)
The Retirement Center of
  the Nation
The Southwest Sun Country
  (about 3,800 hours of
  sunshine a year)
The Sunshine Capital of the
  Southwest
The Sunshine City
The Western Gateway to
  Mexico (65 miles to
  Nogales, Mexico)
The Wonderful Weather
  Land
What the West Is All About

WICKENBURG
  A Bit of the Old West Trans-
    planted in the Twentieth
    Century
  America's Dude Ranch Capi-
    tal
  The Dude Ranch Capital of
    the World
  Dude Ranch Capital, U.S.A.
  The Roundup Capital

WILLCOX
A Good Place to Know, Go, Visit, Stay
The Cattle Capital and Agricultural Center of the Great Southwest
The Cattle Capital of the Nation
The Cattle Capital of the World
The City in the Heart of the Southwest Wonderland

WINSLOW
The Center of Northern Arizona's Scenic Beauty
The City in the Heart of the Nation's Sunniest State
The Gateway to Hopiland and Navajoland (Hopi Indians and Navajo Indians)
The Gateway to Zane Grey's Tonto Basin and Navajoland
The Largest City in Northern Arizona

YOUNGSTOWN
America's Original Retirement Community
The Twin City (with Sun City, Ariz.)

YUMA
The City where You Can Work, Live, Play, the Western Way
The Queen City of the Colorado (River)
The Sunshine Capital of the United States

ARKANSAS

ALMA
The Crossroads for North-South, East-West Traffic

ARKANSAS CITY
Ark City

BENTON
The Gateway to the Bauxite Fields (discovered 1887 in the Ouachita Mountains)

BENTONVILLE
The Gateway to the Northwest

BERRYVILLE
The Center City of the Ozarks
The Turkey Capital of Arkansas (turkey farms)
The Turkey Capital of the Ozarks

BLYTHEVILLE
The City of Churches
The City of Industry and Transportation
The City where Cotton Is King
The City with a Modern Educational System
The Grand Place to Live and Earn a Living
The Home of the National Cotton Picking Contest
The Home of the 97th Bomb Wing
The Place with Excellent Hunting in Season

BULL SHOALS
The Capital of the Big Lake (Bull Shoals Lake)

CAMDEN
South Arkansas' Busy Port City (on Ouachita River)
The Queen City of the Ouachita

CONWAY
The City of Opportunity

CROSSETT
The City of Beautiful Homes

The City of Churches of
All Faiths
The City with a Plan
The City with Attractive
Industrial Sites
The City with Modern Health
Facilities
The Fishing Capital of the
Nation (South)
The Forestry Capital of the
Nation
The Forestry Capital of the
South

DECATUR
The Community of Friendly
People

DOVER
The Gateway to the Ozarks
(between Little Rock and
Fort Smith)
The Home of Ding Dong
Daddy

EL DORADO
The Commercial, Cultural
and Industrial Center of
South Arkansas
The Home of All-Americans
(Jim Mooty, Wayne Harris)
The Home of Business,
Industry and Recreation
The Home of Fine Churches,
Modern Schools
The Home of Miss America,
1964
The Oil Capital of Arkansas
(oil discovered 1921)
The Well Rounded Community

EUREKA SPRINGS
America's Little Switzerland
(mountain resort)
Little Switzerland of the
Ozarks
The "Believe It or Not"
Town
The Capital Resort of the
Ozarks (oldest resort in
the Ozark Region)
The Little Switzerland of
America

The Switzerland of the
Ozarks
The Town of "Up and Down"

FAYETTEVILLE
America's Little Switzerland
(highest point in Arkansas
Ozarks)
Northwest Arkansas' Largest
City
The Athens of Arkansas
The City that Progress Built
The Gateway to Scenic Boston
Mountains
The Gateway to the Boston
Mountains
The Medical Center of North-
west Arkansas

FLIPPIN
The Gateway to Blue Shoals
Lake and Dam

FORREST CITY
The Hoist Capital of America
(Yale and Towne Inc. plant)

FORT SMITH
America's Industrial City
Arkansas' Industrial Center
The Center City
The City of Balance
The City of Your Future
The Growing City of Industry
and Recreation
The Gateway to the Beautiful
Ozark Playground
The Industrial City of
America
The Leading Industrial City
in Arkansas
The Little Gibraltar on the
Arkansas
The Southwestern Factory
City

GENTRY
The Typical Ozark Home
Town

GLENWOOD
The City in the Heart of the
Ouachitas

GRAVETTE
The World's Largest Black
Walnut Factory

GREEN FOREST
The Tomato Capital of the
Ozarks

GREENWOOD
The Good Place to Live

HARRISON
The Gateway to the Ozarks
The Hub of the Ozarks (in
the Arkansas Ozarks)
The Metropolis of a Fast
Growing Commercial
and Agricultural Area
The Ozark Wonderland

HAZEN
The Rice Capital
The Rice Center of the
U.S.A.
The Rice City

HEBER SPRINGS
The Gateway to Giant
Greer's Ferry Lake

HELENA
Arkansas' Only Seaport (on
the Mississippi River)
The City of Industrial Op-
portunity
The Embryonic Center of
Music
The Seaport City
The Twin Cities (with West
Helena)

HOPE
Southwest Arkansas' Most
Conveniently Located
City
The U.S. Watermelon
Capital
The Watermelon Capital
of the U.S.
The Watermelon City

HOT SPRINGS
America's Favorite Spa

America's Greatest Health
and Resort Center
America's Greatest Health
and Rest Center
America's Own Spa (the only
health resort in the U.S.
where the natural hot
waters which flow from
the earth are owned, con-
trolled and endorsed by
the U.S. government)
Arkansas' Largest Health and
Pleasure Resort
One of the World's Greatest
Resort Cities
The Carlsbad of America
The City where the World
Bathes and Plays
The Nation's Health Resort
(famous hot springs and
spas)
The Spa Center of America
The Valley of Vapors
The Vapor City (steam from
the hot springs)

HUNTSVILLE
The Friendly City

JONESBORO
The City Ready for Tomor-
row (home of Arkansas
State College)

KIRBY
The Gateway to Lake Gree-
son and the Daisy State
Park

LAKE VILLAGE
Home of the Big Black Bass

LITTLE ROCK
Arkopolis
The Capital City (population
about 148,500), (only city
in the nation with three
capitals)
The City of Roses
The City of Three Capitals
(three capital buildings
remain, each of a dif-
ferent era)

The Geographic Cultural and
Economic Center

MARIANNA
The Gateway to the St.
Francis

MORRILTON
The Gateway to the Petit
Jean Mountain

MOUNTAIN HOME
The Center of the Most
Popular Resort Section
in the Ozarks
The Fishing Capital of the
Ozarks (White River,
Norfork Lake, Bull
Shoals Lake)
The Gateway to Lake Nor-
folk)
The Home of the Arkansas
Folk Festival

NASHVILLE
The Peach Capital of
Arkansas

PARIS
The Gateway to Mt. Maga-
zine

PINE BLUFF
The City of Gigantic Indus-
tries, Unparalleled
Schools
The City of Magnificent
Churches, Beautiful
Homes
The City of Peace and
Plenty
The Gateway to Southeast
Arkansas
The Trade Center for South-
east Arkansas

ROGERS
The Heartland of the
Beaver Lake Area

RUSSELLVILLE
The Home of Arkansas Polytechnic College

SPRINGDALE
The Agricultural and Indus-
trial Center of Northwest
Arkansas
The Main Street of North-
west Arkansas
The Rodeo of the Ozarks
Town

STUTTGART
The Agricultural Festival
City
The Duck Hunting Capital of
the World
The Fish Farming Research
Center
The Rice and Duck Capital
of the World
The State Rice Branch Ex-
periment Station
The World's Championship
Duck Calling City

TEXARKANA
The Twin Cities (twin cities
on the Arkansas-Texas
border: Texarkana, Ark.,
and Texarkana, Texas)

VAN BUREN
The City on the Move
The Kopper Kettle

WASHINGTON
The Birthplace of Texas
The Cradle of Arkansas
History
The Gateway to Texas
The Home of the Bowie
Knife

WEST HELENA
The Twin Cities (with Helena)

WEST MEMPHIS
The Eastern Gateway into
Arkansas
The Fastest Growing City
in Eastern Arkansas
The Gateway to the Southwest

WILCOX
The Cattle Center

WINSLOW
The Pioneer Resort Town

CALIFORNIA

ALAMEDA
The Garbage City (filled-in
land)
The Isle of Pleasant Living
(eastern shore of San
Francisco Bay)

ALBANY
The City of Homes

ALTADENA
The Community of the
Deodars (trees)

ALTURAS
The Home of the Mule-tail
Deer

ANAHEIM
The Center of a Bustling
Commercial Industrial
and Tourist World
The Center of Commerce
and Industry
The City of Beautiful Parks
The City of Good Living
The Convention Center
The Family City
The Fun Country for Family
Recreation
The Fun N' Convention City
The Home of Disney Land
The Ideal Year 'Round Com-
munity
The Recreation Center

ANGWIN
The City Set on a Hill

ARCADIA
The City of Santa Anita

ATOLIA
The Sin City

ATWATER
The Center for Good Living,
Agriculture, Recreation
and Industry
The City of Beautiful Parks
and Lovely Homes
The City of Diversified Rec-
reation
The City of Good Govern-
ment
The City of Industry and In-
dustrial Development
The City of Inspiring Church
Activities
The City of Modern Schools
The City that Is Near Every-
thing
The Community to Take
Pride In

AVALON
The Port of Friendliness

AZUSA
The Canyon City
The City of the Dams (con-
trol dams)
The Gateway to the San
Gabriels

BAKERSFIELD
The Nashville of the West
(where country stars ob-
tained their start)
The Southern Gateway to the
Sequoia

BALDWIN PARK
The Gateway to the Orange
Empire

BANNING
The Gateway to the Desert
and Idyllwild Mountain
Resort

BEAUMONT
The Center of San Gorgonio
Mountains
The Mountain Pass of Health,
Accessibility, Beauty
The Zone of Ozone

BELMONT
The Hub of the Peninsula

BENICIA
The Athens of California
The City of Industrial Op-
portunity

BERKELEY
The Athens of the West (the
University of California)
The Balanced City

BEVERLY HILLS
The Garden Spot of the
World

BISHOP
The Sportsmans Town
The World Gliding Center

BLUE LAKE
The Gateway to the Great
Mad River Valley
The Place where the Sun-
shine and Sea Meet

BODIE
Shooters' Town (nightly
shootings in wild west
days)

BRISBANE
The City of Stars
The Community Combining
the Best of Two Worlds

BUENO PARK
The Center of the Southland

BURLINGAME
The Entertainment Capital
of the World
One of California's Choicest
Communities

CALIPATRIA
The Lowest Down City in
the Western Hemisphere

CAMBRIA
The Village where the Pines
Meet the Sea

CASTRO VALLEY
The City Big Enough for Op-
portunity - Small Enough
for Friendliness
The Family Community
The Heart of Good Living

CASTROVILLE
The Artichoke Capital of the
World

CATALINA ISLAND
The Outstanding Seaside Resort of the Pacific Coast

CATHEDRAL CITY
The Home of the Coachella
Valley Players (amateur
theatrical group)

CERES
The Center of the Peach
Industry
The City of Community Pride
The City of Growing Industry
The City of Schools
The City of Water and Agri-
culture

CHICO
The Almond Capital of the
World (almond processing
plants)
The Almond Center of the
World (produces 20 per-
cent of the world's supply)

CHOWCHILLA
A Nice Place to Live
The Center of California
The City Between the Sier-
ras and the Sea
The City of Beautiful Homes
The City of Fine Schools
The City of Industry, Agri-
culture and Recreation
The City of Parks, Hospitals
and Churches
The City with a Big Future

CHULA VISTA
California's Fastest Growing
City

The City for Gracious Living
The City where Industry Is
Wanted and Growing
The City where Year-round
Living Is a Pleasure
The City which Tops the
World for Sunshine and
Sociability
The Good Place to Live
The Lemon Capitol of the
World
The Vacation Land

CLAREMONT
A Bit of New England with a
Sombrero on It
Claremont, the Beautiful
The City of Living and
Learning
The College Town amid the
Orange Groves (Pomona
College, Scripps College
for Women, Claremont
Men's College, Claremont
Graduate School, Harvey
Mudd College)

COALINGA
The Heart of the Westside
of Fresno County

COLTON
The Hub City
The Industrial City

COMMERCE
The Model City
The Modern City

COMPTON
The Hub City

CONCORD
The City of Dynamic Opportunity

CORNING
The Center of the Olive
Industry

CORONA
The Circle City (three mile
circular boulevard sur-

rounding the business district)
The City of Business and
Industry
The City of Civic Pride
The City of Recreation for
All Ages
The Lemon Capital

CORONADO
The Community of Beautiful
Homes
The Crowning Gem in Southern
California's Golf Diadem
The Popular Vacation and
Convention Spot

COVINA
The Leading Citrus Center
The Well-planned Balanced
Community

CULVER CITY
The Business Center for
Greater Los Angeles

DEATH VALLEY
America's Bottom
America's Low Spot

DELANO
The City for Business and
Industry
The City for the Future
The City of Recreation
The Community of Opportunity
for Living
The Land of Promise

DEL MONTE
The Twenty-Thousand Acre
Playground

DENAIR
The Community of Rich Land,
Good Water and Mild Climate
The Oasis of the San Joaquin
Valley
The Quiet, Restful, Relaxing
Smog-Free Community

DINUBA
Raisinland, U. S. A.
The Center of the Most Productive Agricultural Area in the Nation
The Community for Camping, Fishing, Skiing and Water Sports
The Year-Round Paradise for Sportsmen

DIXON
The City of Diversified Opportunity
The City for a Pleasant Way of Life
The Fine Community for the Family
The Nugget of the Valley
The Sheep Capital of the State of California

DOWNEY
The City with a Future Unlimited

DUBLIN
The City with a Rich Heritage of American Life
The Crossroads City

EL CERRITO
The City Keyed to Your Way of Living
The City of Gracious Living
The City that Knows where It Is Going
The City with a View
The Dynamic City
The Prime Residential Community in the Bay Area

ELSINORE
The Scenic Health Resort of California

ENCINITAS
The City of Unusual Charm
The Community of Beautiful Homes
The Town with Matchless Climate

ESCONDIDO
The Portal to Palomar (observatory)

EXETER
The City in the Garden of the Sun
The City of Balanced Economy
The City of Industry and Agriculture
The Good Place in Which to Live and Work

FAIRFIELD
Solano County's Twin Cities (with Suisan)
The Heart of Solano County
The Twin Cities (with Suisan)

FONTANA
One of the Most Attractive Communities in Southern California
The Good Place to Live
The Neighborly Friendly Community
The Steel Capital of the West

FORTUNA
The City where Nature Smiles the Year 'Round
The Friendly City

FRESNO
The Agricultural and Recreational Center of California
The Bustling Center of Industry, Agriculture, Wholesale Trade and Shipping
The Gateway to Yosemite Sequoia and King Canyon Parks
The Raisin Center of the World
The Scenic Hub of the Golden State
The Sweet Wine Capital of the World

FULLERTON
The City of Excellence in Living

The City of Hospitality
The Ideal Industrial City of
Orange County

GALT
The Agricultural City with
Industrial Facilities
The Center of a Wonderful
Area of Opportunity
The City which Looks to
the Future with a Great
Deal of Happy Anticipa-
tion
The City with an Exciting
History
The City with a Promising
Future

GARDEN CITY
The Strawberry Festival
City
The Third Largest City in
Orange County

GARDEN GROVE
The Friendly Community
The Planned Growing City

GARDENA
The Little Las Vegas
The Poker City
The Poker-Playing Capital
of the West

GILROY
The Friendly City
The Healthful and Prosperous
Place to Live

GLENDALE
The Jewel City
The Queen of the Valley
(San Fernando Valley)

GLENDORA
The Center of the Citrus
Industry for Southern
California
The Community with a
Congenial Environment
for Generous Living
The Gracious Residential
Community

The Quiet Rural Town

GUERNEVILLE
The "Unplanned" Planned
Community

GUSTINE
The City of Commerce
The City of Industry and
Agriculture
The Community with Pride
The Home of the World's
Largest Walnut Tree

HALF MOON BAY
Spanish Town
The Flower Industry City

HAWTHORNE
The Aircraft Center of the
West
The City of Progress and
Security

HESPERIA
The Friendly Community
The Land of the West

HOLLYWOOD
Filmdom
Filmland
The Big-Headed Burg
The Celluloid City
The Cinema Capital (moving
picture studios opened
1911)
The Cinema Village
The Cinemaland
The Cinematown
The Circle City
The City Beautiful
The City of Galloping Tin-
Types
The Fairyland
The Film Capital
The Film Capital of the
World
The Film City
The Flicker Capital
The Flicker City
The Flicker Lane
The Glamor Capital of the
World

The Glamour City
The Land of Promise
The Movie Village
The Movieland
The Nation's Glamor Capital
The Screenland
The Sinemaland
The Squawkiewood
The Stardom
The Starland
The Studioland
The Tinsel Town

HOLTVILLE
America's Carrot Capital
(in Imperial Valley)
The Carrot Capital
The Center of Imperial
Valley

IMPERIAL
The Heart of Imperial Valley
The New Gold Mine of the
Old West

INDIO
The Center of All Vacation
Fun
The Date Capital of the
United States (produces
about 90 percent of all
dates grown in the United
States)
The Date Capital of the
World
The Desert Wonderland
(Coachella Valley)
The National Date Festival
City
Southern California's Desert
Playground

INGLEWOOD
The Harbor of the Air
(numerous aircraft plants)

ISLETON
The Asparagus Capital of the
World

KERMAN
The City of Industry
The City of Land, Water,

Opportunity and Prosperity
The City of Modern Schools
and Recreation
The Gateway to California's
Newest Frontier
The West Side of Fresno
County

KINGSBURG
The Largest Watermelon
Shipping Center in Cali-
fornia

LAGUNA BEACH
The City of Serene Living
The Riviera of the Pacific
The Winter Paradise

LA JOLLA
America's Riviera
The City of Natural Wonders
The Gem of the Pacific
The Gem of the Pacific Coast
The Jewel of the Pacific
Coast

LAKE TAHOE
(see also Nevada)
America's All-Year Play-
ground
The Cesspool for Gambling
Joints
The City with a Hole in the
Middle
The Coming Vegas
The Recreational Slum
The Sierra "Coney Island" (a
pleasure resort in Brooklyn,
N. Y.)

LANCASTER
The Heart of the Antelope
Valley

LINDSAY
The City in the Garden of
the Sun

LIVINGSTON
The City of Agriculture and
Recreation
The City of Plentiful Civic
Services

The City where the Sun
Ripens the Fruits of
Prosperity

LODI
America's Sherryland
One of California's Historic
Communities
The Center of a Vast
Diversified Recreation
Area
The City of Agriculture and
Industry
The City of Central Location
The City of Classic Archi-
tecture
The City of Community
Facilities
The Exciting Place to Live
The Home of the Flame
Tokay Grape
The Home of the Lodi Grape
Festival
The Home of the National
Wine Show
The Modern Progressive
City

LOMA LINDA
The Gem in the Beautiful
Southern California Setting

LONG BEACH
The City by the Sea
The City of Investments
where Commerce and
Industry Thrive
The Convention Center of
the Pacific Coast
The Gem of Beaches
The Home of the Miss Uni-
verse Pageant
The International City
The Land of Industrial Op-
portunities
The Most Versatile Port on
the West Coast
The Natural Gateway to
Southern California's
Endless Charm
The Pride of the Pacific
The Proud Port of the
Pacific

The Queen of the Beaches
The Star of the Southland
The World Center of oceanology (Battelle Memorial
Institute, Ocean Science
and Engineering, Inc.,
etc.)
The Year 'Round Convention
and Resort Metropolis of
the Pacific
The Year 'Round Playground
of the Pacific

LOS ALTOS
The City of Trees
The Garden Spot of the
World Famous Santa Clara
Valley

LOS ANGELES
America's Gateway to the
Pacific
Cleveland with Palm Trees
El-Ay
Elay
L.A.
Los Diablos
Nineteen Suburbs in Search
of a Metropolis
One Hundred Suburbs in
Search of a City
The Angel City
The Capital of Crackpots
The Catchall of Suckers
The Circus without a Tent
The Citrus Metropolis
The City Built in a Day
The City Built on Sand
The City Metropolis
The City of Angels
The City of Boulevards
The City of Dreadful Joy
The City of Excitement
The City of Flowers
The City of Liquid Sunshine
The City of Make Believe
The City of Sunshine
The Collection of Freeways
in Search of a City
The Community of Trees
The Detroit of Airplanes
The Exciting City
The Exciting World City

The Fabulous City
The Glamor Capital of the
World
The House Built on Sand
The Land of the Afternoon
The Lost Angels
The Mecca of Crackpots
The Metropolis of Isms
The Metropolis of the
Pacific Coast
The Metropolis of the West
The Motion Picture Center
of the World
The Movie City
The Murder City (where
Senator Robert Francis
Kennedy was assassi-
nated)
The Nation's Smog Capital
The Old Pueblo
The Original Site of Cali-
fornication
The Paradise Sullied
The Place where Fun Never
Stops
The Queen of the Cow
Countries
The Seaport of Iowa (face-
tious)
The Second Murder City
(assassination of Senator
R. F. Kennedy)
The Smog City
The Spawning Ground of
Realtors
The Ultimate City (title of
book by Christopher
Rand)
The Upper Sandusky West
The Westernmost Suburb
of Des Moines
The World of Variety
The Year-Round Convention
City
Two Newarks

LOS BANOS
The Center for Agriculture,
Industry and Recreation
The Center for Good Living
The Center for Water,
Industry, Recreation,
Agriculture

The New Crossroads of California

MCFARLAND
The Center of Diversity

MCLOUD
The Blackberry Capital of
the World

MADERA
The Gem City of the Wealthy
San Joaquin Valley

MANTECA
The Butter City (dairy pro-
duction center, Spanish
word for butter)
The City of Varied Industry
The Crossroads of California

MARICOPA
The Gate City (gateway be-
tween the San Joaquin
Valley and the Cuyama
Valley)

MARIPOSA
The Western Gateway City

MARYSVILLE
The Peach Bowl of the
United States

MENLO PARK
The Community Blessed by
Nature and Planned with
Pride

MERCED
The City in the Center of
San Joaquin Valley
The City in the Heart of
California
The Gateway to Yosemite

MILL VALLEY
The Gateway to Muir
Woods

MILLBRAE
The Heart of Fiestaland
Your Place in the Sun

MODESTO
The City that Is Only Two
Hours to the Sierras on
the Sea (on the Tuo-
lumne River)
The Peach Capital of the
World

MONROVIA
The City in Motion
The Gem City of the Foot-
hills

MONTCLAIR
The City on the Go

MONTEBELLO
The City Between the Moun-
tains and the Sea
The City of Flowers
The City of Gardens
The City of Homes
The City of Industry
The Fastest Growing City
in Los Angeles County
(population about 45,700)

MONTEREY
America's Famous Summer
and Winter Resort
The Capital of Old Cali-
fornia (from 1776 to the
end of 1849 and de facto
from 1770-1776)
The City of History and
Romance
The City where America
Began in the West (site
discovered in 1542 by Juan
Rodriguez Cabrillo)
The First American Capital
West of the Rockies
(capital of Alta California
under the Spanish, Mexi-
can and United States
Flags)
The Year Round Golf Capital
of the World

MORGAN HILL
The Dam End of Santa Clara
County
The Land of Opportunity

NAPA
The City Landscaped for
Living, Dedicated to
Progress
The City of Diversified Rec-
reation
The City of Industrial Oppor-
tunity
The Southeastern Entrance
to the Redwood Empire
(97 percent of the world's
great redwoods)
The Table Wine Center of
the World (applied also to
Napa County)

NATIONAL CITY
The City where Summers Are
Mild and Winters Are
Warm

NEVADA CITY
The Gateway to the Great
Tahoe National Forest
The Gateway to the Sports-
man's Paradise

NORCO
The City Living in Rural
Atmosphere

NORTH HOLLYWOOD
The Gateway to the San
Fernando Valley (a part
of the City of Los Angeles)

NORTHRIDGE
The Horse Capital of the
World

OAKDALE
The City in Central Cali-
fornia Convenient to Everything
The City Surrounded by
Great Recreational Oppor-
tunities
The Ladino Clover Center
of America (grazing
for beef cattle, origi-
nally imported from
Italy)
The West at Its Best

OAKLAND
San Francisco's Bedroom
The City of Progress and
Prosperity
The Detroit of the West
(manufacturing center)
The Surprise City
The Western City of Ships
(site of U. S. Army Port
of Embarkation, Naval
Supply Depot, etc.)

OCEANSIDE
The Gateway to Camp
Pendleton
The Gateway to San Luis
Rey Mission

ONTARIO
The City that Charms

ORLAND
The City in California's
Lush Sacramento Valley

OROVILLE
The District Incomparable

PACIFIC GROVE
The Leading Family Resort
Summer and Winter
The Model Family Resort,
Summer and Winter

PALM DESERT
The Bob Hope Desert Golf
Classic City
The Hub of the Coachella
Valley Cove Communities
The Smartest Address on
the Golden Desert
The Winter Golf Mecca

PALM SPRINGS
America's Desert Resort
America's Foremost Desert
Resort
The Capital of Sunshine
The City that Is Just for
Fun
The City where the World
Comes to Play and
Enjoy Life

The Golf Capital of the
World (over 20 challenging
courses)
The Lost Resort
The Oasis in the Desert (in
the Upper Colorado desert)
The Swimming Pool City
(over 4,000 pools)
The Winter Golf Capital of
the World
The World's Winter Golf
Capital
Winter Golf Capital of the
World

PALO ALTO
The City Preserving Its
Heritage, Planning the
Promise of the Future
The City Proud of Its Heri-
tage
The Garden Spot of Peninsular
(at foothills of Coast Range
Mountains)
The Home of Stanford University
The Ideal Home and Recrea-
tional Center
The Outstanding City
The Ultra Modern City

PARAMOUNT
The City of Roses

PASADENA
The City of Roses
The Crown City (at the crown
of the valley)
The Crown City of the Valley
The Crown of the Valley
The Home of the Rose Parade
The Hub of the Fabulous
Gulf Coast
The Town that Roses Built
(famous annual parade on
January first, and football
tournament)

PETALUMA
California's Central Market
for Industrial Products
The Center of Sonoma
County's Agri-Business
Industry

The Egg Basket of the
World (egg production
center)
The Future Manufacturing
Center of the West where
Rail and Water Transpor-
tation Meet (used in 1906)
The Lowell of the West
The Southern Portal to the
Wine Producing Country
The White Leghorn City of
the West
The World's Egg Basket

PICO RIVERA
The Balanced City
The City of Unparalleled
Recreational Facilities
The Crossroads of Los
Angeles County
The Vital City

PIEDMONT
The Queen of the Hills

PISMO BEACH
The City where the Sun
Spends the Winter

PITTSBURG
A Great Place to Live
The City Destined by Its
Site for Prosperity
The City with a Fascinating
History
The City with a Prosperous
Present
The City with an Exciting
Future
The City with Everything
Under the Sun
The Industrial Capital of
California
The Industrial City of the
West (steel plant,
numerous factories)

PLACERVILLE
Hangtown (numerous
hangings in pioneer
days)
The Hub of the Mother
Lode Country

PLEASANTON
The City of Planned Progress

POMONA
The Inland City Beautiful

PORTERVILLE
The Friendly City

PORTOFINO
Southern California's Most
Modern Resort

PORTOLA
The Hub of the Eastern
Plumas Trading Area

REDDING
The Gateway to the Vaca-
tionland of Shasta

REDLANDS
The Busy Business Center
The Gem City
The Gem of the Valley
The Radiant Garden Spot of
California
The Show Place of Southern
California

REDWOOD CITY
The Preferred City on the
Peninsula

RICHMOND
The Fastest Growing Indus-
trial Community (popula-
tion 74, 300)
The Largest City of Contra
Costa County, California

RIDGECREST
The Desert Community

RIPON
The Almond Capitol of
California
The City of Excellent
Schools Among Friendly
People
The City of Relaxed Living
The Community with a Planned
Industrial Growth Pattern

The Home of the Ripon
Almond Blossom Festival

RIVERBANK
The City of Action
The City of Civic Pride
The City of Scenic Beauty

RIVERSIDE
The Center of the Orange
Empire
The City of Exceptional
Beauty
The City of Friendliness
and Beauty
The City of Individuality
and Charm
The Home of the Orange
The Mission City

ROSAMOND
The Gateway to Edwards
(Edwards Air Force
Base)

SACRAMENTO
New Helvetia (founded
August 12, 1839 by
Captain John Augustus
Sutter; first settlement
of white men in interior
California)
Sacto (contraction of word,
first and last syllable of
Sacramento)
The Almond Capital of the
World
The Camellia Capitol of
the World
The Camellia City (first
shipment arrived from
the east in 1852)
The Capital City (popu-
lation about 266, 000)
The City of the Plains
The City of Trees
The City where California
Began (founded August
12, 1839 by Captain
John Augustine Sutter;
first settlement of
white men in interior
California)

The Golden City
The Heart of California
The Land of Romance and
Recreation
The Queen of the Golden
Empire

SAINT HELENA
The City in the Heart of
Colorful Napa Valley
The Premium Wine Capital
of the United States
The Table Wine Center of
the World

SALINAS
The Balanced Community
with the Bright Future
The City that Is

SAN ANSELMO
The Hub

SAN BERNARDINO
The City of Mineral Springs
The Gate City
The Leading Inland City of
the South (on the edge of
the Mojave Desert at the
base of the San Bernardino
Mountains, about sixty
miles inland)
The Playground of Southern
California
San Berdoo

SAN BRUNO
The City with a Future
The Friendliest Spot on the
King's Highway

SAN CARLOS
The City of Good Living

SAN CLEMENTE
The City that Climate Built

SAN DIEGO
America's Only International
Playground
America's Riviera
As Nice as Its Climate
Bag Town (sailors on leave)

California at Its Best
California's First and
   Finest City
California's Plymouth Rock
Golfland, U.S.A. (about
   70 golf courses)
The Air Capital of the West
The Aviation Center of
   America
The Birthplace of California
   (discovered 1542 by
   Cabrillo)
The City Built Around a
   Park
The City by the Sea
The City where California
   and Mexico Meet the
   Blue Pacific
The City where California
   Began (visited in 1539
   by Father Marcos and
   his followers from the
   desert side)
The City with America's
   Finest Year-Around
   Climate
The Gateway to California
The Gateway to the Great
   Life
The Harbor of the Sun
The International Resort
   Area
The Italy of America
The Jewel City of California
The Kingdom of the Sun
The Oceanographic Capital
   of the World
The Place where California
   Began
The Plymouth of the Pacific
   Coast (first permanent
   white settlement on the
   Pacific Coast)
The Plymouth of the West
The Sunniest City in Cali-
   fornia
The Unconventional City
   (did not get the antici-
   pated Republican National
   Convention)
The Vacation Paradise
The World-Famous Zoo
   City

The World's Finest Vacation-
   land
Try San Diego First
Vacationland, U.S.A.

SAN FRANCISCO
America's Most Exciting
   City
America's Most Friendly
   Fascinating City
America's Paris
Everybody's Favorite City
Frisco
Heaven on the Half Shell
The Bagdad by the Bay
The Bay City
The City Beautiful
The City by the Bay
The City by the Golden Gate
The City by the Sea
The City Cosmopolitan
The City for Romantics
The City of a Hundred Hills
The City of Bridges
The City of Firsts
The City of Many Adventures
The City of Miracles
The City of One Hundred
   Hills
The City of the Golden Gate
The City on the Golden Hills
   (title of book by Herb
   Caen and Dong Kingman)
The City that Knows How
The City where the Far East
   Meets the Far West
The Cosmopolitan City
The Cosmopolitan City of
   the West
The Cosmopolitan San Fran-
   cisco
The Cultural Center of the
   West
The Exposition City
The Financial Center of the
   West
The Financial Center of the
   World
The Gateway to the Far
   East
The Gateway to the Orient
The Golden City
The Golden Gate City

The High Rise City
The Market of Three Bar-
barian Tribes
The Mushroom City
The Nation's Western Capital
The Old Gold Hill
The Paris of America
The Paris of the West
The Phoenix of the Pacific
The Poor Man's Paradise
The Port O' Missing Men
The Port of Gold
The Queen City
The Queen City of the Pacific
The Queen City of the Pacific
Coast
The Queen City of the West
The Queen of the Pacific
The Sand Hills of the Eastern
Barbarians
The Suicide Capital of the
United States
The Timeless Wonderland
The True Capital of the
West
The United Nations' Confer-
ence Center (United Na-
tions Conference on Inter-
national Organization of
46 nations opened April
25, 1945)
The Western Gate

SAN JOSE
Business Center of Busy
Northern California
California's First City
The Garden City

SAN LEANDRO
The Cherry City of Cali-
fornia
The Home of Sunshine and
Flowers

SAN LUIS OBISPO
Southern California's Big
"Oh"
The City of the Mountain
Peaks

SAN MARCOS
The City in the Valley of
Discovery

SAN MATEO
The Center of Transportation
to All Points
The City with the Nation's
Most Perfect Year 'Round
Climate
The Growing Center of Ad-
ministrative Offices
The Retail Shopping Center
of the Peninsula

SAN PABLO
The City of Pride and Progress
The Little City with the Big
Inferiority Complex

SAN RAFAEL
The City of Health (St.
Raphael, Patron Saint of
Good Health)
The City where Past and
Future Make a Prosperous
Present
The Heart of Marvelous
Marin County
The Missing City of Marin

SANTA ANA
The City of Resources

SANTA BARBARA
California's Enchanting City
California's World Famous
All-Year Resort
The Channel City
The City by the Sea
The City of Rare Beauty and
Tranquility
The City Proud of Its Historic
Treasures
The City where Hospitality
Is a Tradition
The Hospitable City
The Newport of the Pacific
The Queen of the Missions
(Mission Santa Barbara
founded 1786)
The Riviera of the Pacific

SANTA CLARA
California's First Ranking
Country
California's Great Breeding
Ground for Industry

The Center of Innovative
Technology

SANTA CRUZ
Scenic California's Scenic
Playground
The City where the Red-
woods Meet the Sea
The Land at the End of
the Rainbow
The World's Most Famous
Playground

SANTA MARIA
The Missile Capital of the
West
The Valley of the Gardens
(numerous seed farms)
Your Site in the Sun

SANTA MONICA
The City for Oceans of Fun
The City where the Moun-
tains Meet the Sea
The City where Wilshire
Boulevard Meets the
Pacific
The Convention City of the
World
The Picture Postcard Bay

SANTA PAULA
The Lemon Capital
The Lemon City

SANTA ROSA
The City Designed for Living

SAUSALITO
The Greenwich Village of
the West (literary grounds)

SEASIDE
The Gateway to the Beautiful
Monterey Peninsula

SELMA
The Home of the Peach
The Raisin Capital of the
World

SHAFTER
The Potato Capital

SILVER LAKES
The New Recreational Resort
Community

SOLEDAD
The Gateway to Recreation

SOLVANG
Little Denmark (established
in 1912 as a settlement
for Danes; has Danish
church, college and
schools)

SOUTH GATE
The Model Industry City

SOUTH SAN FRANCISCO
The City where Industry
Makes a Good Neighbor
The Diversified City
The Home of Opportunity
The Hub of Commercial
Activities
The Industrial City

STOCKTON
A Variety of Recreational
Opportunities
California's Inland Harbor
(on Stockton channel and
San Joaquin River)
The Center of California
The City that Has Something
for You
The Gateway to the San
Joaquin Valley
The Heart of America's
Number One Agricultural
Area
The Home of Diamond Wal-
nuts
The Industrial and Distributing
Center of the Pacific Coast
Empire
The Industrial Hub of the
West
The Industrial Link to the
West
The Manufacturing City of
the Pacific
The New Distribution Center
of the West

SUISAN CITY
Solano County's Twin Cities
(with Fairfield)
The Historic Community
The Twin Cities (with Fair-
field, Calif.)

SUNNYVALE
The City with a Built-In
Future

SYLMAR
The Top of the San Fernando
Valley

TAFT
The Oil City

TEHAMA
The Little City of the Big
Trees

TERMINAL ISLAND
A Little Sea by the Sea of
Happy Rest and Reverie

THOUSAND OAKS
The Bel Air of Conejo

TORRANCE
The Modern Industrial City

TRACY
The City where Agriculture
and Industries Meet

TURLOCK
The City Growing with Agri-
culture, Industry and
Education
The City with a Healthy
Climate

TWENTY-NINE PALMS
The Northernmost Oasis in
America

UKIAH
The Home of Bartlett Pears

UPLAND
The City of Good Health,
Living and Business

The Western Shangri-La

VACAVILLE
The City of Excellent Educational Opportunities
The Gateway to the North-
west

VALLEJO
The Navy Town (home of
Mare Island Naval Ship-
yard and California Mari-
time Academy)

VENTURA
The Poinsettia City

VICTORVILLE
The Key City of the High
Desert

VISALIA
The City of Industry

WALNUT CREEK
The Paradise in a Nut Shell

WATERFORD
The City of a Colorful Past
and a Promising Future
The City of Water, Land and
Good Climate
The City where there's Room
to Stretch
The City with an Open Door
to Industry and Progress
The City with Room for
Growth and Space to Relax
The Community Away from
the Crowded Areas
The Window to the Future

WATSONVILLE
The Apple City
The Strawberry Capital of
the World

WEST COVINA
The Headquarters City of
East San Gabriel Valley

WESTMINSTER
The Heart of Orange County

WHITTIER
A Municipal Poem of Beauty,
Sunshine, Health, Pros-
perity and Happiness
The Best Town of Its Age
in this Glorious Climate
The Finest Home and
Cultural Community in
Southern California
The Home Town of Richard
Nixon
The Magic Little City
(founded in 1887 by
Quakers)
The Quaker City (founded
in 1887 by Quakers)
Ye Friendly Towne

WILLITS
The Good Little Town

WILMINGTON
The Heart of the Harbor

YORBA LINDA
The Birthplace of President
Richard Nixon
The Land of Gracious Living

YUBA CITY
The Peach Bowl of the U.S.

COLORADO

ALAMOSA
The City at the Crossroads
of Trans-Americas High-
way and the Navajo Trail

ARVADA
The City of Recreation and
Parks

ASPEN
Ski Capital U.S.A.

AURORA
The Best of Many Worlds
The Gateway to the Rockies

BOULDER
The City where Mountains
and Plains Meet (at the
foot of the Flatirons which
rises 1,000 feet above the
city)
The Gateway to Colorado's
Scenic Region
The Gateway to Roosevelt
National Forest and Rocky
Mountain National Park
The Home of the University
of Colorado
The Wonderland of America

BRIGHTON
Brighton's Future Is Bright

BRUSH
America's Sugar Bowl (Great
Western Beet Sugar Fac-
tory, beet slicing capacity
about 1,600 tons daily)

CENTRAL CITY
The Richest Square Mile on
Earth

COLORADO SPRINGS
The City of Sunshine
The Little Lunnon (London)
(many Britishers live
here)
The Newport of the West

DENVER
The Capital City (population
about 506,000)
The Capital of the Rocky
Mountain Empire
The City in the Clouds
The City of the Plains
The City where Men and
Mountains Meet
The City where there's Fun
for Everyone
The Climate Capital of the
World
The Convention City
The Dynamic Metropolis of
the Rocky Mountain Em-
pire
The Friendly City in the Sky

The Gateway to the Rockies
The Industrial, Commercial
and Cultural Capital
The Little Capital
The Mile High City (alt.
5,280 ft.)
The Mining Town with a
Heart
The Old Roaring Capital of
the Mountainest West
The Queen City of the
Plains
The Queen City of the
Rockies
The Queen City of the West
The Sports Capital of the
West
The Western Capital
The White Collar City

DURANGO
The Switzerland of America
(altitude 6,505 feet)

EMPIRE
The Eastern Approach to
Berthoud Pass

ESTES PARK
Resort Town, U.S.A. (near
Rocky Mountain National
Park)

FORT COLLINS
Eden of the Closest State
to Heaven
The City of Beautiful Parks
The City of Magnificent
Mountains
The City of Panoramic
Boulevards
The City of Plentiful Plains
The Fascinating Foothills
City (about 40 miles
from Fort Collins Moun-
tain Park)
The Gateway to the Poudre
(River)
The Home of the Colorado
Aggies (Colorado Agri-
cultural and Mechanical
College)
The Lamb and Cattle Capital

of the West (large lamb-
feeding center)
The Lilac City
The Safest Spot in the World

FORT MORGAN
The City of Lights
The City where Friendly
People Get Together

GEORGETOWN
The Historic Doorway to
Colorado's Finest See and
Ski Country
The Silver Queen of the
Rockies (at the foot of the
Continental Divide)
The Ski Capital of Colorado
(eight major ski areas
within 20 to 45 minutes
drive)

GLENWOOD SPRINGS
The Kissingen of America

GRAND JUNCTION
America's Most Radioactive
City
The All-American City with
Foresight
The City with Foresight
The Headquarters City
The Hub City of Western
Colorado and Eastern Utah
The Hub of the Scenic West
(Grand Mesa National
Forest)
The Uranium Capital of the
World
The Vacation Center of a
Fabulous Land of Contrasts

IDAHO SPRINGS
The Gold Rush City
The Ideal Location for a
Year-Round Vacation
The Skiing Center of America

LAKEWOOD
The City that Has It All

LEADVILLE
The Cloud City (altitude

Colorado Cities 32

10,188 feet, claimed to
be the highest incorporated
city in the U.S.)
The Magic City
Two Miles High but Miles
Ahead

LIMON
The Gateway to the Rockies

LOVELAND
America's Sweetheart City
(popular mailing address
for valentines)
The Sweetheart Town

MONTE VISTA
The Potato Capital of the
West

OURAY
The Gem City of the
Rockies
The Gem of the Rockies
The Most Spectacular and
Beautiful Part of the
U.S.
The Opal of America
The Switzerland of America

PUEBLO
Colorado's Second City
The City of Fountains
The City of Homes and
Industry
The Fountain City
The Manufacturing City of
the Rocky Mountain
Region
The Steel City of the West
(plant of Colorado Fuel
and Iron Corp.)

RIFLE
The Oil Shale Capital of
the World

ROCKY FORD
The Melon Capital of the
World

SALIDA
Nature's Wonderland

The City Atop the Nation's
Roof Garden (altitude
7,038 feet)
The City in the Valley of
the Arkansas
The City of Dreams
The City on the Highway to
Heaven (altitude 7,038
feet)
The Closest State to Heaven
The Crossroads to Wonder-
land
The Gem City
The Gem of the Ocean
The Heart of the Rockies
The Hospitality City of the
Rockies
The Lovely Gateway to the
Passes
The Portal to the Quint
States
The Roof Garden of America
(altitude 7,038 feet)
The Sportsman's Paradise
The Town with a Heart

STEAMBOAT SPRINGS
Ski Town, U.S.A.
The Gateway to the Routt
National Forest
The Winter and Summer
Playground

STERLING
The Hub of the Denver-Julesburg Oil Production Territory

TRINIDAD
The City where the Santa Fe
Trail of the Prairies
Meets the Mountains of
the Historical West

VAIL
Colorado's Premier Year-
Round Resort
Ten Square Miles of the
World's Finest Skiing
The Baby of the Colorado
Ski Resorts
The City where the Discovery
Is People

The International Village
The International Village of
the Mountain's Base
The Unique Year-round
Resort
The Valley of the Condo-
miniums
The World of Warmth

VICTOR
The City of Mines (near
large producing mines)

WALSH
The Broom Corn Center

WHEAT RIDGE
The Booming Community
with a Balanced Economy
The Carnation Capital of
the World

WINTER PARK
The Powder Snow Capital
of Colorado

CONNECTICUT

ANSONIA
The Industrial Heart of the
Naugatuck Valley

BERLIN
The Pleasant New England
Town

BETHLEHEM
Connecticut's Christmas
Town

BRANFORD
The Gateway to the New
England Shoreline

BRIDGEPORT
The Essen of America
The Industrial Capital of
America
The Industrial Capital of

Connecticut
The Park City
The Proud City
The Recreation Center for
Generations

BRISTOL
Mum City (flowers)
The City of Opportunity
The Clock Center of the
World (numerous clock
factories, site of Ameri-
can Clock and Watch
Museum)

BROOKLYN
The Home of the Israel Putnam State Monument

CLINTON
The Truly Colonial Town

DANBURY
The City in the Country
The Gateway to Candlewood
Lake
The Gateway to New England
The Hat City (numerous hat
factories; first one opened
in 1780)
The Hat City of the World
The Space Age City

DANIELSON
The Crossroads of Industrial
New England

DARIEN
The Bedroom Town
The Residential Town on Long
Island Sound
The Town to Live In

EAST HAMPTON
Jingle Town U.S.A. (made
90 percent of the small
bells, first factory 1808)
The Bell Town (site of bell
factories since 1808)
The Bell Town of America

EAST WINDSOR HILL
The Town to Grow With

FAIRFIELD
A Fine Place to Live

FARMINGTON
The Classic New England
Village
The Mother of Towns (set-
tled 1640)

GREENWICH
The Friendliest Town
(foster children invited
for supper)
The Gateway to New England

GROTON
The Home of the Nuclear
Submarine
The Submarine Capital of
the World
The World's Submarine
Capital (the Nautilus first
atomic-powered submarine
built here and launched
January 21, 1954)

GUILFORD
The City where the Heritage
of the Past Lends Warmth
to the Present
The Shore Village (on Long
Island Sound)
The Shrine of Old Homes

HARTFORD
The Capital City (popula-
tion about 146, 500)
The Charter Oak City (the
constitution of Connecticut
hidden in hollow of an
oak tree)
The City Beautiful
The Convention City of the
East
The East Coast Megalopolis
The Gateway to Connecticut
The Insurance Capital of
the World
The Insurance City (home
office of about 40 in-
surance companies with
combined assets over
12 billion)

The Major Insurance City
The Nation's Insurance
Capital

LITCHFIELD
The Ultimate City
The Williamsburg of the
North

MANCHESTER
The City of Village Charm
(in the valley of the Connecticut River)

MERIDEN
Daffodil Center of Connecticut
The Complete Shopping Center
The Heart of Connecticut
The Silver City (home of
International Silver Co.
and other silverware
manufacturers)
The Silver City of the World

MIDDLETOWN
The Forest City

MYSTIC
The City where Yesterday
Meets Tomorrow
The Cradle of Square Riggers
(famous shipbuilding center
about 1850's)
The Home of Yachtsmen
The Port of Last Call
The Seaport Village (developed
by Marine Historical Asso-
ciation)
Williamsburg of the Sea

NAUGATUCK
The Hub of Connecticut's
Naugatuck River Valley
The Onion City

NEW BRITAIN
The Hardware City (pro-
duction of builders'
hardware)
The Hardware City of the
World
The Wonderful Place to
Live, Work, Play

NEW CANAAN
  The Most Exclusive Residential Town in the East
  The Next Station to Heaven
  The Richest Town in the World

NEW HAVEN
  Connecticut's Elm City
  One of the First American Cities of the Industrial Age
  The City of Elms
  The City of the Future
  The Elm City
  The Gateway to New England
  The Home of the New York Giants
  The Yankee Athens (site of Yale University)

NEW LONDON
  The City Just a Step from the Past, in Step with the Present and Stepping Toward the Future
  The Hills Against the Sky Town
  The Ideal City in All Seasons
  The Submarine Capital of the World
  The Whaling City (industry centered here from 1784 to 1850)
  The Utopia of the North Atlantic

NORWALK
  The Athens of New England
  The Charming Spot in which to Live and Work
  The City of Colonial Charm
  The City of Homes
  The City of Science
  The City of Your Future
  The Clam Town
  The Community of Substance
  The Derby City (first derby hat in the U.S. made here)
  The Fastest Growing Town in New England
  The Gateway of New England

  The Gateway to All New England
  The Hat Town
  The Highest Hub of Fairfield County
  The Home of Yankee Doodle
  The New England Garden Spot
  The Place to Live
  The Progressive City with a Bright Future
  The Rose of New England
  The Shoe and Slipper City
  The Thrifty New England Community Steeped in Colonial Tradition and Democracy
  The Town with a Heart
  The Twin City (with South Norwalk)
  The Well Balanced City with Opportunities for All
  The World's Oyster Capital

NORWICH
  The Rose of New England (famous Memorial Rose Garden honoring World War II dead)

PAWCATUCK
  The Land of Sand, Sea and Sun

ROCKVILLE
  The Loom City

SOUTH NORWALK
  The Twin City (with Norwalk, Conn.)

SOUTH WINDSOR
  The Town with Grow Power

SOUTHBURY
  The Heartland of Colonial Connecticut

STAMFORD
  The City in Step with Tomorrow
  The City of Research
  The Cultural Hub

The Fastest Growing City in
the County (Fairfield
County)
The Fastest Growing Munici-
pality in the State
The Home of the Metered
Maid System
The Impressive Residential
and Research Community
The Lock City (Yale and
Towne factory was located
here)
The Research City

STRATFORD
The City at the Gateway to
New England
The City for Work, Life
or Pleasure
The Town with a Future
(population about 51, 700)

TERRYVILLE
The Lock Town of America

THOMASTON
The Clock City (Seth Thomas
clocks made 1813)

THOMPSON
The Indianapolis of the East
(Thompson Speedway)

TORRINGTON
The Most Accessible City

WALLINGFORD
The Thriving Well Balanced
Industrial Town

WATERBURY
The American Brass City
The Brass Center of the
World
The Brass City (large brass
industry)
The Center of Industrial
Development in Western
Connecticut
The City where Things
Are Happening
The Crossroads of Con-
necticut

The Gateway to the Litchfield
Hills
The Industrial City
The Key City of Naugatuck
Valley

WESTPORT
The Christmas Tree Town
The Town of Homes

WETHERSFIELD
The Rubber City

WILLIMANTIC
The Eastern Connecticut
Center
The Thread City (mill of
American Thread Company)

WILTON
The Town Among the Willows

WINDSOR
Connecticut's First Town
First in Connecticut
The Heart of the New Eng-
land Tobacco Farm Land

WINSTED
The Gateway to the Berk-
shires
The Laurel City (mountain
laurel)

DELAWARE

DOVER
The Capital City (population
about 23, 200, state capital
in 1777)
The Capital of the First
State
The First City of the First
State (became capital
May 12, 1777)
The Home of Latex Rubber

MILFORD
The Heart of Delaware

NEW CASTLE
  The Gateway to the Miss
    Universe Highway

REHOBOTH BEACH
  Delaware's Summer Capital
    (popular summer resort
    on the Atlantic Ocean)
  The Nation's Summer
    Capital (because of the
    large number of vaca-
    tionists from Washington,
    D.C.)
  The Nation's Vacation
    Capital
  Washington-by-the-Sea (near
    Washington, D.C.)

WILMINGTON
  Dupont Town (home of the
    E. I. du Pont de
    Nemours & Co.)
  Dupontonia (see above)
  Quaker Town (formerly
    used because of Quaker
    residents)
  The Chemical Capital of
    the World
  The Financial Center of the
    Del-Mar-Va Peninsula
  The First City of the First
    State (first settlement
    established by the Swedes
    in the territory which
    later was the first to
    ratify the Constitution)
  The Heart of the Harbor
  The Port of Personal
    Service (on Delaware
    River)

DISTRICT OF COLUMBIA

WASHINGTON
  America's First City
  America's Last Colony
  Capital City, U.S.A.
  The Capital City
  The Capital of a Great Nation

The Capital of America
The Capital of Miserable Huts
The Capital of Our Country
The Capital of the Vast Re-
  public
The Center of History in the
  Making
The City Beautiful
The City for Everybody
The City in a Forest
The City of a Thousand
  Thrills
The City of Conversation
The City of Houses Without
  Streets
The City of Inspiration
The City of Lost Footsteps
The City of Magnificent
  Distances (so-called by
  Jose Correo de Serra,
  once Minister from Portu-
  gal)
The City of Receptions
The City of Streets Without
  Houses
The City of Trees Without
  Houses
The City of Washington
The City that Lost Its Magic
The Commercial Empire of
  the United States
The Court City of a Nation
The Crossroads of the World
The Diplomatic Capital of the
  World
The Embryonic Capital
The Enchanted City on the
  Potomac
The Executive City
The Federal Capital
The Federal City
The Federal Seat
The Federal Site
The Federal Town
The Foundling Capital
The Gas House of the Nation
The Grand Emporium of the
  West
The Grand Metropolis
The Great Dismal
The Great Serbonian Bog
The Great White City
The Heart of America

The Magnificent Capital
The Metropolis of the
Country
The Metropolitan City
The Mighty Capital
The Most Beautiful City in
America
The Mud-Hole City
The National Capital
The Nation's Capital
The Nation's Headquarters
The Nation's State
The New Capital
The New City of Washington
The New Settlement
The News Capital of the
World
The Phone Capital of the
World (128 phones for
every 100 people)
The Political Front
The Problem Capitol of the
World
The Second Rome
The Virgin Capital
The Wilderness City
The Wonderland on the
Potomac
The World Center of Inter-
national Activities
The World's Most Beautiful
City
The Young Capital
Washington, B.C.--Before
Corn

FLORIDA

ANNA MARIA
The Choicest Spot in All
Florida
The Island You'll Love

APALACHICOLA
Florida's Friendly Old City
with a New Future
The City of the Friendly
People
The Gateway to the

Apalachicola System
The Gateway to the Inter-
coastal Waterway
The Natural Port City
The Old City with a New
Future
The Oyster Capital of Florida
The Sportman's Paradise

APOPKA
The City Beautiful
The City of Families, Faith
and Friendship
The Fern City of Florida
The Home of the Famous
Large-Mouth Bass
The Plant Capital of Central
Florida (hundreds of acres
of nursery plants)

ARCADIA
Living Gets Better Each Year
in Arcadia and De Soto
County
The City of Character in a
Land of Beauty
The Land of Contrast

ASTATULA
The Center of Central Florida
(on Lake Harris)

AUBURNDALE
The City in the Heart of the
Citrus Belt and Holiday
Highlands

AVON PARK
The City Nature Has En-
dowed with Beauty
The City of Sparkling Blue
Lakes
The City of White Sandy
Beaches
The City with the Mile Long
Mall
The Friendliest Little City
The Jacaranda City with the
Mile Long Mall

BARTOW
The City of Oaks
The City of Oaks and Azaleas

BELLEVIEW
    Florida's Last Frontier
    The City where You Can
        Have Fun and Live Better
    The Gateway to the Tropics
    The Ideal Location for Vaca-
        tion and Home
    The Land of Opportunity
    The Progressive Community
    The Progressive Community
        with a Bright Future
    The Region of Great Natural
        Wonders

BLOUNTSTOWN
    The Agricultural and Timber
        Empire (richest timber
        producing area of Florida)
    The Hub of the Great Apa-
        lachicola Valley
    The Kingdom of Opportunity
    The Paradise of Fishing,
        Hunting and Swimming

BOCA RATON
    The Golden City of the Gold
        Coast
    The Real Garden Spot
    The Splendid Community
    The Water Polo Capital of
        Florida

BONIFAY
    The Ideal Spot for Retire-
        ment
    The Right Climate for Busi-
        ness and Family Living

BONITA SPRINGS
    The Fisherman's Paradise
    The Vacationer's Dream-
        land

BOYNTON BEACH
    A Fine Place to Live
    The Gateway to "Sailfish
        Alley"

BRADENTON
    Florida's Water Wonder-
        land
    South Florida's Oldest
        Pioneer Village

Sun'n Fun Land
The Friendly City
The Twin Cities of the Lower
    Sun-coast (with Sarasota,
    Fla.)

BRANDON
    A Good Place to Live--Better
    The Sightseeing Hub of the
        West Coast of Central
        Florida

BRANFORD
    The City of Beauty
    The City of Beauty on the
        Suwannee River

BROOKSVILLE
    The City of Seven Hills
    The Home of the Tangerine
    The Sunrise of Opportunity

CAPE CANAVERAL
    The Salt Water Trout Capital
        of the World
    The Space Hub

CAPE CORAL
    Florida's Waterfront Water-
        land
    The City of the Future
    The City with a Future
    The Riviera of the Southeast
        U.S.A.
    The Waterfront Wonderland

CAPE KENNEDY
    The Spaceport, U.S.A.
        (rockets, satellites)

CARRABELLE
    A Great Place to Visit, A
        Wonderful Place to Live
    The City in the Heart of
        Florida's Gulf Fishing
    The City where Civic Pride
        Is City-Wide
    The Fisherman's Paradise

CASEY KEY
    Florida's West Coast's
        Finest Vacation Spot

CHATTAHOOCHEE
  Hub City of Good Living
  Hub City of Recreation
  The Hub City of Transpor-
    tation

CHIEFLAND
  The Watermelon Capital
  The Watermelon Center
    Festival

CLEARWATER
  Florida's Newest Conven-
    tion City
  The City where They Come
    to Play and Decide to
    Stay
  The City with a Sparkle
  The Home of the World
    Champion Clearwater
    Bombers
  The Springtime City
  The Winter Home of the
    National League Phila-
    delphia Phillies (baseball
    club)

CLERMONT
  The Gem of the Hills (amid
    17 lakes and hills)
  The Hub of Florida

CLEWISTON
  America's Sweetest Town
    (sugar cane fields)
  Capital of Florida's Sugar
    Industry (largest sugar
    mill in the U.S.)
  The City in the Heart of
    the Everglades
  The Progressive Community
  The Queen City of Florida's
    Sugar Bowl

COCOA
  The Citrus Center (shipping
    point for Indian River
    Citrus fruits)
  The Salt Water Trout Capital
    of the World

COCOA BEACH
  Missile Land, U.S.A.

The Center of Activity for
  America's Space Program
The City at the Portal to the
  Universe
The Cosmopolitan Community
  with the Warmth of a
  Small Town
The Resort Area of Cape
  Kennedy
The Surfing Capital of the
  South (wave formations)
The World's Best Beach

CORAL GABLES
  Florida's Showcase Commu-
    nity
  The City Beautiful (part of
    Greater Miami)
  The City Planned for Perfect
    Living
  The Corporate Capital of
    America

CORAL SPRINGS
  One of the Last Pieces of
    Gold on the Gold Coast

CRESCENT CITY
  The Gateway to the Bass
    Capital of the World

CRESTVIEW
  The Center for Giant Blue-
    berry Bushes
  The Hub City in the Heart of
    Florida's West Country
  The Hub City of Northwest
    Florida
  The Real Paradise for Family
    Living

CROSS CITY
  The City Way Down Upon the
    Suwannee River

DADE CITY
  The Home of the Pioneer
    Florida Museum

DANIA
  The Antiques Center of the
    South
  The City where Life Is

Worth Living
The Cruise Capital of the
World
The Tomato Capital of the
World
The Tomato Center of the
World
The Tourist Mecca and
Antiques Center of the
South

DAVENPORT
Florida's Biggest Little
Town
The Town in the Gateway
to the Beautiful Red
Section of Florida
The Town on the Ridge in
the Heart of Orangeland

DAYTONA BEACH
Florida's Newest Metro-
politan Industrial Area
Florida's Vacation Capital
Florida's Year Round Play-
ground
The All-Year Vacationland
The Fun Capital of the
South
The Ideal Year-Round
Resort
The Prettiest Resort in
the World
The Resort Area
The Summer Fun Capital
of the South (founded
1870)
The World's Largest Family
Resort
The World's Most Famous
Beach (23 miles long,
500 feet wide at low tide)

DE BARY
The Fastest Growing
Friendly Retirement Com-
munity

DEERFIELD BEACH
The City in the Heart of
the Gold Coast
The Heart of the Gold
Coast

The Miracle City of the Gold
Coast
The Northern Gateway to
Broward County

DE LAND
The Athens of Florida (home
of Stetson University)
The City Located in the Very
Heart of Florida
The Home of Stetson Uni-
versity
The Home of Stetson Uni-
versity and Florida Mili-
tary School
The Land of Flowers
The Land of Sunshine

DELRAY BEACH
Florida's Dissimilar Resort
The City in Florida with a
Difference
The Island of Distinctive
Resort Life
The Luxurious City of Tra-
ditional Simplicity

DESTIN
The Billfishing Capital of
Northwest Florida
The City in the Heart of
Northwest Florida's
Miracle Strip
The City where Everybody
Catches Fish
The Luckiest Fishing Village
in the World where Every-
body Catches Fish
The World's Luckiest Fishing
Village (fishing area for
red snapper, etc)
The World's Most Beautiful
Waters and the Whitest
Sand Beaches

DUNEDIN
Florida's Boating Capital on
the Gulf
The City of Beautiful Homes

DUNNELLON
Friendly Dunnellon
Home of Rainbow Springs

(largest in Florida)
Home of the World's Largest
Bass
The Community where Busi-
ness and Pleasure Live
in Complete Harmony
The Community where You
Work and Play the Same
Day
The Kingdom of the Sea
The Kingdom of the Sun
(on the Withlacoochee
River)

EAU GALLIE
The Gateway to the Missile
Test Center
The Gateway to the Space
Program
The Harbor City (land-
locked harbor on the
Indian River)
The Progressive City

EDGEWATER
The City of Progress
The City on Florida's
Famous East Coast and
the Indian River
The Gateway to Nova (Nova
Industrial Area)
The Place in the Sun to
Visit, to Play, to Work,
to Live
The World's Safest Bathing
Beach

ENGLEWOOD
The City where Life Is
Lived Every Day of the
Year
Your Tropical "Home Town"

EUSTIS
The Center of Our Nation's
Playground (on east
shore of Lake Eustis)
The City for a Vacation or
a Lifetime of Real
Living
The City in the Heart of
Central Florida's Water
Wonderland

The Orange Capital of the
World
The Winter and Summer Va-
cation Center of Florida
The World Capital of the
Orange-Growing Industry

EVERGLADES
The Fisherman's Paradise
The Western Water Gate
(the way to 2,100 square
miles of Everglades Na-
tional Park)
The Western Water Gateway
to Everglades National
Park)
The Wonderland of the Ten
Thousand Islands
The Wonderland of the
10,000 Islands and Southern
Collier County

FERNANDINA BEACH
The Buccaneer City (favorite
port for pirates)
The Ocean City (on Amelia
Island)

FORT LAUDERDALE
Florida's Tropical Paradise
The All-Year Vacation City
The Beach that Made Fort
Lauderdale Famous
The Boating Capital of the
World
The City Beautiful
The City of Homes
The City of Sunshine
The Friendly Town
The Gateway to the Ever-
glades
The Heart of the Florida
Lower East Coast
The Home Town in the
American Tropics
The Other Place to Go in
Florida
The Place to Go in Florida
The Place to Let Yourself
Go in Florida
The Sunshine City
The Tropical Wonderland
The Venice of America (more

than 165 miles of lagoons,
canals and rivers flow
within its boundaries)
The World's Most Richly
Endowed Resort Area

FORT MEADE
The City in Florida's Fun-
Filled Holiday Highlands
The City in the Heart of
Florida's Citrus, Phos-
phate, Recreation,
History, Cattle

FORT MYERS
The City of Homes
The City of Palms (Thomas
Alva Edison advocated
the planting of palms
throughout the city)
The City where the Ameri-
can Tropics Begin
The Family Play Area
The Gladioli Capital of the
World
The Jewel City of the
Florida West
The New Resort Area of
Florida

FORT MYERS BEACH
The Safest Beach in the
World
The Tropical Island Wonder-
land in the Gulf of
Mexico (on Estero Island)

FORT PIERCE
Florida's Finest Agricultural
Industrial and Resort
Community
The Capitol of Florida's
Treasure Coast (about
two millions in Spanish
and U.S. gold was re-
covered in 1964)
The City in the Heart of
the World Famous
Indian River Citrus
Country
The Vacationland for the
Whole Family

FORT WALTON
The Heart of Florida's Miracle Strip

FROSTPROOF
The Friendly City of the
Highlands

GAINESVILLE
Florida's Center for Science,
Education, Medicine
North Central Florida's
Shopping Center
North Central Florida's
Shopping Headquarters
The Home of the University
of Florida
The Natural Trading Area
for North Central Florida
The Northern Gateway to
Central Florida
The University City (Univer-
sity of Florida)

GROVELAND
A Good Place to Live, Work
and Play
The City in the Center of
Sunland

HAINES CITY
The City in the Heart of
Florida
The Community where You
Can Live, Work, Relax
The Gateway to the Holiday
Highlands
The Heart of Florida
The Inland Paradise of
Florida
The Picturesque Heart of
Central Florida

HALLANDALE
The City where Your Dreams
of Florida Living Come
True
The Home of the Florida
Derby

HASTINGS
Florida's Potato Capital (multi-
million dollar industry)

HIALEAH
Florida's Fastest Growing
City
The City for Family Living
at Its Best
The Fastest Growing Indus-
trial Area in the South-
east
The South Florida Hub
The Taxpayer's Haven

HIGH SPRINGS
The Ideal Living City in
the Heart of Florida

HOBE SOUND
The Gateway to the Famous
Gold Coast

HOLLY HILL
Small Enough to be Neigh-
borly, Large Enough to
Supply Your Every Need
The City in the Heart of
the Daytona Beach Re-
sort Area
The City with a Heart

HOLLYWOOD
Florida's Golfingest City
The Dream City Come True
The Heart of the Gold Coast
There's Something for Every-
one in Hollywood

HOMESTEAD
The City of Bicycles

IMMOKALEE
The Watermelon Capital
The Watermelon Capital of
Florida

INDIANTOWN
The Community Planned
for Pleasant Living

ISLAMORADA
The City in the Florida
Keys
The Crown Jewel of the
Florida Keys
The Place that Has Everything

The Sportfishing Capital of
the World
The Vacation Paradise for
the Whole Family

JACKSONVILLE
Florida's Gateway City
Florida's Hub of Fun
Jax
The Biggest City in Area in
the Free World (827
square miles)
The Bold New City of the
South
The City of Pleasant Memo-
ries
The City on the Go
The Colorful Key Center for
Defense Activities
The Communication Center
of Florida
The Deep Water Port
The Distribution Center of
the Southeast
The Finance Center of Florida
The Friendly City of Endless
Charm
The Gate City of Florida
(world port and commer-
cial center)
The Gateway City
The Gateway to All Florida
The Hartford of the South
(numerous insurance
companies)
The Hub of Fun
The Hub of History
The Hub of Progress
The Ideal Convention City
The Ideal Place to Work,
Live, Play
The Ideal Year Round Vaca-
tion Spot
The Industrial and Distribu-
tion Center
The Insurance Center of the
South
The Key National Defense Center
The Naval Center of the
South
The Popular Vacationland
The Tourist and Convention
Center

The World's Finest Beach

JAY
The Oil Capital of Florida
(a billion of gallons a
year)

JENSEN BEACH
The Friendly Community in
Martin County
The Sea Turtle Capital of
the World

JUPITER
The First City in Famous
Palm Beach County
The Gateway to Tropical
Florida's First Resort

KEY BISCAYNE
The Island Paradise
The Island Paradise Minutes
from Miama

KEY COLONY BEACH
The Complete Vacation
Resort City
The Gem of Florida's Keys

KEY WEST
America's Devil's Island
America's Singapore
America's Southernmost
City (county seat of
Monroe County)
The Center of America's
Clear Havana Industry
The Cigar Capital of the
World (popular in the
1870's)
The Island City of Old
World Charm
The Island of Contrast
The Nation's Other Capital
(Nixon's home and office)
The Nation's Southernmost
City (near extreme end
of Florida Keys)
The Old Island--The New
Island
The Southernmost City
in the Continental United
States

KISSIMMEE
Florida's Ranch Country
The Cow Capital of Florida

LA BELLE
The City Among the Oaks
The City at the Crossroads
of Southwest Florida
The City where the Fun of
Living Comes "Naturally"
The Tranquil Living in a
Natural Paradise

LAKE ALFRED
One of Florida's Finest
Smaller Communities
The City at the Crossroads
of Holiday Highlands
The City in the Heart of the
Citrus Area

LAKE CITY
Florida's New Gateway
The Forestry Capital of
Florida
The Highway Hub (two inter-
state routes, five primary
highways)
The Hub of North Central
Florida's Scenic Wonder-
land
The Lovely Land of Gracious
Living

LAKE HAMPTON
Florida's Complete Family
Outdoor Recreation Center

LAKE MARY
The Hidden Jewel of Central
Florida
The Village Idea for Retire-
ment, for Raising a Family
and for Placid Everyday
Living
The Village Not for Tourists,
Not for Excitement but for
Modest Tranquil Healthful
Living

LAKE PLACID
The Caladium Capital of the
World (a tropical American

plant of the arum
family)
The Center of the Caladium
Bulb Growing Area
The Economically Stable
Community
The Roof Garden of Florida

LAKE WALES
Florida's Attraction Showcase
The City of the Carillon
(the Bok Tower, 71 bells
weighing from 12 pounds
to 11 tons)

LAKE WEIR
The City for Family Fun in
the Florida Sun
The Very Center of the
Sunshine State
The Year Around Living at
Its Best

LAKE WORTH
The City of Lake Worth
where the Fun Begins
The City where the Tropics
Begin
The Gold Coast in Florida
The Heart of the Palm
Beaches (south of Palm
Beach)
The Recreation Mecca of
the Fabulous Southeastern
Coast of Florida
The Shuffleboard Capital
(32 shuffleboard courts
in the heart of the busi-
ness district)

LAKELAND
Florida's Eighth City
Polk County's Largest City
The City Nearer to Every-
where in Florida
The City of Lakes (19 lakes)
The City where Industry
Finds a Favorable Cli-
mate
The City Wonder-full for
Business
The Distribution Center

for 6,000,000 Floridians
The Heart of the Citrus In-
dustry
The Hub of Florida's Scenic
Wonderland (19 lakes
within city limits)
The Imperial Polk (in Polk
County)
The Vacation for a Lifetime
The Welcome to the City of
Lakes
The World's Citrus Center
(about 90 percent of the
crop is grown here)

LANTANA
The Gem on the Ocean

LARGO
Florida's Most Friendly Com-
munity
The Fair City (site of the
Pinellas County Fair and
Horse Show)
The Hub of Pinellas County

LEESBURG
The Action Center of Florida's
"Holiday Highlands"
The Community where the
Big Bass Bite
The Community with a Heart
in the Heart of Fabulous
Florida
The Watermelon Capital of
Florida

LEHIGH ACRES
Florida's Country Club Town
The Place for Sun, Fun and
Friendship

LONGBOAT KEY
Florida's West Coast Beach
Resort
The Casual Family Beach
Resort in the Center of
Florida's West Coast
The City on the Lazy Blue
Waters of the Gulf of
Mexico
The Everything Island

The World's Finest Natural
White Sand Beaches

MACCLENNY
North Florida's Gretna
Green (numerous mar-
riages performed by
judges)

MAITLAND
Central Florida's Most
Desirable Residential
Community
The Central Florida's City
of Big Opportunity
The Small Town with the
Bustling Activity of a
Growing City

MARATHON
The Fisherman's Paradise
The Heart of the Florida
Keys (second largest
community in Florida
Keys)
The Resort Town where
the Fisherman Is King

MARGATE
The City that Started with
a Plan

MASARYKTOWN
The Egg Center of Florida
(15,000,000 eggs a year)

MELBOURNE
Crossroads to the Universe
The Mid-Way City (midway
between Jacksonville
and Miami Fla.)
The Southern Entry to the
Cape Kennedy area

MERRITT ISLAND
The Launch Pad to Progress

MIAMI
Florida's Magic City
Greater Miami Means More
The Action City
The Air Capital of the
World

The City of Opportunities
The Gateway of the Americas
The Gateway to Latin
America
The Greatest Vacation Spot
of All
The Hub of All South
Florida's Sun-Fun Vacation-
land
The Ideal City for Year-
Round Vacations
The Jewel City of the Sun-
shine State
The Magic City
The Metropolis of South-
eastern Florida
The Paradise of the South
The Playground of the
Americas
The South Sea Isles of
America
The Sunshine Capital of the
World
The Town that Climate Built
The Tropic Metropolis
The Twin Cities (with Miami
Beach)
The Wonder City of the
World
The World's Largest Import-
Export Air Cargo Terminal

MIAMI BEACH
A Fun Festival Place
America's Year Round Play-
ground
The Billion Dollar Sandbar
(book by Polly Redford)
The Capital of Florida's En-
chanting Gold Coast
The City of Magic Islands
and Waterways
The City where the Palms
Meet the Sea
The City where the Welcome's
Warm as the Sunshine
The Convention Center of the
United States
The Fabulous City in the Sun
The Fun and Sun Capital
The Fun Capital
The Gold Coast City
The Great American Resort

The Magic City
The Photogenic Sun Capital
of the East
The Playground of the
Americas
The Riviera of America
The Shangri-La of the
Western Hemisphere
The Sister City in the Sun
The Sun and Fun Capital
of the World
The Twin Cities (with
Miami, Fla.)
The Vacationland of a
Thousand Pleasures
The World's Greatest
Resort
The Year Round Playground
of the Americas
Vacationland, U.S.A.

MONTICELLO
The Garden Spot of North-
west Florida (county
seat of Jefferson County)

MOUNT DORIA
The City with a Touch of
New England

NAPLES
One of the Fastest Growing
Resort Centers
The City on the Gulf (Gulf
of Mexico)
The Conservation City,
U.S.A.
The Gateway to the 10,000
Islands
The Refuge from Resorts

NEW PORT RICHEY
The Gateway to Tropical
Florida

NEW SMYRNA
The World's Largest
Safest Bathing Beach
(on the banks of the
North Indian River)

NEW SMYRNA BEACH
The Sun Shines on Fun in
New Smyrna Beach

NEWBERRY
The Little City of Big Opportunity

NICEVILLE
The Home of Eglin Air Force
Base (with Valparaiso,
Fla.)
Twin Cities on the Bay (with
Valparaiso, Fla.)

OCALA
The Center of the Sunshine
State
The Community where Suc-
cess Begins
The Heart of Florida's Fun-
Land (county seat of
Marion County)
The Heart of Florida's
Thoroughbred Country
The Home of Silver Springs
The Thoroughbred Capital of
Florida (outstanding horse
farms)

OCEAN CITY
The Home of Pure Water

OKEECHOBEE
The Chicago of the South
The Nation's Winter Vege-
table Garden and Sugar
Bowl
The Year-Round Sportsman's
Paradise (on Lake Okee-
chobee)

ORLANDO
Florida's City Beautiful
Florida's Transportation Hub
One of the Ten Fastest
Growing Communities
The Action Center of Florida
The Action City
The Action City Completely
Surrounded by Florida
The Attractions Capital of
the World
The Birthplace of Speed
The City Beautiful
The City Beautiful in the
Heart of Florida

The City of Abundant Cul-
tural Activities
The City of Scenic Beauty
The City of Year-Round
Recreational Opportunities
The City with Unexcelled
Opportunities for Good
Living
The Disney City
The Disney World City
The Fifth Fastest Growing
Metropolitan Area in the
Nation
The Growingest City in the
South
The Hub, the Heart, and
the Center of Florida
The Modern City on the
Move
The Very Heart of Florida
(largest inland city in
Florida)
The Very Heart of the Sun-
shine State

ORMAND-BY-THE-SEA
Retire, Relax, Relive

ORMOND BEACH
The Auto Racing Capital of
the World (old)
The Birthplace of Speed
(automobile races began
about 1902)
The Parrot's Paradise

PAHOKEE
The City with an Area of
Agricultural Achievement
The Garden of the Glades
The Nation's Sugar Bowl
The Sugar Bowl of America
The Winter Vegetable Capi-
tal of the U. S.

PALATKA
The City where Industry
and Recreation Meet
The Bass Capital of the
World
The City where Work and
Play Are Only Minutes
Away

The City with a Future
The Gem City

PALM BAY
The City in the Heart of the
Dynamic Cape Kennedy
Area
The City Programmed for
Progress

PALM BEACH
The Center of a Sportsman's
Paradise
The Golden Coast of Florida
The Home of the Winter
White House
The Mecca for Champions in
Many Fields
The Swing Is to Palm Beach
County
The World's Premier Winter
Resort (a 14 mile island
connected by several
bridges to West Palm
Beach)

PALM SPRINGS
The Delightful Residential
Community in the Heart
of the Palm Beaches
The Garden Spot of the Palm
Beaches
The Ideal Family Community

PALMETTO
The Gateway to Tropical
Florida
The Major Shipping Point for
South Florida Growers
The West Coast Gateway City

PANAMA CITY
The City in Beautiful Bay
County (on St. Andrew
Bay)
The City of Destiny
The City on the Cool Gulf
Coast (an indentation of
the Gulf of Mexico)
The City with the World's
Whitest Beaches
The Fun in the Sun City
The Industrial and Resort
Center

The Pearl of the Florida
  Panhandle
The Year-Round Beachfront
  Condominium Resort

PENSACOLA
  Florida's City of Five Flags
  The Annapolis of the Air
  The Birthplace of U.S.
    Naval Aviation (naval air
    training school opened
    1914)
  The City of Camelias
  The City of Five Flags
  The City of Pleasant Living
  The Cradle of Naval Avia-
    tion
  The Florida Plus City
  The Garden Spot of the
    South
  The Gateway to Florida
  The Gateway to the Gulf
    Coast
  The Gulf Coast City
  The Industrial Center of
    West Florida
  The Metropolis of West
    Florida
  The Nearest Florida Resort
    to Most of the Nation
  The Panama Port
  The Pleasant All-Year Vaca-
    tion Center
  The Scenic City of Five
    Flags at the Top of the
    Gulf of Mexico
  The Typical Resort City

PERRY
  The Eclipse Capital of the
    World (on March 7, 1970,
    40,000 scientists as-
    sembled to see the solar
    eclipse)
  The Gateway to All Florida
    (county seat of Taylor
    country)
  The Pine Tree Capital

PINE ISLAND CENTER
  Florida's Newest Frontier
  The Home of Fishingest
    Bridge

The Home of Florida's
  Fishingest Bridge

PINELLAS PARK
  The Hub of Pinellas County

PLANT CITY
  Just a Real Nice Town
  The Center for Good Clean
    Industry
  The City in the Heart of the
    Great New Central Florida
    Vacationland
  The City Most Convenient to
    All Florida
  The City of Hospitality and
    Charm
  The City where the Sun
    Beams Brighter with "Ole"
    Florida's Hospitality
  The Eastern Gateway to
    Hillsborough County
  The Neighborly Satisfying
    Community for Living
  The Perfect Central Florida
    Location
  The Perfect Place to Live
  The Progressive City
  The Winter Strawberry
    Capital of the World

POMPANO BEACH
  A Study in Contrasts
  The City for Year Round
    Fishing Variety
  The City in the Shadow of
    the Famed Hillsboro Light
  The City of Contrasts
  The City Right in the Center
    of Things
  The City that's a Study in
    Contrasts
  The City where Your Vaca-
    tion Dreams Are Fulfilled
  The Convenient Vacationland
  The Family Oasis of Safe
    Ocean Beaches
  The Gem of the Gold Coast
  The Heart of the Gold Coast
  The Nearest Point of Land
    to the Gulf Stream
  The New Playground of
    America (between Palm

Beach and Miami)
The Perfect Playground for
the Young in Heart
The Sparkling Sand, Golden
Sunshine on the Atlantic
Shore
Truly Izaak Walton's Head-
quarters

PORT EVERGLADES
Florida's Deep Water Harbor
The Cruise Capital of the
South
The Largest Port on the
Lower East Coast
The South's Leading Inter-
national Cruise Port
The South's No. 1 Cruise-
Ship Port

PORT ST. JOE
Florida's Fabulous Frontier
Coast
Florida's Finest Deep Water
Harbor
The City for Reasonable
Living with Plenty of
Elbow Room
The City with a Future
The Constitution City (where
the Florida constitution
was drawn up in 1839)

PUNTA GORDA
The Home of the Famous
Silver King Tarpon
The Sportsman's Paradise
(on Charlotte Harbor)

QUINCY
The City at the Top in
Florida
The City in the Heart of
Florida's Future
The City in the Heart of
Florida's "tall country"
The City of Tobacco
The City where Families
Enjoy Florida Living
in a Beautiful and
Historic Setting
The City where Historic
Pride and Civic Progress

Unite in the Industrial and
Cultural Heart of North-
west Florida
The City where Industry En-
joys Modern Utilities,
Abundant Labor, Favorable
Taxes and Good Govern-
ment
The City where the Old and
the New Combine
The Highest City in Florida
The Industrial Heart of
Florida's Future
The Shade Tobacco Capital
(multi-million dollar crop
of cigar wrapper tobacco)
The Shade-Grown Tobacco
Capital

RIVIERA BEACH
Everything Your Vacation
Heart Desires Can be
Found in Riviera Beach
The Center of the Palm
Beaches (on Singer Island)
The Sun Smiles Happily on
Industry in Riviera Beach
where There Is Every-
thing to Make You Happy

RUSKIN
The Area of Opportunity
The City Centered in the
Heart of the Suncoast
The Place to Live, Relax
and Play ... on Miles of
Water
The Salad Bowl of America
The Salad Bowl of the Nation

ST. AUGUSTINE
America's Oldest City (where
Juan Ponce de Leon
landed on April 3, 1513)
The Ancient City
The Fountain of Youth City
The Nation's Oldest City
(continuous existence since
1565)
The Oldest City in the United
States (permanent white
settlement 1565)
The Summer and Winter

Year 'Round Resort (on
Matanzas Bay)

ST. CLOUD
The Fisherman's Paradise

ST. PETERSBURG
Florida's Second Largest
Tourist City
One of America's Greatest
Playgrounds
The City for Living
The City of Good Living
The City of Homes
The City of the Unburied
Dead
The City on Florida's En-
chanting West Coast
The City with a Million
Ambassadors
The Happy People Place
The Senior Citizens' Capital
of the World
The Sunshine City
Tops in Sun'n Fun

ST. PETERSBURG BEACH
The City on the Gulf of
Mexico

SANFORD
The Celery City
The City of Gracious Living
The Electronic Area of In-
credible Growth
The World's Celery Center
(20% of celery production
in the U.S.)

SARASOTA
Florida's Entertainment
Capital
Florida's Great Gulf Beach
Resort Area
Florida's Unique Vacation
Area
The City of Attractions
The City that Has Every-
thing
The City where Living Is
Delightful
The City where You Work
and Play the Same Day

The Cultural Center of the
Sun Coast
The Fine Place in the World
to Live
The Mecca for Talent
(painters, sculptors,
authors, musicians, archi-
tects, illustrators)
The Relaxing Playspot on
Florida's Semi-Tropical
West Coast
The Ringling City (Circus
Museum)
The Sunshine City
The Twin Cities of the Lower
Sun-coast (with Bradenton,
Fla.)

SEBRING
A Good Place to Visit
A Wonderful Place to Live
The Golfing Capital of Florida
The Hub of the Florida Penin-
sula

SILVER SPRINGS
Nature's Underwater Fairy-
land
One of the Great Natural
Wonders of the World
The Camping Ground of the
Seminole Indians
The Community of Eight
Thrilling Attractions
The Home of World-Famous
Glass Bottom Boats
The Underwater Motion Pic-
ture Capital of the World

SNEADS
The Eastern Gateway to
Jackson County

STARKE
Florida's Winter Strawberry
Market
The Berry Capital of the
World
The Friendly City
The Heart of Florida's Crown
The Heart of Florida's Straw-
berry Market

The Progressive Community
The Strawberry City

STUART
The Sailfish Capital of the
World

SURFSIDE
The Resort where Fun
Never Sets
The Sunny Community of
Leisurely Living and
Happy Holidays

TALLAHASSEE
Florida's Beginning Point
The Capital City (popula-
tion about 89, 500)
The Capital City of Fabu-
lous Florida
The Center of Florida (be-
ginning point for all
Florida maps)
The Southland at Its Best

TAMPA
Florida's Biggest Industrial
City
Florida's Convention Center
Florida's Gulf Coast
Metropolis
Florida's Metropolitan Dis-
tributing Center
Florida's Second Largest
City
Florida's Treasure City
Florida's Year 'Round City
The Center of Florida's
Exciting West Coast
The Cigar Capital of
America
The Cigar City
The City of Diversity
The City where a Wealth
of Pleasure Awaits You
Spring or Summer, Fall
or Winter
The Gateway to the Carib-
bean
The Gateway to World
Ports
The Hub of Florida's West
Coast

The Hub of the Great Orange,
Grapefruit and Winter
Strawberry Producing Sec-
tion in the United States
The Industrial Hub of Florida
The Sightseeing Center of
Florida
The Spanish Town
The Trade Capital of Florida's
West Coast
The Treasure City

TARPON SPRINGS
America's Sponge Diving
Birthplace
Florida's Most Unique City
The Center of the Sponge
Fishing Industry
The City Convenient to All
Florida's Attractions
The City Located in Florida's
Suncoast Area
The City of Clean Industry
The City of Colorful Tradi-
tions of the Mediterranean
with the Best in Florida
Fun
The City of Permanent Home-
sites
The City on Florida's West
Coast
The City of Picturebook
Bayous
The City of Unspoiled Beaches
The Sponge City (sponge
divers)
The Venice of the South
(bordered on three sides
by water, the Gulf of
Mexico, the Anclote River
and Lake Tarpon)

TAVARES
The City Beautiful
The City that Has Everything
for Enjoyable Living
The County Seat of Lovely
Lake County
The Crossroads of Florida

TITUSVILLE
The Best Climate in Eastern
United States

The City of Progress
The Finest Place Under the Sun
The Gateway to the Galaxies (rocket sites)
The Home of the Indian River Citrus
The Missile City
The Tour Entrance to the Kennedy Space Center

TREASURE ISLAND
The City at the Center of a World of Famous Attractions
The Vacationland Without Equal

UMATILLA
The Gateway to Ocala National Forest
The Sportsman's Town (near Florida's best hunting area)

VALPARAISO
Twin Cities on the Bay (with Niceville, Fla.)

VERO BEACH
The City of Homes
The City where Florida's Tropics Begin
The Gem of the Florida East Coast
The Must Stop on the Florida Gold Coast

WAUCHULA
The Cucumber Capital of the World

WEST PALM BEACH
First on the Fun Coast of Florida
Florida's All-Year Resort
The Center of America's Fastest Growing Area
The City where Pleasure Begins
The Fast Growing City
The Metropolitan Center of

Tropical Florida's First Resort Area
Tropical Florida's First Resort

WHITE SPRINGS
The City where the Old Spanish Trail Crosses the Suwannee River

WINTER HAVEN
Central Florida's Lake Region
The Citrus Capital of the World
The Citrus Center of the World
The City of Cypress Gardens
The City of Homes
The City of Hundred Lakes
The Heart of Florida's Citrus Industry
The Holiday Highlands
The Home of Beautiful Cypress Gardens
The Prettiest Little Town This Side of Heaven

WINTER PARK
The City of Gracious Living
The City with Ideal Subtropical Climate
The Community Rich in Agricultural Heritage
The Cultural Center Unexcelled
The Town that Has Become a University (Rollins College)
Your Home Away from Home

ZELLWOOD
The Planned Adult Community
The Vegetable Bowl (major crops are corn, celery, radish, lettuce and beans)

ZEPHYRHILLS
The City of Pure Water

GEORGIA

AIKEN
One of the Most Favorable
Resorts of the South

ALBANY
The Artesian City (numerous
artesian wells)
The City of Opportunity
The Trade Center of South-
west Georgia (seat of
Dougherty County)

ALMA
The Queen City

AMERICUS
Georgia's Mobile Home
Center
The Home of Andersonville

ASHBURN
The Bountiful Country

ATHENS
The Athens You Will Want to
See
The Classic City of the
South (home of the Uni-
versity of Georgia, opened
1801, and named for the
Greek City)
The Home of the University
of Georgia

ATLANTA
One of the Most Accessible
Cities on Earth
The Big Peach
The Business Hub of the
Southeast
The Capital City (population
about 455,000)
The Capital of the New South
The Citadel of the Con-
federacy
The City of Beautiful Homes
and Thriving Industry
The City of Homes
The City of the Modern South
The City Too Busy to Hate
The City Without Limits
The City Without Precedent,
Without Comparison
The Confederate Supply Depot
The Dogwood City
The Federal City
The Fourth Largest Air
Center in the U.S.
The Gate City
The Gate City of the South
The Gate City to the South
The Gateway of the South
The Headquarters City
The Headquarters City of the
Southeast
The Home City
The Hub of the Southeast
The Ideal City (book by R.
Brown)
The Ideal Convention City
The Insurance City
The Key to Industrial Expan-
sion in the Great South-
east
The Manufacturing and In-
dustrial Metropolis of the
Southeast
The Metropolis of a New
South
The New Kind of City
The New National City
The New York of the South
The Queen City of the South
The Railroad City
The San Francisco of Tomor-
row
The Southern Crossroads City
The Sports Capital of the
South (home of the Braves,
Falcons and Chiefs)
The Vanguard of a New Era
of Cities
The Well-balanced Metropolis
The Winter Golf Capital of
America
The World's Great City
The World's Next Great City

AUGUSTA
A Wonderful Place to Live
A Wonderful Place to Live,
to Work, to Play

Georgia's Second Oldest
City
Golf Capital of the U.S.
The Battlefield of the Revo-
lution (American Revolu-
tion)
The Center of a Rich and
Highly Diversified Agri-
cultural Empire
The City of Beautiful
Churches
The City of Beautiful Homes
The Distribution Center of
the Southeast
The Friendly City
The Garden City of the
South
The Gateway of the South-
east
The Golf Capital of America
(site of the Masters Invi-
tation Tournament)
The Heart of Eastern Georgia
and Western South Caro-
lina
The Leading Resort City
The Lowell of the South
(textile manufacturing)
The Progressive City
The Winter Golf Capital of
the World

BAINBRIDGE
Georgia's First Inland Port

BARNESVILLE
The Home of Gordon
College

BAXLEY
The Turpentine Capital of
the World

BLACKSHEAR
The Heart of Tobacco Land

BLAKELEY
The Peanut Capital of the
World

BREMEN
The Clothing Center of the
South

BRUNSWICK
Georgia's Golden Isles
Georgia's Ocean Port
The City of Beauty
The City of Opportunities
The Gateway to Jekyll Island
The Gateway to Your Georgia
Vacationland
The Georgia Vacationland
The Ideal Vacationland
The Progressive City
The Progressive City Plan-
ning Today for the Events
of Tomorrow
The Shrimp Capital of the
World

BUFORD
The Leather City

BULLOCH CROSSROADS
The City where Nature
Smiles and Progress Has
the Right of Way

CAIRO
The Collard and Pickle
Capital

CALHOUN
The Cherokee Indian Capital

CAMILLA
The Hub City

CANTON
The Broiler City

CARROLLTON
The Free State of Carroll
The Friendly City

CEDARTOWN
The Only Cedartown in the
U.S.A.

CLAXTON
The Fruit Cake Capital
The Home of the World-Fa-
mous Claxton Fruit Cake

CLAYTON
Georgia's Mountain Resort

CLEVELAND
The Mountain Gateway

COLLEGE PARK
Atlanta's Airport City

COLUMBUS
The Fountain City
The South's Oldest Industrial
City (planned 1827)

COMMERCE
The Home of Georgia Belle
Peach

CORDELE
The Watermelon Capital of
the World

CORNELIA
The Home of the Big Red
Apple

CUMMING
The Gateway to Lake Lanier

DALTON
The Center of the World's
Tufted Textile Industry
The Gateway to the Chatta-
hoochee National Forest
The Tufted Textile Center
of the World

DAWSON
The Spanish Peanut Center
of the World
The World's Largest Spanish
Peanut Market

DOUGLAS
The Friendly City
The Oldest and Largest To-
bacco Market

DOUGLASVILLE
The Dynamic City

DUBLIN
The City that's 'Dublin' Daily

EAST POINT
A Community Well Planned,
Well Developed, Well
Equipped for Commerce,
Industry and Family Life
A Good Place to Live, to
Work and to Rear Your
Family
The City of Homes and
Industry
The City where People Are
Happy and Industry
Flourishes
The City You Can Be Proud
to Live and Work in
The Diversified Industrial
City
The South's Fastest Growing
City

EASTMAN
The Candy Capital of Georgia

ELBERTON
The Granite Center of the
World
The Granite City

FITZGERALD
The Colony City (settled in
1895 by a colony of Union
veterans)
The Heart of the South
Georgia Empire

FOLKSTON
The Gateway to the Beautiful
Okefenokee Swamp
The Land of the Trembling
Earth

FORT BENNING
The West Point of the South

FORT VALLEY
The Best Pecan Producing
Area in the South
The City of Peaches
The Peach Center

GAINESVILLE
The Broiler Capital of the
World
The Poultry Capital of the
World

GRIFFIN
The Pimiento Center of the
World

HAWKINSVILLE
The City of 13 Highways

HAZLEHURST
The Friendly City

HINESVILLE
The Home of Fort Stewart

JEKYLL ISLAND
America's Year-round
Holiday Island
Georgia's Fabulous Year
Round Beach Resort
Georgia's Island of Friendli-
ness and Hospitality
Georgia's Playground for
Family Fun
Georgia's Year-round
Family Beach Resort
Georgia's Year Round
Family Resort
One of Georgia's Golden
Isles
The Golden Isle in a By-
gone Golden Age
The Island where the Sand
Whispers to the Sea
The Year-round Convention
and Meeting Center
The Year-Round Family
Beach Resort

JESUP
The City Building for Today
and Planning for Tomor-
row
The City of Progress

LA GRANGE
Crossroads of the South
The Largest Cotton Manu-
facturing Center in the
State

LOUISVILLE
The Old Slave Market

LYONS
The Tobacco Center

MACON
The City on the Move
The Friendly City in the
Heart of Georgia
The Heart of Georgia (about
six miles from the geo-
graphical center)
The Heart of the Southeast
The South's Most Beautiful
and Interesting City

MANCHESTER
The Little White House
The Magic City

METTER
The Home of Better Living

MIDWAY
Georgia's Cradle of the
Revolution
The Cradle of the Revolution

MONROE
The Birthplace of the
'Buddy Poppy'

MOULTRIE
A Better Place to Work and
Play
South Georgia's Market Place
The Progressive Community

NASHVILLE
The Bright Leaf Tobacco
Center

NEWNAN
The City of Homes

PEARSON
The Heart of the Turpentine
Industry

PERRY
The Crossroads of Georgia
The Motel City

PINE MOUNTAIN
The Family-style Resort
Center

PLAINS
Peanut City, U.S.A.

QUITMAN
  The Camellia City

ROCKMART
  The City on the Move

ROME
  The City of Fine Educational
    Institutions (Shorter Col-
    lege)
  The City of Seven Hills
  The City of the Seven Hills
    (like Rome, Italy, built
    on seven hills)
  The Hub of Northwest
    Georgia
  The Versatile City

ST. MARYS
  The Second Oldest City in
    the U.S.

ST. SIMONS ISLAND
  The Georgia Vacationland
  The Golden Isles of Georgia
  The Land of the Old South

SANDERSVILLE
  The Kaolin Center of the
    World

SAVANNAH
  America's Most Beautiful
    City
  Georgia's Colonial Capital
  Georgia's Colonial Capital
    City
  Georgia's First City (founded
    1733)
  The City of Historical Charm
  The City of Southern Charm
  The Cradle of Georgia
    (founded Feb. 12, 1773 by
    James Edward Oglethorpe,
    English nobleman, as a
    colony and buffer state
    against the Spaniards in
    Florida)
  The First City of the South
    (settled Feb. 12, 1773 by
    General James Edward
    Oglethorpe)
  The Forest City

The Forest City of the South
The Garden City
The Hostess City of the
  South
The Mother City of Georgia
The New Gateway to World
  Trade
The Sugar Bowl of the South-
  east

SEA ISLAND
  A Great Place to Vacation, a
    Wonderful Place to Live
  The Georgia Vacationland
  The Golden Isles of Georgia
  The Land of the Old South

SMYRNA
  The Jonquil City

STATESBORO
  The Tourist City

SUMMERVILLE
  The City of Young Men

SWAINSBORO
  The Pine Tree Country

SYLVANIA
  The Home of the Famous
    "Jacksonboro Legend"
  The Welcome Station City

SYLVESTER
  The Heart of Hunting Land

THOMASTON
  Tire Cord Capital of the U.S.

THOMASVILLE
  The City of Gracious Living
  The City of Roses
  The Famous Winter Resort
    for Northern Invalids and
    Pleasure Seekers (used
    in 1895)
  The Key Junction to the
    Southeast
  The Most Fashionable Winter
    Resort
  The Original Winter Resort
    of the South

The Rose City (rose gardens
and annual rose show)

THOMSON
The Camellia City of the
South

TIFTON
The Tomato Plant Capital

TOCCOA
The Balanced Community
The Beautiful City
The Furniture, Thread and
Steel City

VALDOSTA
The Airways of America
(near Moody Air Force
Base)
The Azalea City
The Naval Stores Capital
of the World (largest
inland naval stores
market)
The Vale of Beauty

VIDALIA
The Modern Town for
Modern Living

WARM SPRINGS
The Little White House City
(home of Franklin Delano
Roosevelt)

WARNER ROBINS
The Home of Air Material
Command

WASHINGTON
The City of Ante-Bellum
Homes

WAYCROSS
Georgia's "Welcome World"
City
The Center City of Southern
Georgia
The Diversified City
The Gateway to Okefenokee
Swamp

The Land of the Trembling
Earth

WAYNESBORO
The Bird Dog Capital of the
World

WEST POINT
The Home of Textiles

WINDER
The Work Clothing Center
of the World

WOODBURY
The Heart of the Pimento
Country

HAWAII

HILO
The City of Orchids
The Crescent City
The Gateway to the Vol-
canoes
The Orchid Capital of
Hawaii

HONOLULU
The Capital City (popula-
tion about 335,000)
The Center of Pineapple
Industry
The Crossroads of the Pacific
The Exciting City of Welcome

WAIKIKI
The Birthplace of Surfing

IDAHO

AMERICAN FALLS
The Power City (second
largest artificial reservoir
in the United States)

BOISE
The Capital City (population
about 87, 500)
The City of Beautiful
Homes
The City of Trees
The Nation's Largest
Basque Colony
The Pacific Northwest's
Most Progressive Com-
munity
The Pioneer Log Cabin
Village
The Tree City
The Western Mecca for
Enjoyment Unlimited
The Woods

BURLEY
The Best Lighted Town
in the West (light,
power and water obtained
from the Minidoka Pro-
ject)
The Jewel of the Gem
State

CALDWELL
Idaho's Farm Market

COEUR D'ALENE
The Beautiful City by a
Beautiful Lake
The Center of a Resort and
Lumbering Area
The City by the Lake (Lake
Coeur d'Alene)
The Convention and Recrea-
tion Center of the North-
west
The Famous Playground of
the Wondrous Northwest
The Heart of the Emerald
Empire in the North
Idaho Scenic Land
The Only Town in the U. S.
with an Apostrophe in
Its Name

CRAIGMONT
The Second Largest Grain
Shipping Center of the
Northwest

GOODING
The Commercial Center of
Irrigated Idaho

IDAHO CITY
A Gold-Rush Ghost Town

JEROME
The Geographical Center of
Magic Valley

KELLOGG
The Home of Idaho's Greatest
Mines

LEWISTON
Idaho's Oldest Incorporated
City
Idaho's Only Seaport (at the
confluence of the Snake
and Clearwater Rivers)
The Banana Belt City
The First Territorial Capital
(of Idaho)
The Seaport for the Land-
locked State of Idaho

MOSCOW
The City of Homes,
Churches and Fine Schools
(University of Idaho)
The Dry Pea and Lentil
Capital of the World
(seat of legume-rich
Latah County)

NAMPA
The City of Expanding Indus-
try
The Home of the Snake River
Stampede (a rodeo staged
during July)

POCATELLO
The Gate City to the Great
Northwest

PRIEST RIVER
The Gateway to Priest River
Lake Country

SANDPOINT
The Cedar-shipping Center

SUN VALLEY
America's Foremost Year
'Round Sports Center
The All-Year Sports Center
The Gateway to America's
Last Wilderness

TWIN FALLS
Idaho's Finest Residential
Community
One of America's Fastest
Growing Cities (popu-
lation about 22,700)
The Hub of the Magic Val-
ley (headquarters for the
Sawtooth National Forest)

WENDELL
The Center of Gooding
County

ILLINOIS

ABINGDON
The Wagon Capital of the
World

ALTON
The City on Seven Hills
The City Planners' Dream
The City that Came Back
(Anti-abolitionist riot
1837, abolitionist Elijah
P. Lovejoy killed and
printing presses de-
stroyed)
Tusselburgh (evidently re-
ferring to above)

ARCOLA
The Broom Town

AUBURN
The Redwood City of Illinois

BATAVIA
The Rock City (limestone
quarries)

BERWYN
The Dormitory City

BLOOMINGTON
It's Pleasant to Live In
The Hub of Illinois
The Prairie City
The Twin City (with Normal,
Ill.)

BYRON
The Hudson of the West (on
Rock River)

CAIRO
The Goose Capital of the
World
The River City

CALUMET CITY
The Sister City (with Ham-
mond, Ind.)
The Sun Town

CANTON
A Good Place to Live, Work,
Play

CARBONDALE
The Crossroads of the Continent (division headquarters
for the Illinois Central
Railroad)

CARTHAGE
The Colorful Captivating
Community

CENTRALIA
The Gateway to Egypt (name
applied to southern quarter
of Illinois, Egyptian motifs
on several buildings)
The Oil Center of Illinois
The Population Center, U.S.A.

CHAMPAIGN
The Twin Cities (with Ur-
bana, Ill.)

CHICAGO
America's No. 1 Contrary
City

America's Riviera
Chi
Hogopolis
Old Chi
Pigopolis
Prokopolis
The Big Potato
The Big Town
The Breezy Town
The Capital of the Convention World (1,000 trade shows, expositions, etc. annually)
The City Beautiful
The City by the Lake
The City of Big Shoulders
The City of Extremes
The City of Innovation and Culture
The City of Many Cities
The City of Superlatives
The City of the Lakes
The City of the Lakes and Prairies
The City of 35,000 Hotel Rooms
The City of Winds
The City that Works
The City with Two Faces
The Convention Capital of the World
The Convention City
The Cornopolis
The Country's Greatest Rail Center
The Crime Capital
The Gangland
The Garden City
The Gem of the Prairies
The Golf Capital of the Midwest
The Hog Butcher for the World
The Home of the Loop
The Host City of the Nation
The Hub of American Merchandising
The Industrial Hub of the United States
The International Crossroads of the World
The Lake City

The Leading Convention City in the Country
The Meat-Packing Capital of the World
The Metropolis of the West
The Midland Metropolis
The Midwest Golf Capital
The Midwest Metropolis
The Mighty Metropolis
The Miracle City of the Midwest
The Nation's No. 1 Convention City
The Phoenix City
The Pork City
The Prairie
The Queen of the Lakes
The Second City Syndrome
The Something for Everyone City
The Western Metropolis
The White City
The Windy City
The Wonderful Town
The World's Busiest Airport City
The World's Fair City
The World's Largest Railroad Center
The World's Railroad Capital
The World's Railroad Mecca

DECATUR
Playtown, U.S.A.
The Diversified Manufacturing Center
The Soybean Capital of the World (numerous processing mills)
The Soybean Center
The World-Known Processing Center for Corn and Soybeans

DE KALB
The Barb City (barb wire invented and manufactured here)
The Barbed Wire Capital of the World (barb wire invented and manufactured there in 1873)

DIXON
  The Petunia Capital of the
  World

DUNDEE
  Santa's Village

EAST MOLINE
  America's Farm Implement
  Capital (plant of Inter-
  national Harvester Co.)
  The Quad Cities (with
  Moline, Ill., Rock Island,
  Ill., and Davenport,
  Iowa)

EFFINGHAM
  The Heart of the U.S.A.

ELGIN
  The Community with Its
  Sites Set on Tomorrow

EUREKA
  The Pumpkin Capital of the
  World

EVANSTON
  The Finest New England
  Village in the Middle
  West
  The Historical City of
  Homes
  The Ideal Home Community

GALENA
  The City Time Forgot
  The Crescent City of the
  Northwest

GALESBURG
  The College City (Knox
  College)
  The World's Greatest Mule
  Market

GREENVILLE
  The Busy Friendly Growing
  City
  The City of Churches of
  All Faiths
  The City of Industrial
  Sites

The City of Modern Industry
The City of Modern Schools
The City with Recreation for
  Everyone
The Home of Greenville
  College
The Up-to-date Farming
  Center

GRIGGSVILLE
  The Purple Martin Capital of
  the World (numerous in-
  sect-devouring purple
  martins)
  The World's Largest Cardinal
  Gardens

HARVARD
  America's Milk Center (Star-
  line Model Dairy Farm)
  The Liveliest Town of Its
  Size in the World
  The Milk Capital of the
  World
  The Milk Center of the World

JOLIET
  One of Illinois' Top Industrial
  Cities
  The Industrial City
  The Pittsburgh of the West
  (several hundred manu-
  facturing plants)

KEWANEE
  The Hog Capital of the
  World

LOMBARD
  The Lilac Town

MC HENRY
  The Western Gateway to
  the Chain O'Lakes

MACOMB
  The World's Largest Art
  Pottery City (site of the
  Haeger Potteries, Inc.)

MATTOON
  The Center of Agricultural,
  Commercial, Industrial

Oil Transportation
The Center of Agriculture,
Commerce, Industry, Oil,
and Transportation
The City Noted for Diversi-
fication

METROPOLIS
The City of Roses

MOLINE
The Farm Machinery Capital
of America
The Plow City (John Deere
began plow manufacture
in 1847)
The Quad Cities (with East
Moline, Ill., Rock Is-
land, Ill., and Davenport,
Iowa)
The Tri-Cities (with Rock
Island, Ill., and Daven-
port, Iowa)

MONMOUTH
The Prime Beef Capital
The Prime Beef Center of
the World

MOOSEHEART
The City of Childhood
(children's home of Loyal
Order of Moose)

MOUNDS
The Goose Capital of the
World

NAUVOO
The City Beautiful (on the
east bank of the Missis-
sippi River)

NORMAL
The Twin City (with Bloomington, Ill.)

NORTHBROOK
The Fastest Town on Skates
(home of Anne Henning
and Diane Holum,
Olympic winner at Sap-
poro, Japan, 1972)

The Speed Skating Capital of
the World

OAK PARK
The Saints Rest (settled in
1833)

PANA
City of Roses
One of the World's Largest
Rose Growing Centers
The Rose Center

PEKIN
The Celestial City

PEORIA
Illinois' Second City (popu-
lation about 121,000)
The Bright Spot of America
The Center of Midwest
Friendliness
The City Pledged to Progress
The Progressive City
The Whiskey Town (site of
the world's largest dis-
tillery, Hiram Walker &
Sons)

PLANO
The Biggest Industrial Little
City in the World

PRINCETON
The City where Tradition
Meets Progress

PULLMAN
The City of Brick (part of
Chicago)

QUINCY
The Gem City
The Gem City in the Heart
of the Great Mississippi
Valley
The Gem City of Mid-America
The Gem City of the Middle
West
The Gem City of the West
The Model City
The Most Beautiful of All
Western Cities

ROCK ISLAND
The Quad Cities (with East
Moline, Ill., Moline,
Ill., and Davenport,
Iowa)
The Tri-Cities (with Moline,
Ill., and Davenport,
Iowa)

ROCKFORD
Illinois' Second Industrial
City
Illinois' Second Largest
City
The City at the Top in
Illinois
The City of Beautiful Homes
The Crossroads of the Mid-
dle West
The Forest City
The Nation's Second Largest
Machine-tool Center
The Rich Agricultural and
Industrial Heartland of
Mid-America

SHELBYVILLE
The City in the Heart of
the Kaskasie Valley
The City where the Action Is
The Friendly City

SPARTA
The Comic Book Capital of
the World

SPRINGFIELD
A Great American Shrine
(Lincoln Tomb State
Memorial)
A Progressive American
City
An Important Convention
and Conference City
City of Churches (about
120)
Illinois' Capital City (se-
lected 1837)
The Capital City (popu-
lation about 96,200)
The City of Flowers
The Flower City
The Home of Abraham
Lincoln

STEGER
The Piano Center of America

STERLING
The City of Trees
The Heart of American
Hardware

TAYLORVILLE
The Soybean Capital of the
World (formerly used)

URBANA
The Twin Cities (with Champaign, Ill.)

VANDALIA
Wilderness Capital of
Lincoln's Land (capital of
Illinois from 1820 to 1839)

VILLA GROVE
The Pancake Capital of the
World

WEST FRANKFORT
The Geographic Center of
Industrial Southern Illinois
The Heart of a Dispersed
City of Towns

WESTCHESTER
The Gateway to the Tollroads

INDIANA

ALBION
The Heart of the Indiana
Lake Country

ANDERSON
Mid-America's Industrial
Center

ANGOLA
Mid-America's Finest Vacationland
The Center of Activity (the
boundaries of three states,

Indiana, Ohio and Michigan, meet at the northeast tip of Starke County of which Angola is the county seat)

ATTICA
The Gem City of the Wabash (on the Wabash and Erie Canal)

BEDFORD
The Home of the Nation's Building Stone
The Stone City (the heart of the Indiana limestone district)

BLOOMINGTON
The Gateway to Scenic Southern Indiana

BOONVILLE
The Lincoln City

BRAZIL
The Clay City (about a dozen factories making clay products from local clay)

CARROLLTOWN
Tailholt (featured in James Whitcomb Riley's poem "The Little Town O'Tailholt")

COLUMBUS
The Athens of the Prairie (many innovative architectural achievements)
The City of Better Living

CONNERSVILLE
Little Detroit (five makes of automobiles once manufactured there)

CRAWFORDSVILLE
The Athens of America (referring to the literary figures who once lived in the town,

General Lew Wallace, Maurice Thompson, Meredith Nicholson, etc.)
The Athens of Indiana
The Athens of the Hoosier State
The Home of Ben Hur (General Lew Wallace's study)
The Hoosier Athens (Wabash College)

DANVILLE
The Gable Town (gabled roofs)

ELKHART
The Band City (produces over 60 percent of band instruments)
The Band Instrument Center of the Country
The Lake Capital of the Hoosier State
The Musical Instrument Capital of the World (band instruments manufactured)
The World's Largest Mobile Home Manufacturing Center

EVANSVILLE
The Air Crossroads of America
The City in the Valley of Opportunity
The City of Opportunity
The Refrigeration Capital of the World

FORT WAYNE
Indiana's Busiest, Happiest City
The Birthplace of Night Baseball (game played under "rays of electric light" on June 2, 1882)
The Center of the World's Magnet Wire Production
The City of Industrial and Commercial Opportunities
The Gateway to the Northern Indiana Lake Region
The Gateway to the West

The Hub of the Great North-
Central Industrial and
Agricultural America
The Summit City

FOUNTAIN CITY
Grand Central Station of
the Underground Railroad
(home of Quaker Levi
Coffin, major terminus
of Underground Railroad
during the Civil War)

FRANKFORT
The City Substantial

FRENCH LICK
America's Greatest Health
and Pleasure Resort
(mineral waters, Pluto
water bottled here,
luxury hotels)
America's Sports Mecca
The Carlsbad of America
The Home of the Famous
Pluto Mineral Springs

GARY
America's Magic City (it
didn't exist at the turn
of the century)
The Century of Industry
The Gateway to Indiana
Dunes
The Gateway to Vast Farm
and Industrial Markets
The Magic City
The Playground of the
Dunes
The Steel City (U.S. Steel
Corp. mill)
The Steel-Making City

GENEVA
The Limberlost Country
(the Limberlost swamp
region made famous in
the books of Gene Strat-
ton Porter)

GOSHEN
The Maple City

GREENSBURG
The City with a Future
The Tower Tree City (the
tower of the courthouse
contains a growing tree)

GREENWOOD
The Town of Happy Homes

HAMMOND
The Sister Community (with
Calumet City, Ill.)
The Town of the Fearless

INDIANAPOLIS
America's Greatest Inland
City
The Capital City (population
about 741,000)
The City that Has the Re-
sources to Fit Your Busi-
ness Needs
The Crossroads of America
The Hoosier Capital
The Hoosier City
The Hub of the Nation-wide
Transportation System
(7 interstate highways,
6 major railroads, 6 air-
lines, 125 truck lines)
The Logical Convention City
The Opportunity City
The Railroad City

JASPER
The Chair and Desk City
The Nation's Wood Capital
(manufacture of wood of-
fice furniture)
The Town that Made Garbage
Illegal

JEFFERSONVILLE
Indiana's Gateway City
(terminal of the American
Commercial Barge Line)
The Falls Cities (with New
Albany, Ind., and Louis-
ville, Ky.)

KOKOMO
The City of Firsts

The City of the First Automobile

LAFAYETTE
The Star City (on the Wa-
bash River)
The Twin Cities (with West
Lafayette, Ind.)

LA PORTE
Indiana's Finest Home Town
The City of Lakes (seven
lakes partially in the
city)
The Home of Iowa's Only
Future Farmer of Ameri-
cas-Agricultural Museum
(FFA-AG)
The Maple City
The Town where People
Count Most

LEBANON
The Friendliest City in the
State

LEESBURG
The Gateway of the Lake
Region (Tippecanoe Lake)

LOGANSPORT
The City of Bridges (situated at the confluence of
the Wabash and Eel
Rivers)

MADISON
The City 'Neath the Hills
(on the Ohio River)

MARION
The Queen City of the Gas
Belt (gas and oil dis-
covered in 1880's)

MARTINSVILLE
The Artesian City (artesian
wells supply mineral
water)

MICHIGAN CITY
Indiana's Summer Playground

The Capital of Duneland (located in the famous sand
dune country at the southern end of Lake Michigan)
The Largest Resort Center
in Indiana
The Vacationland with Complete Facilities

MIDDLETOWN
The Typical American City

MISHAWAKA
The City in the Valley of
Promise

MITCHELL
The Home of Astronaut Virgil
(Gus) Grissom
The Largest Small City in
Indiana (population about
4,100)

MONTPELIER
The Oil City

MORGANTOWN
The Gateway to Brown County

MUNCIE
Magic Muncie
Middletown U.S.A. (two books
about Muncie by sociolo-
gists Robert S. and Helen
M. Lynd entitled Middle-
town and Middletown in
Transition)
The City of Magic
The City of Pride
The El Dorado of the West
The Friendly City
The Home of the Industrial
Genii
The Magic City
The Magic Town
The Mainspring of the Mid-
west
The Typical American
City (on the White
River, population about
76,500)

NEW ALBANY
A Good Place to Live,
Work and Play
The Falls Cities (with Jef-
fersonville, Ind., and
Louisville, Ky.)
The Home of the Robert E.
Lee (the famous steam-
boat was built there)
The Plywood Capital of the
World
The Plywood Center of the
Nation
The Real Hoosier City

NEW CASTLE
The City with a Planned
Future
The City of Roses

NEW HARMONY
The Athens of America (on
Wabash River)

PAOLI
The Crossroads of Southern
Indiana

PERU
The Circus City (winter head-
quarters of numerous
circuses)
The Circus City of the
World
The Thriving Pleasant City
The Truly Complete Com-
munity

PLAINFIELD
The Friendly Folk's Village
The Village of Friendly Folk

RICHMOND
The Eastern Gateway to
Indiana
The Quaker City of the
West (founded 1806 by
the Society of Friends)
The Rose Center of the
United States

ROANOKE
The Athens of Indiana (Roanoke

Classical Seminary, con-
sidered ultimate in culture
in 1860's)

ROCKVILLE
The Covered Bridge Capital
of the World (38 bridges
in Parke County)

SALEM
The Athens of the West

SEYMOUR
The Crossroads of America
The Crossroads of Southern
Indiana
The Gateway of Southern
Indiana (between the White
River and the Vernon Fork
of the Muscatatuck)

SHELBYVILLE
The City in the Heart of
Kaskasie Valley

SOUTH BEND
The Future Workshop of the
Middle West
The Major World Tool and
Die Training Center

TERRE HAUTE
Boomtown, U.S.A. (derisive
title for numerous gas
explosions in 1963)
The Pittsburgh of the Big
West
The Sin Center
The Switzerland of America
The Sycamore City

VINCENNES
The Beautiful and Historic
City
The Citadel of the Old North-
west (fort erected here in
1732)
The City in a Rich Agricul-
tural Area
The City of Diversified Indus-
tries
The City of Fine Schools
(Vincennes Univ.)

The City on the Banks of
the Wabash
The City with Important
Transportation Facilities

WABASH
The First Electrically Lighted
City in the World
The Rock City (Wabash River
over white stones and
rocks)

WARSAW
The Gateway to the Indiana
Lake Area (Winona,
Center and Pike)

WASHINGTON
The Garden Spot of Southern
Indiana

WEST LAFAYETTE
The Twin Cities (with
Lafayette, Ind.)

WINONA LAKE
The Home of Conventions

IOWA

ALGONA
The Friendly City
The Gateway to West Bend
Grotto

ATLANTIC
The Center of Nationwide
Rail and Truck Connec-
tions
The City in the Heart of
the Cattle and Corn
Country
The City of Beautiful Parks
and Playgrounds
The Hub City of Southwest
Iowa

AUDUBON
The City of Progress, Our

Past and Our Future
The City where the T-Bone
Special Starts

BURLINGTON
A Great Place for Living
The Orchard City
The Porkopolis of Iowa

CEDAR FALLS
The Garden City
The Garden City of Iowa
The Home of Quaker Oats
The Lawn City

CEDAR RAPIDS
Healthful, Hospitals and
Humane
Picturesque, Progressive
and Prosperous
The Gracious Well-Planned
City for Pleasant Living
or Working
The Metropolis of Industry
The Parlor City
The Rapid City (swift rapids)

CHARLES CITY
The Birthplace of the Farm
Tractor
The City of Opportunity

DAVENPORT
Dynamic Davenport
The City of Beauty
The City where the West
Begins
The Eastern Gateway of Iowa
The Port of Hospitality on
the Great Father of Waters
The Progressive City with
the Rich Heritage and
Charm of the Old River
Days
The Quad Cities (with East
Moline, Moline, and Rock
Island, Ill.)
The Queen City
The Tri-Cities (with Moline
and Rock Island, Ill.)

DECORAH
The Switzerland of Iowa

DENVER
The Pheasant Country

DES MOINES
Great Today--Greater
Tomorrow
Iowa's Industrial, Finan-
cial and Commercial
Center
Iowa's Own City
The Action Capital of the
Midwest
The Capital City (popu-
lation about 194,100;
capital in 1857)
The Center of the Midwest
and the Country (250
miles from Minneapolis
and St. Paul; 140 miles
from Omaha; 340 miles
from Chicago; 300 miles
from St. Louis and
200 miles from Kansas
City)
The City of Certainties
The Farm Capital of
America
The Insurance City
The Largest Insurance
Center in the West
(about fifty insurance
companies)

DE WITT
The Prime Beef Center
of the World

DUBUQUE
Family Fun and Action
Iowa's Industrial, Scenic
and Cultured City
The City for Family Fun
and Action
The City of Progress
The Heidelberg of
America (Germanic
influence in architecture
and schools)
The Key City
The Key City of Iowa
The Little Heidelberg of
America
The Queen City of the
Northwest

FORT DODGE
The Gypsum City (one of the
largest gypsum producing
centers)

FORT MADISON
The City with a Blueprint for
Civic and Industrial Im-
provement

IOWA CITY
The Athens of America
The Athens of Iowa

JEFFERSON
The Community f Hospitable
People
The Home of t.e Mahanay
Memorial Carillon Tower

KEOKUK
A Good Place to Live, Work
and Do Business
The City that Holds the Key
to Mid-America
The City that Is Attracting
New Industry
The Gate City (foot of the
Mississippi River)
The Home of George M.
Verity
The Power City (Keokuk
Dam drains about 120,000
square mile area)
The Progressive City

LE CLAIRE
The Birthplace of Buffalo
Bill Cody

MARSHALLTOWN
A Good Place to Live and
Work
The City of Progress with
Pride and Purpose
The Convention City of Iowa

MASON CITY
The Friendly and Progres-
sive City
The Home of the "Music
Man" (Meredith
Wilson)

MONONA
The Heart of the Corn
Country

MUSCATINE
The Pearl City (pearl button
production)
The Port City of the Corn
Belt

NEW HAMPTON
The Petunia Capital

NEWTON
The Home Laundry Appliance
Center of the World

OTTUMWA
The City that Has a Future
Because It Has a Plan
Today's City with Tomor-
row's Vision

PLEASANTVILLE
The Rose City

ST. DONATUS
The Picturesque Old World
Village

SHENANDOAH
The World's Largest Seed
and Nursery Center

SIOUX CITY
The City of David
The City of Distinction
The City where the Industrial
East Meets the Agricul-
tural West
The Foremost Industrial
Center of Iowa
The Home Market for the
Great Northwest
The Industrial City of Iowa
The Livestock, Grain and
Industrial Capital of the
Great Northwest
The World's Central Live
stock Market

WAUKON
The City of Friendly

People and Nice Homes
The City of Good Schools
and Churches
The Town in the Heart of
Iowa's Scenic Vacation
Land

WEBSTER
Main Street, USA

KANSAS

ABILENE
The Biggest Little City
(population about 6,600)
The Center of the Great
Kansas Agricultural Em-
pire
The City of the Plains (on
Smoky Hill River)
The Gem of the Plains
The Good Size Town for
Knowing Your Neighbor
The Greyhound City (about
sixty percent of America's
greyhound dogs born and
bred here)
The Growing City of Oppor-
tunity
The Heart of History and
Romance in Kansas
The Health Center and Prin-
cipal Trade Center of
North Central Kansas

ARKANSAS CITY
The Ark City (on Mississippi
River)
The City in the Heart of
Roger Babson's Magic
Circle
The Important Transportation
Center

AUGUSTA
The Agricultural Community
The City Dedicated to
Growth and Prosperity

BLUE RAPIDS
The Peaceful Friendly Town
The Town at the Headwaters
of Tuttle Creek Lakes
The Town with a Future
The Vacation Headquarters

BURLINGAME
The City where the Trail
Meets Rail (Santa Fe
Trail)

CALDWELL
The Queen City of the Border

CAWKER CITY
The Biggest Little Town in
Kansas

CEDAR VALE
The Quail Haven

CHANUTE
The City in the Land of
Friendship
The City of Established
Industry
The Major Market of the
Midwest

COFFEYVILLE
The Cow Town (settled in
1870, formerly used)

COLBY
The Golden Buckle on the
Wheat Belt (the heart of
the wheat belt)

CONCORDIA
The City of Concord
The City of Good Schools
The City that Is Big
Enough to Serve You
and Small Enough to
Know You
The City with Unity in the
Community
The Medical Center of
North Central Kansas

DODGE CITY
The Biggest Little City in
the U.S.A. (population
about 16,300)
The Buckle on the Kansas
Wheat Belt
The Cowboy Capital
The Cowboy Capital of the
World
The Home of World Famous
Front Street and Boot Hill
The Queen City of the Cow
Towns
The Queen of the Cow Towns
The Shipping Center of the
Southwest
The Wickedest Little City in
America

EMPORIA
The City where Progress Is
Our Constant Endeavor
The Educational Center of
the West (site of Kansas
State Teachers College
and College of Emporia)
The Loveliest Site in the
World for a Town

FORT LEAVENWORTH
The City where the History
of the West Begins (fort
erected in 1827 as protec-
tion from Indians)

GARDEN CITY
The Family Town
The Garden Spot of the West

GOODLAND
The Heart of the Wheat Land

GREAT BEND
The Oil Capital in the Heart
of the Wheat Belt (oil
wells)

HUGOTON
The Gas Capital of the World
The Natural Gas Capital of
the U.S.

HUTCHINSON
The Clean City
The Friendly City

The Gracious City
The Proud City
The Salt City (extensive
salt beds underlying the
city)
The Well Groomed City
The Well Mannered City

INDEPENDENCE
The Buckle on the Oil Belt
(oil and gas)
The City where the Accent
Is on Family
The Queen City of South-
east Kansas

KINGMAN
The Catfish Capital of
Kansas

KINSLEY
Half Way and a Place to
Stay (between Dodge
City and Great Bend)

LA CROSSE
An Ideal Location for
Industry
The County Seat of Rush
County
The Home of the Post
Rock Museum

LAWRENCE
Midway, U.S.A.

LEAVENWORTH
The City where Progress
Profits Growth
The City where the Story
of the West Began
The Cottonwood City
The First City of Kansas
The Sight-Seeing City of
the Middle West

LIBERAL
The Pancake Center
The Pancake Center of the
World

MANHATTAN
The City where People

Play and Prosper
The Complete Community
The Home Town
The Kansas Water Sports
Capital

MEDICINE LODGE
The Crossroads of North
America
The Home of Carrie Nation

MISSION
The Skyline City

NORTON
The Pheasant Capital of
Kansas

OGDEN
The Last Place on the Map

OLATHE
The Cowboy Boot Capital
(boot factories)

OSAWATOMIE
The City of Choice Industrial
Sites
The City of Historical Interest
The Cradle of the Civil War
The Home of John Brown
Memorial Park
The Progressive City

OVERBROOK
Don't Overlook Overbrook

PRATT
The Better Community for
Better Living
The Home of the Kansas
State Fish Hatchery
The Home of the Miss Kansas
Pageant
The Trade Center

SALINA
Non-Stop to Everywhere
Salina Has More of Every-
thing
The City on the Move
The City where North and
South Meet East and West

The Convention City
The Distributing Center for
Central and Western
Kansas
The Fourth Largest City in
Kansas
The Home of Schilling Air
Force Base
The Hub of the Inter-State
Highway System
The Metropolis of Central
and Northwest Kansas
The Proven Progressive
City

SHAWNEE
The Gateway of Kansas

SMITH CENTER
The "Home on the Range"
Birthplace

TOPEKA
The Capital City (population
about 126,500)
The Center of the Nation

VICTORIA
The Cathedral of the Plains
(St. Fidelis Church)

WELLINGTON
The Wheat Capital of the
World

WICHITA
Kansas' Premier City
One of the World's Great
Airplane Manufacturing
Centers (Beech, Boeing,
Cessna, etc.)
The Air Capital (four major
airlines unite)
The Air Capital of America
The Air Capital of the
Nation
The Air Capital of the
World
The City of Conventions
The City of Industry
The Cow Capital
The Magic Mascot of the
Plains

The Peerless Princess of
the Plains
The Petroleum Capital of
Kansas

WILLIAMSTOWN
Billtown

KENTUCKY

ASHLAND
The Busy Friendly City
The City where Coal Meets
Iron (steel mill)

BARDSTOWN
The Bourbon Capital of the
World
The Second Oldest Town in
Kentucky
The Town of Tradition

BOWLING GREEN
Southern Kentucky's Largest
Shopping Center
The City where Folks Are
Not Too Busy to Be
Friendly
The Confederate State Capital
of Kentucky (during the
Confederate occupation)

CAVE CITY
The Gateway to the Mam-
mouth Cave

CORBIN
The Hub of the Valley of
Parks (near Cumberland
Falls, Lake Cumberland
and Levi Jackson Wilder-
ness Road State Park)

COVINGTON
The Dixie Gateway (at con-
fluence of Ohio and Licking
Rivers opposite Cincin-
nati, Ohio)
The X-Ray City

FLORENCE
  The City where Hospitality
  of the South Begins

FRANKFORT
  Kentucky's Capital
  The Bluegrass Capital (se-
  lected in 1792)
  The Capital City (popula-
  tion about 24,700)
  The Diversified Community
  The Heart of America
  The Heart of Kentucky
  The Historic Frankfort
  (founded in 1786)

HARLAN
  The Coal Capital of Kentucky

HARRODSBURG
  The Birthplace of Western
  America

HENDERSON
  The Gateway to the Greatest
  Vacation Land in Mid-
  America
  The Land of Outdoor Fun

HORSE CAVE
  The Economic Center of
  the Cave Area

LEXINGTON
  Kentucky's Blue Grass
  Capital
  One of the Nation's Largest
  Spring Lamb Producing
  Centers
  One of the South's Foremost
  Educational Centers
  The Athens of the West
  (University of Kentucky)
  The Belle City of the Blue-
  grass Regions
  The Bluegrass Capital
  The Capital of the Blue-
  grass Region
  The Capital of the Horse
  World
  The Chief City of the Blue-
  grass Region
  The Dimple of the Bluegrass

The Heart of Kentucky's
  Bluegrass Region (about
  1,200 square miles)
The Retail, Wholesale,
  Industrial, Medical Insti-
  tutional Center of Kentucky
The Thoroughbred, Standard-
  breed and Saddle Horse
  Center of America
The Trade Center of the
  Rich Blue Grass, Tobacco
  and Livestock Region
The World's Largest Loose-
  Leaf Tobacco Market

LOUISVILLE
  Derby Town (the site of the
  Kentucky Derby)
  The Bustling River Port
  The City by the Falls (Ohio
  River)
  The City of Beautiful
  Churches
  The City of Conflict
  The City of Homes
  The City of the Falls
  The Convention City
  The Falls Cities (with Jef-
  fersonville and New Albany,
  Ind.)
  The Falls City (on the Ohio
  River)
  The Gateway City (on the
  Ohio River)
  The Gateway to the South
  The Growing Industrial,
  Financial and Educational
  Center
  The Home of the Kentucky
  Derby
  The Metropolis of the New
  South
  The Nation's Thoroughfare

MURRAY
  The Birthplace of Radio
  (Nathan B. Stubblefield
  radio pioneer)
  The Friendliest Little
  "Big Town" in Ken-
  tucky (population about
  14,200)

OWENSBORO
  The Heart of the Big River
    Country

PADUCAH
  America's Newest Industrial
    Center
  The Capital of Western
    Kentucky
  The Medical Center

WINCHESTER
  The Center of the Blue
    Grass Area

LOUISIANA

ALEXANDRA
  The Crossroads of Louisiana
    (on the Red River)
  The Geographical Crossroads
    of Louisiana
  The Heart of Louisiana
  The Hub City (center of the
    industrial area of the
    state)
  The Twin Cities on the Red
    River in the Heart of
    Louisiana (with Pineville)

BASTROP
  The Fastest Growing Indus-
    trial Center in the South
  The Industrial Center of
    Louisiana

BATON ROUGE
  America's Most Beautiful
    Capitol
  Louisiana's Fastest Growing
    City
  The Capital City (population
    about 183,100)
  The Chemical Center of the
    South
  The City where the Sea
    Starts (northernmost point
    on the Mississippi River
  The Dynamic Center of

the Great River Road
The Farthest Inland Deep
  Water Port
The Growth Center of the
  Mississippi
The Home of Louisiana State
  University
The Seventh Largest Seaport
  in the U.S.

BOGALUSA
  The Magic City of the Green
    Empire (founded 1906)

BOSSIER CITY
  The City Situated in Strategic
    Northwest Louisiana
  The Growingest City in
    Louisiana

BREAUX BRIDGE
  The Crawfish Capital of the
    World

BURAS
  The Center of the Louisiana
    Orange Industry

CROWLEY
  The Rice Capital of Louisiana
  The Rice Capital of the World
  The Rice Center of America
  The Rice City of America

EAST BATON ROUGE
  The Capital Parish of the
    State Named for Louis
    and Anna

FORT JESSUP
  The Cradle of the Mexican
    War (troops from the fort
    were sent to Texas during
    the Revolution from
    Mexico)

FRANKLIN
  The Cleanest City in
    Louisiana

GONZALEZ
  Jambalaya Capital of the
    World

The City of Southern
Friendliness and Charm

GRAND ISLE
The Playground of New
Orlean's People

HAMMOND
The Strawberry Capital of
America

HODGE
The Biggest Little Town in
the South

HOUMA
The Oyster Center of the
State
The Venice of America

IBERVILLE
The Heart of the Sugar
Bowl (book title)

INDEPENDENCE
Little Italy

JENNINGS
Louisiana's Cleanest City
The Cradle of Louisiana
Oil (the first oil well in
the state flowed Sept.
21, 1901)
The Garden Spot of Loui-
siana

LAFAYETTE
The Azalea Trail City
The City in the Heart of
South Central Louisiana
(on the Vermillion
River)
The French Louisiana
The Hub of Southwestern
Louisiana

LAKE CHARLES
The Rice Capital of Loui-
siana
The Sea Gate to the Southwest (on the Calcasieu
River, 37 miles from
the Gulf of Mexico)

MARKSVILLE
The Fishing Shangri-La of
the South

MINDEN
The Home of Champions
(athletic teams and the
Louis-Annes precision drill
team)

MONROE
The Metropolis of the World's
Largest Gas Field
The Twin Cities (with West
Monroe)
The Twin Cities of the Oua-
chita (with West Monroe)

NATCHITOCHES
The Up-to-Date Oldest Town
in Louisiana (French
trading post established
in 1714)

NEW IBERIA
The Little Arcady of South-
western Louisiana
The Pepper Sauce Capital of
the World
The Queen City of the Teche
(a stream flowing into the
Atchafalaya Bayou)

NEW ORLEANS
America's Most Hedonistic
City
America's Most Interesting
City
The Air Hub of the Americas
The Alexandria of America
The City Care Forgot
The City of Charm
The City of Contrasts
The City of the Mardi Gras
The City with the Old French
Town
The Convention City
The Crawfish Town
The Creole City
The Crescent City (it curves
around the Mississippi)
The Gateway to the World
The Global Center of

the New South
The Great South Gate
(entrance to the Gulf of
Mexico)
The Gulf City (on the Gulf
of Mexico)
The Heart of America's
New Commercial Frontier
The Heart of Dixie
The Hub of the Americas
The International City
The Key of the Great
Valley
The Mardi Gras City
The Mardi Gras Metropolis
The Metropolis of the
South
The Old French Town
The Paris of America
The Queen of the South
The South's Greatest City
(founded in 1718; popu-
lation about 569,200)
The Winter Capital of
America

PINEVILLE
The Crossroads of Louisiana
The Twin Cities on the Red
River in the Heart of
Louisiana (with Alexandria)

PORT ALLEN
The Gateway to the West

RAYNE
The Frog Market of the
Nation

RUSTON
The Friendly City of Many
Opportunities
The Land of Good Living

ST. FRANCISVILLE
The Town Two Miles Long
and Two Yards Wide
(population about 1,600)

SHREVEPORT
The Capital City of the
Land of Ark-La-Tex
The City of Churches

The City on the Grow
The New City in the Old
South (incorporated 1839)
The Pipeline Capital of
America (during the oil
and gas boom of the 1920's
and 1930's)
The Pivot City of the Central
South
The Pivot City of the South
The Queen City of the Ark-
La-Tex (located geographi-
cally near the borders of
Texas and Arkansas)

SLIDELL
The City Geared to Space-
Age Families
The City of Good Living
The City with a Bright Future

WEST MONROE
The Twin Cities (with Monroe,
La.)
The Twin Cities of the Oua-
chita (with Monroe, La.)

_____

MAINE

_____

AROOSTOOK
The City of Pine, Potatoes
and People (book)

AUBURN
The City of Homes
The Industrial Heart of
Maine
The Shire City of Andros-
coggin County
The Shoe City (about 15
shoe factories)
The Twin Cities (with
Lewiston)

AUGUSTA
The Capital City (population
about 21,900)
The City of Manifold Ad-
vantages

The City of Year-Around
    Recreation

BANGOR
    The Center of Maine
    The Gateway to the North
        Woods
    The Greatest Lumber
        Market in the World
        (not claimed now)
    The Lumber City
    The Metropolis of the
        Northeast
    The Queen City (population
        about 32,200)
    The Queen City of the East
    The Twin Cities (with
        Brewer; Bangor on the
        east bank, Brewer on
        the west bank of the
        Penobscot River)

BAR HARBOR
    Maine's Most Famous
        Coast Resort (on Mount
        Desert Island, on French-
        man Bay)
    The Lobster Center of the
        World

BATH
    Maine's Shipbuilding City
    The Cradle of Ships
    The Shipbuilding Capital
    The Shipping City (on the
        Kennebec River, claims
        to have launched more
        ships than any other
        place in the world)

BELFAST
    The Biggest Little City in
        Maine
    The Broiler Capital of
        Maine
    The Broiler Capital of New
        England
    The Broiler Center
    The Capital of the Broiler
        Industry
    The Shire City of Waldo
        County

BELGRADE
    Maine's Most Beautiful Vaca-
        tion Region
    The Recreational Center of
        Central Maine
    The Vacation Spot from June
        Through October

BETHEL
    The Gateway to Maine from
        the White Mountains
    The Ideal Place in which to
        Live, Work and Play (in
        the Rangeley Lake area,
        on the Androscoggin River)
    The Quiet New England
        Village

BIDDEFORD
    The City where Life Is
        Different
    The Gateway to Maine (on
        the Saco River)
    The Major Market of York
        County (with Saco, Me.)
    The Nation's Best Recrea-
        tional Area - Four Season
        Fun
    The Twin Cities (with Saco,
        Me., opposite sides of
        the Saco River)

BINGHAM
    The City where Historic
        Yesterday Greets Dynamic
        Tomorrow

BOOTHBAY
    The Boatbuilding and Fishing
        Center
    The Resort and Artist's
        Colony

BOOTHBAY HARBOR
    The Artist's Paradise
    The Boating and Yachting
        Center
    The Boating Capital of New
        England
    The City where the Trees
        Meet the Sea
    The Home of the World
        Record Cod

The Town Rich in Historic
Beauty
The Yachting Capital of New
England

BREWER
The Twin Cities (with
Bangor, Me., opposite
sides of the Penobscot
River)

BRIDGTON
Every Season There's a
Reason to Visit
The Four Seasons Vacation-
land (Cumberland Co.)
The Vacation Fun Spot of
Western Maine (12 lakes
in the town)
The Wonderland of Lakes

BRUNSWICK
The Home of Bowdoin
College

CALAIS
The International City
(International Bridge to
St. Stephens, New Bruns-
wick, Canada)

CAMDEN
The City where the Mountains
Meet the Sea (on Penob-
scot Bay)
The Gem of Penobscot Bay
The Prettiest Spot in Maine
The Thriving Lively Town
The Town Rich in Year-
Round Recreational and
Cultural Diversions

CARIBOU
The Center of the World's
Potato Empire
The Hub of Aroostook
County
The Hub of Five Seasons
of Activity
The Northeastern-most
City in the U.S.

CHERRYFIELD
The Sportsman's Paradise

CHINA
The Family Vacation Resort

DAMARISCOTTA
The Twin Towns (with New-
castle, Me.)
The Twin Villages (with Newcastle; Damariscotta on
the east bank of the Damariscotta River opposite
Newcastle)

DENMARK
A Place to Live, Work or
Play

EASTPORT
The Sardine Capital of the
U.S.
The Sardine City

ELLSWORTH
The City at the Crossroads
Down East
The Gateway to the Bar
Harbor Region and At-
lantic Canada

FARMINGTON
The City in Maine's Blue
Mountain Region
The Gateway to a Year
'Round Vacation
The Gateway to Rangeley and
Sugarloaf
The Gateway to the Rangeley
Lakes
The Hunter's Paradise
The Shire Town and Hub of
the County (Franklin
County)
The Shopping Center of Frank-
lin County

FORT KENT
The Gateway to Canada's St.
Lawrence Seaway (at the
junction of the Fish and
St. John River)
The Gateway to the Allagash
Country
The Gateway to the Fish
River Chain of Lakes

The Terminus of the Alla-
gash Canoe Trip

FREEPORT
The Birthplace of Maine
(where the commis-
sioners of the District
of Maine and the Com-
monwealth of Massa-
chusetts signed an agree-
ment for the separation)

FRYEBURG
The Friendly Prosperous
Town
The Place for Vacations
Year 'Round and for
Year 'Round Living

GREEN LAKE
The Gateway to the Bar
Harbor region (2,900
lakes)

GREENVILLE
The Four-Season Resort
and Trading Center for
Moosehead Region, Alla-
gash Wilderness Water-
way and Baxter State
Park

HALLOWELL
The Antique Center of Maine

HARRISON
A Family Community for
Your Maine Vacation
The Friendly Village

HOULTON
One of the Nation's Best
Locations
The Capital of Aroostook
County
The Garden of Maine
(Aroostook County agri-
cultural center)
The Shopping Center of
Northern Maine
The Town Just Rite for
Your Plant Site
You'll Like Living in Houlton

JACKMAN
The Gateway to Real Vaca-
tion Pleasure
The Switzerland of Maine

KENNEBEC
The Heart of the Nations
Vacationland

KENNEBUNK
The "Maine" Idea in Recreation

KENNEBUNKPORT
The Famous Seafaring Town

KINGFIELD
The Little City in the Woods

KITTERY
The Gateway to Maine

LAKEWOOD
The Broadway Colony in the
Heart of Maine (Lakewood
Playhouse and Summer
colony)
The Ideal Summer Resort

LEWISTON
The Home City
The Ideal Working City
The Industrial Center
The Industrial Heart of
Maine
The Progressive, Prosperous
and Peaceful Community
The Spindle City (largest
textile manufacturing center
in Maine; the home of
Bates Mfg. Co.)
The Textile Center
The Twin Cities (with Auburn,
Me.)
The Working City

MANCHESTER
The Queen City of Maine

MILLINOCKET
The City in the Heart of
Maine's Vacationland
The Gateway to Famous

Recreation Areas
The Gateway to Mt. Katah-
din
The Magic City
The Vacation Spot in Northern
Maine

MONHEGAN
The Fortunate Island (in
Knox County, island in
the Atlantic Ocean)

MONHEGAN ISLAND
The Cradle of New England

MOSCOW
The City where Historic
Yesterday Greets Dynamic
Tomorrow

MOUNT KATAHDIN
America's Alarm City

NAPLES
The Center of the Sebago-
Long Lake Resort Region
of Long Lake
The Heart of the Region

NEWCASTLE
The Twin Towns (with
Damariscotta, Me.)
The Twin Villages (on the
west bank of the
Damariscotta River oppo-
site Damariscotta on the
east bank)

NORWAY
Maine's Fastest Growing
Industrial and Recrea-
tional Area
The Fastest Growing Com-
munity in Maine
The Snowshoe Town of
America

OGUNQUIT
Ogunquit Is the Sea
The Beautiful Place by the
Sea (scenic three-mile
beach whose Indian name
means "beautiful place by
the sea")

OLD ORCHARD BEACH
Sun and Fun! Sand 'N Sea!
The All-Round Playground
(seashore resort)
The City of Sun and Fun,
Sand 'N Sea
The Cleanest Beach in the
World
The Finest Beach in the
World (700 feet wide at
low tide)
The Playground of the Nation
The Playground of Vacation-
land

OLD TOWN
The Canoe City (industrial
city on the Penobscot
River where world-famed
canoes are manufactured)

PARIS
Maine's Fastest Growing In-
dustrial and Recreational
Area
The City on the Hill
The Fastest Growing Com-
munity in Maine (popu-
lation about 300)
The Rockhound's Paradise

PATTEN
The Northern Gateway to the
Natural Paradise Baxter
Park
The Unspoiled Beauty Spot of
Northern Maine

PEAKS ISLAND
The Island of Easy Living
(part of Portland, Maine)

PENOBSCOT
The City of Historic Beauty
The City of Solid Comfort

PITTSFIELD
The Center of Progress in
Maine (on the Sebasticook
River)

PORTLAND
A Wonderful Place to Live,
to Work and Play

America's Sunrise Gateway
The Beautiful City by the
   Sea
The Beautiful Town that
   Is Seated by the Sea
The Forest City
The Gateway to Vacation-
   land
The Hill City
The Largest City and Com-
   mercial Center of Maine
The Vacation City on Casco
   Bay

PRINCETON
   The Gateway to the Grand
      Lakes Area

RANGELEY
   The Summer Capital of
      Golf in the U.S.
   The Trading Center for
      the Rangeley Lakes Chain
   The Year-Round Resort

RAYMOND
   The Tall Tower Town

ROCKLAND
   The Lobster Capital of the
      World
   The Metropolis of the
      Penobscot Bay Region

RUMFORD
   Maine's Outstanding Winter
      Sports Center

SACO
   The City where Life Is
      Different
   The Gateway to Maine (on
      the Saco River)
   The Major Market of York
      County (with Biddeford,
      Me.)
   The Twin Cities (with
      Biddeford)

SANFORD
   The Up and Coming City
      (in York County, popu-
      lation about 10,500)

SCARBOROUGH
   Maine's Most Beautiful Un-
      spoiled Sandy Beach on
      Pront's Neck

SEARSPORT
   The Fastest Growing Deep
      Water Seaport in Maine
      (Penobscot Bay)
   The Home of Old Sea Cap-
      tains
   The Home of World Famous
      Sea Captains

SEBAGO LAKE
   The Town of Sandy Beaches

SKOWHEGAN
   The Friendliest Town in
      New England (on the
      Kennebec River, (popu-
      lation about 6,600)
   The Place to Live, Play
      and Work
   The Place to Watch

SOUTH BERWICK
   The Parish of Unity

STOCKTON SPRINGS
   The Home of the World's
      Largest Black Walnut
      Processing Plant
   The Home of the World-
      Famous Stockton Cheese

STRONG
   The Toothpick Center of
      Maine

VINALHAVEN
   Maine's Most Enchanting
      Island

WATERVILLE
   The Bullhead Capital of the
      World
   The Elm City
   The Site of Colby College
      Nestled in Maine Country-
      side
   The Wool City

WELLS
One of New England's Most
Famous Coast Resorts
The Fine Resort Area on
the Coast

WISCASSET
The Modern Town Rich in
History (historic homes
built in the 1790's and
early 1800's)

YARMOUTH
The Coastal Town of Charm
and Beauty (on Casco Bay)
The Town on the Shore of
Historic Casco Bay

YORK
Maine in a Nutshell
The Southern Gateway to
Maine

MARYLAND

ANNAPOLIS
Crabtown (crab fishing)
The Ancient City (Capital of
Maryland in 1694)
The Athens of America
The Capital City (popula-
tion about 34,200)
The City where Land and
Water Meet
The Crab City
The Crabtown-on-the Bay
(crab fishing)
The First Peace Time
Capital of the United
States
The Gateway to the South
The Heart of Maryland
The Modern City with a
Colonial Setting
The Venice of America
(many creeks and streams)

BALTIMORE
Maryland's Largest City

(population about 847,000)
The Aviation Center of the
East
The Birthplace of the Star
Spangled Banner
The City of Promise
The City of Tomorrow
The Convention City
The Mobtown (lawless ele-
ment which prevailed par-
ticularly during the Civil
War)
The Monumental City (first
city to erect a monument
to George Washington,
cornerstone laid July 4,
1815)
The National Anthem City
(where the Star Spangled
Banner was written)
The Nation's Most Hospitable
City

BETHESDA
The Western Gateway to the
Nation's Capital

BETTERTON
The Jewel of the Upper
Chesapeake

CHESTERTOWN
The City on the Chester

CHEVY CHASE
The Suburb of Washington

COLUMBIA
The City of the Future
The New City for People and
Business

CRISFIELD
The Seafood Capital of the
World (on Tangier Sound,
part of Chesapeake Bay)

CUMBERLAND
The Heart of the Potomac
Highlands (eastern end of
Georges Creek)
The Queen City
The Transportation City

EASTON
  The Colonial Capital of
    the Eastern Shore
    (unofficial)
  The Newport of the
    Eastern Shore

ELKTON
  Gretna Green
  Gretna Green of
    Maryland
  Head of Elk

FREDERICK
  The City in Mary-
    lands Historic Heart-
    land
  The Heart of Industry
  The Hub of History

GREENBELT
  The Cooperative Com-
    munity

OCEAN CITY
  A City There's a Lot to
    Like About
  Maryland's Playground
  The City Just for Fun
  The Fort Lauderdale
    of the Eastern
    Shore
  The White Marlin Capital
    of the World
  There's a Lot to Like
    About Ocean City

POCOMOKE CITY
  Home of the National
    Bass Round-Up

REHOBETH
  Golftown, U.S.A.

SALISBURY
  The Central City
    of the Eastern
    Shore
  The Tennis Capital
    of the World (U.S.
    Indoor Tennis
    Tournaments are
    held here)

MASSACHUSETTS

AGAWAM
  The Mother of Springfield
    (original settlement 1634)

AMESBURY
  The Carriage Center of the
    World

AMHERST
  The Distinguished and
    Friendly Community
  The Seat of Amherst College
  The Town with Traditional
    New England Hospitality

ASHFIELD
  The Little Switzerland

BEDFORD
  Wilderness Town

BELLINGHAM
  The Growing Community Cen-
    tered in a Growing Market

BERNARDSTON
  The Clown Capital of the
    World (headquarters of the
    Clown Club of America)

BEVERLY
  The Birthplace of the Ameri-
    can Navy (the schooner
    "Hannah" was armed, out-
    fitted and commissioned by
    George Washington in 1775
    as the first ship of the
    American Navy)
  The City in the Country by
    the Sea
  The Garden City
  The Heart of the Famous
    North Shore (on the At-
    lantic Ocean)
  The Historic City in the
    County by the Sea
  The Home Port of the
    First Armed Schooner
    "Hannah"

BOLTON
  The Residential Community

BOSTON
  Beantown
  Bostonia
  The American Athens
  The Athens
  The Athens of America
  The Athens of the New World
  The Athens of the United States
  The Athens of the West
  The Baked Beans City
  The Bay Horse
  The Birthplace of Freedom
  The Bitches' Heaven
  The Capital City (population 601,000)
  The Capital of New England
  The City of Baked Beans
  The City of Bean Eaters
  The City of Contrasts
  The City of Firsts
  The City of Kind Hearts
  The City of Notions
  The City of Paul Revere
  The Classic City
  The College Capital of the World
  The Cradle of Liberty
  The Cradle of the American Revolution
  The Historic Capital of Massachusetts
  The Historical City
  The Home of Baked Beans
  The Home of the Freedom Trail
  The Home of the Homeless Ballet
  The Hub
  The Hub of New England
  The Hub of the Commonwealth
  The Hub of the Solar System (so called by Oliver Wendell Holmes)
  The Hub of the Universe (statement attributed to Oliver Wendell Holmes)
  The Hub Town
  The Literary Emporium
  The Major Cultural Center of the World

  The Metropolis of New England
  The Modern Athens
  The Mother City of America
  The Panhandler's Heaven
  The Puritan City
  The Puritan Zion
  The Tri-Mountain City (the three hills on which it was originally built)
  Tremont

BRAINTREE
  The Future Industrial Capital of the South Shore

BROCKTON
  The City of Shoes (shoe products)
  The Industrial City
  The Shoe City

BROOKLINE
  The Richest Town in the World
  The Town of Millionaires (a residential suburb of Boston)

CAMBRIDGE
  The Athens of America
  The Center of History, Education and Industry
  The Geographical Center of the Metropolitan Boston Area
  The Hub of a New World (title of book by Christopher Rand)
  The Outstanding American City
  The University City (Harvard University, Radcliffe College, Massachusetts Institute of Technology, etc.)

CHATHAM
  The First Stop of the East Wind (on Cape Cod)
  The Town where Summer Is Air-Conditioned (Atlantic Ocean on one side, Nantucket Sound on the other)

CHELSEA
The City of Transformations

CHESTERFIELD
The Friendly Town

CHICOPEE
The City of Elms
The Fastest Growing City
in New England
The Future Minded City
(population about 62, 500)
The Hub of Fast Trans-
portation

CLINTON
The Industrial and Com-
mercial Center

CONCORD
The Cradle of Liberty
(battle fought April 19,
1775)
The Golden Age Haven

DEDHAM
The Birthplace of Democracy
The Sober-Minded (settled
in 1636)

DEERFIELD
The Historic Village

DENNIS
The Heart of Cape Cod

DUXBURY
The Mayflower Town

EASTHAM
Vacationland, U.S.A.

EVERETT
The Industrial Half-Sister

FALL RIVER
The Border City
The City Built on Yarn
and Water
The City of Falling
Water
The Home of the U.S.S.
Massachusetts

The Scholarship City (numerous scholarships offered)
The Spindle City (cotton and
textile mills)

FALMOUTH
The Naples of America

FITCHBURG
The Mercantile Center
The Paper Manufacturing
City
The Quality City

FOXBORO
The City on the Crossroads
of the Expressways
The Ideal Location for Commerce

FRAMINGHAM
The Diversified Manufacturing
Community

FRANKLIN
Industry Need Not Wish in
Franklin

GARDNER
The Chair Capital of the
World
The Chair City (furniture
manufacturing companies
and large chair in the
town square)

GLOUCESTER
America's First and Most
Historic Fishing Port
The Ocean Paradise

GREAT BARRINGTON
The Shopping Center of
Southern Berkshire
Country
The Winter Playground

GREENFIELD
The Dream-town
The Well-balanced Community

HAVERHILL
America's Oldest Industrial
City

The Place by the Winding
River
The Queen Shoe City of
the World
The Shoe Town

HOLYOKE
A City in the Country
The City at the Heart of
Industrial New England
The City of Diversified
Industries
The City of Uninterrupted
Electric Power
The Fine Writing Paper
Center of the World
The Industrial City
The Largest Industrial
City in Western Massa-
chusetts
The Paper City (better-
grade writing paper
produced)
The Paper City of the
World

HUDSON
The City where "Growth"
Is in High Gear
The Crossroads of Industrial
Development

HYANNIS
The Main Street of the
South Shore

IPSWICH
The Birthplace of American
Independence
The Home of the Famous
Ipswich Clam

LANCASTER
An Agricultural and Resi-
dential Town

LAWRENCE
The City where Modern
America Began
The City where Visitors
Meet Hospitality
The Immigrant City
The Textile Capital of

the World
The Worsted Mill Capital of
the World

LEOMINSTER
The Baby City (became a
city in 1915)
The Comb City (in 1845 had
24 factories making combs)

LEXINGTON
The Birthplace of American
Liberty
The Cradle of Liberty
(Minute Men resisted
British troops, April 19,
1775)

LOWELL
The City of Magic
The City of Spindles
The Manchester of America
(Manchester, England,
cotton manufacturing city)
The Modern American Athens
(Lowell Technical Institute)
The Spindle City (cotton and
woolen mills)

LUDLOW
The Industrial Center

LYNN
Shoe Capital of the World
The Center of Distribution
The City of Shoes
The City of Soles
The Machine City
The Shoe City (manufacturing
began 1635)

MALDEN
The Ideal City
The Proud City with a Bright
Future

MARBLEHEAD
The Birthplace of the Ameri-
can Navy
The City where Tradition
Lingers
The Greatest Town for
Fishing in New England

(seacoast on Massachusetts Bay and Atlantic Ocean)
The Yachting Capital of the World
The Yachting Center of the World

MARTHA'S VINEYARD
One Hundred Square Miles of Picturesque Pleasure
The Friendly Island (in Atlantic Ocean)

MELROSE
The City of Homes and Gracious Living

MIDDLETOWN
Santa's Lookout

MONTAGUE
The Typical Puritan Town

NANTUCKET
The Far Away Island (30 miles off the Massachusetts coast in the Atlantic Ocean)
The Far Away Land (30 miles off the mainland in the Atlantic Ocean)
The Island of Enchantment

NEW BEDFORD
The Economy Gateway
The Gateway to Cape Cod
The Leading Scallop Port of the World
The Trading Center
The Whaling Capital of the World
The Whaling City (at one time the greatest whaling port in the world)

NEW SEABURY
America's Most Honored Community

NEWBURYPORT
Historic Newburyport

The Birthplace of the United States Coast Guard
The City of Captains' Houses
The City of Industry
The City with a Blending of Past and Present on the Banks of the Merrimac
The Yankee City

NEWTON
The Commuter's Haven (a suburb of Boston, Mass.)
The Garden City
The Tin Horn Village

NORTHAMPTON
The Heart of the Pioneer Valley
The Meadow City

NORTON
The Typical New England City

OAK BLUFFS
The City for Fun in the Sun

ORANGE
The Home of Minute Tapioca
The Sport Parachuting Center of the United States of America

ORLEANS
The City Forty Miles at Sea

PEABODY
The Largest Leather City (numerous tanneries producing many types of leather)
The Leather City (tanneries)

PITTSFIELD
The Center of Culture
The City of Culture
The Heart of the Berkshires (on the Housatonic River)
The Heart of the Famous Berkshire Hills
The Industrial City
The Middle Town of New England
The Mill Town

The Show Country of New
England
The Vacation Land in the
Center of the Berkshires
The Youthful Community

PLAINVILLE
The World's Largest
Specialty Jewelry Manu-
facturing Center

PLYMOUTH
America's Home Town
Pilgrim Land
Plymouth Offers Progress
The City where the Old
Meets the New
The Corner Stone of a
Nation
The First Town of America
(December 1620, Pil-
grims made first perma-
nent settlement north of
Virginia)
The Home of Historic
Plimoth Plantation
The Hometown of America
The Land of the Pilgrims,
Sun and Sand
The Nation's Birthplace
The Town where There Is
Fun for the Entire
Family

PROVINCETOWN
The Port of the Pilgrims
The Tip of Cape Cod (pro-
jects into Cape Cod Bay
and Atlantic Ocean, first
landing place of Pilgrims,
Nov. 11, 1620)

QUINCY
Enlightening, Entertaining,
Exciting
The Birthplace of Liberty
The Birthplace of the
Second and Sixth Presi-
dents (John Adams and
his son, John Quincy
Adams)
The City of Presidents
The City where American

Independence Began
The City with a Proud Heri-
tage and a Sparkling
Future
The Fastest Growing City in
Massachusetts
The Granite City
The Shipbuilding City

ROCKPORT
The Artist's Paradise
The City at the Tip of Cape
Ann
The Most Popular Summer
Resort in New England
The Quaint Seacoast Town at
the Tip of Cape Ann

SALEM
New England's Treasure
House
The Center of the Beautiful
North Shore of Massa-
chusetts
The City of Homes
The City of Peace
The City of Witches (famous
witchcraft trials in colonial
days about 1692)
The City where History
Blends with Progress
The Historic City
The Most Historic City in
the East
The Most Historic Community
The Paradise of New Eng-
land
The Witch City
The Witchcraft City

SALISBURY BEACH
Five Miles of Smiles, Sea,
Sand and Fun
New England's Playground on
the Atlantic
The Jones Beach of New
England

SANDWICH
The Home of Sandwich
Glass (manufactured
from 1825 to 1887)

SAUGUS
   The Birthplace of America's
   Iron and Steel Industry

SCITUATE
   The Vacation or Year
   Round Home City (on the
   Atlantic Ocean)

SHELBURNE FALLS
   The Town of Tumbling
   Waters (center of the
   hydroelectric plants of
   the New England Power
   Company)

SOMERVILLE
   The City of Hills
   The City of Homes
   The Heart of New England

SOUTH EGREMONT
   No Other Place Quite
   Like It
   The Complete Resort

SOUTH LEE
   The Small Village in the
   Berkshires

SOUTHBRIDGE
   The Eye of the Common-
   wealth (ophthalmic
   products)
   The Heart of New England

SPRINGFIELD
   A Host without Parallel
   One of the Most Accessible
   Cities in the Eastern
   States
   The Best Convention Point
   in the East
   The City of Homes
   The City Rich in Tradition
   and Opportunity
   The City where There's
   Something for Everybody
   The Convention City
   The Crossroads of New
   England
   The Dean of the 27 Spring-
   fields in the U.S.A.

The Distribution Center of
   the Northeast
The Home of More Than
   4,000 Commercial
   Travelers
The Metropolis of Western
   Massachusetts
The Rifle City (National
   Armory established April
   2, 1794)

STERLING
   An Appealing Residential-
   Agricultural Community

STOCKBRIDGE
   The Village Nestled in the
   Storied Berkshire Hills

STURBRIDGE
   The Home of the Famous
   Old Sturbridge Village

SUDBURY
   The Puritan Village

TANGLEWOOD
   America's First Summer
   Festival

TAUNTON
   The Christmas City
   The Cradle of American
   Liberty (a Liberty Pole
   was erected October 1774)
   The Largest City for Its
   Size (population about
   45,400)
   The Stove City

VINEYARD HAVEN
   The Place where Life Is
   Real Throughout the Year
   The Port of Entry and Busi-
   ness Center

WALTHAM
   The City of Five-Score
   Industries
   The Heartland of Industry and
   Electronics
   The Precision City

WAREHAM
  The City where Strangers
    Become Friends
  The City where the Land
    Meets the Water
  The Place to Live, Relax
    and Play--Night and Day

WELLESLEY
  The Town of Schools--and
    a College (Wellesley
    College for women, Bab-
    son Institute for men)

WESTBORO
  The Crossroads of New
    England

WESTFIELD
  The Big Little City Growing
    Bigger Yearly
  The City with a Future
  The Whip City (manufac-
    turers of whips)

WEST SPRINGFIELD
  The Site of the Eastern
    States' Exposition

WEYMOUTH
  An Aggregate of Villages

WILLIAMSTOWN
  The Village Beautiful

WINCHENDON
  The City in the Center of
    New England
  The Toy Town (manu-
    facturing center)

WOBURN
  The Home of a Yankee
    Count
  The Tanning City

WOODS HOLE
  America's Naples (on the
    southwestern tip of
    Cape Cod)

WORCESTER
  The Birthplace of Modern
    Rocketry

  The City in the Heart of
    Massachusetts Vacation-
    land
  The City of Diversified Indus-
    tries
  The City of Prosperity
  The Faithful City (from its
    motto "Floreat Semper
    Civitas Fidelis")
  The Heart of Massachusetts
  The Heart of the Bay State
  The Heart of the Common-
    wealth
  The Heart of the Massachu-
    setts Vacationland
  The Population Center
  The Population Center, the
    Highway Center and the
    Rail Center of New England

MICHIGAN

ADRIAN
  The Maple City of Michigan
    (shade trees)

ANN ARBOR
  The Research Capital of the
    Midwest
  The Research Center of the
    Midwest (University of
    Michigan)

BATTLE CREEK
  The Best Known City in the
    World (population about
    37,000)
  The Best Known City of Its
    Size in the World
  The Breakfast Food City
  The Cereal Food Center of
    the World
  The Health City
  The Health Food City

BAY CITY
  The City where the Sum-
    mer Trails Begin (on
    Lake Huron)

BEAVERTON
 The City Growing with
  Plastics

BELDING
 The Land of Chief Wabasis

BELLAIRE
 America's "Bit O'Ireland"
  in County O'Antrim

BELLEVILLE
 The Happy Town

BENTON HARBOR
 Michigan's Most Famous
  Summer Resort
 The Heart of the Fruit
  Belt
 The Twin-Cities (with St.
  Joseph)

BLANEY PARK
 The Playground of Paul
  Bunyon (Bunyon Museum)

BOYNE CITY
 The All-Season Vacationland

BRIGHTON
 The Center of Sixty-One
  Lakes

BRONSON
 The City the Depression
  Passed Up

CADILLAC
 The Friendliest Area in
  Northern Lower Michigan

CLARE
 The Gateway to the North

COLON
 The Magic City (the home
  of Harry Blackstone,
  magician)

DEARBORN
 Michigan's Dynamic City
 Michigan's Fastest Growing
  City

Michigan's Fastest Growing
 Community
The City of Advantages

DETROIT
 Detroit the Beautiful
 Dynamic Detroit
 Fordtown (Ford Motor Com-
  pany)
 God's Greatest City
 Renaissance by the River
 The Auto City
 The Automobile Capital of the
  World
 The Automobile City
 The Automobile City of the
  World
 The Automotive Capital of
  the World
 The Beautiful City of the
  Straits
 The City of Destiny
 The City of Future Magnifi-
  cence
 The City of Progress
 The City of Straits (on the
  strait connecting Lake
  Saint Clair and Lake Erie)
 The City of Twentieth Century
  America
 The Dynamic City
 The Greatest Automobile
  Capital
 The Most Beautiful City
 The Motor Capital of the
  World
 The Motor City
 The Overgrown Small Town
 The Renaissance City

EATON RAPIDS
 The Wool City

ELK RAPIDS
 The City for a Vacation of a
  Lifetime
 The Entrance to the Chain-O-
  Lakes

FLINT
 The Automobile Center
  (Buick, Chevrolet com-
  panies, etc.)

The Country Music Capital
of the North
The Home of Buick
The Vehicle City (largest
General Motors plant)

FRANKFORT
The Gateway to the Pro-
posed Sleeping Bear
National Park
The Gliding and Soaring
Center of the United
States

GAYLORD
The Ski Capitol of Michigan

GLADSTONE
The All Year Round Vaca-
tion Center

GRAND RAPIDS
The City in the Heart of
250 Sparkling Lakes and
Streams
The City of Happy Homes
The Furniture Capital of
America
The Furniture Center of
the World (high-grade
furniture)
The Furniture City
The Gateway to the Water
Wonderland
The Hub of West Michigan

GRAYLING
The Source of the Au Sable
(Au Sable River)

HAMTRAMCK
The Polish City (Polish
community, a part of
Detroit)

HARRISON
The City where the North
Begins

HOLLAND
The City of Tulips
The Clean, Colorful Tulip
City on Scenic Lake Macatawa

The Dutch City (settled in
1847 by the Dutch)
The Tulip Capital
The Tulip Center of America
The Tulip City

HONOR
The Gateway to Sleeping Bear
Dunes

HOUGHTON
America's First Mining Capital (site of Michigan College of Mining)

IRONWOOD
The Center of the Gogebic
Iron Range (open pits and
underground mines)
The Gateway City to the West

JACKSON
Jacksonopolis
The City of Roses
The Home of Illuminated
Cascades (about 500 acres
outside the city limits,
illuminated cascades,
winding canals and lagoons)
The Prison City
The Rose City

KALAMAZOO
The Celery City

LAKE CITY
The Center of a Marvelous
Natural Playground

LANSING
The Capital City (population
about 134,400)
The City in the Forest

LIVONIA
The City where Ambition
Meets Opportunity

MACKINAC ISLAND
The Bermuda of the North
(island 3 miles long, 2
miles wide)
The Fudge Capital of the World

The Showplace of the Lakes
The Summer Wonderland
(state park, resort)

MACKINAW CITY
The Gateway to Mackinac
Island and the Upper
Peninsula of Michigan

MANISTEE
The Salt City (salt deposits)

MANISTIQUE
The Motel City of the Top
O'Lake Michigan

MARQUETTE
The Center of All There Is
to See in the Upper
Peninsula
The Four Season's Play-
ground
The Queen City of Lake
Superior
The Queen City of the
Northland

MARSHALL
The Historic City of
Hospitality

MEARS
The Gateway to the Sand
Dune Mountains

MESICK
The Mushroom Capital

MORLEY
The Gateway to the Water
Wonderland

MOUNT CLEMENS
America's Bath City
(famous mineral springs)
The Health City (mineral
waters)

MOUNT PLEASANT
The Oil Capital

MUNSING
The Gateway to Pictured

Rocks (37 miles of cliffs
and odd formations about
5 miles northeast)
The Naples of America

MUSKEGON
The Gambling Queen
The Lumber City (47 lumber
mills)
The Lumber City of the
World
The Lumber Queen
The Lumber Queen of the
World
The Red Light Queen
The Saloon Queen
The Sawdust City

NEW BALTIMORE
Live and Play in Anchor
Bay
The Gateway to Michigan

NEWAYGO
America's Little Switzerland

NILES
The Four Flags City (the
only locality in Michigan
under four flags, France
England, Spain and the
United States)

OWOSSO
The Friendly City

PETOSKEY
Northern Michigan's Shopping
Center

PONTIAC
The City where Industry Is
First

ROCKFORD
The Biggest Little City in
Michigan (population about
2,400)

ROGERS CITY
The Limestone City (lime-
stone quarries)

ROYAL OAK
The City of Homes
(suburb of Detroit)
The Gateway to Eastern
Michigan

SAGINAW
The City of Opportunities
The Industrial Center
The Timber Capital of
the World

ST. JOHNS
The Hub of Michigan

ST. JOSEPH
The Twin Cities
(with Benton Harbor,
Mich.)

ST. LOUIS
The Geographical Center
of Michigan

SAULT STE. MARIE
Soo (Soo Locks, St.
Mary's Falls Ship
Canal)
The Gateway of Lake
Superior

SUTTONS
The Alpine Village

TAWAS CITY
Perchville, U.S.A.

TRAVERSE CITY
The Cherry Capital of
the World
The Cherry City

WAYLAND
The Cow Town

WAYNE
The Center of Civic and
Industrial Opportunity

WHITE CLOUD
The City where the
North Begins and the
Pure Waters Flow

WHITE ROCK
Michigan's Most Renowned
Phantom City

WHITEHALL
The City for Every Vacation
Pleasure

WYANDOTTE
The City of Good Homes
The Heart of Down River's
Chemical Empire
(numerous chemical plants)

MINNESOTA

AITKIN
The Turkey Capital

ALEXANDRIA
The Bass Capital of the
World
The Best Vacation and
Recreation Area Anywhere
The Birthplace of America
The City with Accommoda-
tions to Suit Your Desire
The City with Entertainment
for Everyone
The Entrance to Viking Land
The Home of the Runestone
The Home of the World's
Largest Viking
The Lake Region Playground
The Land of the Vikings

ANOKA
The Halloween Capital of the
World

AURORA
The City Down on the Mesabi
(on eastern edge of the
Mesabi iron range)

BAGLEY
The Gateway to Itasca
Park

BARNUM
An Arrowhead Egg
Basket (poultry raising
industry)

BEAVER BAY
A North Shore Haven
(at the mouth of the
Beaver River)

BECKER
The Sunfish Capital of the
World

BEMIDJI
One of America's Fifty
Best Vacation Spots
Paul Bunyan's Playground
The Headwaters of the
Mississippi
The Home of Bemidji
State College
The Home of Forestry
Products
The Home of Paul Bunyan

BENA
The City where the
Partridge Finds a
Refuge

BLACKDUCK
The Hunter's Rendezvous
(on Blackduck Lake)
The Lake Region in
Minnesota
The Recreational Sportland
of Minnesota
The Unexcelled Water
Sport Region

BLOOMINGTON
The City with a Future

BRAINERD
Paul Bunyan's Capital
(27-foot animated
Bunyan statue)
The Capital of the Paul
Bunyan Playground
The Home Town of Paul
Bunyan
The Hub City

BUHL
The Springs of Health and
Pits of Wealth (open pit
mines)

CARLTON
The Birthplace of the Northern
Pacific (where the first
spike was driven)

CASS LAKE
The Capital of the Chippewa
Nation (Indian tribe)
The Permanent Home of the
Pine

CLOQUET
The Modern Phoenix (built
on the ashes of an earlier
town)

COLERAINE
The Model Village (popu-
lation about 1,100)

COOK
The Home of the Christmas
Tree Industry

CROOKSTON
The City in the Agriculturally
Rich Red River Valley
The City of Churches of All
Faiths
The City of Exceptional
Transportation and Power
Facilities
The City of Golf, Beautiful
Parks
The City of Industry and
Industrial Sites
The City of Playgrounds and
Recreation
The City with Excellent
Medical Facilities
The City with Modern School
Systems
The City with the World's
Largest Ox Cart (in the
Pioneer Museum)
The Gateway to Fabulous
Hunting and Fishing
The Large Retail and Whole-
sale Distributing Center

CROSBY
The Cuyuna Capital (cuyuna
iron range)

DEER RIVER
The Gateway to the Chip-
pewa National Forest

DETROIT LAKES
The Sunfish Capital of the
World

DULUTH
Minnesota's Mini-San Fran-
cisco
The Air-Conditioned City
The Air-Conditioned Duluth
The Center of the Universe
(population about 93, 900)
The City of Destiny
The City on a Mountain
The City where the Prairie
Meets the Sea (Lake
Superior)
The Coolest Summer City
The Gateway to the World
The Gateway to the World
through the St. Lawrence
Seaway
The Hay Fever Relief
Haven of America
The Metropolis of the Un-
salted Seas
The Old Maid City, Looking
Under Her Bed Every
Night for an Ocean
The Ore and Grain Port
The Popular Convention City
The Recreational, Industrial
City
The Summer City
The Twin Ports (with
Superior, Wisc.)
The Westernmost Port on
America's Fourth Seacoast
The Year 'Round Playground
The Zenith City of the Un-
salted Sea (its position
on the Great Lakes)

EAST GRAND FORKS
The Potato Capital of the
World

ELY
The Canoe Outfitting Capital
of the World
The Capital of the Vermilion
Range (Vermilion iron
range)
The City where the Wilder-
ness Begins)
The Gate to the Sportsman's
Eden
The Gateway to the Sports-
man's Eden

EVELETH
The Hill Top City (alt.
1, 574 ft.)
The Hockey Capital of the
Nation

FAIRMONT
The Walleye Capital of the
World

FARIBAULT
The Athens of the Northwest
The Nation's Peony Capital
(20, 000 flowers in bloom)
The Peony Center of the
World (won peony prize
at the Century of Progress
Exposition 1933)

FERGUS FALLS
The City Beautiful in the
Land O'Lakes
The City in Otter Tail
Country
The City of Camping and
Hunting
The City of Recreation
The City of Winter and
Water Sports
The Dairying City
The Queen City of the Otter
Trail Empire

GILBERT
The Village of Destiny

GLENWOOD
The Annual Waterama
City

Minnesota's Summer and
Winter Playground
The Most Beautiful City
in the State
The Vacation Area
The Winter Fishing Capital

GRAND MARAIS
The Place where Lake
Meets Forest (on Lake
Superior)

GRAND PORTAGE
The Gateway to Isle
Royale National Park
The Oldest Settlement
in Minnesota (central
depot of the North-
west Company in
1792)

HIBBING
America's Iron Capital
America's Mining Capital
The Iron Ore Capital of
the World (population
about 15,500)
The Richest Village on
Earth
The Town that Moved Over-
night

HOVLAND
The Lake Trout Capital

INTERNATIONAL FALLS
The Trail's End (across
the Rainy River from
Fort Frances, Ontario,
Canada)

LAKE CITY
The Birthplace of Water
Skiing (1922)

LAMBERTON
The Area Trade Center
The Grain Center

LITTLE FALLS
The Small Boat Capital
of the World

LONG PRAIRIE
The Largest Little Pig
Market

LONGVILLE
The Turtle Center of the
World

MILLE LACS
The Walleye Capital of the
World

MINNEAPOLIS
America's Safest Big City
The Center of the Flour
Milling Industry
The City in Touch with
Tomorrow
The City of Industry
The City of Lakes
The City of Lakes and Mills
(title of book)
The City of Lakes and Parks
The City of Opportunity
The City to Watch
The Dual Cities (with St.
Paul)
The Fast-Growing Nerve
Center for America's
Great Northland Empire
The Flour City (extensive
milling)
The Flour Milling Capital of
the World
The Gateway City
The Gateway to the North-
west
The Milltown
The Sawdust City
The Twin Cities (with St.
Paul)
The Twin City (with St. Paul)
The Twins (with St. Paul)

MOOSE LAKE
The Southern Gateway (be-
tween Superior and St.
Paul)

MORRIS
The City for Education and
Research

The City of Eight Beautiful
Churches
The City with Excellent
Hunting and Fishing
The Heart of West Central
Minnesota
The Home of North Central
Soil and Water Conser-
vation Research Field
Station
The Little City with Big
Schools
The Modern Baseball Park
City
The Progressive Business
Community
The Shopping Center for
50,000 Minnesotans
The State Recreation Area

MOUNTAIN LAKE
The Birthplace of the
Mesabi

NISSWA
The Four Season Vacation-
land

NORTHFIELD
America's Holstein Capital
The City of Cows, Col-
leges and Contentment
(St. Olaf and Carleton
College)
The Holstein Capital of
America

OWATONNA
The Butter Capital of the
World
The Typical American City

PARK RAPIDS
The Center of All-Year Fun
The Center of Unexcelled
Water Sports
The City at the Headwaters
of the Mississippi River
The City for Summer or
Winter Vacation
The Vacation Region of
Minnesota
The Winter Wonderland

PRINCETON
The City of Flowers

PROCTOR
The Hub

REDWOOD FALLS
Hunting Headquarters
Southwestern Minnesota's
Finest Shopping Center
The Center of the Sioux
Uprising (1862)
The Center with Recreation
for Everyone
The Progressive Agricultural
Region
The Scenic City of Southern
Minnesota

ROCHESTER
The Busiest Potential
Metropolitan Market

ST. CLOUD
The Busy Gritty Granite City
The City of Diversified
Industry
The City of Extraordinary
Health-Care Services
The City of Industrial
Progress
The City where the Missis-
sippi Becomes Mighty
The Granite City (first
quarry opened 1868)
The Major Medical Center
The Talked-about City

ST. PAUL
Pig's Eye
The Boston of the West
The Capital City (population
about 291,000)
The City in the Land of
Lakes
The Dual Cities (with Min-
neapolis)
The Gateway to the Famed
Northwoods
The Gateway to the North-
west
The Gem City
The Ideal American City

The North Star City
The Saintly City
The Twin Cities (with
  Minneapolis)
The Twin City (with Min-
  neapolis)
The Twins (with Minne-
  apolis)
The Winter Sport Capital
  of the Nation

SAUK CENTRE
The Home of the Original
  Main Street (Sinclair
  Lewis' book)

SIBLEY
The End of the World

SLAYTON
The Hub City

THIEF RIVER FALLS
The Capital of U.S. Snow-
  mobiling
The Snowmobile Capital
  of the U.S.

VIRGINIA
The Queen City of the
  Iron Range
The Queen City of the
  Range

WADENA
The Vacation Land

WALKER
The Excellent Hunting
  Paradise
The Home of the Walleyed
  Pike
The Leech Lake Area
  Paradise
The Muskie Capital of the
  World
The Paradise for the
  Sportsman and the
  Family
The Vacationer's Paradise
  (in the Chippewa
  National Forest)
The Water Sports Paradise

WATERVILLE
The Bullhead Capital of the
  World

WINONA
Minnesota's Outdoor Play-
  ground
The Gate City (on Mississippi
  River)

WORTHINGTON
The Business Heart of South-
  western Minnesota
The Turkey Capital of Minne-
  sota
The Turkey Capital of the
  World

MISSISSIPPI

BAY ST. LOUIS
The Praline Capital of the
  World

BILOXI
America's Riviera (27 mile
  sand beach)
Heart of the Fabulous Gulf
  Coast Country
Mississippi's Great Resort
  and Historic Center
Nation's Seafood Center
The Center of a Bustling
  Seafood Industry
The Fisherman's Paradise
The Mother of New Orleans
The Oldest French City in
  the United States
The Thriving Tourist Capitol
The Year 'Round Resort and
  Convention Center

BROOKHAVEN
The Homeseeker's Paradise
The Hospitality Capital of
  the New South
The Industrial Paradise
The Perfect Place for
  Growing Up

CANTON
The Historic Town of the
Old South--Now a Pro-
gressive City

CLARKSDALE
The Golden Buckle on the
Cotton Belt

CLEVELAND
So Near to So Much
The City of Opportunity
The Home of Delta State
College
The Hub of the Delta

COLUMBUS
The Beautiful City
The City of Diversified
Industries
The City where Industrial and
Agricultural Activities Are
Blended with Dairying and
Livestock Production
The City with an Important
Asset to Industrial Ex-
pansion (Tennessee-
Tombigbee Waterway)
The City with Over 100
Ante-Bellum Homes
The City with the Oldest
State College for Women
(Mississippi State Col-
lege for Women)
The Friendly City
The Historical City with a
Progressive Outlook
The Town with the Most to Offer

CORINTH
The City that Smiles Back
The City where Dixie
Welcomes You

CRYSTAL SPRINGS
Tomatopolis of the World

GLOSTER
It's a Fine Place to Live

GREENVILLE
Mississippi's Largest River
Port

One of Mississippi's Fastest
Growing Cities
The City where Main Street
Meets the River and Joins
Main Street Mid-America
The Fast Growing City
The Largest River Port in
Mississippi
The Metropolis of the Mis-
sissippi Delta
The Port City of the Delta
The Service Center to Main-
stream U.S.A.

GREENWOOD
One of the World's Largest
Long-staple Cotton
Markets
The City in the Heart of
Mississippi's Rich Delta
The City with a Future
The City with an Aristocratic
Past
The City with an Exciting
Future
The Medical Center of the
Mississippi Delta (loca-
tion of Greenwood-Leflore
Hospital)
The Sportsman's Paradise

GRENADA
The Heart of North Missis-
sippi and Beautiful
Grenada Lake

GULFPORT
America's Riviera (on Gulf
of Mexico)
Mississippi's Gateway to the
Sea
The All Year Playground of
the Old South
The Central City of the
Metropolitan Mississippi
Gulf Coast
The City in the Center of
Mid-America's Riviera
Year 'Round Resort
The City in the Center where
the Action Is
The City where Your Ship
Comes In

The City with a Future
The Home of Mississippi's
Annual Deep Sea Fishing
Rodeo (the largest deep
sea fishing event in the
world)
The Hospitality City

HAZLEHURST
The Center of Copiah,
Mississippi's Most
Diversified County

HOLLY SPRINGS
The Athens of the South
The City of Roses
The Educational, Cultural
and Business Center

JACKSON
A City of Rich Cultural
and Residential Charm
Chimneyville
One of the Fastest Growing
Cities in the Nation
One of the South's Fastest
Growing Cities
The Agricultural Capital
The Balanced Community
of Opportunity and
Happy Homes
The Capital City (popula-
tion about 171,000)
The Capital of America's
State of Opportunity
The Center of Commerce
and Agriculture
The Center of Year 'Round
Recreation
The City at the Crossroads
of the Old and New South
The City of Fine Homes,
Churches, and Schools
The City that Means Busi-
ness and the Good Life
Too
The City where a New
South Is in the Making
The City where the Old
South and the New South
Meet
The Crape Myrtle City
The Crossroads of the

Old and the New South
The Crossroads of the South
The Educational Capital
The Friendly City
The Industrial Capital
The Oil Capital
The Oil Center for Missis-
sippi
The Vivid Capital of the Old
South

LAUREL
Magnolia's Largest Industrial
City
Mississippi's Industrial City
(canning, sweet potato,
starch manufacturing,
masonite)
The Chemurgic City (pine
lumber converted into
masonite)
The Magnolia's State Industrial City
The Oil Capital of Mississippi

LONG BEACH
The Friendly City

MCCOMB
The Camellia City of
America
The Charm Circle of the
South
The City of Camellias

MERIDIAN
The Heart of the New South

MOSS POINT
The Payroll Town

NATCHEZ
The Bluff City (alluvial bluffs
overlooking the Missis-
sippi River)
The City on the Mississippi
where the Old South Still
Lives
The City where the Charm,
Culture and Traditions
of the Old South Blend
in a Modern City

The City where the Old
South Still Lives
The Historic City of
America (explored in
1682 by La Salle)

OXFORD
The City for Golf, Fishing,
Hunting
The City for Swimming
and Motor Sports
The Good Place to Live
The Home of "Ole Miss"
(The University of Mis-
sissippi)
The Home of the Famous
Chambers Ranges
The Home of the University
of Mississippi
The Important Agricultural
Center
The Recreation Capital of
the World

PASCAGOULA
Mississippi's Industrial
Seaport
The Industrial and Recrea-
tional Paradise

PASS CHRISTIAN
Nature's Gift to the Gulf
Coast
The City where You Can
Live and Enjoy Life

PICAYUNE
The Gateway to the Future
in Space
The Tung Oil Center of
America
The Tung Tree Capital of
the World

POPLARVILLE
One of the Banner Agri-
cultural Counties in the
South

STARKVILLE
The Dairy Center of the
South

TUPELO
Mississippi's Best Example
of the New South
Mississippi's Finest Example
of the New South
The Capital of the Great
Chickasaw Nation
The City where Industry,
Agriculture and Cultural
Life All Balance
The City without City Limits
The City without Limits
The Community Working To-
gether for the Future
The First TVA City (first
contract with the Tennes-
see Valley Authority to
purchase electricity signed
November 11, 1933)
The Former Capital of the
Chickasaw Nation

VICKSBURG
One of the Most Rapidly
Developing Industrial
Cities
The City of Growing Indus-
trial and Commercial Im-
portance
The City Proud of Its
History
The City with One of the
Leading Medical Centers
in the South
The Gibraltar of America
(on the Mississippi River,
reputed to have been an
impregnable fortification in
the War of Secession, fell
July 4, 1863 after seige of
one year)
The Gibraltar of Louisiana
The Gibraltar of the Con-
federacy
The Gibraltar of the South
The Hill City (206 feet
altitude)
The Key City
The Leading Industries
Center of Lumber Pro-
cessing and Metal
Working

WEST POINT
The Point of Opportunity

YAZOO CITY
Mississippi's Thriving
Industrial Center
The City where the Delta
Begins
The Gateway to the Delta
(low flat on the Yazoo
River)
The Oil Capital of Mis-
sissippi

MISSOURI

ASH GROVE
The Area Shopping Cross-
roads
The Friendly Community,
the Home of Friendly
People

AURORA
The Tri-County Trading
Center

BOLIVAR
The Largest Shopping
Center in the Pomme
de Terre Area

BOONEVILLE
The Gateway to Mount
Magazine
The Gateway to the
Northern Section of the
Ozark National Forest

BUTLER
The West Gate to the Land-
O-Lakes

CAPE GIRARDEAU
The City of Roses

CARTHAGE
The City at the Cross-

roads of Mid-America
The Crossroads of Mid-
America
The Home of World Famous
Carthage Marble
The Ideal Place to Stay or
Play
The Marble City
The Pure Bred Jersey
Capital of America

CASSVILLE
The City of Seven Valleys
The Hub of the Scenic
Ozarks (near Roaring
River State Park)
The Once Confederate Capital
of America (1861)

CLINTON
The Queen City of the Golden
Valley
The Sportsman's Paradise

COLUMBIA
The Athens of the Midwest
(home of the University
of Missouri)
The City in the Center of
Things
The Convention City

CRANE
The Home of 'Old Hickory'
Ham and Bacon

DE SOTO
The Fountain City (numerous
artesian wells)

EL DORADO SPRINGS
The City where Gracious
Living and Fine Churches
Offer a Life of Content-
ment for Businessman,
Worker, Retired and the
Sportsman
The Land of Lakes Shopping
Center
The Wonder City in the
Middle of the Land of
Lakes

ELDON
The Gateway to Lake of
the Ozarks (12 miles
from Bagnell Dam)

ELLINGTON
Missouri's Finest Deer,
Squirrel, Quail and
Coon Hunting City
The City on the Ozarks
Frontier Trail
The Excellent Fishing and
Water Sports City
The Hub of the Ozarks

FAYETTE
The Mother of Counties
(organized January 13,
1816 from which 46
counties were formed,
36 in Missouri and 10
in Iowa)

FORSYTH
The Twin Lakes Capital of
of the Ozarks (Lake
Taneycomo and Bull
Shoals Lake)

GREENFIELD
The Headwaters of Stockton
Lake

HANNIBAL
The Bluff City (Cardiff
Hill and Lovers' Leap)
The Boyhood Home of Mark
Twain
The Capital of Youth (Tom
and Huck monument,
Mark Twain's characters)
The St. Petersburg of Tom
Sawyer

HOUSTON
The Big Little Town
The County Seat of Texas
County in Missouri
The Home Town of
Emmett Kelly (clown)
The Town in the Land of
the Pineys

INDEPENDENCE
The City where the West
Begins (starting place in
1849 of Santa Fe and
Oregon Trails)
The Gateway to the West
The Queen City of the Trails

JEFFERSON CITY
Jeff City (named for Thomas
Jefferson)
The Capital City (population
about 32,800)
The Convention City

JOPLIN
The Center of Mid-American
Industrial Progress
The Chemical City
The City Growing Out of
Yesterday Into Tomorrow
The Crossroads of America
The Crossroads of Mid
America
The Fastest Growing Chemi-
cal Center in the Great
Midwest
The Gateway to the Ozarks
The Town that "Jack" Built

KANSAS CITY
The City of Fountains
The City of Progress and
Contrasts
The City of the Future
The City of Wheat
The Gateway to the West and
the Southwest
The Greatest Primary Winter
Wheat Market
The Heart of America
The Heart of the United
States of America
The Home of the Athletics
(baseball team)
The Metropolis of the Mis-
souri Valley
The Mushroomopolis
The Nation's Largest Winter
Wheat Market
The Overgrown Cow Town
The Steak Center of the

the Nation (Kansas City
Livestock Exchange and
Stockyards)

KNOB NOSTER
The Gateway to the White-
man Air Force Base

LAKE OZARK
America's Fastest Growing
Vacation Area
America's Favorite Family
Vacation Area

LAMAR
The Birthplace of Harry S
Truman

LEBANON
Near to Everything Every-
where

LINCOLN
Benton County's Fastest
Growing City

LOWRY CITY
The City where the Ozarks
Meet the Plains

MARCELINE
The Magic City

MARSHALL
The Center of a Lively
Industrial and Agricultural
Trade Area
The City Beautiful
The City with a Great Po-
tential for Growth
The Mother of the West

MEXICO
The Capital of Little Dixie
The Fire Clay and Horse
Capital of the World
The Fireclay Capital (manu-
factures clay products)
The Fireclay Capital of
the World
The Saddle Horse Capital
of the World

The World's Saddle Horse
Capital

MOBERLY
Missouri's Magic City
The City in the Heart of the
Heartland
The City of Lakes, Fishing,
Boating, Swimming
The City of Modern Building
and Industry
The City with 100 Years of
Progress
The Home of Moberly Grey-
hounds (basketball cham-
pions)
The Important Railroad and
Truck Center
The Magic City
The Prosperous Agricultural
Area

MONETT
The Big "M" of the Ozarks
The Gateway to Outdoor
Fishing and Hunting Ac-
tivities

MOUND CITY
The Duck Mecca of the Midwest

NEOSHO
The City of Springs
The Excellent Hunting Area
for Deer, Quail and Small
Game
The Flower Box City
The Flowerbox City
The Important Dairy Center
(Pet Milk plant)
The Vacation Headquarters

NEVADA
The Bushwacker's Capital
(headquarters of several
Confederate detachments
in the War of Secession)

NOEL
The Christmas City

OSCEOLA
A Key Spot in the Future
of Kaysinger Reservoir
The Home of the World's
Finest Catfish

PARIS
The Gateway to the North
Central Section of the
Ozark National Forest
The Northern Gateway to
Mount Magazine and the
Magazine Recreational
Area

PIERCE CITY
A Diversified Agricultural
and Industrial Com-
munity

POPLAR BLUFF
The Eastern Gateway to
the Ozarks

RICHMOND HEIGHTS
The City of Homes

ROCKAWAY BEACH
The Perfect Vacation Spot

ROGERSVILLE
The Coon Capital of the
World

ROLLA
The Child of the Railroad
(a stopping off place
on the St. Louis-San
Francisco Railroad)
The Scientific Center

ST. CHARLES
The First Capital of Mis-
souri (1821-1826)
The Hub of Missouri's
Booming Area
The Last Outpost of
Civilization

STE GENEVIEVE
The Oldest City West
of the Mississippi

ST. JOSEPH
The City Worth While
The Home of Jesse James

ST. LOUIS
America's Great Central
Market and Tourist City
America's Shoe Capital
Paincourt
The Child of the River
The City of a Thousand
Sights
The City of Culture and
Entertainment
The City of Learning
The City of the French
The Convention City
The Family City
The Future Great City of
the World
The Gateway Arch City
The Gateway of the West
The Gateway to Space
The Gateway to the American
West
The Gateway to the Centers
of the Aerospace Industry
The Gateway to the West
The Great River City (on the
Mississippi River)
The Heart of the Midwest
The Historical and Cultural
Center
The Holiday City
The Home of the World's
Largest Brewery (An-
heuser-Busch Brewery)
The Hub of American Inland
Navigation
The Hub of the New High-
Speed Interstate Highway
System
The Largest Metropolis in
the Mississippi Valley
The Memphis of the American
Nile
The Mound City
The Parent of the West
The Parking Lot City
The Pride of the Mississippi
Valley
The Queen of the Mississippi

The Shoe Capital of America
The Showboat City
The Solid City
The Vacation City
The Vatican City

SARCOXIE
The Peony Capital of the
World

SEDALIA
A Good Place to Live,
Work and Enjoy Life
The City where North and
South Meet East and
West
The Convention City
The Gateway to the Lake
of the Ozarks
The Gateway to the Land
O'Lakes
The Home of the State Fair
The Queen City of the
Prairies

SENECA
The Northeastern Gateway
to the Grand Lake Resort
Area

SILVER DOLLAR CITY
Missouri's Historic Crafts
and Entertainment Capital
The Capital of the Ozarks

SOUTH WEST CITY
The Busy Agricultural Community

SPRINGFIELD
The Dairy, Agricultural and
Industrial Center
The Gateway to Four Ozark
Vacation Areas
The Gateway to the Southern
Ozarks
The Paris of the Ozarks
The Queen City of the
Ozarks

STOCKTON
A Wonderful Place to Rear

Your Family Beneath Wide-
Open Missouri Skies
The Best Town in the State
by a Damsite
The City at the Water's Edge
The City where "Fish Are
Jumpin' and the Livin' Is
Easy"
The City where Game in Its
Wild State Abounds
The City where You Can Live
in the City Limits and Be
on the Lake
The City where You Have the
Splendor of Four Seasons
The Haven to Retire in,
Away from the Rush

TRENTON
The City with a Future

UNIONVILLE
The Feeder Calf Capital of
the World

WARSAW
The City of Opportunity,
Recreation, Retirement
The Gunstock Capital of the
World
The Most Opportune Locality
of the Middle West
The Spoonbill Capital of the
World

WASHINGTON
Missouri's Most Industrially
Diversified Small City
The Corncob Pipe Capital of
the World
The Place to Live
The Williamsburg of the Mid
West

WEST PLAINS
The Area's Leading Agri-
cultural Trade Center
The County Seat of Hovell
County
The Feeder Pig Capital of
the World
The Fourth Largest Stock

Market in the State
The Heart of the Ozarks
The Land of Milk and
Honey
The Largest City in South
Central Missouri and
Northern Kansas
The Largest Feeder Pig
Market in the Midwest

WESTPORT
The Gateway to the Early
West

WILLOW SPRINGS
The Gateway to the South

WINDSOR
The North Gateway to the
Kaysinger Dam and
Reservoir Area

MONTANA

ANACONDA
The City on the Top of the
Rockies
The Home of the Largest
Copper Producing
Smelter and Smoke-
stack in the World (585
feet, Anaconda Mining
Co.)
The St. Moritz of the
Rockies (winter sport
resort)
The Smelter City (one of
the largest non-ferrous
producing plants)

BILLINGS
A Great Intermountain
Transportation Center
America's Ideal Vacation
Land
Montana's Only Billion
Dollar Market
The Capital of the Midland
Empire
The City in the Heart of the
Nation's Famous Dude
Ranch Country
The City in the Mountain
Country
The Civics Center of the
Midland Empire
The Commercial Center of
the Midland Empire
The Fun Capital of the Vaca-
tion State
The Gateway to America's
Wonderland
The Gateway to the West (on
the west bank of the
Yellowstone River)
The Land of Shining Mountains
The Magic City
The Midland Empire City
The Midland Empire Magic
City
The Queen City of the Mid-
land Empire
The Silver Dollar City
The Star of the Big Sky
Country
The Sun City of the Big Sky
Country

BROADUS
The Biggest Little Town in
the West (population about
800)

BUTTE
One of America's Most
Unique Cities
One of the Most Colorful
Cities in America
The Black Heart of Montana
The Center of Montana's
Wonderland
The Copper City (numerous
large copper mines)
The Heart of Montana's
Magic-land
The Important Center of
Copper Mining
The Only Electric Lighted
Cemetery in the United
States
The Richest Hill on Earth
(one of the world's

greatest mining cities)
The World's Greatest
Mining Camp

COLUMBIA FALLS
The Industrial Hub of Flathead Valley

CULBERTSON
The Hub of the Safflower
Industry

CUT BANK
Montana's Friendly Com-
munity
The Oil Capital of Montana
(about 1,200 oil wells
and 100 gas wells)

EUREKA
The Christmas Tree Capital
of the Nation
The Christmas Tree Capital
of the World

FORSYTH
The City of Trees
The Tree City

GLENDIVE
The City with a Future to
Share
The Gateway to the Historic
Northwest (seat of Daw-
son County)

GREAT FALLS
Montana's Largest and
Friendliest City (popula-
tion about 58,500)
The Electric City (hydro-
electric power plant on
the Missouri River)
The Niagara of the West
(hydro electric plants
on the Great Falls of
the Missouri)

HELENA
The Capital City (popula-
tion about 23,600)
The Last Chance Gulf (its
name in 1864)

The Queen of the Mountains

JORDAN
The Lonesomest Town in
the World (population
about 500)

KALISPELL
The Center of a Land of En-
chantment (the Swan Range
on the east, the Whitefish
Range to the north)
The Hub of the Beautiful Flat-
head Valley
The Northwest Montana's
Business and Shopping
Center

LAUREL
The Frontier of Industrial
Opportunity
The Hub of Montana's Vast
Vacationland
The Scenic Gateway
The Sportsman's Paradise

LIBBY
Nature's Play Ground

LIVINGSTON
The Home of the Original
Trout Derby (National
Trout Derby)

MILES CITY
The Cow Capital of Montana
The Cow Capital of the West
(about 25 percent of Mon-
tana's cattle and sheep)

MISSOULA
The Garden City
The Medical Center of
Western Montana
The Place to Enjoy Yourself

PHILIPSBURG
The Year-Round Sportsman's
Paradise

RED LODGE
The Resort Center

ST. MARY
   The Eastern Gateway to
   Glacier National Park

SHELBY
   The Gateway to Alaska

SIDNEY
   The Heart of the Yellowstone Valley

WEST GLACIER
   The Western Entrance to
   Glacier National Park

WOLF POINT
   The Shopping Center of
   Northeast Montana

NEBRASKA

ALLIANCE
   The Cattle Capital of
   Nebraska

AUBURN
   The City for Fishing and
   Hunting
   The City for Water Sports
   The County Seat of Nemaha
   County
   The Historical Area
   The Quail Capital of
   Nebraska
   The Thirty Acre Industrial
   Tract

BASSETT
   The Home of Famous Sand
   Hill Beef

BEATRICE
   The City of Agriculture
   The City of Industry
   The Prosperous City of
   Beauty and Good
   Living
   The Site of the first U.S.
   Homestead

BLAIR
   The City where Commerce,
   Farming, Industry and
   Education Thrive Together
   The Eastern Gateway to
   Nebraskaland

BOYS TOWN
   The City of Little Men (home
   for destitute boys)

BROWNVILLE
   Historic Brownville, where
   Nebraska Begins (three
   miles north of the Kansas
   border)

BURWELL
   The Friendliest Little City
   in Nebraska

CHADRON
   Nebraskaland's Big Game
   Capital
   The Southern Gateway to the
   Black Hills

CRAWFORD
   The Big Game Capital of
   Nebraska
   The City in the Heart of the
   Pine Ridge

FREMONT
   A Good Place to Live, Work
   and Play
   The City where Agriculture
   and Industry Meet
   The Midwest's Most Progres-
   sive City
   The Trade Center of Mid-
   East Nebraska

GERING
   The Best Lighted City in the
   World
   The City in the Heart of
   Irrigation

GOTHENBURG
   The City in the Heart of the
   Irrigated Platte Valley
   The Pony Express City

GRAND ISLAND
A Good Place to Work and
  Live
Nebraska's Third City
The Progressive City

HASTINGS
The City of Friendly Folks
The City of Liquid Gold
  (abundant water supply)
The Crossroads of the Nation
The Fastest Growing City
  in the State
The Growing City
The Queen City

KEARNEY
The Gateway to the East
The Gateway to the West
The Halfway Point--San
  Francisco to Boston
The Hub of the Nation
  (center of Platte Valley)
The Midway City

LINCOLN
The Capital City (population
  about 158, 500)
The City Worthy of a Noble
  Name
The Cornhusker Capital City
The Hartford of the West
  (insurance companies)
The Holy City
The Lilac City
The Loveliest Modern City
  in Mid-America

MCCOOK
The Center of a Fisher-
  man's Paradise
The Center of the Great
  Lakes of Nebraska
The O.K. City
The Oil Capital of South-
  west Nebraska
The Retail Center of
  Southwest Nebraska
  and Northeast Kansas

MINDEN
The Christmas City
The Home of Harold Warp's
  Pioneer Village

NEBRASKA CITY
The Arbor Lodge City (home
  of J. Sterling Morton,
  founder of Arbor Day)
The Center of Midwest Apple
  Area
The Evergrowing Industrial
  Center
The Historic City
The Town that Gave the
  World a Great Idea
  (Arbor Day)

NORFOLK
Nebraska's Game Paradise
North Nebraska's Largest
  City
The Host City (Northeast
  Nebraska)
The Southern Gateway to the
  Lewis and Clark Lake

NORTH PLATTE
The City in the Middle of
  Everywhere
The City where the Rodeo
  Was Born
The Home of Buffalo Bill

OGALLALA
Nebraska's Sport Center
The Cowboy Capital of
  Nebraska (the end of the
  Old Texas Trail terminal)
The Electronics Capital of
  the Midwest
The Gateway to the Nebraska
  Panhandle
The Home of Lake Mc-
  Conaugy and Kingsley Dam
The Official Cowboy Capital
  of Nebraska

OMAHA
Boy's Town
The City of Recreation and
  Culture
The Crossroads of the Nation
The Gate City of the West
The Gateway City
The Gateway to Nebraska's
  Vacationland
The Gateway to the West
The Market Town

The New York of Nebraska
The Queen of the Prairie
The Steak Capital of the
World
The World's Largest Live-
stock and Meat Packing
Center

ORD
The Agriculture Center
The Center for Recreation
The Heart of Nebraska Land
The Important Popcorn
Center
The Industrial Site Center
The Town in the Beautiful
North Coup Valley

PERU
The Home of State Teachers
College

PLAINVIEW
Nebraska's Friendly City

SCOTTS BLUFF
The Service Center for
Industrial Agriculture

SIDNEY
The City where the Hospi-
tality of the Old West
Remains
The Home of Historical
Fort Sidney
The Recreation Hub of the
Historical Colorful West

SUPERIOR
The Metropolis of South
Central Nebraska

VALENTINE
The City with a Heart
The Heart City of the
Sandhills
The Home of the Original
Long Horns
Valentine Has Everything
Your One-Stop Sports Para-
dise

WAHOO
The City of Opportunity

The Heart of the Nation
The Home of Good Indians

WILBER
The Czech Capital of
Nebraska

YORK
The City at the Crossroads
of Nebraskaland's Best
Hunting Country
The City where There Are
No Strangers--Just New
Friends

NEVADA

AUSTIN
The Silver Boom Town

BEATTY
The Chicago of Nevada
The Chicago of the West
The Gateway to Death
Valley

BOULDER CITY
The Garden City of Clark
County
The Garden City of Southern
Nevada
The Gateway to the Lake
Mead Recreational Area

CALIENTE
The Former Railroad Com-
munity

CARLIN
The Railroad Town
The Western Entrance to
Scenic Canyons

CARSON CITY
The Capital City
The Gateway to Lake Tahoe
and Yosemite Valley
The Smallest Capital in
America (population about
22,500)

ELKO
   The Cattle Country
   The Commerce and Govern-
      mental Center
   The Early Mormon Ranching
      Community
   The Metropolis of Eastern
      Nevada (population about
      7,600)
   The Ranching Center

ELY
   The Center of the Most Im-
      portant Mining Area in
      the United States
   The Gateway to Scenic Ad-
      venture

FALLON
   The Center for Western
      Nevada Agriculture
   The Heart of Western
      Nevada's Agricultural
      Region
   The Oasis of Nevada

GARDNERVILLE
   The Twin Cities (with
      Minden, Nev.)

GENOA
   The Oldest Town in Nevada
      (settled in 1845 by
      Mormon emigrants)

HAWTHORNE
   The Headquarters for
      Fishermen

HENDERSON
   The Chief Industrial Com-
      munity in Nevada
   The Industrial Center

LAKE TAHOE
   (see Lake Tahoe, Calif.)

LAS VEGAS
   Nevada's Largest City
   One of America's Fastest
      Growing Cities
   Playtown, U.S.A.
   The All-Season Convention-

Vacation Location
   The All-Year Resort and
      Recreation Center
   The Big Apple of the Desert
   The Booming Convention City
   The Broadway of the Desert
      (lighted main street)
   The City Built on Gambling
   The City of Chance
   The City of Destiny
   The City of Little Wedding
      Churches
   The City of Luck
   The City that Has Everything
      for Everyone--Anytime
   The City that Is Still a
      Frontier Town (used 1939)
   The City that Never Sleeps
   The City that Swings Twenty-
      four Hours a Day
   The City where the Action Is
   The City where the Fun Be-
      gins and Never Ends
   The City without Clocks (book
      by Ed Reid)
   The Con City
   The Convention Capital of
      the West
   The Desert Babylon
   The Early West in Modern
      Splendor
   The Entertainment Capital of
      the World
   The Fastest Growing Metro-
      politan Area in the Nation
   The Favored Vacation Package
      of Western America
   The Fun Capital of the World
   The Gambler's Mecca
   The Gambler's Paradise on
      Earth
   The Gateway to Lake Mead
      and Hoover Dam
   The Gateway to Pleasure
   The Gateway to the Grand
      Canyon
   The Glamor and Action Capital
      of the World
   The Great Convention-Vaca-
      tion Location
   The Green Felt Jungle
      (book by Ed Reid and
      Ovid Demaris)

The Hub City of the Scenic
Southwest
The Hub of a Vast Scenic
and Sports Wonderland
The Land of Roulette
Wheels
The Leading Entertainment
Mecca
The Luxury Resort Town
The Metropolis of Southern
Nevada
The Monte Carlo of the
West
The Nation's Great New
Convention City
The Never-Closed Casino
City
The New American Mecca
The Place where Every
Day's a Holiday
The Play Around the Clock
Time
The Playground of the
Desert
The Playground of the
"Now" Set
The Playground of the
World
The Scenic Sportland
The Sin City
The Sinful City
The Spectacular Convention
Center
The Splendor of the West
The Sun, Fun and Action
Town
The Town Blessed by an
Ideal Year-Round Climate
The Twenty-Four Hour
Gambling City
The World Famous Resort
and Convention Center
The World Renowned Strip
The World's Largest
Gambling Center
The Year-Round Center for
Major Spectator Events

LOVELOCK
Nevada's Nile Valley
The Agricultural Town

MINDEN
The Twin Cities (with
Gardnerville, Nev.)

MOUNTAIN CITY
The Early Mountain Town

RENO
The Biggest Little City in
the World (population
about 84,000)
The Center of Summer and
Winter Sports
The City where the Action Is
The Twin Cities by the
Truckee (with Sparks,
Nev.)

SPARKS
One of the Fastest Growing
Communities in the West
The City with Promise
The Rail City
The Twin Cities by the
Truckee (with Reno, Nev.)

TONOPAH
The Queen of the Silver
Camps (1900's)
The Silver Town

VIRGINIA CITY
The City of Illusion (novel
by Vardis Fisher)
The City that Saved the Union
(silver from the Comstock
mines shipped to President
Lincoln bolstered the
buying power of the Union
army)
The Home of the Comstock
Lode (one of the richest
fissure vein deposits of
gold and silver ever found)
The Queen of the Comstock
Lode
The World's Liveliest Ghost
Town

WELLS
The Gateway to the Ruby
Mountains

WINNEMUCCA
The Center for Ranching

___

NEW HAMPSHIRE

___

ASHLAND
The Nice Place to Live

BERLIN
The Chemical City
The City for the Full Life
The City in the White
Mountains
The City that Trees Built
The First Ski Club City

BETHLEHEM
The Heart of the White
Mountains

BOW
The Birthplace of Mary
Baker Eddy

CENTER SANDWICH
The Place Convenient to
the Lakes and Mountains

CLAREMONT
The Site of Two of New
Hampshire's Oldest
Churches

COLEBROOK
The Town on the Connecticut
River in Scenic Northern
New Hampshire

CONCORD
The Capital City (popula-
tion about 30,200)

DIXVILLE
The Rooftop of New Hamp-
shire
The Switzerland of America

DOVER
The Easterly Gateway to
the Lakes and White
Mountains Regions
The First Permanent Settlement in New Hampshire
The Garrison City (the
guardian fort and defender
of the state)

EXETER
The Historical Center on the
Connecticut River in
Scenic Northern New
Hampshire

FITZWILLIAM
The Picturesque Village South
of Mount Monadnock

FRANKLIN
Gateway to the White Moun-
tains
The Birthplace of Daniel
Webster
The Friendly City on the Move

GILFORD
The Place to Live, Work and
Play

GLEN
The City in the Center of the
White Mountains

HAMPTON BEACH
The City where Your Vaca-
tion Dreams Take Shape
The Favorite Family Seaside
Resort (on the Atlantic
Ocean)

HANOVER
The Home of Dartmouth College

HENNIKER
The Only Henniker on Earth

INTERVALE
The Summer and Winter Resort

JACKSON
The Exclusive Summer and
Winter Resort in the White
Mountains

JEFFERSON
Santa's Village

KEENE
The City with the Widest
Paved Street in the
World
The Garden Spot of the Uni-
verse
The Town Situated in the
Beautiful Ashuelot River
Valley

LACONIA
The City in the Heart of
the Lakes Region
The City of the Lakes
The City on the Lakes (on
Lake Winnipesaukee,
overlooks four lakes)
The City with the Panoramic
View of the Beautiful
New Hampshire Lakes
Area

LANCASTER
The Friendly Town in the
Friendly State
Santa's Village

LINCOLN
The Town in the Heart of
the White Mountains

LITTLETON
The World Capital of
Stereograph Production

LYME
The Truly Charming New
England Town

MANCHESTER
The City in the Very Heart
of New England
The City of Opportunity
The Manchester of America
The Queen City
The Queen City of New
Hampshire
The Queen City of the
Merrimack Valley (on
the Merrimack River)

The Queen City of the State
with All Modern Facilities

MEREDITH
The Latchkey to the White
Mountains
The Town that Is Going
Places

MERRIMACK
The Fastest Growing Town
in Hillsboro County

MOUNT WASHINGTON
The Goliath of All North-
eastern North America
The Top of New England

NASHUA
The Gate City (on the Nashua
River)
The Gate City of New Hamp-
shire)

NEW LONDON
The Home of Colby College

NEWPORT
The City of the Sun
The Sunshine Town

NORTH CONWAY
All-Year Sports Headquarters
The Center of the Largest
Eastern Ski Area
The Most Complete Year
'Round Resort Town in the
White Mountains
The Village of Skis
The Year 'Round Vacation
Town in the White Moun-
tains

NORTHFIELD
The Twin Towns of the New
Hampshire Lakes Region
(with Tilton)

NORTH WALPOLE
Steamtown, U.S.A.

PORTSMOUTH
An Old Town by the Sea

New England's Great Sea-
shore Resort
The New World Port (only
natural deepwater harbor
between the ports of
Portland, Me., and
Boston, Mass.)
The Port City (New Hamp-
shire's only seaport)

ROCHESTER
The City of Friendly People
The City of Governors
The Gateway to Vacation-
land

RUMNEY
The Crutch Capital of the
World (crutch manu-
facturing)

SEABROOK
The Coastal Gateway to
New Hampshire

SUNAPEE
The City where Skiing Is
an Adventure
The Leading New Hamp-
shire Resort on Beautiful
Sunapee Lake

TAMWORTH
The Place where Lakes
Meet Mountains

TILTON
The Boy's Town of New
England (Spaulding Youth
Center)
The Twin Towns of the New
Hampshire Lake Regions
(with Northfield)

WATERVILLE VALLEY
The Recreation Center of
New Hampshire
The Recreation Convention
Center of New Hampshire

WEIRS BEACH
The Complete Four Season
Resort

The Vacation Center of Beauti-
ful Lake Winnipesaukee
The Vacation Crossroads of
New England

WINNIPESAUKEE
The Smile of the Great Spirit
(name used by the Indians
for Lake Winnipesaukee)

WOLFEBORO
The Oldest Summer Resort
in America (founded 1759)

WONALANCET
The Sled Dog Center of the
U.S. (location of Chinook
Kennels)

WOODSTOCK
The Summer Resort Near
Many Scenic Points of
Interest

NEW JERSEY

ASBURY PARK
Health City, U.S.A.
One of America's Foremost
All Year Resorts
The All Year Home Town
The Beauty Spot of the North
Jersey Coast (on the At-
lantic Ocean)
The City-by-the-Sea
The Commercial Center of
the North Jersey Coast
The Nation's Great All-Year
Resort
The Nation's Great All-Year
Resort City-by-the-Sea
The Nation's Great Resort
City-by-the-Sea
The Queen of Ocean Resorts
The Resort of Enjoyment

ATLANTIC CITY
America's Bagdad by the Sea
(on the Atlantic Ocean)

America's Number One
Resort for Year-Round
Health and Pleasure
America's Ocean Playground
The Biggest Little City in
America
The City of Fun and Frolic
The City of Health and
Recreation
The City where the Action Is
The City with More of
Everything
The Coastline of Health and
Happiness
The Four Season Resort for
Health, Rest and Pleasure
The Host with the Most
The Mecca of the Millions
The More than Just the
Sea and the Shore
The Number One Host of
the Jersey Coast
The Oldest Newest Most
Perfect Year-Round Re-
sort in America
The Playground of the World
The Queen of Resorts
The Showplace of the Nation
The Skyline of Romance
The Vacation Capital of the
Nation
The Vacation City Supreme
The World's Playground
The Year 'Round Vacation
Playland

AVALON
The City Cooler by a Mile
The Gem of the Jersey
Coast

BAYONNE
The Oil City (refineries
and tanks, pipeline to
Longview, Texas)

BELMAR
The Fisherman's Paradise
The Modern Little City

BERGEN
The Foreign Car Capital of
the U.S.

BRADLEY BEACH
The Favorite Family Resort
Since 1893
The Friendly Resort City

CAMDEN
The Capital of Radio (home
of the RCA-Victor Manu-
facturing Co.)
The Home of National Industries

CAPE MAY
America's Most Distinctive
Seashore Vacationland
America's Oldest Seashore
Resort
The Nation's Oldest Seashore
Resort (settled about 1664)

CHERRY HILL
The Place of Personal
Prestige and Practical
Advantages

DOVER
The Business Heart of the
Lakeland Area
The Home of the Garden
State Philharmonic Sym-
phony Orchestra
The Pittsburgh of New Jersey
(industrial area)

EAST BRUNSWICK
The Center of the World's
Biggest Market
The City Pointing the Way
for Industry
The Gateway to a Fabulous
Market
The Hub of Commerce

EAST WINDSOR
The Gateway to Everywhere

EDGEWATER
Bergen County's Only Deepwater Port

ELIZABETH
Betsytown (humorous varient)
The Rail and Harbor City

FRANKLIN
    The Fluorescent Mineral
    Capital of the World
    (Franklin Mineral Mu-
    seum)

GARFIELD
    The City of Industrial
    Peace

GLASSBORO
    The Summit Town (where
    President L. B. Johnson
    conferred with Soviet
    Premier Kosygin)

HAMMONTON
    The Garden City of Beauty
    The Garden Spot of the
    Garden State

HARVEY CEDARS
    America's Greatest Family
    Resort
    The High Point of Long
    Beach Island

HOBOKEN
    The Gibraltar of Democracy
    The Little Eden
    The Mile Square City .

JERSEY CITY
    The American City of Op-
    portunity
    The City that Has Every-
    thing for Industry

KEARNY
    The Heart of America's
    Industrial War Front

LACEY TOWNSHIP
    The Home of New Jersey's
    First Nuclear Generating
    Plant

LAMBERTVILLE
    The Gateway to the Pennsyl-
    vania Dutch Country

LAVALLETTE
    The Complete Resort

LONG BEACH TOWNSHIP
    The Pride of Magic Long
    Beach Island
    The Town Unmatched in
    Growth, Beauty, Home

LONG BRANCH
    America's First Seashore
    Resort (summer home of
    President Garfield)
    The City on the Crest
    The Friendly City
    The Summer Capital of the
    Presidents

LOWER TOWNSHIP
    The Gateway to the South

MADISON
    The Rose City (rose-growing
    center)

METUCHEN
    The Brainy Borough

MILLVILLE
    The Holly City of America

MORRISTOWN
    The Military Capital of the
    Colonies

MOUNT LAUREL
    The Balanced Community

NEW BRUNSWICK
    The Industrial and Cultural
    Center of New Jersey

NEWARK
    One of America's Outstanding
    Cities
    The Birmingham of America
    The City of Industry
    The Mail-Order Fraud
    Capital of the Nation
    The Milwaukee of the East
    (production of beer and ale)

NORTH WILDWOOD
    The Seashore with the Suburban
    Look
    Something to Write Home About

OCEAN BEACH
The Seashore Community
of Modern Summer Cot-
tages

OCEAN CITY
America's First Choice in
Family Resorts
America's Greatest Family
Resort (on island between
Great Egg Harbor and
Atlantic City)
The City for Family People
The City where You Enjoy
the Best Things in Life

OCEAN GATE
The Perfect Year-Round
Wonderland

OCEAN GROVE
God's Square Mile of Health
and Happiness
Neptune Township's Ocean
Front
The First Choice in Family
Resorts

PARAMUS
The Merchandising Mecca
of New Jersey

PARSIPPANY
Parsippany Means Business
The Modern Municipality for
Modern Industry

PATERSON
The American Lyons (a
mill town producing nylon,
rayon, silk, wool and
textile dyes)
The Cotton Town of the
U.S.A.
The Cradle of American
Industry (planned as an
industrial town by Alex-
ander Hamilton and So-
ciety for Establishing
Useful Manufactures
1791)
The Federal City (Alexander
Hamilton and others

planned this city expecting
it to serve as the capital
of the U.S.)
The Lyons of America
The Silk City (silk manu-
facturing)

PEARL RIVER
The Town of Friendly People

PERTH AMBOY
The City by the Sea (on
Raritan Bay)
The Clay Center
The Shopping Center of the
Raritan Bay Area

PLAINFIELD
The Queen City in the Garden
State
The Queen City of New
Jersey

PRINCETON
The Most Beautiful College
Town in America (Prince-
ton University)

RARITAN
The Crossroads of the
Eastern Market
The Friendly Town of
Friendly People

ROXBURY
A Nice Place to Live and
Work

SAYREVILLE
The Home of Nationally Known
Industries

SEA ISLAND CITY
The City of Family Fun in
the Sun

SEA ISLE CITY
The City with a Smile
The Island of Contentment
The Sea and Sand Vacationland

SEASIDE HEIGHTS
The Place to Play by Night

and Day
The Vacation Capital of
Ocean County

SECAUCUS
New Jersey's First Suburb

SHORE ACRES
The Venice of the New
Jersey Shore (because of
its many lagoons)

SMITHVILLE
The Town where the Memory
Lingers On

STONE HARBOR
The Clean and Quiet Resort
The Finest in Tennis on the
Jersey Coast
The Seashore at Its Best
The Venice of America (sea-
shore community, sheltered
waterways)

TRENTON
The Capital City (population
about 97, 500)

UNION CITY
The Home of the American
Embroidery Industry

UPPER TOWNSHIP
The Haven for Fishermen
and Hunters

VENTNOR CITY
The All-Year Residential
Resort

VINELAND
The Dandelion Capital
The Poultry Center

WEST CALDWELL
An Ideal Community in
which to Live, Work
and Play

WEST PORTAL
Little Switzerland

WILDWOOD
Five Miles of Health and Hap-
piness
The City for Summer Vacation
and All Year
The Family Vacation Spot
The Tent City (popular summer
resort, tents replaced by
solid buildings)
The World's Finest and Safest
Bathing Beach (on Atlantic
Ocean)

WILDWOOD CREST
The Perfect Family Vacation
Spot
Wildwood Crest for Pleasure
and Rest

WOODBRIDGE
New Jersey's Dynamic Location

NEW MEXICO

ACOMA
The Sky City (steep cliffs)

ALAMOGORDO
The City where the Atomic
Age Dawned (July 16, 1945)
The City where the Space Age
Began
The City with the Largest
Solar Observatory
The City with the Stimulating
Cultural Environment
The City with the World's
Highest Golf Course
The Nation's Oldest Continually
Active Parish
The Only International Street-
car Line City (crosses into
Mexico)
The Rocket City (near site of
first man-made atomic ex-
plosion of July 16, 1945 at
White Sands Proving Ground)

The Southernmost U.S.
Ski Area

ALBUQUERQUE
One of the World's Leading
Convention Centers
The Duke City (the Duke
of Albuquerque created
by Henry IV of Castile,
brother of Queen Eliza-
beth)
The Fastest Growing Metro-
politan City in the Nation
The Growing City
The Hot Air Balloon Capital
of the World
The Marketing and Trading
Center
The Metropolis of New
Mexico
The Miracle in the South-
west
The Transportation and
Traffic Center of New
Mexico

CARLSBAD
The Cavern City (about 25
miles from Carlsbad
Caverns National Park)

CHAMA
The Snowmobile Capital of
the Southwest

CLAYTON
The Friendly Town

CLOVIS
The Cattle Capital of the
Southwest

DULCE
The Home of the Jicarilla
Apache Tribe

FARMINGTON
The Energy Capital of the
West (producer of gas,
and oil, terminus of
two natural gas pipe-
lines)

GALLUP
The Indian Capital (site of
the Intertribal Indian
Ceremonial)
The Indian Capital of the
World

GRANTS
The Uranium Capital of the
World (processing mills
for uranium)

JEMEZ PUEBLO
Track and Field Town, U.S.A.

LOS ALAMOS
The Atomic City
The Capital of the Atomic
Age (Los Alamos Scientific
Laboratory)

LOVINGTON
The City where Oil and Water
Mix (the Oil Patch area
and fertile soil)

MOUNTAINAIR
The Gateway to Ancient Cities

RATON
The Gate City

ROSWELL
Retire in Roswell for a Life
of Health and Happiness

RUIDOSO
The Last Frontier

SANTA FE
New Mexico's Capital City
The Ancient City
The Capital City (population
about 46,200)
The Capital City Different
The Center of Prehistoric,
Historic and Scenic Interest
The City Different
The City of Holy Faith
The Oldest and Quaintest
City in the United States
(believed to have been

settled by Indians in
1210 and by Europeans
in 1610)
The Royal City

SILVER CITY
The Gateway to the Gila
Wilderness (headquarters
for Gila National Forest)

TAOS
The Art Center of the
Southwest
The Northern New Mexico's
Most Unique Vacationland

TUCUMCARI
A Wonderful Place of Rec-
reational Enjoyment

NEW YORK

ALBANY
The Beautiful Historic
Capital of the Empire
State
The Birthplace of the Union
The Capital City (population
about 109,000)
The Capital of the Empire
State
The City of Homes
The Cradle of the American
Union (Benjamin Franklin
proposed a federal union
of 13 colonies at the
congress of 1754)
The Edinburgh of America
The Governmental, Educa-
tional Recreational
Center
The Historic and Colorful
Capital of the Empire
State
The Hub of the Empire
State's Capital District
The Oldest Chartered City
in the United States (an
exaggerated claim)

The Oldest City in the United
States Operating Under Its
Original Charter

AMSTERDAM
The Carpet City
The Carpet City of the
World (the foremost manu-
facturing city for carpets
and rugs)
The City of Diversified In-
dustries
The City of Rugs
The Foot of the Adirondacks
(on the Mohawk River and
the New York Barge Canal)

AUBURN
The Cordage City (cord manufacturing)

AURIESVILLE
The Land of the Crosses

AUSABLE CHASM
One of the Great Scenic
Wonders of the United
States
The Grand Canyon of the
East (scenic attraction)
The Yosemite of the East

BEMUS POINT
The Muskie Capital of New
York
The Village Right in the
Middle of Things on
Beautiful Chautaqua Lake

BINGHAMTON
The Bran Town
The Hub of Cultural and
Commercial Life
The Parlor Town
The Triple Cities (with Endi-
cott and Johnson City)

BOLTON LANDING
The Place for All Seasons
A Vacation for Every Budget

BRANT LAKE
The Center of the Summer-

time World in the Great
North Woods

BREWSTER
The Hub of the Harlem
Valley

BROOKLYN
The Bedroom of New York
(one of the boroughs of
New York City, pri-
marily a residential
sector)
The Church City
The City of Churches
The City of Homes
The Dormitory of New York
The Greatest City's
Greatest Borough

BUFFALO
An Overgrown Village
One of America's Most Im-
portant Inland Fort
Centers
The Beautiful City of Homes,
Diversified Business and
Progressive Outlook
The Bison City (the scien-
tific name for buffalo)
The Center of America's
Greatest Market
The Center of Industrial
and Atomic Development
The City of Flour (flour
and feed milling)
The City of Good Neighbors
The City of Homes
The City of Progressive
Outlook
The City of Trees
The Electric City of the
Future
The First and Last Major
U.S. Port of Call on
the Seaway Route
The Flour City
The Flour Milling Capital
of the World
The Gateway City to Canada
The Gateway to Canada
The Gateway to Picturesque
Canada

The Gateway to the Heart-
land of America
The Gateway to the World's
Richest Market
The Go-Ahead City Along the
Niagara Frontier
The Heart of the World
Famous Niagara Region
The Hub of the Niagara
Frontier
The Metropolis in a Forest
of Trees (more than
40,000 city-owned trees)
The Mistake by the Lake
The Most Accessible City
on the North American
Continent
The National, Industrial,
Scientific, Educational
and Cultural Center
The Pathway to Progress
The Queen City of the Great
Lakes
The Queen City of the Lakes
The Rail Center
The Second Largest Railroad
Center in the United
States (12 freight termi-
nals, 5 passenger termi-
nals)
The Snow Basket of the
Empire State
The Transport Center of the
Nation
The Wonder City of America

CANANDAIGUA
The Chosen Spot in the
Beautiful Finger Lakes

CAPE VINCENT
Gateway to the Thousand
Islands
The Black Bass Capital of
the World
The Home of the Gamey
Black Bass

CARTHAGE
The Gateway to the Adiron-
dacks and the 1,000
Island Region

CHAZY
The Home of the Mac Intosh
Apple

CITY ISLAND
The Hub of New York's
Boating Center

COHOES
The City of the Mills

COLD SPRING HARBOR
Bungtown

COLTON
The Center of the St. Lawrence Valley Vacationland

CONEY ISLAND
Sodom by the Sea (title of
book by Oliver Pilat and
Jo Ranson)

COOPERSTOWN
The Birthplace of Baseball
The Heart of the Leather-
stocking Land
The Home of Baseball
(where Abner Doubleday
introduced the game)
The Home of James Feni-
more Cooper
The Village of Great Mu-
seums (the Baseball Mu-
seum, the Farmers Mu-
seum, etc.)
The Village of Museums
The Village where Nature
Smiles

CORNING
The Crystal City (Steuben
Glass Center and Steuben
factory)
The Major Glass Center
(the 200-inch lens for
Mt. Palomar's Telescope
was made here)

CORTLAND
The County Seat of Cortland
County

The Typewriter Capital of
the World

DUNKIRK
New York's Lake Erie Vaca-
tionland in Beautiful
Chautauqua County

ELLENVILLE
Ellenville is Everythingville

ELMIRA
The Center of Commerce
The Glider Capital of America
The Glider Capital of the
World

ENDICOTT
The Triple Cities (with Binghamton and Johnson City)

FORT ANNE
The Gateway to the North

FREDONIA
The Most Beautiful Village in
New York State (a description by Chauncey M. De-
pew)

FULTON
The Power City

GARDEN CITY
The Cathedral Town (Protes-
tant Episcopal Cathedral
of the Incarnation, in the
Sea of the Episcopal
Diocese)

GENEVA
The Heart of the Finger Lakes
Vacationland

GLENS FALLS
Hometown, U.S.A.
The Gateway to the Adiron-
dacks

GOSHEN
The Cradle of the Trotter
(two famous trotting tracks)

GOWANDA
Growing Gowanda

GREENPORT
The Community that Has
Everything

HAMBURG
The Town that Friendship
Built

HAMPTON
Long Island's World Famous
Ocean Playground

HAMPTON BAYS
Long Island's Ocean Play-
ground

HANCOCK
The Switzerland of the
Catskills

HARRIMAN
The Gateway to the Southern
Catskills

HEMPSTEAD
The Hub of Nassau
The Hub of Nassau County

HYDE PARK
The Home of Franklin
Delano Roosevelt (national
shrine)

INDIAN LAKE
The Heart of the Adiron-
dacks

ISLIP
The Industrial Dynamo
The Residential Haven
The Town with a Split
Personality

ITHACA
The City Pretty as a
Picture Post Card
The Educational Center

JOHNSON CITY
The Shoe City (site of

Endicott-Johnson Corp.,
shoe factory)
The Triple Cities (with Binghamton and Endicott)

KINDERHOOK
The Village Beautiful

KINGSTON
New York's First Capital
New York State's First
Capital
The Colonial City (first capi-
tal of New York State,
1777)
The First Capital of New
York
The Gateway to the Catskills
(Catskill Mountains)

LAKE GEORGE
America's Family Playground
Storytown, U.S.A.
The Queen of America's
Lakes
The Queen of American
Lakes
The Queen of the American
Lakes
The Resort Area Family Play-
ground
The Resort Area of the Adi-
rondacks
The Summer Paradise

LAKE LUZERNE
The Center of the Ranch-
Resort Country
The Gateway to the Adiron-
dacks (Adirondack Moun-
tains)
The Heart of the Dude Ranch
Country
The Land of Lovely Lakes
The Year Around Vacationland

LAKE PLACID
America's Most Complete
Resort
America's Switzerland (in
the Adirondack Mountains
on Mirror Lake)
Nation's Finest Winter

Sports Center
New York State's Complete
    All-Season Resort
One of America's Oldest
    Playgrounds
The Four Season Resort
The Golfers' and Vaca-
    tioners' Paradise
The Olympic Village
The Summer Vacationland
    and Winter Wonderland
The Switzerland of
    America

LOCKPORT
The Buying Center for
    Thousands
The Hub of the Great
    Niagara Fruit Belt
The Well-Balanced Com-
    munity

LONG BEACH
America's Healthiest City
The City by the Sea (the
    Atlantic Ocean)
The Ideal Vacation Resort
The Ideal Vacation Resort
    and Year 'Round Resi-
    dential Community

LONG LAKE
The Magnificent Mountain
    Wonderland

MALONE
The Big Little City
The City Famous for
    Friendliness
The Community of Oppor-
    tunity
The Star of the North

MANCHESTER
The Center of the Mega-
    lopolis

MASSENA
The Aluminum City
    (Aluminum Company of
    America's smelting plant)
The Gateway of the North
The Gateway to Vacationland

The Heart of the Famous St.
    Lawrence Seaway
The Heart of Vacationland
The Home of the St. Law-
    rence Seaway
The Seaway Vacationland

MATTITUCK
The Friendly Village
The Village that Has Every-
    thing

MEDINA
The Garden Center of the
    Empire State

MEXICO
The Mother of Towns

MIDDLETOWN
The Gateway to Upstate

MONROE
The Lake Region
The Place where There Is
    Everything for Everyone

MONTAUK
A Lifetime of Vacation Living
America's Riviera
The Miami Beach of the
    North
The Place for Those Who
    Want to Get Away from
    It All--But Not Too Far
The Place where the End Is
    Just the Beginning

MONTICELLO
The Catskills and County
    Crossroads of the Center
    for Action
The Home of the Mighty M
    (Monticello Raceway)

NEWARK
The Rose Capital of America
    (rose cultivation, annual
    rose festival)

NEW ROCHELLE
The City Alive
The City of Huguenots (settled

by the Huguenots in 1689)
The Park City
The Queen City of the
Sound (Long Island Sound)

NEW YORK CITY
America's Leading Tourist
Resort
America's Mecca
Father Knickerbocker (re-
ferring to the type of
trousers worn by the
early Dutch settlers)
Gotham (name given to
New York City by Wash-
ington Irving in the
Salamagundi Papers,
1807)
The Babylonian Bedlam (al-
lusion to the confusion
of tongues at Babel,
described in Genesis XI)
The Bagdad of the Subway
The Bagdad on the Hudson
The Banking Center of the
World
The Big Apple
The Big Burg
The Big City
The Big Town
The Biggest Gateway to
Immigrants
The Burg
The Business Capital of the
Nation
The Business Capital of the
World
The Capital of Finance
The Capital of the World
The Center of the World
(Trygve Lie, first United
Nations general secretary,
on Sept. 7, 1962)
The City
The City at the Crossroads
of High Diplomacy
The City of Cities (book
by Hulbert Foother)
The City of Friendly People
The City of Golden Dreams
The City of Islands (the
borough of Manhattan
and numerous other small
islands within the city limits)
The City of Light
The City of Orchestras
(music center and "Tin
Pan Alley")
The City of Skyscrapers
(the tallest building in the
world; the Empire State
Building, the Chrysler
Building, 60 Wall Tower,
etc.)
The City of Superlatives
The City of the World
The City of Towers
The City that Belongs to the
World
The City that Never Sleeps
The City with Everything
The Cleanest Big City in the
World
The Coliseum City
The Commercial Capital of
America
The Commercial Emporium
The Corporate Capital of
America
The Crossroads of the World
The Cuisine Capital of the
World
The Cultural Capital of
America
The Cultural Center of the
Nation
The Cultural City
The Empire City
The Entertainment Capital of
the World
The Fashion Capital of the
World
The Fear City
The Financial Capital of the
World
The Financial Hub
The First City of the World
(the most populated city
in the United States, ap-
proximately 8 million)
The Friendly City
The Frog and Toe
The Front Office of American
Business
The Fun City
The Fun City on the Hudson

The Greatest All-Year
Round Vacation City
The Greatest Industrial
Center in the World
The Headquarters of World
Banking
The Hong Kong of the
Hudson
The Host of the World
The Hub City of the World
The Hub of Transport
The Information City
The Land of Surprising
Contrasts
The Mecca for Young
Adults
The Mecca of Telephone
Men
The Media City
The Melting Pot (drama by
Israel Zangwill, 1908)
The Metropolis
The Metropolis of a Conti-
nent
The Metropolis of America
The Metropolitan City
The Mighty Manhattan
The Modern Gomorrah (one
of the cities of the plains
destroyed by fire and
brimstone because of
wickedness, mentioned
in the Old Testament)
The Money Town
The Most Colorful Exciting
City in the World
The Movie-Making City
The Nation's First City
The Nation's Greatest City
The Nation's Largest Com-
munications Center
The Nation's Largest Port
The Port of Many Ports
The Printing Capital of the
World
The Restaurant City
The Science City
The Seat of Empire (named
in 1784 by George
Washington)
The Super City
The University of Telephony
The Vacation City

The Wonder City
The Wonder City of the
World
The Wonderful Town
The World Capital of Fashion
The World's Capital City
The World's Fair City
The World's Financial
Capital
The World's Metropolis
The World's Most Exiting
All Year Round Vacation
Center

NIAGARA FALLS
America's Scenic Wonderland
Nature's Mighty Masterpiece
The Cataract City (descriptive)
The City of Business
The City of Fine Schools
The City of Homes
The City of Industry
The City of Scenic Marvels
The Honeymoon Capital of the
World
The Honeymoon City (a
favorite vacation spot for
honeymoon couples)
The Honeymooner's Paradise
The King of Power
The Nearby Wonder of the
World
The Power City (hydroelectric
stations)
The Power City of Scenic
Wonders
The Powerhouse of the
Niagara Frontier
The Quality City
The Queen of Beauty
The Scenic Gateway to
America

NORTH POLE
Santa's Workshop (toy factory)
Village of Breathtaking Beauty
and Enchantment
Village of Enchantment

NORTH TONAWANDA
The Twin Cities of Oppor-
tunity at the Heart of the
Niagara Frontier (with
Tonawanda)

OGDENSBURG
A Community on the Move
for a Century and a Half
with More to Offer for
the Future
An Entire City of Friendly
People
Enjoyment in History Re-
lived
The City Historical and
Enjoyable
The Friendliest City on any
International Border
The Gateway to International
Fun for the Entire Family

OLD FORGE
The Year 'Round Vacation-
land

OLEAN
The Heart of the Enchanted
Mountains
The Home of the Miss New
York State Pageant

ONEIDA
A Bit of America at Its
Best

ONEONTA
The City of Hills (west of
the Catskill Mountain
region)
The Manufacturing City

OSWEGO
The Seaport of Central New
York

OYSTER BAY
The Home of Theodore
Roosevelt

PERU
The Home of the Mac
Intosh Apple

PORT CHESTER
The Sin City

POTSDAM
The Business and Cultural

Center of the St. Lawrence
Valley
The Education, Cultural,
Business Distribution
Center of the St. Lawrence
Valley
The Manufacturing Center

POUGHKEEPSIE
The Home of Vassar College
The Industrial City
The Queen City of the Hudson

QUEENSBURY
The Better Place in which
to Live, Visit or Do
Business
The Home of the Lake George
Opera Festival

RHINEBECK
Violet Town

RIPLEY
The Gretna Green (on Lake
Erie)

RIVERHEAD
The Gateway to the Hamptons
The Hub of Eastern Long
Island
The Ideal Town in which to
Live, Work, Shop and
Play
The Town where Your Sum-
mer Fun Begins

ROCHESTER
Lake Ontario's Westernmost
American Seaport
The Aquaduct City
The Camera Center
The Camera City
The City Built by Hands
The City of Giant Industry
The City of Great Industry
The City of Homes
The City of Many Industries
The City of Quality Products
The City of Varied Industries
The City where the Seaway
Meets the Thruway
The Emerging Metropolis

The Flour City
The Flower City
The Friendliest City
The Gateway to Vacation-
land
The Home of One of the
Nation's Largest Skilled
Technical Work Forces
The Kodak City
The Lilac Festival City
The Photo Capital of the
World
The Photographic and Opti-
cal Center of the World
The Photography Capital
The Power City
The Quality City
The Snapshot City
The Water-Power City
(book by Blake McKelvey)
The World's Largest Lilac
Center

ROME
The Copper City (about 10
percent of the copper
factories of the U.S.)

RYE
America's Premier Play-
ground
The Border Town

SARANAC LAKE
The Little City in the
Adirondacks

SARATOGA SPRINGS
America's Most Wonderful
Spa
Fun Country, U.S.A.
The Baden-Baden of America
The Capital of Thorough-
bred Racing
The Convention City
The Home of America's
Greatest Spa
The Home of Health,
History and Horse
The Inevitable Spa City
The Peerless Summer, Winter
and Health Resort of
America

The Playground of High So-
ciety
The Queen of the Spas
The Spa City

SCHENECTADY
Dorp
Old Dorp
The City of Flourishing
Industries
The City of Magic
The City that Lights and
Hauls the World
The Electric City (site of the
General Electric Co.)
The Electrical City (site of
the General Electric Co.)
The Gateway to the West
(on the Mohawk River)
The Magic City

SCHROON LAKE
The Cultural Center of the
Adirondacks
The Family Vacationland
The Heart of the Adirondack
Vacationland
The Playground of the
Adirondacks (summer re-
sort)

SHARON SPRINGS
America's Mountain Spring
(White sulphur spring four
barrels a minute)
The Baden-Baden of America

SHELTER ISLAND
The Vacationer's Paradise

SKANEATELES
The Teasel Capital of the
Country (a teasel is a
large thistle used for
raising nap on wool)

SOMERS
The Birthplace of the Ameri-
can Circus
The Circus Capital
The Cradle of the American
Circus

SOUTHAMPTON
  The Oldest English Settle-
    ment in New York State
    (founded in 1640)

SPECULATOR
  The City in the Lake
    District of the Adirondacks
  The Land of Beautiful Lakes
  The Vacationland of Un-
    limited Enjoyment

STONY CREEK
  The Biggest Small Town in
    New York State
  The Dude Ranch Capital of
    the East

SYRACUSE
  The Central City
  The City of Conventions
  The City of Isms
  The City of Salt
  The City of the Plains
  The City that Salt Built
    (book by Lilian Steele
    Munson)
  The Crossroads of New
    York State
  The Crossroads of the
    World's Richest Market
  The Electronics Capital of
    the World
  The Fair City
  The Heart of New York
    State
  The Hub of New York State
  The Hub of the Empire
    State
  The Ideal Residential City
  The Salt City (salt springs
    and salt brine)
  The Telegraphic Hub
  The Venice of America

THERESA
  The Gateway to Twelve
    Beautiful Lakes

TICONDEROGA
  America's Most Historic
    Town
  The Home of the Christmas Club

The Home of the International
  Paper Company
The Land where History Was
  Made

TONAWANDA
  The Twin Cities of Oppor-
    tunity at the Heart of the
    Niagara Frontier (with
    North Tonawanda)

TROY
  The Collar City (factories
    manufacturing Arrow shirts
    and collars)
  The Tide-Water City (at head
    of the Hudson River)

TRUMANSBURG
  The City in the Heart of the
    Finger Lakes

TUPPER LAKE
  The Crossroads of the Adi-
    rondacks

UTICA
  The Beautiful City of Homes
    in the Historic Mohawk
    Valley
  The City of the Crossroads
    of the Empire State
  The City of Successful Diversi-
    fied Industry
  The City with a Past, Present
    and Future
  The Crossroads of New York
  The Gateway to the Adirondacks
  The Heart of America's
    Richest Market
  The Hub of the Empire State
  The Total Community Com-
    mitted to Building a Vital
    City
  The Watering-Pot of America
  Utica Makes It Happen

WALTON
  The Foothills of the Cat-
    skills
  The Heart and Hub of Dela-
    ware County

WARRENSBURG
  The Queen Village of the
  Adirondacks

WATERTOWN
  The City of Pleasant Living
  and Industry
  The City where Industry
  Thrives
  The Gateway to the St.
  Lawrence Power and
  Seaway
  The Gateway to the Thousand
  Islands
  The Hydro-Electric City
  The Metropolis of Northern
  New York
  The Woolworth Town (Frank
  H. Woolworth established
  the first 5 and 10 cent
  store here)

WATKINS GLEN
  The Heart of the Lake
  Country
  The Home of Road Racing
  in America
  The Vacation Center
  Your Vacation Center

WELLS
  A Truly Year 'Round Vacation Land

WEST POINT
  The Gibraltar of the Hudson

WESTPORT
  The City where the Adirondacks Meet Lake Cham-
  plain

WHITE PLAINS
  The Center for Medicine
  The Heart of Westchester
  (Westchester County)
  The Hub of Major Employ-
  ment, Education and
  Commercial Center

WHITEHALL
  The Birthplace of the U.S.
  Navy

WILLIAMSVILLE
  The Gateway to Niagara Falls

WOODSTOCK
  Upstate Greenwich Village

YONKERS
  The City Next to the Greatest
  City in the World
  The City of Graceful Living
  The Queen City of the Hudson
  The Terrace City

NORTH CAROLINA

ASHEVILLE
  One of the Leading Health
  and Tourist Resorts of
  the East
  The Capital City of the Land
  of the Sky
  The City in the Land of the
  Sky (altitude 2,250 feet)
  The City in the Sky
  The City where Spring Spends
  the Winter
  The Convention Center in the
  Land of the Sky
  The Land of the Sky (altitude
  1,980 feet to 3,020 feet)
  The Popular Convention
  City
  The Preeminent Vacation
  Center

BELMONT
  The City in the Heart of the
  Piedmont Crescent

BLOWING ROCK
  The Heart of North Carolina's
  Holiday Highland
  The Southern Holiday High-
  land

BOONE
  The Home of the "Horn of
  the West" (historical drama
  story of Daniel Boone)

The Horn of the West
The Hub of the "Holiday
Highlands"
The Roof of Eastern America
(8,333 feet)

BREVARD
The Home of the Brevard
Music Center
The Music Center of the
South (Brevard Music
Center)
The Popular Summer Resort

BURLINGTON
The Home of State's First
Industrial Training
Center

CAPE CARTERET
The Land of Leisure Living
The Variety Vacation Land

CAROLINA BEACH
The States Largest Ocean-
side Resort Town

CHAPEL HILL
The Capital of the Southern
Mind (University of
North Carolina)

CHARLOTTE
Carolina's Queen City
The Action City
The City of Churches
The City where the South-
east Gets Its Money
The Flourishing Chief
City of the Carolinas
The Heart of the Piedmont
The Home City
The Hornets' Nest
The Queen City
The Spearhead of the New
South

CHEROKEE
The Gateway to the Great
Smoky Mountains Na-
tional Park

CLAYTON
The Tobacco and Farming
Center

CONCORD
The Gateway to the Friendly
City

DRAPER
The Tri-City (with Leaks-
ville and Spray, N.C.)

DURHAM
The City of the South

EDENTON
The Cradle of the Colony
(one of the oldest commu-
nities)
The South's Prettiest Town

FAIRMONT
The Liveliest Town in Robeson County

FAYETTEVILLE
The City of Historical Heritage

FRANKLIN
The Gem Capital of the
World (numerous ruby
mines)

GASTONIA
The Pacemaker of the Pied-
mont
What We Make Makes Us

GOLDSBORO
The Community of Progress
The Friendly City of
Progress
The Heart of Eastern North
Carolina

GREENSBORO
The Center of the Greatest
Manufacturing Area in
the South
The City of Charm
The Pivot of the Piedmont

HATTERAS
The Blue Marlin Capital
of the World

HATTERAS ISLAND
The Graveyard of the At-
lantic

HAVELOCK
The Gateway to Cherry
Point

HENDERSON
The Bird Sanctuary
The City where Hospitality
Never Ceases
The City with a Future
The Gateway to the South
(North Carolina's Most
Northern City)
One of the Leading Tobacco
Markets for Bright Leaf
Tobacco

HENDERSONVILLE
The City of Four Glorious
Seasons
The Dancingest Town in
the United States
(numerous street and
other public dances)
The Flower, Fruit, Vege-
table Center
The Resort City of Blue
Ridge
The Summer and Health
Resort
Your Cool Mountain Vaca-
tionland

HICKORY
The Best Balanced City

HIGH POINT
The Furniture City (about
90 furniture factories)
The Furniture City of
the World
The Furniture Production
Center of the U.S.
The Industrial City

HIGHLANDS
The Highest Incorporated
Town in Eastern America

HIWASSEE DAM
The Vacationland of the Sky

JACKSONVILLE
The City on the Go

KANNAPOLIS
The Towel City (site of
Cannon Mills)

LEAKSVILLE
The Tri-City (with Spray and
Draper, N.C.)

LEXINGTON
The City Four-Dimensional
The Winter Golf Capital of
America

LITTLE SWITZERLAND
A Beauty Spot of the Blue
Ridge

MURPHY
The Great Smokies' Mountain
Lake Neighbor
The Land of Lakes and Trout
Streams
The Land of the Sky
The Mountain Lake Vacation-
land
The Southern Gateway to the
Great Smokies

NEW BERN
The All-Year Resort Center
The Historic Center of North
Carolina
The Hub of Coastal Carolina
The Land of Enchanting
Waters

NEWPORT
The Town with Old-Fashioned
Courtesy

OCRACOKE
North Carolina's Pleasure
Island

PINEHURST
Golftown, U.S.A.
The Golf Capital of the
United States

RALEIGH
The Capital City (popu-
lation about 144,000)
The City of Oaks
The Oak City
The Trading Center

ROANOKE RAPIDS
The Northeastern North
Carolina Industrial
Center

ROCKY MOUNT
The Gate to the Old South
(on the Tar River)

SANFORD
The Brick Capital of the
United States
The City where Business
and Friendship Thrive
The Gateway to the Famous
Sandhills
The Heart of North Carolina

SEALEVEL
The Home of the Green
Sea Horse

SOUTHERN PINES
The Mid-South Resort

SPRAY
The Tri-City (with Leaks-
ville and Draper, N.C.)

SPRUCE PINE
The Mineral City (feldspar
and kaolin)

STATESVILLE
The City of Progress
The Crossroads of Tomor-
row

SWANSBORO
An Area Rich in Historical
Attractions

The Friendly City by the Sea
where River, Sound and
Ocean Meet

THOMASVILLE
The American Chair Center
The Chair Capital of the
World
The Chair City (furniture
manufacturing since 1870)

TRYON
The City in the Famous
Thermal Belt of North
Carolina
The Friendliest Town in
America (in the Blue
Ridge Mountains)

WAYNESVILLE
The Gateway to the Great
Smoky Mountains State
Park
The Vacation and Health
Resort

WELDON
Rockfish Capital
The Rock Fish Capital of the
World (on the Roanoke
River)

WHITE LAKE
The Nation's Safest Beach

WILLIAMSTON
The Heart of East Carolina

WILLISTON
Clam Capital, U.S.A.

WILSON
The Greatest Show in To-
baccoland (bright-leaf
tobacco market)

WINSTON-SALEM
The Camel City (a brand
cigarette manufactured
by the R. J. Reynolds
Tobacco Company)
The City Founded Upon
Cooperation

The City of Culture, History,
Industry
The City of History, Culture,
Education, Industry
The Twin Cities (Winston
and Salem consolidated
in 1913)
The Twin City (Winston
and Salem consolidated
in 1913)

WRIGHTSVILLE BEACH
Northernmost Ice-Free Port

NORTH DAKOTA

BISMARCK
The Capital City (population
about 37,500)
The Capital of Opportunity
The City Beside the Broad
Missouri
The Fastest Growing City
in the Northwest
The Medical Center of
North Dakota
The Skyscraper City of the
Prairies (17-story
capitol)
The Tourist Capital of
North Dakota

DEVILS LAKE
The Heart of the Nation's
Durham Producing Center
The Satanic City (a synonym
for devil)

DICKINSON
A Good Place to Visit, a
Good Place to Live
North Dakota's Queen City
The City that Is Big Enough
to Serve You, Yet Small
Enough to Know You
The Gateway of America's
Scenic Wonderland
The Gateway to the West
The Queen City

The Queen City of the
Prairies
The Threshold of Theodore
Roosevelt National
Memorial Park

ENDERLIN
The City that Is Friendly,
Progressive, Alive
The Tri-County City that Is
Friendly, Progressive,
Alive

FARGO
A Fine Residential Center
An Important Livestock
Center
The Bread Basket of the
World
The Distribution Center for
the Great Northwest
The Food Basket of the
World
The Gateway City
The Gateway City to the
Bread Basket of the World
The Land of Business Oppor-
tunity
The Mainline City (by air,
rail and highway)
The Metropolis of North
Dakota
The Natural Location for
Agricultural Industry

GARRISON
Mid-America's Fast Growing
Exciting New Playground
The Aquatic Wonderland
The Busy Friendly Growing
City
The Cattle Ranching City
The City in the Heart of
Sunny North Dakota
The City of Diversified
Farming
The City of Many Churches
The City of Modern Schools
The Fishing and Hunting
Headquarters for Gigantic
Lake Garrison
The Golfing and Fishing
Paradise

GRAFTON
  Every Year a Growth Year
    for Grafton
  Growing Grafton Leads
    North Dakota
  The Agricultural Breadbasket
    Center of North America
  The Center of the Red River
    Valley Bread Basket
  The Nation's No. 3 Potato
    Center, Soon the First
  The True Center of the
    Rich Red River Valley

GRAND FORKS
  The City with a Heart
  The Heart of North Dakota
  The Home of the University
    of North Dakota
  The Only Grand Forks in
    the Nation

JAMESTOWN
  Jimtown
  The City with a Future
  The Home of the World's
    Largest Buffalo

LAKOTA
  The Durum Center of the
    World

LARIMORE
  The Shelterbelt Capital of
    the World

MARMARTH
  The City of Trees

MEDORA
  The City where the Wild
    West Kicks Up Its Heels
  The Cow Town

MINOT
  It's Easy to Get Here,
    Pleasant to Stay
  North Dakota's Favorite
    Convention City
  The Continental Crossroads
  The Gateway to Garrison
    Dam
  The Hub of Recreational

  North Dakota
  The Magic City (referring to
    its fast growth)

NEW TOWN
  The Old West's Newest City

PETERSBURG
  The Flax Center of North
    Dakota

RUGBY
  The Gateway to the Interna-
    tional Peace Garden
  The Geographical Center of
    North America

STANLEY
  The Gateway to Garrison Dam
    and Roosevelt National
    Memorial Park

STANTON
  The Home of Sakakawea
  The Most Historic Spot in
    North Dakota
  The Power City

TIOGA
  The Oil Capital of North
    Dakota

VALLEY CITY
  The City Beautiful
  The Good Place to Live and
    Enjoy Life
  The Milling Center
  The North Dakota Winter
    Show Center
  The Turkey and Dairy Pro-
    cessing Center

WALFORD CITY
  The City for Recreation and
    Relaxation
  The City with Abundant Grain
  The City with Churches of
    All Faiths
  The City with Excellent
    Hunting and Fishing
  The City with Good Schools
    and Modern Medical
    Facilities

The City with Water Sports
The Gateway to the North
Unit of the Theodore
Roosevelt National
Memorial Park

WILLISTON
A Good Place to Work,
Live and Play
The Capitol of a Great
Empire
The City where the Best
Begins

OHIO

AKRON
Rubber's Home Town
The Center of the World's
Rubber Manufacturing
The City of Opportunity
The Heart of America's
Workshop
The Rubber Capital of the
United States (numerous
factories producing tires
and other rubber pro-
ducts)
The Rubber Capital of the
World
The Rubber City
The Summit City (950 feet
altitude, highest point
of old Ohio and Erie
Canal)
The Tire Capital of the
World
The Tire City of the United
States

ALLIANCE
The Carnation City

AMHERST
The World's Sandstone
Center

BAINBRIDGE
The Cradle of Dental

Education (school for
dentists opened in 1826
by Dr. John Harris)

BARBERTON
The Largest Industrial City
of Its Size in Ohio
The Magic City

BEREA
The Grindstone City

BERLIN
The Heart of Amish Terri-
tory Swiss Cheese

BOWLING GREEN
The City of Opportunity

BUSINESSBURG
The Switzerland of Ohio

CADIZ
The Proudest Small Town in
America (population about
3,100)

CANTON
The Gateway to the Midwest

CEDAR POINT
The Atlantic City of the
Great Lakes
The Atlantic City of the
Middle West (resort area
on Sandusky Bay)
The Disneyland of the Mid-
west

CHILLICOTHE
Ohio's First Capital

CINCINNATI
America's Paris
Pigopolis
Porkopolis
The Athens of the Middle
West
The Beautiful City
The Birmingham of America
The City of Personality
The City of Rivers and Hills
The City on Seven Hills

The Conservative Cincinnatti
The Contented City
The Crossroads of the
  Nation
The Floral City
The Gateway to the South
The Paris of America
The Queen City
The Queen City of the Ohio
The Queen City of the Ohio
  River
The Queen City of the West
The Queen of the West
The Ragtown (manufacture
  of cloaks and suits often
  referred to in the trade
  as "rags")

CLEVELAND
  Lake Erie's Vacation City
  The Advertising Center
  The Best Location in the
    Nation
  The Capital City of a Great
    Trade Empire
  The City that Cooperates
  The Fifth City (in 1920
    census)
  The First City in American
    Spirit
  The Forest City
  The Industrial Heart of
    America
  The Lighting Capital of
    the World (General
    Electric Company's
    lamp division)
  The Mistake on the Lake
  The Modern Athens
  The Overgrown Country
    Town
  The Queen of Lake Erie
  The University of Light
    (General Electric
    Company's lamp di-
    vision)
  The Vacation City

COLUMBIANA
  The Biggest Little Town
    in Ohio

COLUMBUS
  Ohio's Beautiful Capital
  The Capital City (population
    about 582,000)
  The City of Beauty, Industry,
    Sports, Education
  The City where Train and
    Plane Meet
  The Friendly Progressive
    and Dominant City
  The Middle of Marketing
    America
  The Rich Prosperous Market
    Area
  The Rose Capital of the World

CONNEAUT
  The Plymouth of the Western
    Reserve (first settlers in
    Ohio, July 4, 1796)

CRESTLINE
  The Railroad Center Since
    1850

DAYTON
  The Aviation City
  The Birthplace of Aviation
    (Wright-Patterson Air
    Force Base)
  The Cash Register City (Na-
    tional Cash Register Co.
    factory)
  The City Beautiful
  The City of Beauty
  The City of Industry
  The City of Progress
  The Cradle of Aviation
    (Wright-Patterson Air
    Force Base)
  The Cradle of Creativity
  The Crossroads of Your
    National Market
  The Gem City
  The Gem City of Ohio
  The Home of the Wright
    Brothers
  The Pioneering Center of
    Aviation
  The World Famous Manu-
    facturing Center

DEFIANCE
The City of Industry, Agriculture, Education, Patriotism, Scenic Beauty and Civic Pride

DELPHOS
The Heart of Industrial America

DENNISON
The Clay Pipe Center of the World

DOVER
The Home of Warther Museum (world famous carvings)

EAST CLEVELAND
The Lighting Headquarters of the World

EAST LIVERPOOL
The Ceramic City (leading pottery center)
The Pottery Center

ELYRIA
The City of Beauty and Unlimited Opportunities
The City of Diversified Products
The Growth Market in Lorain County

EUCLID
The Fastest Growing City in Ohio (used in 1930)

FAIRBORN
Ohio's Most Progressive City

FOSTORIA
The City with a Great Future
The Great Railroad Center

FREMONT
The City of Varied Industries

The Cutlery Center of America

GALLIPOLIS
The City of the Gauls (settled by the French in 1790)

HAMILTON
The Postmark of Distinctive Trademarks (Gen. Arthur St. Clair built Fort Hamilton in 1791)

HAYDENVILLE
The Ideal Town

JEFFERSON
The Philadelphia of the West

KENT
The Tree City

LAKESIDE
The Chautauqua of the Great Lakes (summer conference grounds on the southern shore of Lake Erie)

LAKEWOOD
The City of Homes

LIMA
A City of Fine Homes and Streets
The Hub of a $500,000 Trading Area
The Pipeline Center of the Nation

LORAIN
One of the Fastest Growing Areas in the Nation

MANSFIELD
The City in the Heart of Industrial America
The Fun Center of Ohio (year-round reception program)

MARIETTA
A Town for Those in Love with Life

Ohio's First City
Ohio's Oldest and Most
Beautiful City (settled
by 48 people in 1788)
The Birthplace of the
Northwest Territory
The City of Diversified
Industries
The City of Many Cultural
Advantages
The Most Historic City in
the Northwest Terri-
tory (first civil govern-
ment in the Northwest
Territory when Arthur
St. Clair took the oath
of governor in 1788)

MARION
The Shovel City of the
World

MAUMEE
The Progressive Community
Hewn from a Wilderness

MONTGOMERY
The Village of Lovely
Homes and Friendly
People

NEWARK
The Mound Builders' City

NILES
The Birthplace of McKinley
(President William
McKinley born Jan. 29,
1843)
The Haven for Industry,
Commerce and Good
Living

NORWALK
The Maple City

PERRYSBURG
The Progressive Community
Hewn from a Wilderness

PORTSMOUTH
The City Proud of the
Past and Preparing for
the Future
The City where Southern
Hospitality Begins (on the
Ohio River)
The Steel City (iron and
steel factory built 1872)

SABINA
The Eden of Ohio

SALEM
Ohio's City of Friends
The Quaker City (founded in
1801 by Quakers)

SANDUSKY
The Gateway to Lake Erie
The Gateway to the Ohio
Lake Erie Islands (on
Sandusky Bay of Lake
Erie)

SIDNEY
The Industrial City

SPRINGFIELD
The Champion City
The City of Progress
The Flower City
The Hub of Historic Ohio
The Hub of Historical Ohio
The Progressively Growing
Well-Seasoned City

STEUBENVILLE
The Best Town Site on the
Ohio (on the Ohio River,
population about 28,100)

STRONGSVILLE
The Crossroads of the Nation
(20 miles southeast of
downtown Cleveland)

SUGARCREEK
The Little Switzerland of
Ohio (headquarters of
Ohio's Swiss Cheese As-
sociation)
The Swiss Cheese Center
of Ohio (numerous
factories)

TOLEDO
One of America's Great
Cities
One of the Busiest Fresh-
water Ports in the World
(on the Maumee River
flowing into Lake Erie)
The Busiest Freshwater
Port in the World
The Central Gateway of the
Great Lakes
The City Serving the In-
dustrial Farming Com-
mercial Heart of America
The City where Coal and
Iron meet
The City where the Seaway
Meets the Turnpike
The Corn City
The Glass Capital of the
World (numerous glass
factories)
The Glass Center (factories
of Owens-Illinois Glass
Co., Ford Glass Co.,
Libby-Owens, etc.)
The Mud Hen City
The Nation's Most Dynamic
and Valuable Entity
The Pivot City of the Great
Lakes (on Lake Erie)
The Second Largest Port
on the Great Lakes
The Third Largest Rail
Center in the Nation
The World's Largest Coal-
Shipping Port
The World's Largest Coal
Shipper

UHRICHSVILLE
The Clay Pipe Center of
the World

UPPER SANDUSKY
The Friendly Community
of Beauty and Industry
The Home of the Wyandot
Indians
The Indian Village (home
of Wyandot Indians)

VAN WERT
The Nation's Peony Center

The Peony City of America

WARREN
The Home of Little Steel
(steel mills)

YOUNGSTOWN
The Capital City
The Capital City of a Great
Industrial Empire
The Center of Ohio's Sixth
Largest Metropolitan Area
The Center of the Industrial
Northeast
The City of Business and
Industry
The City of Cultural, Edu-
cational and Recreational
Opportunities for All
The City of Progress
The Gateway to the Old
Western Reserve
The Land of Flowing Springs
The Recreational, Educa-
tional and Cultural Center
of Northeastern Ohio
The Steel-Built City
The Steel City

ZANESVILLE
America's Typical City
The Capital City (Ohio's
capital from 1810-1812)
The Pottery City (pottery,
tile, glass manufac-
turing)
The "Y" Bridge City (bridge
built in the form of the
letter "Y")

_____

OKLAHOMA

_____

ADA
The City Destined to Lead
Southern Oklahoma

ALTUS
The All American City
The City of Growing Indus-
trial Activity

The City with a Future to
Share

ARDMORE
The Capital of South
Central Oklahoma

BARTLESVILLE
America's Ideal Family
Center
The City with a Future

BOISE CITY
The Center of an Empire

CHANDLER
The Largest Pecan Shipping
Center in America
The Pecan Capital of the
World

CLAREMORE
The Best Known Little City
in America (population
about 9,100)

COALGATE
There's More than Coal in
Coalgate

DRUMRIGHT
The Friendliest Town in
Oklahoma
The Gateway to the Lakes
The Pipeline Capital of the
World

DURANT
The Heart of the Red River
Valley
The Queen of the Three
Valleys

ELK CITY
The Broom Corn Capital of
the World
The City in the Heart of
the Anadarko Basin
The Gas Capital of the
World
The Largest Broom Corn
Shipping Point in the
Country

EL RENO
The Heart of the Canadian
Valley

ENID
The Queen City of the
Cherokee Strip

GROVE
The Friendly Community
The Spot for a Home and
Life of Joy

GUTHRIE
The Birthplace of Oklahoma
(first state capital 1907)
The Fraternal Capital of the
Southwest (largest Scottish
Rite Temple)

HEAVENER
The Best Fishing in Oklahoma

HUGO
The Circus Town, U.S.A.

JOY
The Oil Capital
The Oil Capital of the
United States

KENTON
The Cowboy Capital (used before
Oklahoma became a state)

KETCHUM
The Home of the First Fully
Automatic Non-Attended
Dial Telephone Switchboard
in the United States

KINGFISHER
The Buckle of the Wheat Belt

KONAWA
The City of Progress

LAWTON
The City of Convention Facili-
ties
The City of the Annual Easter
Pageant
The Fort Sill Artillery and
Missile Center

The Home of the Museum of
the Great Plains
The Post City (U.S. Army
and Fort Lawton)
The Rollicking, Hilarious
Tent and Shack City
The Wildlife Refuge Center

MCALESTER
The City with Oklahoma's
Largest Coal Field
The City with the Largest
Man-made Reservoir in
the World (Eufaula)

MANGUM
The Friendly City

MARIETTA
The County Seat of Love
County

MIDWEST CITY
America's Model City
The Home of the Tinker
Air Force Base

MUSKOGEE
Port City Mid-America
The City of Beauty
The City of History
The Established City
The Heartland of Green
County

NOWATA
The Home of Championship
Cowboys
The World's Largest Shal-
low Oil Field

OKLAHOMA CITY
The Biggest Little City in
the World
The Capital City (population
about 378,000)
The Capital of Soonerland
The Central City of the
Great Southwest
The City of 1,000 Lakes
(actually 1,514 lakes
ranging from a few
acres to 100,000

acre-foot Elm Creek
Reservoir)
The Hub of the Great South-
west
The Industrial Frontier of
America
The Land of Perpetual
Prosperity
The Sedate Capital of the
Bible Belt
The Town where Oil Derricks
Loom in Almost Any Yard
The Town where the Office
Ledger Has Replaced the
Horse Pistol

OKMULGEE
The City where Oil Flows,
Gas Blows and Glass Glows

PONCA CITY
The City Built on Oil, Soil
and Toil

POTEAU
The Home of the Frontier
Sports Arena

PRYOR
The Gateway from South and
West to Ozark Playgrounds

SALINA
The Oldest White Settlement
in the State (founded by
Pierre Chouteaux, explorer,
in 1796)

SALLISAW
The City of History and
Industry

SAPULPA
The Capital City of Creek
County

SEILING
The Little Louisville of the
Southwest

SHAWNEE
The Red Bud City of Okla-
homa

SNYDER
The Granite City
The Home of World's
Finest Granite

TAHLEQUAH
The Former Capital of the
Cherokee Indian Nation

TALITHINA
Just a Swell Place to Live
and Play

TEXOLA
The Land of Greer (organized
as Greer County in 1860)

TULSA
America's Most Beautiful
City
America's Most Livable
City
The Aerospace Capital of
Oklahoma
The City Beautiful
The City for All Seasons
of the Year
The City that Has It Now
The City with a Personality
The Fair Little City
The Great Outdoor Recrea-
tion City
The Home of Diamond
Products
The Home of the Interna-
tional Petroleum Expo-
sition
The Magic City
The Main Street of America
The Most Eastern Western
Metropolis
The Most Northern Southern
City
The Oil Capital
The Oil Capital of the South-
west
The Oil Capital of the
World
The Water Capital of the
Southwest
The Young Man's Capital
of the World

VINITA
The Ozark's Western Gate-
way (on the Texas Road,
formerly the Osage Trace)
The Second Oldest Settle-
ment in Oklahoma

WAGONER
The Queen of the Prairies

WEATHERFORD
The Bird Hunter's Paradise
The Community a Whole Lot
to Like About
The Gypsum City
The Productive Agricultural
Community

WOODWARD
The Greatest Market in Northwest Oklahoma

OREGON

ALBANY
The Center of Space-age
Metals Development
The Community of Fine
Homes, Schools and
Churches
The Gateway to the Santiam
Vacation and Recreation
Area
The Hole in the Ground
(altitude 216 feet; the
current washed away a
section near the mouth
of the Calapooya River)
The Hub City
The Hub of the Willamette
Valley
The Rye Grass Capital of the
World
The Site of the World's
Championship Timber
Carnival
The Smart Shopping Center
for the Central Willamette
Valley

ASHLAND
The American Carlsbad
(mineral springs)
The City of Spas (lithia
water mineral springs)
The Gateway
The Granite City (marble
works 1865)
The Home Town of Southern
Oregon

ASTORIA
The First Port on the
Columbia
The Salmon City (on the
Columbia River)

AURORA
The Dutchtown (founded in
1857 by Dr. William
Keil and German settlers)

BAKER
The Denver of Oregon
The Friendly City on the
Oregon Trail
The Gold Coast of Oregon
(gold discovered on
Griffin Creek 1861)
The Switzerland of America

COOS BAY
The Lumber Port of the
World
The World's Largest Lumber
Shipping Port

COQUILLE
The Gem City of Cedar
Empire (on the Coquille
River)

CORNELIUS
The Corntown

CORVALLIS
The Heart of the Valley
(Willamette Valley)
The Ideal Community

DIAMOND LAKE
Gem of the Cascades
The Home of the Rainbow
Trout

ENTERPRISE
The Gateway to Wallowa National Forest

EUGENE
Northwest's Custom Tailored
Convention City
Oregon's Second Market
Skinner's Mudhold (Eugene
F. Skinner established his
land claim in 1846 near
the Eugene and Willamette
Rivers)
The Distribution Hub of South-
west Oregon
The Spokane of Oregon
Western Oregon's Leading
Industrial and Marketing
Center

FOREST GROVE
Oregon's Own Homebase for
Fun, Culture and Scenic
Splendor
The City Between the City
and the Sea

GARIBALDI
Little Holland (numerous
dikes)

GRESHAM
The Friendly City

HILLSBORO
The Filbert Center of the
United States

JACKSONVILLE
The Best Preserved Pioneer
Community in the Pacific
Northwest

LA GRANDE
The Hub of Northeast Oregon
(foot of Blue Mountains)

LAKEVIEW
The Tallest Town in Oregon
(elevation 4,800 feet)

LANCASTER
The Fightin'est Town on the
River

MCMINNVILLE
The Walnut City

MEDFORD
The Bustling Western City
(population about 31,900)
The Fun Capitol of Southern
Oregon
The Land of Incredible
Beauty and Great Liva-
bility
The Pear City (annual pear
pack of the district about
4,000 carloads)
The Vacationland Unlimited

NEWBERG
The Quaker City (founded
by Quakers)

NEWPORT
The Dungeness Crab Capital
of the World

NORTH BEND
The City of Progress (city
government 1903)

ONTARIO
The Brightest Spot in Eastern
Oregon
The Capital of Eastern
Oregon

OREGON CITY
The City of Firsts

PENDLETON
The Round-Up City (Pendleton's first round-up, 1912)

PORTLAND
America's Newest Convention
City
Little Stumptown (contemp-
tuously so-called in the
early days by non-resi-
dents because there were
so many stumps in the
streets, sometimes painted
white so they could be
seen in the dark)
The Beautiful City of Roses

The Capital of the Land of
Out-Doors
The City in the Evergreen
Playground
The City of Homes
The City of Roses
The City on the Willamette
The Convention City
The Country's Largest
Lumber Shipping Center
The Lumber Industry's
Capital
The Lumber Manufacturing
Center of the Pacific
Northwest
The Metropolis of the State
of Oregon
The Rose City
The Spinster City
The Sub-Treasury of the
Pacific Northwest
The Summer Capital

PRINEVILLE
The Agate Capital of the U.S.
(agates, jasper, chalced-
ony, quartz crystals, etc.)
The Country where the Cli-
mate Invites You Out-of-
Doors
The Cowboy Capital of Oregon
The Feel Younger Country

REDMOND
Tailhold
The Hub of Central Oregon

ROSEBURG
The Lumber Capital of the
Nation
The Lumber City
The Timber Capital of the
Nation
The Timber Capital of the
World

SALEM
An All American City of the
Great Northwest
Oregon's Beautiful Capital
City
The Capital City (population
about 73,000)

The Capital City of Good
Living, Commerce and
Industry
The Charmed Land of Un-
equalled Beauty
The Cherry City
The City of Diversified
Industry
The City of Orderly Growth
The City of Unexcelled Op-
portunities for Business
and Industry
The City where Advantages
Abound for Business
The Fisherman's Paradise
The Fishermen's Playground
The Gateway to the Great
Northwest Market
The Happy City Life
The Heart of the Pacific
Wonderland

SEASIDE
The Playground of the
Northwest

STAYTON
The Green Bean Center

TILLAMOOK
The Land of Cheese, Trees
and Ocean Breeze (on
the Pacific Ocean)

WOODBURN
The Berry City

PENNSYLVANIA

ALIQUIPPA
The Dynamic Area of Growth
The Focal Point of Industrial
America
The Phenomenal Example of
American Growth

ALLENTOWN
The Cement City
The Center of Commerce

and Industry
The Center of the Atlantic
Seaboard Megalopolis
The City on the Move with
a Glowing Future Dedi-
cated to Gracious Living
The Clean City
The Community of Gracious
People
The Highly Diversified Manu-
facturing Center
The Hub of the Common-
wealth's Third Largest
Industrial Complex
The Hub of the Greater
Lehigh Valley
The Lehigh Valley City
The Queen City
The Queen City of the Lehigh
Valley (on the Lehigh
River)
The Scrapple City
The Socially Attractive Com-
munity
The Thriving City in Pennsyl-
vania's Dynamic Lehigh
Valley

ALTOONA
The City of Home Owners
The Mountain City (altitude
about 1,170 feet, east
base of Allegheny Moun-
tains)
The Pleasant Place to Live
and Work
The Railroad City (shops and
yards of Pennsylvania
Railroad)

AMBLER
One of Pennsylvania's Fastest
Growing Communities
The Hub of Homes and In-
dustries

BEDFORD
The Mineral Springs City
(resort area popular
since 1795)
The Resort and Convention
Playground of the Alle-
ghenies

The World's Best Little
Town

BEDFORD SPRINGS
The Carlsbad of America

BELLEFONTE
The City of Governors
The City of the Belles

BERLIN
The Scenic City (in Brothers
Valley)

BERWICK
The Car Shop City (Ameri-
can Car and Foundry
plant)

BETHLEHEM
Allentown's Sister City
America's Christmas City
The Christmas City
The Christmas City of the
U. S. A.
The City where the Action Is
The City with a Historic
Past, an Enlightened
Present and a Dynamic
Future
The Community with a Rich
Heritage
The Fastest Growing City
in Pennsylvania
The Historic Bethlehem
The Hub of the Great
Lehigh Valley
The Natural Tourist and
Convention Center
The Outstanding Fast-
Growing City
The Star City with a Great
Future
The Steel City (Bethlehem
Steel Co., plant and
coke works)
The Unique and Distinctive
Community
The Vibrant and Virile
American City

BLOOMSBURG
An Ideal Place to Work
and Live

BLOSSBURG
The Tannery City

BRADFORD
The Growing Industrial Center
of Northwestern Pennsyl-
vania
The High Grade Oil Metropo-
lis of the World
The Metropolitan Center of
McKean County
The Natural Gas City

BREEZEWOOD
The Gateway to the South
The Town of Motels

BUSHKILL
The Niagara of Pennsylvania
(300-foot series of falls)

CARLISLE
The City of Molly Pitcher
(grave of Molly Pitcher,
heroine of Battle of Mon-
mouth)
The Crossroads of American
History
The Crossroads of History
The Crystal Center of the
World (manufacturing of
quartz crystals for radio
sets, etc.)

CHESTER
The Ship-Building City (on
the Delaware River)

COATESVILLE
A Good Place in which to
Work and Live

CONNELLSVILLE
The Bituminous City
The Iron Ore City

COUDERSPORT
The Ice Mine City (a vertical
shaft 40 feet deep, 8 feet
wide and 10 feet long
containing ice formations
during the spring, con-
tinuing through the summer

and disappearing in the
winter)

DOWNINGTOWN
The Gateway to the Pennsylvania Dutch Country

DOYLESTOWN
Home of the Mercer
Museum

EAST LIBERTY
Stringtown on the Pike

EASTON
The Transportation City

EBENSBURG
The Lookout City (altitude
2,022 feet)

ELKLAND
The Dairy City

ELLWOOD CITY
A Good Place to Live,
Work and Play
Ellwood City Encourages
Enterprise
The City of Diversified
Industry

EMPORIUM
The Land of the Endless
Mountains

EPHRATA
The Community where
Living Is at Its Best
The Home of Miss America
1954

ERIE
The City of Diversified
Industry and Commerce
The Gem City of the Lakes
The Harbor City (only
lake port in Pennsylvania,
located on Lake Erie)

GETTYSBURG
The Battlefield City (bloodiest
battle of the War of

Secession, July 1-3, 1863,
loss 23,001 men)
The Great Place to Visit
The Nation's Greatest Historic
Shrine

GREENSBURG
The City Progressive
The Community Progressive
The Tunnel City (bituminous
coal mines)

HANOVER
The Shoe City

HARRISBURG
Pennsylvania's Capital City
The Capital City (population
about 62,600)
The Capital City of the Key-
stone State
The Center of the Northeast
The City Beautiful, Romantic
and Historic
The City that Puts Business
on the Go
The Courteous Capital City
The Heart of Distribution
The Heart of the Common-
wealth
The Host City to Conventions
The Hub of the Interstate and
U.S. Highways
The State City
The Transportation King of
the Mid-East

HAZLETON
Pennsylvania's Highest City
The "Can Do" City
The Crossroads of Tomorrow

HERSHEY
Chocolate Town, U.S.A.
(Hershey Chocolates)
Progress Through Vision
The Chocolate City
The Chocolate Crossroads of
the World
The Chocolate Town
The Golf Capital of Pennsyl-
vania

HOLLIDAYSBURG
    The Canal City (in the 1830's
    a canal and railroad
    terminus)
    The Portage City (to Johns-
    town, Pa.)

HUMMELSTOWN
    The Brownstone City

HUNTINGDON
    Pennsylvania's New Vacation-
    land
    The Scenic Land of the
    Standing Stone (upright
    stone column [tribal
    totem pole] which is the
    symbol of the Indian
    lore)

INDIANA
    The Christmas Tree Capital
    of the World

JEANNETTE
    The Friendly City with a
    Future
    The Glass City

JERSEY SHORE
    The Fair Play City (settled
    in 1785)

JOHNSONBURG
    The Paper City (Castanea
    Paper Company)

JOHNSTOWN
  ‧ The City from Trail Dust
    to Star Dust
    The Cradle of the Steel
    Industry
    The Flood City (disastrous
    flood May 31, 1889)
    The Flood Free City
    The Friendly City

KANE
    Air Conditioned by Nature
    (2,200 feet above the
    sea)
    The Ice Box of Pennsyl-
    vania

The Summit City (2,013 feet
    altitude)
The Weedless City (the city
    ordinance requires elimina-
    tion of weeds)
The Winter Sports City
The Year-Round Health and
    Recreational Resort

LANCASTER
    America's Garden Spot
    America's Oldest Inland City
    One of America's Top Twenty
    Tourist Attractions
    Pennsylvania's Above-Average
    Market of Industry and
    Agriculture
    Pennsylvania's Economic
    Bright Spot
    The Arsenal (rifles and can-
    nons were forged during
    the Revolutionary War)
    The Bread-Basket (during the
    Revolutionary War the
    farmlands supplied the
    Army)
    The Buying Center of a
    Quarter Million People
    The City Fast-Growing,
    Diversified
    The City in the Heart of
    Pennsylvania Dutch Country
    The Heart of Pennsylvania
    Dutch Country
    The Metropolis of "Dutchland"
    The Oldest Inland City in the
    United States
    The Pretzel City
    The Red Rose City

LATROBE
    The Birthplace of Professional
    Football

LEBANON
    The Iron Mountain City (Cor-
    nall ore mines in opera-
    tion since 1742, largest
    iron mines in eastern U.S.)

LEWISBURG
    The College City (Bucknell Uni-
    versity established 1846)

LOCK HAVEN
The Eastern Gateway to
Bucktail State Park
The Private Flying Capital
of the World (head-
quarters of the Piper
Airplane Company)
The Sawdust City (lumbering)

MCKEESPORT
The City in the Heart of
Industrial America
The Tube City (plant of
National Tube Co.)

MANHEIM
The Rose City (on December
4, 1772 "Baron" von
Stiegel, a trustee of the
Manheim Lutheran Congre-
gation deeded a plot of
ground to them with the
stipulation that "in the
month of June forever here-
after the rent of one red
rose if the same shall be
lawfully demanded" shall
be paid)

MAUCH CHUNK
The Switchback City (since
1827 site of first switchback railway)
The Switzerland of America

MEADVILLE
The Hub of Industrial
America

MECHANICSBURG
Big City Benefits with Small
Town Advantages

MERCER
The Hub of Highways

MONROEVILLE
The Gateway to Pittsburgh
The Nation's Residential
Research Center
The Residential Research
Center of the
Nation

MOUNT CARMEL
The Center of Eastern Penn-
sylvania
The Friendly Community for
Progressive Industry

MOUNT JOY
The Garden Spot of Pennsyl-
vania
The Hub of the Richest
Farming District of the
U.S.
The Ideal Industrial Town
The Town where Natural
Beauty and Industry Meet
to Create

NAZARETH
The City where Industry
Prospers, You Will Too

NEW CASTLE
The City with Its Sights on
Its Future
The Gateway to the Miss Uni-
verse Highway (U.S. 301)

NEW KENSINGTON
The Aluminum City (Aluminum
Company of America plant)
The Center of Allegheny
Valley's Business and In-
dustrial Activity
The City of Growing Industries

NORRISTOWN
The Aqueduct City

OIL CITY
The Derrick City (site of
derricks used since 1860
discovery of oil)

PHILADELPHIA
A Glorious Past ... A Bril-
liant Present ... Looking
Forward to an Exciting
Future
America's Bicentennial City
America's Convention City
America's Great Convention
City
Philly

The Athens of Colonial
America
The Birthplace of American
Independence
The Birthplace of American
Liberty (Declaration of
Independence signed
July 4, 1776)
The Birthplace of the Nation
The City for All Seasons
The City of Brotherly Love
The City of Churches
The City of Firsts
The City of Homes
The City of Penn (William
Penn settled in 1682)
The Cradle of Democracy
The Cradle of Liberty
The Cradle of the Revolu-
tion
The Gateway to the United
States
The Great American City
The Modern City of Great
Historical Interest
The Nation's Birthplace
The Native City of Benjamin
Franklin
The Pacesetter of Progress
The Quaker City (settled
by William Penn and
Quaker colony)
The Quakertown
The Rebel Capital
The Sleepy Town
The World's Greatest Work-
shop
The World's Largest Fresh-
Water Port

PITTSBURGH
A City Excitingly Alive and
Progressive
America's Most Progressive
City
One of the Most Beautiful
Cities in the Nation
One of the World's Greatest
Industrial Research
Centers
The Arsenal for the Nation
The Big Smoke
The Big Smoky

The Biggest Inland Port in
America
The Birmingham of America
The Birthplace of American
Film
The Bustling Steel, Coal,
Glass and Aluminum
Center
The Center for the Arts
The Center of Beautiful Hill-
top Views
The Center of Eastern Steel
Making
The City of Bridges (Liberty
Bridge, Smithfield St.
Bridge, Ft. Pitt Bridge,
etc.)
The City of Contrasts
The City of Four National
Pro Teams
The City of Steel (U.S.
Steel Corp.)
The City of the Longest Sun-
day
The City of the Unexpected
The City of 250,000 Trees
The City Reborn
The City where the Old Has
Given Way to the New
The Coal City
The Computer Center
The Forge of the Universe
The Forks of the Ohio
The Gateway Between East
and West
The Gateway Center
The Gateway to the West
The Greatest Steel City in
the World
The Home of the Nickelodeon
The Industrial City of the
West
The Iron City
The Most Bridged City in
the World
The Nation's Busiest Inland
Port
The Nuclear Center
The Overlooked City
The Renaissance City of
America
The Research Center
The Smoky City

The Special Library Capital
of the World
The Steel Capital of the
World
The Steel City
The Steel Town
The University Center
The Workshop of the World
(headquarters of more
than 100 major corpora-
tions)
The World's Workshop

POTTSVILLE
The Coal City (southern
gateway to the anthra-
cite region)

READING
Penn's Town (founded in
1748 by Thomas and
Richard Penn, sons of
William Penn)
The Brewing City
The Capital of Pennsylvania
German Land
The Center of the World's
Best Market
The City of Progress
The Industrial Metropolis
The Pretzel City (J. T.
Adams Pretzel Bakery,
established 1873)
The Textile City

ROCHESTER
The Gateway to the West
where the Ohio and the
Beaver Rivers Meet

SCRANTON
America's Year 'Round
Playground
The Anthracite Capital of
the World (coal mines)
The Anthracite Center of
the World
The Anthracite City
The City of Black Diamonds
(coal)
The Electric City (first
electric streetcar
line on which fares

were collected, 1886)
The Friendly City
The Wonderful Convention
City
The World's Largest Anthra-
cite Coal Mining City

SMETHPORT
The Bucktail City (Bucktail
Regiment organized in
1861 by Gen. Thomas L.
Kane)

SOMERSET
Eastern Gateway to Laurel
Highlands
Growing Progressive Com-
munity
The Community of the Future
The Frosty City
The Roof Garden of Penn-
sylvania (Mt. Davis, alti-
tude 3,240 feet)
The Summer and Winter
Paradise

STATE COLLEGE
The Educational-Cultural
Community
The Penn State City (site of
Pennsylvania State College)

STROUDSBURG
The Gateway to the Poconos
(about fourteen miles from
the heart of the Pocono
Mountains)

TITUSVILLE
The Gateway to the Galaxies
The Town that Outlives and
Outgrew the Oil Boom (first
successful oil well drilled
1859, Drake well)

UNION CITY
The Chair Center of the
World

UNIONTOWN
The City of Coal Kings
The Coke City

WARREN
  The City of Industrial Op-
    portunity

WASHINGTON
  The City of Homes, Educa-
    tion and Industry
  The Crossroads of the
    Nation

WAYNESBURG
  The Catacomb City

WELLSBORO
  The Canyon City (Pine
    Creek Gorge, the Grand
    Canyon of Pennsylvania)
  The Pennsylvania Athens

WEST CHESTER
  An Alluring Attractive
    Suburban Municipality
  The Athens of Pennsylvania
  The Heart of Historic
    America
  The Shopping Center of
    Chester County

WILKES-BARRE
  The Black Diamond City
    (coal)
  The Diamond City
  The Heart of the Valley
    that Warms a Nation
    (Wyoming Valley)

WILKINSBURG
  The City of Churches

WILLIAMSPORT
  The Birthplace and Home
    of Little League Baseball
  The Lumber City
  The Queen City
  The Sawdust City of America
    (sawmills in the 1900's)
  The Scenic Capital of
    Central Pennsylvania
    (on the west branch of
    the Susquehanna River)

YORK
  The Castle City

The City of Diversified
  Industry and Civic Achieve-
  ment
The Community of Craftsmen
The Distribution Point,
  U.S.A.
The First Capital of the
  United States
The Nation's First Capital
The Plough-Share City
The White Rose City (refers
  to symbol of York in
  struggle against Lancaster
  in the struggle (1455-1471)
  for possession of the
  English throne)

RHODE ISLAND

BRISTOL
  The City where Things Are
    Shipshape and Bristol Fast

CENTRAL FALLS
  The Twin Cities (with Paw-
    tucket, R.I.)

CUMBERLAND
  The Mineral Pocket of New
    England (iron, copper and
    other minerals have been
    found within its borders)

EAST GREENWICH
  The Heart of Rhode Island

GALILEE
  The Tuna Capital of the
    World

JAMESTOWN
  A Safe Place for Children
  The City where the Breezes
    Blow (on Conanicut
    Island)

JOHNSTON
  The Friendly City
  The Friendly Town

LINCOLN
   Historic and Scenic Lincoln

MIDDLETOWN
   The Resort Town on Rhode
      Island
   The Woods (on Aquidneck
      Island between Newport
      and Portsmouth)

NARRAGANSETT
   The Resort Town on Rhode
      Island

NEWPORT
   America's City of History
   America's First Resort
      (in the 1720's a famous
      vacation resort of Caro-
      lina and West Indies
      planters and merchants)
   America's First Vacation-
      land
   America's Oldest Summer
      Resort
   America's Society Capital
   Rhode Island's Most
      Historic Town
   The Capital of Vacation
      Land
   The City by the Sea
   The City of Contrasts
   The Famed America's
      Cup Racing City
   The Historic Showplace of
      America
   The Home of Tennis,
      Mansions and the
      America's Cup Race
   The Naval Center
   The Queen of Summer
      Resorts
   The Queen of the Resorts
   The Queen of World Resorts
   The Sailing Capital of the
      World (Newport-Bermuda
      race, Annapolis-Newport
      race, England-Newport
      Trans-Atlantic Single-
      handed race, America's
      Cup race)
   The Summer Capital of
      Society

   The Summer Resort
   The Tennis Town
   The Town Famous for Its
      Great Mansions
   The Yachting Capital of the
      World
   Xanadu by the Sea

NEW SHOREHAM
   America's Bermuda (on
      Block Island)
   The Bermuda of the North
   The Fisherman's Paradise
      of the North Atlantic

NORTH KINGSTOWN
   The Home of the Atlantic
      Sea Bees

PAWTUCKET
   The Birthplace of America's
      Cotton Industry
   The Birthplace of the Ameri-
      can Cotton Industry
      (Samuel Slater established
      his mill in 1790)
   The Cradle of the American
      Textile Industry
   The Heart of the Blackstone
      Valley
   The Land of Sea, Sand and
      Sun
   The Twin Cities (with Central
      Falls, R.I.)

PORTSMOUTH
   The Home for Your Business
   The Home for Your Family
   The Home of the Portsmouth
      Compact
   The Vacation Center

PROVIDENCE
   America in Miniature
   The Bee-hive of Industry
   The Big Money Center You
      Never Heard Much About
   The Capital City (popu-
      lation about 163,000)
   The Center of U.S. Jewelry
      Production
   The Cradle of American

Independence
The Cultural and Economic
Center of Southeastern
New England
The First City of America's
First Vacationland
The Gateway of Southern
New England
The Modern City with a
Proud Heritage
The Perry Davis' Pain
Killer City
The Roger Williams City
(founded in 1636 by
Roger Williams)
The Southern Gateway of
New England

WARWICK
The Growing City Con-
venient to Recreation
Areas

WEEKAPAUG
The Place for Excellent
Surf Bathing

WESTERLY
The Land of Sand, Sea and
Sun

WICKFORD
The Art Center of Rhode
Island
The Venice of America
(on Narragansett Bay)

SOUTH CAROLINA

ABBEVILLE
The Cradle and the Grave
of the Confederacy
(secession movement
originated Nov. 22, 1860,
last cabinet meeting of
President Jefferson Davis
May 2, 1865)

AIKEN
One of the Most Fashionable
Winter Resorts of the
South
One of the Most Favorable
Winter Resorts of the
South
The City in the Land of the
Pines
The Polo Capital of the
Nation
The Polo Capital of the
South
The Sports Center of the
South (steeplechase and
horse show annual events)

ALLENDALE
The Tourist Mecca of the
South (numerous tourist
accommodations)

ANDERSON
A Place to Live, a Place
to Work
The City of Hospitality
The Electric City (first town
in the south to have an
unlimited hydro-electric
power)

BATESBURG
The Only Twin-Cities in
South Carolina (with Lees-
ville, S.C.)

BEAUFORT
The Capital of the Sea
Islands
The City in the Heart of the
Coastal Sea Islands
The Eighteenth Century Sea-
port
The Gateway to the Carolina
Sea Islands
The Home of Parris Island
(U.S. Marine Corps East
Coast Recruit Depot)
The Nation's Most Historic
Area
The Newport of the South
The Pleasant Place

BELTON
The Place where Friendly
People Come to Stay

CAESAR'S HEAD
  The Summer Resort in the
  Blue Ridge Mountains

CAYCE
  The Gateway to Mountains
  and Seashore (about
  three hours from each)

CHARLESTON
  America's Most Historic
  City
  The Air Capital of the
  Carolinas
  The Capital of the Carolinas
  The Capital of the Coastal
  Empire of South Carolina
  The Capital of the Planta-
  tions
  The City by the Sea
  The City of Churches
  The City of History and
  Romance
  The City of Secession (first
  ordinance of secession,
  1860)
  The County Seat of Growing
  Charleston County
  The Cradle of Secession
  The Earthquake City
  The Historic Seaport City
  The Historical City of the
  South
  The Holy City
  The Palmetto City
  The Plumb Line Port to
  Panama
  The Queen City of the Sea
  The Queen City of the
  South
  The Quintessenial Strong-
  hold of the American
  Blueblood

CHERAW
  The Prettiest Town in
  Dixie

COLUMBIA
  South Carolina's Capital
  City
  The Capital City (population
  about 99,000)

The Gateway to the South
The Golden Rule City

CONWAY
  The City by the Waccamaw
  The Gateway to the Grand
  Strand

DARLINGTON
  The Pearl of the Pee Dee

DILLON
  The Gateway to the Palmetto
  State

ELLENTON
  The H-Bomb's Home Town

FLORENCE
  The Home of South Carolina's
  Little Arlington (veterans
  of five wars buried in the
  national cemetery established
  in 1868)
  The Magic City

GAFFNEY
  The Hub of the Southeast

GREENVILLE
  The Textile Center of the
  World (textile finishing and
  garment production)

GREENWOOD
  The Gate City of the Pied-
  mont
  The Industrial Center of
  Western Carolina
  The Natural Shopping Center
  The Widest Street in the
  World

HARTSVILLE
  The City of Lovely Gardens
  The Ideal Spot to Relax

LATTA
  The Gateway to the Palmetto
  State

LEESVILLE
  The Only Twin-Cities in

South Carolina (with
Batesburg, S.C.)

MANNING
The Prettiest Small Town
Between New York and
Miami

MULLINS
The Tobacco Capital of
South Carolina

MYRTLE BEACH
The Hub City of the Famed
Grand Strand
The Seaside Golf Capital of
the U.S.A.
The Sun Fun Capital
The Sun Fun City

NEWBERRY
The City of Friendly
Folks

ROCK HILL
The City without Cob-
webs

SIMPSONVILLE
The Heart and Center of
the Golden Strip

SPARTANBURG
The Crossroads of the
New South
The Hub City of the South-
east
The South's Largest Pro-
ducer of Cotton Cloth

SUMMERTON
The Home of the World's
Only Landlocked Striped
Rock Bass

SUMMERVILLE
The Flower Town in the
Pines

SUMTER
The Gamecock City
(named for General

Thomas Sumter "the game-
cock of the Revolution")

SOUTH DAKOTA

ABERDEEN
A Good Place to Live
The Convention Hub of the
Dakotas
The Hub City (in the James
River Valley)
The Hub City of the Dakotas
(four railroads in the
area resemble the spokes
of a wheel)
The Quint City (birthplace of
the quintuplets born to
Mrs. Andrew Fisher on
Sept. 14, 1963)
The Railroad Hub of the
Dakotas

BELLE FOURCHE
The Home of the Famed
Black Hills Round-Up
The Northern Gateway to the
Black Hills

BRITTON
The City of the Continental
Divide

BROOKINGS
The Home City
The Home of South Dakota
State College

CANTON
The Gateway to the Newton
Hills State Park

CUSTER CITY
The Town where the Action Is
The Town with a Gunsmoke
Flavor

DE SMET
The Little Town on the
Prairie

DEADWOOD
  The Historic City of the
    Black Hills (gold dis-
    coveries about 1876)
  The Twin Cities of the
    Northern Black Hills of
    South Dakota

EDGEMONT
  The Home of the Black
    Hills Uranium Industry
  The Uranium Center of
    South Dakota (uranium
    and vanadium extraction
    mills)

FAITH
  South Dakota's Prairie
    Oasis

FAULKTON
  The Heart of the South
    Dakota Pheasant Country

FORT THOMPSON
  The Paddlefish Capital of
    the World

HOT SPRINGS
  The City in a Valley where
    Recuperation, Rehabilita-
    tion, Rest and Relaxation
    with Recreation and Scenic
    Beauty Abound
  The City of Healing Waters
    (mineral springs)
  The Southern Gateway to
    the Black Hills

HOWARD
  The Pheasant Paradise of
    America

HURON
  The Center of the World's
    Largest Irrigation Power
    Navigation Flood Control
    Project
  The Central City of South
    Dakota
  The City with Future
    Unlimited
  The Convention Headquarters

for the Dakotas
  The Fair City (site of the
    South Dakota State Fair)
  The Natural City (geographi-
    cally nearest both the
    center of population of
    the entire state and popu-
    lation center of that
    portion of the state lying
    east of the Missouri
    River)
  The Pheasant Capital of the
    World

KADOKA
  The Gateway to the Badlands
  The Gateway to the Badlands
    and Pine Ridge Indian
    Reservation

KEYSTONE
  The Friendly Place
  The Home of the World-
    Famous Mount Rushmore
    National Memorial

LAKE ANDES
  The Fish City (site of state
    fish hatchery)

LEAD
  Over a Mile High, a Mile
    Long, a Mile Wide and a
    Mile Deep
  The Mile High City
  The Mile High City of the
    Black Hills
  The Twin Cities of the
    Northern Black Hills of
    South Dakota

MADISON
  The City of Lakes and Parks
  The City that Says "Welcome
    Neighbor"
  The Land of Longtails
  The Water City (Lake Madi-
    son and Lake Herman)

MARTIN
  The Metropolis of the
    Pine Ridge Reservation
    Country

MILBANK
The Granite City (Milbank
granite quarries)

MITCHELL
A Pleasant Place to Visit
A Wonderful Place to Live
South Dakota's City of Op-
portunity
South Dakota's Opportunity
City
The Educational Centre
The Home of the World's
Only Corn Palace
The Marketing and Shopping
Center
The Medical Center
The Recreational Center

MOBRIDGE
The Bridge City on Lake
Oahe
The Northern Pike Capital
of the World

ONIDA
The Wheat Capital

PIERRE
A Real Western City
The Capital City (population
about 10, 300)
The Center of Commerce
The Center of Great Wealth
The Center of the Sunshine
State
The City in the Center of
Hunting Lands
The City in the Heart of
Western Ranch Land
The Coming City of the
Great Northwest
The Future Great City
The Gateway to the Black
Hills
The Home of Friendly
People
The Home of the Giant
Oahe Dam
The Metropolis of the
Northwest
The Rail Center of the
Northwest

The Railroad Center
The Railroad Town
The Site of the Oahe Dam

PLATTE
The Doorway to the South
Dakota Great Lakes

RAPID CITY
The Denver of South Dakota
The Eastern Gateway to the
Black Hills
The Eastern Gateway to the
Mountainous Black Hills
where East Meets West
and the Friendly Hospi-
tality
The Fastest Growing City in
the Upper Midwest
The Gate City
The Gateway City of the Hills
The Gateway to the Black
Hills

REDFIELD
The Birthplace of South
Dakota's Pheasant Hunting

SIOUX FALLS
The Crossroads of the Nation
The Gateway to the Dakotas
The Gateway to the West
The Growing City
The Pheasant Capital of the
World
The Pheasant City, U.S.A.
The Progressive City
The Progressive Gateway City
to the Dakotas
The Queen City

SPEARFISH
Home of the World-Famous
Black Hills Passion Play
The Queen City
The Queen City of the Hills
(the Black Hills)

SPENCER
The Granite City
The Greatest Little
Town in the Midwest

STURGIS
The Key City of the Black
Hills

VERMILLION
The Home of the University
of South Dakota
The University City (Uni-
versity of South Dakota)

WALL
The Gateway to the Bad-
lands National Park
The Northern Gateway to
the Badlands National
Monument

WATERTOWN
South Dakota's Newest
Convention City
The Lake City (on Lake
Kampeska)

WEBSTER
The Gateway to Coteau
Lake Region
The Gateway to the Lake
Region
The Petunia Capital of the
World

WINNER
The Gateway to the Black
Hills

YANKTON
The City where Your Dream
Vacation Can Become a
Reality
The Gateway to South Dakota's
Vacation Wonderland
The Mother City
The Mother City of the
Dakotas (oldest city in
Dakota territory, terri-
torial capital 1861)
The Port of Entry to the
Missouri Great Lakes
The Recreation Paradise
on Beautiful Lewis and
Clark Lake

TENNESSEE

ALCOA
The Twin Cities (with Maryville, Tenn.)

ATHENS
The City where Business
and Industry Thrive and
People Enjoy a Wide
Variety of Year Around
Recreation
The Progressive City

BRISTOL
The City in the Heart of
Eastern America (see also
Virginia)
The Outdoorman's Paradise
The Shopping Center of the
Appalachians (see also
Virginia)
The Tri-Cities (with Johnson
City and Kingsport, Tenn.)
Twin Cities (with Bristol,
Va.)

CARTHAGE
The City on the Banks of the
Scenic Cumberland River

CHATTANOOGA
One of America's Most Inter-
esting Cities
The Chief Industrial City of
the South (more than 500
manufacturers)
The Dynamo of Dixie
The Gate City
The Mountain City
The Scenic Center of the
South
The Scenic City
The Year-Round Attraction
City

CLARKSVILLE
One of the Fastest Developing
Areas in the Nation
One of the World's Largest

Markets for Dark Fired
Tobacco
The Balanced American
City
The Queen City of the
Cumberland

CLEVELAND
A Good Place to Aim For

COLUMBIA
The Mule Capital of the
World

COOKEVILLE
The Home of the Tennessee
Technological University
The Hub City of Upper
Cumberland

COPPERHILL
The Painters' Paradise

CROSSVILLE
Natures Own Air Conditioning
The Crossroads of the
South

DYERSBURG
The City Thriving from the
Fertile Banks of Ole
Man River

ERWIN
The Gateway to the Smoky
Mountains

GATLINBURG
The Convention Center of
the Great Smokies
The Convention City of the
Great Smokies
The Fastest Growing
Mountain Resort
The Gateway Resort Town
of Your Smokies
The Gateway to the Great
Smokies (the Great
Smoky Mountains Na-
tional Park)
The Gateway to the Smokies
The Handicraft Capital of
the United States

The Host Resort to the
Nation

GLEASON
Taterville
The Tater Town

GREENVILLE
One of the Country's Leading
Burley Markets

HENDERSONVILLE
The Community Full of
History
The Progressive Community

JACKSON
The Home of Casey Jones

JOHNSON CITY
The Gateway to the Smokies
The Tri-Cities (with Bristol
and Kingsport, Tenn.)

KINGSPORT
The City of Diversified Industry (planned 1916)
The Tri-Cities (with Bristol
and Johnson City, Tenn.)

KNOXVILLE
The Capital of Big Orange
Country
The City of the Great
Smokies
The City where Lakes and
Mountains Meet
The Four-Season Vacation
Center
The Gateway to the Great
Lakes of the South
The Gateway to the Great
Smoky Mountains National
Park
The Gateway to the Smokies
The Home of the University
of Tennessee
The Major Research and Edu-
cational Center
The Marble City
The Metropolis of East
Tennessee
The Queen City of the Moun-
tains

LAFAYETTE
The Gateway to the Scenic
Cumberland Mountains

MCMINNVILLE
The Friendly City

MANCHESTER
The County Seat of Historic
Coffee County
The Home of Old Stone
Fort

MARYVILLE
The Twin Cities (with Alcoa,
Tenn.)

MEMPHIS
Babylon on the Bluff
Big Shelby
Crumptown
Homicide Headquarters
Queen of the American Nile
Sodom of the South
The Beautiful City
The Birth of the "Blues"
The Bluff City
The Boom Town on the
River
The Capital of the Mid-
South
The City at the Crossroads
of the South
The City Beautiful
The City of Hospitality
The City of Manageable
Size
The City of Opportunity
The City of Tradition
The City that Balks at
Changes
The Cleanest City, the
Safest City and the
Quietest City in the
Country
The Commercial Metropolis
of West Tennessee
The Convention City in the
Heart of the South
The Cotton Capital of the
World
The Cotton Center
The Crossroads of

the Mid-South
The First City
The Gateway to the South
The Home of King Cotton
The Important Hub for Rail
The Innkeeper's City
The Largest Spot Cotton
Market and Hardwood
Lumber Market in the
World
The Murder Capital of
America
The Nation's Cleanest City
The Place of Good Abode
The Progressive City
The Tri-State Capital (Arkan-
sas-Tennessee-Mississippi)
The World's Largest Hard-
wood Lumber Market
The World's Largest Spot
Cotton Market

MILAN
The City of Diversified Agri-
culture
The City with a Modern
School System
The City with Abundant TVA
Power
The City with Excellent
Transportation
The Progressive Community

MORRISTOWN
The City Always Expanding
The City Rich in History
The Cleanest City in the
United States
The Home of the Tennessee
Valley Industrial District
The Lakeway to the Smokies
The Vacation Wonderland

MURFREESBORO
One of the Fastest Growing
Cities in the South
The City with a Blueprint
for Living
The Exact Geographic Center
of the State
The Friendly Community
The Home of the Middle Ten-
nessee State University

NASHVILLE
Music City, U.S.A. (origi-
nation point of Grand
Old Opry and other shows)
Tennessee's Beauty Spot
The Athens of the South
(Nashville contains a
replica of the Parthenon)
The Capital City (population
about 469,000)
The Capital City of Indus-
trial Progress
The Capital City of
Tennessee
The Choice Place to Live
and Work
The Church Center
The City Beautiful
The City of Diversified
Interests
The City of Opportunity
The City of Rocks
The Commercial Capital of
the Central South
The Country Music Capital
of the World
The Dimple of the Universe
The Gateway of the South
The Home of Grand Old
Opry
The Home of the "Nash-
ville Sound"
The Iris City
The Plus City
The Rock City
The Wall Street of the
South

NEWPORT
The Gateway to the Smokies

OAK RIDGE
The Atomic Capital of the
World
The Atomic City
The Atomic Energy City
(manufacture of atomic
bomb)
The Birthplace of the
Atomic Age
The City of the Atom
The City on the Move

PORTLAND
The Best Town to Live In
The Home of the Middle
Tennessee Strawberry
Festival
The Imperfect Town

SAVANNAH
The Home of the National
Catfish Derby
The Place where Sportsmen
Meet
The World's Finest Catfish
Waters

SHELBYVILLE
The Walking Horse Capital
of the World

TATE SPRINGS
The Carlsbad of America

TULLAHOMA
The Queen City of the High-
land Rim
The Thermopylae of Middle
Tennessee (winter head-
quarters of Gen. Braxton
Bragg fell to Union
General Rosecrans on
July 3, 1863)

TEXAS

ABILENE
Texas' Only Atlas Missile
Sites
The Athens of the West
(Hardin-Simmons Univer-
sity, McMurray and Abi-
lene Christian colleges)
The Key City of West Texas

ALICE
The Hub City of South Texas
The Hub City of the South
Texas Oil Industry
The Sweetheart of South Texas

ALPINE
The Roof Garden of Texas
(altitude 4,484 feet)
The Roof Garden Resort of
Texas

ALVIN
The Center of the Action in
the Tremendous Houston-
Gulf Coast
The Crossroads to the Gulf

AMARILLO
The City of Diversified
Industry and Agriculture
The City where We Fly
360 Days a Year
The Metropolis of an Agri-
cultural Empire
The Metropolis of the Pan-
handle
The Plains Empire City
The Queen City of the
Panhandle
The Queen City of the
Plains
The Young City Going Places

ARANSAS PASS
The City with the World's
Largest Shrimping Facili-
ties
The Shrimporee City
The Thriving Community

ARLINGTON
The City in the Heart of
America's Future

AUSTIN
The Big Heart of Texas
The Boom Town Without
Oil
The Capital City (population
about 307,000)
The City of the Violet
Crown (located on violet-
crowned hills)
The Friendly City
The Fun-tier Capital of
Texas
The Good Life in Texas
The Ideal Home City

BANDERA
The Dude Ranch Capital of
Texas
The Switzerland of Texas

BAY CITY
The Deep South of Texas (on
Bay Prairie)

BEAUMONT
The Birthplace of the Modern
Oil Industry
The City where Great East
Texas Meets the Sea
The City where Main Street
Meets the World
The Industrial City
The Industrial Giant of Far
Southwest Texas
The Port City
The Queen of the Neches (on
the Sabine-Neches water-
way)

BENJAMIN
The Big Cattle Country

BORGER
The Boomtown
The Industrial Center of the
Panhandle

BRADY
The Heart of Texas

BRENHAM
The Heart of Your Texas
Market

BROWNFIELD
The Queen City of the South

BROWNSVILLE
The Capital of the Rio Grande
Valley
The City "Electric" with
Growth and Change
The City on the Border by
the Sea
The City where Mexico Meets
Uncle Sam (across the
river is Matamoras,
Mexico)

The City with a Blend of
Two Cultures and Two
Counties
The International Trade
Center
The Metropolis of the
Magic Valley
The Truly International
City

CAMBELLTON
The Thriving Supply
Point

CANTON
The Capital of the "Free
State" of Van Zandt
County
The Home of the Famous
"First Monday" Trades
Day

CARRIZO SPRINGS
The Hub of the Winter
Garden (in Dimmit
County)

CHARLOTTE
The Prosperous Center
of a Rich Farming
District

CHILDRESS
The City of the Plains
(county seat of Childress
County)

CLEBURNE
The Gateway to Lake
"Whitney"

CLEVELAND
The Entrance to Sam Houston
National Forest
The Gateway to the Lakes

COLUMBUS
The City of Live Oaks

COOPER
The Vetch Capital of the
World

CORPUS CHRISTI
Texas's Sparkling City by the
Sea
The City where Texas Meets
the Sea (on Corpus Christi
Bay)
The City where Your Ship
Will Come In
The Fastest Growing City in
Texas (population about
210, 000)
The Gateway to Padre Island
The Jewel on the Gulf of
Mexico
The Metropolis of the Richest
Part of Texas
The Sparkling City by the Sea
The Sun City

COTULLA
The Main Street of North
America

CROCKETT
Paradise in the Pines

CRYSTAL CITY
The Spinach Capital of the
World
The World's Spinach Capital
(a statue of Popeye stands
in Popeye Park)

CUERO
The Turkey Capital of the
World

DALLAS
Athens of the Southwest
Big "D"
The All-American Town
The Bright Spot
The City Deep in the Heart
of Texas
The City of Homes
The City of Opportunity
The City of the Hour
The City with a Future
The Electronics Aerospace
Center
The Fastest Growing City
The Financial Center of the
Southwest

The High Point for Travel
Fun
The Metropolis of North
Texas
The Metropolis of the
Southwest
The Murder Capital of the
World (so-called after
the assassination of
President John Fitzgerald
Kennedy)
The Rich Busy Pride of
Texas
The Southwest Metroplex
(with Fort Worth)
The Southwestern Head-
quarters of American
Business
The Southwest's Leading
Financial Manufacturing
and Distribution Center
The Sports Center of the
Southwest
The Time of Your Life City

DEL RIO
The Queen City of the Rio
Grande

DENISON
Texas' First Stop
The Gate City (in north-
eastern Grayson
County)
The Home of Denison
Dam
The Home of Eisenhower's
Birthplace
The Home of Eisenhower's
Birthplace and Denison
Dam-Lake Texoma

DENTON
The City Half a World from
the "Hubbub"
The City Half an Hour from
the Hub
The City on the Move
The Fun Place

DICKINSON
The City of Fine Homes,
Churches and Schools

DUNCAN
The Oil Well Cementing Capital of the World

EDGEWOOD
The Center of the Rich Gas
and Sulphur Fields

EDINBURG
The City on the Grow
The City where the Rio
Grande Valley Begins
The Educational Center of the
Valley (Rio Grande Valley)
The Gateway City
The Gateway to the Rio
Grande Valley

EL PASO
The City in the Southwest
Sun Country
The Crossroads City
The Crossroads of America
The Crossroads of the
Americas
The Exciting International
City
The Gateway to Mexico
The Host City of the Sunland
Empire
The Hub of the International
Southwest
The International City
The Largest City in the
Most Favored Climate
Area in America

FALFURREAS
The Largest Unincorporated
Town in the U.S. (1929)

FORT WORTH
The Arsenal of Democracy
The Banking City
The Chicago of the Southwest
The City of Beautiful Heights
The City of Delight
The City of Insurance Interests
The City of Lakes
The City of Western Charm
and Hospitality
The City where the West
Begins

The City Worth Looking
Into
The Cow Town (largest
livestock marketing and
processing center south
of Kansas City)
The Fort Town
The Friendly City
The Friendly City of the
Southwest
The Fun Spot of the South-
west
The Gateway to the West
The Gateway to West Texas
The Hub of Banking and
Insurance Interests
The Lake City
The Medical Center (17
hospitals and 85 private
clinics)
The Panther City
The Queen City of the
Plains
The Queen City of the
Prairies
The Second Largest Aircraft
Production Center in the
Country
The Southwest Metroplex
(with Dallas)
The Stage Coach Town (the
first stagecoach line in
Texas connected Fort
Worth with West Texas)
The World's Greatest Store-
house of Raw Material

GAINESVILLE
Circus Town, U.S.A.

GALVESTON
America's Port of Quickest
Dispatch
The City of Hospitality
The Island They Wrote the
Song About
The Old Lady of the Sea
The Oldest Port in the
West Gulf
The Oleander City
The Oleander City by the
Sea
The Oleander City of Texas

The Port and Playground of
the Southwest (on Gulf of
Mexico)
The Port of the Southwest
The Queen City
The Seaport of the West
The Space Port USA
The Treasure Island of the
Southwest

GARLAND
The City of Neighbors
The Wonderful Place to Live
and Work

GLADEWATER
The City in the Heart of the
East Texas Oil Fields

GONZALES
A Great Place to Live
The City where the Fight for
Texas Liberty Began
The Lexington of Texas (Oct.
2, 1835, the first shots
of the revolution against
Mexico)
The Mecca for History Lovers
The Opportunity for History
The Playground for Vaca-
tioners

GRAND PRAIRIE
Hometown, U.S.A.
The Center of the Aircraft
Industry
The Gateway to Six Flags
Over Texas

HARLINGEN
The Growing City of the
Lower Rio Grande Valley
of Texas
The Growingest City in the
Rio Grande Valley
The Key City in the Lower
Rio Grande Valley
The Medical Referral Center
of South Texas
The Retirement Center

HENDERSON
The Crape Myrtle City

HEREFORD
The City Without a Toothache (low dental decay rate)

HILLTOP LAKES
America's Most Complete Resort

HOUSTON
America's Growingest City
Babylon on the Bayou
Land of the Big Rich
Nature's Gift to Texas
Southwest's Foremost Educational Center
Space City, U.S.A.
Space Headquarters, U.S.A.
The Astrodome City
The Bayou City
The Booming Oil Rich City
The City of Gracious Living
The City of Magnolias
The City that Built Its Seaport
The Command Post for the Nation's Manned Space Exploration
The Cultural Center of the Southwest
The Energy Capital
The Energy Capital of the United States
The Energy Capital of the World
The Fashion Capital of the Nation
The Fastest Growing of the Nation's Major Cities
The First City in Texas
The First Cotton Port
The Giant of the Golden Bend
The Headquarters of the International Oil Tool Trade
The Home of America's Greatest Petrochemical Industry Complex
The Home of Astronauts
The Land of the Big Inch (oil pipeline)
The Land of the Big Rich

The Largest City in the South
The Largest City in the Southwest
The Leading Commercial Financial and Distribution Center
The Leading Industrial City of the Southwest
The Leading Spot Cotton Market
The Magnolia City
The Metropolis of the West
The Miracle City
The Monument to Southwestern Economic Growth
The Murder Capital of the World
The Nation's Most Exciting New Convention Center
The Natural Gas Pipeline Capital of the Nation
The Newest Most Prosperous Fastest-Growing Urban Industrial Center in America
The Number One City in the Southwest
The Oil Center of the World
The Petroleum World Center
The Sassy New Pittsburgh of the Southern Rim
The Seamy Little Swamp Town
The Space Center
The World's Heart Transplant Capital
The World's Petroleum Capital

HUGHES SPRINGS
The Home of the East Texas Peach Festival
The Peach City

HUNTSVILLE
The Mount Vernon of Texas (last home and burial place of Sam Houston)

HURST
The Strategic Geographical Location for Industry

IRVING
The Now City

JACKSONVILLE
The Tourist Mecca of East
Texas

JASPER
The Gateway to East Texas'
Enchanting Vacationland

JEFFERSON
The Gateway to Texas
The Living Page from
Texas History
The Williamsburg of Texas

JOHNSON CITY
The Home Town of Lyndon
B. Johnson
The Peach Center of Texas

JOURDANTON
The Dairyland of Texas
The Watermelon Town

JUNCTION
The Yosemite of Texas

KERRVILLE
The Capital City of the
Hill County Playland
The Capital of the Hill
Country
The City in the Heart 'o
the Hills
The City on the Grow
The Educational and Cul-
tural Center
The Vacation Paradise of
the Texas Hill Country
The Year-Round Playground

KILEEN
The Gateway to Ft. Hood

KINGSVILLE
The Spot Forever Texas

KOUNTZE
The Big Light in the Big
Thicket

LAREDO
The Gate City (on the Rio
Grande River which sepa-
rates it from Nuevo
Laredo, Texas)
The Gateway City
The Gateway to Mexico
The Ideal Vacation for a
Two-Nation Vacation
The Major Inland Port Serving
Mexico and Latin America

LIBERTY
The Hub of the Industrial
Gulf Coast

LLANO
The Deer Capital of Texas

LONE STAR
The City of Youth, Industry,
Recreation
The City to Grow With

LOS FRESNOS
The Biggest Little City in the
Valley

LUBBOCK
Texas' Largest Isolated
Market
The Cottonseed Oil Capital of
the World
The Home of Texas Tech
(Texas Technological Col-
lege)
The Hub City of the South
Plains
The Hub of Agriculture
The Hub of Beauty
The Hub of Civic Pride
The Hub of Education
The Hub of Industry and Oil
The Hub of Livestock Pro-
cessing
The Hub of the Plains
(county seat of Lubbock
County)
The Industrial, Agricultural
and Educational Center of
the South Plains of
Texas

LULING
  The Toughest Town in Texas
    (formerly used)

MABANK
  The Friendliest Town on
    the Lake

MCALLEN
  The City of Palms
  The Garden of the Golden
    Grapefruit
  The Gateway to Mexico

MCKINNEY
  The Home of Prosperous
    Agriculture Business and
    Industry

MARLIN
  The Bluebonnet Capital
  The Southwest's Greatest
    Health Resort

MARSHALL
  The Athens of Texas
  The City where the Con-
    temporary Combines
    with the Historic
  The City with Something
    for Everyone
  The Gateway to the Great
    Southwest
  The Golden Gateway to the
    Great Gulf Southwest
  The Home of Lady Bird
    Johnson
  The Hub of Transportation
  The Industrial Rocket
    Center
  The Oil, Gas, Steel,
    Chemical, Clay, Lumber
    Center
  The Recreation and Industrial
    Center of East Texas
  The Sportsman's Playground

MESQUITE
  People Prefer Mesquite
  The City of Elegance

MIDLAND
  The City of Fine Homes

The City of Progress and Op-
    portunity
  The City where the Golfing's
    Great
  The Financial Center
  The Headquarters City of
    the Permian Basin
  The Oil Center
  The Recreation Center

MILANO
  The City of Varied Industries

MINEOLA
  The Gateway to the Pines
  The Watermelon Center

MINERAL WELLS
  The City at the Crossroads
    of Texas
  The Finest for Hunting,
    Fishing and Skin-Diving
  The Gateway to Possum
    Kingdom Lake
  The Place to Live, Work
    and Play
  The World Famous Bath and
    Scientific Massage Center

MISSION
  The Home of the Texas
    Grapefruit (Ruby Red)

NACOGDOCHES
  The City in the Heart of the
    Piney Woods of East
    Texas
  The City of Friendly People
  The City where History and
    Progress Join Hands
  The City with a Great Past
    and a Great Future
  The Historic Center of East
    Texas
  The Thriving and Progres-
    sive Community

ODESSA
  A City where Growth Has
    Become a Habit
  America's Newest Industrial
    Frontier
  The City of Change

The City of Dreams
The New Industrial Frontier
of the Southwest
The Oil City of the Southwest (Penn field opened
1929, Crowden field 1930)

ORANGE
The City where Water Means
Pleasure, Progress and
Prosperity
The Gateway to Texas and
the Astrodome
The Water Wonderland

PALACIOS
The Encampment City

PALESTINE
The Home of Texas Dogwood
Trails
The Homesteader's Paradise
(in the center of Ander-
son County)

PAMPA
The City at the Top O'
Texas
The City where Wheat Grows
and Oil Flows
The Friendly City

PANNA MARIA
The Polish City in Texas
(established 1854 by
Catholic Poles)

PARIS
The City Beautiful
The City in Beautiful North-
east Texas
The Crape Myrtle City of
Texas
The Industrial Center of the
Red River Valley
The Medical Center of
Northeast Texas

PASADENA
The Hub of the Fabulous
Golden Gulf Coast
The Industrial Center of
the South

PEARSALL
The Land of Diversification

PECOS
The World's First Rodeo

PERRYTON
The Oil and Gas Center of
the Great Anadarko Basin
The Wheat Heart of the
Nation

PHARR
The City of Palms
The Industrial Frontier of the
Magic Lower Rio Grande
Valley of Texas

PITTSBURG
The Home of East Texas'
Peach Festival

PLANO
The Manufacturing Research
and Development Center
of the Southwest

PORT ARTHUR
The City of Homes
We Oil the World

POTEET
The Strawberry Capital of
Texas

RANGER
The City of Flowing Gold (oil
wells)

RICHARDSON
A City Conducive to Education
A Wonderful Place to Live
and Work
One of America's Best
Planned Cities
The Electronic City of the
Southwest

ROBY
The Best in the West
The Good Home Town

ROCKPORT
The Toast of the Coast

SAN ANGELO
  The City of Angels
  The Nation's Sheep Capital

SAN ANTONIO
  One of America's Four
    Unique Cities
  St. Anthony's Town (mission
    authorized 1716)
  The Alamo City (March 6,
    1837 Alamo siege cli-
    maxed)
  The Citadel of History
  The City in the Sun
  The City of Contrast and
    Romance
  The City of Contrasts
  The City of Flaming Ad-
    venture
  The City of Missions
  The City where Life Is
    Different
  The Cradle of Texas Liberty
  The Fiesta City
  The Free State of Bexar
  The Gateway City in the Sun
  The Gateway to Mexico
  The Gateway to Old Mexico
  The Hemis Fair City
  The Mission City
  The Mother City of an
    Empire
  The Old Garrison
  The Venice of the Prairie
    (canals winding through
    the streets)
  The Winter Playground of
    America
  Unsainted Anthony
  When You See San Antonio,
    You See Texas

SAN AUGUSTINE
  The Cradle of Texas
  The Oldest American Town
    in Texas

SAN BENITO
  The City on the Grow
  The Resaca City

SAN FELIPE
  The Birthplace of Anglo-

American Settlement in
  Texas (1823)

SAN SABA
  The Pecan Capital of the
    World

SCHULENBURG
  A Thriving Town where
    Prosperity and Content-
    ment Go Hand-in-Hand

SHAMROCK
  The Greenest Spot in the
    Golden Spread of Texas

SHERMAN
  The Athens of Texas

SMITHVILLE
  The Heart of the Megapolis

STONEWALL
  The Home of LBJ (President
    Lyndon Baines Johnson)
  The Peach Capital of Texas

STOWELL
  The Hub of the Industrial
    Gulf Coast

SURFSIDE
  The Gateway to Gulf of
    Mexico

SWEETWATER
  The City Dedicated to Indus-
    trial Development
  The City of Economic Progress
  The City where People Like
    People
  The Complete City
  The Last of the Western
    Frontier
  The West Texas Industrial
    City
  The World's Largest Rattle-
    snake Roundup City

TASCOSA
  The Cowboy Capital of the
    Plains

TEMPLE
The Population Center of
Texas

TERLINGUA
Chili Capital of the World

TEXARKANA
The Gateway to Arkansas
The Twin Cities (with
Texarkana, Ark.; twin
cities on the Arkansas-
Texas border)

TEXAS CITY
The Port of Opportunity
The Trading Post of Yester-
day-A Great Industrial
Center Today

TOMBALL
The Farm Community
The Home of the Cougars

TRINITY
The City with Natural
Beauty the Year 'Round
The Headquarters of Lake
Livingston

TYLER
The Distribution Center for
Four States
The Floral Metropolis of
East Texas
The Heart of East Texas
The Rose Capital
The Rose Capital of
America
The Rose Capital of the
World
The Wonderful Place to
Live

UVALDE
The City Beautiful
The Heart of the Best
Sheep and Goat Country
in Texas
The Honey Capital of the
United States
The Honey Capital of the
World

The Town of Many Oppor-
tunities

VERNON
The City Beautiful

VICTORIA
The City with a Future for
All Industry

WACO
The Athens of Texas (home
of Baylor University)
The City on the Grow
The Heart of the Texas
Funtier
The Hub of Texas
The Palace of King Cotton
The Queen of the Brazos
(on the Brazos River)
The Target of Opportunity

WEATHERFORD
The Versatile City
The Watermelon Capital of
the World

WEST COLUMBIA
The Birthplace of a Republic
(the first congress of the
Republic of Texas assem-
bled on October 3, 1836
at Columbia)
The First Capital of the Republic of Texas

WINNIE
The Home of Texas Rice
Festival
The Home of the Largest
Catfish Farm in Texas
The Rice and Catfish Capital
of Texas

YOAKUM
A City of Homes, Schools
and Churches
The City by Accident
The Hub City of South Texas
(in western Lavaca
County)
The Tomato Capital of South
Central Texas

YORKTOWN
    The Home of the Little
        World's Fair
    The Little World's Fair
        City

UTAH

BRIDGERLAND
    Everybody's Playground

BRIGHAM CITY
    The City of Peaches (peach
        production)
    The Cleanest and Friendliest
        City in the West
    The Gateway to the Bear
        River Migratory Bird
        Refuge
    The Gateway to the World's
        Largest Bird Refuge
    The Nearest City to the
        Golden Spike Site

CORINNE
    The Burg on the Bear (Bear
        River)
    The Gentile City

HANKSVILLE
    The Gateway to Hite and
        Glen Canyon

HURRICANE
    The Gateway to Zion Na-
        tional Park

KANAB
    The Gateway to the Grand
        Canyon (on south)
    The Little Hollywood (a
        favorite movie location)

MOAB
    The Uranium Capital of the
        World (discovery by
        Charles Steen in 1952)

OGDEN
    The City of Diversified
        Industry
    The City where Business
        and Happy Living Flourish
    The Transportation Hub of
        the West
    The West's Fastest-Growing
        Transportation and Indus-
        trial Center

PAROWAN
    The Mother of the South
        (base for colonization of
        other places in southern
        region of Utah)

PRICE
    The Gateway to the Canyon-
        lands and Highlands of
        Southeastern Utah
    The Heart of a Hunter's
        Paradise

PROVO
    The Center of Scenic Utah
    The City of Beauty, Progress
        and Culture
    The Freedom City
    The Gateway to Mountainland
    The Gateway to Utah's Fa-
        mous Mountainland
    The Gateway to Vacation-
        Land
    The Host to the West's
        Scenic Wonder-Ways
    The Pioneer Mormon City
    The Wonderful Place to Play

ST. GEORGE
    The City where the Summer
        Spends the Winter
    The Gateway to Zion National
        Park

SALT LAKE CITY
    Deseret
    The Capital City (population
        about 172,000)
    The Center of Scenic America
    The City by the Great Salt
        Lake
    The City of Opportunities
    The City of the Saints (home
        of the Church of Jesus
        Christ of Latter-day Saints)

The Crossroads of the West
The Great Salt Lake City
The Mormon City
The Mormon Metropolis
The Mormon's Mecca
The New Jerusalem
The Utah Zion
Zion

SALTAIR
The Coney Island of the
West

SPRINGVILLE
The Art City (Springville
Museum of Art)

TORREY
The Gateway to Capitol
Reef National Monument

WENDOVER
The Big Little City on the
Desert

VERMONT

BARRE
The Friendly Place to Live
and Work
The Granite Center of the
World (granite quarries)

BARTON
The Hub of the Northeast
Kingdom
The Place for Home,
Industry, Recreation

BASIN HARBOR
The Popular Summer Resort
on Lake Champlain

BELLOWS FALLS
The Community on the
Move

BENNINGTON
The Historical Town in
Southwestern Vermont
The Southwestern Gateway to
the Historic Four Season
Vacationland
The Williamsburg of the
North
Vermont's Most Historic
Town (British expedition
defeated August 16, 1777
by General John Stark)

BRANDON
The Quiet Historical New
England Village

BRATTLEBORO
The City where Vermont
Begins (on the Connecti-
cut River)
The Organ Town (organ pro-
duction)
The Southeastern Gateway to
Vermont

BURLINGTON
The City of Homes and Parks
The Land of Amazing Variety
and Contrasts
The Queen City
The Queen City of Vermont
The Southern Gateway to
Vermont's Largest City
The Year 'Round Vacation-
land
Vermont's Largest City

CHESTER
The Home of the National
Survey (Map Company)

HARDWICK
The Granite Center

KILLINGTON
The Four Mountains of Fun
The Four Seasons Resort
The World Capital of Learning
to Ski

LUDLOW
Ludlow Is a Snow Town,
Ludlow Is a Fun Town,
Ludlow Has Everything

The Growing Village Sur-
rounded by Mountains and
Small Lakes

LYNDONVILLE
Nature's Palladium
The Four Season Playground
in the Heart of the Green
Mountains
The Gateway to the North-
east Kingdom

MANCHESTER
The Famous Four Season
Recreation Area in the
Heart of Vermont's
Green Mountains
The Four Season Resort
and Cultural Center
This Pleasant Land Among
the Mountains

MIDDLEBURY
The Beautiful Colonial Vil-
lage in Western Vermont
The Home of World Famous
Middlebury College

MONTPELIER
The Capital City (population
about 8,400)
The Capital City of the
Green Mountain State
The Green Mountain City
The Insurance and Granite
Center

NEWPORT
The City in the Northeast
Kingdom
The Four Season Com-
munity
The Holiday Harbor of
Vermont

PLYMOUTH
The Birthplace of Calvin
Coolidge (July 4, 1872)

PROCTOR
The Marble Capital of the
United States (home of
Vermont Marble Company)

RUTLAND
The Center of the Marble
Industry
The Community on the Move
The Heart of the Green
Mountains
The Marble City (large
marble quarries)
The Year Around Playground
Vermont's Second Largest
City

ST. ALBANS
The Railroad City (yards and
shops of the Central Ver-
mont Railway)

ST. JOHNSBURY
The Maple Center of the
World
The Maple Sugar Center of
the World
The Scale Manufacturing
Center of the World
The Ski Crossroads of the
World

SOUTH BURLINGTON
The Southern Gateway to
Vermont's Largest City

SPRINGFIELD
Precision Valley
Progress Through Precision
The Black River Area of
Vermont
The Black River Valley Area
of Vermont
The Black River Valley of
Vermont
The Cradle of Industry
The Cradle of Invention
The Four Season Area
The Gateway to Picturesque
Precision Valley
The Home of Precision
The Home of Yankee In-
genuity
The Industrial Center of
Vermont
The Modern and Progressive
Town
The Springboard into the Four
Season Area

STOWE
    Snow or No, Go to Stowe,
        Any Season, Many
        Reasons
    Stowe Is the Place to Be
    The All Year Round Vacation-
        land
    The Cool and Sunny Paradise
    The Gateway to Smuggler's
        Notch (between Mt. Mans-
        field and the Sterling
        Mountains)
    The Ski Capital of the East
        (a single and two double
        chair lifts, three T-bar
        lifts, etc.)
    The Skier's Heaven
    The Snow Paradise
    The Year-round Resort
        Capital of New England--
        Where the Fun Stays After
        the Snow Is Gone
    There Is Only One Stowe

WAITSFIELD
    The Peaceful Valley in the
        Heart of the Green
        Mountains

WATERBURY
    The City Located in the
        Heart and Center of
        Vermont
    The Gateway to the Mount
        Mansfield Area
    The Recreation Crossroads
        of Vermont
    Vermont's Recreation
        Crossroads

WELLS RIVER
    The Crossroads of Northern
        New England

WHITE RIVER JUNCTION
    The Gateway to the Green
        Mountain State

WINDSOR
    The Arsenal of the Union
        (in Civil War)
    The Birthplace of the Re-
        public of Vermont

WINOOSKI
    The Mill City (former tex-
        tile and woodworking fac-
        tories)

WOODSTOCK
    One of the Most Beautiful and
        Popular Vermont Towns

VIRGINIA

ALBERTA
    The Land of the Pines

ALEXANDRIA
    The Heart of the Nation's
        Heritage
    The Historic Home Town of
        General George Washington
    The Home Town of George
        Washington

ALTAVISTA
    The First Four-Way Test
        Town in the World
    The Friendly Community in
        Piedmont County
    The Young Town with a Pro-
        gressive Attitude

APPALACHIA
    The Center of the Coal Fields

ARLINGTON
    The Bedroom of Washington
        (residential area of many
        persons working in the
        nation's capital)
    The City of the Slain (Arling-
        ton National Cemetery)
    The Resting Place of the Un-
        known American Hero (in
        Arlington National Ceme-
        tery)

ASHLAND
    The Slash Town (1848 health
        resort Slash Cottage)

BEDFORD
   The Mineral Springs City
   (limestone, sulphur,
   iron and sweet water
   springs) (see also Pa.)

BERRYVILLE
   Battletown (name applied to
   local tavern where fights
   were frequent)

BLACKSBURG
   A Good Place to Live and
   Work
   The City in Pace with the
   Space Age
   The City where Industry
   and Education Meet (home
   of Virginia Polytechnic
   Institute)
   The Community that Builds
   Health Minds and Bodies
   The Space Age Community

BLACKSTONE
   The Heart of the Old Do-
   minion
   The Lunchstone

BLUEFIELD
   Nature's Air-Conditioned
   City (adjoining Bluefield,
   W. Va.)
   Twin Cities (with Bluefield,
   W. Va.)

BOYKINS
   Tarrara City

BRISTOL
   The City in the Heart of
   Eastern America (see
   also Tennessee)
   The Shopping Center of the
   Appalachians (see also
   Tennessee)
   Twin Cities (with Bristol,
   Tenn.)

BUCKROE BEACH
   Virginia's Seaside Playground

CHARLOTTESVILLE
   Jefferson's Country (in Albe-
   marle County)
   The Fairest Georgian City
   of the New World
   The Heart of Historic Virginia
   The Home of the Albemarle
   Pippin (extensive peach and
   apple orchards)

CHASE CITY
   Christiansville

CHESAPEAKE
   The City Destined to be One
   of the Great Cities of the
   Southeast
   The City of History and
   Culture
   The City of Opportunity
   The City with Room to Grow
   and Grow

CHINCOTEAGUE
   The Sportsman's Paradise
   (on the eastern shore of
   Chincoteague Bay)

CHRISTIANSBURG
   The Gateway to the Southwest
   (on the Blue Ridge Plateau)

CLARKSVILLE
   Nature's Unspoiled Wonder-
   land
   The Friendliest Town on
   Earth
   The Old Mart (tobacco
   market)
   Virginia's Vacation Paradise
   on Beautiful Buggs Island
   Lake

CLIFTON FORGE
   The City that's Scenic, Busy
   and Friendly

CLINCHPORT
   The Frog Level

COLONIAL BEACH
   Las Vegas on the Potomac

(river resort on Potomac
River)

COLONIAL HEIGHTS
The City Located in the
Heart of Virginia's
Industry
The City on the Highway of
Progress
The Most Promising Indus-
trial Community of the
Future

CULPEPER
A Beautiful Community in
Beautiful Virginia
A High and Pleasant Situation
The Hub of Northern Virginia

DAMASCUS
The Gateway to Three Local
Slogan States: Virginia,
Tennessee, North Caro-
lina

DANVILLE
Danville Invites You to Make
Our City Your City
The Bright Leaf Tobacco
Market of the World
The Capital City of South
Side Virginia
The Capital City of Southern
Virginia
The Church City
The City of Churches (over
100 sanctuaries of various
denominations)
The City on the Dan (Dan
River)
The Fine Place to Live and
Work
The Home of the Dan River
Mills (largest single-unit
textile mill in the world)
The Home of the World's
Largest Single-Unit Tex-
tile Mill
The Last Capital of the
Confederacy (April 3-10,
1865 occupied by Jefferson
Davis and his cabinet after
the evacuation of Richmond)

The Tobacco City
The World's Best Tobacco
Market
Virginia's Largest Market for
Bright Leaf Tobacco

DRAKES BRANCH
Ducks' Puddle

DUNGANNON
Bumgannon

EDINBURG
The Granary of the Con-
federacy

FALLS CHURCH
A Good Place to Work ...
In and From

FREDERICKSBURG
America's Most Historic
City (numerous battles
between 1861-1865)
George Washington's Boyhood
Home
The Boyhood Home of George
Washington
The Cockpit of the Civil
War
The Friendly City
The Gateway to Historyland
The Land of Washington
The Most Historic City in
America

FRONT ROYAL
Northern Entrance to the
Skyline Drive, Shenandoah
National Park
The City where the Shenan-
doah National Park
Begins
The City where the Skyline
Drive Begins

GLOUCESTER
America's Daffodil Capital
The Land of Life Worth
Living

GRETNA
The Junction

HAMILTON
Harmony

HAMPTON
America's Oldest English
Colony
Crab Town (oyster and
fishing industry)
The Oldest Continuous
English Speaking Settle-
ment in America (settled
in 1610)

HAMPTON ROADS
The World's Greatest Harbor
(the James, Nansemond
and Elizabeth Rivers flow
into Chesapeake Bay)

HARRISONBURG
The City with the Planned
Future
The Turkey Capital of the
East
The Turkey Capital of the
Nation
The World's Turkey Capital
Virginia's Biggest Little
City (population about
16,300)

HILLSVILLE
The Hill Town

HOLLAND
Holland's Corner

HOPEWELL
The Chemical Capital of
Virginia
The Wonder City (on the
James River)
Virginia's Inland Port

INDEPENDENCE
Pinhook

JAMESTOWN
The Birthplace of the
Nation (English colony,
permanent settlement
in 1607)
The First English Colony

LEXINGTON
The Athens of Virginia (home
of Washington and Lee University)
The Shrine of the South (home
of Virginia Military Institute, burial place of Stonewall Jackson, etc.)

LYNCHBURG
Lunchburg (humorous)
The Center of Historic
Virginia
The Center of Old Virginia
The City of Charming Houses
The City of Friendliness,
Culture and Traditions
The City of Hills (overlooking
the James River)
The City of Industry and Op-
portunity
The City where Good Living
Is the Custom
The Community of Culture
and Traditions
The Friendly City
The Hill City
The Industrial, Geographical
Historic and Transporta-
tion Center of Virginia
The Modern City
The Progressive Metropolis

MANASSAS
The Town Rich in History

MARTINSVILLE
The Furniture City (numerous
furniture factories)
The Sweatshirt Capital of the
World

MATHEWS
The Midway Garden Spot of
the Atlantic Coast

MOUNT VERNON
The Home of Our First
President

NANSEMOND
The World's Largest Peanut
Market

Virginia's Fastest Growing
Industrial Community

NEW MARKET
The Travel Center of the
World Renowned Shenan-
doah Valley
The Western Gateway to
the Skyline Drive

NEWPORT NEWS
The City of Ships and Ship-
building
The World's Greatest
Harbor (James River)

NORFOLK
The Capital of the Most
Historic Resort Area in
America
The Center of the Mid-
Atlantic
The City By the Sea
The City for All Seasons
The City that Does Things
The Industrial Vacation
and Seafood Shopping
Center
The Marine Metropolis of
Virginia
Vacationland, U.S.A.

PENNINGTON GAP
The Gap (in Cumberland
Mountains)

PETERSBURG
America's Most Historic
City
The City Industrially Sound
and Historically Great
The City of Industrial Op-
portunity
The City where Nineteenth
Century America Lives
The City with a Past
The Cockade City (Captain
Richard Mc Roe and
his company of volun-
teers wore a cockade)
The Cockade of the Union
(nickname given by
President James Madison--

50,000 Confederate troops
defended the city for ten
months against 113,000
Federal besiegers)
The Crossroads of History

PORTSMOUTH
The Best Natural Harbor in
the World
The Hub of Historic Shrines
The Hub of the Scenic His-
toric Tidewater Region at
the Base of Chesapeake
Bay
The Industrial Center
The Modern City
The Navy's First City of the
Sea (Norfolk Naval Ship-
yard)

PULASKI
The Gem City

RICHMOND
America's Fastest Growing
Industrial City
An Interesting Past, a
Prosperous Present, an
Unlimited Future
Byrd Town (foundation laid
in 1733 by William Byrd II)
One of the World's Largest
Manufacturers of Ciga-
rettes
The Capital City (population
about 233,000)
The Capital of the Confederacy
The Capital of the Old South
The City of Great Men and
Great Times
The City of Monuments
The City of Romance and
Rebellion
The City of Seven Hills
The City on the James
The City that's Looking
Ahead
The City with Some of
America's Greatest Memo-
ries
The Cockade City
The Confederate Capital
The Gateway to the South

The Good Times Capital
The Modern Rome
The Monument City
The Nine Hills
The Queen City of the South
The Queen on the James
(James River)
The Tobacco Capital of the
World

ROANOKE
The Coal Capital of the
Southwest
The Magic City
The Magic City of the South
The Magic City of Virginia
The Master City
The Shopping Center of
Western Virginia
The Star City of the South
(mammoth man-made
star shining atop Mill
Mountain)
Virginia's Mountain Capital

RODA
The Happy Hollow

ROSLYN
The Gateway to Virginia

SINGERS GLEN
The Glen

SMITHFIELD
The Ham Town
The Hickory Smoking Capital
of the World
The Home of the Smithfield
Ham

SOUTH HILL
The Third Largest Tobacco
Market in Virginia

STAUNTON
The Birthplace of Woodrow
Wilson
The Queen City of the
Shenandoah Valley

SUFFOLK
The Fastest Growing Area

in Virginia
The Home of Planters Pea-
nuts
The Peanut City (processing
plant of Planters Peanuts)
The World's Largest Peanut
Center
Virginia's Fast Growing In-
dustrial Community

TAZEWELL
The City on the Trail of the
Lonesome Pine

TOMS BROOK
The Brook

VICTORIA
The City in the Heart of
Southside Virginia
The Town of Hospitality and
Progress

VINTON
Virginia's Dogwood Capital

VIRGINIA BEACH
A Whole New World with
Every Sunrise
America's Historyland Play-
ground
The City where Fun and
History Meet the Sea
The City where the Pines
Meet the Sea
The Fun and Sun Playground
The Fun Shines Brightest in
the Summer Time
The Garden Spot for Golf
The Land of Play and Plenty
The Resort Center
The Vacationist's Paradise
Virginia's Atlantic City

WACHAPREAGUE
The Oldest Sport Fishing
Center in Virginia

WAYNESBORO
A Wonderful Place to Visit
and a Better Place to
Live
The City where the Blue

Ridge Parkway Joins the
Skyline Drive
The Hub of Scenic and His-
toric Western Virginia

WILLIAMSBURG
The Capital of Colonial
Virginia
The City that Turned Back
Time
The Colonial Capital of
Virginia
The Community where the
Future May Learn from
the Past
The Historic City
The Restored Colonial City
(a project supported by
John D. Rockefeller, Jr.)
Virginia Colony's Elegant
Old Capital

WINCHESTER
The Apple Capital
The Apple Capital in the
Beautiful Shenandoah
Valley
The Apple Capital of the
World
The City in the Beautiful
Shenandoah Valley
The City in the Heart of
the Shenandoah Valley of
Virginia
The City Rich in History
with a Wealth of Charm
The City where the South
Begins at the Gateway
to the Beautiful Shenan-
doah Valley
The Gateway to Old Virginia
The Home of the Apple
Blossom Festival
The Home of the World-
Famous Annual Shenan-
doah Apple Blossom
Festival
The Northern Gateway to
the Beautiful Shenandoah
Valley
The Northern Gateway
to the Shenandoah
Valley

WYTHEVILLE
The Hub of Southwest Vir-
ginia

YORKTOWN
The City where Independence
Was Born
The Waterloo of the Revolu-
tion (October 19, 1781
General Cornwallis sur-
rendered)

WASHINGTON

ABERDEEN
The Lumbering and Fishing
Center
The Plank Island
The Twin Cities (with Ho-
quiam, Grays Harbor)

ANACORTES
The Magic City (on Fidalgo
Island)
The Principal Shopping Center
The Ship Harbor
The Squaw Harbor

AUBURN
The Slaughter House (named
for Lt. W. A. Slaughter,
renamed Auburn in 1893)

BANGOR
The Three Spits

BELLINGHAM
The Tulip City (tulip cultiva-
tion)

BREMERTON
The Home of the Pacific Fleet
(Puget Sound Navy Yard)
The Home of the Puget Sound
Naval Shipyard
The String Town

BUCKLEY
The City of Good Water (on
the White River)

BURLEY
The Circle City

CAMAS
The City of Paper (Crown-
Zellerbach mills)

CARBONADO
The Model Mining Com-
munity (ceased operations
about 1920)

CARNATION
The Home of Contented
Cows (Carnation Milk
Products Company Farms)
The Milk City

CASHMERE
The Home of Aplets, the
Confection of the Fairies
(apple juice flavored en-
riched by walnuts and
spices)

CENTRALIA
The Heart of Washington's
Timber Belt
The Hub City (junction of
the Chehalis and Skookum-
chuck Rivers)
The Hub City of South-
western Washington

CHEHALIS
The Friendly City

CHELAN
The Deep Water (Lake
Chelan, bottom 400 feet
below sea level)

CHENEY
The Depot Springs

CLARKSTON
Jawbone Flats (original
name, changed in 1900
to Clarkston)

COLBY
The Coal Bay

COLFAX
The Wheat Capital of America

CONCONULLY
The Money Hole (a mountain
recess settled in 1886 by
prospectors)

COULEE CITY
The Engineers' Town (junction point of the railroad
and stage lines)

COUPEVILLE
One of the Oldest Cities in
Washington
The Port of Sea Captains
(first of whom was Captain
Thomas Coupe who settled
in 1852)

COYLE
The Fisherman's Harbor

DAVENPORT
The City where Wheat Is
King (second largest wheat
producing county in the
U.S.)
The Important Cattle Center

DAYTON
The City of Shady Walks and
Pleasant Lawns

EDMONDS
The Princess City of Puget
Sound (between Seattle
and Everett)

ELLENSBURG
The Robbers' Roost (original
name in 1867)
The Rodeo City (rodeo held
on Labor Day weekend)

ENUMCLAW
The Home of the Evil Spirits

EVERETT
The Airplane Manufacturing
Center

The City of Smokestacks
The Gateway to the Olympic
National Park
The Industrial City of
Smokestacks
The Lumbering Center
The Western Terminus of
U.S. Highway No. 2

FALL CITY
The Falls (on the Snoqualmie River)
The Landing (original name)

FERNDALE
The Gem of the Nooksack
Valley (on the Nooksack
River)

FRUITLAND
The Robbers' Roost (early
rendezvous for cattle
thieves and desperadoes)

GRANITE FALLS
The Portage (the Stillaquamish River and the Pilchuck River)

HILLYARD
The Horse Plains

HOQUIAM
The Board Foot (saw mills)
The Cape Cod of the West
The Twin Cities (with Aberdeen, the Grays Harbor
Cities)

INDEX
The Tourist's Paradise
(near Snoqualmie National
Forest)

KAHLOTUS
The Hole-in-the-Ground
(Indian word, town on
Washtucna Lake)

KALAMA
The City where Rail Meets
Water (Northern Pacific
Railroad at confluence of

Columbia and Kalama
Rivers)
The Town where Rail Meets
Water (the Northern Pacific
and the Columbia River)

KENNEWICK
The Grassy Place (irrigated
farmlands)
The Tri-Cities (with Richland
and Pasco)

KITTITAS
The Land of Bread

LA CONNER
The Venice of Puget Sound
(sloughs and marshes)

LATAH
The Hangman Creek

LEAVENWORTH
The Bavarian Village
The World's Largest Salmon
Hatchery Site

LONGVIEW
The City Practical that Vision
Built (first planned city in
the northwest, dedicated
1923)
The First Planned City in the
Pacific Northwest

MCCLEARY
The Typical Pacific Northwest
Logging Community

MANETTE
The String Town

MARYSVILLE
The Home of the Strawberry
Festival

MASON CITY
The All-Electric Community
(pre-fabricated)

MAZAMA
Goat Creek

MESA
  The Table-Land

MONROE
  Park Place
  The Gateway to Stevens
    Pass
  The Model Municipality

MONTESANTO
  Mount Zion
  The Birthplace of Tree
    Farms

MUKILTEO
  Good Camping Ground

OCOSTA
  Ocosta by the Sea (on
    Grays Harbor)

OLYMPIA
  An Important Commercial
    City
  The Bear's Place (domicile
    of the brown bear)
  The Capital City (population
    about 25,800)
  The Capital of the Ever-
    green State

ORCAS
  The Gem of the San Juans

ORONDO
  The Town which Held the
    Key

PAHA
  The Big Water

PALISADES
  The Beulah Land

PALOUSE
  The Grass Lands

PASCO
  The Tri-Cities (with Rich-
    land and Kennewick)

PATAHA
  Favorsburg (town site

plotted in 1882 by "Vine"
  Favor)
Waterstown (former name)

POMONA
  The Roman Goddess of Fruit
    Trees (whose name was
    Pomona)

PORT ANGELES
  Our Lady of the Angels
  The City where the Mountains
    Meet the Sea (between the
    Olympic range and Strait
    of Juan de Fuca)
  The Popular Tourist Center

PORT GAMBLE
  Boston
  The Brightness of the Noonday
    Sun

PORT MADISON
  The Oleman House

PORT TOWNSEND
  The Key City (a key city on
    Port Townsend Bay in the
    sailing boat era)
  The Key City of Puget Sound
    (on the Olympic Peninsular)
  The Port of Entry (on the
    Olympic Peninsula where
    the Straight of Juan de Fuca
    joins Puget Sound)

PULLMAN
  The Home of State College of
    Washington
  The Three Forks

PUYALLUP
  The Generous People

QUILCENE
  The Salt Water People

RENTON
  The Jet Transport Capital of
    the World (Boeing plant)

RICHLAND
  The Town the Atom Built

(Hanford Engineer Works)
The Tri-Cities (with Kennewick and Pasco)

RUBY
The Babylon of Washington
Territory (a lawless wide
open town when formed)

SEATTLE
The American Gateway to
Alaska and the Orient
The Boating Capital of the
World
The Cannery City
The City of Eternal Views
(vistas of lakes, moun-
tains and sound waters)
The City of Homes
The City of Seven Hills
The Commercial Center in
the Pacific Northwest
The Cosmopolitan Seaport
The Evergreen Playground
The Gateway to Alaska
The Gateway to the Orient
The Great Sports Resort
Community
The International Melting
Pot
The Little Portage (between
Puget Sound and Lake
Washington)
The Major World Seaport
The Metropolis of the
Pacific Northwest
The Most Scenic City on
the Continent
The Nation's Most Beautiful
City
The Northwest Gateway
The Queen City
The Queen City of the
Northwest
The Queen City of the
Sound
The Visually Exciting City
The World Port
The World's Greatest Hali-
but Port

SEQUIM
The Smooth Water
The Still Water

SHELTON
Christmas Town, U.S.A.
(famous for its Christmas
tree crop)
The Strong Water

SKAMOKAWA
Little Venice (on Skamokawa
Creek)
The Smoke on the Water

SNOHOMISH
The Hub (at the confluence
of the Pilchuck and Sno-
homish Rivers)

SPOKANE
America's Most Exciting City
The Absolute Center of Out-
doorland, U.S.A.
The Center of the Vast In-
land Empire
The Friendly City
The Gateway to the Inland
Empire
The Heart of the Inland
Empire
The Heart of the Lumber
Country
The Home of the Mining
Barons
The Inland Empire of the
Pacific Northwest
The Medical Center (14
hospitals)
The Metropolis of the Inland
Empire
The Minneapolis of the West
The Most Handsome, Re-
surgent and Progressive
Showcase City
The 1974 World's Fair City
The Outdoor Recreation City
The Trading Center of the
Inland Empire

SPRINGDALE
The Squire City

STEILACOOM
The Oldest Historical City
on Puget Sound

SULTAN
    The Western Gateway to
    Stevens Pass

SUNNYSIDE
    The Holy City (Christian
    Cooperative Movement
    settlement in 1898)

TACOMA
    The Center of Industry
    The City of Destiny
    The City of Fine Hotels
    The City with a Snow-
    Capped Mountain in Its
    Dooryard
    The Commencement City
    The Evergreen Playground
    The Forest Products
    Capital of America
    The Gateway to Mount
    Ranier
    The Lumber Capital
    The Lumber Capital of
    America
    The Lumber Capital of
    the World
    The Nearest Metropolitan
    Center to All Five Gate-
    ways of Ranier National
    Park
    The Second Major City on
    Puget Sound
    The Third Largest City in
    Washington

TOUCHET
    The White Stallion (original
    name designated by
    Lewis and Clark)

TUKWILA
    The Land of Hazel Nuts

TUMWATER
    The Falls (on the Deschutes
    River)
    The New Market
    The Waterfalls

UNION
    Another Clyde City
    The Venice of the Pacific

UTSALADDY
    The Land of Berries

VANCOUVER
    Columbia City (on the Colum-
    bia River)
    The Oldest City in the State
    The Oldest Community in
    Washington

VASHON
    The Metropolis of Vashon
    Island (midway between
    Seattle and Tacoma)

WALLA WALLA
    The Center of Activity for
    All of Southeastern
    Washington and North-
    eastern Oregon
    The City of Beautiful Trees
    and Ideal Climate
    The City of Friendly People
    The Cradle of Pacific North-
    west History
    The Place of Many Waters

WATERVILLE
    The Jumper's Flats (claim
    jumping)
    The Sour Dough Flats

WENATCHEE
    The Apple Capital
    The Apple Capital of the
    World
    The Gateway to the Valley of
    Perfect Apples
    The Home of Apple Blossom
    Festival

WESTPORT
    The Nationally Known Deep
    Sea Salmon Fishing Center

WILBUR
    The Goosetown (in 1888
    Samuel Wilbur Condit
    shot a tame gander be-
    lieving it was a wild goose)

WILLAPA
    The Venice of the North-

west (on the Willapa
River)

WINTHROP
The Partially Restored
Pioneer Mining Village

WISHRAM
The Food Emporium

YAKIMA
The Eastern Gateway to
Mt. Ranier National
Park
The Fruit Bowl of the Nation
The Seat Capital of the
World

WEST VIRGINIA

BECKLEY
The Smokeless Coal Capital
of the World (center of
coal mining and natural
gas region)

BLUEFIELD
Nature's Air-Conditioned
City
The Air Conditioned City
(adjoining Bluefield, Va.)
The City where the Moun-
tains Meet the Sky
The Gateway to the Great
Coal Fields of Southern
West Virginia
The Metropolis of the
Southern West Virginia
Coal Fields
Twin Cities (with Bluefield,
Va.)

CHARLESTON
The Capital City (population
about 67,400)
The Chemical City (produces
calcium chlorine, iodine,
etc.)

ELKINS
The Vacation Capital of the
Appalachian Highlands (on
the Tygarts Valley River)

HUNTINGTON
The Gateway City (south-
western section of W. Va.)

MARTINSBURG
The Chief Industrial City of
the Eastern Panhandle

MIDDLEWAY
The Wizard's Clip

MORGANTOWN
The Home of West Virginia
University (founded 1867)

MOUNDSVILLE
The City of Industrial Poten-
tialities
The Handmade Glass City

PARKERSBURG
The City of Wonderful Living
with Industrial Prosperity

SHEPHERDSTOWN
The Oldest Town in West
Virginia (established 1732)

SOUTH CHARLESTON
The Chemical Center of the
World

TUNNELTON
The Coal Center

WELCH
Little New York (closely built
congested area)

WHEELING
The Chief City of West
Virginia (population about
45,000)
The City of Beautiful Parks
(Oglebay Park, largest in
W. Va.)
The City of Historic Lore (first

visitor, Captain de Bien-
ville, 1749)
The City of Magnificent
Stores
The City of Nails
The City of Thriving Indus-
tries
The Nail City
The Trading Center

WISCONSIN

ANTIGO
The City where Potatoes
Are King (potato-growing
region)

APPLETON
The Crescent City

BARABOO
The Capital of the American
Circus

BELOIT
A Metropolitan Community
of Opportunity
One of Wisconsin's Fastest
Growing Cities

CLINTONVILLE
The Home of Four Wheel
Drive Trucks

COLBY
The Midget City

CRIVITZ
The Gateway to the Lakes
and Streams of the
Thunder Mountain Region
(on the Peshtigo River)

DELAVAN
The Circus Capital of
America in the Nineteenth
Century
The Cradle of the American
Circus

DE PERE
America's Number One Small
City (on the Fox River)
The City of Historic Charm
The Home of the Norbertines
(St. Norbert College)

EAU CLAIRE
The City Blessed in Many
Ways
The City of the Green Light
The Friendly Door to Wis-
consin's Indianhead Country
The Key City of Central
Northwest Wisconsin
The Sawdust City

EDGERTON
The Tobacco City

FOND DU LAC
The Fountain City

GREEN BAY
The Cheese Storage Capital
of the World
The Home of the Packers
(stadium and playing field
of the professional foot-
ball team known as the
Green Bay Packers)
The Packers Town
The Port of Distinction
Titletown, U.S.A. (because
of Packers, championship
football team)

HAYWARD
The Musky Capital (excellent
musky fishing)

IRON RIVER
The Blueberry Capital of the
Nation
The Gateway to the Ottawa
National Forest (over 900
miles of trout streams and
552 lakes)

KAUKAUNA
The Electric City (municipally
owned and operated hydro-
electric power and water

facilities)
The Friendly City
The Lion of the Fox River
Valley

KENOSHA
The Gateway to the World

LA CROSSE
The Gateway City (on the
Mississippi River at the
confluence of the Black
and La Crosse Rivers)
The Gateway to the Coulee
Country
The Gateway to the Mid-
west

LAKE GENEVA
The Newport of Chicago
Society (a summer resi-
dential colony which re-
ceived its impetus in
1871 as a result of the
Chicago fire)

MADISON
The Capital City (population
about 173,000)
The City Built on an Isth-
mus (between Lakes Monona
and Mendota)
The City of Beautiful Homes
and Thriving Industry
The City of Parks
The City on the Square
The Cultural Center
The Four Lake City
The Four Lakes City
(Lakes Mendota, Monona,
Waubesa and Kegonsa)
The Home of the University
of Wisconsin
The Ideal Convention and
Vacation City
The Key Shopping and Manu-
facturing Center
The Lake City
The Most Beautiful Little
City in America
The Recreational Center

MANITOWOC
The Clipper City (a ship-
building center where
clipper ships were built
from 1860 to 1880)

MARINETTE
The Queen City (named for
Queen Marinette of the
Menominee Indian tribe)
The White Pine Producing
Center of the World (1830
to 1890)

MARSHFIELD
The Crossroads of Wisconsin
The Modern City

MENASHA
The Twin Cities (with Neenah,
Wis.)

MERRILL
The City of Parks
The Natural Trading Center

MILWAUKEE
America's Machine Shop
Great for Business, Great
for Living and Growing
Greater
Milwaukee the Beautiful
The American Munich
The Beer Capital of America
(numerous breweries)
The Beer City
The Blonde Beauty of the
Lakes
The Brewing Capital of the
World (Blatz Brewery,
Pabst Brewery, etc.)
The Bright Spot
The City Beautiful
The City of Fountains
The City of Homes
The City of New World Vigor
The City of Old World Charm
The City where Beer Is
Famous
The Cream City (from the
color of bricks manu-
factured there)

The Cream White City of
the Unsalted Seas
The Deutsch-Athens (German
immigrants)
The Fair White City
The Foam City
The Friendly City
The German Athens
(German immigrants)
The Home of the Braves
The Industrial City
The July Capital of the
World
The Machine Shop of
America
The Major Port of Call
on America's New
Fourth Seacoast
The Middlewest Center
for Diversified Manu-
facture
The Railway Metropolis
of the West
There's More in Milwaukee
Wisconsin's Beautiful
Capitol City

MINERAL POINT
The Shake-Rag City
(Shake Rag Street where
women waved rags and
dishcloths to summon
miners on an opposite
hill to return for
dinner)

MONROE
America's Swiss Cheese
Capital (about 300 fac-
tories)
The Swiss Cheese Capital
of the United States
(numerous factories)

NEENAH
The Paper City (numerous
paper mills)
The Paper City of the
World (numerous paper
producing mills)
The Twin Cities (with
Menasha, Wis.)

NEW GLARUS
Little Switzerland (numerous
Swiss colonist descendants)

NEW RICHMOND
The City Beautiful

OCONOMOWOC
The Place where the Waters
Meet (mineral springs)

ORFORDVILLE
The Grass Roots of America

OSHKOSH
The City of Industry, Recrea-
tion, Business
The City of Opportunity
The Heart of the Fox Valley
Area
The Sawdust City

PARK FALLS
The City in the Center of the
Beautiful North Woods
The City in the Heart of the
Chequamegon National
Forest
The Fun Town (popular recrea-
tion area)
The Vacation Wonderland
The Vacationland of Northern
Wisconsin
The Wonderland City in the
North Woods

PLYMOUTH
The Cheese Capital of the
World

PORTAGE
The City where the North
Begins

PORT WING
The Hub of Lake Superior's
Beautiful South Shore Drive

PRAIRIE DU CHIEN
America's Wild Life Pre-
server
The Gateway to the

Winneshiek (Winneshiek
Bluff)
The Historical City (seen
in 1673 by Joliet and
Marquette)

PRENTICE
The Friendly Village (population about 500)

RACINE
Kringleville (after the Dane's
favorite pastry)
The Belle City
The Belle City of the Lakes
(on Lake Michigan)
The City of Advantages
The Czech Bethlehem
(Bohemian settlement)
The Danish Capital of the
United States (one-third
of its population of
Danish descent)
Wisconsin's Second City
(population about
90,700)

RHINELANDER
The Capital of the Heart
O' the Lakes (trading
center for hunters,
campers, fishermen)
The Gateway to the World's
Most Concentrated Lake
Region (22 lakes, 11
trout streams, 2 rivers)
The Home of the Hodag
(beast of frightening ap-
pearance)
The Hub of the Northwest
Resorts Area
The Snowmobile Capital of
the World

RIPON
The Birthplace of the Re-
publican Party (organized
Feb. 28, 1854)
The City of the Twin Spires
(the spires on College
Hill of the Grace Lu-
theran and Congregational
Churches)

The Republican Party City

ROSENDALE
The Peony Center of the Midwest

SHEBOYGAN
The Bratwurst Capital of the
World (German settlement)
The Chair City (industry de-
clined about 1918)
The Cheese City
The City of Cheese, Chairs,
Children and Churches
(seldom used after 1940)
The City of Elms
The City of Four C's
The City of Home Owners
The Evergreen City
Wurst City of the World
(smoked sausage and brat-
wurst production)

STEVENS POINT
The City of Wonderful Water
(on Plover and Wisconsin
Rivers)

STURGEON BAY
The Canal City (canal con-
necting Green Bay with
Lake Michigan)
The Cherry Tree City
(1,000,000 cherry trees)

SUPERIOR
America's Most Westerly In-
land Port (at head of Lake
Superior)
America's Second Port (on
Lake Superior)
The City of One Hundred
Lakes and Streams
The City of Smiles
The City of the Northland
The City where Spring Spends
the Summer
The Consumer Cooperative
Center of the United States
The Eye of the Northwest
The Four Season City
The Hub of North America
The Playground of Presidents

The Summer Capital of
America (on Lake Superior)
The Transportation Center
of North America (grain
center and shipping termi-
nus for copper and iron)
The Twin Ports (with
Duluth, Minn.)

THREE LAKES
The Midwest's Winter
Sports Mecca

TOMAH
The Gateway to the Wisconsin Cranberry Country

TWO RIVERS
The Coolest Spot in Wis-
consin

VIROQUA
The Tobacco Center

WAUKESHA
The City with a Future
The Hub of the Fastest
Growing County in the
State
The Spring City (medicinal
springs)

WAUPUN
The City of Sculpture

WAUSAU
The Forest City

WEST ALLIS
The City of Homes and
Diversified Industries
The Saratoga of the West
(medicinal springs)

WISCONSIN DELLS
America's Scenic Wonder-
land (on the Wisconsin
River, lined by rock
formations)

WISCONSIN RAPIDS
The Geographic Heart of the
State (on the Wisconsin
River)

WYOMING

AFTON
The Switzerland of America
(6,134 feet altitude)

BASIN
Bean Town (marketing center
for the bean crop)
The Garden City (a tree and
shrub planting campaign
was instituted in 1910)

CASPER
The Convention City
The Geographic Center of the
Oil Industry in the Rocky
Mountains
The Growing City
The Hub
The Hub City (seat of Natrona
County)
The Magic City of the Plains
The Oil Capital of the Rockies
(oil fields, 3 major oil
refineries, 400 oil affiliated
concerns)
The Oil City
The Progress City of the
Rockies
Wyoming's Most Progressive
City (population about
39,200)

CHEYENNE
Hell on Wheels (formerly used)
The Capital City (population
about 43,500)
The Home of Frontier Days
The Magic City of the Plains
The Magic City of the West

DOUGLAS
The Tent Town (name con-
ferred in 1886 when the
town was founded)

DUBOIS
The Rock Capital of the
Nation

EVANSTON
The Most Typical Western
City in Wyoming

GILLETTE
The Coal Boom Town
The Modern Boom Town
The Oil Boom Town
The Sharpest Town in the
West

GLENDO
Wyoming's Big Little Town

GLENROCK
The Oil City (oil refinery)

JACKSON
The Dude Ranch and Resort
Center
The Last of the Old West
and the Best of the New
The New Height in Ameri-
can Skiing (in Teton
National Forest, 4,135
feet vertical rise)

KEMMERER
The Gateway to Western
Wyoming's Wonderland

LANDER
The Apple City
The Big Mountain Country
The City in the Heart of
the Big Mountain Country
The City where the Rails
and the Trails Begin
(western terminus of the
Chicago and Northwestern
Railway)
The Gateway to the Largest
Wilderness Area in the
U.S.
The Paradise of Outdoor
Recreation
The Push Root City

LARAMIE
The Athens of Wyoming
(home of the University
of Wyoming)
The Center for Medicine

Bow National Forest
Recreation Area
The Gateway to the Snowy
Range
The Gem City

LOVELL
The City of Roses
The Rose Town

LUSK
The Land of Prairie and
Beautiful Hills

PINEDALE
The Gateway to the Bridger
Wilderness

POWELL
The City where Oil and
Water Mix
The Friendly Little City in
the Prosperous Shoshone
Valley
The Home of Northwest Com-
munity College
The Oasis in Mountain Country

ROCK SPRINGS
The City of Industry in the
Land of Sage and Sun
The Gateway to Yellowstone
and Teton National Parks

SARATOGA
America's Newest Family
Playground
The Small Town with a Big
Welcome
The Town where the Trout
Leap in Main Street

SHERIDAN
The Center of the Dude Ranch
Industry
The City in "The Big Horns"
The City in the Heart of
"The Big Horns"
The City in the Shadow of
the Big Horn
The City where the West
Remains
The Community of Hospitality

The Headquarters of the
  Big Horn National Forest
The Optimist City

SHOSHONI
  The Hunting Capital of
    Wyoming

THERMOPOLIS
  The Center of the West
  The City of Health and
    Recreation
  The City of Heat (thermal
    springs)

The Health Center of the
  West (hot springs)
The Home of the World's
  Largest Mineral Hot
  Springs
The Hospitality Town
The Recreation Center of
  the West
The World's Largest
  Mineral Hot Springs
  (13,000 gallons flow per
  minute)
Wyoming's Year 'Round
  Health and Scenic Center

Absolute Center of Outdoorland,
U. S. A. Spokane, Wash.
Action Capital of the Midwest.
Des Moines, Iowa
Action Center of Florida's
"Holiday Highlands. " Lees-
burg, Fla.
Action City. Charlotte, N. C.
Action City. Miami, Fla.
Action City. Orlando, Fla.
The Action City Completely
Surrounded by Florida.
Orlando, Fla.
Advertising Center. Cleveland,
Ohio
Aerospace Capital of Oklahoma.
Tulsa, Okla.
Agate Capital of the U. S.
Prineville, Ore.
Aggregate of Villages. Wey-
mouth, Mass.
Agricultural and Industrial Cen-
ter of Northwest Arkansas.
Springdale, Ark.
Agricultural and Recreational
Center of California. Fres-
no, Calif.
Agricultural and Residential
Town. Lancaster, Mass.
Agricultural and Timber Em-
pire. Blountstown, Fla.
Agricultural Breadbasket Center
of North America. Grafton,
N. D.
Agricultural Capital. Jackson,
Miss.
Agricultural City with Indus-
trial Facilities. Galt, Calif.
Agricultural Community. Au-
gusta, Kan.
Agricultural Festival City.
Stuttgart, Ark.

Agricultural Town. Lovelock,
Nev.
Agriculture Center. Ord, Neb.
Air Capital. Wichita, Kan.
Air Capital of America. Wich-
ita, Kan.
Air Capital of the Carolinas.
Charleston, S. C.
Air Capital of the Nation.
Wichita, Kan.
Air Capital of the West. San
Diego, Calif.
Air Capital of the World.
Miami, Fla.
Air Capital of the World. Wich-
ita, Kan.
Air-Conditioned by Nature. Kane,
Pa.
Air-Conditioned Capital of
America. Phoenix, Ariz.
Air-Conditioned City. Blue-
field, W. Va.
Air-Conditioned City. Duluth,
Minn.
Air-Conditioned Duluth. Duluth,
Min.
Aircraft Center of the West.
Hawthorne, Calif.
Air Crossroads of America.
Evansville, Ind.
Air Crossroads of the World.
Anchorage, Alaska
Air Hub of the Americas. New
Orleans, La.
Airplane Manufacturing Center.
Everett, Wash.
Airways of America. Valdosta,
Ga.
Alabama's City in Motion. Mo-
bile, Ala.
Alabama's Only Port City.
Mobile, Ala.

205

Alamo City. San Antonio, Tex.
Alaska's Capital City. Juneau,
Alaska
Alaska's First City. Ketchikan,
Alaska
Alaska's Friendly City. Cor-
dova, Alaska
Alaska's Little Norway. Peters-
burg, Alaska
Alaska's Most Scenic Historic
Playground. Sitka, Alaska
Alaska's Number One Tourist
City. Sitka, Alaska
Alaska's Scenic Capital. Juneau,
Alaska
Alex City. Alexander City,
Ala.
Alexandria of America. New
Orleans, La.
All America City. Altus,
Okla.
All American City of the Great
Northwest. Salem, Ore.
All-American City with Fore-
sight. Grand Junction,
Colo.
All-American Town. Dallas,
Tex.
All-Electric Community.
Mason City, Wash.
All-Round Playground. Old
Orchard Beach, Me.
All-Season Convention Vaca-
tion Location. Las Vegas,
Nev.
All-Season Vacationland. Boyne
City, Mich.
All Year Home Town. Asbury
Park, N. J.
All Year Playground of the
Old South. Gulfport,
Miss.
All Year Residential Resort.
Ventnor City, N. J.
All-Year Resort and Recrea-
tion Center. Las Vegas,
Nev.
All-Year Resort Center. New
Bern, N. C.
All Year Round Vacation Cen-
ter. Gladstone, Mich.
All Year Round Vacationland.
Stowe, Vt.

All-Year Sports Center. Sun
Valley, Idaho
All-Year Sports Headquarters.
North Conway, N. H.
All Year Vacation City. Fort
Lauderdale, Fla.
All-Year Vacationland. Day-
tona Beach, Fla.
Allentown's Sister City. Beth-
lehem, Pa.
Alluring Attractive Suburban
Municipality. West Chester,
Pa.
Almond Capital of the World.
Chico, Calif.
Almond Capital of the World.
Sacramento, Calif.
Almond Capitol of California.
Ripon, Calif.
Almond Center of the World.
Chico, Calif.
Alpine Village. Suttons Bay,
Mich.
Aluminum City. Massena,
N. Y.
Aluminum City. Muscle Shoals,
Ala.
Aluminum City. New Kensing-
ton, Pa.
America in Miniature. Provi-
dence, R. I.
America's Alarm City. Mount
Katahdin, Me.
America's All-Year Playground.
Lake Tahoe, Calif.
America's Bagdad by the Sea.
Atlantic City, N. J.
America's Bath City. Mount
Clemons, Mich.
America's Bermuda. New
Shoreham, R. I.
America's Bicentennial City.
Philadelphia, Pa.
America's "Bit O'Ireland" in
County O'Antrim. Bellaire,
Mich.
America's Bottom. Death Val-
ley, Calif.
America's Carrot Capital.
Holtville, Calif.
America's Christmas City.
Bethlehem, Pa.
America's City of History.
Newport, R. I.

America's Convention City.
Philadelphia, Pa.
America's Daffodil Capital.
Gloucester, Va.
America's Desert Resort
Palm Springs, Calif.
America's Devil's Island.
Key West, Fla.
America's Dude Ranch
Capital. Wickenburg, Ariz.
America's Family Playground.
Lake George, N.Y.
America's Famous Summer
and Winter Resort.
Monterey, Calif.
America's Farm Implement
Capital. East Moline, Ill.
America's Fastest Growing
Industrial City. Richmond,
Va.
America's Fastest Growing
Vacation Area. Lake
Ozark, Mo.
America's Favorite Family
Vacation Area. Lake
Ozark, Mo.
America's Favorite Spa.
Hot Springs, Ark.
America's Favorite Sun and
Fun Vacationland. Phoenix,
Ariz.
America's First and Most
Historic Fishing Port.
Gloucester, Mass.
America's First Choice in
Family Resorts. Ocean
City, N.J.
America's First City.
Washington, D.C.
America's First City of Sun-
shine. Tucson, Ariz.
America's First Mining
Capital. Houghton, Mich.
America's First Resort.
Newport, R.I.
America's First Seashore
Resort. Long Branch,
N.J.
America's First Summer
Festival. Tanglewood,
Mass.
America's First Vacationland.
Newport, R.I.

America's Foremost Desert
Resort. Palm Springs,
Calif.
America's Foremost Year
'Round Sports Center. Sun
Valley, Idaho
America's Garden Spot. Lan-
caster, Pa.
America's Gateway to the
Pacific. Los Angeles, Calif.
America's Great Central Market.
and Tourist City. St. Louis,
Mo.
America's Great Convention
City. Philadelphia, Pa.
America's Greatest Family Re-
sort. Harvey Cedars, N.J.
America's Greatest Family Re-
sort. Ocean City, N.J.
America's Greatest Health and
Pleasure Resort. French
Lick, Ind.
America's Greatest Health and
Resort Center. Hot Springs,
Ark.
America's Greatest Health and
Rest Center. Hot Springs,
Ark.
America's Greatest Inland City.
Indianapolis, Ind.
America's Healthiest City.
Long Beach, N.Y.
America's Historyland Play-
ground. Virginia Beach, Va.
America's Holstein Capital.
Northfield, Minn.
America's Home Town. Ply-
mouth, Mass.
America's Ideal Family Center.
Bartlesville, Okla.
America's Ideal Vacation Land.
Billings, Mont.
America's Industrial City.
Fort Smith, Ark.
America's Iron Capital. Hib-
bing, Minn.
America's Last Colony. Wash-
ington, D.C.
America's Leading Tourist Re-
sort. New York, N.Y.
America's Little Switzerland.
Eureka Springs, Ark.

America's Little Switzerland.
Fayetteville, Ark.
America's Little Switzerland.
Newaygo, Mich.
America's Low Spot. Death
Valley, Calif.
America's Machine Shop.
Milwaukee, Wis.
America's Magic City. Gary,
Ind.
America's Mecca. New
York, N.Y.
America's Milk Center.
Harvard, Ill.
America's Mining Capital.
Hibbing, Minn.
America's Model City. Midwest City, Okla.
America's Most Beautiful
Capitol. Baton Rouge, La.
America's Most Beautiful
City. Savannah, Ga.
America's Most Beautiful
City. Tulsa, Okla.
America's Most Complete
Resort. Hilltop Lakes, Tex.
America's Most Complete
Resort. Lake Placid, N.Y.
America's Most Distinctive
Seashore Vacationland.
Cape May, N.J.
America's Most Exciting City.
San Francisco, Calif.
America's Most Exciting City.
Spokane, Wash.
America's Most Friendly
Fascinating City. San
Francisco, Calif.
America's Most Hedonistic
City. New Orleans, La.
America's Most Historic City.
Charleston, S.C.
America's Most Historic City.
Fredericksburg, Va.
America's Most Historic City.
Petersburg, Va.
America's Most Historic Town.
Ticonderoga, N.Y.
America's Most Honored Community. New Seabury,
Mass.
America's Most Interesting
City. New Orleans, La.

America's Most Livable City.
Tulsa, Okla.
America's Most Progressive
City. Pittsburgh, Pa.
America's Most Radioactive
City. Grand Junction, Colo.
America's Most Scenic Capital.
Juneau, Alaska
America's Most Westerly Inland
Port. Superior, Wis.
America's Most Wonderful Spa.
Saratoga Springs, N.Y.
America's Mountain Spring.
Sharon Springs, N.Y.
America's Naples. Woods Hole,
Mass.
America's Newest Convention
City. Portland, Ore.
America's Newest Family Playground. Saratoga, Wyo.
America's Newest Industrial
Center. Paducah, Ky.
America's Newest Industrial
Frontier. Odessa, Tex.
America's No. 1 Contrary City.
Chicago, Ill.
America's Number One Resort
for Year-Round Health and
Pleasure. Atlantic City,
N.J.
America's No. 1 Small City.
De Pere, Wis.
America's Ocean Playground.
Atlantic City, N.J.
America's Oldest City. St.
Augustine, Fla.
America's Oldest English Colony.
Hampton, Va.
America's Oldest Industrial
City. Haverhill, Mass.
America's Oldest Inland City.
Lancaster, Pa.
America's Oldest Seashore
Resort. Cape May, N.J.
America's Oldest Summer Resort. Newport, R.I.
America's Only International
Playground. San Diego,
Calif.
America's Original Retirement
Community. Youngstown, Ariz.
America's Own Spa. Hot Springs,
Ark.

America's Paris. Cincinnati, Ohio

America's Paris. San Francisco, Calif.

America's Port of Quickest Dispatch. Galveston, Tex.

America's Premier Playground. Rye, N.Y.

America's Riviera. Biloxi, Minn.

America's Riviera. Chicago, Ill.

America's Riviera. Gulfport, Miss.

America's Riviera. La Jolla, Calif.

America's Riviera. Montauk, N.Y.

America's Riviera. San Diego, Calif.

America's Safest Big City. Minneapolis, Minn.

America's Scenic Wonderland. Niagara Falls, N.Y.

America's Scenic Wonderland. Wisconsin Dells, Wis.

America's Second Port. Superior, Wis.

America's Sherryland. Lodi, Calif.

America's Shoe Capital. St. Louis, Mo.

America's Singapore. Key West, Fla.

America's Society Capital. Newport, R.I.

America's Southernmost City. Key West, Fla.

America's Sponge Diving Birthplace. Tarpon Springs, Fla.

America's Sports Mecca. French Lick, Ind.

America's Sugar Bowl. Brush, Colo.

America's Sunrise Gateway. Portland, Me.

America's Sweetest Town. Clewiston, Fla.

America's Sweetheart City. Loveland, Colo.

America's Swiss Cheese Capital. Monroe, Wis.

America's Switzerland. Lake Placid, N.Y.

America's Typical City. Zanesville, Ohio

America's Wild Life Preserver. Prairie du Chien, Wis.

America's Year 'Round Holiday Island. Jekyll Island, Ga.

America's Year 'Round Playground. Miami Beach, Fla.

America's Year 'Round Playground. Scranton, Pa.

American Athens. Boston, Mass.

American Brass City. Waterbury, Conn.

American Carlsbad. Ashland, Ore.

American Chair Center. Thomasville, No. Car.

American City of Opportunity. Jersey City, N.J.

American Gateway to Alaska and the Orient. Seattle, Wash.

American Lyons. Paterson, N.J.

American Munich. Milwaukee, Wis.

Ancient and Honorable Pueblo. Tucson, Ariz.

Ancient City. Annapolis, Md.

Ancient City. St. Augustine, Fla.

Ancient City. Santa Fe, N.M.

Angel City. Los Angeles, Calif.

Annapolis of the Air. Pensacola, Fla.

Annie's Town. Anniston, Ala.

Annual Waterama City. Glenwood, Minn.

Another Clyde City. Union, Wash.

Anthracite Capital of the World. Scranton, Pa.

Anthracite Center of the World. Scranton, Pa.

Anthracite City. Scranton, Pa.

Antique Center of Maine. Hallowell, Me.

Antiques Center of the South. Dania, Fla.

Appealing Residential-Agricultural Community. Sterling, Mass.

Apple Capital. Wenatchee, Wash.

Apple Capital. Winchester, Va.

Apple Capital in the Beautiful Shenandoah Valley. Winchester, Va.

Apple Capital of the World. Wenatchee, Wash.

Apple Capital of the World. Winchester, Va.

Apple City. Lander, Wyo.

Apple City. Watsonville, Calif.

Aquatic Wonderland. Garrison, N.D.

Aqueduct City. Norristown, Pa.

Aqueduct City. Rochester, N.Y.

Arbor Lodge City. Nebraska City, Neb.

Area of Opportunity. Ruskin, Fla.

Area Rich in Historical Attractions. Swansboro, No. Car.

Area Shopping Crossroads. Ash Grove, Mo.

Area Trade Center. Lamberton, Minn.

Area's Leading Agricultural Trade Center. West Plains, Mo.

Arizona's Copper Capital. Bisbee, Ariz.

Arizona's First Capital. Prescott, Ariz.

Arizona's Gateway to Sonora, Mexico. Santa Cruz Co., Ariz.

Arizona's Second Largest City. Tucson, Ariz.

Arizona's Third Largest City. Mesa, Ariz.

Ark City. Arkansas City, Ark.

Arkansas' Industrial Center. Fort Smith, Ark.

Arkansas' Largest Health and

Pleasure Resort. Hot Springs, Ark.

Arkansas' Only Seaport. Helena, Ark.

Arkopolis. Little Rock, Ark.

Arrowhead Egg Basket. Barnum, Minn.

Arsenal. Lancaster, Pa.

Arsenal for the Nation. Pittsburgh, Pa.

Arsenal of Democracy. Fort Worth, Tex.

Arsenal of the Union. Windsor, Vt.

Art Center of Rhode Island. Wickford, R.I.

Art Center of the Southwest. Taos, N.M.

Art City. Springville, Utah

Artesian City. Albany, Ga.

Artesian City. Martinsville, Ind.

Artichoke Capital of the World. Castroville, Calif.

Artist's Paradise. Boothbay Harbor, Me.

Artist's Paradise. Rockport, Mass.

Asparagus Capital of the World. Isleton, Calif.

Astrodome City. Houston, Texas

Athens. Boston, Mass.

Athens of Alabama. Tuscaloosa, Ala.

Athens of America. Annapolis, Md.

Athens of America. Boston, Mass.

Athens of America. Cambridge, Mass.

Athens of America. Crawfordsville, Ind.

Athens of America. Iowa City, Iowa

Athens of America. New Harmony, Ind.

Athens of Arkansas. Fayetteville, Ark.

Athens of California. Benicia, Calif.

Athens of Colonial America. Philadelphia, Pa.

Athens of Florida. De Land,
Fla.
Athens of Indiana. Crawfords-
ville, Ind.
Athens of Indiana. Roanoke,
Ind.
Athens of Iowa. Iowa City,
Iowa
Athens of New England.
Norwalk, Conn.
Athens of Pennsylvania.
West Chester, Pa.
Athens of Texas. Marshall,
Texas
Athens of Texas. Sherman,
Texas
Athens of Texas. Waco,
Texas
Athens of the Hoosier State.
Crawfordville, Ind.
Athens of the Middle West.
Cincinnati, Ohio
Athens of the Midwest.
Columbia, Mo.
Athens of the New World.
Boston, Mass.
Athens of the Northwest.
Fairbault, Minn.
Athens of the Prairie.
Columbus, Ind.
Athens of the South. Holly
Springs, Miss.
Athens of the South. Nash-
ville, Tenn.
Athens of the Southwest.
Dallas, Tex.
Athens of the United States.
Boston, Mass.
Athens of the West. Abilene,
Tex.
Athens of the West. Berkeley,
Calif.
Athens of the West. Boston,
Mass.
Athens of the West. Lexing-
ton, Ky.
Athens of the West. Salem,
Ind.
Athens of Virginia. Lexington,
Va.
Athens of Wyoming. Laramie,
Wyo.

Athens You Will Want to See.
Athens, Ga.
Atlanta's Airport City. College
Park, Ga.
Atlantic City of the Great Lakes.
Cedar Point, Ohio
Atlantic City of the Middle
West. Cedar Point, Ohio
Atomic Capital of the World.
Oak Ridge, Tenn.
Atomic City. Los Alamos,
N. M.
Atomic City. Oak Ridge, Tenn.
Atomic Energy City. Oak
Ridge, Tenn.
Attractions Capital of the World.
Orlando, Fla.
Auto City. Detroit, Mich.
Auto Racing Capital of the
World. Ormond Beach, Fla.
Automobile Capital of the World.
Detroit, Mich.
Automobile Center. Flint,
Mich.
Automobile City. Detroit,
Mich.
Automobile City of the World.
Detroit, Mich.
Automotive Capital of the World.
Detroit, Mich.
Aviation Center of America.
San Diego, Calif.
Aviation Center of the East.
Baltimore, Md.
Aviation City. Dayton, Ohio
Azalea City. Valdosta, Ga.
Azalea Trail City. Lafayette,
La.

Baby City. Leominster, Mass.
Baby of the Colorado Ski Re-
sorts. Vail, Colo.
Babylon of Washington Terri-
tory. Ruby, Wash.
Babylon on the Bayou. Houston,
Texas
Babylon on the Bluff. Memphis,
Tenn.
Babylonian Bedlam. New York,
N. Y.

Bad Birmingham. Birmingham, Ala.

Baden-Baden of America. Saratoga, N.Y.

Baden-Baden of America. Saratoga Springs, N.Y.

Baden-Baden of America. Sharon Springs, N.Y.

Bagdad by the Bay. San Francisco, Calif.

Bagdad of the Subway. New York, N.Y.

Bagdad on the Hudson. New York, N.Y.

Bag Town. San Diego, Calif.

Baked Beans City. Boston, Mass

Balanced American City. Clarksville, Tenn.

Balanced City. Berkeley, Calif.

Balanced City. Pico Rivera, Calif.

Balanced Community. Mount Laurel, N.J.

Balanced Community. Toccoa, Ga.

Balanced Community of Opportunity and Happy Homes. Jackson, Miss.

Balanced Community with the Bright Future. Salinas, Calif.

Banana Belt City. Lewiston, Idaho

Band City. Elkhart, Ind.

Band Instrument Center of the Country. Elkhart, Ind.

Banking Center of the World. New York, N.Y.

Banking City. Fort Worth, Tex.

Barb City. De Kalb, Ill.

Barbed Wire Capital of the World. De Kalb, Ill.

Bass Capital of the World. Alexandria, Minn.

Bass Capital of the World. Palatka, Fla.

ı Battlefield City. Gettysburg, Pa.

Battlefield of the Revolution. Augusta, Ga.

Battletown. Berryville, Va.

Bavarian Village. Leavenworth, Wash.

Bay City. San Francisco, Calif.

Bay Horse. Boston, Mass.

Bayou City. Houston, Tex.

Beach that Made Fort Lauderdale Famous. Fort Lauderdale, Fla.

Bean Town. Basin, Wyo.

Beantown. Boston, Mass.

Bear's Place. Olympia, Wash.

Beautiful and Historic City. Vincennes, Ind.

Beautiful City. Cincinnati, Ohio

Beautiful City. Columbus, Miss.

Beautiful City. Memphis, Tenn.

Beautiful City. Toccoa, Ga.

Beautiful City by a Beautiful Lake. Coeur d'Alene, Idaho

Beautiful City by the Sea. Portland, Me.

Beautiful City of Homes, Diversified Business and Progressive Outlook. Buffalo, N.Y.

Beautiful City of Homes in the Historic Mohawk Valley. Utica, N.Y.

Beautiful City of Roses. Portland, Ore.

Beautiful City of the Straits. Detroit, Mich.

Beautiful Colonial Village in Western Vermont. Middlebury, Vt.

Beautiful Community in Beautiful Virginia. Culpeper, Va.

Beautiful Historic Capital of the Empire State. Albany, N.Y.

Beautiful Place by the Sea. Ogunquit, Me.

Beautiful Town that Is Seated by the Sea. Portland, Me.

Beauty Spot of the Blue Ridge. Little Switzerland, N.C.

Beauty Spot of the North Jersey Coast. Asbury Park, N.J.

Bedroom of New York. Brooklyn, N.Y.

Bedroom of Washington. Arlington, Va.

Bedroom Town. Darien, Conn.
Bee-Hive of Industry. Provi-
dence, R. I.
Beer Capital of America.
Milwaukee, Wis.
Beer City. Milwaukee, Wis.
Bel Air of Conejo. Thousand
Oaks, Calif.
"Believe It or Not" Town.
Eureka Springs, Ark.
Bell Town. East Hampton,
Conn.
Bell Town of America. East
Hampton, Conn.
Belle City. Racine, Wis.
Belle City of the Bluegrass
Regions. Lexington, Ky.
Belle City of the Lakes.
Racine, Wis.
Benton County's Fastest
Growing City. Lincoln,
Mo.
Bergen County's Only Deep-
water Port. Edgewater,
N. J.
Bermuda of the North. Macki-
nac Island, Mich.
Bermuda of the North. New
Shoreham, R. I.
Berry Capital of the World.
Starke, Fla.
Berry City. Woodburn, Ore.
Best Balanced City. Hickory,
N. C.
Best Climate in Eastern United
States. Titusville, Fla.
Best Convention Point in the
East. Springfield, Mass.
Best Fishing in Oklahoma.
Heavener, Okla.
Best in the West. Roby, Tex.
Best Known City in the World.
Battle Creek, Mich.
Best Known City of Its Size
in the World. Battle Creek,
Mich.
Best Known Little City in
America. Claremore,
Okla.
Best Lighted City in the
World. Gering, Neb.
Best Lighted Town in the West.
Burley, Idaho

Best Location in the Nation.
Cleveland, Ohio
Best Natural Harbor in the
World. Portsmouth, Va.
Best of Many Worlds. Aurora,
Colo.
Best Pecan Producing Area in
the South. Fort Valley, Ga.
Best Preserved Pioneer Com-
munity in the Pacific North-
west. Jacksonville, Ore.
Best Town in the State by a
Damsite. Stockton, Mo.
Best Town of Its Age in This
Glorious Climate. Whittier,
Calif.
Best Town Site on the Ohio.
Steubenville, Ohio
Best Town to Live In. Port-
land, Tenn.
Best Vacation and Recreation
Area Anywhere. Alexandria,
Minn.
Betsytown. Elizabeth, N. J.
Better Community for Better
Living. Pratt, Kan.
Better Place in which to Live,
Visit or Do Business.
Queensbury, N. Y.
Better Place to Work and Play.
Moultrie, Ga.
Beulah Land. Palisades, Wash.
Big Apple. New York, N. Y.
Big Apple of the Desert. Las
Vegas, Nev.
Big Burg. New York, N. Y.
Big Cattle Country. Benjamin,
Tex.
Big City. New York, N. Y.
Big City Benefits with Small
Town Advantages. Mechanics-
burg, Pa.
Big "D". Dallas, Tex.
Big Game Capital of Nebraska.
Crawford, Neb.
Big Heart of Texas. Austin,
Tex.
Big Light in the Big Thicket.
Kountze, Tex.
Big Little City. Malone, N. Y.
Big Little City Growing
Bigger Yearly. Westfield,
Mass.

Big Little City on the Desert.
Wendover, Utah
Big Little Town. Houston,
Mo.
Big "M" of the Ozarks.
Monett, Mo.
Big Money Center You Never
Heard Much About. Provi-
dence, R. I.
Big Mountain Country. Lander,
Wyo.
Big Peach. Atlanta, Ga.
Big Potato. Chicago, Ill.
Big Shelby. Memphis, Tenn.
Big Smoke. Pittsburgh, Pa.
Big Smoky. Pittsburgh, Pa.
Big Town. Chicago, Ill.
Big Town. New York, N. Y.
Big Water. Paha, Wash.
Biggest City in Area in the
Free World. Jacksonville,
Fla.
Biggest Gateway to Immigrants.
New York, N. Y.
Biggest Industrial Little City
in the World. Plano, Ill.
Biggest Inland Port in America.
Pittsburgh, Pa.
Biggest Little City. Abilene,
Kan.
Biggest Little City in America.
Atlantic City, N. J.
Biggest Little City in Maine.
Belfast, Me.
Biggest Little City in Michigan.
Rockford, Mich.
Biggest Little City in the
U. S. A. Dodge City, Kan.
Biggest Little City in the
Valley. Los Fresnos, Tex.
Biggest Little City in the
World. Oklahoma City,
Okla.
Biggest Little City in the
World. Reno, Nev.
Biggest Little Town in Kansas.
Cawker City, Kan.
Biggest Little Town in Ohio.
Columbiana, Ohio
Biggest Little Town in the
South. Hodge, La.
Biggest Little Town in the
West. Broadus, Mont.

Biggest Small Town in New
York State. Stony Creek,
N. Y.
Big-Headed Burg. Hollywood,
Calif.
Billfishing Capital of Northwest
Florida. Destin, Fla.
Billion Dollar Sandbar. Miami
Beach, Fla.
Billtown. Williamstown, Kan.
Bird Dog Capital of the World.
Waynesborg, Ga.
Bird Hunter's Paradise.
Weatherford, Okla.
Bird Sanctuary. Henderson,
N. C.
Birmingham of America. Cin-
cinnati, Ohio
Birmingham of America. Newark,
N. J.
Birmingham of America. Pitts-
burg, Pa.
Birth of the "Blues". Memphis,
Tenn.
Birthplace and Home of Little
League Baseball. Williams-
port, Pa.
Birthplace of a Republic. West
Columbia, Tex.
Birthplace of America. Alex-
andria, Minn.
Birthplace of American Film.
Pittsburgh, Pa.
Birthplace of America's Cotton
Industry. Pawtucket, R. I.
Birthplace of America's Iron
and Steel Industry. Saugus,
Mass.
Birthplace of American Inde-
pendence. Ipswich, Mass.
Birthplace of American Inde-
pendence. Philadelphia, Pa.
Birthplace of American Liberty.
Lexington, Mass.
Birthplace of American Liberty.
Philadelphia, Pa.
Birthplace of Anglo-American
Settlement in Texas. San
Felipe, Texas
Birthplace of Aviation. Dayton,
Ohio
Birthplace of Baseball. Coopers-
town, N. Y.

Birthplace of Buffalo Bill
Cody. Le Claire, Iowa
Birthplace of California. San
Diego, Calif.
Birthplace of Calvin Coolidge.
Plymouth, Vt.
Birthplace of Daniel Webster.
Franklin, N.H.
Birthplace of Democracy.
Dedham, Mass.
Birthplace of Dixie. Mont-
gomery, Ala.
Birthplace of Freedom. Boston,
Mass.
Birthplace of Harry S. Truman.
Lamar, Mo.
Birthplace of Liberty. Quincy,
Mass.
Birthplace of McKinley.
Niles, Ohio
Birthplace of Maine. Freeport,
Me.
Birthplace of Mary Baker Eddy.
Bow, N.H.
Birthplace of Modern Rocketry.
Worcester, Mass.
Birthplace of Night Baseball.
Fort Wayne, Ind.
Birthplace of Oklahoma. Guthrie,
Okla.
Birthplace of President Richard
M. Nixon. Yorba Linda,
Calif.
Birthplace of Professional
Football. Latrobe, Pa.
Birthplace of Radio. Murray,
Ky.
Birthplace of South Dakota's
Pheasant Hunting. Redfield,
S.D.
Birthplace of Speed. Ormond
Beach, Fla.
Birthplace of Surfing. Waikiki,
Hawaii
Birthplace of Texas. Washington,
Ark.
Birthplace of the American
Circus. Somers, N.Y.
Birthplace of the American
Cotton Industry. Pawtucket,
R.I.
Birthplace of the American Navy.
Beverly, Mass.

Birthplace of the Atomic Age.
Oak Ridge, Tenn.
Birthplace of the 'Buddy Poppy'.
Monroe, Ga.
Birthplace of the Farm Tractor.
Charles City, Iowa
Birthplace of the Mesabi. Moun-
tain Lake, Minn.
Birthplace of the Modern Oil
Industry. Beaumont, Tex.
Birthplace of the Nation.
Jamestown, Va.
Birthplace of the Nation. Phila-
delphia, Pa.
Birthplace of the Northern
Pacific. Carlton, Minn.
Birthplace of the Northwest
Territory. Marietta, Ohio
Birthplace of the Republic of
Vermont. Windsor, Vt.
Birthplace of the Republican
Party. Ripon, Wis.
Birthplace of the Second and
Sixth Presidents. Quincy,
Mass.
Birthplace of the Star Spangled
Banner. Baltimore, Md.
Birthplace of the Union. Albany,
N.Y.
Birthplace of the United States
Coast Guard. Newburyport,
Mass.
Birthplace of the U.S. Navy.
Whitehall, N.Y.
Birthplace of Tree Farms.
Montesanto, Wash.
Birthplace of U.S. Naval Avia-
tion. Pensacola, Fla.
Birthplace of Water Skiing.
Lake City, Minn.
Birthplace of Western America.
Harrodsburg, Ky.
Birthplace of Woodrow Wilson.
Staunton, Va.
Bison City. Buffalo, N.Y.
Bit of America at Its Best.
Oneida, N.Y.
Bit of New England with a
Sombrero on It. Claremont,
Calif.
Bit of the Old West Trans-
planted in the Twentieth Cen-
tury. Wickenburg, Ariz.

Bitches' Heaven. Boston, Mass.
Bituminous City. Connellsville, Pa.
Black Bass Capital of the World. Cape Vincent, N. Y.
Black Diamond City. Wilkes-Barre, Pa.
Black Heart of Montana. Butte, Mont.
Black River Area of Vermont. Springfield, Vt.
Black River Valley Area of Vermont. Springfield, Vt.
Black River Valley of Vermont. Springfield, Vt.
Blackberry Capital of the World. McLoud, Calif.
Blonde Beauty of the Lakes. Milwaukee, Wis.
Blue Marlin Capital of the World. Hatteras, N. C.
Blueberry Capital of the Nation. Iron River, Wis.
Bluebonnet Capital. Marlin, Tex.
Bluegrass Capital. Frankfort, Ky.
Bluegrass Capital. Lexington, Ky.
Bluff City. Eufaula, Ala.
Bluff City. Hannibal, Mo.
Bluff City. Memphis, Tenn.
Bluff City. Natchez, Miss.
Bluff City of the Chattahoochee. Eufaula, Ala.
Board Foot. Hoquiam, Wash.
Boatbuilding and Fishing Center. Boothbay, Me.
Boating and Yachting Center. Boothbay Harbor, Me.
Boating Capital of New England. Boothbay Harbor, Me.
Boating Capital of the World. Fort Lauderdale, Fla.
Boating Capital of the World. Seattle, Wash.
Boat Racing Capital of the South. Guntersville, Ala.
Bob Hope Desert Golf Classic City. Palm Desert, Calif.
Bold New City of the South. Jacksonville, Fla.

Boom Town on the River. Memphis, Tenn.
Boom Town without Oil. Austin, Tex.
Booming Community with a Balanced Economy. Wheat Ridge, Colo.
Booming Convention City. Las Vegas, Nev.
Booming Oil Rich City. Houston, Tex.
Boomtown. Borger, Tex.
Boomtown, U.S.A. Terre Haute, Ind.
Border City. Fall River, Mass.
Border Town. Rye, N. Y.
Boston. Port Gamble, Wash.
Boston of the West. St. Paul, Minn.
Bostonia. Boston, Mass.
Bountiful Country. Ashburn, Ga.
Bourbon Capital of the World. Bardstown, Ky.
Boyhood Home of George Washington. Fredericksburg, Va.
Boyhood Home of Mark Twain. Hannibal, Mo.
Boy's Town. Omaha, Neb.
Boy's Town of New England. Tilton, N. H.
Brainy Borough. Metuchen, N. J.
Bran Town. Binghamton, N. Y.
Brass Center of the World. Waterbury, Conn.
Brass City. Waterbury, Conn.
Bratwurst Capital of the World. Sheboygan, Wis.
Bread-Basket. Lancaster, Pa.
Bread-Basket of the World. Fargo, N. D.
Breakfast Food City. Battle Creek, Mich.
Breezy Town. Chicago, Ill.
Brewing Capital of the World. Milwaukee, Wis.
Brewing City. Reading, Pa.
Brick Capital of U.S.A. Sanford, N. C.
Bride of the Mountains. Talladega, Ala.

Bridge City on Lake Oahe.
Mobridge, So. Dak.
Bright Leaf Tobacco Center.
Nashville, Ga.
Bright Leaf Tobacco Market
of the World. Danville,
Va.
Bright Spot. Dallas, Tex.
Bright Spot. Milwaukee, Wis.
Bright Spot of America.
Peoria, Ill.
Brightest Spot in Eastern
Oregon. Ontario, Ore.
Brightness of the Noonday
Sun. Port Gamble, Wash.
Brighton's Future Is Bright.
Brighton, Colo.
Broadway Colony in the Heart
of Maine. Lakewood, Me.
Broadway of the Desert. Las
Vegas, Nev.
Broiler Capital of Maine.
Belfast, Me.
Broiler Capital of New Eng-
land. Belfast, Me.
Broiler Capital of the World.
Gainesville, Ga.
Broiler Center. Belfast, Me.
Broiler City. Canton, Ga.
Brook. Toms Brook, Va.
Brooklyn of the South. Annis-
ton, Ala.
Broom Corn Capital of the
World. Elk City, Okla.
Broom Corn Center. Walsh,
Colo.
Broom Town. Arcola, Ill.
Brownstone City. Hummels-
town, Pa.
Buccaneer City. Fernandina
Beach, Fla.
Buckle on the Kansas Wheat
Belt. Dodge City, Kan.
Buckle of the Wheat Belt.
Kingfisher, Okla.
Buckle on the Oil Belt.
Independence, Kan.
Bucktail City. Smethport, Pa.
Bullhead Capitol of the World.
Waterville, Minn.
Bumgannon. Dungannon, Va.
Bungtown. Cold Spring Harbor,
N.Y.

Burg. New York, N.Y.
Burg on the Bear. Corinne,
Utah
Bushwackers' Capital. Nevada,
Mo.
Busiest Freshwater Port in the
World. Toledo, Ohio
Business and Cultural Center
of the St. Lawrence Valley.
Potsdam, N.Y.
Business Capital of the Nation.
New York, N.Y.
Business Capital of the World.
New York, N.Y.
Business Center for Greater
Los Angeles. Culver City,
Calif.
Business Center of Busy North-
ern California. San Jose,
Calif.
Business, Finance, Industry,
Shopping and Transportation
Hub. Flagstaff, Ariz.
Business Heart of Southwestern
Minnesota. Worthington,
Minn.
Business Heart of the Lakeland
Area. Dover, N.J.
Business Hub of the Southeast.
Atlanta, Ga.
Business Potential Metropolitan
Market. Rochester, Minn.
Bustling Center of Industry,
Agriculture, Wholesale Trade
and Shipping. Fresno, Calif.
Bustling Resort City in the
Desert. Tucson, Ariz.
Bustling River Port. Louis-
ville, Ky.
Bustling Steel, Coal, Glass and
Aluminum Center. Pitts-
burgh, Pa.
Bustling Western City. Medford,
Ore.
Busy Agricultural Community.
Southwest City, Mo.
Busy Business Center. Red-
lands, Calif.
Busy Friendly City. Ashland,
Ky.
Busy Friendly Growing
City. Garrison, N.D.

Busy Friendly Growing City.
Greenville, Ill.
Busy Gritty Granite City.
St. Cloud, Minn.
Butter Capital of the World.
Owatonna, Minn.
Butter City.   Manteca, Calif.
Buying Center for Thousands.
Lockport, N.Y.
Buying Center of a Quarter
Million People.   Lancaster,
Pa.
Byrd Town.   Richmond, Va.

Caladium Capital of the World.
Lake Placid, Fla.
California at Its Best.   San
Diego, Calif.
California's Central Market
for Industrial Products.
Petaluma, Calif.
California's Enchanting City.
Santa Barbara, Calif.
California's Fastest Growing
City.   Chula Vista, Calif.
California's First and Finest
City.   San Diego, Calif.
California's First City.   San
Jose, Calif.
California's First Ranking
Country.   Santa Clara, Calif.
California's Great Breeding
Ground for Industry.   Santa
Clara, Calif.
California's Inland Harbor.
Stockton, Calif.
California's Plymouth Rock.
San Diego, Calif.
California's World-Famous
All-Year Resort.   Santa
Barbara, Calif.
Camel City.   Winston-Salem,
N.C.
Camellia Capitol of the World.
Sacramento, Cal.
Camellia City.   Greenville,
Ala.
Camellia City.   Quitman,
Ga.
Camellia City.   Sacramento,
Calif.

Camellia City of America.
McComb, Miss.
Camellia City of the South.
Thomson, Ga.
Camera Center.   Rochester,
N.Y.
Camera City.   Rochester, N.Y.
Camping Ground of the Seminole
Indians.   Silver Springs, Fla.
'Can Do' City.   Hazleton, Pa.
Canal City.   Hollidaysburg, Pa.
Canal City.   Sturgeon Bay,
Wis.
Candy Capital of Georgia.   East-
man, Ga.
Canned Salmon Capital of the
World.   Ketchikan, Alaska
Cannery City.   Seattle, Wash.
Cannon City.   Kannapolis, N.C.
Canoe City.   Old Town, Me.
Canoe Outfitting Capital of the
World.   Ely, Minn.
Canyon City.   Azusa, Calif.
Canyon City.   Wellsboro, Pa.
Cape Cod of the West.   Hoquiam,
Wash.
Capital City.   Albany, N.Y.
Capital City.   Annapolis, Md.
Capital City.   Atlanta, Ga.
Capital City.   Augusta, Me.
Capital City.   Austin, Tex.
Capital City.   Baton Rouge, La.
Capital City.   Bismarck, N.D.
Capital City.   Boise, Idaho
Capital City.   Boston, Mass.
Capital City.   Carson City, Nev.
Capital City.   Charleston,
W. Va.
Capital City.   Cheyenne, Wyo
Capital City.   Columbia, S.C.
Capital City.   Columbus, Ohio
Capital City.   Concord, N.H.
Capital City.   Denver, Colo.
Capital City.   Des Moines, Iowa
Capital City.   Dover, Del.
Capital City.   Frankfort, Ky.
Capital City.   Harrisburg, Pa.
Capital City.   Hartford, Conn.
Capital City.   Helena, Mont.
Capital City.   Honolulu, Hawaii
Capital City.   Indianapolis, Ind.
Capital City.   Jackson, Miss.
Capital City.   Jefferson City, Mo.

Capital City. Juneau, Alaska
Capital City. Lansing, Mich.
Capital City. Lincoln, Neb.
Capital City. Little Rock,
  Ark.
Capital City. Madison, Wis.
Capital City. Montgomery,
  Ala.
Capital City. Montpelier, Vt.
Capital City. Nashville, Tenn.
Capital City. Oklahoma City,
  Okla.
Capital City. Olympia, Wash.
Capital City. Phoenix, Ariz.
Capital City. Pierre, S.D.
Capital City. Providence, R.I.
Capital City. Raleigh, N.C.
Capital City. Richmond, Va.
Capital City. Sacramento,
  Calif.
Capital City. St. Paul, Minn.
Capital City. Salem, Ore.
Capital City. Salt Lake City,
  Utah
Capital City. Santa Fe, N.M.
Capital City. Springfield, Ill.
Capital City. Tallahassee, Fla.
Capital City. Topeka, Kan.
Capital City. Trenton, N.J.
Capital City. Washington, D.C.
Capital City. Youngstown,
  Ohio
Capital City. Zanesville, Ohio
Capital City Different. Santa
  Fe, N.M.
Capital City of a Great Indus-
  trial Empire. Youngstown,
  Ohio
Capital City of a Great Nation.
  Washington, D.C.
Capital City of a Great Trade
  Empire. Cleveland, Ohio
Capital City of Alaska. Juneau,
  Alaska
Capital City of Arizona.
  Phoenix, Ariz.
Capital City of Creek County.
  Sapulpa, Okla.
Capital City of Fabulous
  Florida. Tallahassee, Fla.
Capital City of Good Living,
  Commerce and Industry.
  Salem, Ore.

Capital City of Industrial Pro-
  gress. Nashville, Tenn.
Capital City of Southern Vir-
  ginia. Danville, Va.
Capital City of Southside Vir-
  ginia. Danville, Va.
Capital City of Tennessee.
  Nashville, Tenn.
Capital City of the Country with
  a Copper Bottom. Globe,
  Ariz.
Capital City of the Green Moun-
  tain State. Montpelier, Vt.
Capital City of the Hill County
  Playland. Kerrville, Tex.
Capital City of the Keystone
  State. Harrisburg, Pa.
Capital City of the Land of
  Ark-La-Tex. Shreveport,
  La.
Capital City of the Land of
  the Sky. Asheville, N.C.
Capital City, U.S.A. Washing-
  ton, D.C.
Capital of America. Washington,
  D.C.
Capital of America's State of
  Opportunity. Jackson, Miss.
Capital of an Empire. Juneau,
  Alaska
Capital of Aroostook County.
  Houlton, Me.
Capital of Big Orange Country.
  Knoxville, Tenn.
Capital of Colonial Virginia.
  Williamsburg, Va.
Capital of Crackpots. Los
  Angeles, Calif.
Capital of Duneland. Michigan
  City, Ind.
Capital of Eastern Oregon.
  Ontario, Ore.
Capital of Finance. New York,
  N.Y.
Capital of Florida's Enchanting
  Gold Coast. Miami Beach,
  Fla.
Capital of Florida's Sugar In-
  dustry. Clewiston, Fla.
Capital of Little Dixie. Mexico,
  Mo.
Capital of Miserable Huts.
  Washington, D.C.

Capital of New England. Boston,
Mass.
Capital of Old California.
Monterey, Calif.
Capital of Opportunity. Bismarck, N.D.
Capital of Our Country. Washington, D.C.
Capital of Pennsylvania German-Land. Reading, Pa.
Capital of Radio. Camden,
N.J.
Capital of Soonerland. Oklahoma City, Okla.
Capital of South Central Oklahoma. Ardmore, Okla.
Capital of Sunshine. Palm
Springs, Calif.
Capital of the American Circus.
Baraboo, Wis.
Capital of the Atomic Age.
Los Alamos, N.M.
Capital of the Big Lake. Bull
Shoals, Ark.
Capital of the Blue-Grass
Region. Lexington, Ky.
Capital of the Broiler Industry.
Belfast, Me.
Capital of the Carolinas.
Charleston, S.C.
Capital of the Chippewa Nation.
Cass Lake, Minn.
Capital of the Coastal Empire
of South Carolina. Charleston, S.C.
Capital of the Confederacy.
Richmond, Va.
Capital of the Convention World.
Chicago, Ill.
Capital of the Empire State.
Albany, N.Y.
Capital of the Evergreen Club.
Olympia, Wash.
Capital of the First State.
Dover, Del.
Capital of the "Free State" of
Van Zandt County. Canton,
Tex.
Capital of the Great Chicksaw
Nation. Tupelo, Miss.
Capital of the Heart O' the
Lakes. Rhinelander,
Wis.

Capital of the Hill Country.
Kerrville, Tex.
Capital of the Horse World.
Lexington, Ky.
Capital of the Land of Outdoors.
Portland, Ore.
Capital of the Midland Empire.
Billings, Mont.
Capital of the Mid-South.
Memphis, Tenn.
Capital of the Most Historic
Resort Area in America.
Norfolk, Va.
Capital of the New South.
Atlanta, Ga.
Capital of the Old South.
Richmond, Va.
Capital of the Ozarks. Silver
Dollar City, Mo.
Capital of the Paul Bunyan
Playground. Brainerd, Mich.
Capital of the Plantations.
Charleston, S.C.
Capital of the Rio Grande Valley. Brownsville, Tex.
Capital of the Rocky Mountain
Empire. Denver, Colo.
Capital of the Sea Islands.
Beaufort, S.C.
Capital of the Southern Mind.
Chapel Hill, N.C.
Capital of the Vast Republic.
Washington, D.C.
Capital of the Vermilion Range.
Ely, Minn.
Capital of the World. New
York, N.Y.
Capital of Thoroughbred
Racing. Saratoga Springs,
N.Y.
Capital of U.S. Snowmobiling.
Thief River Falls, Minn.
Capital of Vacationland. Newport, R.I.
Capital of Western Kentucky.
Paducah, Ky.
Capital of Youth. Hannibal,
Mo.
Capital Parish of the State
Named for Louis and Anna.
East Baton Rouge, La.
Capital Resort of the Ozarks.
Eureka Springs, Ark.

Capitol City. Little Rock, Ark.
Capitol of a Great Empire.
Williston, N. D.
Capitol of Florida's Treasure
Coast. Fort Pierce, Fla.
Car Shop City. Berwick, Pa.
Carlsbad of America. Bedford Springs, Pa.
Carlsbad of America. French
Lick, Ind.
Carlsbad of America. Hot
Springs, Ark.
Carlsbad of America. Tate
Springs, Tenn.
Carnation Capital of the World.
Wheat Ridge, Colo.
Carnation City. Alliance,
Ohio
Carolina's Queen City.
Charlotte, No. Car.
Carpet City. Amsterdam,
N. Y.
Carpet City of the World.
Amsterdam, N. Y.
Carriage Center of the World.
Amesbury, Mass.
Carrot Capital. Holtville,
Calif.
Cash Register City. Dayton,
Ohio
Castle City. York, Pa.
Casual Family Beach Resort
in the Center of Florida's
West Coast. Longboat Key,
Fla.
Catacomb City. Waynesburg,
Pa.
Cataract City. Niagara Falls,
N. Y.
Catchall of Suckers. Los
Angeles, Calif.
Catfish Capital of Kansas.
Kingman, Kans.
Cathedral of the Plains. Victoria, Kan.
Cathedral Town. Garden City,
N. Y.
Catskills and County Crossroads of the Center for
Action. Monticello, N. Y.
Cattle Capital and Agricultural
Center of the Great Southwest. Willcox, Ariz.

Cattle Capital of Nebraska.
Alliance, Neb.
Cattle Capital of the Nation.
Willcox, Ariz.
Cattle Capital of the Southwest.
Clovis, N. M.
Cattle Capital of the World.
Willcox, Ariz.
Cattle Center. Willcox, Ariz.
Cattle Country. Elko, Nev.
Cattle Ranching City. Garrison,
N. D.
Cavern City. Carlsbad, N. M.
Cedar-shipping Center. Sandpoint, Idaho
Celery City. Kalamazoo, Mich.
Celery City. Sanford, Fla.
Celestial City. Pekin, Ill.
Celluloid City. Hollywood, Calif.
Cement City. Allentown, Pa.
Centennial City. Fairbanks,
Alaska
Center City. Fort Smith, Ark.
Center City of Southern Georgia.
Waycross, Ga.
Center City of the Ozarks.
Berryville, Ark.
Center for Agriculture, Industry
and Recreation. Los Banos,
Calif.
Center for Giant Blueberry
Bushes. Crestview, Fla.
Center for Good Clean Industry.
Plant City, Fla.
Center for Good Living. Los
Banos, Calif.
Center for Good Living, Agriculture, Recreation and Industry. Atwater, Calif.
Center for Medicine. White
Plains, N. Y.
Center for Medicine Bow National Forest Recreation Area.
Laramie, Wyo.
Center for Ranching. Winnemucca, Nev.
Center for Recreation. Ord,
Neb.
Center for the Arts. Pittsburgh, Pa.
Center for Water, Industry,
Recreation, Agriculture.
Los Banos, Calif.

Center for Western Nevada
Agriculture. Fallon, Nev.
Center of a Bustling Com-
mercial Industrial and
Tourist World. Anaheim,
Calif.
Center of a Bustling Seafood
Industry. Biloxi, Miss.
Center of a Fisherman's
Paradise. McCook, Neb.
Center of a Land of Enchant-
ment. Kalispell, Mont.
Center of a Lively Industrial
and Agricultural Trade
Area. Marshall, Mo.
Center of a Marvelous Natural
Playground. Lake City,
Mich.
Center of a Resort and Lum-
bering Area. Coeur d'Alene,
Idaho
Center of a Rich and Highly
Diversified Agricultural
Empire. Augusta, Ga.
Center of a Sportsman's
Paradise. Palm Beach,
Fla.
Center of a Vast Diversified
Recreation Area. Lodi, Calif.
Center of a Wonderful Area of
Opportunity. Galt, Calif.
Center of Activity. Angola,
Ind.
Center of Activity for All of
Southeastern Washington and
Northeastern Oregon. Walla
Walla, Wash.
Center of Activity for Ameri-
ca's Space Program. Cocoa
Beach, Fla.
Center of Agricultural, Com-
mercial, Industrial Oil Trans-
portation. Mattoon, Ill.
Center of Agriculture, Com-
merce, Industry Oil and
Transportation. Mattoon, Ill.
Center of All There Is to See
in the Upper Peninsula.
Marquette, Mich.
Center of All Vacation Fun.
Indio, Calif.
Center of All-Year Fun. Park
Rapids, Minn.

Center of Allegheny Valley's
Business and Industrial Ac-
tivity. New Kensington, Pa.
Center of America's Fastest
Growing Area. West Palm
Beach, Fla.
Center of America's Greatest
Market. Buffalo, N.Y.
Center of an Empire. Boise
City, Okla.
Center of California. Chowchilla,
Calif.
Center of California. Stockton,
Calif.
Center of Central Florida.
Astatula, Fla.
Center of Civic and Industrial
Opportunity. Wayne, Mich.
Center of Commerce. Elmira,
N.Y.
Center of Commerce. Pierre,
S.D.
Center of Commerce and Cul-
ture. Jackson, Miss.
Center of Commerce and In-
dustry. Allentown, Pa.
Center of Commerce and In-
dustry. Anaheim, Calif.
Center of Copiah, Mississippi's
Most Diversified County.
Hazlehurst, Miss.
Center of Culture. Pittsfield,
Mass.
Center of Distribution. Lynn,
Mass.
Center of Diversity. McFar-
land, Calif.
Center of Eastern Pennsylvania.
Mount Carmel, Pa.
Center of Eastern Steel Making.
Pittsburgh, Pa.
Center of Everything in Northern
Arizona. Flagstaff, Ariz.
Center of Florida. Tallahassee,
Fla.
Center of Florida's Exciting
West Coast. Tampa, Fla.
Center of Gooding County.
Wendell, Idaho
Center of Great Wealth. Pierre,
S.D.
Center of Historic Virginia.
Lynchburg, Va.

Center of History, Education
and Industry. Cambridge,
Mass.
Center of History in the
Making. Washington, D. C.
Center of Imperial Valley.
Holtville, Calif.
Center of Industrial and Atomic
Development. Buffalo,
N. Y.
Center of Industrial Develop-
ment in Western Connecti-
cut. Waterbury, Conn.
Center of Industry. Gary,
Ind.
Center of Industry. Tacoma,
Wash.
Center of Innovation and
Culture. Chicago, Ill.
Center of Innovative Tech-
nology. Santa Clara, Calif.
Center of Maine. Bangor,
Me.
Center of Mid-American In-
dustrial Progress. Joplin,
Mo.
Center of Midwest Apple Area.
Nebraska City, Neb.
Center of Midwest Friendli-
ness. Peoria, Ill.
Center of Montana's Wonder-
land. Butte, Mont.
Center of Nationwide Rail and
Truck Connections. At-
lantic, Iowa
Center of North Arizona's
Scenic Vacationland.
Flagstaff, Ariz.
Center of Northern Arizona's
Scenic Beauty. Winslow,
Ariz.
Center of Ohio's Sixth Metro-
politan Areas. Youngstown,
Ohio
Center of Old Virginia.
Lynchburg, Va.
Center of Our Nation's Play-
ground. Eustis, Fla.
Center of Prehistoric, His-
toric and Scenic Interest.
Santa Fe, N. M.
Center of Progress in Maine.
Pittsfield, Me.

Center of San Gorgonio Moun-
tains. Beaumont, Calif.
Center of Scenic America.
Salt Lake City, Utah
Center of Scenic Southeast
Alaska. Wrangell, Alaska
Center of Scenic Utah. Provo,
Utah
Center of Sixty-One Lakes.
Brighton, Mich.
Center of Sonoma Country's
Agri-Business Industry.
Petaluma, Calif.
Center of Southeast Alaska's
Vacationland. Petersburg,
Alaska
Center of Summer and Winter
Sports. Reno, Nev.
Center of the Action in the
Tremendous Houston-Gulf.
Coast. Alvin, Tex.
Center of the Aircraft Industry.
Grand Prairie, Tex.
Center of the Atlantic Seaboard
Megalopolis. Allentown, Pa.
Center of the Beautiful North
Shore of Massachusetts.
Salem, Mass.
Center of the Blue Grass Area.
Winchester, Ky.
Center of the Caladium Bulb
Growing Area. Lake Placid,
Fla.
Center of the Citrus Industry
for Southern California.
Glendora, Calif.
Center of the Coal Fields.
Appalachia, Va.
Center of the Dude Ranch In-
dustry. Sheridan, Wyo.
Center of the Flour Milling
Industry. Minneapolis, Minn.
Center of the Gogebic Iron
Range. Ironwood, Mich.
Center of the Great Kansas
Agricultural Empire. Abi-
lene, Kan.
Center of the Great Lakes of
Nebraska. McCook, Neb.
Center of the Greatest Manu-
facturing Area in the
South. Greensboro,
N. C.

Center of the Industrial North-
east. Youngstown, Ohio
Center of the Largest Eastern
Ski Area. North Conway,
N.H.
Center of the Louisiana Orange
Industry. Buras, La.
Center of the Marble Industry.
Rutland, Vt.
Center of the Megalopolis.
Manchester, N.Y.
Center of the Mid-Atlantic.
Norfolk, Va.
Center of the Midwest and
the Country. Des Moines,
Iowa
Center of the Most Important
Mining Area in the United
States. Ely, Nevada
Center of the Most Popular
Resort Section in the
Ozarks. Mountain Home,
Ark.
Center of the Most Productive
Agricultural Area in the
Nation. Dinuba, Calif.
Center of the Nation. Topeka,
Kan.
Center of the Nation's Greatest
Concentration of Varied
Natural Attractions. Pres-
cott, Ariz.
Center of the Northeast.
Harrisburg, Pa.
Center of the Olive Industry.
Corning, Calif.
Center of the Orange Empire.
Riverside, Calif.
Center of the Palm Beaches.
Riviera Beach, Fla.
Center of the Peach Industry.
Ceres, Calif.
Center of the Pineapple
Industry. Honolulu, Hawaii
Center of the Ranch-Resort
Country. Lake Luzerne,
N.Y.
Center of the Red River Valley
Bread Basket. Grafton,
N.D.
Center of the Rich Gas
and Sulphur Fields. Edge-
wood, Tex.

Center of the St. Lawrence
Valley Vacationland. Colton,
N.Y.
Center of the Sebago-Long Lake
Resort Region of Long Lake.
Naples, Me.
Center of the Sioux Uprising.
Redwood Falls, Minn.
Center of Space-age Metals
Development. Albany, Ore.
Center of the Southland. Bueno
Park, Calif.
Center of the Sponge Fishing
Industry. Tarpon Springs,
Fla.
Center of the Summer-Time
World in the Great North
Woods. Brant Lake, N.Y.
Center of the Sunshine State.
Ocala, Fla.
Center of the Sunshine State.
Pierre, S.D.
Center of the Universe. Duluth,
Minn.
Center of the Vast Inland Em-
pire. Spokane, Wash.
Center of the West. Thermo-
polis, Wyo.
Center of the World. New York,
N.Y.
Center of the World's Best
Market. Reading, Pa.
Center of the World's Biggest
Market. East Brunswick,
N.J.
Center of the World's Largest
Irrigation, Power Navigation
Flood Control Project.
Huron, S.D.
Center of the World's Magnet
Wire Production. Ft. Wayne,
Ind.
Center of the World's Potato
Empire. Caribou, Me.
Center of the World's Rubber
Manufacturing. Akron, Ohio
Center of the World's Tufted
Textile Industry. Dalton, Ga.
Center of Transportation to
All Points. San Mateo,
Calif.
Center of Unexcelled Water
Sports. Park Rapids, Minn.

Center of U.S. Jewelry Pro-
duction. Providence, R.I.
Center of Yavapai. Prescott,
Ariz.
Center of Year 'Round Recre-
ation. Jackson, Miss.
Center with Recreation for
Everyone. Redwood Falls,
Minn.
Central City. Syracuse, N.Y.
Central City of South Dakota.
Huron, S.D.
Central City of the Eastern
Shore. Salisbury, Md.
Central City of the Great
Southwest. Oklahoma City,
Okla.
Central City of the Metropoli-
tan Mississippi Gulf Coast.
Gulfport, Miss.
Central Florida's City of Big
Opportunity. Maitland, Fla.
Central Florida's Lake Region.
Winter Haven, Fla.
Central Florida's Most Desir-
able Residential Community.
Maitland, Fla.
Central Gateway of the Great
Lakes. Toledo, Ohio
Ceramic City. East Liver-
pool, Ohio
Cereal Food Center of the
World. Battle Creek,
Mich.
Cesspool for Gambling Joints.
Lake Tahoe, Calif.
Chair and Desk City. Jasper,
Ind.
Chair Capital of the World.
Gardner, Mass.
Chair Capital of the World.
Thomasville, N.C.
Chair Center of the World.
Union City, Pa.
Chair City. Gardner, Mass.
Chair City. Sheboygan, Wis.
Chair City. Thomasville,
N.C.
Champion City. Springfield,
Ohio
Channel City. Santa Barbara,
Calif.

Charm Circle of the South.
McComb, Miss.
Charm Spot of the Deep South.
Mobile, Ala.
Charmed Land of Unequalled
Beauty. Salem, Ore.
Charming Spot in which to Live
and Work. Norwalk, Conn.
Charter Oak City. Hartford,
Conn.
Chautauqua of the Great Lakes.
Lakeside, Ohio
Cheese Capital of the World.
Plymouth, Wis.
Cheese City. Sheboygan, Wis.
Cheese Storage Capital of the
World. Green Bay, Wis.
Chemical Capital of the World.
Wilmington, Del.
Chemical Capital of Virginia.
Hopewell, Va.
Chemical Center of the South.
Baton Rouge, La.
Chemical Center of the World.
South Charleston, W. Va.
Chemical City. Berlin, N.H.
Chemical City. Charleston,
W. Va.
Chemical City. Joplin, Mo.
Chemurgic City. Laurel,
Miss.
Cherokee-Indian Capital. Cal-
houn, Ga.
Cherry Capital of the World.
Traverse City, Mich.
Cherry City. Salem, Ore.
Cherry City. Traverse City,
Mich.
Cherry City of California.
San Leandro, Calif.
Cherry Tree City. Sturgeon
Bay, Wis.
Chi. Chicago, Ill.
Chicago of Nevada. Beatty,
Nev.
Chicago of the North. Anchorage,
Alaska
Chicago of the South. Okee-
chobee, Fla
Chicago of the Southwest. Fort
Worth, Tex.
Chicago of the West. Beatty,
Nev.

Chief City of the Bluegrass
Region. Lexington, Ky.
Chief City of West Virginia.
Wheeling, W. Va.
Chief Industrial City of the
Eastern Panhandle. Mar-
tinsburg, W. Va.
Chief Industrial City of the
South. Chattanooga, Tenn.
Chief Industrial Community
in Nevada. Henderson,
Nev.
Child of the Railroad. Rolla,
Mo.
Child of the River. St.
Louis, Mo.
Chili Capital of the World.
Terlingua, Tex.
Chimneyville. Jackson, Miss.
Chocolate City. Hershey, Pa.
Chocolate Crossroads of the
World. Hershey, Pa.
Chocolate Town. Hershey, Pa.
Chocolate Town, U.S.A.
Hershey, Pa.
Choice Place to Live and Work.
Nashville, Tenn.
Choicest Spot in All Florida.
Anna Maria, Fla.
Chosen Spot in the Beautiful
Finger Lakes. Canan-
daigua, N.Y.
Christiansville. Chase City,
Va.
Christmas City. Bethlehem,
Pa.
Christmas City. Minden, Neb.
Christmas City. Noel, Mo.
Christmas City. Taunton, Mass.
Christmas City of the U.S.A.
Bethlehem, Pa.
Christmas Town, U.S.A.
Shelton, Wash.
Christmas Tree Capital of the
Nation. Eureka, Mont.
Christmas Tree Capital of the
World. Eureka, Mont.
Christmas Tree Capital of the
World. Indiana, Pa.
Christmas Tree Town. West-
port, Conn.
Church Center. Nashville,
Tenn.

Church City. Brooklyn, N.Y.
Church City. Danville, Va.
Cigar Capital of America.
Tampa, Fla.
Cigar Capital of the World.
Key West, Fla.
Cigar City. Tampa, Fla.
Cinema Capital. Hollywood,
Calif.
Cinemaland. Hollywood, Calif.
Cinematown. Hollywood, Calif.
Cinema Village. Hollywood,
Calif.
Cinnabar Capitol. Terlingua,
Tex.
Circle City. Corona, Calif.
Circle City. Hollywood, Calif.
Circus Capital. Somers, N.Y.
Circus Capital of America in
the Nineteenth Century.
Delavan, Wis.
Circus City. Burley, Wash.
Circus City. Peru, Ind.
Circus City of the World. Peru,
Ind.
Circus Town, U.S.A. Gaines-
ville, Tex.
Circus Town, U.S.A. Hugo,
Okla.
Circus without a Tent. Los
Angeles, Calif.
Citadel of History. San Antonio,
Tex.
Citadel of the Confederacy.
Atlanta, Ga.
Citadel of the Old Northwest.
Vincennes, Ind.
Citrus Capital of the World.
Winter Haven, Fla.
Citrus Center. Cocoa, Fla.
Citrus Center of the World.
Winter Haven, Fla.
Citrus Metropolis. Los Angeles,
Calif.
City. New York, N.Y.
City Alive. New Rochelle, N.Y.
City Always Expanding. Morris-
town, Tenn.
City Among the Oaks. La Belle,
Fla.
City as Nice as Its Climate.
San Diego, Calif.

City at the Center of a World
of Famous Attractions.
Treasure Island, Fla.
City at the Crossroads Down
East. Ellsworth, Me.
City at the Crossroads of High
Diplomacy. New York,
N.Y.
City at the Crossroads of Holi-
day Highlands. Lake Alfred,
Fla.
City at the Crossroads of Mid-
America. Carthage, Mo.
City at the Crossroads of
Nebraskaland's Best Hunting
Country. York, Neb.
City at the Crossroads of
Texas. Mineral Wells, Tex.
City at the Crossroads of the
Empire State. Utica, N.Y.
City at the Crossroads of
Southwest Florida. La
Belle, Fla.
City at the Crossroads of the
Old and New South. Jack-
son, Miss.
City at the Crossroads of the
South. Memphis, Tenn.
City at the Crossroads of
Trans-America's Highway
and the Navajo Trail.
Alamosa, Colo.
City at the Gateway to New
England. Stratford, Conn.
City at the Headwaters of the
Mississippi River. Bemidji,
Minn.
City at the Heart of Industrial
New England. Holyoke, Mass.
City at the Portal to the Uni-
verse. Cocoa Beach, Fla.
City at the Tip of Cape Ann.
Rockport, Mass.
City at the Top in Florida.
Quincy, Fla.
City at the Top in Illinois.
Rockford, Ill.
City at the Top O'Texas.
Pampa, Tex.
City at the Water's Edge.
Stockton, Mo.
City Atop the Nation's Roof
Garden. Salida, Colo.

City Beautiful. Apopka, Fla.
City Beautiful. Birmingham,
Ala.
City Beautiful. Chicago, Ill.
City Beautiful. Coral Gables,
Fla.
City Beautiful. Dayton, Ohio
City Beautiful. Fort Lauder-
dale, Fla.
City Beautiful. Hartford, Conn.
City Beautiful. Hollywood,
Calif.
City Beautiful. Marshall, Mo.
City Beautiful. Memphis, Tenn.
City Beautiful. Milwaukee,
Wis.
City Beautiful. Nashville, Tenn.
City Beautiful. Nauvoo, Ill.
City Beautiful. New Richmond,
Wis.
City Beautiful. Orlando, Fla.
City Beautiful. Paris, Tex.
City Beautiful. San Francisco,
Calif.
City Beautiful. Tavares, Fla.
City Beautiful. Tulsa, Okla.
City Beautiful. Uvalde, Tex.
City Beautiful. Valley City,
N.D.
City Beautiful. Vernon, Tex.
City Beautiful. Washington,
D.C.
City Beautiful in the Heart of
Florida. Orlando, Fla.
City Beautiful in the Land O'
Lakes. Fergus Falls, Minn.
City Beautiful, Romantic and
Historic. Harrisburg, Pa.
City Beside the Broad Mis-
souri. Bismarck, N.D.
City Between the City and the
Sea. Forest Grove, Ore.
City Between the Mountains
and the Sea. Montebello,
Calif.
City Between the Sierras and
the Sea. Chowchilla, Cal.
City Big Enough for Oppor-
tunity - Small Enough for
Friendliness. Castro Valley,
Calif.
City Blessed in Many Ways.
Eau Claire, Wis.

City Building for Today and
Planning for Tomorrow.
Jesup, Ga.
City Built Around a Park.
San Diego, Calif.
City Built by Hands.
Rochester, N. Y.
City Built in a Day. Los
Angeles, Calif.
City Built on an Isthmus.
Madison, Wis.
City Built on Gambling. Las
Vegas, Nev.
City Built on Oil, Soil and
Toil. Ponca City, Okla.
City Built on Sand. Los
Angeles, Calif.
City Built on Yarn and Water.
Fall River, Mass.
City by Accident. Yoakum,
Tex.
City by the Bay. Mobile, Ala.
City by the Bay. San Fran-
cisco, Calif.
City by the Falls. Louisville,
Ky.
City by the Golden Gate. San
Francisco, Calif.
City by the Great Salt Lake.
Salt Lake City, Utah.
City by the Lake. Chicago, Ill.
City by the Lake. Coeur
d'Alene, Idaho
City-by-the-Sea. Asbury Park,
N. J.
City by the Sea. Charleston,
S. C.
City by the Sea. Long Beach,
Calif.
City by the Sea. Long Beach,
N. Y.
City by the Sea. Newport, R. I.
City by the Sea. Norfolk, Va.
City by the Sea. Perth Am-
boy, N. J.
City by the Sea. San Diego,
Calif.
City by the Sea. San Fran-
cisco, Calif.
City by the Sea. Santa Bar-
bara, Calif.
City by the Sea in Beautiful
Southeastern Alaska.
Sitka, Alaska

City by the Waccamaw. Con-
way, S. C.
City Care Forgot. New Orleans,
La.
City Centered in the Heart of
the Suncoast. Ruskin, Fla.
City Conducive to Education.
Richardson, Tex.
City Convenient to All Florida's
Attractions. Tarpon Springs,
Fla.
City Cooler by a Mile. Avalon,
N. J.
City Cosmopolitan. San Fran-
cisco, Calif.
City Dedicated to Growth and
Prosperity. Augusta, Kans.
City Dedicated to Industrial De-
velopment. Sweetwater, Tex.
City Deep in the Heart of Texas.
Dallas Tex.
City Designed for Living. Santa
Rosa, Calif.
City Destined by Its Site for
Prosperity. Pittsburg, Calif.
City Destined to be One of the
Great Cities of the Southeast.
Chesapeake, Va.
City Destined to Lead Southern
Oklahoma. Ada, Okla.
City Different. Santa Fe, N. M.
City Down on the Mesabi.
Aurora, Minn.
City "Electric" with Growth and
Change. Brownsville, Tex.
City Excitingly Alive and Pro-
gressive. Pittsburgh, Pa.
City Famous for Friendliness.
Malone, N. Y.
City Fast-Growing, Diversified.
Lancaster, Pa.
City for a Pleasant Way of
Life. Dixon, Calif.
City for a Vacation of a Life-
time. Elk Rapids, Mich.
City for a Vacation or a Life-
Time of Real Living. Eustis,
Fla.
City for All Seasons. Mobile,
Ala.
City for All Seasons. Norfolk,
Va.
City for All Seasons. Phila-
delphia, Pa.

City for All Seasons of the Year. Tulsa, Okla.

City for Business and Industry. Delano, Calif.

City for Education and Research. Morris, Minn.

City for Every Vacation Pleasure. Whitehall, Mich.

City for Everybody. Washington, D. C.

City for Family Fun and Action. Dubuque, Iowa

City for Family Fun in the Florida Sun. Lake Weir, Fla.

City for Family Living at Its Best. Hialeah, Fla.

City for Fishing and Hunting. Auburn, Neb.

City for Family People. Ocean City, N. J.

City for Fun in the Sun. Oak Bluffs, Mass.

City for Golf, Fishing, Hunting. Oxford, Miss.

City for Gracious Living. Chula Vista, Calif.

City for Living. St. Petersburg, Fla.

City for Oceans of Fun. Santa Monica, Calif.

City for Reasonable Living with Plenty of Elbow Room. Port St. Joe, Fla.

City for Recreation and Relaxation. Walford City, N. D.

City for Romantics. San Francisco, Calif.

City for Summer or Winter Vacation. Park Rapids, Minn.

City for Summer Vacation and All Year. Wildwood, N. J.

City for Swimming and Motor Sports. Oxford, Miss.

City for the Full Life. Berlin, N. H.

City for the Future. Delano, Calif.

City for Water Sports. Auburn, Neb.

City for Work, Life or Pleasure. Stratford, Conn.

City for Year Round Fishing Variety. Pompano Beach, Fla.

City Forty Miles at Sea. Orleans, Mass.

City Founded Upon Cooperation. Winston-Salem, N. C.

City Four Dimensional. Lexington, N. C.

City From Trail Bust to Star Dust. Johnstown, Pa.

City Geared to Space-Age Families. Slidell, La.

City Growing Out of Yesterday into Tomorrow. Joplin, Mo.

City Growing with Agriculture, Industry and Education. Turlock, Calif.

City Growing with Plastics. Beaverton, Mich.

City Half a World from the "Hubbub". Denton, Tex.

City Half an Hour from the Hub. Denton, Tex.

City Historical and Enjoyable. Ogdensburg, N. Y.

City in a Forest. Washington, D. C.

City in a Rich Agricultural Area. Vincennes, Ind.

City in a Valley where Recuperation, Rehabilitation, Rest and Relaxation with Recreation and Scenic Beauty Abound. Hot Springs, S. D.

City in Arizona's Valley of the Sun. Phoenix, Ariz.

City in Beautiful Bay County. Panama City, Fla.

City in Beautiful Northeast Texas. Paris, Tex.

City in California's Lush Sacramento Valley. Orland, Calif.

City in Central California Convenient to Everything. Oakdale, Calif.

City in Florida with a Difference. Delray Beach, Fla.

City in Florida's Fun-Filled Holiday Highlands. Fort Meade, Fla.

City in Maine's Blue Mountain
Region. Farmington, Me.
City in Maryland's Historic
Heartland. Frederick, Md.
City in Motion. Monrovia,
Calif.
City in Otter Tail County.
Fergus Falls, Minn.
City in Pace with the Space
Age. Blacksburg, Va.
City in Step with Tomorrow.
Stamford, Conn.
City in the Agriculturally
Rich Red River Valley.
Crookston, Minn.
City in the Beautiful Shenan-
doah Valley. Winchester,
Va.
City in "The Big Horns".
Sheridan, Wyo.
City in the Center of Hunting
Lands. Pierre, S.D.
City in the Center of Mid-
America's Riviera Year
'Round Resort. Gulfport,
Miss.
City in the Center of New
England. Winchendon,
Mass.
City in the Center of San
Joaquin Valley. Merced,
Calif.
City in the Center of Sunland.
Groveland, Fla.
City in the Center of the
Beautiful North Woods.
Park Falls, Wis.
City in the Center of the
Most Amazing and Beautiful
Country in the World.
Flagstaff, Ariz.
City in the Center of the White
Mountains. Glen, N.H.
City in the Center of Things.
Columbia, Mo.
City in the Center where the
Action Is. Gulfport, Miss.
City in the Clouds. Denver,
Colo.
City in the Country. Dan-
bury, Conn.
City in the Country. Holyoke,
Mass.

City in the Country by the
Sea. Beverly, Mass.
City in the Evergreen Play-
ground. Portland, Ore.
City in the Famous Thermal
Belt of North Carolina.
Tryon, N.C.
City in the Florida Keys.
Islamorada, Fla.
City in the Forest. Lansing,
Mich.
City in the Garden of the Sun.
Bowie, Ariz.
City in the Garden of the Sun.
Exeter, Calif.
City in the Garden of the Sun.
Lindsay, Calif.
City in the Heart of America's
Future. Arlington, Tex.
City in the Heart of Arizona
Vacationland. Mesa, Ariz.
City in the Heart of California.
Merced, Calif.
City in the Heart of Central
Florida's Water Wonderland.
Eustis, Fla.
City in the Heart of Coconino
National Forest. Flagstaff,
Ariz.
City in the Heart of Colorful
Napa Valley. St. Helena,
Calif.
City in the Heart of Eastern
America. St. Helena, Calif.
City in the Heart of Florida.
Haines City, Fla.
City in the Heart of Florida's
Citrus, Phosphate, Recrea-
tion, History, Cattle. Fort
Meade, Fla.
City in the Heart of Florida's
Gulf Fishing. Carrabelle,
Fla.
City in the Heart of Florida's
Future. Quincy, Fla.
City in the Heart of Florida's
"Tall Country". Quincy,
Fla.
City in the Heart of Industrial
America. McKeesport, Pa.
City in the Heart of Industrial
America. Mansfield, Ohio
City in the Heart of Irrigation.

Gering, Neb.
City in the Heart of Kaskasie
Valley. Shelbyville, Ind.
City in the Heart of Maine's
Vacationland. Millinocket,
Me.
City in the Heart of Massa-
chusetts Vacationland.
Worcester, Mass.
City in the Heart of Missis-
sippi's Rich Delta. Green-
wood, Miss.
City in the Heart of North-
west Florida's Miracle
Strip. Destin, Fla.
City in the Heart of Penn-
sylvania Dutch Country.
Lancaster, Pa.
City in the Heart of Roger
Babson's Magic Circle.
Arkansas City, Kans.
City in the Heart of South
Central Louisiana. Lafa-
yette, La.
City in the Heart of Southside
Virginia. Victoria, Va.
City in the Heart of Sunny
North Dakota. Garrison,
N.D.
City in the Heart of the
Anadarko Basin. Elk City,
Okla.
City in the Heart of "The
Big Horns". Sheridan,
Wyo.
City in the Heart of the Big
Mountain Country. Lander,
Wyo.
City in the Heart of the Cattle
and Corn Country. Atlantic,
Iowa
City in the Heart of the Che-
quamegon National Forest.
Park Falls, Wis.
City in the Heart of the Citrus
Area. Lake Alfred, Fla.
City in the Heart of the Citrus
Belt and Holiday Highlands.
Auburndale, Fla.
City in the Heart of the
Coastal Sea Islands.
Beaufort, S.C.
City in the Heart of the

Daytona Beach Resort Area.
Holly Hill, Fla.
City in the Heart of the Dy-
namic Cape Kennedy Area.
Palm Bay, Fla.
City in the Heart of the East
Texas Oil Fields. Glade-
water, Tex.
City in the Heart of the Ever-
glades. Clewiston, Fla.
City in the Heart of the Finger
Lakes. Trumansburg, N.Y.
City in the Heart of the Gold
Coast. Deerfield, Fla.
City in the Heart of the Great
New Central Florida Vaca-
tionland. Plant City, Fla.
City in the Heart of the Heart-
land. Moberly, Mo.
City in the Heart of the Irri-
gated Platte Valley. Gothen-
burg, Neb.
City in the Heart O' the Hills.
Kerrville, Tex.
City in the Heart of the Kas-
kasie Valley. Shelbyville,
Ill.
City in the Heart of the Lakes
Region. Laconia, N.H.
City in the Heart of the
Miracle Strip. Destin, Fla.
City in the Heart of the Na-
tion's Famous Dude Ranch
Country. Billings, Mont.
City in the Heart of the Na-
tion's Sunniest State. Wins-
low, Ariz.
City in the Heart of the Ouachi-
tas. Glenwood, Ark.
City in the Heart of the Pied-
mont Crescent. Belmont,
N.C.
City in the Heart of the Pine
Ridge. Crawford, Neb.
City in the Heart of the Piney
Woods of East Texas.
Nacogdoches, Tex.
City in the Heart of the Shenan-
doah Valley of Virginia.
Winchester, Va.
City in the Heart of the South-
west Wonderland. Wilcox,
Ariz.

City in the Heart of the
World Famous Indian River
Citrus Country. Fort
Pierce, Fla.
City in the Heart of Two
Hundred and Fifty Sparkling
Lakes and Streams. Grand
Rapids, Mich.
City in the Heart of Western
Ranch Land. Pierre, S.D.
City in the Lake District of
the Adirondacks. Speculator,
N.Y.
City in the Land of Chief
Wabasis. Belding, Mich.
City in the Land of Friend-
ship. Chanute, Kans.
City in the Land of Lakes.
St. Paul, Minn.
City in the Land of the Pines.
Aiken, S.C.
City in the Land of the Sky.
Asheville, N.C.
City in the Middle of Every-
where. North Platte,
Neb.
City in the Mountain Country.
Billings, Mont.
City in the Northeast Kingdom.
Newport, Vt.
City in the Pines. Flagstaff,
Ariz.
City in the Shadow of the Big
Horn. Sheridan, Wyo.
City in the Shadow of the
Famed Hillsboro Light.
Pompano Beach, Fla.
City in the Sky. Asheville,
N.C.
City in the Southwest Sun
Country. El Paso, Tex.
City in the Sun. San Antonio,
Tex.
City in the Valley of Discovery.
San Marcos, Calif.
City in the Valley of Oppor-
tunity. Evansville, Ind.
City in the Valley of Promise.
Mishawaka, Ind.
City in the Valley of the
Arkansas. Salida, Colo.
City in the Valley of the Sun.
Glendale, Ariz.

City in the Very Heart of New
England. Manchester, N.H.
City in the White Mountains.
Berlin, N.H.
City in Touch with Tomorrow.
Minneapolis, Minn.
City Industrially Sound and
Historically Great. Peters-
burg, Va.
City Just a Step from the Past,
in Step with the Present and
Stepping Toward the Future.
New London, Conn.
City Just for Fun. Ocean
City, Md.
City Keyed to Your Way of
Living. El Cerrito, Calif.
City Landscaped for Living,
Dedicated to Progress.
Napa, Calif.
City Living in Rural Atmosphere.
Norco, Calif.
City Located in Florida's Sun-
coast Area. Tarpon Springs,
Fla.
City Located in the Heart and
Center of Vermont. Water-
bury, Vt.
City Located in the Heart of
Virginia's Industry. Colonial
Heights, Va.
City Located in the Very Heart
of Florida. De Land, Fla.
City Metropolis. Los Angeles,
Calif.
City Most Convenient to
All Florida. Plant City,
Fla.
City Nature Has Endowed with
Beauty. Avon Park, Fla.
City Nearer to Everywhere in
Florida. Lakeland, Fla.
City 'Neath the Hills. Madi-
son, Ind.
City Next to the Greatest City
in the World. Yonkers,
N.Y.
City Noted for Diversification.
Mattoon, Ill.
City of a Colorful Past and a
Promising Future. Water-
ford, Calif.

City of a Hundred Hills.
San Francisco, Calif.
City of a Thousand Sights.
St. Louis, Mo.
City of a Thousand Thrills.
Washington, D. C.
City of Abundant Cultural Ac-
tivities. Orlando, Fla.
City of Achievement. Decatur,
Ala.
City of Action. Riverbank,
Calif.
City of Advantages. Dear-
born, Mich.
City of Advantages. Racine,
Wis.
City of Agriculture. Beatrice,
Neb.
City of Agriculture and
Industry. Lodi, Calif.
City of Agriculture and Recrea-
tion. Livingston, Cal.
City of Angels. Los Angeles,
Calif.
City of Angels. San Angelo,
Tex.
City of Ante-Bellum Homes.
Washington, Ga.
City of Attractions. Sarasota,
Fla.
City of Baked Beans. Boston,
Mass.
City of Balance. Fort Smith,
Ark.
City of Balanced Economy.
Exeter, Calif.
City of Bean Eaters. Boston,
Mass.
City of Beautiful Churches.
Augusta, Ga.
City of Beautiful Churches.
Louisville, Ky.
City of Beautiful Churches,
Homes and Buildings.
Florence, Ala.
City of Beautiful Heights.
Fort Worth, Tex.
City of Beautiful Hilltop Views.
Pittsburgh, Pa.
City of Beautiful Homes.
Augusta, Ga.
City of Beautiful Homes.
Boise, Idaho

City of Beautiful Homes. Chow-
chilla, Cal.
City of Beautiful Homes.
Crossett, Ark.
City of Beautiful Homes.
Dunedin, Fla.
City of Beautiful Homes.
Rockford, Ill.
City of Beautiful Homes and
Thriving Industry. Atlanta,
Ga.
City of Beautiful Homes and
Thriving Industry. Madison,
Wis.
City of Beautiful Lakes. Ana-
heim, Calif.
City of Beautiful Parks. Fort
Collins, Colo.
City of Beautiful Parks.
Wheeling, W. Va.
City of Beautiful Parks and
Lovely Homes. Atwater,
Calif.
City of Beautiful Parks and
Playgrounds. Atlantic, Iowa
City of Beautiful Trees and
Ideal Climate. Walla Walla,
Wash.
City of Beauty. Branford, Fla.
City of Beauty. Brunswick, Ga.
City of Beauty. Davenport,
Iowa
City of Beauty. Dayton, Ohio
City of Beauty. Montgomery,
Ala.
City of Beauty. Muskogee,
Okla.
City of Beauty and Unlimited
Opportunities. Elyria, Ohio
City of Beauty, Industry, Sports,
Education. Columbus, Ohio
City of Beauty on the Suwannee
River. Branford, Fla.
City of Beauty, Progress and
Culture. Provo, Utah
City of Better Living. Colum-
bus, Ind.
City of Bicycles. Homestead,
Fla.
City of Black Diamonds. Scran-
ton, Pa.
City of Boulevards. Los Angeles,
Calif.

City of Brick. Pullman, Ill.
City of Bridges. Logansport, Ind.
City of Bridges. Pittsburgh, Pa.
City of Bridges. San Francisco, Calif.
City of Brotherly Love. Philadelphia, Pa.
City of Business. Niagara Falls, N. Y.
City of Business and Industry. Corona, Cal.
City of Business and Industry. Youngstown, Ohio
City of Camellias. McComb, Miss.
City of Camellias. Pensacola, Fla.
City of Camping and Hunting. Fergus Falls, Minn.
City of Captains' Houses. Newburyport, Mass.
City of Central Location. Lodi, Calif.
City of Certainties. Des Moines, Iowa
City of Chance. Las Vegas, Nev.
City of Change. Odessa, Tex.
City of Character in a Land of Beauty. Arcadia, Fla.
City of Charm. Greensboro, N. C.
City of Charm. New Orleans, La.
City of Charming Houses. Lynchburg, Va.
City of Cheese, Chairs, Children and Churches. Sheboygan, Wis.
City of Childhood. Mooseheart, Ill.
City of Choice Industrial Sites. Osawatomie, Kan.
City of Churches. Anniston, Ala.
City of Churches. Blytheville, Ark.
City of Churches. Brooklyn, N. Y.
City of Churches. Charleston, S. C.
City of Churches. Charlotte, N. C.
City of Churches. Danville, Va.
City of Churches. Ozark, Ala.
City of Churches. Philadelphia, Pa.
City of Churches. Shreveport, La.
City of Churches. Springfield, Ill.
City of Churches. Wilkinsburg, Pa.
City of Churches of All Faiths. Crookston, Minn.
City of Churches of All Faiths. Crossett, Ark.
City of Churches of All Faiths. Greenville, Ill.
City of Cities. New York, N. Y.
City of Civic Pride. Corona, Cal.
City of Civic Pride. Riverbank, Calif.
City of Classic Architecture. Lodi, Calif.
City of Clean Industry. Tarpon Springs, Fla.
City of Coal Kings. Uniontown, Pa.
City of Colonial Charm. Norwalk, Conn.
City of Colorful Traditions of the Mediterranean with the Best in Florida Fun. Tarpon Springs, Fla.
City of Commerce. Gustine, Cal.
City of Community Facilities. Lodi, Calif.
City of Community Pride. Ceres, Calif.
City of Concord. Concordia, Kan.
City of Conflict. Louisville, Ky.
City of Contrast and Romance. San Antonio, Tex.
City of Contrasts. Boston, Mass.
City of Contrasts. Huntsville, Ala.

City of Contrasts. New Orleans, La.
City of Contrasts. Newport, R. I.
City of Contrasts. Pittsburgh, Pa.
City of Contrasts. Pompano Beach, Fla.
City of Contrasts. San Antonio, Tex.
City of Contrasts. Seward, Alaska
City of Contrasts. Syracuse, N. Y.
City of Convention Facilities. Lawton, Okla.
City of Conventions. Syracuse, N. Y.
City of Conventions. Wichita, Kan.
City of Conversation. Washington, D. C.
City of Cows, Colleges and Contentment. Northfield, Minn.
City of Cultural, Educational and Recreational Opportunities for All. Youngstown, Ohio
City of Culture. Pittsfield, Mass.
City of Culture and Entertainment. St. Louis, Mo.
City of Culture, History, Industry. Winston-Salem, N. C.
City of Cypress Gardens. Winter Haven, Fla.
City of David. Sioux City, Iowa
City of Delight. Fort Worth, Tex.
City of Destiny. Detroit, Mich.
City of Destiny. Duluth, Minn.
City of Destiny. Las Vegas, Nev.
City of Destiny. Panama City, Fla.
City of Destiny. Tacoma, Wash.
City of Distinction. Sioux City, Iowa
City of Diversified Agriculture. Milan, Tenn.

City of Diversified Farming. Garrison, N. D.
City of Diversified Industries. Amsterdam, N. Y.
City of Diversified Industries. Columbus, Miss.
City of Diversified Industries. Holyoke, Mass.
City of Diversified Industries. Marietta, Ohio
City of Diversified Industries. Vincennes, Ind.
City of Diversified Industries. Worcester, Mass.
City of Diversified Industries and Civic Achievement. York, Pa.
City of Diversified Industry. Ellwood City, Pa.
City of Diversified Industry. Kingsport, Tenn.
City of Diversified Industry. Ogden, Utah
City of Diversified Industry. St. Cloud, Minn.
City of Diversified Industry. Salem, Ore.
City of Diversified Industry and Agriculture. Amarillo, Tex.
City of Diversified Industry and Commerce. Erie, Pa.
City of Diversified Interests. Nashville, Tenn.
City of Diversified Opportunity. Atwater, Calif.
City of Diversified Opportunity. Dixon, Calif.
City of Diversified Products. Elyria, Ohio
City of Diversified Recreation. Atwater, Calif.
City of Diversified Recreation. Napa, Calif.
City of Diversity. Tampa, Fla.
City of Dreadful Joy. Los Angeles, Calif.
City of Dreams. Odessa, Tex.
City of Dreams. Salida, Colo.
City of Dynamic Opportunity. Concord, Calif.
City of Economic Progress. Sweetwater, Tex.

City of Eight Beautiful Churches.
Morris, Minn.
City of Elegance. Mesquite,
Tex.
City of Elms. Chicopee, Mass.
City of Elms. New Haven,
Conn.
City of Elms. Sheboygan, Wis.
City of Established Industry.
Chanute, Kans.
City of Eternal Views.
Seattle, Wash.
City of Excellence in Living.
Fullerton, Calif.
City of Excellent Educational
Opportunities. Vacaville,
Calif.
City of Excellent Schools
Among Friendly People.
Ripon, Calif.
City of Exceptional Beauty.
Riverside, Calif.
City of Exceptional Transpor-
tation and Power Facilities.
Crookston, Minn
City of Excitement. Los
Angeles, Calif.
City of Exciting Contrasts.
Barrow, Alaska
City of Executives. Birming-
ham, Ala.
City of Expanding Industry.
Nampa, Idaho
City of Extraordinary Health-
Care Services. St. Cloud,
Minn.
City of Extremes. Chicago,
Ill.
City of Falling Water. Fall
River, Mass.
City of Families, Faith and
Friendship. Apopka, Fla.
City of Family Fun in the
Sun. Sea Island City, N.J.
City of Fine Educational Insti-
tutions. Rome, Ga.
City of Fine Homes. Midland,
Tex.
City of Fine Homes and
Streets. Lima, Ohio
City of Fine Homes,
Churches and Schools.
Dickinson, Tex.

City of Fine Homes, Churches
and Schools. Jackson, Miss.
City of Fine Hotels. Tacoma,
Wash.
City of Fine Schools. Chow-
chilla, Cal.
City of Fine Schools. Niagara
Falls, N.Y.
City of Fine Schools. Vin-
cennes, Ind.
City of Firsts. Boston, Mass.
City of Firsts. Kokomo, Ind.
City of Firsts. Oregon City,
Ore.
City of Firsts. Philadelphia,
Pa.
City of Firsts. San Francisco,
Calif.
City of Five Flags. Mobile,
Ala.
City of Five Flags. Pensacola,
Fla.
City of Five-Score Industries.
Waltham, Mass.
City of Flaming Adventure.
San Antonio, Tex.
City of Flour. Buffalo, N.Y.
City of Flourishing Industries.
Schenectady, N.Y.
City of Flowers. Los Angeles,
Calif.
City of Flowers. Montebello,
Calif.
City of Flowers. Princeton,
Minn.
City of Flowers. Springfield,
Ill.
City of Flowers and Sunshine.
Los Angeles, Calif.
City of Flowing Gold. Ranger,
Tex.
City of Fountains. Kansas
City, Mo.
City of Fountains. Milwaukee,
Wis.
City of Fountains. Pueblo,
Colo.
City of Four C's. Sheboygan,
Wis.
City of Four Glorious Seasons.
Hendersonville, N.C.
City of Four National Pro Teams.
Pittsburgh, Pa.

City of Friendliness and Beauty. Riverside, Calif.

City of Friendliness, Culture and Traditions. Lynchburg, Va.

City of Friendly Folks. Hastings, Neb.

City of Friendly Folks. Newberry, S.C.

City of Friendly People. Nacogdoches, Tex.

City of Friendly People. New York, N.Y.

City of Friendly People. Rochester, N.H.

City of Friendly People. Walla Walla, Wash.

City of Friendly People and Nice Homes. Waukon, Iowa

City of Fun and Frolic. Atlantic City, N.J.

City of Future Magnificence. Detroit, Mich.

City of Galloping Tintypes. Hollywood, Calif.

City of Gardens. Montebello, Calif.

City of Giant Industry. Rochester, N.Y.

City of Gigantic Industries, Unparalleled Schools. Pine Bluff, Ark.

City of Golden Dreams. New York, N.Y.

City of Golf, Beautiful Parks. Crookston, Minn.

City of Good Government. Atwater, Calif.

City of Good Health, Living and Business. Upland, Calif.

City of Good Homes. Wyandotte, Mich.

City of Good Living. Anaheim, Calif.

City of Good Living. St. Petersburg, Fla.

City of Good Living. San Carlos, Calif.

City of Good Living. Slidell, La.

City of Good Neighbors. Buffalo, N.Y.

City of Good Schools. Concordia, Kans.

City of Good Schools and Churches. Waukon, Iowa

City of Good Water. Buckley, Wash.

City of Governors. Bellefonte, Pa.

City of Governors. Huntsville, Ala.

City of Governors. Rochester, N.H.

City of Gracious Living. El Cerrito, Calif.

City of Gracious Living. Houston, Tex.

City of Gracious Living. Huntsville, Ala.

City of Gracious Living. Sanford, Fla.

City of Gracious Living. Thomasville, Ga.

City of Gracious Living. Winter Park, Fla.

City of Gracious Living. Yonkers, N.Y.

City of Great Industry. Rochester, N.Y.

City of Great Men and Great Times. Richmond, Va.

City of Growing Industrial Activity. Altus, Okla.

City of Growing Industrial and Commercial Importance. Vicksburg, Miss.

City of Growing Industries. New Kensington, Pa.

City of Growing Industry. Ceres, Calif.

City of Happy Homes. Grand Rapids, Mich.

City of Healing Waters. Hot Springs, S.D.

City of Health. San Rafael, Calif.

City of Health and Recreation. Atlantic City, N.J.

City of Health and Recreation. Thermopolis, Wyo.

City of Health, History,

Hospitality. Tombstone,
Ariz.
City of Heat. Thermopolis,
Wyo.
City of Hills. Lynchburg, Va.
City of Hills. Oneonta, N.Y.
City of Hills. Somerville,
Mass.
City of Historic Beauty.
Penobscot, Me.
City of Historic Charm. De
Pere, Wis.
City of Historic Lore. Wheel-
ing, W. Va.
City of Historical Charm.
Savannah, Ga.
City of Historical Heritage.
Fayetteville, N.C.
City of Historical Interest.
Osawatomie, Kan.
City of History. Muskogee,
Okla.
City of History and Culture.
Chesapeake, Va.
City of History and Industry.
Sallisaw, Okla.
City of History and Romance.
Charleston, S.C.
City of History and Romance.
Monterey, Calif.
City of History, Culture, Edu-
cation, Industry. Winston-
Salem, N.C.
City of Holy Faith. Santa
Fe, N.M.
City of Home Owners. Al-
toona, Pa.
City of Home Owners. She-
boygan, Wis.
City of Homes. Albany, Calif.
City of Homes. Albany, Ga.
City of Homes. Atlanta, Ga.
City of Homes. Auburn, Me.
City of Homes. Brooklyn, N.Y.
City of Homes. Buffalo, N.Y.
City of Homes. Dallas, Tex.
City of Homes. Fort Lauder-
dale, Fla.
City of Homes. Fort Myers,
Fla.
City of Homes. Lakewood, Ohio
City of Homes. Louisville,
Ky.

City of Homes. Milwaukee,
Wis.
City of Homes. Montebello,
Calif.
City of Homes. Newnan, Ga.
City of Homes. Niagara Falls,
N.Y.
City of Homes. Norwalk, Conn.
City of Homes. Philadelphia, Pa.
City of Homes. Port Arthur, Tex.
City of Homes. Portland, Ore.
City of Homes. Richmond
Heights, Mo.
City of Homes. Rochester, N.Y.
City of Homes. Royal Oak,
Mich.
City of Homes. St. Petersburg,
Fla.
City of Homes. Salem, Mass.
City of Homes. Seattle, Wash.
City of Homes. Somerville,
Mass.
City of Homes. Springfield,
Mass.
City of Homes. Vero Beach,
Fla.
City of Homes. Winter
Haven, Fla.
City of Homes. Winter Park,
Fla.
City of Homes and Diversified
Industries. West Allis, Wis.
City of Homes and Gracious
Living. Melrose, Mass.
City of Homes and Industry.
East Point, Ga.
City of Homes and Industry.
Pueblo, Colo.
City of Homes and Parks.
Burlington, Vt.
City of Homes, Churches and
Fine Schools. Moscow,
Idaho
City of Homes, Education and
Industry. Washington, Pa.
City of Homes, Schools and
Churches. Yoakum, Tex.
City of Hospitality. Anderson,
S.C.
City of Hospitality. Decatur,
Ala.
City of Hospitality. Fullerton,
Calif.

City of Hospitality. Galveston, Tex.

City of Hospitality. Memphis, Tenn.

City of Hospitality and Charm. Plant City, Fla.

City of Houses without Streets. Washington, D. C.

City of Huguenots. New Rochelle, N. Y.

City of Hundred Lakes. Winterhaven, Fla.

City of Illusion. Virginia City, Nev.

City of Individuality and Charm. Riverside, Calif.

City of Industrial and Commercial Opportunities. Fort Wayne, Ind.

City of Industrial Opportunity. Benicia, Calif.

City of Industrial Opportunity. Helena, Ark.

City of Industrial Opportunity. Napa, Calif.

City of Industrial Opportunity. Petersburg, Va.

City of Industrial Opportunity. Warren, Pa.

City of Industrial Peace. Garfield, N. J.

City of Industrial Potentialities. Moundsville, W. Va.

City of Industrial Progress. St. Cloud, Minn.

City of Industrial Sites. Greenville, Ill.

City of Industry. Beatrice, Neb.

City of Industry. Dayton, Ohio

City of Industry. Kerman, Calif.

City of Industry. Minneapolis, Minn.

City of Industry. Montebello, Calif.

City of Industry. Newark, N. J.

City of Industry. Newburyport, Mass.

City of Industry. Niagara Falls, N. Y.

City of Industry. Visalia, Calif.

City of Industry. Wichita, Kan.

City of Industry, Agriculture and Recreation. Chowchilla, Calif.

City of Industry, Agriculture, Education, Patriotism, Scenic Beauty and Civic Pride. Defiance, Ohio

City of Industry and Agriculture. Exeter, Calif.

City of Industry and Agriculture. Gustine, Calif.

City of Industry and Industrial Development. Atwater, Calif.

City of Industry and Industrial Sites. Crookston, Minn.

City of Industry and Opportunity. Lynchburg, Va.

City of Industry and Transportation. Blytheville, Ark.

City of Industry in the Land of Sage and Sun. Rock Springs, Wyo.

City of Industry, Recreation, Business. Oshkosh, Wis.

City of Inspiration. Washington, D. C.

City of Inspiring Church Activities. Atwater, Calif.

City of Insurance Interests. Fort Worth, Tex.

City of Investments where Commerce and Industry Thrive. Long Beach, Calif.

City of Islands. New York, N. Y.

City of Isms. Syracuse, N. Y.

City of Kind Hearts. Boston, Mass.

City of Lake Worth where the Fun Begins. Lake Worth, Fla.

City of Lakes. Fort Worth, Tex.

City of Lakes. La Porte, Ind.

City of Lakes. Lakeland, Fla.

City of Lakes. Minneapolis, Minn.

City of Lakes and Mills. Minneapolis, Minn.

City of Lakes and Parks.
Madison, So. Dak.
City of Lakes and Parks.
Minneapolis, Minn.
City of Lakes, Fishing,
Boating, Swimming.
Moberly, Mo.
City of Land, Water, Oppor-
tunity and Prosperity.
Kerman, Calif.
City of Learning. St. Louis,
Mo.
City of Light. New York,
N. Y.
City of Lights. Fort Morgan,
Colo.
City of Liquid Gold. Hastings,
Neb.
City of Liquid Sunshine. Los
Angeles, Calif.
City of Little Wedding Churches.
Las Vegas, Nev.
City of Living and Learning.
Claremont, Calif.
City of Little Men. Boys
Town, Neb.
City of Live Oaks, Columbus,
Tex.
City of Lost Footsteps. Wash-
ington, D. C.
City of Lovely Gardens. Harts-
ville, S. C.
City of Luck. Las Vegas, Nev.
City of Magic. Lowell, Mass.
City of Magic. Muncie, Ind.
City of Magic. Schenectady,
N. Y.
City of Magic Islands and Water-
ways. Miami Beach, Fla.
City of Magnificent Churches,
Beautiful Homes. Pine Bluff,
Ark.
City of Magnificent Distances.
Washington, D. C.
City of Magnificent Mountains.
Fort Collins, Colo.
City of Magnificent Stores.
Wheeling, W. Va.
City of Magnolias. Houston, Tex.
City of Make Believe. Los
Angeles, Calif.
City of Manageable Size.
Memphis, Tenn.

City of Manifold Advantages.
Augusta, Me.
City of Many Adventures. San
Francisco, Calif.
City of Many Churches. Gar-
rison, N. D.
City of Many Cities. Chicago,
Ill.
City of Many Cultural Advan-
tages. Marietta, Ohio
City of Many Industries.
Rochester, N. Y.
City of Mineral Springs. San
Bernardino, Calif.
City of Mines. Victor, Colo.
City of Miracles. San Fran-
cisco, Calif.
City of Missions. San Antonio,
Tex.
City of Modern Building and
Industry. Moberly, Mo.
City of Modern Industry.
Greenville, Ill.
City of Modern Schools. At-
water, Calif.
City of Modern Schools. Gar-
rison, N. D.
City of Modern Schools. Green-
ville, Ill.
City of Modern Schools and
Recreation. Kerman, Calif.
City of Molly Pitcher. Carlisle,
Pa.
City of Monuments. Richmond,
Va.
City of Nails. Wheeling, W. Va.
City of Natural Wonders. La
Jolla, Calif.
City of Neighbors. Garland, Tex.
City of New World Vigor. Mil-
waukee, Wisc.
City of Notions. Boston, Mass.
City of Oaks. Bartow, Fla.
City of Oaks. Raleigh, N. C.
City of Oaks. Tuscaloosa, Ala.
City of Oaks and Azaleas. Bar-
tow, Fla.
City of Old World Charm. Mil-
waukee, Wisc.
City of One Hundred Hills. San
Francisco, Calif.
City of One Hundred Lakes.
Winter Haven, Fla.

City of One Hundred Lakes
and Streams. Superior,
Wis.

City of One Thousand Lakes.
Oklahoma City, Okla.

City of Opportunities. Brunswick, Ga.

City of Opportunities. Miami,
Fla.

City of Opportunities. Saginaw,
Mich.

City of Opportunities. Salt
Lake City, Utah

City of Opportunity. Akron,
Ohio

City of Opportunity. Albany,
Ga.

City of Opportunity. Bowling
Green, Ohio

City of Opportunity. Bristol,
Conn.

City of Opportunity. Charles
City, Iowa

City of Opportunity. Chesapeake, Va.

City of Opportunity. Cleveland,
Miss.

City of Opportunity. Conway,
Ark.

City of Opportunity. Dallas,
Tex.

City of Opportunity. Evansville, Ind.

City of Opportunity. Manchester, N.H.

City of Opportunity. Memphis,
Tenn.

City of Opportunity. Minneapolis, Minn.

City of Opportunity. Montgomery, Ala.

City of Opportunity. Nashville,
Tenn.

City of Opportunity. Oshkosh,
Wis.

City of Opportunity. Wahoo,
Neb.

City of Opportunity, Recreation,
Retirement. Warsaw, Mo.

City of Orchestras. New York,
N.Y.

City of Orchids. Hilo, Hawaii

City of Orderly Growth. Salem,
Ore.

City of Outstanding Educational
Advantages. Florence, Ala.

City of Palms. Fort Myers,
Fla.

City of Palms. McAllen, Tex.

City of Palms. Pharr, Tex.

City of Panoramic Boulevards.
Fort Collins, Colo.

City of Paper. Camas, Wash.

City of Parks. Madison, Wis.

City of Parks. Merrill, Wis.

City of Parks, Hospitals and
Churches. Chowchilla, Calif.

City of Paul Revere. Boston,
Mass.

City of Peace. Salem, Mass.

City of Peace and Plenty. Pine
Bluff, Ark.

City of Peaches. Brigham City,
Utah

City of Peaches. Fort Valley,
Ga.

City of Penn. Philadelphia, Pa.

City of People. Demopolis, Ala.

City of Permanent Homesites.
Tarpon Springs, Fla.

City of Personality. Cincinnati,
Ohio

City of Picturebook Bayous.
Tarpon Springs, Fla.

City of Pine, Potatoes and
People. Aroostook, Me.

City of Pines and Flowers.
Dothan, Ala.

City of Planned Progress.
Pleasanton, Calif.

City of Playgrounds and Recreation. Crookston, Minn.

City of Pleasant Living. Pensacola, Fla.

City of Pleasant Living and
Industry. Watertown, N.Y.

City of Pleasant Memories.
Jacksonville, Fla.

City of Plentiful Civic Services.
Livingston, Calif.

City of Plentiful Plains. Fort
Collins, Colo.

City of Presidents. Quincy,
Mass.

City of Pride. Muncie, Ind.

City of Pride and Progress.
San Pablo, Calif.

City of Progress. Dayton, Ohio

City of Progress. Detroit, Mich.

City of Progress. Dubuque, Iowa

City of Progress. Edgewater, Fla.

City of Progress. Jesup, Ga.

City of Progress. Konawa, Okla.

City of Progress. North Bend, Ore.

City of Progress. Reading, Pa.

City of Progress. Springfield, Ohio

City of Progress. Statesville, N.C.

City of Progress. Titusville, Fla.

City of Progress. Youngstown, Ohio

City of Progress and Contrasts. Kansas City, Mo.

City of Progress and Opportunity. Midland, Tex.

City of Progress and Opportunity. Phenix City, Ala.

City of Progress and Prosperity. Oakland, Calif.

City of Progress and Security. Hawthorne, Calif.

City of Progress, Our Past and Our Future. Audubon, Iowa

City of Progress with Pride and Purpose. Marshalltown, Iowa

City of Progressive Outlook. Buffalo, N.Y.

City of Promise. Baltimore, Md.

City of Prosperity. Worcester, Mass.

City of Pure Water. Zephyrhills, Fla.

City of Quality Products. Rochester, N.Y.

City of Rare Beauty and Tranquility. Santa Barbara, Calif.

City of Receptions. Washington, D.C.

City of Recreation. Delano, Calif.

City of Recreation. Fergus Falls, Minn.

City of Recreation and Culture. Omaha, Neb.

City of Recreation and Parks. Arvada, Colo.

City of Recreation for All Ages. Corona, Calif.

City of Relaxed Living. Ripon, Calif.

City of Research. Stamford, Conn.

City of Resources. Santa Ana, Calif.

City of Rich Cultural and Residential Charm. Jackson, Miss.

City of Rivers and Hills. Cincinnati, Ohio

City of Rocks. Nashville, Tenn.

City of Romance and Rebellion. Richmond, Va.

City of Roses. Cape Girardeau, Mo.

City of Roses. Holly Springs, Miss.

City of Roses. Jackson, Mich.

City of Roses. Little Rock, Ark.

City of Roses. Lovell, Wyo.

City of Roses. Metropolis, Ill.

City of Roses. New Castle, Ind.

City of Roses. Pana, Ill.

City of Roses. Paramount, Calif.

City of Roses. Pasadena, Calif.

City of Roses. Portland, Ore.

City of Roses. Thomasville, Ga.

City of Rugs. Amsterdam, N.Y.

City of Salt. Syracuse, N.Y.

City of Santa Anita. Arcadia, Calif.

City of Scenic Beauty. Orlando, Fla.

City of Scenic Beauty. Riverbank, Calif.

City of Scenic Marvels.
Niagara Falls, N.Y.
City of Schools. Ceres, Calif.
City of Science. Norwalk,
Conn.
City of Sculpture. Waupun,
Wis.
City of Secession. Charleston, S.C.
City of Seclusion. Seldovia,
Alaska
City of Serene Living. Laguna
Beach, Calif.
City of Seven Hills. Brooksville, Fla.
City of Seven Hills. Richmond,
Va.
City of Seven Hills. Rome,
Ga.
City of Seven Hills. Seattle,
Wash.
City of Seven Valleys. Cassville, Mo.
City of Seven Wonders. Flagstaff, Ariz.
City of Shady Walks and Pleasant
Lawns. Dayton, Wash.
City of Ships and Shipbuilding.
Newport News, Va.
City of Shoes. Brockton, Mass.
City of Shoes. Lynn, Mass.
City of Six Flags. Mobile, Ala.
City of Skyscrapers. New York,
N.Y.
City of Smiles. Superior, Wis.
City of Smokestacks. Everett,
Wash.
City of Soles. Lynn, Mass.
City of Solid Comfort. Penobscot, Me.
City of Southern Charm. Savannah, Ga.
City of Southern Friendliness
and Charm. Gonzales, La.
City of Sparkling Blue Lakes.
Avon Park, Fla.
City of Spas. Ashland, Ore.
City of Spindles. Lowell,
Mass.
City of Springs. Neosho, Mo.
City of Stars. Brisbane, Calif.
City of Steel. Pittsburgh, Pa.
City of Straits. Detroit, Mich.

City of Streets without Houses.
Washington, D.C.
City of Sucessful Diversified
Industry. Utica, N.Y.
City of Sun and Fun, Sand 'N
Sea. Old Orchard Beach,
Me.
City of Sunshine. Colorado
Springs, Colo.
City of Sunshine. Fort Lauderdale, Fla.
City of Sunshine. Los Angeles,
Calif.
City of Sunshine. Tucson,
Ariz.
City of Sunshine and Silver.
Tombstone, Ariz.
City of Superlatives. Chicago,
Ill.
City of the Annual Easter
Pageant. Lawton, Okla.
City of the Atom. Oak Ridge,
Tenn.
City of the Belles. Bellefonte,
Pa.
City of the Big Shoulders.
Chicago, Ill.
City of the Carillon. Lake
Wales, Fla.
City of the Continental Divide.
Britton, S.D.
City of the Dams. Azusa,
Calif.
City of the Falls. Louisville,
Ky.
City of the First Automobile.
Kokomo, Ind.
City of the French. St. Louis,
Mo.
City of the Friendly People.
Apalachicola, Fla.
City of the Future. Cape Coral,
Fla.
City of the Future. Columbia,
Md.
City of the Future. Kansas
City, Mo.
City of the Future. New Haven,
Conn.
City of the Gauls. Gallipolis,
Ohio
City of the Golden Gate. San
Francisco, Calif.

City of the Great Smokies.
Knoxville, Tenn.
City of the Green Light.
Eau Claire, Wis.
City of the Hour. Dallas,
Tex.
City of the Lakes. Chicago,
Ill.
City of the Lakes. Laconia,
N.H.
City of the Lakes and Prairies.
Chicago, Ill.
City of the Longest Sunday.
Pittsburgh, Pa.
City of the Mardi Gras. New
Orleans, La.
City of the Mills. Cohoes,
N.Y.
City of the Modern South.
Atlanta, Ga.
City of the Mountain Peaks.
San Luis Obispo, Calif.
City of the Northland. Su-
perior, Wis.
City of the People. Demopolis,
Ala.
City of the Plains. Abilene,
Kan.
City of the Plains. Childress,
Tex.
City of the Plains. Denver,
Colo.
City of the Plains. Sacra-
mento, Calif.
City of the Plains. Syracuse,
N.Y.
City of the Saints. Salt Lake
City, Utah
City of the Seven Hills. Rome,
Ga.
City of the Slain. Arlington,
Va.
City of the South. Durham,
N.C.
City of the Straits. Detroit,
Mich.
City of the Sun. Newport, N.H.
City of the Twin Spires.
Ripon, Wis.
City of the Unburied Dead.
St. Petersburg, Fla.
City of the Unexpected. Pitts-
burgh, Pa.

City of the Violet Crown.
Austin, Tex.
City of the World. New York,
N.Y.
City of 13 Highways. Hawkins-
ville, Ga.
City of 35,000 Hotel Rooms.
Chicago, Ill.
City of Three Capitals. Little
Rock, Ark.
City of Thriving Industries.
Wheeling, W. Va.
City of Tobacco. Quincy, Fla.
City of Tomorrow. Baltimore,
Md.
City of Towers. New York,
N.Y.
City of Tradition. Memphis,
Tenn.
City of Transformations.
Chelsea, Mass.
City of Trees. Boise, Idaho
City of Trees. Buffalo, N.Y.
City of Trees. Forsyth, Mont.
City of Trees. Los Altos,
Calif.
City of Trees. Marmarth, N.D.
City of Trees. Sacramento,
Calif.
City of Trees. Sterling, Ill.
City of Trees without Houses.
Washington, D.C.
City of Tulips. Holland, Mich.
City of Twentieth Century
America. Detroit, Mich.
City of 250,000 Trees. Pitts-
burgh, Pa.
City of Unexcelled Opportunities
for Business and Industry.
Salem, Ore.
City of Uninterrupted Electric
Power. Holyoke, Mass.
City of Unparalleled Recrea-
tional Facilities. Pico
Rivera, Calif.
City of Unspoiled Beaches.
Tarpon Springs, Fla.
City of Unusual Charm. En-
cinitas, Calif.
City of Varied Industries.
Fremont, Ohio
City of Varied Industries.
Milano, Tex.

City of Varied Industries.
Rochester, N. Y.
City of Varied Industry.
Manteca, Calif.
City of Village Charm. Man-
chester, Conn.
City of Washington. Wash-
ington, D. C.
City of Water and Agriculture.
Ceres, Calif.
City of Water, Land and
Good Climate. Waterford,
Calif.
City of Western Charm and
Hospitality. Fort Worth,
Tex.
City of Wheat. Kansas City,
Mo.
City of White Sandy Beaches.
Avon Park, Fla.
City of Winds. Chicago, Ill.
City of Winter and Water
Sports. Fergus Falls,
Minn.
City of Witches. Salem,
Mass.
City of Wonderful Living with
Industrial Prosperity.
Parkersburg, W. Va.
City of Wonderful Water.
Stevens Point, Wis.
City of Year-Around Recrea-
tion. Augusta, Me.
City of Year-Round Recrea-
tional Opportunities. Or-
lando, Fla.
City of Young Men. Sum-
merville, Ga.
City of Your Future. Fort
Smith, Ark.
City of Your Future. Nor-
walk, Conn.
City of Youth, Industry,
Recreation. Lone Star,
Tex.
City on a Mountain. Duluth,
Minn.
City on Florida's Enchanting
West Coast. St. Peters-
burg, Fla.
City on Florida's Famous East
Coast and the Indian River.
Edgewater, Fla.

City on Florida's West Coast.
Tarpon Springs, Fla.
City on Seven Hills. Alton,
Ill.
City on Seven Hills. Cincin-
nati, Ohio
City on the Banks of the Scenic
Cumberland River. Carthage,
Tenn.
City on the Banks of the Wa-
bash. Vincennes, Ind.
City on the Border by the Sea.
Brownsville, Tex.
City on the Chester. Chester-
town, Md.
City on the Cool Gulf Coast.
Panama City, Fla.
City on the Crest. Long Branch,
N. J.
City on the Crossroads of the
Expressways. Foxboro,
Mass.
City on the Dan. Danville, Va.
City on the Go. Jacksonville,
N. C.
City on the Go. Montclair,
Calif.
City on the Golden Hills. San
Francisco, Calif.
City on the Grow. Edinburg,
Tex.
City on the Grow. Kerrville,
Tex.
City on the Grow. San Benito,
Tex.
City on the Grow. Shreveport,
La.
City on the Grow. Waco, Tex.
City on the Gulf. Naples, Fla.
City on the Gulf of Mexico.
St. Petersburg Beach, Fla.
City on the Highway of Pro-
gress. Colonial Heights, Va.
City on the Highway to Heaven.
Salida, Colo.
City on the Hill. Paris, Me.
City on the James. Richmond,
Va.
City on the Lakes. Laconia,
N. H.
City on the Lazy Blue Waters
of the Gulf of Mexico.
Longboat Key, Fla.

City on the Mississippi where
the Old South Still Lives.
Natchez, Miss.
City on the Move.   Denton,
Tex.
City on the Move.   Macon, Ga.
City on the Move.   Oak Ridge,
Tenn.
City on the Move.   Rockmart,
Ga.
City on the Move.   Salina, Kan.
City on the Move.   Van Buren,
Ark.
City on the Move with a Glowing
Future Dedicated to Gracious
Living. Allentown, Pa.
City on the Ozarks Frontier
Trail. Ellington, Mo.
City on the Square.   Madison,
Wis.
City on the Top of the Rockies.
Anaconda, Mont.
City on the Trail of the Lone-
some Pine. Tazewell, Va.
City on the Willamette.   Port-
land, Ore.
City Planned for Perfect Living.
Coral Gables, Fla.
City Planners' Dream.   Alton,
Ill.
City Pledged to Progress.
Peoria, Ill.
City Pointing the Way for
Industry.   East Brunswick,
N.J.
City Practical that Vision Built.
Longview, Wash.
City Preserving Its Heritage,
Planning the Promise of
the Future.   Palo Alto, Calif.
City Pretty as a Picture Post
Card. Ithaca, N.Y.
City Programmed for Progress.
Palm Bay, Fla.
City Progressive.   Greens-
burg, Pa.
City Proud of Its Heritage.
Palo Alto, Calif.
City Proud of Its Historic
Treasures.   Santa Barbara,
Calif.
City Proud of Its History.
Vicksburg, Miss.

City Proud of the Past and
Preparing for the Future.
Portsmouth, Ohio
City Ready for Tomorrow.
Jonesboro, Ark.
City Reborn.   Pittsburgh, Pa.
City Rich in History.   Morris-
town, Tenn.
City Rich in History with a
Wealth of Charm.   Win-
chester, Va.
City Rich in Tradition and Op-
portunity.   Springfield, Mass.
City Rich in Western Tradition.
Prescott, Ariz.
City Right in the Center of
Things.   Pompano Beach,
Fla.
City Serving the Industrial
Farming Commercial Heart
of America.   Toledo, Ohio
City Set on a Hill.   Angwin,
Calif.
City Situated in Strategic North-
West Louisiana.   Bossier
City, La.
City Substantial.   Frankfort,
Ind.
City Surrounded by Great Rec-
reational Opportunities.
Oakdale, Calif.
City that Balks at Changes.
Memphis, Tenn.
City that Belongs to the World.
New York, N.Y.
City that Built Its Seaport.
Houston, Tex.
City that Came Back.   Alton, Ill.
City that Charms.   Ontario,
Calif.
City that Climate Built.   San
Clemente, Calif.
City that Cooperates.   Cleveland,
Ohio
City that Does Things.   Norfolk,
Va.
City that Has a Future Because
It Has a Plan.   Ottumwa,
Iowa
City that Has Everything.
Sarasota, Fla.
City that Has Everything for En-
joyable Living. Tavares, Fla.

City that Has Everything for
Everyone--Anytime. Las
Vegas, Nev.
City that Has Everything for
Industry. Jersey City,
N.J.
City that Has Everything
Under the Sun. Phoenix,
Ariz.
City that Has It All. Lake-
wood, Colo.
City that Has It Now. Tulsa,
Okla.
City that Has Something for
You. Stockton, Calif.
City that Has the Resources to
Fit Your Business Needs.
Indianapolis, Ind.
City that Holds the Key to
Mid-America. Keokuk,
Iowa
City that Is. Salinas, Calif.
City that Is Attracting New
Industry. Keokuk, Iowa
City that Is Big Enough to
Serve You, Yet Small
Enough to Know You. Con-
cordia, Kan.
City that Is Big Enough to
Serve You, Yet Small
Enough to Know You.
Dickinson, N.D.
City that Is Friendly, Pro-
gressive, Alive. Enderlin,
N.D.
City that Is Just for Fun.
Palm Springs, Calif.
City that Is Near Everything.
Atwater, Calif.
City that Is Only Two Hours
to the Sierras or the Sea.
Modesto, Calif.
City that Is Still a Frontier
Town. Las Vegas, Nev.
City that Knows How. San
Francisco, Calif.
City that Knows where It Is
Going. El Cerrito, Calif.
City that Lights and Hauls
the World. Schenectady,
N.Y.
City that Lost Its Magic.
Washington, D.C.

City that Means Business and
the Good Life Too. Jack-
son, Miss.
City that Never Sleeps. Las
Vegas, Nev.
City that Never Sleeps. New
York, N.Y.
City that Progress Built.
Fayetteville, Ark.
City that Puts Business on the
Go. Harrisburg, Pa.
City that Salt Built. Syracuse,
N.Y.
City that Saved the Union.
Virginia City, Nev.
City that Says Welcome Neigh-
bor. Madison, S.D.
City that Smiles Back. Corinth,
Miss.
City that Started with a Plan.
Margate, Fla.
City that Swings Twenty-four
Hours a Day. Las Vegas,
Nev.
City that Trees Built. Berlin,
N.H.
City that Turned Back Time.
Williamsburg, Va.
City that Works. Chicago, Ill.
City that's a Study in Contrasts.
Pompano Beach, Fla.
City that's 'Dublin' Daily. Dub-
lin, Ga.
City that's Looking Ahead.
Richmond, Va.
City that's Scenic, Busy and
Friendly. Clifton Forge, Va.
City the Depression Passed Up.
Bronson, Mich.
City there's a Lot to Like About.
Ocean City, Md.
City Thriving from the Fertile
Banks of Ole Man River.
Dyersburg, Tenn.
City Time Forgot. Galena, Ill.
City to Grow with. Lone Star,
Tex.
City to Watch. Minneapolis,
Minn.
City Too Busy to Hate. At-
lanta, Ga.
City Way Down Upon the Suwan-
nee River. Cross City, Fla.

City where a New South Is in
the Making. Jackson, Miss.

City where a Wealth of Pleasure
Awaits You Spring or Sum-
mer, Fall or Winter.
Tampa, Fla.

City where Advantages Abound
for Business. Salem, Ore.

City where Agriculture and
Industries Meet. Tracy,
Calif.

City where Agriculture and
Industry Meet. Fremont,
Neb.

City where Ambition Meets
Opportunity. Livonia,
Mich.

City where America Began in
the West. Monterey, Calif.

City where American Independence Began. Quincy,
Mass.

City where Beer Is Famous.
Milwaukee, Wis.

City where Business and
Friendship Thrive. Sanford,
N. C.

City where Business and Happy
Living Flourish. Ogden,
Utah

City where Business and In-
dustry Thrive and People
Enjoy a Wide Variety of
Year Around Recreation.
Athens, Tenn.

City where California and
Mexico Meet the Blue
Pacific. San Diego, Calif.

City where California Began.
Sacramento, Calif.

City where California Began.
San Diego, Calif.

City where Civic Pride is
City-Wide. Carrabelle, Fla.

City where Coal and Iron
Meet. Toledo, Ohio

City where Coal Meets Iron.
Ashland, Ky.

City where Commerce,
Farming, Industry and
Education Thrive Together.
Blair, Neb.

City where Cotton Is King.
Blytheville, Ark.

City where Dixie Welcomes
You. Corinth, Miss.

City where Everybody Catches
Fish. Destin, Fla.

City where Families Enjoy
Florida Living in a Beautiful
and Historic Setting. Quincy,
Fla.

City where "Fish Are Jumpin'
and the Livin' Is Easy".
Stockton, Mo.

City where Florida's Tropics
Begin. Vero Beach, Fla.

City where Folks Are Not Too
Busy to Be Friendly.
Bowling Green, Ky.

City where Friendly People
Get Together. Fort Morgan,
Col.

City where Fun and History
Meet the Sea. Virginia
Beach, Va.

City where Gambling Reigns
Supreme. Las Vegas, Nev.

City where Game in Its Wild
State Abounds. Stockton, Mo.

City where Good Living Is the
Custom. Lynchburg, Va.

City where Gracious Living and
Fine Churches Offer a Life
of Contentment for Businessman, Worker, Retired and
the Sportsman. El Dorado
Springs, Mo.

City where Great East Texas
Meets the Sea. Beaumont,
Tex.

City where Growth Has Become
a Habit. Odessa, Tex.

City where "Growth" Is in High
Gear. Hudson, Mass.

City where Historic Pride and
Civic Progress Unite in the
Industrial and Cultural Heart
of Northwest Florida.
Quincy, Fla.

City where History and Progress
Join Hands. Nacogdoches,
Tex.

City where History Blends with
Progress. Salem, Mass.

City where Historic Yesterday
Greets Dynamic Tomorrow.
Bingham, Me.
City where Historic Yesterday
Greets Dynamic Tomorrow.
Moscow, Me.
City where Hospitality Is a
Tradition. Santa Barbara,
Calif.
City where Hospitality Never
Ceases. Henderson, N. C.
City where Hospitality of the
South Begins. Florence,
Ky.
City where Independence Was
Born. Yorktown, Va.
City where Industrial and Agri-
cultural Activities Are
Blended with Dairying and
Livestock Production.
Columbus, Miss.
City where Industry, Agri-
culture, and Cultural Life
All Balance. Tupelo, Miss.
City where Industry and Educa-
tion Meet. Blacksburg, Va.
City where Industry and Recrea-
tion Meet. Palatka, Fla.
City where Industry Enjoys
Modern Utilities, Abundant
Labor, Favorable Taxes
and Good Government.
Quincy, Fla.
City where Industry Finds a
Favorable Climate. Lake-
land, Fla.
City where Industry Is First.
Pontiac, Mich.
City where Industry Is Wanted
and Growing. Chula Vista,
Calif.
City where Industry Makes a
Good Neighbor. South San
Francisco, Calif.
City where Industry Profits.
Atmore, Ala.
City where Industry Prospers,
You Will Too. Nazareth,
Pa.
City where Industry Thrives.
Watertown, N. Y.
City where It's June in

January Along the Romantic
Apache Trail. Mesa, Ariz.
City where Lakes and Moun-
tains Meet. Knoxville, Tenn.
City where Land and Water
Meet. Annapolis, Md.
City where Life Is Different.
Biddeford, Me.
City where Life Is Different.
Saco, Me.
City where Life Is Different.
San Antonio, Tex.
City where Life Is Lived Every
Day of the Year. Engle-
wood, Fla.
City where Life Is Worth
Living. Dania, Fla.
City where Living Is Delightful.
Sarasota, Fla.
City where Main Street Meets
the River and Joins Main
Street Mid-America. Green-
ville, Miss.
City where Main Street Meets
the World. Beaumont, Tex.
City where Men and Mountains
Meet. Denver, Colo.
City where Mexico Meets Uncle
Sam. Brownsville, Tex.
City where Modern America
Began. Lawrence, Mass.
City where Mountains and Plains
Meet. Boulder, Colo.
City where Nature Smiles and
Progress Has the Right of
Way. Bulloch Crossroads,
Ga.
City where Nature Smiles the
Year 'Round. Fortuna, Calif.
City where Nineteenth Century
America Lives. Petersburg,
Va.
City where North and South
Meet East and West. Salina,
Kan.
City where North and South
Meet East and West. Sedalia,
Mo.
City where Oil and Water Mix.
Lovington, N. M.
City where Oil and Water Mix.
Powell, Wyo.

City where Oil Flows, Gas Blows and Glass Glows. Okmulgee, Okla.

City where Past and Future Make a Prosperous Present. San Rafael, Calif.

City where People Are Happy and Industry Flourishes. East Point, Ga.

City where People Like People. Sweetwater, Tex.

City where People Like to Live. Homer, Alaska

City where People Play and Prosper. Manhattan, Kan.

City where Pleasure Begins. West Palm Beach, Fla.

City where Potatoes Are King. Antigo, Wis.

City where Progress and Pleasures Are Partners. Douglas, Ariz.

City where Progress Is Our Constant Endeavor. Emporia, Kans.

City where Progress Profits Growth. Leavenworth, Kan.

City where Rail Meets Water. Kalama, Wash.

City where River, Air, Rail and Highway Meet. Decatur, Ill.

City where Scenic Grandeur, History, Legend and a Bustling Modern Economy Are Blended into Everyday Life. Sitka, Alaska

City where She Danced. Salome, Ariz.

City where Skiing Is an Adventure. Sunapee, N.H.

City where Southern Hospitality Begins. Portsmouth, Ohio

City where Spring Spends the Summer. Superior, Wis.

City where Spring Spends the Winter. Asheville, N.C.

City where Strangers Become Friends. Wareham, Mass.

City where Summer Winters. Chandler, Ariz.

City where Summer Winters. Phoenix, Ariz.

City where Summers Are Mild and Winters Are Warm. National City, Calif.

City where Texas Meets the Sea. Corpus Christi, Tex.

City where the Accent Is on Family. Independence, Kan.

City where the Action Is. Atlantic City, N.J.

City where the Action Is. Bethlehem, Pa.

City where the Action Is. Reno, Nev.

City where the Action Is. Shelbyville, Ill.

City where the Adirondacks Meet Lake Champlain. Westport, N.Y.

City where the American Tropics Begin. Fort Meyers, Fla.

City where the Atomic Age Dawned. Alamogordo, N.M.

City where the Blue Ridge Parkway Joins the Skyline Drive. Waynesboro, Va.

City where the Breezes Blow. Jamestown, R.I.

City where the Charm, Culture and Tradition of the Old South Blend in a Modern City. Natchez, Miss.

City where the Contemporary Combines with the Historic. Marshall, Texas

City where the Delta Begins. Yazoo City, Miss.

City where the Discovery Is People. Vail, Colo.

City where the Far East Meets the Far West. San Francisco, Calif.

City where the Fight for Texas Liberty Begins. Gonzales, Tex.

City where the Fun Begins and Never Ends. Las Vegas, Nev.

City where the Fun of Living Comes "Naturally". La Belle, Fla.

City where the Golfing's Great. Midland, Tex.

City where the Heritage of the Past Lends Warmth to the Present. Guilford, Conn.

City where the History of the West Begins. Fort Leavenworth, Kan.

City where the Hospitality of the Old West Remains. Sidney, Neb.

City where the Industrial East Meets the Agricultural West. Sioux City, Iowa

City where the Land Meets the Water. Wareham, Mass.

City where the Mighty Smithy Stands. Birmingham, Ala.

City where the Mississippi Becomes Mighty. St. Cloud, Minn.

City where the Mountain Meets the Sea. Santa Monica, Calif.

City where the Mountains Meet the Sea. Camden, Me.

City where the Mountains Meet the Sea. Port Angeles, Wash.

City where the Mountains Meet the Sky. Bluefield, W. Va.

City where the North Begins. Harrison, Mich.

City where the North Begins. Portage, Wis.

City where the North Begins and the Pure Waters Flow. White Cloud, Mich.

City where the Old and the New Combine. Quincy, Fla.

City where the Old Has Given Way to the New. Pittsburgh, Pa.

City where the Old Meets the New. Plymouth, Mass.

City where the Old South and the New South Meet. Jackson, Miss.

City where the Old South Still Lives. Natchez, Miss.

City where the Old Spanish Trail Crosses the Suwannee River. White Springs, Fla.

City where the Ozarks Meet the Plains. Lowry City, Mo.

City where the Palms Meet the Sea. Miami Beach, Fla.

City where the Partridge Finds a Refuge. Bena, Minn.

City where the Pines Meet the Sea. Virginia Beach, Va.

City where the Prairie Meets the Sea. Duluth, Minn.

City where the Rails and the Trails Begin. Lander, Wyo.

City where the Redwoods Meet the Sea. Santa Cruz, Calif.

City where the Rio Grande Valley Begins. Edinburg, Tex.

City where the Rodeo Was Born. North Platte, Neb.

City where the Santa Fe Trail of the Prairies Meets the Mountains of the Historical West. Trinidad, Colo.

City where the Sea Starts. Baton Rouge, La.

City where the Seaway Meets the Thruway. Rochester, N.Y.

City where the Seaway Meets the Turnpike. Toledo, Ohio

City where the Shenandoah National Park Begins. Front Royal, Va.

City where the Skyline Drive Begins. Front Royal, Va.

City where the South Begins at the Gateway to the Beautiful Shenandoah Valley. Winchester, Va.

City where the Southeast Gets Its Money. Charlotte, N.C.

City where the Space Age Began. Alamogordo, N.M.

City where the Story of the West Began. Leavenworth, Kans.

City where the Summer Spends the Winter. St. George, Utah

City where the Summer Trails Begin. Bay City, Mich.

City where the Sun Beams Brighter with "Ole" Florida's Hospitality. Plant City, Fla.

City where the Sun Ripens the Fruits of Prosperity. Livingston, Calif.

City where the Sun Spends the Winter. Pismo Beach, Calif.

City where the T-Bone Special Starts. Audubon, Iowa

City where the Trail Ends and the Sea Begins. Homer, Alaska

City where the Trail Meets Rail. Burlingame, Kan.

City where the Trees Meet the Sea. Boothbay Harbor, Me.

City where the Tropics Begin. Lake Worth, Fla.

City where the Welcome's Warm as the Sunshine. Miami Beach, Fla.

City where the West Begins. Davenport, Iowa

City where the West Begins. Fort Worth, Tex.

City where the West Begins. Independence, Mo.

City where the West Begins. Williston, N. D.

City where the West Remains. Sheridan, Who.

City where the Wild West Kicks Up Its Heels. Medora, N. D.

City where the Wilderness Begins. Ely, Minn.

City where the World Bathes and Plays. Hot Springs, Ark.

City where the World Comes to Play and Enjoy Life. Palm Springs, Calif.

City where There Are No Strangers ... Just New Friends. York, Neb.

City where There Is Always Something to Do and See Under Sunny Skies. Tucson, Ariz.

City where There's Fun for Everyone. Denver, Colo.

City where There's Room to Stretch. Waterford, Calif.

City where There's Something for Everyone. Springfield, Mass.

City where They Come to Play and Decide to Stay. Clearwater, Fla.

City where Things Are Happening. Waterbury, Conn.

City where Things Are Shipshape and Bristol Fast. Bristol, R. I.

City where Tradition Lingers. Marblehead, Mass.

City where Tradition Meets Progress. Princeton, Ill.

City where Train and Plane Meet. Columbus, Ohio

City where Vermont Begins. Brattleboro, Vt.

City where Visitors Meet Hospitality. Lawrence, Mass.

City where Water Means Pleasure, Progress and Prosperity. Orange, Tex.

City where We Fly 360 Days a Year. Amarillo, Tex.

City where Wheat Grows and Oil Flows. Pampa, Tex.

City where Wheat Is King. Davenport, Wash.

City where Wilshire Boulevard Meets the Pacific. Santa Monica, Calif.

City where Winter Wears a Tan. Tucson, Ariz.

City where Work and Play Are Only Minutes Away. Palatka, Fla.

City where Year-Round Living Is a Pleasure. Chula Vista, Calif.

City where Yesterday Meets Tomorrow. Mystic, Conn.

City where You Can Have Fun and Live Better. Belleview, Fla.

City where You Can Live and Enjoy Life. Pass Christian, Miss.

City where You Can Live in the City Limits and Be on the Lake. Stockton, Mo.

City where You Can Work,
Live, Play, the Western
Way. Yuma, Ariz.
City where You Enjoy the
Best Things in Life. Ocean
City, N. J.
City where You Have the
Splendor of Four Seasons.
Stockton, Mo.
City where You Work and
Play the Same Day.
Sarasota, Fla.
City where Your Dream Vaca-
tion Can Become a Reality.
Yankton, S. D.
City where Your Dreams of
Florida Living Come True.
Hallandale, Fla.
City where Your Ship Comes In.
Gulfport, Miss.
City where Your Ship Will Come
In. Corpus Christi, Tex.
City where Your Vacation
Dreams Are Fulfilled.
Pompano Beach, Fla.
City where Your Vacation
Dreams Take Shape.
Hampton Beach, N. H.
City which Looks to the Future
with a Great Deal of Happy
Anticipation. Galt, Calif.
City which Tops the World for
Sunshine and Sociability.
Chula Vista, Calif.
City with a Big Future. Chow-
chilla, Calif.
City with a Blend of Two
Cultures and Two Counties.
Brownsville, Tex.
City with a Blending of Past
and Present on the Banks of
the Merrimac. Newbury-
port, Mass.
City with a Blueprint for Civic
and Industrial Improvement.
Fort Madison, Iowa
City with a Blueprint for Living.
Murfreesboro, Tenn.
City with a Bright Future.
Slidell, La.
City with a Built-in Future.
Sunnyvale, Calif.

City with a Difference. Tucson,
Ariz.
City with a Fascinating History.
Pittsburg, Calif.
City with a Future. Bartles-
ville, Okla.
City with a Future. Blooming-
ton, Minn.
City with a Future. Cape Coral,
Fla.
City with a Future. Dallas,
Tex.
City with a Future. Greensburg,
Ind.
City with a Future. Greenwood,
Miss.
City with a Future. Gulfport,
Miss.
City with a Future. Henderson,
N. C.
City with a Future. Jamestown,
N. D.
City with a Future. Palatka,
Fla.
City with a Future. Port St.
Joe, Fla.
City with a Future. San Bruno,
Calif.
City with a Future. Trenton,
Mo.
City with a Future. Waukesha,
Wis.
City with a Future. Westfield,
Mass.
City with a Future for All In-
dustry. Victoria, Tex.
City with a Future to Share.
Altus, Okla.
City with a Future to Share.
Glendive, Mont.
City with a Future Unlimited.
Downey, Calif.
City with a Great Civic Pride
and a Sound Business Cli-
mate. Alexander City, Ala.
City with a Great Future.
Fostoria, Ohio
City with a Great Past and a
Great Future. Nacogdoches,
Tex.
City with a Great Potential for
Growth. Marshall, Mo.

City with a Healthy Climate.
Turlock, Calif.
City with a Heart.   Grand
Forks, N. D.
City with a Heart.   Holly Hill,
Fla.
City with a Heart.   Valentine,
Neb.
City with a Heart in the
Heart of Dixie.   Birming-
ham, Ala.
City with a Historic Past, an
Enlightened Present and a
Dynamic Future.   Bethle-
hem, Pa.
City with a Hole in the Middle.
Lake Tahoe, Calif.
City with a Million Ambassa-
dors.   St. Petersburg, Fla.
City with a Modern Educational
System.   Blytheville, Ark.
City with a Modern School
System.   Milan, Tenn.
City with a Past.   Peters-
burg, Va.
City with a Past, Present and
Future.   Utica, N. Y.
City with a Personality.
Tulsa, Okla.
City with a Plan.   Crossett,
Ark.
City with a Planned Future.
New Castle, Ind.
City with a Promising Future.
Galt, Calif.
City with a Prosperous Present.
Pittsburg, Calif.
City with a Proud Heritage
and a Sparkling Future.
Quincy, Mass.
City with a Rich Heritage
of American Life.   Dublin,
Calif.
City with a Smile.   Sea Isle
City, N. J.
City with a Snow-Capped
Mountain in Its Dooryard.
Tacoma, Wash.
City with a Sparkle.   Clear-
water, Fla.
City with a Touch of New
England.   Mount Doria,
Fla.

City with a View.   El Cerrito,
Calif.
City with Abundant Grain.   Wal-
ford City, N. D.
City with Abundant TVA Power.
Milan, Tenn.
City with Accommodations to
Suit Your Desire.   Alex-
andria, Minn.
City with America's Finest
Year-Around Climate.   San
Diego, Calif.
City with an Area of Agricul-
tural Achievement.   Pahokee,
Fla.
City with an Aristocratic Past.
Greenwood, Miss.
City with an Exciting Future.
Greenwood, Miss.
City with an Exciting Future.
Pittsburg, Calif.
City with an Exciting History.
Galt, Calif.
City with an Important Asset
to Industrial Expansion.
Columbus, Miss.
City with an Open Door to
Industry and Progress.
Waterford, Calif.
City with Attractive Industrial
Sites.   Crossett, Ark.
City with Churches of All
Faiths.   Walford, City, N. D.
City with Entertainment for
Everyone.   Alexandria, Minn.
City with Everything.   New
York, N. Y.
City with Everything.   Tucson,
Ariz.
City with Everything Under the
Sun.   Pittsburg, Calif.
City with Excellent Hunting and
Fishing.   Morris, Minn.
City with Excellent Hunting and
Fishing.   Walford City, N. D.
City with Excellent Medical
Facilities.   Crookston, Minn.
City with Excellent Transpor-
tation.   Milam, Tenn.
City with Foresight.   Grand
Junction, Colo.
City with Future Unlimited.
Huron, S. D.

City with Good Schools and
Modern Medical Facilities.
Walford City, N.D.

City with Ideal Subtropical
Climate. Winter Park,
Fla.

City with Important Transportation Facilities. Vincennes,
Ind.

City with Its Sights on Its
Future. New Castle, Pa.

City with Modern Health
Facilities. Crossett, Ark.

City with Modern School
Systems. Crookston, Minn.

City with More of Everything.
Atlantic City, N.J.

City with Natural Beauty the
Year 'Round. Trinity, Tex.

City with Oklahoma's Largest
Coal Field. McAlester,
Okla.

City with 100 Years of
Progress. Moberly, Mo.

City with One of the Leading
Medical Centers in the
South. Vicksburg, Miss.

City with Opportunity for All.
Decatur, Ala.

City with Over 100 Ante-Bellum Homes. Columbus,
Miss.

City with Promise. Sparks,
Nev.

City with Recreation for
Everyone. Greenville, Ill.

City with Room for Growth
and Space to Relax. Waterford, Calif.

City with Room to Grow and
Grow. Chesapeake, Va.

City with Room to Stretch and
Grow In. Atmore, Ala.

City with Small Town Hospitality. Trussville, Ala.

City with Some of America's
Greatest Memories. Rich-
mond, Va.

City with Something for
Everyone. Marshall, Tex.

City with the Largest Man-
Made Reservoir in the
World. McAlester, Okla.

City with the Largest Solar
Observatory. Alamogordo,
N.M.

City with the Mile Long Mall.
Avon Park, Fla.

City with the Nation's Most
Perfect Year 'Round
Climate. San Mateo,
Calif.

City with the Old French Town.
New Orleans, La.

City with the Oldest State College for Women. Columbus,
Miss.

City with the Panoramic View
of the Beautiful New Hampshire Lakes Area. Laconia,
N.H.

City with the Planned Future.
Harrisonburg, Va.

City with the Stimulating Cultural Environment. Alamo-
gordo, N.M.

City with the Widest Paved
Street in the World. Keene,
N.H.

City with the World's Highest
Golf Course. Alamogordo,
N.M.

City with the World's Largest
Ox Cart. Crookston, Minn.

City with the World's Largest
Shrimping Facilities. Aransas Pass, Tex.

City with the World's Whitest
Beaches. Panama City, Fla.

City with Two Faces. Chicago,
Ill.

City with Unexcelled Opportunities for Good Living.
Orlando, Fla.

City with Unity in the Community. Concordia, Kan.

City with Water Sports. Walford, City, N.D.

City without a Toothache.
Hereford, Tex.

City without City Limits.
Tupelo, Miss.

City without Clocks. Las
Vegas, Nev.

City without Cobwebs. Rock
Hill, So. Car.

City without Limits. Atlanta, Ga.

City without Limits. Tupelo, Miss.

City without Precedent, without Comparison. Atlanta, Ga.

City Wonder-Full for Business. Lakeland, Fla.

City Worth Looking Into. Fort Worth, Tex.

City Worth While. St. Joseph, Mo.

City Worthy of a Noble Name. Lincoln, Neb.

City You Can be Proud to Live and Work In. East Point, Ga.

Civics Center of the Midland Empire. Billings, Mont.

Clam Capital, U.S.A. Williston, No. Car.

Clam Town. Norwalk, Conn.

Claremont, the Beautiful. Claremont, Calif.

Classic City. Boston, Mass.

Classic City of the South. Athens, Ga.

Classic New England Village. Farmington, Conn.

Clay Center. Perth Amboy, N.J.

Clay City. Brazil, Ind.

Clay Pipe Center of the World. Dennison, Ohio

Clay Pipe Center of the World. Uhrichsville, Ohio

Clean and Quiet Resort. Stone Harbor, N.J.

Clean City. Allentown, Pa.

Clean City. Hutchinson, Kan.

Clean Colorful Tulip City on Scenic Lake Macatawa. Holland, Mich.

Cleanest and Friendliest City in the West. Brigham City, Utah

Cleanest Beach in the World. Old Orchard Beach, Me.

Cleanest Big City in the World. New York, N.Y.

Cleanest City in Louisiana. Franklin, La.

Cleanest City in the United States. Morristown, Tenn.

Cleanest City, the Safest City and the Quietest City in the Country. Memphis, Tenn.

Cleveland with Palm Trees. Los Angeles, Calif.

Climate Capital of the World. Denver, Colo.

Clipper City. Manitowoc, Wis.

Clock Center of the World. Bristol, Conn.

Clock City. Thomaston, Conn.

Closest State to Heaven. Salida, Colo.

Clothing Center of the South. Bremen, Ga.

Cloud City. Leadville, Colo.

Clown Capital of the World. Bernardston, Mass.

Coal Bay. Colby, Wash.

Coal Boom Town. Gillette, Wyo.

Coal Capital of Kentucky. Harlan, Ky.

Coal Capital of the Southwest. Roanoke, Va.

Coal Center. Tunnelton, W. Va.

Coal City. Pittsburgh, Pa.

Coal City. Pottsville, Pa.

Coastal Gateway to New Hampshire. Seabrook, N.H.

Coastal Town of Charm and Beauty. Yarmouth, Me.

Coastline of Health and Happiness. Atlantic City, N.J.

Cockade City. Petersburg, Va.

Cockade City. Richmond, Va.

Cockade of the Union. Petersburg, Va.

Cockpit of the Civil War. Fredericksburg, Va.

Coke City. Uniontown, Pa.

Coliseum City. New York, N.Y.

Collar City. Troy, N.Y.

Collard and Pickle Capital. Cairo, Ga.

Collection of Freeways in Search of a City. Los Angeles, Calif.

College Capital of the World. Boston, Mass.

College City. Galesburg, Ill.
College City. Lewisburg, Pa.
College Town Amid the Orange
Groves. Claremont, Calif.
Colonial Capital of the Eastern
Shore. Easton, Md.
Colonial Capital of Virginia.
Williamsburg, Va.
Colonial City. Kingston, N.Y.
Colony City. Fitzgerald, Ga.
Colorado's Premier Year-Round
Resort. Vail, Colo.
Colorado's Second City.
Pueblo, Colo.
Colorful Captivating Community.
Carthage, Ill.
Colorful Key Center for De-
fense Activities. Jackson-
ville, Fla.
Columbia City. Vancouver,
Wash.
Comb City. Leominster, Mass.
Comic Book Capital of the
World. Sparta, Ill.
Coming City of the Great
Northwest. Pierre, S.D.
Coming Vegas. Lake Tahoe,
Calif.
Command Post for the Nation's
Manned Space Exploration.
Houston, Tex.
Commencement City. Tacoma,
Wash.
Commerce and Governmental
Center. Elko, Nevada
Commercial Capital of America.
New York, N.Y.
Commercial Capital of the
Central South. Nashville,
Tenn.
Commercial Center in the
Pacific Northwest. Seattle,
Wash.
Commercial Center of Irrigated
Idaho. Gooding, Idaho
Commercial Center of the
Midland Empire. Billings,
Mont.
Commercial Center of the
North Jersey Coast. Asbury
Park, N.J.
Commercial, Cultural and
Industrial Center of South

Arkansas. El Dorado,
Ark.
Commercial Empire of the
United States. Washington,
D.C.
Commercial Emporium. New
York, N.Y.
Commercial Metropolis of West
Tennessee. Memphis, Tenn.
Communication Center of
Florida. Jacksonville, Fla.
Community a Whole Lot to Like
About. Weatherford, Okla.
Community Away from the
Crowded Areas. Waterford,
Calif.
Community Blessed by Nature
and Planned with Pride.
Menlo Park, Calif.
Community Combining the Best
of Two Worlds. Brisbane,
Calif.
Community for Camping, Fishing,
Skiing and Water Sports.
Dinuba, Calif.
Community Full of History.
Hendersonville, Tenn.
Community Nestled in the
Shadow of the Superstition
Mountains. Apache Junction,
Ariz.
Community of Beautiful Homes.
Coronado, Calif.
Community of Beautiful Homes.
Encinitas, Calif.
Community of Craftsmen. York,
Pa.
Community of Culture and Tra-
ditions. Lynchburg, Va.
Community of Eight Thrilling
Attractions. Silver Springs,
Fla.
Community of Fine Homes,
Schools and Churches. Al-
bany, Ore.
Community of Friendly People.
Decatur, Ark.
Community of Gracious People.
Allentown, Pa.
Community of Hospitable People.
Jefferson, Iowa
Community of Hospitality.
Sheridan, Wyo.

Community of Opportunity.
Malone, N.Y.
Community of Opportunity for
Living. Delano, Calif.
Community of Progress.
Goldsboro, N.C.
Community of Rich Land, Good
Water and Mild Climate.
Denair, Calif.
Community of Substance. Nor-
walk, Conn.
Community of the Deodars.
Altadena, Calif.
Community of the Future.
Somerset, Pa.
Community of Trees. Los
Altos, Calif.
Community on the Move.
Bellows Falls, Vt.
Community on the Move.
Rutland, Vt.
Community on the Move for
a Century and a Half with
More to Offer for the
Future. Ogdensburg, N.Y.
Community Planned for
Pleasant Living. Indian-
town, Fla.
Community Progressive.
Greensburg, Pa.
Community Rich in Agricultural
Heritage. Winter Park,
Fla.
Community that Builds Health
Minds and Bodies. Blacks-
burg, Va.
Community that Has Everything.
Greenport, N.Y.
Community to Take Pride In.
Atwater, Calif.
Community Well Planned, Well
Developed, Well Equipped
for Commerce, Industry and
Family Life. East Point,
Ga.
Community where Business and
Pleasure Live in Complete
Harmony. Dunnellon, Fla.
Community where Living Is at
Its Best. Ephrata, Pa.
Community where Success
Begins. Ocala, Fla.

Community where the Big Bass
Bite. Leesburg, Fla.
Community where the Future
May Learn from the Past.
Williamsburg, Va.
Community where You Can
Live, Work, Relax. Haines
City, Fla.
Community where You Work and
Play the Same Day. Dun-
nellon, Fla.
Community with a Congenial
Environment for Generous
Living. Glendora, Calif.
Community with a Heart in the
Heart of Fabulous Florida.
Leesburg, Fla.
Community with a Planned In-
dustrial Growth Pattern.
Ripon, Calif.
Community with a Rich Heritage.
Bethlehem, Pa.
Community with Its Sites Set on
Tomorrow. Elgin, Ill.
Community with Pride. Gustine,
Calif.
Community Working Together
for the Future. Tupelo,
Miss.
Commuter's Haven. Newton,
Mass.
Complete City. Sweetwater,
Tex.
Complete Community. Man-
hattan, Kan.
Complete Four Season Resort.
Weirs Beach, N.H.
Complete Resort. Lavallette,
N.J.
Complete Resort. South Egre-
mont, Mass.
Complete Shopping Center.
Meriden, Conn.
Complete Vacation Resort City.
Key Colony Beach, Fla.
Computer Center. Pittsburgh,
Pa.
Con City. Las Vegas, Nev.
Concentrator City. Miami,
Ariz.
Coney Island of the West.
Saltair, Utah

Confederate Capital. Richmond, Va.
Confederate State Capital of Kentucky. Bowling Green, Ky.
Confederate Supply Depot. Atlanta, Ga.
Connecticut's Christmas Town. Bethlehem, Conn.
Connecticut's Elm City. New Haven, Conn.
Connecticut's First Town. Windsor, Conn.
Conservation City, U. S. A. Naples, Fla.
Conservative Cincinnati. Cincinnati, Ohio
Constitution City. Port St. Joe, Fla.
Consumer Cooperative Center of the United States. Superior, Wis.
Contented City. Cincinnati, Ohio
Continental Crossroads. Minot, N. D.
Convenient Vacationland. Pompano Beach, Fla.
Convention and Recreation Center of the Northwest. Coeur D'Alene, Idaho
Convention Capital of the West. Las Vegas, Nev.
Convention Capital of the World. Chicago, Ill.
Convention Center. Anaheim, Calif.
Convention Center in the Land of the Sky. Asheville, No. Car.
Convention Center of the Great Smokies. Gatlinburg, Tenn.
Convention Center of the Pacific Coast. Long Beach, Calif.
Convention Center of the United States. Miami Beach, Fla.
Convention City. Baltimore, Md.
Convention City. Casper, Wyo.

Convention City. Chicago, Ill.
Convention City. Columbia, Mo.
Convention City. Denver, Colo.
Convention City. Jefferson City, Mo.
Convention City. Juneau, Alaska
Convention City. Louisville, Ky.
Convention City. New Orleans, La.
Convention City. Portland, Ore.
Convention City. St. Louis, Mo.
Convention City. Salina, Kan.
Convention City. Saratoga Springs, N. Y.
Convention City. Sedalia, Mo.
Convention City. Springfield, Mo.
Convention City in the Heart of the South. Memphis, Tenn.
Convention City of Iowa. Marshalltown, Iowa
Convention City of the East. Hartford, Conn.
Convention City of the Great Smokies. Gatlinburg, Tenn.
Convention City of the World. Santa Monica, Calif.
Convention Headquarters for the Dakotas. Huron, S. D.
Convention Hub of the Dakotas. Aberdeen, S. D.
Cool and Sunny Paradise. Stowe, Vt.
Coolest Spot in Wisconsin. Two Rivers, Wis.
Coolest Summer City. Duluth, Minn.
Coon Capital of the World. Rogersville, Mo.
Cooperative Community. Greenbelt, Md.
Copper City. Butte, Mont.
Copper City. Rome, N. Y.
Copper City. Valdez, Alaska
Cordage City. Auburn, N. Y.
Corn City. Toledo, Ohio
Corncob Pipe Capital of the World. Washington, Mo.
Corner Stone of a Nation. Plymouth, Mass.

Cornhusker Capital City.
Lincoln, Neb.
Cornopolis. Chicago, Ill.
Corntown. Cornelius, Ore.
Corporate Capital of America.
Coral Gables, Fla.
Corporate Capital of America.
New York, N.Y.
Cosmopolitan City. San
Francisco, Calif.
Cosmopolitan City of the West.
San Francisco, Calif.
Cosmopolitan Community with
the Warmth of a Small
Town. Cocoa Beach, Fla.
Cosmopolitan San Francisco.
San Francisco, Calif.
Cosmopolitan Seaport. Seattle,
Wash.
Cotton Capital of the World.
Memphis, Tenn.
Cotton Center. Memphis,
Tenn.
Cottonseed Oil Capital of the
World. Lubbock, Tex.
Cotton Town of the U.S.A.
Paterson, N.J.
Cottonwood City. Leavenworth,
Kan.
Country Music Capital of the
North. Flint, Mich.
Country Music Capital of the
World. Nashville, Tenn.
Country where the Climate
Invites You Out-of-Doors.
Prineville, Ore.
Country's Greatest Rail Center.
Chicago, Ill.
Country's Largest Lumber
Shipping Center. Portland,
Ore.
County Seat of Coconimo
County. Flagstaff, Ariz.
County Seat of Cortland
County. Cortland, N.Y.
County Seat of Growing
Charleston County. Charles-
ton, S.C.
County Seat of Historic Coffee
County. Manchester,
Tenn.
County Seat of Hovell County.
West Plains, Mo.

County Seat of Love County.
Marietta, Okla.
County Seat of Lovely Lake
County. Tavares, Fla.
County Seat of Nemaha County.
Auburn, Neb.
County Seat of Rush County.
La Crosse, Kan.
County Seat of Texas County.
Houston, Mo.
Court City of a Nation. Wash-
ington, D.C.
Courteous Capital City. Harris-
burg, Pa.
Covered Bridge Capital of the
World. Rockville, Ind.
Cow Capital. Wichita, Kan.
Cow Capital of Florida. Kis-
simmee, Fla.
Cow Capital of Montana. Miles
City, Mont.
Cow Capital of the West. Miles
City, Mont.
Cow Town. Coffeyville, Kan.
Cow Town. Fort Worth, Tex.
Cow Town. Medora, N.D.
Cow Town. Wayland, Mich.
Cow Town of the South. Mont-
gomery, Ala.
Cowboy Boot Capital. Olathe,
Kan.
Cowboy Capital. Dodge City,
Kan.
Cowboy Capital. Kenton, Okla.
Cowboy Capital. Prescott,
Ariz.
Cowboy Capital of Nebraska.
Ogallala, Neb.
Cowboy Capital of Oregon.
Prineville, Ore.
Cowboy Capital of the Plains.
Tascosa, Tex.
Cowboy Capital of the World.
Dodge City, Kan.
Crab City. Annapolis, Md.
Crab Town. Hampton, Va.
Crabtown. Annapolis, Md.
Crabtown-on-the-Bay. Annapolis,
Md.
Cradle and Grave of the Con-
federacy. Abbeville, S.C.
Cradle of American Independence.
Providence, R.I.

Cradle of American Industry.
Paterson, N.J.
Cradle of American Liberty.
Taunton, Mass.
Cradle of Arkansas History.
Washington, Ark.
Cradle of Aviation. Dayton,
Ohio
Cradle of Creativity. Dayton,
Ohio
Cradle of Democracy. Phila-
delphia, Pa.
Cradle of Dental Education.
Bainbridge, Ohio
Cradle of Georgia. Savannah,
Ga.
Cradle of Industry. Spring-
field, Vt.
Cradle of Invention. Spring-
field, Vt.
Cradle of Liberty. Boston,
Mass.
Cradle of Liberty. Concord,
Mass.
Cradle of Liberty. Lexington,
Mass.
Cradle of Liberty. Phila-
delphia, Pa.
Cradle of Louisiana Oil.
Jennings, La.
Cradle of Naval Aviation.
Pensacola, Fla.
Cradle of New England. Mon-
hegan Island, Me.
Cradle of Pacific Northwest
History. Walla Walla, Wash.
Cradle of Secession. Charles-
ton, S.C.
Cradle of Ships. Bath, Me.
Cradle of Square Riggers.
Mystic, Conn.
Cradle of Texas. San Augus-
tine, Tex.
Cradle of Texas Liberty. San
Antonio, Tex.
Cradle of the American Circus.
Delavan, Wis.
Cradle of the American Circus.
Somers, N.Y.
Cradle of the American Revo-
lution. Boston, Mass.
Cradle of the American Textile
Industry. Pawtucket, R.I.

Cradle of the American Union.
Albany, N.Y.
Cradle of the Civil War. Osa-
watamie, Kans.
Cradle of the Colony. Edenton,
N.C.
Cradle of the Confederacy.
Montgomery, Ala.
Cradle of the Mexican War.
Fort Jessup, La.
Cradle of the Revolution. Mid-
way, Ga.
Cradle of the Revolution. Phila-
delphia, Pa.
Cradle of the Steel Industry.
Johnstown, Pa.
Cradle of the Trotter. Goshen,
N.Y.
Crape Myrtle City. Henderson,
Tex.
Crape Myrtle City. Jackson,
Miss.
Crape Myrtle City of Texas.
Paris, Tex.
Crawfish Capital of the World.
Breaux Bridge, La.
Crawfish Town. New Orleans,
La.
Cream City. Milwaukee, Wis.
Cream White City of the Un-
salted Seas. Milwaukee,
Wis.
Creole City. New Orleans, La.
Crescent City. Appleton, Wis.
Crescent City. Hilo, Hawaii
Crescent City. New Orleans,
La.
Crescent City of the Northwest.
Galena, Ill.
Crime Capital. Chicago, Ill.
Crosspads of the Nation. Wash-
ington, Pa.
Crossroads City. Dublin, Calif.
Crossroads City. El Paso,
Tex.
Crossroads for North-South
East-West Traffic. Alma,
Ark.
Crossroads of Alaska. Tok,
Alaska
Crossroads of America. El
Paso, Tex.

Crossroads of America.
Indianapolis, Ind.
Crossroads of America.
Joplin, Mo.
Crossroads of America.
Seymour, Ind.
Crossroads of American
History. Carlisle, Pa.
Crossroads of California.
Manteca, Calif.
Crossroads of Connecticut.
Waterbury, Conn.
Crossroads of Florida.
Tavares, Fla.
Crossroads of Georgia.
Perry, Ga.
Crossroads of History.
Carlisle, Pa.
Crossroads of History.
Petersburg, Va.
Crossroads of Industrial
Development. Hudson,
Mass.
Crossroads of Industrial
New England. Danielson,
Conn.
Crossroads of Los Angeles
County. Pico Rivera,
Calif.
Crossroads of Louisiana.
Alexandria, La.
Crossroads of Louisiana.
Pineville, La.
Crossroads of Mid-America.
Carthage, Mo.
Crossroads of Mid America.
Joplin, Mo.
Crossroads of New England.
Springfield, Mass.
Crossroads of New England.
Westboro, Mass.
Crossroads of New York.
Utica, N.Y.
Crossroads of New York State.
Syracuse, N.Y.
Crossroads of North America.
Medicine Lodge, Kans.
Crossroads of Northern New
England. Wells River, Vt.
Crossroads of Southern Indiana.
Paoli, Ind.
Crossroads of Southern Indiana.
Seymour, Ind.

Crossroads of the Adirondacks.
Tupper Lake, N.Y.
Crossroads of the Americas.
El Paso, Tex.
Crossroads of the Continent.
Carbondale, Ill.
Crossroads of the Eastern
Market. Raritan, N.J.
Crossroads of the Mid-South.
Memphis, Tenn.
Crossroads of the Middle West.
Rockford, Ill.
Crossroads of the Nation.   Cin-
cinnati, Ohio
Crossroads of the Nation.
Hastings, Neb.
Crossroads of the Nation.
Omaha, Neb.
Crossroads of the Nation.
Sioux Falls, S.D.
Crossroads of the Nation.
Strongsville, Ohio
Crossroads of the Pacific.
Honolulu, Hawaii
Crossroads of the New South.
Spartanburg, S.C.
Crossroads of the Old and the
New South. Jackson, Miss.
Crossroads of the South.
Crossville, Tenn.
Crossroads of the South. Jack-
son, Miss.
Crossroads of the South. La
Grange, Ga.
Crossroads of the West. Salt
Lake City, Utah
Crossroads of the World.
Anchorage, Alaska
Crossroads of the World. New
York, N.Y.
Crossroads of the World.
Washington, D.C.
Crossroads of the World's
Richest Market. Syracuse,
N.Y.
Crossroads of Tomorrow.
Hazleton, Pa.
Crossroads of Tomorrow.
Statesville, N.C.
Crossroads of Wisconsin.
Marshfield, Wis.
Crossroads of Your National
Market. Dayton, Ohio

Crossroads to the Gulf. Alvin,
Tex.
Crossroads to the Universe.
Melbourne, Fla.
Crossroads to Wonderland.
Salida, Colo.
Crown City. Pasadena, Calif.
Crown City of the Valley.
Pasadena, Calif.
Crown Jewel of the Florida
Keys. Islamorada, Fla.
Crown of the Valley. Pasa-
dena, Calif.
Crowning Gem in Southern
California's Golf Diadem.
Coronado, Calif.
Cruise Capital of the South.
Port Everglades, Fla.
Cruise Capital of the World.
Dania, Fla.
Crumptown. Memphis, Tenn.
Crutch Capital of the World.
Rumney, N.H.
Crystal Center of the World.
Carlisle, Pa.
Crystal City. Corning, N.Y.
Cucumber Capital of the
World. Wauchula, Fla.
Cuisine Capital of the World.
New York, N.Y.
Cultural and Economic Center
of Southeastern New Eng-
land. Providence, R.I.
Cultural Capital of America.
New York, N.Y.
Cultural Center. Madison,
Wis.
Cultural Center of the Adi-
rondacks. Schroon Lake,
N.Y.
Cultural Center of the Nation.
New York, N.Y.
Cultural Center of the South-
west. Houston, Tex.
Cultural Center of the Sun
Coast. Sarasota, Fla.
Cultural Center of the West.
San Francisco, Calif.
Cultural Center Unexcelled.
Winter Park, Fla.
Cultural City. New York, N.Y.
Cultural Hub. Stamford,
Conn.

Cutlery Center of America.
Fremont, Ohio
Cuyuna Capital. Crosby, Minn.
Czech Bethlehem. Racine, Wis.
Czech Capital of Nebraska.
Wilber, Neb.

Daffodil Center of Connecticut.
Meriden, Conn.
Dairy, Agricultural and Indus-
trial Center. Springfield,
Mo.
Dairy Center of the South.
Starkville, Miss.
Dairy City. Elkland, Pa.
Dairying City. Fergus Falls,
Minn.
Dairyland of Texas. Jourdan-
ton, Tex.
Dam End of Santa Clara County.
Morgan Hill, Calif.
Dancingest Town in the United
States. Hendersonville, N.C.
Dandelion Capital. Vineland,
N.J.
Danish Capital of the United
States. Racine, Wis.
Danville Invites You to Make
Our City Your City. Dan-
ville, Va.
Date Capital of the United
States. Indio, Calif.
Dean of the 27 Springfields in
the U.S.A. Springfield,
Mass.
Deep South of Texas. Bay City,
Tex.
Deep Water. Chelan, Wash.
Deep Water Port. Jackson-
ville, Fla.
Deer Capital of Texas. Llano,
Tex.
Delaware's Summer Capital.
Rehoboth Beach, Del.
Delightful Residential Com-
munity in the Heart of the
Palm Beaches. Palm
Springs, Fla.
Denver of Oregon. Baker, Ore.
Denver of South Dakota. Rapid
City, S.D.

Depot Springs. Cheney, Wash.
Derby City. Norwalk, Conn.
Derby Town. Louisville, Ky.
Derrick City. Oil City, Pa.
Deseret. Salt Lake City, Utah
Desert Babylon. Las Vegas,
Nev.
Desert Community. Ridge-
crest, Calif.
Desert Wonderland. Indio,
Calif.
Detroit of Airplanes. Los
Angeles, Calif.
Detroit of the West. Oakland,
Calif.
Detroit the Beautiful. Detroit,
Mich.
Deutsch-Athens. Milwaukee,
Wis.
Diamond City. Wilkes-Barre,
Pa.
Dimple of the Bluegrass.
Lexington, Ky.
Dimple of the Universe. Nash-
ville, Tenn.
Diplomatic Capital of the World.
Washington, D. C.
Disney City. Orlando, Fla.
Disney World City. Orlando,
Fla.
Disneyland of the Midwest.
Cedar Point, Ohio
Distinguished and Friendly
Community. Amherst,
Mass.
Distributing Center for Central
and Western Kansas. Salina,
Kan.
Distribution Center for Four
States. Tyler, Tex.
Distribution Center for
6,000,000 Floridians.
Lakeland, Fla.
Distribution Center for the
Great Northwest. Fargo,
N. D.
Distribution Center of the
Southeast. Augusta, Ga.
Distribution Center of the
Southeast. Jacksonville, Fla.
Distribution Center of the
Northeast. Springfield,
Mass.

Distribution Hub of Southwest
Oregon. Eugene, Ore.
Distribution Point, U. S. A.
York, Pa.
District Incomparable. Oroville,
Calif.
Diversified Agricultural and
Industrial Community. Pierce
City, Mo.
Diversified City. South San
Francisco, Calif.
Diversified City. Waycross, Ga.
Diversified Community. Frank-
fort, Ky.
Diversified Industry City. East
Point, Ga.
Diversified Manufacturing Cen-
ter. Decatur, Ill.
Diversified Manufacturing Com-
munity. Framingham, Mass.
Dixie City. Montgomery, Ala.
Dixie Gateway. Covington, Ky.
Dogwood City. Atlanta, Ga.
Don't Overlook Overbrook.
Overbrook, Kan.
Doorway to the South Dakota
Great Lakes. Platte, So.
Dak.
Dormitory City. Berwyn, Ill.
Dormitory of New York.
Brooklyn, N. Y.
Dorp. Schenectady, N. Y.
Dream City Come True. Holly-
wood, Fla.
Dream Town. Greenfield,
Mass.
Druid City. Tuscaloosa, Ala.
Dry Pea and Lentil Capital of
the World. Moscow, Idaho
Dual Cities. Minneapolis, and
St. Paul, Minn.
Duck Hunting Capital of the
World. Stuttgart, Ark.
Duck Mecca of the Midwest.
Mound City, Mo.
Ducks' Puddle. Drakes Branch,
Va.
Dude Ranch and Resort Center.
Jackson, Wyo
Dude Ranch Capital of Texas.
Bandera, Tex.
Dude Ranch Capital of the East.
Stony Creek, N. Y.

Dude Ranch Capital of the
World. Wickenburg, Ariz.
Dude Ranch Capital, U.S.A.
Wickenburg, Ariz.
Duke City. Albuquerque,
N.M.
Dungeness Crab Capital of
the World. Newport, Ore.
Dupont Town. Wilmington,
Del.
Dupontonia. Wilmington, Del.
Durum Center of the World.
Lakota, No. Dak.
Dutch City. Holland, Mich.
Dutchtown. Aurora, Ore.
Dynamic Area of Growth.
Aliquippa, Pa.
Dynamic Center of the Great
River Road. Baton Rouge,
La.
Dynamic City. Detroit, Mich.
Dynamic City. Douglas-
ville, Ga.
Dynamic City. El Cerrito,
Calif.
Dynamic Davenport. Daven-
port, Iowa
Dynamic Detroit. Detroit,
Mich.
Dynamic Metropolis of the
Rocky Mountain Empire.
Denver, Colo.
Dynamo of Dixie. Chatta-
nooga, Tenn.

Early Mormon Ranching Com-
munity. Elko, Nevada
Early Mountain Town. Moun-
tain City, Nev.
Early West in Modern Splen-
dor. Las Vegas, Nev.
Earthquake City. Charleston,
S.C.
East Coast Megalopolis.
Hartford, Conn.
Easterly Gateway to the Lakes
and White Mountains Region.
Dover, N.H.
Eastern Approach to Berthoud
Pass. Empire, Colo.
Eastern Connecticut Center.

Willimantic, Conn.
Eastern Gateway into Arkansas.
West Memphis, Arkansas
Eastern Gateway of Iowa.
Davenport, Iowa
Eastern Gateway to Bucktail
State Park. Lock Haven,
Pa.
Eastern Gateway to Glacier
National Park. St. Mary,
Mont.
Eastern Gateway to Hillsborough
County. Plant City, Fla.
Eastern Gateway to Indiana.
Richmond, Ind.
Eastern Gateway to Jackson
County. Sneads, Fla.
Eastern Gateway to Laurel
Highlands. Somerset, Pa.
Eastern Gateway to Mt. Ranier
National Park. Yakima,
Wash.
Eastern Gateway to Nebraska-
land. Blair, Neb.
Eastern Gateway to the Black
Hills. Rapid City, S.D.
Eastern Gateway to the Moun-
tainous Black Hills where
East Meets West and the
Friendly Hospitality. Rapid
City, S.D.
Eastern Gateway to the Ozarks.
Poplar Bluff, Mo.
Eastern Shore of Mobile Bay.
Fairhope, Ala.
Eclipse Capital of the World.
Perry, Fla.
Economic Center of the Cave
Area. Horse Cave, Ky
Economically Stable Community.
Lake Placid, Fla.
Economy Gateway. New Bed-
ford, Mass.
Eden of Ohio. Sabina, Ohio
Eden of the Closest State to
Heaven. Fort Collins, Colo.
Edinburgh of America. Albany,
N.Y.
Educational and Cultural Center.
Kerrville, Tex.
Educational Capital. Jackson,
Miss.
Educational Center. Ithaca, N.Y.

Educational Center. Mitchell, S. D.

Educational Center of the Valley. Edinburg, Tex.

Educational Center of the West. Emporia, Kan.

Educational, Cultural and Business Center. Holly Springs, Miss.

Education, Cultural, Business Distribution Center of the St. Lawrence Valley. Potsdam, N. Y.

Educational- Cultural Community. State College, Pa.

Egg Basket of the World. Petaluma, Calif.

Egg Center of Florida. Masaryktown, Fla.

Eighteenth Century Seaport. Beaufort, S. C.

El-Ay. Los Angeles, Calif.

Elay. Los Angeles, Calif.

El Dorado of the West. Muncie, Ind.

Electric City. Anderson, S. C.

Electric City. Great Falls, Mont.

Electric City. Kaukauna, Wis.

Electric City. Schenectady, N. Y.

Electric City. Scranton, Pa.

Electric City of the Future. Buffalo, N. Y.

Electrical Center of America. Sheffield, Ala.

Electrical City. Schenectady, N. Y.

Electronic Area of Incredible Growth. Sanford, Fla.

Electronic Center of the Southwest. Fort Huachuca, Ariz.

Electronic City of the Southwest. Richardson, Tex.

Electronics Aerospace Center. Dallas, Tex.

Electronics Capital of the Midwest. Ogallala, Neb.

Electronics Capitol of the World. Syracuse, N. Y.

Ellenville Is Everythingville. Ellenville, N. Y.

Ellwood City Encourages Enterprise. Ellwood City, Pa.

Elm City. New Haven, Conn.

Elm City. Waterville, Me.

Embryonic Capital. Washington, D. C.

Embryonic Center of Music. Helena, Ark.

Emerging Industrial Center. Birmingham, Ala.

Emerging Metropolis. Rochester, N. Y.

Empire City. New York, N. Y.

Encampment City. Palacios, Tex.

Enchanted City on the Potomac. Washington, D. C.

End of the World. Sibley, Minn.

Energy Capital. Houston, Tex.

Energy Capital of the U. S. Houston, Tex.

Energy Capital of the West. Farmington, N. M.

Energy Capital of the World. Houston, Tex.

Engineers' Town. Coulee City, Wash.

Enjoyment in History Relived. Ogdensburg, N. Y.

Enlightening, Entertaining, Exciting. Quincy, Mass.

Entertainment Capital of the World. Burlingame, Calif.

Entertainment Capital of the World. Las Vegas, Nev.

Entertainment Capital of the World. New York, N. Y.

Entire City of Friendly People. Ogdensburg, N. Y.

Entrance to Sam Houston National Forest. Cleveland, Tex.

Entrance to the Chain-O-Lakes. Elk Rapids, Mich.

Entrance to Viking Land. Alexandria, Minn.

Eskimo Village. Kotzebue, Alaska

Essen of America. Bridgeport, Conn.

Established City. Muskogee,
Okla.
Evergreen City. Sheboygan,
Wis.
Evergreen Playground. Seat-
tle, Wash.
Evergreen Playground.
Tacoma, Wash.
Evergrowing Industrial Center.
Nebraska City, Neb.
Every Season there's a Reason
to Visit. Bridgton, Me.
Everybody's Favorite City.
San Francisco, Calif.
Everybody's Playground.
Bridgerland, Utah.
Everything Island. Longboat
Key, Fla.
Everything Your Vacation
Heart Desires Can Be
Found in Riviera Beach.
Riviera Beach, Fla.
Exact Geographic Center of
the State. Murfreesboro,
Tenn.
Excellent Fishing and Water
Sports City. Ellington,
Mo.
Excellent Hunting Area for
Deer, Quail and Small
Game. Neosho, Mo.
Excellent Hunting Paradise.
Walker, Minn.
Exciting City. Los Angeles,
Calif.
Exciting City of Welcome.
Honolulu, Hawaii.
Exciting International City.
El Paso, Tex.
Exciting Place to Live. Lodi,
Calif.
Exciting World City. Los
Angeles, Calif.
Exclusive Summer and Winter
Resort in the White
Mountains. Jackson, N.H.
Executive City. Washington,
D.C.
Exposition City. San Fran-
cisco, Calif.
Eye of the Commonwealth
Southbridge, Mass.

Eye of the Northwest. Superior,
Wis.

Fabulous City. Los Angeles,
Calif.
Fabulous City in the Sun.
Miami Beach, Fla.
Fair City. Huron, S.D.
Fair City. Largo, Fla.
Fair City. Syracuse, N.Y.
Fair Little City. Tulsa, Okla.
Fair Play City. Jersey Shore,
Pa.
Fair White City. Milwaukee,
Wis.
Fairest Georgian City of the
New World. Charlottesville,
Va.
Fairyland. Hollywood, Calif.
Faithful City. Worcester, Mass.
Falls. Fall City, Wash.
Falls. Tumwater, Wash.
Falls Cities. Jeffersonville,
Ind.
Falls Cities. Louisville, Ky.
Falls Cities. New Albany, Ind.
Falls City. Louisville, Ky.
Famed America's Cup Racing
City. Newport, R.I.
Famed Gold Rush Town. Nome,
Alaska
Family City. Anaheim, Calif.
Family City. St. Louis, Mo.
Family Community. Castro
Valley, Calif.
Family Community for Your
Maine Vacation. Harrison,
Me.
Family Fun and Action. Du-
buque, Iowa
Family Oasis of Safe Ocean
Beaches. Pompano Beach,
Fla.
Family Play Area. Fort
Myers, Fla.
Family-Style Resort Center.
Pine Mountain, Ga.
Family Town. Garden City,
Kan.
Family Vacation Resort. China,
Me.

Family Vacation Spot. Wild-
wood, N.J.
Family Vacationland. Schroon
Lake, N.Y.
Famous Four Season Recrea-
tion Area in the Heart of
Vermont's Green Mountains.
Manchester, Vt.
Famous Playground of the
Wondrous Northwest.
Coeur d'Alene, Idaho
Famous Seafaring Town.
Kennebunkport, Me.
Famous Winter Resort for
Northern Invalids and
Pleasure Seekers. Thomas-
ville, Ga.
Far Away Island. Nantucket,
Mass.
Far Away Land. Nantucket,
Mass.
Farm Capital of America.
Des Moines, Iowa
Farm Community. Tomball,
Tex.
Farm Machinery Capital of
America. Moline, Ill.
Farthest Inland Deep Water
Port. Baton Rouge, La.
Fascinating Foothills City.
Fort Collins, Colo.
Fashion Capital of the Nation.
Houston, Tex.
Fashion Capital of the World.
New York, N.Y.
Fast Growing City. Green-
ville, Miss.
Fast Growing City. West Palm
Beach, Fla.
Fast Growing Industrial Com-
munity. Richmond, Calif.
Fast-Growing Nerve Center
for America's Great North-
land Empire. Minneapolis,
Minn.
Fastest Growing Area in Vir-
ginia. Suffolk, Va.
Fastest Growing Chemical
Center in the Great Mid-
west. Joplin, Mo.
Fastest Growing City. Dallas,
Tex.
Fastest Growing City in

Eastern Arkansas. West
Memphis, Ark.
Fastest Growing City in Los
Angeles County. Montebello,
Calif.
Fastest Growing City in Massa-
chusetts. Quincy, Mass.
Fastest Growing City in New
England. Chicopee, Mass.
Fastest Growing City in Ohio.
Euclid, Ohio
Fastest Growing City in Pennsyl-
vania. Bethlehem, Pa.
Fastest Growing City in Texas.
Corpus Christi, Tex.
Fastest Growing City in the
County. Stamford, Conn.
Fastest Growing City in the
Northwest. Bismarck, N.D.
Fastest Growing City in the
State. Hastings, Neb.
Fastest Growing City in the
Upper Midwest. Rapid City,
S.D.
Fastest Growing Community in
Maine. Norway, Me.
Fastest Growing Community in
Maine. Paris, Me.
Fastest Growing Deep Water
Seaport in Maine. Sears-
port, Me.
Fastest Growing Friendly Re-
tirement Community. De-
Bary, Fla.
Fastest Growing Industrial
Area in the Southeast.
Hialeah, Fla.
Fastest Growing Industrial
Center in the South. Bas-
trop, La.
Fastest Growing Metropolitan
City in the Nation. Albu-
querque, N.M.
Fastest Growing Metropolitan
Area in the Nation. Las
Vegas, Nev.
Fastest Growing Mountain Re-
sort. Gatlinburg, Tenn.
Fastest Growing Municipality
in the State. Stamford, Conn.
Fastest Growing of the Nation's
Major Cities. Houston,
Tex.

Fastest Growing Town in Hillsboro County. Merrimack, N.H.

Fastest Growing Town in New England. Norwalk, Conn.

Fastest Town on Skates. Northbrook, Ill.

Father Knickerbocker. New York, N.Y.

Favored Vacation Package of Western America. Las Vegas, Nev.

Favorite Family Resort Since 1893. Bradley Beach, N.J.

Favorite Family Seaside Resort. Hampton Beach, N.H.

Favorsburg. Pataha, Wash.

Fear City. New York, N.Y.

Federal Capital. Washington, D.C.

Federal City. Atlanta, Ga.

Federal City. Paterson, N.J.

Federal City. Washington, D.C.

Federal Seat. Washington, D.C.

Federal Site. Washington, D.C.

Federal Town. Washington, D.C.

Feeder Calf Capital of the World. Unionville, Mo.

Feeder Pig Capital of the World. West Plains, Mo.

Feel Younger Country. Prineville, Ore.

Fern City of Florida. Apopka, Fla.

Fiesta City. San Antonio, Tex.

Fifth City. Cleveland, Ohio

Fifth Fastest Growing Metropolitan Area in the Nation. Orlando, Fla.

Fightin'est Town on the River. Lancaster, Ore.

Filbert Center of the United States. Hillsboro, Ore.

Film Capital. Hollywood, Calif.

Film Capital of the World. Hollywood, Calif.

Film City. Hollywood, Calif.

Filmdom. Hollywood, Calif.

Filmland. Hollywood, Calif.

Financial Capital of the World. New York, N.Y.

Financial Center. Midland, Tex.

Financial Center of Alaska. Anchorage, Alaska

Finance Center of Florida. Jacksonville, Fla.

Financial Center of the Del-Mar-Va Peninsula. Wilmington, Del.

Financial Center of the Southwest. Dallas, Tex.

Financial Center of the West. San Francisco, Calif.

Financial Center of the World. San Francisco, Calif.

Financial Hub. New York, N.Y.

Fine Community for the Family. Dixon, Calif.

Fine Place in the World to Live. Sarasota, Fla.

Fine Place to Live. Boynton, Beach, Fla.

Fine Place to Live. Fairfield, Conn.

Fine Place to Live and Work. Danville, Va.

Fine Residential City. Fargo, N.D.

Fine Resort Area on the Coast. Wells, Me.

Fine Writing Paper Center of the World. Holyoke, Mass.

Finest Beach in the World. Old Orchard Beach, Me.

Finest for Hunting, Fishing and Skin-Diving. Mineral Wells, Tex.

Finest Home and Cultural Community in Southern California. Whittier, Calif.

Finest in Tennis on the Jersey Coast. Stone Harbor, N.J.

Finest New England Village in the Middle West. Evanston, Ill.

Finest Place Under the Sun. Titusville, Fla.

Fire Clay and Horse Capital of the World. Mexico, Mo.

Fireclay Capital. Mexico, Mo.
Fireclay Capital of the World.
Mexico, Mo.
First American Capital West
of the Rockies. Monterey,
Calif.
First and Last Major U.S.
Port of Call on the Seaway
Route. Buffalo, N.Y.
First Capital City. Sitka,
Alaska
First Capital of Arizona.
Prescott, Ariz.
First Capital of Missouri.
St. Charles, Mo.
First Capital of New York.
Kingston, N.Y.
First Capital of the Republic
of Texas. West Columbia,
Tex.
First Capital of the State.
Huntsville, Ala.
First Capital of the United
States. York, Pa.
First Choice in Family Re-
sorts. Ocean City, N.J.
First City. Ketchikan,
Alaska
First City. Memphis, Tenn.
First City in Alaska. Ketchi-
kan, Alaska
First City in American Spirit.
Cleveland, Ohio
First City in Famous Palm
Beach County. Jupiter, Fla.
First City in Texas. Houston,
Tex.
First City of America's First
Vacationland. Providence,
R.I.
First City of Kansas. Leaven-
worth, Kan.
First City of the First State.
Wilmington, Del.
First City of the South. Sa-
vannah, Ga.
First City of the World. New
York, N.Y.
First Cotton Port. Houston,
Tex.
First Electrically Lighted City
in the World. Wabash,
Ind.

First English Colony. James-
town, Va.
First Four-Way Test Town in
the World. Altavista, Va.
First in Connecticut. Windsor,
Conn.
First on the Fun Coast of
Florida. West Palm Beach,
Fla.
First Peace Time Capital of
the United States. Annapolis,
Md.
First Permanent Settlement in
New Hampshire. Dover, N.H.
First Planned City in the Pacific
Northwest. Longview, Wash.
First Port on the Columbia.
Astoria, Ore.
First Ski-Club City. Berlin,
N.H.
First Stop of the Eastwind.
Chatham, Mass.
First Territorial Capital.
Lewiston, Idaho
First Town of America. Ply-
mouth, Mass.
First TVA City. Tupelo, Miss.
Fish City. Lake Andes, S.D.
Fish Farming Research Center.
Stuttgart, Ark.
Fisherman's Harbor. Coyle,
Wash.
Fisherman's Paradise. Belmar,
N.J.
Fisherman's Paradise. Biloxi,
Miss.
Fisherman's Paradise. Bonita
Springs, Fla.
Fisherman's Paradise. Car-
rabelle, Fla.
Fisherman's Paradise. Ever-
glades, Fla.
Fisherman's Paradise. Mara-
thon, Fla.
Fisherman's Paradise. St.
Cloud, Fla.
Fisherman's Paradise. Salem,
Ore.
Fisherman's Paradise of the
North Atlantic. New Shore-
ham, R.I.
Fisherman's Playground.
Salem, Ore.

Fishing and Hunting Head-
quarters for Gigantic Lake
Garrison. Garrison, N.D.
Fishing Capital of the Nation
(South). Crossett, Ark.
Fishing Capital of the Ozarks.
Mountain Home, Ark.
Fishing Shangri-La of the
South. Marksville, La.
Five Miles of Health and Hap-
piness. Wildwood, N.J.
Five Miles of Smiles, Sea,
Sand and Fun. Salisbury
Beach, Mass.
Five Star City in the Valley
of the Sun. Chandler, Ariz.
Flax Center of North Dakota.
Petersburg, N.D.
Flicker Capital. Hollywood,
Calif.
Flicker City. Hollywood,
Calif.
Flicker Lane. Hollywood,
Calif.
Flood City. Johnstown, Pa.
Flood Free City. Johnstown,
Pa.
Floral City. Cincinnati, Ohio
Floral Metropolis of East
Texas. Tyler, Tex.
Florida Plus City. Pensacola,
Fla.
Florida's All-Year Resort.
West Palm Beach, Fla.
Florida's Attraction Showplace.
Lake Wales, Fla.
Florida's Beginning Point.
Tallahassee, Fla.
Florida's Biggest Industrial
City. Tampa, Fla.
Florida's Biggest Little Town.
Davenport, Fla.
Florida's Boating Capital on
the Gulf. Dunedin, Fla.
Florida's Center for Science,
Education, Medicine.
Gainesville, Fla.
Florida's City Beautiful.
Orlando, Fla.
Florida's City of Five Flags.
Pensacola, Fla.
Florida's Complete Family
Outdoor Recreation

Center. Lake Hampton,
Fla.
Florida's Convention City.
Tampa, Fla.
Florida's Country Club Town.
Lehigh Acres, Fla.
Florida's Deep Water Harbor.
Port Everglades, Fla.
Florida's Dissimilar Resort.
Delray Beach, Fla.
Florida's Eighth City. Lake-
land, Fla.
Florida's Entertainment Capital.
Sarasota, Fla.
Florida's Fabulous Frontier
Coast. Port St. Joe, Fla.
Florida's Fastest Growing City.
Hialeah, Fla.
Florida's Finest Agricultural,
Industrial and Resort Com-
munity. Fort Pierce, Fla.
Florida's Finest Deep Water
Harbor. Port St. Joe, Fla.
Florida's Friendly Old City-
with a New Future. Apala-
chicola, Fla.
Florida's Gateway City. Jack-
sonville, Fla.
Florida's Golfingest City.
Hollywood, Fla.
Florida's Great Gulf Beach Re-
sort Area. Sarasota, Fla.
Florida's Gulf Coast Metropolis.
Tampa, Fla.
Florida's Hub of Fun. Jackson-
ville, Fla.
Florida's Last Frontier. Belle-
view, Fla.
Florida's Magic City. Miami,
Fla.
Florida's Metropolitan Dis-
tributing Center. Tampa,
Fla.
Florida's Most Friendly Com-
munity. Largo, Fla.
Florida's Most Unique City.
Tarpon Springs, Fla.
Florida's New Gateway. Lake
City, Fla.
Florida's Newest Convention
City. Clearwater, Fla.
Florida's Newest Frontier.
Pine Island Center, Fla.

Florida's Newest Metropolitan
Industrial Area. Daytona
Beach, Fla.
Florida's Potato Capital.
Hastings, Fla.
Florida's Ranch Country.
Kissimmee, Fla.
Florida's Second Largest City.
Tampa, Fla.
Florida's Second Largest
Tourist City. St. Peters-
burg, Fla.
Florida's Showcase Community.
Coral Gables, Fla.
Florida's Transportation Hub.
Orlando, Fla.
Florida's Treasure City.
Tampa, Fla.
Florida's Tropical Paradise.
Fort Lauderdale, Fla.
Florida's Unique Vacation
Area. Sarasota, Fla.
Florida's Vacation Capital.
Daytona Beach, Fla.
Florida's Water Wonderland.
Bradentown, Fla.
Florida's Waterfront Wonder-
land. Cape Coral, Fla.
Florida's West Coast Beach
Resort. Longboat Key,
Fla.
Florida's West Coast's
Finest Vacation Spot.
Casey Key, Fla.
Florida's Winter Strawberry
Market. Starke, Fla.
Florida's Year 'Round City.
Tampa, Fla.
Florida's Year Round Play-
ground. Daytona Beach,
Fla.
Flour City. Buffalo, N.Y.
Flour City. Minneapolis,
Minn.
Flour City. Rochester, N.Y.
Flour Milling Capital of the
World. Buffalo, N.Y.
Flour Milling Capital of the
World. Minneapolis,
Min.
Flourishing Chief City of
the Carolinas. Charlotte,
N.C.

Flower Box City. Neosho, Mo.
Flower City. Rochester, N.Y.
Flower City. Springfield, Ill.
Flower City. Springfield, Ohio
Flower, Fruit, Vegetable Center.
Hendersonville, N.C.
Flower Industry City. Half
Moon Bay, Calif.
Flower Town in the Pines.
Summerville, S.C.
Flowerbox City. Neosho, Mo.
Fluorescent Mineral Capital of
the World. Franklin, N.J.
Foam City. Milwaukee, Wis.
Focal Point of Industrial
America. Aliquippa, Pa.
Food Basket of the World.
Fargo, N.D.
Food Emporium. Wishram,
Wash.
Foot of the Adirondacks. Am-
sterdam, N.Y.
Football Capital of the South.
Birmingham, Ala.
Foothills of the Catskills.
Walton, N.Y.
Fordtown. Detroit, Mich.
Foreign Car Capital of the U.S.
Bergen, N.J.
Foremost Industrial Center of
Iowa. Sioux City, Iowa
Forest City. Cleveland, Ohio
Forest City. Middletown,
Conn.
Forest City. Portland, Me.
Forest City. Rockford, Ill.
Forest City. Savannah, Ga.
Forest City. Wausau, Wis.
Forest City of the South.
Savannah, Ga.
Forest Products Capital of
America. Tacoma, Wash.
Forestry Capital of Florida.
Lake City, Fla.
Forestry Capital of the Nation.
Crossett, Ark.
Forestry Capital of the South.
Crossett, Ark.
Forge of the Universe. Pitts-
burg, Pa.
Forks of the Ohio. Pittsburgh,
Pa.
Former Capital of the Cherokee

Indian Nation. Tahlequah,
Okla.
Former Capital of the Chicka-
saw Nation. Tupelo, Miss.
Former Railroad Community.
Caliente, Nev.
Fort Lauderdale of the Eastern
Shore. Ocean City, Md.
Fort Sill Artillery and Mis-
sile Center. Lawton,
Okla.
Fort Town. Fort Worth,
Tex.
Fortunate Island. Monhegan,
Me.
Foundling Capital. Washington,
D. C.
Fountain City. Columbus, Ga.
Fountain City. De Soto, Mo.
Fountain City. Fond du Lac,
Wis.
Fountain City. Pueblo, Colo.
Fountain of Youth City. St.
Augustine, Fla.
Four Flags City. Niles, Mich.
Four Lake City. Madison,
Wis.
Four Lakes City. Madison,
Wis.
Four Leaf Clover City.
Decatur, Ala.
Four Mountains of Fun. Killing-
ton, Vt.
Four Season Area. Springfield,
Vt.
Four Season City. Superior,
Wis.
Four Season Community. New-
port, Vt.
Four Season Playground in the
Heart of the Green Mountains.
Lyndonville, Vt.
Four Season Resort. Lake
Placid, N. Y.
Four Season Resort and Cul-
tural Center. Manchester,
Vt.
Four-Season Resort and Trading
Center for Moosehead Region,
Allagash Wilderness Water-
way and Baxter State Park.
Greenville, Me.
Four Season Resort for Health,

Rest and Pleasure. Atlantic
City, N. J.
Four-Season Vacation Center.
Knoxville, Tenn.
Four Season Vacationland.
Nisswa, Minn.
Four Season's Playground.
Marquette, Mich.
Four Seasons Resort. Killing-
ton, Vt.
Four Seasons Vacationland.
Bridgton, Me.
Fourth Largest Air Center in
the U. S. Atlanta, Ga.
Fourth Largest City in Kansas.
Salina, Kan.
Fourth Largest Stock Market
in the State. West Plains,
Mo.
Fraternal Capital of the South-
west. Guthrie, Okla.
Free State of Bexar. San
Antonio, Tex.
Free State of Carroll. Carroll-
ton, Ga.
Freedom City. Provo, Utah
French Louisiana. Lafayette,
La.
Friendliest Area in Northern
Lower Michigan. Cadillac,
Mich.
Friendliest City. Rochester,
N. Y.
Friendliest City in the State.
Lebanon, Ind.
Friendliest City on any Inter-
national Border. Ogdensburg,
N. Y.
Friendliest Little "Big Town"
in Kentucky. Murray, Ky.
Friendliest Little City. Avon
Park, Fla.
Friendliest Little City in
Nebraska. Burwell, Neb.
Friendliest Spot on the King's
Highway. San Bruno, Calif.
Friendliest Town. Greenwich,
Conn.
Friendliest Town in America.
Tryon, N. C.
Friendliest Town in New
England. Skowhegan,
Me.

Friendliest Town in Oklahoma.
Drumright, Okla.
Friendliest Town on Earth.
Clarksville, Va.
Friendliest Town on the Lake.
Mabank, Tex.
Friendly and Progressive City.
Mason City, Iowa.
Friendly City.   Albertville,
Ala.
Friendly City.   Algona, Iowa
Friendly City.   Augusta, Ga.
Friendly City.   Austin, Tex.
Friendly City.   Bradenton, Fla.
Friendly City.   Carrollton, Ga.
Friendly City.   Chehalis, Wash.
Friendly City.   Columbus,
Miss.
Friendly City.   Cordova,
Alaska
Friendly City.   Douglas, Ga.
Friendly City.   Fort Worth,
Tex.
Friendly City.   Fortuna, Calif.
Friendly City.   Fredericks-
burg, Va.
Friendly City.   Gilroy, Calif.
Friendly City.   Gresham, Ore.
Friendly City.   Hazlehurst,
Ga.
Friendly City.   Huntsville, Ark.
Friendly City.   Hutchinson,
Kans.
Friendly City.   Jackson, Miss.
Friendly City.   Johnston, R.I.
Friendly City.   Johnstown, Pa.
Friendly City.   Kaukauna, Wis.
Friendly City.   Long Beach,
Miss.
Friendly City.   Long Branch,
N.J.
Friendly City.   Lynchburg, Va.
Friendly City.   McMinnville,
Tenn.
Friendly City.   Mangum, Okla.
Friendly City.   Milwaukee, Wis.
Friendly City.   Muncie, Ind.
Friendly City.   New York, N.Y.
Friendly City.   Owosso, Mich.
Friendly City.   Pampa, Tex.
Friendly City.   Porterville,
Calif.
Friendly City.   Scranton, Pa.
Friendly City.   Shelbyville, Ill.

Friendly City.   Spokane, Wash.
Friendly City.   Starke, Fla.
Friendly City by the Sea where
River, Sound and Ocean Meet.
Swansboro, N.C.
Friendly City in the Heart of
Georgia. Macon, Ga.
Friendly City in the Heart of
the Old West. Douglas,
Ariz.
Friendly City in the Sky.
Denver, Colo.
Friendly City of Endless Charm.
Jacksonville, Fla.
Friendly City of Many Oppor-
tunities. Ruston, La.
Friendly City of Progress.
Goldsboro, N.C.
Friendly City of the Higulands.
Frostproof, Fla.
Friendly City of the Southwest.
Fort Worth, Tex.
Friendly City on the Move.
Franklin, N.H.
Friendly City on the Oregon
Trail. Baker, Ore.
Friendly City with a Future.
Jeannette, Pa.
Friendly Community.   Garden
Grove, Calif.
Friendly Community.   Grove,
Okla.
Friendly Community.   Hesperia,
Calif.
Friendly Community.   Murfrees-
boro, Tenn.
Friendly Community for Progres-
sive Industry. Mount Carmel,
Pa.
Friendly Community in Martin
County. Jensen Beach, Fla.
Friendly Community in Pied-
mont County. Altavista, Va.
Friendly Community of Beauty
and Industry. Upper San-
dusky, Ohio
Friendly Community, the Home
of Friendly People. Ash
Grove, Mo.
Friendly Door to Wisconsin's
Indianhead Country. Eau
Claire, Wis.
Friendly Dunnellon. Dunnellon,
Fla.

Friendly Fabulous Flagstaff.
Flagstaff, Ariz.
Friendly Folk's Village.
Plainfield, Ind.
Friendly Frontier City. Fair-
banks, Alaska
Friendly Island. Martha's
Vineyard, Mass.
Friendly Little City in the
Prosperous Shoshone
Valley. Powell, Wyo.
Friendly Place. Keystone,
S. D.
Friendly Place to Live and
Work. Barre, Vt.
Friendly Progressive and
Dominant City. Columbus,
Ohio
Friendly Prosperous Town.
Fryeburg, Me.
Friendly Resort City. Bradley
Beach, N. J.
Friendly Town. Chesterfield,
Mass.
Friendly Town. Clayton,
N. M.
Friendly Town. Fort Lauder-
dale, Fla.
Friendly Town. Johnston,
R. I.
Friendly Town of Friendly
People. Raritan, N. J.
Friendly Village. Harrison,
Me.
Friendly Village. Mattituck,
N. Y.
Friendly Village. Prentice,
Wis.
Frisco. San Francisco, Calif.
Frog and Toe. New York,
N. Y.
Frog Level. Clinchport, Va.
Frog Market of the Nation.
Rayne, La.
Front Door Entrance to an
Alaska Vacation. Anchorage,
Alaska
Front Office of American
Business. New York, N. Y.
Frontier of Industrial Oppor-
tunity. Laurel, Mont.
Frosty City. Somerset,
Pa.

Fruit Bowl of the Nation.
Yakima, Wash.
Fruit Cake Capital. Claxton,
Ga.
Fudge Capital of the World.
Mackinac Island, Mich.
Fun and Sun Capital. Miami
Beach, Fla.
Fun and Sun Playground. Vir-
ginia Beach, Va.
Fun Capital. Miami Beach,
Fla.
Fun Capital of the South.
Daytona Beach, Fla.
Fun Capital of the Vacation
State. Billings, Mont.
Fun Capital of the World.
Las Vegas, Nev.
Fun Capitol of Southern Ore-
gon. Medford, Ore.
Fun Center of Ohio. Mans-
field, Ohio
Fun City. New York, N. Y.
Fun-City-on-the-Hudson. New
York, N. Y.
Fun Country for Family Rec-
reation. Anaheim, Calif.
Fun Country, U. S. A. Sara-
toga Springs, N. Y.
Fun Festival Place. Miami
Beach, Fla.
Fun in the Sun City. Panama
City, Fla.
Fun 'N Convention City. Ana-
heim, Calif.
Fun 'N Excitement Center.
Scottsdale, Ariz.
Fun Place. Denton, Tex.
Fun Shines Brightest in the
Summer Time. Virginia
Beach, Va.
Fun Spot of the Southwest.
Fort Worth, Tex.
Fun-Tier Capital of Texas.
Austin, Tex.
Fun Town. Park Falls, Wis.
Furniture Capital of America.
Grand Rapids, Mich.
Furniture Center of the World.
Grand Rapids, Mich.
Furniture City. Grand Rapids,
Mich.
Furniture City. High Point, N. C.

FURNITURE 276 Cities

Furniture City. Martinsville, Va.

Furniture City of the World. High Point, N.C.

Furniture Production Center of the U.S. High Point, N.C.

Furniture, Thread and Steel City. Toccoa, Ga.

Future Great City. Pierre, S.D.

Future Great City of the World. St. Louis, Mo.

Future Industrial Capital of the South Shore. Braintree, Mass.

Future Manufacturing Center of the West where Rail and Water Transportation Meet. Petaluma, Calif.

Future Minded City. Chicopee, Mass.

Future Workshop of the Middle West. South Bend, Ind.

Gable Town. Danville, Ind.

Gambler's Mecca. Las Vegas, Nev.

Gambler's Paradise on Earth. Las Vegas, Nev.

Gambling Queen. Muskegon, Mich.

Gamecock City. Sumter, S.C.

Gangland. Chicago, Ill.

Gap. Pennington Gap, Va.

Garbage City. Alameda, Calif.

Garden Center of the Empire State. Medina, N.Y.

Garden City. Basin, Wyo.

Garden City. Beverly, Mass.

Garden City. Cedar Falls, Iowa

Garden City. Chicago, Ill.

Garden City. Missoula, Mont.

Garden City. Newton, Mass.

Garden City. San Jose, Calif.

Garden City. Savannah, Ga.

Garden City of Beauty. Hammonton, N.J.

Garden City of Clark County. Boulder City, Nev.

Garden City of Iowa. Cedar Falls, Iowa

Garden City of Southern Nevada. Boulder City, Nev.

Garden City of the South. Augusta, Ga.

Garden of Maine. Houlton, Me.

Garden of the Glades. Pahokee, Fla.

Garden of the Golden Grapefruit. McAllen, Tex.

Garden Spot for Golf. Virginia Beach, Va.

Garden Spot of Louisiana. Jennings, La.

Garden Spot of Northwest Florida. Monticello, Fla.

Garden Spot of Pennsylvania. Mount Joy, Pa.

Garden Spot of Southern Indiana. Washington, Ind.

Garden Spot of the Garden State. Hammonton, N.J.

Garden Spot of the Palm Beaches. Palm Springs, Fla.

Garden Spot of the Peninsula. Palo Alto, Calif.

Garden Spot of the South. Pensacola, Fla.

Garden Spot of the Universe. Keene, N.H.

Garden Spot of the West. Garden City, Kan.

Garden Spot of the World. Beverly Hills, Calif.

Garden Spot of the World Famous Santa Clara Valley. Los Altos, Calif.

Garrison City. Dover, N.H.

Gas Capital of the World. Elk City, Okla.

Gas Capital of the World. Hugoton, Kan.

Gas House of the Nation. Washington, D.C.

Gate City. Atlanta, Ga.

Gate City. Chattanooga, Tenn.

Gate City. Denison, Tex.

Gate City. Keokuk, Iowa

Gate City. Laredo, Tex.

Gate City. Maricopa, Calif.

Gate City. Nashua, N.H.

Gate City. Rapid City, S.D.

Gate City. Raton, N.M.
Gate City. San Bernardino,
Calif.
Gate City. Winona, Minn.
Gate City of Florida. Jackson-
ville, Fla.
Gate City of New Hampshire.
Nashua, N. H.
Gate City of the Piedmont.
Greenwood, S. C.
Gate City of the South. At-
lanta, Ga.
Gate City of the West. Omaha,
Neb.
Gate City to the Great North-
west. Pocatello, Idaho
Gate City to the South. At-
lanta, Ga.
Gate to the Old South. Rocky
Mount, N. C.
Gate to the Sportsman's Eden.
Ely, Minn.
Gateway. Ashland, Ore.
Gateway Arch City. St.
Louis, Mo.
Gateway Between East and
West. Pittsburgh, Pa.
Gateway Center. Pittsburgh,
Pa.
Gateway City. Edinburg, Tex.
Gateway City. Fargo, N. D.
Gateway City. Huntington,
W. Va.
Gateway City. Jacksonville,
Fla.
Gateway City. La Crosse,
Wis.
Gateway City. Laredo, Tex.
Gateway City. Louisville, Ky.
Gateway City. Minneapolis,
Minn.
Gateway City. Seward, Alaska
Gateway City for the Far
North. Fairbanks, Alaska
Gateway City in the Sun. San
Antonio, Tex.
Gateway City to Canada.
Buffalo, N. Y.
Gateway City to the Bread
Basket of the World. Fargo,
N. D.
Gateway City to the Hills.
Rapid City, S. D.

Gateway City to the West. Iron-
wood, Mich.
Gateway from South and West
to Ozark Playgrounds.
Pryor, Okla.
Gateway of America's Scenic
Wonderland. Dickinson,
N. D.
Gateway of Kansas. Shawnee,
Kan.
Gateway of Lake Superior. Sault
Ste. Marie, Mich.
Gateway of New England. Nor-
walk, Conn.
Gateway of Southern Indiana.
Seymour, Ind.
Gateway of Southern New Eng-
land. Providence, R. I.
Gateway of the Adirondacks.
Utica, N. Y.
Gateway of the Americas.
Miami, Fla.
Gateway of the Lake Region.
Leesburg, Ind.
Gateway of the North. Mas-
sena, N. Y.
Gateway of the South. Atlanta,
Ga.
Gateway of the South. Nash-
ville, Tenn.
Gateway of the Southeast.
Augusta, Ga.
Gateway of the West. St. Louis,
Mo.
Gateway of Vast Farm and In-
dustrial Markets. Gary, Ind.
Gateway of West Texas. Fort
Worth, Tex.
Gateway Port of Alaska.
Ketchikan, Alaska
Gateway Resort Town of Your
Smokies. Gatlinburg, Tenn.
Gateway to a Fabulous Market.
East Brunswick, N. J.
Gateway to a Year 'Round Vaca-
tion. Farmington, Me.
Gateway to Adventure. Ketchi-
kan, Alaska
Gateway to Adventure on North
America's Spectacular
Marine Highway. Ketchikan,
Alaska
Gateway to Alabama's Gulf Coast.
Foley, Ala.

Gateway to Alaska. Ketchi-
kan, Alaska
Gateway to Alaska. Seattle,
Wash.
Gateway to Alaska. Shelby,
Mont.
Gateway to All Florida. Jack-
sonville, Fla.
Gateway to All Florida. Perry,
Fla.
Gateway to All New England.
Norwalk, Conn.
Gateway to America's Last
Wilderness. Sun Valley,
Idaho
Gateway to America's Wonder-
land. Billings, Mont.
Gateway to Ancient Cities.
Mountainair, N. M.
Gateway to Arizona's Scenic
and Recreational Area.
Globe, Ariz.
Gateway to Arkansas. Texar-
kana, Tex.
Gateway to Blue Shoals Lake
and Dam. Flippin, Ark.
Gateway to Brown County.
Morgantown, Ind.
Gateway to California. San
Diego, Calif.
Gateway to California's Newest
Frontier. Kerman, Calif.
Gateway to Camp Pendleton.
Oceanside, Calif.
Gateway to Canada. Buffalo,
N. Y.
Gateway to Canada's St. Law-
rence Seaway. Fort Kent,
Me.
Gateway to Candlewood Lake.
Danbury, Conn.
Gateway to Cape Cod. New
Bedford, Mass.
Gateway to Capitol Reef Na-
tional Monument. Torrey,
Utah
Gateway to Cherry Point.
Havelock, N. C.
Gateway to Chiricahua National
Monument. Bowie, Ariz.
Gateway to Colorado's
Scenic Region. Boulder,
Colo.

Gateway to Connecticut. Hart-
ford, Conn.
Gateway to Coteau Lake Region.
Webster, S. D.
Gateway to Death Valley.
Beatty, Nev.
Gateway to East Texas' Enchant-
ing Vacationland. Jasper,
Tex.
Gateway to Eastern Michigan.
Royal Oak, Mich.
Gateway to Edwards. Rosa-
mond, Calif.
Gateway to Egypt. Centralia,
Ill.
Gateway to Everywhere. East
Windsor, N. J.
Gateway to Fabulous Hunting
and Fishing. Crookston,
Minn.
Gateway to Famous Recreation
Areas. Millinocket, Me.
Gateway to Florida. Pensacola,
Fla.
Gateway to Fort Huachuca.
Bisbee, Ariz.
Gateway to Ft. Hood. Kileen,
Tex.
Gateway to Four Ozark Vaca-
tion Areas. Springfield, Mo.
Gateway to Garrison Dam.
Minot, N. D.
Gateway to Garrison Dam and
Roosevelt National Memorial
Park. Stanley, N. D.
Gateway to Giant Greer's Ferry
Lake. Heber Springs, Ark.
Gateway to Glacier Bay Na-
tional Monument. Juneau,
Alaska
Gateway to Historyland.
Fredericksburg, Va.
Gateway to Hite and Glen Can-
yon. Hanksville, Utah
Gateway to Hopiland and Navajo-
land. Winslow, Ariz.
Gateway to Hoover Dam. King-
man, Ariz.
Gateway to Indiana Dunes.
Gary, Ind.
Gateway to International Fun
for the Entire Family.
Ogdensburg, N. Y.

Gateway to Isle Royal National
Park. Grand Portage,
Minn.
Gateway to Itasca Park. Bag-
ley, Minn.
Gateway to Jekyll Island.
Brunswick, Ga.
Gateway to Kenai Peninsula.
Seward, Alaska
Gateway to Lake Erie. San-
dusky, Ohio
Gateway to Lake Greeson and
the Daisy State Park.
Kirby, Ark.
Gateway to Lake Lanier.
Cumming, Ga.
Gateway to Lake Mead and
Hoover Dam. Las Vegas,
Nev.
Gateway to Lake Norfolk.
Mountain Home, Ark.
Gateway to Lake of the
Ozarks. Eldon, Mo.
Gateway to Lake Tahoe and
Yosemite Valley. Carson
City, Nev.
Gateway to Lake "Whitney".
Cleburne, Tex.
Gateway to Latin America.
Miami, Fla.
Gateway to Mackinac Island
and Upper Peninsula of
Michigan. Mackinaw City,
Mich.
Gateway to Maine. Bidde-
ford, Me.
Gateway to Maine. Kittery,
Me.
Gateway to Maine. Saco, Me.
Gateway to Maine from the
White Mountains. Bethel,
Me.
Gateway to Mexico. El Paso,
Tex.
Gateway to Mexico. Laredo,
Tex.
Gateway to Mexico. McAllen,
Tex.
Gateway to Mexico. San
Antonio, Tex.
Gateway to Mexico's Great
West Coast. Nogales,
Ariz.

Gateway to Michigan. New
Buffalo, Mich.
Gateway to Monument Valley.
Kayenta, Ariz.
Gateway to Mt. Katahdin. Mil-
linocket, Me.
Gateway to Mt. Magazine.
Paris, Ark.
Gateway to Mount Magazine.
Booneville, Mo.
Gateway to Mount Ranier.
Tacoma, Wash.
Gateway to Mountainland.
Provo, Utah
Gateway to Mountains and Sea-
shore. Cayce, S.C.
Gateway to Muir Woods. Mill
Valley, Calif.
Gateway to Nebraska's Vaca-
tionland. Omaha, Neb.
Gateway to New England. Dan-
bury, Conn.
Gateway to New England.
Greenwich, Conn.
Gateway to New England. New
Haven, Conn.
Gateway to Niagara Falls.
Williamsville, N.Y.
Gateway to Nova. Edgewater,
Fla.
Gateway to Ocala National
Forest. Umatilla, Fla.
Gateway to Okefenokee Swamp.
Waycross, Ga.
Gateway to Old Mexico. San
Antonio, Tex.
Gateway to Old Virginia. Win-
chester, Va.
Gateway to Outdoor Fishing and
Hunting Activities. Monett,
Mo.
Gateway to Padre Island.
Corpus Christi, Tex.
Gateway to Pictured Rocks.
Munising, Mich.
Gateway to Picturesque Canada.
Buffalo, N.Y.
Gateway to Picturesque Pre-
cision Valley. Springfield, Vt.
Gateway to Pittsburgh. Mon-
roeville, Pa.
Gateway to Pleasure. Las Vegas,
Nev.

Gateway to Possum Kingdom
Lake. Mineral Wells, Tex.
Gateway to Priest River Lake
Country. Priest River,
Idaho
Gateway to Rangeley and Sugar-
loaf. Farmington, Me.
Gateway to Real Vacation
Pleasure. Jackman, Me.
Gateway to Recreation. Sole-
dad, Calif.
Gateway to Roosevelt Na-
tional Forest and Rocky
Mountain National Park.
Boulder, Colo.
Gateway to "Sailfish Alley."
Boynton Beach, Fla.
Gateway to Salt and Fresh-
water Fishing, Hunting,
Scenic Beauty and Fun.
Ketchikan, Alaska
Gateway to San Luis Rey Mis-
sion. Oceanside, Calif.
Gateway to Scenic Adventure.
Ely, Nev.
Gateway to Scenic Boston
Mountains. Fayetteville,
Ark.
Gateway to Scenic Southern
Indiana. Greater Bloom-
ington, Ind.
Gateway to Six Flags Over
Texas. Grand Prairie,
Tex.
Gateway to Sleeping Bear
Dunes. Honor, Mich.
Gateway to Smuggler's Notch.
Stowe, Vt.
Gateway to Sonoyta, Mexico,
and the Gulf of Lower Cali-
fornia. Ajo, Ariz.
Gateway to South Dakota's
Vacation Wonderland.
Yankton, S.D.
Gateway to Southeast Arkansas.
Pine Bluff, Ark.
Gateway to Space. St. Louis, Mo.
Gateway to Stevens Pass.
Monroe, Wash.
Gateway to Texas. Jefferson,
Tex.
Gateway to Texas. Washing-
ton, Ark.

Gateway to Texas and the As-
trodome. Orange, Tex.
Gateway to the (See also under
"Gateway of" and "Gateway
to")
Gateway to the Adirondacks.
Glens Falls, N.Y.
Gateway to the Adirondacks.
Lake Luzerne, N.Y.
Gateway to the Adirondacks.
Utica, N.Y.
Gateway to the Adirondacks and
the 1000 Island Region.
Carthage, N.Y.
Gateway to the Allagash County.
Fort Kent, Me.
Gateway to the American West.
St. Louis, Mo.
Gateway to the Apalachicola
System. Apalachicola, Fla.
Gateway to the Arctic. Fair-
banks, Alaska
Gateway to the Badlands.
Kadoka, S.D.
Gateway to the Badlands and
the Pine Ridge Indian Reser-
vation. Kadoka, S.D.
Gateway to the Badlands Na-
tional Park. Wall, S.D.
Gateway to the Bar Harbor
Region. Green Lake, Me.
Gateway to the Bar Harbor
Region and Atlantic Canada.
Ellsworth, Me.
Gateway to the Bass Capital of
the World. Crescent City,
Fla.
Gateway to the Bauxite Fields.
Benton, Ark.
Gateway to the Bear River
Migratory Bird Refuge.
Brigham, Utah
Gateway to the Beautiful Monte-
rey Peninsula. Seaside,
Calif.
Gateway to the Beautiful Oke-
fenokee Swamp. Folkston,
Ga.
Gateway to the Beautiful Ozark
Playground. Fort Smith, Ark.
Gateway to the Berkshires.
Winsted, Conn.
Gateway to the Black Hills.
Pierre, S.D.

Gateway to the Black Hills.
Rapid City, S. D.
Gateway to the Black Hills.
Winner, S. D.
Gateway to the Boston
Mountains. Fayetteville,
Ark.
Gateway to the Bridger Wilder-
ness. Pinedale, Wyo
Gateway to the Canyonlands
and Highland of Southeastern
Utah. Price, Utah
Gateway to the Caribbean.
Tampa, Fla.
Gateway to the Carolina Sea
Islands. Beaufort, S. C.
Gateway to the Catskills.
Kingston, N. Y.
Gateway to the Centers of the
Aerospace Industry. St.
Louis, Mo.
Gateway to the Chattahoochee
National Forest. Dalton,
Ga.
Gateway to the Chippewa Na-
tional Forest. Deer River,
Minn.
Gateway to the Coulee Country.
La Crosse, Wisc.
Gateway to the Dakotas. Sioux
Falls, S. D.
Gateway to the Delta. Yazoo
City, Miss.
Gateway to the Desert and
Idyllwild Mountain Resort.
Banning, Calif.
Gateway to the Early West.
Westport, Mo.
Gateway to the East. Kearney,
Neb.
Gateway to the Everglades.
Fort Lauderdale, Fla.
Gateway to the Fabulous Desert
Lake Region. Apache
Junction, Ariz.
Gateway to the Famed North-
woods. St. Paul, Minn.
Gateway to the Famous Gold
Coast. Hobe Sound, Fla.
Gateway to the Famous Sand-
hills. Sanford, N. C.
Gateway to the Far East. San
Francisco, Calif.

Gateway to the Fish River Chain
of Lakes. Fort Kent, Me.
Gateway to the Friendly City.
Concord, N. C.
Gateway to the Future in Space.
Picayune, Miss.
Gateway to the Galaxies. Titus-
ville, Fla.
Gateway to the Gila Wilderness.
Silver City, N. M.
Gateway to the Golden Interior.
Skagway, Alaska
Gateway to the Grand Canyon.
Kanab, Utah
Gateway to the Grand Canyon.
Las Vegas, Nev.
Gateway to the Grand Lakes
Area. Princeton, Me.
Gateway to the Grand Strand.
Conway, S. C.
Gateway to the Great Coal
Fields of Southern West Vir-
ginia. Bluefield, W. Va.
Gateway to the Great Lakes of
the South. Knoxville, Tenn.
Gateway to the Great Life. San
Diego, Calif.
Gateway to the Great Mad River
Valley. Blue Lake, Calif.
Gateway to the Great Northwest
Market. Salem, Ore.
Gateway to the Great Smokies.
Gatlinburg, Tenn.
Gateway to the Great Smoky
Mountains National Park.
Cherokee, N. C.
Gateway to the Great Smoky
Mountains National Park.
Knoxville, Tenn.
Gateway to the Great Smoky
Mountains National Park.
Waynesville, N. C.
Gateway to the Great Southwest.
Marshall, Tex.
Gateway to the Great Tahoe
National Forest. Nevada
City, Calif.
Gateway to the Greatest Vaca-
tionland in Mid-America.
Henderson, Ky.
Gateway to the Green Mountain
State. White River Junction,
Vt.

Gateway to the Gulf Coast.
Pensacola, Fla.
Gateway to the Gulf of Mexico.
Surfside, Tex.
Gateway to the Hamptons.
Riverhead, N.Y.
Gateway to the Heartland of
America. Buffalo, N.Y.
Gateway to the Historic
Northwest. Glendive, Mont.
Gateway to the Holiday High-
lands. Haines City, Fla.
Gateway to the Indiana Lake
Area. Warsaw, Ind.
Gateway to the Inland Empire.
Spokane, Wash.
Gateway to the Intercoastal
Waterway. Apalachicola,
Fla.
Gateway to the Interior.
Valdez, Alaska
Gateway to the International
Peace Garden. Rugby,
N.D.
Gateway to the Lake Mead
Recreational Area. Boulder
City, Nev.
Gateway to the Lake of the
Ozarks. Sedalia, Mo.
Gateway to the Lake Region.
Webster, S.D.
Gateway to the Lakes. Cleve-
land, Tex.
Gateway to the Lakes. Drum-
right, Okla.
Gateway to the Lakes and
Streams of the Thunder
Mountain Region. Crivitz,
Wis.
Gateway to the Land O'Lakes.
Sedalia, Mo.
Gateway to the Largest Wilder-
ness Area in the U.S.
Lander, Wyo
Gateway to the Litchfield
Hills. Waterbury, Conn.
Gateway to the Mammoth Cave.
Cave City, Ky.
Gateway to the Midwest.
Canton, Ohio
Gateway to the Midwest.
La Crosse, Wis.
Gateway to the Miss Universe

Highway. New Castle,
Pa.
Gateway to the Missile Test
Center. Eau Gallie, Fla.
Gateway to the Mount Mansfield
Area. Waterbury, Vt.
Gateway to the Nebraska Pan-
handle. Ogallala, Neb.
Gateway to the New England
Shoreline. Branford, Conn.
Gateway to the Newton Hills
State Park. Canton, S.D.
Gateway to the North. Clare,
Mich.
Gateway to the North. Fort
Anne, N.Y.
Gateway to the North Central
Section of the Ozark Na-
tional Forest. Paris, Mo.
Gateway to the North Unit of
the Theodore Roosevelt Na-
tional Memorial Park. Wal-
ford City, N.D.
Gateway to the North Woods.
Bangor, Me.
Gateway to the Northeast King-
dom. Lyndonville, Vt.
Gateway to the Northern Indiana
Lake Region. Fort Wayne,
Ind.
Gateway to the Northern Sec-
tion of the Ozark National
Forest. Booneville, Mo.
Gateway to the Northwest.
Bentonville, Ark.
Gateway to the Northwest.
Minneapolis, Minn.
Gateway to the Northwest. St.
Paul, Minn.
Gateway to the Northwest.
Vacaville, Calif.
Gateway to the Ohio Lake Erie
Islands. Sandusky, Ohio
Gateway to the Old Western
Reserve. Youngstown, Ohio
Gateway to the Old Western
Reserve. Zanesville, Ohio
Gateway to the Olympic Na-
tional Park. Everett, Wash.
Gateway to the Orange Empire.
Baldwin Park, Calif.
Gateway to the Orient. San
Francisco, Calif.

Gateway to the Orient. Seattle,
Wash.
Gateway to the Ottawa National
Forest. Iron River, Wis.
Gateway to the Ozarks. Dover,
Ark.
Gateway to the Ozarks. Har-
rison, Ark.
Gateway to the Ozarks. Jop-
lin, Mo.
Gateway to the Palmetto State.
Dillon, S.C.
Gateway to the Palmetto State.
Latta, S.C.
Gateway to the Pennsylvania
Dutch Country. Downing-
town, Pa.
Gateway to the Pennsylvania
Dutch Country. Lambert-
ville, N.J.
Gateway to the Petit Jean
Mountain. Morrilton, Ark.
Gateway to the Petrified
Forest National Park. Hol-
brook, Ariz.
Gateway to the Pines. Mine-
ola, Tex.
Gateway to the Poconos.
Stroudsburg, Pa.
Gateway to the Poudre. Fort
Collins, Colo.
Gateway to the Proposed
Sleeping Bear National Park.
Frankfort, Mich.
Gateway to the Rangeley Lakes.
Farmington, Me.
Gateway to the Rio Grande
Valley. Edinburg, Tex.
Gateway to the Rockies.
Aurora, Colo.
Gateway to the Rockies.
Denver, Colo.
Gateway to the Rockies.
Limon, Colo.
Gateway to the Routt National
Forest. Steamboat Springs,
Colo.
Gateway to the Ruby Moun-
tains. Wells, Nev.
Gateway to the St. Francis.
Marianna, Ark.
Gateway to the St. Lawrence

Power and Seaway. Water-
town, N.Y.
Gateway to the Salt River Chain
of Lakes. Apache Junction,
Ariz.
Gateway to the San Fernando
Valley. North Hollywood,
Calif.
Gateway to the San Gabriels.
Azusa, Calif.
Gateway to the San Joaquin
Valley. Stockton, Calif.
Gateway to the Sand Dune
Mountains. Mears, Mich.
Gateway to the Santiam Vaca-
tion and Recreation Area.
Albany, Ore.
Gateway to the Scenic Cumber-
land Mountains. Lafayette,
Tenn.
Gateway to the Smokies. Gat-
linburg, Tenn.
Gateway to the Smokies. John-
son City, Tenn.
Gateway to the Smokies. Knox-
ville, Tenn.
Gateway to the Smokies. New-
port, Tenn.
Gateway to the Smoky Mountains.
Erwin, Tenn.
Gateway to the Snowy Range.
Laramie, Wyo.
Gateway to the South. Annapo-
lis, Md.
Gateway to the South. Breeze-
wood, Pa.
Gateway to the South. Cin-
cinnati, Ohio
Gateway to the South. Colum-
bia, S.C.
Gateway to the South. Hender-
son, N.C.
Gateway to the South. Louis-
ville, Ky.
Gateway to the South. Lower
Township, N.J.
Gateway to the South. Memphis,
Tenn.
Gateway to the South. Rich-
mond, Va.
Gateway to the South. Willow
Springs, Mo.

Gateway to the Southern Cat-
skills. Harriman, N.Y.
Gateway to the Southern
Ozarks. Springfield, Mo.
Gateway to the Southwest.
Christiansburg, Va.
Gateway to the Southwest.
West Memphis, Ark.
Gateway to the Space Pro-
gram. Eau Gallie, Fla.
Gateway to the Sportsman's
Eden. Ely, Minn.
Gateway to the Sportsman's Para-
dise. Nevada City, Calif.
Gateway to the Stikine.
Wrangell, Alaska
Gateway to the Ten Thousand
Islands. Naples, Fla.
Gateway to the Thousand Is-
lands. Cape Vincent, N.Y.
Gateway to the Thousand Is-
lands. Watertown, N.Y.
Gateway to the Tollroads.
Westchester, Ill.
Gateway to the Tropics.
Belleview, Fla.
Gateway to the United States.
Philadelphia, Pa.
Gateway to the Vacationland
of Shasta. Redding, Calif.
Gateway to the Valley of Per-
fect Apples. Wenatchee,
Wash.
Gateway to the Valley of the
Sun. Phoenix, Ariz.
Gateway to the Volcanoes.
Hilo, Hawaii
Gateway to the Water Wonder-
land. Grand Rapids, Mich.
Gateway to the Water Wonder-
land. Morley, Mich.
Gateway to the West. Billings,
Mont.
Gateway to the West. Dickin-
son, N.D.
Gateway to the West. Fort
Wayne, Ind.
Gateway to the West. Fort
Worth, Tex.
Gateway to the West. Inde-
pendence, Mo.
Gateway to the West. Kearney,
Neb.

Gateway to the West. Omaha,
Neb
Gateway to the West. Pitts-
burgh, Pa.
Gateway to the West. Port
Allen, La.
Gateway to the West. St. Louis,
Mo.
Gateway to the West. Schenec-
tady, N.Y.
Gateway to the West. Sioux
Falls, S.D.
Gateway to the West and South-
west. Kansas City, Mo.
Gateway to the West where the
Ohio and the Beaver Rivers
Meet. Rochester, Pa.
Gateway to Western Wyoming's
Wonderland. Kemmerer,
Wyo.
Gateway to the White Mountains.
Franklin, N.H.
Gateway to the White Mountains
of Eastern Arizona. Springer-
ville, Ariz.
Gateway to the Whiteman Air
Force Base. Knob Noster,
Mo.
Gateway to the Winneshiek.
Prairie du Chien, Wis.
Gateway to the Wisconsin Cran-
berry Country. Tomah,
Wisc.
Gateway to the World. Duluth,
Minn.
Gateway to the World. Kenosha,
Wis.
Gateway to the World. New
Orleans, La.
Gateway to the World through
the St. Lawrence Seaway.
Duluth, Minn.
Gateway to the World's Largest
Bird Refuge. Brigham City,
Utah
Gateway to the World's Most
Concentrated Lake Region.
Rhinelander, Wis.
Gateway to the World's Richest
Market. Buffalo, N.Y.
Gateway to the Yukon. Skag-
way, Alaska

Gateway to Three Local Slogan
States, Virginia, Tennessee,
North Carolina. Damascus,
Va.
Gateway to Tropical Florida.
New Port Richey, Fla.
Gateway to Tropical Florida.
Palmetto, Fla.
Gateway to Tropical Florida's
First Resort. Jupiter, Fla.
Gateway to Twelve Beautiful
Lakes. Theresa, N.Y.
Gateway to Upstate. Middle-
town, N.Y.
Gateway to Utah's Famous
Mountainland. Provo, Utah
Gateway to Vacationland.
Massena, N.Y.
Gateway to Vacationland.
Portland, Me.
Gateway to Vacationland.
Provo, Utah
Gateway to Vacationland.
Rochester, N.H.
Gateway to Vacationland.
Rochester, N.Y.
Gateway to Vast Farm and
Industrial Markets. Gary,
Ind.
Gateway to Virginia. Roslyn,
Va.
Gateway to Wallowa National
Forest. Enterprise, Ore.
Gateway to "Wanderland" in
Mohave County, Arizona.
Kingman, Ariz.
Gateway to West Bend Grotto.
Algona, Iowa
Gateway to West Texas. Fort
Worth, Tex.
Gateway to World Ports.
Tampa, Fla.
Gateway to Yellowstone and
Teton National Parks.
Rock Springs, Wyo.
Gateway to Yosemite. Merced,
Calif.
Gateway to Yosemite Sequoia
and King Canyon Parks.
Fresno, Calif.
Gateway to Your Georgia Va-
cationland. Brunswick, Ga.

Gateway to Zane Grey's Tonto
Basin and Navajoland.
Winslow, Ariz.
Gateway to Zion National Park.
Hurricane, Utah
Gateway to Zion National Park.
St. George, Utah
Gem Capital of the World.
Franklin, N.C.
Gem City. Dayton, Ohio
Gem City. Laramie, Who.
Gem City. Palatka, Fla.
Gem City. Pulaski, Va.
Gem City. Quincy, Ill.
Gem City. Redlands, Calif.
Gem City. St. Paul, Minn.
Gem City. Salida, Colo.
Gem City in Arizona's Valley of
the Sun. Mesa, Ariz.
Gem City in the Heart of the
Great Mississippi Valley.
Quincy, Ill.
Gem City of Cedar Empire.
Coquille, Ore.
Gem City of Mid-America.
Quincy, Ill.
Gem City of Ohio. Dayton,
Ohio
Gem City of Southern Alabama.
Andalusia, Ala.
Gem City of the Foothills. Los
Gatos, Calif.
Gem City of the Foothills.
Monrovia, Calif.
Gem City of the Lakes. Erie,
Pa.
Gem City of the Middle West.
Quincy, Ill.
Gem City of the Rockies. Ouray,
Colo.
Gem City of the Wabash. At-
tica, Ind.
Gem City of the Wealthy San
Joaquin Valley. Madera,
Calif.
Gem City of the West. Quincy,
Ill.
Gem in the Beautiful Southern
California Setting. Loma
Linda, Calif.
Gem of Beaches. Long Beach,
Calif.

Gem of Florida's Keys.   Key
Colony Beach, Fla.
Gem of Penobscot Bay.   Cam-
den, Me.
Gem of the Cascades.   Dia-
mond Lake, Ore.
Gem of the Florida East
Coast.   Vero Beach, Fla.
Gem of the Gold Coast.
Pompano Beach, Fla.
Gem of the Hills.   Clermont,
Fla.
Gem of the Jersey Coast.
Avalon, N.J.
Gem of the Nooksack Valley.
Ferndale, Wash.
Gem of the Ocean.   Salida,
Colo.
Gem of the Pacific.   La Jolla,
Calif.
Gem of the Pacific Coast.
La Jolla, Calif.
Gem of the Plains.   Abilene,
Kan.
Gem of the Prairies.   Chicago,
Ill.
Gem of the Rockies.   Ouray,
Colo.
Gem of the San Juans.   Orcas,
Wash.
Gem of the Valley.   Redlands,
Calif.
Gem on the Ocean.   Lantana,
Fla.
Generous People.   Puyallup,
Wash.
Gentile People.   Corinne, Utah
Geographic Center of Industrial
Southern Illinois.   West
Frankfort, Ill.
Geographic Center of the Oil
Industry in the Rocky
Mountains.   Casper, Wyo.
Geographic Cultural and Eco-
nomic Center.   Little Rock,
Ark.
Geographic Heart of the State.
Wisconsin Rapids, Wis.
Geographical Center of Magic
Valley.   Jerome, Idaho
Geographical Center of
Michigan.   St. Louis,
Mich.

Geographical Center of North
America.   Rugby, N.D.
Geographical Center of the
Metropolitan Boston Area.
Cambridge, Mass.
Geographical Center of the
South.   Huntsville, Ala.
Geographical Crossroads of
Louisiana.   Alexandria, La.
George Washington's Boyhood
Home.   Fredericksburg, Va.
Georgia Vacationland.   Bruns-
wick, Ga.
Georgia Vacationland.   Sea Is-
land, Ga.
Georgia Vacationland.   St.
Simons Island, Ga.
Georgia's Colonial Capital.
Savannah, Ga.
Georgia's Colonial Capital City.
Savannah, Ga.
Georgia's Cradle of the Revo-
lution.   Midway, Ga.
Georgia's Fabulous Year Round
Beach Resort.   Jekyll Is-
land, Ga.
Georgia's First City.   Savannah,
Ga.
Georgia's First Inland Port.
Bainbridge, Ga.
Georgia's Golden Isles.   Bruns-
wick, Ga.
Georgia's Island of Friendli-
ness and Hospitality.   Jekyll
Island, Ga.
Georgia's Mobile Home Center.
Americus, Ga.
Georgia's Mountain Resort.
Clayton, Ga.
Georgia's Ocean Port.   Bruns-
wick, Ga.
Georgia's Playground for Family
Fun.   Jekyll Island, Ga.
Georgia's Second Oldest City.
Augusta, Ga.
Georgia's "Welcome World"
City.   Waycross, Ga.
Georgia's Year-Round Family
Beach Resort.   Jekyll Is-
land, Ga.
Georgia's Year Round Family
Resort.   Jekyll Island,
Ga.

German Athens. Milwaukee,
Wis.

Giant of the Golden Bend.
Houston, Tex.

Gibraltar of America. Vicksburg, Miss.

Gibraltar of Democracy. Hoboken, N.J.

Gibraltar of Louisiana. Vicksburg, Miss.

Gibraltar of the Confederacy.
Vicksburg, Miss.

Gibraltar of the Hudson.
West Point, N.Y.

Gibraltar of the South.
Vicksburg, Miss.

Gladioli Capital of the World.
Fort Myers, Fla.

Glamor Capital of the World.
Hollywood, Calif.

Glamor Capital of the World.
Los Angeles, Calif.

Glamour and Action Capital of
the World. Las Vegas, Nev.

Glamour City. Hollywood,
Calif.

Glass Capital of the World.
Toledo, Ohio

Glass Center. Toledo, Ohio

Glass City. Jeannette, Pa.

Glen. Singers Glen, Va.

Glider Capital of America.
Elmira, N.Y.

Glider Capital of the World.
Elmira, N.Y.

Gliding and Soaring Center
of the United States.
Frankfort, Mich.

Global Center of the New
South. New Orleans, La.

Glorious Past ... A Bril-
liant Present ... Looking
Forward to an Exciting
Future. Philadelphia, Pa.

Go-Ahead City Along the
Niagara Frontier. Buffalo,
N.Y.

Goat Creek. Mazama, Wash.

God's Greatest City. Detroit,
Mich.

God's Square Mile of Health
and Happiness. Ocean
Grove, N.J.

Gold Coast City. Miami
Beach, Fla.

Gold Coast in Florida. Lake
Worth, Fla.

Gold Coast of Oregon. Baker,
Ore.

Gold-Rush Ghost Town. Idaho
City, Idaho

Golden Age Haven. Concord,
Mass.

Golden Buckle on the Cotton
Belt. Clarksdale, Miss.

Golden Buckle on the Wheat
Belt. Colby, Kan.

Golden City. Sacramento,
Calif.

Golden City. San Francisco,
Calif.

Golden City of the Gold Coast.
Boca Raton, Fla.

Golden Coast of Florida. Palm
Beach, Fla.

Golden Gate City. San Francisco, Calif.

Golden Gateway to the Great
Gulf Southwest. Marshall,
Tex.

Golden Heart of Alaska. Fairbanks, Alaska

Golden Heart Metropolis of the
Interior. Fairbanks, Alaska

Golden Heart of the North.
Fairbanks, Alaska

Golden Isle in a By-Gone Golden
Age. Jekyll Island, Ga.

Golden Isles of Georgia. St.
Simons Island, Ga.

Golden Isles of Georgia. Sea
Islands, Ga.

Golden Rule City. Columbia,
S.C.

Goldrush City. Idaho Springs,
Colo.

Golf Capital of America.
Augusta, Ga.

Golf Capital of Pennsylvania.
Hershey, Pa.

Golf Capital of the Midwest.
Chicago, Ill.

Golf Capital of the U.S.
Augusta, Ga.

Golf Capital of the United States.
Pinehurst, N.C.

Golf Capital of the World.
  Palm Springs, Calif.
Golfers' and Vacationers' Para-
  dise. Lake Placid, N.Y.
Golfing and Fishing Paradise.
  Garrison, N.D.
Golfing Capital of Florida.
  Sebring, Fla.
Golfland, U.S.A. San Diego,
  Calif.
Golftown, U.S.A. Pinehurst,
  N.C.
Golftown, U.S.A. Rehobeth,
  Md.
Goliath of All North-Eastern
  North America. Mount
  Washington, N.H.
Good Camping Ground. Mukil-
  teo, Wash.
Good Home Town. Roby, Tex.
Good Life in Texas. Austin,
  Tex.
Good Little Town. Willits,
  Calif.
Good Place in which to Live
  and Work. Exeter, Calif.
Good Place in which to Work
  and Live. Coatesville, Pa.
Good Place to Aim For. Cleve-
  land, Tenn.
Good Place to Know, Go, Visit,
  Stay. Willcox, Ariz.
Good Place to Live. Aber-
  deen, S.D.
Good Place to Live. Chula
  Vista, Calif.
Good Place to Live. Fontana,
  Calif.
Good Place to Live. Oxford,
  Miss.
Good Place to Live and Enjoy
  Life. Valley City. N.D.
Good Place to Live and Work.
  Blacksburg, Va.
Good Place to Live and Work.
  Marshalltown, Iowa
Good Place to Live--Better.
  Brandon, Fla.
Good Place to Live, to Work
  and to Rear Your Family.
  East Point, Ga.
Good Place to Live, Work and
  Do Business. Keokuk, Iowa

Good Place to Live, Work and
  Enjoy Life. Sedalia, Mo.
Good Place to Live, Work and
  Play. Canton, Ill.
Good Place to Live, Work and
  Play. Ellwood City, Pa.
Good Place to Live, Work and
  Play. Fremont, Neb.
Good Place to Live, Work and
  Play. Groveland, Fla.
Good Place to Live, Work and
  Play. New Albany, Ind.
Good Place to Visit. Sebring,
  Fla.
Good Place to Visit, A Good
  Place to Live. Dickinson,
  N.D.
Good Place to Work and Live.
  Grand Island, Neb.
Good Place to Work ... In and
  From. Falls Church, Va.
Good Place to Work, Live and
  Play. Williston, N.D.
Good Size Town for Knowing
  Your Neighbor. Abilene, Kan.
Good Times Capital. Richmond,
  Va.
Goose Capital of the World.
  Cairo, Ill.
Goose Capital of the World.
  Mounds, Ill.
Goosetown. Wilbur, Wash.
Gotham. New York, N.Y.
Governmental, Educational,
  Recreational Center. Albany,
  N.Y.
Gracious City. Hutchinson,
  Kan.
Gracious Residential Community.
  Glendora, Calif.
Gracious Well-Planned City for
  Pleasant Living or Working.
  Cedar Rapids, Iowa
Grain Center. Lamberton,
  Minn.
Granary of the Confederacy.
  Edinburg, Va.
Grand Canyon of the East.
  Ausable Chasm, N.Y.
Grand Central Station of the
  Underground Railroad.
  Fountain City, Ind.

Grand Emporium of the West.
Washington, D. C.
Grand Metropolis. Washington,
D. C.
Grand Place to Live and Earn
a Living. Blytheville, Ark.
Granite Center. Hardwick, Vt.
Granite Center of the World.
Barre, Vt.
Granite Center of the World.
Elberton, Ga.
Granite City. Ashland, Ore.
Granite City. Elberton, Ga.
Granite City. Milbank, S. D.
Granite City. Quincy, Mass.
Granite City. St. Cloud, Minn.
Granite City. Snyder, Okla.
Granite City. Spencer, S. D.
Grass Lands. Palouse, Wash.
Grass Roots of America. Or-
fordville, Wis.
Grassy Place. Kennewick,
Wash.
Graveyard of the Atlantic.
Hatteras, N. C.
Great American City. Phila-
delphia, Pa.
Great American Resort. Miami
Beach, Fla
Great American Shrine. Spring-
field, Ill.
Great Convention-Vacation Lo-
cation. Las Vegas, Nev.
Great Dismal. Washington,
D. C.
Great for Business, Great for
Living and Growing Greater.
Milwaukee, Wis.
Great Intermountain Transporta-
tion Center. Billings, Mont.
Great Outdoor Recreation City.
Tulsa, Okla.
Great Place for Living. Bur-
lington, Iowa
Great Place to Live. Gonzalez,
Tex.
Great Place to Live. Pittsburg,
Calif.
Great Place to Vacation, A
Wonderful Place to Live.
Sea Island, Ga.
Great Place to Visit. Gettys-
burg, Pa.

Great Place to Visit, A Wonder-
ful Place to Live. Carra-
belle, Fla.
Great Railroad Center. Fos-
toria, Ohio
Great River City. St. Louis,
Mo.
Great Salt Lake City. Salt Lake
City, Utah
Great Serbonian Bog. Wash-
ington, D. C.
Great Smokies' Mountain Lake
Neighbor. Murphy, N. C.
Great South Gate. New Orleans,
La.
Great Sports Resort Community.
Seattle, Wash.
Great Today--Greater Tomor-
row. Des Moines, Iowa
Great White City. Washington,
D. C.
Greater Miami Means More.
Miami, Fla.
Greatest All-Year Round Vaca-
tion City. New York, N. Y.
Greatest Automobile Capital.
Detroit, Mich.
Greatest City's Greatest Borough.
Brooklyn, N. Y.
Greatest Industrial Center in
the World. New York, N. Y.
Greatest Little Town in the
Midwest. Spencer, S. D.
Greatest Lumber Market in the
World. Bangor, Me.
Greatest Market in Northwest
Oklahoma. Woodward, Okla.
Greatest Primary Winter Wheat
Market. Kansas City, Mo.
Greatest Show in Tobaccoland.
Wilson, N. C.
Greatest Steel City in the World.
Pittsburgh, Pa.
Greatest Town for Fishing in
New England. Marblehead,
Mass.
Greatest Vacation Spot of All.
Miami, Fla.
Green Bean Center. Stayton,
Ore.
Green Felt Jungle. Las Vegas,
Nev.
Green Mountain City. Mont-
pelier, Vt.

Green Spot in Arizona's Famous
Valley of the Sun. Chandler,
Ariz.
Greenest Spot in the Golden
Spread of Texas. Shamrock,
Tex.
Greenwich Village of the West.
Sausalito, Calif.
Gretna Green. Elkton, Md.
Gretna Green. Ripley, N.Y.
Gretna Green of Maryland.
Elkton, Md.
Greyhound City. Abilene, Kan.
Grindstone City. Berea, Ohio
Growing Center of Administra-
tive Offices. San Mateo,
Calif.
Growing City. Albuquerque,
N.M.
Growing City. Casper, Wyo.
Growing City. Hastings, Neb.
Growing City. Sioux Falls,
S.D.
Growing City Convenient to
Recreation Areas. War-
wick, R.I.
Growing City of Industry and
Recreation. Fort Smith,
Ark.
Growing City of Opportunity.
Abilene, Kan.
Growing City of the Lower Rio
Grande Valley of Texas.
Harlingen, Tex.
Growing Community Centered
in a Growing Market.
Bellingham, Mass.
Growing Gowanda. Gowanda,
N.Y.
Growing Grafton Leads North
Dakota. Grafton, N.D.
Growing Industrial Center of
Northwestern Pennsylvania.
Bradford, Pa.
Growing Industrial, Financial
and Educational Center.
Louisville, Ky.
Growing Progressive Commu-
nity. Somerset, Pa.
Growing Village Surrounded
by Mountains and Small
Lakes. Ludlow, Vt.
Growingest City in

Louisiana. Bossier City,
La.
Growingest City in the Rio
Grande Valley. Harlingen,
Tex.
Growingest City in the South.
Orlando, Fla.
Growth Center of the Missis-
sippi. Baton Rouge, La.
Growth Market in Lorain
County. Elyria, Ohio
Guided Missile Research and
Space Flight Center. Hunts-
ville, Ala.
Gulf City. Mobile, Ala.
Gulf City. New Orleans, La.
Gulf Coast City. Pensacola,
Fla.
Gunstock Capital of the World.
Warsaw, Mo.
Gypsum City. Fort Dodge,
Iowa
Gypsum City. Weatherford,
Okla.

H-Bomb's Home Town. Ellen-
ton, S.C.
Half Way and a Place to Stay.
Kinsley, Kan.
Halfway Point. Kearney, Neb.
Halloween Capital of the World.
Anoka, Minn.
Ham Town. Smithfield, Va.
Handicraft Capital of the United
States. Gatlinburg, Tenn.
Handmade Glass City. Mounds-
ville, W.Va.
Hangman Creek. Latah, Wash.
Hangtown. Placerville, Calif.
Happy Hollow. Roda, Va.
Happy Life City. Salem, Ore.
Happy People Place. St.
Petersburg, Fla.
Happy Town. Belleville, Mich.
Harbor City. Eau Gallie,
Fla.
Harbor City. Erie, Pa.
Harbor of the Air. Inglewood,
Calif.
Harbor of the Sun. San Diego,
Calif.

Hardware City. New Britain, Conn.

Hardware City of the World. New Britain, Conn.

Harmony. Hamilton, Va.

Hartford of the South. Jacksonville, Fla.

Hartford of the West. Lincoln, Neb.

Hat City. Danbury, Conn.

Hat City of the World. Danbury, Conn.

Hat Town. Norwalk, Conn.

Haven for Fishermen and Hunters. Upper Township, N.J.

Haven for Industry, Commerce and Good Living. Niles, Ohio

Haven to Retire in, Away from the Rush. Stockton, Mo.

Hay Fever Relief Haven of America. Duluth, Minn.

Head of Elk. Elkton, Md.

Headquarters City. Atlanta, Ga.

Headquarters City. Grand Junction, Colo.

Headquarters City of East San Gabriel Valley. West Covina, Calif.

Headquarters City of the Permian Basin. Midland, Tex.

Headquarters City of the Southeast. Atlanta, Ga.

Headquarters for Fishermen. Hawthorne, Nev.

Headquarters of Lake Livingston. Trinity, Tex.

Headquarters of the Big Horn National Forest. Sheridan, Wyo.

Headquarters of the International Oil Tool Trade. Houston, Tex.

Headquarters of World Banking. New York, N.Y.

Headwaters of Stockton Lake. Greenfield, Mo.

Headwaters of the Mississippi. Bemidji, Minn.

Health Center and Principal Trade Center of North Central Kansas. Abilene, Kan.

Health Center of the West. Thermopolis, Wyo.

Health City. Battle Creek, Mich.

Health City. Mount Clemens, Mich.

Health City, U.S.A. Asbury Park, N.J.

Health Food City. Battle Creek, Mich.

Healthful and Prosperous Place to Live. Gilroy, Calif.

Healthful, Hospitals and Humane. Cedar Rapids, Iowa

Heart and Center of the Golden Strip. Simpsonville, S.C.

Heart and Hub of Delaware County. Walton, N.Y.

Heart City of the Sandhills. Valentine, Neb.

Heart of a Dispersed City of Towns. West Frankfort, Ill.

Heart of a Great State. Columbus, Ohio

Heart of a Hunter's Paradise. Price, Utah

Heart of Alabama. Montevallo, Ala.

Heart of America. Frankfort, Ky.

Heart of America. Kansas City, Mo.

Heart of America. Washington, D.C.

Heart of American Hardware. Sterling, Ill.

Heart of America's Industrial War Front. Kearny, N.J.

Heart of America's New Commercial Frontier. New Orleans, La.

Heart of America's Number One Agricultural Area. Stockton, Calif.

Heart of America's Workshop. Akron, Ohio

Heart of Amish Territory Swiss Cheese. Berlin, Ohio

Heart of California. Sacramento, Calif.

Heart of Cape Cod. Dennis, Mass.

Heart of Connecticut. Meriden, Conn.

Heart of Delaware. Milford, Del.

Heart of Distribution. Harrisburg, Pa.

Heart of Dixie. New Orleans, La.

Heart of Down River's Chemical Empire. Wyandotte, Mich.

Heart of East Carolina. Williamston, N. C.

Heart of East Texas. Tyler, Tex.

Heart of Eastern Georgia and Western South Carolina. Augusta, Ga.

Heart of Eastern North Carolina. Goldsboro, N. C.

Heart of Fiestaland. Millbrae, Calif.

Heart of Florida. Haines City, Fla.

Heart of Florida's Citrus Industry. Winter Haven, Fla.

Heart of Florida's Crown. Starke, Fla.

Heart of Florida's Fun-Land. Ocala, Fla.

Heart of Florida's Miracle Strip. Fort Walton, Fla.

Heart of Florida's Strawberry Market. Starke, Fla.

Heart of Florida's Thoroughbred Country. Ocala, Fla.

Heart of Georgia. Macon, Ga.

Heart of Good Living. Castro Valley, Calif.

Heart of Historic America. West Chester, Pa.

Heart of Historic Virginia. Charlottesville, Va.

Heart of History and Romance in Kansas. Abilene, Kan.

Heart of Hunting Land. Sylvester, Ga.

Heart of Imperial Valley. Imperial, Calif.

Heart of Industrial America. Delphos, Ohio

Heart of Industry. Frederick, Md.

Heart of Kentucky. Frankfort, Ky.

Heart of Kentucky's Blue Grass Region. Lexington, Ky.

Heart of Louisiana. Alexandria, La.

Heart of Marvelous Marin County. San Rafael, Calif.

Heart of Maryland. Annapolis, Md.

Heart of Massachusetts. Worcester, Mass.

Heart of Montana's Magicland. Butte, Mont.

Heart of Nebraska Land. Ord, Neb.

Heart of New England. Somerville, Mass.

Heart of New England. Southbridge, Mass.

Heart of New York State. Syracuse, N. Y.

Heart of North Carolina. Sanford, N. C.

Heart of North Carolina's Holiday Highland. Blowing Rock, N. C.

Heart of North Dakota. Grand Forks, N. D.

Heart of North Mississippi and Beautiful Grenada Lake. Grenada, Miss.

Heart of Orange County. Westminster, Calif.

Heart of Rhode Island. East Greenwich, R. I.

Heart of Solano County. Fairfield, Calif.

Heart of Texas. Brady, Tex.

Heart of the Adirondack Vacationland. Schroon Lake, N.Y.

Heart of the Adirondacks. Indian Lake, N. Y.

Heart of the American Riviera. Foley, Ala.

Heart of the Antelope Valley. Lancaster, Calif.

Heart of the Bay State. Worcester, Mass.

Heart of the Berkshires. Pittsfield, Mass.

Heart of the Best Sheep and Goat Country in Texas. Uvalde, Tex.

Heart of the Big River Country.
Owensboro, Ky.
Heart of the Blackstone Valley.
Pawtucket, R. I.
Heart of the Canadian Valley.
El Reno, Okla.
Heart of the Citrus Industry.
Lakeland, Fla.
Heart of the Commonwealth.
Harrisburg, Pa.
Heart of the Commonwealth.
Worcester, Mass.
Heart of the Corn Country.
Monona, Iowa
Heart of the Dude Ranch
County. Lake Luzerne,
N. Y.
Heart of the Emerald Empire
in the North Idaho Scenic
Land. Coeur d'Alene,
Idaho
Heart of the Enchanted Moun-
tains. Olean, N. Y.
Heart of the Fabulous Gulf
Coast Country. Biloxi,
Miss.
Heart of the Famous Berk-
shire Hills. Pittsfield,
Mass.
Heart of the Famous North
Shore. Beverly, Mass.
Heart of the Famous St. Law-
rence Seaway. Massena,
N. Y.
Heart of the Finger Lakes
Vacationland. Geneva, N. Y.
Heart of the Florida Keys.
Marathon, Fla.
Heart of the Florida Lower
East Coast. Fort Lauder-
dale, Fla.
Heart of the Fox Valley Area.
Oshkosh, Wis.
Heart of the Fruit Belt.
Benton Harbor, Mich.
Heart of the Gold Coast.
Deerfield Beach, Fla.
Heart of the Gold Coast.
Hollywood, Fla.
Heart of the Gold Coast.
Pompano Beach, Fla.
Heart of the Green Mountains.
Rutland, Vt.

Heart of the Harbor. Wilming-
ton, Del.
Heart of the Indiana Lake
Country. Albion, Ind.
Heart of the Inland Empire.
Spokane, Wash.
Heart of the Lake Country.
Watkins Glen, N. Y.
Heart of the Leatherstocking
Land. Cooperstown, N. Y.
Heart of the Lumber Country.
Spokane, Wash.
Heart of the Massachusetts
Vacationland. Worcester,
Mass.
Heart of the Megapolis. Smith-
ville, Tex.
Heart of the Midwest. St.
Louis, Mo.
Heart of the Nation. Wahoo,
Neb.
Heart of the Nation's Durham
Producing Center. Devils
Lake, N. D.
Heart of the Nation's Heritage.
Alexandria, Va.
Heart of the Nation's Vacation-
land. Kennebec, Me.
Heart of the New England
Tobacco Farmland. Windsor,
Conn.
Heart of the New South.
Meridian, Miss.
Heart of the Old Dominion.
Blackstone, Va.
Heart of the Old Southwest.
Tucson, Ariz.
Heart of the Ozarks. West
Plains, Mo.
Heart of the Pacific Wonderland.
Salem, Ore.
Heart of the Palm Beaches.
Lake Worth, Fla.
Heart of the Pennsylvania
Dutch Country. Lancaster,
Pa.
Heart of the Piedmont. Char-
lotte, N. C.
Heart of the Pimento Country.
Woodbury, Ga.
Heart of the Pioneer Valley.
Northampton, Mass.
Heart of the Potomac Highlands.
Cumberland, Md.

Heart of the Red River Valley.
Durant, Okla.
Heart of the Region. Naples,
Me.
Heart of the Rockies. Salida,
Colo.
Heart of the Romantic South-
west in the Valley of the
Sun. Mesa, Ariz.
Heart of the Scenic Southwest.
Tucson, Ariz.
Heart of the South Dakota
Pheasant Country. Faulk-
ton, S. D.
Heart of the South Georgia
Empire. Fitzgerald, Ga.
Heart of the Southeast. Macon,
Ga.
Heart of the Sugar Bowl.
Iberville, La.
Heart of the Sun Country.
Phoenix, Ariz.
Heart of the Texas Funtier.
Waco, Tex.
Heart of the Turpentine In-
dustry. Pearson, Ga.
Heart of the U. S. A. Effing-
ham, Ill.
Heart of the United States of
America. Kansas City, Mo.
Heart of the Valley. Corvallis,
Ore.
Heart of the Valley that Warms
a Nation. Wilkes-Barre, Pa.
Heart of the Westside of Fresno
County. Coalinga, Calif.
Heart of the Wheat Land.
Goodland, Kan.
Heart of the White Mountains.
Bethlehem, N. H.
Heart of the World Famous
Niagara Region. Buffalo,
N. Y.
Heart of the Yellowstone Val-
ley. Sidney, Mont.
Heart of Tobacco Land. Black-
shear, Ga.
Heart of Vacationland. Mas-
sena, N. Y.
Heart of Washington's Timber
Belt. Centralia, Wash.
Heart of West Central Minne-
sota. Morris, Minn.

Heart of Westchester. White
Plains, N. Y.
Heart of Western Nevada's Agri-
cultural Region. Fallon, Nev.
Heart of Your Texas Market.
Brenham, Tex.
Heartland of Colonial Connecticut.
Southbury, Conn.
Heartland of Green County.
Muskogee, Okla.
Heartland of Industry and Elec-
tronics. Waltham, Mass.
Heartland of the Beaver Lake
Area. Rogers, Ark.
Heaven on the Half Shell. San
Francisco, Calif.
Heidelberg of America. Du-
buque, Iowa
Helicopter Capital of the World.
Ozark, Ala.
Helicopter City. Ozark, Ala.
Hell on Wheels. Cheyenne,
Wyo.
Hells Forty Acres. San Carlos,
Ariz.
Hemisfair City. San Antonio,
Tex.
Hickory Smoking Capital of the
World. Smithfield, Va.
Hidden Jewel of Central Florida.
Lake Mary, Fla.
High and Pleasant Situation.
Culpeper, Va.
High Grade Oil Metropolis of
the World. Bradford, Pa.
High Point for Travel Fun.
Dallas, Tex.
High Point of Long Beach Island.
Harvey Cedars, N. J.
High Rise City. San Francisco,
Calif.
Highest City in Florida. Quincy,
Fla.
Highest Hub of Fairfield County.
Norwalk, Conn.
Highest Incorporated Town in
Eastern America. Highlands,
N. C.
Highly Diversified Manufacturing
Center. Allentown, Pa.
Highway Hub. Lake City, Fla.
Hill City. Lynchburg, Va.
Hill City. Portland, Me.

Hill City. Vicksburg, Miss.
Hill Top City. Eveleth, Minn.
Hill Town. Hillsville, Va.
Hills Against the Sky Town.
  New London, Conn.
Historic and Colorful Capital
  of the Empire State. Al-
  bany, N.Y.
Historic and Scenic Lincoln.
  Lincoln, R.I.
Historic Bethlehem. Bethlehem,
  Pa.
Historic Brownville, where
  Nebraska Begins. Brown-
  ville, Neb.
Historic Capital of Massa-
  chusetts. Boston, Mass.
Historic Center of East Texas.
  Nacogdoches, Tex.
Historic Center of North Caro-
  lina. New Bern, N.C.
Historic City. Nebraska City,
  Neb.
Historic City. Salem, Mass.
Historic City. Williamsburg,
  Va.
Historic City in the County by
  the Sea. Beverly, Mass.
Historic City of America.
  Natchez, Miss.
Historic City of Hospitality.
  Marshall, Mich.
Historic City of the Black Hills.
  Deadwood, S.D.
Historic Community. Suisun
  City, Calif.
Historic Doorway to Colorado's
  Finest See and Ski Country.
  Georgetown, Colo.
Historic Frankfort. Frankfort,
  Ky.
Historic Gateway. Sitka,
  Alaska
Historic Heart of the Southwest.
  Tucson, Ariz.
Historic Home Town of General
  George Washington.
  Alexandria, Va.
Historic Newburyport. New-
  buryport, Mass.
Historic Seaport City.
  Charleston, S.C.
Historic Showplace of America.
  Newport, R.I.

Historic Town of the Old South
  ... Now a Progressive City.
  Canton, Miss.
Historic Village. Deerfield,
  Mass.
Historical and Cultural Center.
  St. Louis, Mo.
Historical Area. Auburn, Neb.
Historical Center on the Con-
  necticut River in Scenic
  Northern New Hampshire.
  Exeter, N.H.
Historical City. Boston, Mass.
Historical City. Prairie du
  Chien, Wis.
Historical City of Homes.
  Evanston, Ill.
Historical City of the South.
  Charleston, S.C.
Historical City with a Progres-
  sive Outlook. Columbus,
  Miss.
Historical Town in Southwestern
  Vermont. Bennington, Vt.
Hockey Capital of the Nation.
  Eveleth, Minn.
Hog Butcher for the World.
  Chicago, Ill.
Hog Capital of the World. Ke-
  wanee, Ill.
Hogopolis. Chicago, Ill.
Hoist Capital of America. For-
  rest City, Ark.
Hole in the Ground. Albany,
  Ore.
Hole in the Ground. Kahlotus,
  Wash.
Holiday City. St. Louis, Mo.
Holiday Harbor of Vermont.
  Newport, Vt.
Holiday Highlands. Winter
  Haven, Fla.
Holland's Corner. Holland, Va.
Holly City of America. Mill-
  ville, N.J.
Holstein Capital of America.
  Northfield, Minn.
Holy City. Charleston, S.C.
Holy City. Lincoln, Neb.
Holy City. Sunnyside, Wash.
Home City. Atlanta, Ga.
Home City. Brookings, S.D.
Home City. Charlotte, N.C.

Home City. Lewiston, Me.
Home for Your Business.
Portsmouth, R. I.
Home for Your Family.
Portsmouth, R. I.
Home Laundry Appliance Center
of the World. Newton,
Iowa
Home Market for the Great
Northwest. Sioux City,
Iowa
Home of a Yankee Count.
Woburn, Mass.
Home of Abraham Lincoln.
Springfield, Ill.
Home of Air Material Com-
mand. Warner Robins, Ga.
Home of All-Americans. El
Dorado, Ark.
Home of America's Greatest
Petrochemical Industry
Complex. Houston, Tex.
Home of America's Greatest
Spa. Saratoga Springs,
N. Y.
Home of Andersonville.
Americus, Ga.
Home of Aplets, the Confec-
tion of the Fairies. Cash-
mere, Wash.
Home of Apple Blossom Festi-
val. Wenatchee, Wash.
Home of Arkansas Polytechnic
College. Russellville, Ark.
Home of Astronaut Virgil
(Gus) Grissom. Mitchell,
Ind.
Home of Astronauts. Houston,
Tex.
Home of Baked Beans. Boston,
Mass.
Home of Bartlett Pears.
Ukiah, Calif.
Home of Baseball. Coopers-
town, N. Y.
Home of Beautiful Cypress
Gardens. Winter Haven,
Fla.
Home of Bemidji State Col-
lege. Bemidji, Minn.
Home of Ben Hur. Crawfords-
ville, Ind.

Home of Better Living. Met-
ter, Ga.
Home of Bowdoin College.
Brunswick, Me.
Home of Buffalo Bill. North
Platte, Neb.
Home of Buick. Flint, Mich.
Home of Business, Industry and
Recreation. El Dorado, Ark.
Home of Carrie Nation. Medi-
cine Lodge, Kans.
Home of Casey Jones. Jackson,
Tenn.
Home of Champions. Minden,
La.
Home of Championship Cowboys.
Nowata, Okla.
Home of Colby College. New
London, N. H.
Home of Contented Cows.
Carnation, Wash.
Home of Conventions. Winona
Lake, Ind.
Home of Dartmouth College.
Hanover, N. H.
Home of Delta State College.
Cleveland, Miss.
Home of Denison Dam. Deni-
son, Tex.
Home of Diamond Products.
Tulsa, Okla.
Home of Diamond Walnuts.
Stockton, Calif.
Home of Ding Dong Daddy.
Dumas, Ark.
Home of Disneyland. Anaheim,
Calif.
Home of East Texas' Peach
Festival. Pittsburg, Tex.
Home of Elgin Air Force Base.
Niceville, Fla.
Home of Eisenhower's Birth-
place. Denison, Tex.
Home of Eisenhower's Birth-
place and Denison Dam-Lake
Texoma. Denison, Tex.
Home of Famous Sand Hill Beef.
Bassett, Neb.
Home of Fine Churches, Modern
Schools. El Dorado, Ark.
Home of Fishingest Bridge.
Pine Island Center, Fla.
Home of Florida's Fishingest

Bridge. Pine Island Center,
Fla.
Home of Florence State Col-
lege. Florence, Ala.
Home of Forestry Products.
Bemidji, Minn.
Home of Fort Rucker, the
Army Aviation Center.
Ozark, Ala.
Home of Fort Stewart. Hines-
ville, Ga.
Home of Four Wheel Drive
Trucks. Clintonville, Wis.
Home of Franklin Delano
Roosevelt. Hyde Park,
N. Y.
Home of Friendly People.
Pierre, S. D.
Home of Frontier Days.
Cheyenne, Who.
Home of George M. Verity.
Keokuk, Iowa
Home of Georgia Belle Peach.
Commerce, Ga.
Home of Good Indians. Wa-
hoo, Neb.
Home of Gordon College.
Barnesville, Ga.
Home of Greenville College.
Greenville, Ill.
Home of Harold Warp's
Pioneer Village. Minden,
Neb.
Home of Health, History and
Horses. Saratoga Springs,
N. Y.
Home of Helen Keller. Tus-
cumbia, Ala.
Home of Historic Plimoth
Plantation. Plymouth,
Mass.
Home of Historical Fort Sid-
ney. Sidney, Neb.
Home of Hospitality. Jasper,
Ala.
Home of Idaho's Greatest
Mines. Kellogg, Idaho
Home of Illuminated Cascades.
Jackson, Mich.
Home of Iowa's Only Future
Farmer of Americas-Agri-
cultural Museum. La Porte,
Ind.

Home of James Fenimore
Cooper. Cooperstown, N. Y.
Home of Jesse James. Saint
Joseph, Mo.
Home of John Brown Memorial
Park. Osawatomie, Kan.
Home of King Cotton. Memphis,
Tenn.
Home of Lady Bird Johnson.
Marshall, Tex.
Home of Lake McConaugy and
Kingsley Dam. Ogallala,
Neb.
Home of Latex Rubber. Dover,
Del.
Home of Little Steel. Warren,
Ohio
Home of Louisiana State Uni-
versity. Baton Rouge, La.
Home of L. B. J. Stonewall,
Tex.
Home of Minute Tapioca.
Orange, Mass.
Home of Miss America 1954.
Ephrata, Pa.
Home of Miss America 1964.
El Dorado, Ark.
Home of Mississippi's Annual
Deep Sea Fishing Rodeo.
Gulfport, Miss.
Home of Moberly Greyhounds.
Moberly, Mo.
Home of More than 4,000 Com-
mercial Travellers. Spring-
field, Mass.
Home of National Industries.
Camden, N. J.
Home of Nationally Known In-
dustries. Sayreville, N. J.
Home of New Jersey's First
Nuclear Generating Plant.
Lacey Township, N. J.
Home of North Central Soil and
Water Conservation Research
Field Station. Morris, Minn.
Home of Northwest Community
College. Powell, Wyo.
Home of 'Old Hickory' Ham and
Bacon. Crane, Mo.
Home of Old Sea Captains.
Searsport, Me.
Home of Old Stone Fort. Man-
chester, Tenn.

Home of 'Ole Miss.' Oxford, Miss.
Home of One of the Nation's Largest Skilled Technical Work Forces. Rochester, N.Y.
Home of Opportunity. South San Francisco, Calif.
Home of Our First President. Mount Vernon, Va.
Home of Parris Island. Beaufort, S.C.
Home of Paul Bunyan. Bemidji, Minn.
Home of Planters Peanuts. Suffolk, Va.
Home of Precision. Springfield, Vt.
Home of Prosperous Agriculture Business and Industry. McKinney, Tex.
Home of Pure Water. Ocean City, Fla.
Home of Quaker Oats. Cedar Rapids, Iowa
Home of Rainbow Springs. Dunnellon, Fla.
Home of Road Racing in America. Watkins Glen, N.Y.
Home of Sakakawea. Stanton, N.D.
Home of Sandwich Glass. Sandwich, Mass.
Home of Santa Claus. North Pole, Alaska
Home of Schilling Air Force Base. Salina, Kan.
Home of Silver Springs. Ocala, Fla.
Home of South Carolina's Little Arlington. Florence, S.C.
Home of South Dakota State College. Brookings, S.D.
Home of Stanford University. Palo Alto, Calif.
Home of State College of Washington. Pullman, Wash.
Home of State Teachers College. Peru, Neb.
Home of State's First

Industrial Training Center. Burlington, N.C.
Home of Stetson University. De Land, Fla.
Home of Stetson University and Florida Military School. De Land, Fla.
Home of Sunshine and Flowers. San Leandro, Calif.
Home of Ten Thousand Friendly People. Flagstaff, Ariz.
Home of Tennis, Mansions and the America's Cup Race. Newport, R.I.
Home of Texas Dogwood Trails. Palestine, Tex.
Home of Texas Rice Festival. Winnie, Tex.
Home of Texas Tech. Lubbock, Tex.
Home of Textiles. West Point, Ga.
Home of the Albemarle Pippin. Charlottesville, Va.
Home of the American Embroidery Industry. Union City, N.J.
Home of the Apple Blossom Festival. Winchester, Va.
Home of the Arkansas Folk Festival. Mountain Home, Ark.
Home of the Atlantic Sea Bees. North Kingstown, R.I.
Home of the Athletics. Kansas City, Mo.
Home of the Big Black Bass. Lake Village, Ark.
Home of the Big Red Apple. Cornelia, Ga.
Home of the Black Hills Uranium Industry. Edgemont, S.D.
Home of the Boll Weevil Monument. Enterprise, Ala.
Home of the Bowie Knife. Washington, Ark.
Home of the Braves. Milwaukee, Wis.
Home of the Brevard Music Center. Brevard, N.C.
Home of the Christmas Club. Ticonderoga, N.Y.

Home of the Christmas Tree
Industry. Cook, Minn.
Home of the Coachella Valley
Players. Cathedral City,
Calif.
Home of the Colorado Aggies.
Fort Collins, Colo.
Home of the Comstock Lode.
Virginia City, Nev.
Home of the Cougars. Tom-
ball, Tex.
Home of the Dan River Mills.
Danville, Va.
Home of the East Texas Peach
Festival. Hughes Springs,
Tex.
Home of the Evil Spirits. Enum-
claw, Wash.
Home of the Fabulous Sun
Devil Athletic Team and
Arizona State University.
Tempe, Ariz.
Home of the Famed Black Hills
Round-Up. Belle Fourche,
S.D.
Home of the Famous Chambers
Ranges. Oxford, Miss.
Home of the Famous "First
Monday" Trades Day. Can-
ton, Tex.
Home of the Famous Ipswich
Clam. Ipswich, Mass.
Home of the Famous "Jackson-
Boro Legend." Sylvania,
Ga.
Home of the Famous Large-
Mouth Bass. Apopka,
Fla.
Home of the Famous Old
Sturbridge Village. Stur-
bridge, Mass.
Home of the Famous Pluto
Mineral Springs. French
Lick, Ind.
Home of the Famous Silver
King Tarpon. Punta Gorda,
Fla.
Home of the First Fully Auto-
matic Non-Attended Dial
Telephone Switchboard in
the United States. Ketchum,
Okla.

Home of the Flame Tokay
Grape. Lodi, Calif.
Home of the Florida Derby.
Hallandale, Fla.
Home of the Freedom Trail.
Boston, Mass.
Home of the Frontier Sports
Arena. Poteau, Okla.
Home of the Gamey Black Bass.
Cape Vincent, N.Y.
Home of the Garden State
Philharmonic Symphony
Orchestra. Dover, N.J.
Home of the Giant Oahe Dam.
Pierre, S.D.
Home of the Grand Ole Opry.
Nashville, Tenn.
Home of the Green Sea Horse.
Sealevel, N.C.
Home of the Hodag. Rhine-
lander, Wis.
Home of the Homeless Ballet.
Boston, Mass.
Home of the "Horn of the West."
Boone, N.C.
Home of the Indian River Citrus.
Titusville, Fla.
Home of the Industrial Genii.
Muncie, Ind.
Home of the International Paper
Company. Ticonderoga, N.Y.
Home of the International
Petroleum Exposition. Tulsa,
Okla.
Home of the Israel Putnam State
Monument. Brooklyn, Conn.
Home of the Jicarilla Apache
Tribe. Dulce, N.M.
Home of the Jubilee. Fairhope,
Ala.
Home of the Kansas State Fish
Hatchery. Pratt, Kan.
Home of the Kentucky Derby.
Louisville, Ky.
Home of the Lake George Opera
Festival. Queensbury, N.Y.
Home of the Largest Catfish
Farm in Texas. Winnie, Tex.
Home of the Largest Copper
Producing Smelter and Smoke-
stack in the World. Ana-
conda, Mont.

Home of the Little World's
Fair. Yorktown, Tex.
Home of the Lodi Grape Festi-
val. Lodi, Calif.
Home of the Loop. Chicago,
Ill.
Home of the Mac Intosh Apple.
Chazy, N.Y.
Home of the Mac Intosh Apple.
Peru, N.Y.
Home of the Mahanay Memorial
Carillon Tower. Jefferson,
Iowa
Home of the Mercer Museum.
Doylestown, Pa.
Home of the Metered Maid
System. Stamford, Conn.
Home of the Middle Tennessee
State University. Murfrees-
boro, Tenn.
Home of the Middle Tennessee
Strawberry Festival. Port-
land, Tenn.
Home of the Mighty M. Monti-
cello, N.Y.
Home of the Mining Barons.
Spokane, Wash.
Home of the Miss Kansas
Pageant. Pratt, Kan.
Home of the Miss New York
State Pageant. Olean, N.Y.
Home of the Miss Universe
Pageant. Long Beach, Calif.
Home of the Mule-Tail Deer.
Alturas, Calif.
Home of the Museum of the
Great Plains. Lawton,
Okla.
Home of the "Music Man."
Mason City, Iowa
Home of the "Nashville Sound."
Nashville, Tenn.
Home of the National Bass
Round-Up. Pocomoke City,
Md.
Home of the National Cotton
Picking Contest. Blythe-
ville, Ark.
Home of the National Peanut
Festival. Dothan, Ala.
Home of the National Survey.
Chester, Vt.
Home of the National Wine
Show. Lodi, Calif.

Home of the Nation's Building
Stone. Bedford, Ind.
Home of the New York Giants.
New Haven, Conn.
Home of the Nickelodeon.
Pittsburgh, Pa.
Home of the 97th Bomb Wing.
Blytheville, Ark.
Home of the Norbertines. De
Pere, Wis.
Home of the Nuclear Submarine.
Groton, Conn.
Home of the Orange. River-
side, Calif.
Home of the Original Long
Horns. Valentine, Neb.
Home of the Original Main
Street. Sauk Centre, Minn.
Home of the Original Trout
Derby. Livingston, Mont.
Home of the Pacific Fleet.
Bremerton, Wash.
Home of the Packers. Green
Bay, Wis.
Home of the Peach. Selma,
Calif.
Home of the Pioneer Florida
Museum. Dade City, Fla.
Home of the Portsmouth Com-
pact. Portsmouth, R.I.
Home of the Post Rock Mu-
seum. La Crosse, Kan.
Home of the Puget Sound Naval
Shipyard. Bremerton, Wash.
Home of the Rainbow Trout.
Diamond Lake, Ore.
Home of the Ripon Almond Blos-
som Festival. Ripon, Calif.
Home of the Robert E. Lee.
New Albany, Ind.
Home of the Rose Parade.
Pasadena, Calif.
Home of the Runestone. Alex-
andria, Minn.
Home of the St. Lawrence Sea-
way. Massena, N.Y.
Home of the Smithfield Ham.
Smithfield, Va.
Home of the Snake River Stam-
pede. Nampa, Idaho.
Home of the State Fair. Sedalia,
Mo.
Home of the Strawberry Festival.
Marysville, Wash.

Home of the Tangerine.
Brooksville, Fla.
Home of the Tennessee Tech-
nological University. Cooke-
ville, Tenn.
Home of the Tennessee Valley
Industrial District. Mor-
ristown, Tenn.
Home of the Texas Grapefruit.
Mission, Tex.
Home of the Tinker Air Force
Base. Midwest City, Okla.
Home of the U.S.S. Massa-
chusetts. Fall River, Mass.
Home of the University of
Arizona. Tucson, Ariz.
Home of the University of
Colorado. Boulder, Colo.
Home of the University of
Florida. Gainesville, Fla.
Home of the University of
Georgia. Athens, Ga.
Home of the University of
Mississippi. Oxford, Miss.
Home of the University of
North Dakota. Grand Forks,
N.D.
Home of the University of
South Dakota. Vermillion,
S.D.
Home of the University of
Tennessee. Knoxville, Tenn.
Home of the University of
Wisconsin. Madison, Wis.
Home of the Walleyed Pike,
Walker, Minn.
Home of the Winter White
House. Palm Beach, Fla.
Home of the World Champion
Clearwater Bombers.
Clearwater, Fla.
Home of the World-Famous
Annual Shenandoah Apple
Blossom Festival. Win-
chester, Va.
Home of the World-Famous
Black Hills Passion Play.
Spearfish, S.D.
Home of the World-Famous
Glass Bottom Boats.
Silver Springs, Fla.
Home of the World-Famous
Claxton Fruit Cake.
Claxton, Ga.

Home of the World-Famous
Mount Rushmore National
Memorial. Keystone, S.D.
Home of the World-Famous
Stockton Cheese. Stockton
Springs, Me.
Home of the World Record Cod.
Boothbay Harbor, Me.
Home of the World's Finest
Catfish. Osceola, Mo.
Home of the World's Finest
Granite. Snyder, Okla.
Home of the World's Largest
Bass. Dunnellon, Fla.
Home of the World's Largest
Bear. Kodiak, Alaska
Home of the World's Largest
Black Walnut Processing
Plant. Stockton Springs,
Me.
Home of the World's Largest
Brewery. St. Louis, Mo.
Home of the World's Largest
Buffalo. Jamestown, N.D.
Home of the World's Largest
Mineral Hot Springs.
Thermopolis, Wyo.
Home of the World's Largest
Single-Unit Textile Mill.
Danville, Va.
Home of the World's Largest
Viking. Alexandria, Minn.
Home of the World's Largest
Walnut Tree. Gustine,
Calif.
Home of the World's Only Corn
Palace. Mitchell, S.D.
Home of the World's Only Land-
Locked Striped Rock Bass.
Summerton, S.C.
Home of the Wright Brothers.
Dayton, Ohio
Home of the Wyandot Indians.
Upper Sandusky, Ohio
Home of Theodore Roosevelt.
Oyster Bay, N.Y.
Home of Vassar College.
Poughkeepsie, N.Y.
Home of Vulcan. Birmingham,
Ala.
Home of Warther Museum.
Dover, Ohio
Home of West Virginia

University. Morgantown,
W. Va.
Home of World Famous Carth-
age Marble. Carthage, Mo.
Home of World Famous Front
Street and Boot Hill. Dodge
City, Kan.
Home of World Famous Middle-
bury College. Middlebury,
Vt.
Home of World Famous Sea
Captains. Searsport, Me.
Home of Yachtsmen. Mystic,
Conn.
Home of Yankee Doodle. Nor-
walk, Conn.
Home of Yankee Ingenuity.
Springfield, Vt.
"Home on the Range" Birth-
place. Smith Center, Kan.
Home Port of the First Armed
Schooner "Hannah." Beverly,
Mass.
Home Town. Manhattan, Kan.
Home Town in the American
Tropics. Fort Lauderdale,
Fla.
Home Town of Emmett Kelly.
Houston, Mo.
Home Town of George Washing-
ton. Alexandria, Va.
Home Town of Lyndon B.
Johnson. Johnson City, Tex.
Home Town of Paul Bunyan.
Brainerd, Minn.
Home Town of Richard Nixon.
Whittier, Calif.
Home Town of Southern Ore-
gon. Ashland, Ore.
Homeseeker's Paradise.
Brookhaven, Miss.
Hometown of America. Ply-
mouth, Mass.
Hometown, U.S.A. Glens
Falls, N.Y.
Hometown, U.S.A. Grand
Prairie, Tex.
Homocide Headquarters.
Memphis, Tenn.
Homesteader's Paradise.
Palestine, Tex.
Honey Capital of the United
States. Uvalde, Tex.

Honey Capital of the World.
Uvalde, Tex.
Honeymoon Capital of the World.
Niagara Falls, N.Y.
Honeymoon City. Niagara Falls,
N.Y.
Honeymooner's Paradise.
Niagara Falls, N.Y.
Hong Kong of the Hudson. New
York, N.Y.
Hoosier Athens. Crawfords-
ville, Ind.
Hoosier Capital. Indianapolis,
Ind.
Hoosier City. Indianapolis, Ind.
Horn of the West. Boone, N.C.
Hornets' Nest. Charlotte, N.C.
Horse Capital of the World.
Northridge, Calif.
Horse Plains. Hillyard, Wash.
Hospitality Capital of the New
South. Brookhaven, Miss.
Hospitable City. Santa Barbara,
Calif.
Hospitality Center of Alaska.
Petersburg, Alaska
Hospitality City. Gulfport, Miss.
Hospitality City of the Rockies.
Salida, Colo.
Hospitality Town. Thermopolis,
Wyo.
Host City. Norfolk, Neb.
Host City of the Nation. Chi-
cago, Ill.
Host City of the Sunland Em-
pire. El Paso, Tex.
Host City to Conventions. Har-
risburg, Pa.
Host of the World. New York,
N.Y.
Host Resort to the Nation.
Gatlinburg, Tenn.
Host to the West's Scenic Won-
der-Ways. Provo, Utah
Host with the Most. Atlantic
City, N.J.
Host without Parallel. Spring-
field, Mass.
Hostess City of the South.
Savannah, Ga.
Hot Air Balloon Capital of
the World. Albuquerque,
N.M.

Hottest Town. Quartzsite,
Ariz.
House Built on Sand. Los
Angeles, Calif.
Hub. Boston, Mass.
Hub. Casper, Wyo.
Hub. Proctor, Minn.
Hub. San Anselmo, Calif.
Hub. Snohomish, Wash.
Hub City. Aberdeen, S.D.
Hub City. Albany, Ore.
Hub City. Alexandria, La.
Hub City. Anchorage, Alaska
Hub City. Brainerd, Minn.
Hub City. Camilla, Ga.
Hub City. Casper, Wyo.
Hub City. Centralia, Wash.
Hub City. Colton, Calif.
Hub City. Compton, Calif.
Hub City. Robertsdale, Ala.
Hub City. Slayton, Minn.
Hub City in the Heart of
Florida's West Country.
Crestview, Fla.
Hub City of Good Living.
Chattahooche, Fla.
Hub City of Northwest Florida.
Crestview, Fla.
Hub City of Recreation.
Chattahoochee, Fla.
Hub City of South Texas. Alice,
Tex.
Hub City of South Texas.
Yoakum, Tex.
Hub City of Southwest Iowa.
Atlantic, Iowa
Hub City of Southwestern
Washington. Centralia,
Wash.
Hub City of the Dakotas.
Aberdeen, S.D.
Hub City of the Famed Grand
Strand. Myrtle Beach, S.C.
Hub City of the Scenic South-
west. Las Vegas, Nev.
Hub City of the South Plains.
Lubbock, Tex.
Hub City of the South Texas
Oil Industry. Alice, Tex.
Hub City of the Southeast.
Spartanburg, S.C.
Hub City of the World. New
York, N.Y.

Hub City of Transportation.
Chattahoochee, Fla.
Hub City of Upper Cumberland.
Cookeville, Tenn.
Hub City of Western Colorado
and Eastern Utah. Grand
Junction, Colo.
Hub of a $500,000,000 Trading
Area. Lima, Ohio
Hub of a New World. Cam-
bridge, Mass.
Hub of a Vast Scenic and Sports
Wonderland. Las Vegas,
Nev.
Hub of Agriculture. Lubbock,
Tex.
Hub of All South Florida's Sun-
Fun Vacationland. Miami,
Fla.
Hub of American Inland Naviga-
tion. St. Louis, Mo.
Hub of American Merchandising.
Chicago, Ill.
Hub of Arizona's Lumber Indus-
try. Flagstaff, Ariz.
Hub of Aroostook County.
Caribou, Me.
Hub of Banking and Insurance
Interests. Fort Worth, Tex.
Hub of Beauty. Lubbock, Tex.
Hub of Central Oregon. Red-
mond, Ore.
Hub of Civic Pride. Lubbock,
Tex.
Hub of Coastal Carolina. New
Bern, N.C.
Hub of Commerce. East Bruns-
wick, N.J.
Hub of Commercial Activities.
South San Francisco, Calif.
Hub of Connecticut's Nauga-
tuck River Valley. Nauga-
tuck, Conn.
Hub of Cultural and Commercial
Life. Binghamton, N.Y.
Hub of Eastern Long Island.
Riverhead, N.Y.
Hub of Education. Lubbock,
Tex.
Hub of Fast Transportation.
Chicopee, Mass.
Hub of Five Seasons of Activity.
Caribou, Me.

Hub of Florida. Clermont,
Fla.
Hub of Florida's Scenic Won-
derland. Lakeland, Fla.
Hub of Fun. Jacksonville,
Fla.
Hub of Historic Ohio. Spring-
field, Ohio
Hub of Historic Shrines. Ports-
mouth, Va.
Hub of Historical Ohio. Spring-
field, Ohio
Hub of History. Frederick,
Md.
Hub of History. Jacksonville,
Fla.
Hub of Homes and Industries.
Ambler, Pa.
Hub of Illinois. Bloomington,
Ill.
Hub of Industrial America.
Meadville, Pa.
Hub of Industry and Oil. Lub-
bock, Tex.
Hub of Lake Superior's Beautiful
South Shore Drive. Port
Wing, Wis.
Hub of Livestock Processing.
Lubbock, Tex.
Hub of Major Employment,
Education and Commercial
Center. White Plains, N.Y.
Hub of Michigan. St. Johns,
Mich.
Hub of Missouri's Booming
Area. St. Charles, Mo.
Hub of Montana's Vast Vaca-
tion Land. Laurel, Mont.
Hub of Nassau. Hempstead,
N.Y.
Hub of Nassau County. Hemp-
stead, N.Y.
Hub of New England. Boston,
Mass.
Hub of New York State.
Syracuse, N.Y.
Hub of New York's Boating
Center. City Island, N.Y.
Hub of North America.
Superior, Wis.
Hub of North Central Florida's
Scenic Wonderland. Lake
City, Fla.

Hub of Northeast Oregon. La
Grande, Ore.
Hub of Northern Virginia. Cul-
peper, Va.
Hub of Northwest Georgia.
Rome, Ga.
Hub of Pinellas County. Largo,
Fla.
Hub of Pinellas County. Pinel-
las Park, Fla.
Hub of Progress. Jacksonville,
Fla.
Hub of Recreational North
Dakota. Minot, N.D.
Hub of Scenic and Historic
Western Virginia. Waynes-
boro, Va.
Hub of Southwest Alabama.
Monroeville, Ala.
Hub of Southwest Virginia.
Wytheville, Va.
Hub of Southwestern Louisiana.
Lafayette, La.
Hub of Texas. Waco, Tex.
Hub of the Americas. New
Orleans, La.
Hub of the Beautiful Flathead
Valley. Kalispell, Mont.
Hub of the Chattahoochee Valley.
Phenix City, Ala.
Hub of the Coachella Valley
Cove Communities. Palm
Desert, Calif.
Hub of the Commonwealth.
Boston, Mass.
Hub of the Commonwealth's
Third Largest Industrial
Complex. Allentown, Pa.
Hub of the Delta. Cleveland,
Miss.
Hub of the Denver-Julesburg
Oil Production Territory.
Sterling, Colo.
Hub of the Eastern Plumas
Trading Area. Portola,
Calif.
Hub of the Empire State.
Syracuse, N.Y.
Hub of the Empire State.
Utica, N.Y.
Hub of the Empire State's
Capital District. Albany,
N.Y.

Hub of the Fabulous Golden
Gulf Coast. Pasadena, Tex.
Hub of the Fabulous Gulf Coast.
Pasadena, Calif.
Hub of the Fastest Growing
County in the State. Wauke-
sha, Wis.
Hub of the Florida Peninsula.
Sebring, Fla.
Hub of the Great Apalachicola
Valley. Blountstown, Fla.
Hub of the Great Niagara
Fruit Belt. Lockport, N.Y.
Hub of the Great North-Central
Industrial and Agricultural
America. Fort Wayne, Ind.
Hub of the Great Lehigh Val-
ley. Bethlehem, Pa.
Hub of the Great Orange,
Grapefruit and Winter Straw-
berry Producing Section in
the United States. Tampa,
Fla.
Hub of the Great Southwest.
Oklahoma City, Okla.
Hub of the Great Southwest.
Phoenix, Ariz.
Hub of the Greater Lehigh
Valley. Allentown, Pa.
Hub of the Harlem Valley.
Brewster, N.Y.
Hub of the Highways. Mercer,
Pa.
Hub of the "Holiday Highlands".
Boone, N.C.
Hub of the Industrial Gulf
Coast. Liberty, Tex.
Hub of the Industrial Gulf
Coast. Stowell, Tex.
Hub of the International South-
west. El Paso, Tex.
Hub of the Interstate and U.S.
Highways. Harrisburg, Pa.
Hub of the Inter-State Highway
System. Salina, Kan.
Hub of the Kenai Peninsula.
Soldatna, Alaska
Hub of the Magic Valley.
Twin Falls, Idaho
Hub of the Mother Lode
Country. Placerville, Calif.
Hub of the Nation. Kearney,
Neb.

Hub of the Nation-Wide Trans-
portation System. Indianapo-
lis, Ind.
Hub of the New High-Speed
Interstate Highway System.
St. Louis, Mo.
Hub of the Niagara Frontier.
Buffalo, N.Y.
Hub of the North Alabama Re-
sort Areas. Decatur, Ala.
Hub of the Northeast Kingdom.
Barton, Vt.
Hub of the Northwest Resorts
Area. Rhinelander, Wis.
Hub of the Ozarks. Ellington,
Mo.
Hub of the Ozarks. Harrison,
Ark.
Hub of the Peninsula. Belmont,
Calif.
Hub of the Plains. Lubbock,
Tex.
Hub of the Powerful Tennessee
Valley. Huntsville, Ala.
Hub of the Richest Farming
District of the United States.
Mount Joy, Pa.
Hub of the Safflower Industry.
Culbertson, Mont.
Hub of the Scenic Historic
Tidewater Region at the Base
of Chesapeake Bay. Ports-
mouth, Va.
Hub of the Scenic Ozarks. Cass-
ville, Mo.
Hub of the Scenic West. Grand
Junction, Colo.
Hub of the Solar System. Boston,
Mass.
Hub of the Southeast. Atlanta,
Ga.
Hub of the Southeast. Gaffney,
S.C.
Hub of the Southwest's Sun
Country. Tucson, Ariz.
Hub of the Universe. Boston,
Mass.
Hub of the Valley of Parks.
Corbin, Ky.
Hub of the Willamette Valley.
Albany, Ore.
Hub of the Winter Garden.
Carrizo, Tex.

Hub of Thlingit Totem Land.
Wrangell, Alaska
Hub of Transport. New York,
N. Y.
Hub of Transportation. Mar-
shall, Tex.
Hub of West Michigan. Grand
Rapids, Mich.
Hub, the Heart, and the
Center of Florida. Orlando,
Fla.
Hub Town. Boston, Mass.
Hudson of the West. Byron,
Ill.
Hunter's Paradise. Farming-
ton, Me.
Hunter's Rendezvous. Black-
duck, Minn.
Hunting Capital of Wyoming.
Shoshoni, Wyo.
Hunting Headquarters. Red-
wood Falls, Minn.
Hydro-Electric City. Water-
town, N. Y.

Ice Box of Pennsylvania.
Kane, Pa.
Ice Mine City. Coudersport,
Pa.
Idaho's Farm Market. Cald-
well, Idaho
Idaho's Finest Residential
Community. Twin Falls,
Idaho
Idaho's Oldest Incorporated
City. Lewiston, Idaho
Idaho's Only Seaport. Lewis-
ton, Idaho
Ideal American City. St.
Paul, Minn.
Ideal City. Atlanta, Ga.
Ideal City. Malden, Mass.
Ideal City for Year-Round
Vacations. Miami, Fla.
Ideal City in All Seasons.
New London, Conn.
Ideal Community. Corvallis,
Ore.
Ideal Community in which
to Live, Work, and Play.
West Caldwell, N. J.

Ideal Convention and Vacation
City. Madison, Wis.
Ideal Convention City. Atlanta,
Ga.
Ideal Convention City. Jackson-
ville, Fla.
Ideal Family Community. Palm
Springs, Fla.
Ideal Home and Recreational
Center. Palo Alto, Calif.
Ideal Home City. Austin, Tex.
Ideal Home Community. Doug-
las, Alaska
Ideal Home Community.
Evanston, Ill.
Ideal Industrial City of Orange
County. Fullerton, Calif.
Ideal Industrial Town. Mount
Joy, Pa.
Ideal Living City in the Heart
of Florida. High Springs,
Fla.
Ideal Location for a Year-Round
Vacation. Idaho Springs,
Colo.
Ideal Location for Commerce.
Foxboro, Mass.
Ideal Location for Industry.
La Crosse, Kan.
Ideal Location for Vacation and
Home. Belleview, Fla.
Ideal Place in which to Live,
Work and Play. Bethel, Me.
Ideal Place to Stay or Play.
Carthage, Mo.
Ideal Place to Work and Live.
Bloomsburg, Pa.
Ideal Place to Work, Live,
Play. Jacksonville, Fla.
Ideal Residential City. Syra-
cuse, N. Y.
Ideal Spot for Retirement.
Bonifay, Fla.
Ideal Spot to Relax. Hartsville,
S. C.
Ideal Summer Resort. Lake-
wood, Me.
Ideal Town. Haydenville, Ohio
Ideal Town in which to Live,
Work, Shop and Play.
Riverhead, N. Y.
Ideal Vacation for a Two-Nation
Vacation. Laredo, Tex.

Ideal Vacation Resort. Long
Beach, N.Y.
Ideal Vacation Resort and Year
'Round Residential Com-
munity. Long Beach, N.Y.
Ideal Vacationland. Bruns-
wick, Ga.
Ideal Working City. Lewiston,
Me.
Ideal Year Round Community.
Anaheim, Calif.
Ideal Year Round Resort.
Daytona Beach, Fla.
Ideal Year Round Vacation
Spot. Jacksonville, Fla.
Illinois' Capital City. Spring-
field, Ill.
Illinois' Second City. Peoria,
Ill.
Illinois' Second Industrial
City. Rockford, Ill.
Illinois' Second Largest City.
Rockford, Ill.
Immigrant City. Lawrence,
Mass.
Imperfect Town. Portland,
Tenn.
Imperial Polk. Lakeland, Fla.
Important Agricultural Center.
Oxford, Miss.
Important Cattle Center.
Davenport, Wash.
Important Center of Copper
Mining. Butte, Mont.
Important Commercial City.
Olympia, Wash.
Important Convention and
Conference City. Spring-
field, Ill.
Important Dairy Center.
Neosho, Mo.
Important Hub for Rail.
Memphis, Tenn.
Important Livestock Center.
Fargo, N.D.
Important Popcorn Center.
Ord, Neb.
Important Railroad and Truck
Center. Moberly, Mo.
Important Transportation
Center. Arkansas City,
Kan.
Impressive Residential and

Research Community. Stam-
ford, Conn.
Indian Capital. Gallup, N.M.
Indian Capital of the World.
Gallup, N.M.
Indian Village. Upper Sandusky,
Ohio
Indiana's Busiest, Happiest
City. Fort Wayne, Ind.
Indiana's Finest Home Town.
La Porte, Ind.
Indiana's Gateway City. Jef-
fersonville, Ind.
Indiana's Summer Playground.
Michigan City, Ind.
Indianapolis of the East.
Thompson, Conn.
Industrial, Agricultural and
Educational Center of the
South Plains of Texas.
Lubbock, Tex.
Industrial and Commercial
Center. Clinton, Mass.
Industrial and Cultural Center
of New Jersey. New
Brunswick, N.J.
Industrial and Distributing
Center of the Pacific Coast
Empire. Stockton, Calif.
Industrial and Distribution
Center. Jacksonville, Fla.
Industrial and Recreational
Center of East Alabama.
Alexander City, Ala.
Industrial and Recreational
Paradise. Pascagoula, Miss.
Industrial and Resort Center.
Panama City, Fla.
Industrial and Trading Center
of East Alabama. Opelika,
Ala.
Industrial Capital. Jackson,
Miss.
Industrial Capital of America.
Bridgeport, Conn.
Industrial Capital of California.
Pittsburg, Calif.
Industrial Capital of Connecti-
cut. Bridgeport, Conn.
Industrial Center. Henderson,
Nev.
Industrial Center. Lewiston,
Me.

Industrial Center. Ludlow, Mass.

Industrial Center. Portsmouth, Va.

Industrial Center. Saginaw, Mich.

Industrial Center of Louisiana. Bastrop, La.

Industrial Center of the Great South. Birmingham, Ala.

Industrial Center of the Panhandle. Borger, Tex.

Industrial Center of the Red River Valley. Paris, Tex.

Industrial Center of the South. Pasadena, Tex.

Industrial Center of the Southeast. Birmingham, Ala.

Industrial Center of Vermont. Springfield, Vt.

Industrial Center of West Florida. Pensacola, Fla.

Industrial Center of Western Carolina. Greenwood, S.C.

Industrial City. Beaumont, Tex.

Industrial City. Brockton, Mass.

Industrial City. Colton, Calif.

Industrial City. High Point, N.C.

Industrial City. Holyoke, Mass.

Industrial City. Joliet, Ill.

Industrial City. Milwaukee, Wis.

Industrial City. Pittsfield, Mass.

Industrial City. Poughkeepsie, N.Y.

Industrial City. Sidney, Ohio

Industrial City. South San Francisco, Calif.

Industrial City. Waterbury, Conn.

Industrial City Beautiful. Birmingham, Ala.

Industrial City of America. Fort Smith, Ark.

Industrial City of Dixie. Birmingham, Ala.

Industrial City of Iowa. Sioux City, Iowa

Industrial City of North Alabama. Huntsville, Ala.

Industrial City of Smokestacks. Everett, Wash.

Industrial City of the South. Birmingham, Ala.

Industrial City of the West. Pittsburg, Calif.

Industrial City of the West. Pittsburgh, Pa.

Industrial, Commercial and Cultural Capital. Denver, Colo.

Industrial Dynamo. Islip, N.Y.

Industrial Frontier of America. Oklahoma City, Okla.

Industrial Frontier of the Magic Lower Rio Grande Valley of Texas. Pharr, Tex.

Industrial, Geographical Historic and Transportation Center of Virginia. Lynchburg, Va.

Industrial Giant of Far Southwest Texas. Beaumont, Tex.

Industrial Half-Sister. Everett, Mass.

Industrial Heart of America. Cleveland, Ohio

Industrial Heart of Florida's Future. Quincy, Fla.

Industrial Heart of Maine. Auburn, Me.

Industrial Heart of Maine. Lewiston, Me.

Industrial Heart of the Naugatuck Valley. Ansonia, Conn.

Industrial Hub of Flathead Valley. Columbia Falls, Mont.

Industrial Hub of Florida. Tampa, Fla.

Industrial Hub of the United States. Chicago, Ill.

Industrial Hub of the West. Stockton, Calif.

Industrial Link to the West. Stockton, Calif.

Industrial Metropolis. Reading, Pa.

Industrial Paradise. Brookhaven, Mass.

Industrial Rocket Center. Marshall, Tex.

Industrial Site Center. Ord, Neb.

Industrial Vacation and Seafood Shopping Center. Norfolk, Va.

Industry Need Not Wish in Franklin. Franklin, Mass.

Inevitable Spa City. Saratoga Springs, N. Y.

Information City. New York, N. Y.

Inland City Beautiful. Pomona, Calif.

Inland Empire of the Pacific Northwest. Spokane, Wash.

Inland Metropolis. Birmingham, Ala.

Inland Paradise of Florida. Haines City, Fla.

Innkeeper's City. Memphis, Tenn.

Insurance and Granite Center. Montpelier, Vt.

Insurance Capital of the World. Hartford, Conn.

Insurance Center of the South. Jacksonville, Fla.

Insurance City. Atlanta, Ga.

Insurance City. Des Moines, Iowa

Insurance City. Hartford, Conn.

Interesting Past, a Prosperous Present, an Unlimited Future. Richmond, Va.

International City. Calais, Me.

International City. El Paso, Tex.

International City. Long Beach, Calif.

International City. New Orleans, La.

International Crossroads of the World. Chicago, Ill.

International Melting Pot. Seattle, Wash.

International Polar Air Crossroads of the World. Anchorage, Alaska

International Resort Area. San Diego, Calif.

International Trade Center. Brownsville, Tex.

International Village. Vail, Colo.

International Village of the Mountain's Base. Vail, Colo.

Iowa's Industrial, Financial and Commercial Center. Des Moines, Iowa

Iowa's Industrial, Scenic and Cultured City. Dubuque, Iowa

Iowa's Own City. Des Moines, Iowa

Iris City. Nashville, Tenn.

Iron City. Bessemer, Ala.

Iron City. Pittsburgh, Pa.

Iron City on the Tennessee River. Sheffield, Ala.

Iron Mountain City. Lebanon, Pa.

Iron Ore Capital of the World. Hibbing, Minn.

Iron Ore City. Connellsville, Pa.

Island City of Old World Charm. Key West, Fla.

Island of Contentment. Sea Isle City, N. J.

Island of Contrast. Key West, Fla.

Island of Distinctive Resort Life. Delray Beach, Fla.

Island of Easy Living. Peaks Island, Me.

Island of Enchantment. Nantucket, Mass.

Island Paradise. Key Biscayne, Fla.

Island Paradise Minutes from Miami. Key Biscayne, Fla.

Island They Wrote the Song About. Galveston, Tex.

Island where the Sand Whispers to the Sea. Jekyll Island, Ga.

Island You'll Love. Anna Maria, Fla.

Isle of Pleasant Living. Alameda, Calif.

Italy of America. San Diego, Calif.

It's a Fine Place to Live. Gloster, Miss.

It's Easy to Get Here, Pleasant
to Stay. Minot, N.D.
It's Pleasant to Live In.
Bloomington, Ill.

Jacaranda City with the Mile
Long Mall. Avon Park,
Fla.
Jacksonopolis. Jackson,
Mich.
Jambalaya Capital of the
World. Gonzales, La.
Jawbone Flats. Clarkston,
Wash.
Jax. Jacksonville, Fla.
Jeff City. Jefferson City,
Mo.
Jefferson's Country. Charlottes-
ville, Va.
Jet Transport Capital of the
World. Renton, Wash.
Jewel City. Glendale, Calif.
Jewel City of California. San
Diego, Calif.
Jewel City of the Sunshine
State. Miami, Fla.
Jewel City of the Florida
West Coast. Fort Myers,
Fla.
Jewel of the Gem State.
Burley, Idaho
Jewel of the Pacific Coast.
La Jolla, Calif.
Jewel of the Upper Chesapeake.
Betterton, Md.
Jewel on the Gulf of Mexico.
Corpus Christi, Tex.
Jimtown. Jamestown, N.D.
Jingle Town, U.S.A. East
Hampton, Conn.
Jones Beach of New England.
Salisbury Beach, Mass.
Jonquil City. Smyrna, Ga.
July Capital of the World.
Milwaukee, Wis.
Jumper's Flats. Waterville,
Wash.
Junction. Gretna, Va.
Just a Real Nice Town.
Plant City, Fla.
Just a Swell Place to Live
and Play. Talithina, Okla.

Kansas City of Alaska. Fair-
banks, Alaska
Kansas' Premier City. Wichita,
Kan.
Kansas Water Sports Capital.
Manhattan, Kan.
Kaolin Center of the World.
Sandersville, Ga.
Kentucky's Blue Grass Capital.
Lexington, Ky.
Kentucky's Capital. Frankfort,
Ky.
Key City. Dubuque, Iowa
Key City. Port Townsend,
Wash.
Key City. Vicksburg, Miss.
Key City in the Lower Rio
Grande Valley. Harlingen,
Tex.
Key City of Central Northwest
Wisconsin. Eau Claire, Wis.
Key City of Iowa. Dubuque,
Iowa
Key City of Naugatuck Valley.
Waterbury, Conn.
Key City of Puget Sound. Port
Townsend, Wash.
Key City of Southern California.
Riverside, Calif.
Key City of the Black Hills.
Sturgis, S.D.
Key City of the High Desert.
Victorville, Calif.
Key City of West Texas.
Abilene, Tex.
Key City to the West Coast of
Mexico. Nogales, Ariz.
Key Junction to the Southeast.
Thomasville, Ga.
Key National Defense Center.
Jacksonville, Fla.
Key of the Great Valley. New
Orleans, La.
Key Shopping and Manufacturing
Center. Madison, Wis.
Key Spot in the Future of Kay-
singer Reservoir. Osceola,
Mo.
Key to Industrial Expansion in
the Great Southeast. Atlanta,
Ga.
King Crab Capital of the World.
Kodiak, Alaska

King of Power. Niagara Falls,
N. Y.
Kingdom of Opportunity.
Blountstown, Fla.
Kingdom of the Sea. Dunnel-
lon, Fla.
Kingdom of the Sun. Dunnel-
lon, Fla.
Kingdom of the Sun. San
Diego, Calif.
Kissingen of America. Glen-
wood Springs, Colo.
Kodak City. Rochester, N. Y.
Kopper Kettle. Van Buren,
Ark.
Kringleville. Racine, Wis.

L. A. Los Angeles, Calif.
Ladino Clover Center of
America. Oakdale, Calif.
Lake Capital of the Hoosier
State. Elkhart, Ind.
Lake City. Chicago, Ill.
Lake City. Fort Worth, Tex.
Lake City. Madison, Wis.
Lake City. Watertown, S. D.
Lake Erie's Vacation City.
Cleveland, Ohio
Lake Ontario's Westernmost
American Seaport.
Rochester, N. Y.
Lake Region. Monroe, N. Y.
Lake Region in Minnesota.
Blackduck, Minn.
Lake Region Playground.
Alexandria, Minn.
Lake Trout Capital. Hovland,
Minn.
Lakeway to the Smokies.
Morristown, Tenn.
Lamb and Cattle Capital of
the West. Fort Collins,
Colo.
Land at the End of the Rain-
bow. Santa Cruz, Calif.
Land of Amazing Variety and
Contrasts. Burlington, Vt.
Land of Beautiful Lakes.
Speculator, N. Y.
Land of Berries. Utsaladdy,
Wash.

Land of Bread. Kittitas, Wash.
Land of Business Opportunity.
Fargo, N. D.
Land of Cheese, Trees and
Ocean Breeze. Tillamook,
Ore.
Land of Chief Wabasis. Belding,
Mich.
Land of Contrast. Arcadia,
Fla.
Land of Crosses. Auriesville,
N. Y.
Land of Diversification. Pear-
sall, Texas
Land of Enchanting Waters.
New Bern, N. C.
Land of Flowers. De Land,
Fla.
Land of Flowing Springs.
Youngstown, Ohio
Land of Good Living. Ruston,
La.
Land of Gracious Living. Yorba
Linda, Calif.
Land of Greer. Texola, Okla.
Land of Incredible Beauty and
Great Livability. Medford,
Ore.
Land of Hazel Nuts. Tukwila,
Wash.
Land of Industrial Opportunities.
Long Beach, Calif.
Land of Lakes and Trout
Streams. Murphy, N. C.
Land of Lakes Shopping Center.
El Dorado Springs, Mo.
Land of Leisure Living. Cape
Carteret, N. C.
Land of Life Worth Living.
Gloucester, Va.
Land of Longtails. Madison,
S. D.
Land of Lovely Lakes. Lake
Luzerne, N. Y.
Land of Milk and Honey. West
Plains, Mo.
Land of Opportunity. Belle-
view, Fla.
Land of Opportunity. Morgan
Hill, Calif.
Land of Outdoor Fun. Hender-
son, Ky.
Land of Perpetual Harvest.
Glendale, Ariz.

Land of Perpetual Prosperity.
Oklahoma City, Okla.
Land of Play and Plenty.
Virginia Beach, Va.
Land of Prairie and Beautiful
Hills. Lusk, Wyo.
Land of Promise. Delano,
Calif.
Land of Promise. Hollywood,
Calif.
Land of Romance and Recrea-
tion. Sacramento, Calif.
Land of Roulette Wheels.
Las Vegas, Nev.
Land of Sand, Sea and Sun.
Pawcatuck, Conn.
Land of Sand, Sea and Sun.
Westerly, R. I.
Land of Shining Mountains.
Billings, Mont.
Land of Sunshine. De Land,
Fla.
Land of Surprising Contrasts.
New York, N. Y.
Land of the Afternoon. Los
Angeles, Calif.
Land of the Big Inch.
Houston, Tex.
Land of the Endless Mountains.
Emporium, Pa.
Land of the Old South. St.
Simons Island, Ga.
Land of the Old South. Sea
Island, Ga.
Land of the Pilgrims, Sun
and Sand. Plymouth, Mass.
Land of the Pines. Alberta,
Va.
Land of the Sky. Asheville,
N. C.
Land of the Sky. Murphy,
N. C.
Land of the Trembling Earth.
Folkston, Ga.
Land of the Trembling Earth.
Waycross, Ga.
Land of the Vikings. Alexan-
dria, Minn.
Land of the West. Hesperia,
Calif.
Land of Washington. Frede-
ricksburg, Va.
Land where History Was

Made. Ticonderoga,
N. Y.
Landing. Fall City, Wash.
Large Retail and Wholesale
Distributing Center. Crooks-
ton, Minn.
Largest Broom Corn Shipping
Point in the Country. Elk
City, Okla.
Largest City and Commercial
Center of Maine. Portland,
Me.
Largest City for Its Size.
Taunton, Mass.
Largest City in Northern Ari-
zona. Winslow, Ariz.
Largest City in South Central
Missouri and Northern Kansas.
West Plains, Mo.
Largest City in the Largest
State. Anchorage, Alaska
Largest City in the Most Favored
Climate Area in America.
El Paso, Tex.
Largest City in the South.
Houston, Tex.
Largest City in the Southwest.
Houston, Tex.
Largest City of Contra Costa
County. Richmond, Calif.
Largest Cotton Manufacturing
Center in the State. La
Grange, Ga.
Largest Feeder Pig Market in
the Midwest. West Plains,
Mo.
Largest Ghost Town in America.
Jerome, Ariz.
Largest Industrial City in
Western Massachusetts.
Holyoke, Mass.
Largest Industrial City of Its
Size in Ohio. Barberton,
Ohio
Largest Insurance Center in the
West. Des Moines, Iowa
Largest Leather City. Peabody,
Mass.
Largest Little Pig Market.
Long Prairie, Minn.
Largest Metropolis in the
Mississippi Valley. St.
Louis, Mo.

Largest Pecan Shipping Center in America. Chandler, Okla.

Largest Port in the Lower East Coast. Port Everglades, Fla.

Largest Resort Center in Indiana. Michigan City, Ind.

Largest River Port in Mississippi. Greenville, Miss.

Largest Shopping Center in the Pomme de Terre Area. Bolivar, Mo.

Largest Small City in Indiana. Mitchell, Ind.

Largest Spot Cotton Market and Hardwood Lumber Market in the World. Memphis, Tenn.

Largest Unincorporated Town in the U.S. Falfurrias, Tex.

Largest Watermelon Shipping Center in California. Kingsburg, Calif.

Las Vegas on the Potomac. Colonial Beach, Va.

Last Capital of the Confederacy. Danville, Va.

Last Chance Gulf. Helena, Mont.

Last Frontier. Ruidoso, N.M.

Last of the Old West and the Best of the New. Jackson, Wyo.

Last of the Western Frontier. Sweetwater, Tex.

Last Outpost of Civilization. St. Charles, Mo.

Last Place on the Map. Ogden, Kan.

Launch Pad to Progress. Merritt Island, Fla.

Laurel City. Winsted, Conn.

Lawn City. Cedar Falls, Iowa

Leading Citrus Center. Covina, Calif.

Leading Commercial Financial and Distribution Center. Houston, Tex.

Leading Convention City in the Country. Chicago, Ill.

Leading Entertainment Mecca. Las Vegas, Nev.

Leading Family Resort Summer and Winter. Pacific Grove, Calif.

Leading Industrial City in Arkansas. Fort Smith, Ark.

Leading Industrial City of the Southwest. Houston, Tex.

Leading Industries Center of Lumber Processing and Metal Working. Vicksburg, Miss.

Leading Island City of the South. San Bernardino, Calif.

Leading New Hampshire Resort on Beautiful Sunapee Lake. Sunapee, N.H.

Leading Resort City. Augusta, Ga.

Leading Scallop Port of the World. New Bedford, Mass.

Leading Spot Cotton Market. Houston, Tex.

Leather City. Buford, Ga.

Leather City. Peabody, Mass.

Leech Lake Area Paradise. Walker, Minn.

Lehigh Valley City. Allentown, Pa.

Lemon Capital. Corona, Calif.

Lemon Capital. Santa Paula, Calif.

Lemon Capital of the World. Chula Vista, Calif.

Lemon Center. Santa Paula, Calif.

Lettuce Center of the Nation. Aguila, Ariz.

Lexington of Texas. Gonzalez, Tex.

Lifetime of Vacation Living. Montauk, N.Y.

Lighting Capital of the World. Cleveland, Ohio

Lighting Headquarters of the World. East Cleveland, Ohio

Lilac City. Fort Collins, Colo.

Lilac City. Lincoln, Neb.

Lilac Festival City. Rochester, N.Y.

Lilac Town. Lombard, Ill.

Limberlost Country. Geneva, Ind.

Limestone City. Rogers City, Mich.

Lincoln City. Boonville, Ind.

Lion of the Fox River Valley. Kaukauna, Wis.

Literary Emporium. Boston, Mass.

Little Arcady of Southwestern Louisiana. New Iberia, La.

Little Capital. Denver, Colo.

Little City in the Adirondacks. Saranac Lake, N.Y.

Little City in the Woods. Kingfield, Me.

Little City of Big Opportunity. Newberry, Fla.

Little City of Charm. Mesa, Ariz.

Little City of the Big Trees. Tehama, Calif.

Little City with Big Schools. Morris, Minn.

Little City with the Big Inferiority Complex. San Pablo, Calif.

Little Denmark. Solvang, Calif.

Little Detroit. Connersville, Ind.

Little Eden. Hoboken, N.J.

Little Gibraltar on the Arkansas. Fort Smith, Ark.

Little Heidelberg of America. Dubuque, Iowa

Little Holland. Garibaldi, Ore.

Little Hollywood. Kanab, Utah

Little Italy. Independence, La.

Little Las Vegas. Gardena, Calif.

Little Louisville of the Southwest. Seiling, Okla.

Little Lunnon (London). Colorado Springs, Colo.

Little New York. Welch, W. Va.

Little Norway of Alaska. Petersburg, Alaska

Little Portage. Seattle, Wash.

Little Sea by the Sea of Happy Rest and Reverie. Terminal Island, Calif.

Little Stumptown. Portland, Ore.

Little Switzerland. Ashfield, Mass.

Little Switzerland. New Glarus, Wis.

Little Switzerland. West Portal, N.J.

Little Switzerland of America. Eureka Springs, Ark.

Little Switzerland of Ohio. Sugarcreek, Ohio

Little Switzerland of the Ozarks. Eureka Springs, Ark.

Little Town on the Prairie. De Smet, S.D.

Little Venice. Skamokawa, Wash.

Little White House. Manchester, Ga.

Little White House City. Warm Springs, Ga.

Little World's Fair City. Yorktown, Tex.

Live and Play in Anchor Bay. New Baltimore, Mich.

Liveliest Resort Area. Phoenix, Ariz.

Liveliest Town in Robeson County. Fairmont, N.C.

Liveliest Town of Its Size in the World. Harvard, Ill.

Livestock, Grain and Industrial Capital of the Great Northwest. Sioux City, Iowa

Living Gets Better Each Year in Arcadia and De Soto County. Arcadia, Fla.

Living Page from Texas History. Jefferson, Tex.

Lobster Capital of the World. Rockland, Me.

Lobster Center of the World. Bar Harbor, Me.

Lock City. Stamford, Conn.

Lock Town of America. Terryville, Conn.

Logical Convention City. Indianapolis, Ind.

London Bridge Town. Lake
Havasu City, Ariz.
Lonesomest Town in the World.
Jordan, Mont.
Long Island's Ocean Play-
ground. Hampton Bays,
N.Y.
Long Island's World Famous
Ocean Playground. Hamp-
ton, N.Y.
Lookout City. Ebensburg, Pa.
Loom City. Rockville, Conn.
Los Diablos. Los Angeles,
Calif.
Lost Angels. Los Angeles,
Calif.
Lost Resort. Palm Springs,
Calif.
Louisiana's Cleanest City.
Jennings, La.
Louisiana's Fastest Growing
City. Baton Rouge, La.
Loveliest Modern City in
Mid-America. Lincoln,
Neb.
Loveliest Site in the World
for a Town. Emporia,
Kan.
Loveliest Village of the Plains.
Auburn, Ala.
Lovely Gateway to the Passes.
Salida, Colo.
Lovely Land of Gracious
Living. Lake City, Fla.
Lowell of the South. Augusta,
Ga.
Lowell of the West. Peta-
luma, Calif.
Lowest Down City in the
Western Hemisphere. Cali-
patria, Calif.
Luckiest Fishing Village in the
World where Everybody
Catches Fish. Destin, Fla.
Ludlow Is a Snow Town, Lud-
low Is a Fun Town, Ludlow
Has Everything. Ludlow,
Vt.
Lumber Capital. Tacoma,
Wash.
Lumber Capital of Alaska.
Wrangell, Alaska
Lumber Capital of America.
Tacoma, Wash.

Lumber Capital of the Nation.
Roseburg, Ore.
Lumber Capital of the World.
Tacoma, Wash.
Lumber City. Bangor, Me.
Lumber City. Muskegon, Mich.
Lumber City. Roseburg, Ore.
Lumber City. Williamsport,
Pa.
Lumber City of the World.
Muskegon, Mich.
Lumber Export Capital of Alaska.
Wrangell, Alaska
Lumber Industry's Capital.
Portland, Ore.
Lumber Manufacturing Center
of the Pacific Northwest.
Portland, Ore.
Lumber Port of the World.
Coos Bay, Ore.
Lumber Queen. Muskegon,
Mich.
Lumber Queen of the World.
Muskegon, Mich.
Lumbering and Fishing Center.
Aberdeen, Wash.
Lumbering Center. Everett,
Wash.
Lunchburg. Lynchburg, Va.
Lunchstone. Blackstone, Va.
Luxurious City of Traditional
Simplicity. Delray Beach,
Fla.
Luxury Resort Town. Las
Vegas, Nev.
Lyons of America. Paterson,
N.J.

Machine City. Lynn, Mass.
Machine Shop of America. Mil-
waukee, Wis.
Magic City. Anacortes, Wash.
Magic City. Anniston, Ala.
Magic City. Barberton, Ohio
Magic City. Billings, Mont.
Magic City. Birmingham, Ala.
Magic City. Colon, Mich.
Magic City. Florence, S.C.
Magic City. Gary, Ind.
Magic City. Leadville, Colo.
Magic City. Manchester, Ga.

Magic City. Marceline, Mo.
Magic City. Miami, Fla.
Magic City. Miami Beach, Fla.
Magic City. Millinocket, Me.
Magic City. Minot, N.D.
Magic City. Moberly, Mo.
Magic City. Muncie, Ind.
Magic City. Roanoke, Va.
Magic City. Schenectady, N.Y.
Magic City. Tulsa, Okla.
Magic City of the Green Empire. Bogalusa, La.
Magic City of the Plains. Casper, Wyo.
Magic City of the Plains. Cheyenne, Wyo.
Magic City of the South. Birmingham, Ala.
Magic City of the South. Roanoke, Va.
Magic City of the West. Cheyenne, Wyo.
Magic City of Virginia. Roanoke, Va.
Magic Little City. Whittier, Calif.
Magic Mascot of the Plains. Wichita, Kan.
Magic Muncie. Muncie, Ind.
Magic Town. Muncie, Ind.
Magnificent Capital. Washington, D.C.
Magnificent Mountain Wonderland. Long Lake, N.Y.
Magnolia City. Houston, Tex.
Magnolia State's Industrial City. Laurel, Miss.
Magnolia's Largest Industrial City. Laurel, Miss.
Mail-Order Fraud Capital of the Nation. Newark, N.J.
Main Street of America. Tulsa, Okla.
Main Street of North America. Cotulla, Tex.
Main Street of Northwest Arkansas. Springdale, Ark.
Main Street of the South Shore. Hyannis, Mass.
Main Street, USA. Webster City, Iowa
"Maine" Idea in Recreation. Kennebunk, Me.

Maine in a Nutshell. York, Me.
Maine's Fastest Growing Industrial and Recreational Area. Norway, Me.
Maine's Fastest Growing Industrial and Recreational Area. Paris, Me.
Maine's Most Beautiful Unspoiled Sandy Beach on Pront's Neck. Scarborough, Me.
Maine's Most Beautiful Vacation Region. Belgrade, Me.
Maine's Most Famous Coast Resort. Bar Harbor, Me.
Maine's Most Enchanting Island. Vinalhaven, Me.
Maine's Outstanding Winter Sports Center. Rumford, Me.
Maine's Shipbuilding City. Bath, Me.
Mainline City. Fargo, N.D.
Mainspring of the Midwest. Muncie, Ind.
Major Cultural Center of the World. Boston, Mass.
Major Glass Center. Corning, N.Y.
Major Inland Port Serving Mexico and Latin America. Laredo, Tex.
Major Insurance City. Hartford, Conn.
Major Market of the Midwest. Chanute, Kans.
Major Market of York County. Biddeford, Me.
Major Market of York County. Saco, Me.
Major Medical Center. St. Cloud, Minn.
Major Port of Call on America's New Fourth Seacoast. Milwaukee, Wis.
Major Research and Educational Center. Knoxville, Tenn.
Major Shipping Point for South Florida Growers. Palmetto, Fla.
Major World Seaport. Seattle, Wash.
Major World Tool and Die Training Center. South Bend, Ind.

Manchester of America.
Lowell, Mass.
Manchester of America.
Manchester, N. H.
Manufacturing and Industrial
Metropolis of the South-
east. Atlanta, Ga.
Manufacturing Center. Pots-
dam, N. Y.
Manufacturing City. Oneonta,
N. Y.
Manufacturing City of the
Pacific. Stockton, Calif.
Manufacturing City of the
Rocky Mountain Regions.
Pueblo, Colo.
Manufacturing Research and
Development Center of the
Southwest. Plano, Tex.
Maple Center of the World.
St. Johnsbury, Vt.
Maple City. Goshen, Ind.
Maple City. La Porte, Ind.
Maple City. Norwalk, Ohio
Maple City of Michigan.
Adrian, Mich.
Maple Sugar Center of the
World. St. Johnsbury, Vt.
Marble Capital of the United
States. Proctor, Vt.
Marble City. Carthage, Mo.
Marble City. Knoxville, Tenn.
Marble City. Rutland, Vt.
Marble City. Sylacauga, Ala.
Mardi Gras City. New Or-
leans, La.
Mardi Gras Metropolis. New
Orleans, La.
Marine Metropolis of Virginia.
Norfolk, Va.
Market of Three Barbarian
Tribes. San Francisco, Calif.
Market Town. Omaha, Neb.
Marketing and Shopping Center.
Mitchell, S. D.
Marketing and Trading Center.
Albuquerque, N. M.
Maryland's Largest City.
Baltimore, Md.
Maryland's Playground. Ocean
City, Md.
Maryland's Playground.
Roanoke, Va.

Master City. Roanoke, Va.
Mayflower Town. Duxbury,
Mass.
Meadow City. Las Vegas,
N. M.
Meadow City. Northampton,
Mass.
Meat-Packing Capital of the
World. Chicago, Ill.
Mecca for Champions in Many
Fields. Palm Beach, Fla.
Mecca for History Lovers.
Gonzalez, Tex.
Mecca for Talent. Sarasota,
Fla.
Mecca for Young Adults. New
York, N. Y.
Mecca of Crackpots. Los
Angeles, Calif.
Mecca of Telephone Men. New
York, N. Y.
Mecca of the Millions. Atlantic
City, N. J.
Media City. New York, N. Y.
Medical Center. Fort Worth,
Tex.
Medical Center. Mitchell, S. D.
Medical Center. Paducah, Ky.
Medical Center. Spokane, Wash.
Medical Center of North America.
Bismarck, N. D.
Medical Center of North Central
Kansas. Concordia, Kan.
Medical Center of Northeast
Texas. Paris, Tex.
Medical Center of Northwest
Arkansas. Fayetteville, Ark.
Medical Center of the Missis-
sippi Delta. Greenwood, Miss.
Medical Center of Western Mon-
tana. Missoula, Mont.
Medical Referral Center of
South Texas. Harlingen, Tex.
Melon Capitol of the World.
Rocky Ford, Colo.
Melting Pot. New York, N. Y.
Memphis of the American Nile.
St. Louis, Mo.
Mercantile Center. Fitchburg,
Mass.
Merchandising Mecca of New
Jersey. Paramus, N. J.
Metropolis. New York, N. Y.

Metropolis in a Forest of
Trees. Buffalo, N.Y.
Metropolis of a Continent.
New York, N.Y.
Metropolis of a Fast Growing
Commercial and Agri-
cultural Area. Harrison,
Ark.
Metropolis of a New South.
Atlanta, Ga.
Metropolis of America.
New York, N.Y.
Metropolis of an Agricultural
Empire. Amarillo, Tex.
Metropolis of Central and
Northwest Kansas. Salina,
Kan.
Metropolis of "Dutchland."
Lancaster, Pa.
Metropolis of Eastern Nevada.
Elko, Nev.
Metropolis of East Tennessee.
Knoxville, Tenn.
Metropolis of Industry. Cedar
Rapids, Iowa
Metropolis of Isms. Los
Angeles, Calif.
Metropolis of New England.
Boston, Mass.
Metropolis of New Mexico.
Albuquerque, N.M.
Metropolis of North Dakota.
Fargo, N.D.
Metropolis of North Texas.
Dallas, Tex.
Metropolis of Northern New
York. Watertown, N.Y.
Metropolis of South Central
Nebraska. Superior, Neb.
Metropolis of Southeastern
Florida. Miami, Fla.
Metropolis of Southern
Nevada. Las Vegas, Nev.
Metropolis of the Country.
Washington, D.C.
Metropolis of the Desert.
Phoenix, Ariz.
Metropolis of the Inland
Empire. Spokane, Wash.
Metropolis of the Magic
Valley. Brownsville, Tex.
Metropolis of the Mississippi
Delta. Greenville, Miss.

Metropolis of the Missouri
Valley. Kansas City, Mo.
Metropolis of the New South.
Louisville, Ky.
Metropolis of the Northeast.
Bangor, Me.
Metropolis of the Northwest.
Pierre, S.D.
Metropolis of the Pacific Coast.
Los Angeles, Calif.
Metropolis of the Pacific
Northwest. Seattle, Wash.
Metropolis of the Panhandle.
Amarillo, Tex.
Metropolis of the Penobscot
Bay Region. Rockland, Me.
Metropolis of the Pine Ridge
Reservation Country. Martin,
S.D.
Metropolis of the Richest Part
of Texas. Corpus Christi,
Tex.
Metropolis of the South. New
Orleans, La.
Metropolis of the Southern West
Virginia Coal Fields. Blue-
field, W. Va.
Metropolis of the Southwest.
Dallas, Tex.
Metropolis of the State of Ore-
gon. Portland, Ore.
Metropolis of the Unsalted
Seas. Duluth, Minn.
Metropolis of the West. Chi-
cago, Ill.
Metropolis of the West.
Houston, Tex.
Metropolis of the West. Los
Angeles, Calif.
Metropolis of the World's
Largest Gas Field. Monroe,
La.
Metropolis of Vashon Island.
Vashon, Wash.
Metropolis of West Florida.
Pensacola, Fla.
Metropolis of Western Massa-
chusetts. Springfield,
Mass.
Metropolitan Center of Mc-
Kean County. Bradford,
Pa.
Metropolitan Center of Tropical

Florida's First Resort Area.
W. Palm Beach, Fla.
Metropolitan City. New York,
N. Y.
Metropolitan City. Washing-
ton, D. C.
Metropolitan Community of Op-
portunity. Beloit, Wis.
Miami Beach of the North.
Montauk, N. Y.
Michigan's Dynamic City.
Dearborn, Mich.
Michigan's Fastest Growing
City. Dearborn, Mich.
Michigan's Fastest Growing
Community. Dearborn,
Mich.
Michigan's Most Famous Sum-
mer Resort. Benton Har-
bor, Mich.
Michigan's Most Renowned
Phantom City. White Rock,
Mich.
Mid-America's Fast Growing
Exciting New Playground.
Garrison, N. D.
Mid-America's Finest Vaca-
tionland. Angola, Ind.
Mid-America's Industrial
Center. Anderson, Ind.
Mid-South Resort. Southern
Pines, N. C.
Mid-Way City. Melbourne,
Fla.
Middle of Marketing America.
Columbus, Ohio
Middle Town of New England.
Pittsfield, Mass.
Middletown, U. S. A. Muncie,
Ind.
Middlewest Center for Diver-
sified Manufacture. Mil-
waukee, Wis.
Midget City. Colby, Wis.
Midland Empire City. Bil-
lings, Mont.
Midland Metropolis. Chicago,
Ill.
Midway City. Kearney, Neb.
Midway Garden Spot of the
Atlantic Coast. Mathews,
Va.
Midway, U. S. A. Lawrence,
Kan.

Midwest Golf Capital. Chi-
cago, Ill.
Midwest Metropolis. Chicago,
Ill.
Midwest's Most Progressive
City. Fremont, Neb.
Midwest's Winter Sports Mecca.
Three Lakes, Wis.
Mighty Capital. Washington,
D. C.
Mighty Manhattan. New York,
N. Y.
Mighty Metropolis. Chicago,
Ill.
Mile High City. Denver, Colo.
Mile High City. Lead, S. D.
Mile High City. Prescott, Ariz.
Mile High City of Health.
Prescott, Ariz.
Mile High City of the Black
Hills. Lead, S. D.
Mile Square City. Hoboken,
N. J.
Military Capital of the Colonies.
Morristown, N. J.
Milk Capital of the World.
Harvard, Ill.
Milk Center of the World.
Harvard, Ill.
Milk City. Carnation, Wash.
Mill City. Winooski, Vt.
Million Dollar Camp. Tok,
Alaska
Milling Center. Valley City,
N. D.
Mill Town. Pittsfield, Mass.
Milltown. Minneapolis, Minn.
Milwaukee the Beautiful. Mil-
waukee, Wis.
Milwaukee of the East. Newark,
N. J.
Mineral City. Spruce Pine,
N. C.
Mineral City of the South.
Birmingham, Ala.
Mineral Pocket of New England.
Cumberland, R. I.
Mineral Springs City. Bed-
ford, Pa.
Mineral Springs City. Bed-
ford, Va.
Mining Town with a Heart.
Denver, Colo.

Minneapolis of the West.
Spokane, Wash.
Minnesota's Mini-San Fran-
cisco. Duluth, Minn.
Minnesota's Outdoor Play-
ground. Winona, Minn.
Minnesota's Summer and
Winter Playground. Glen-
wood, Minn.
Miracle City. Anchorage,
Alaska
Miracle City. Houston, Tex.
Miracle City in the Desert.
Phoenix, Ariz.
Miracle City of the Gold
Coast. Deerfield Beach,
Fla.
Miracle City of the Midwest.
Chicago, Ill.
Miracle in the Southwest.
Albuquerque, N.M.
Missile Capital of the West.
Santa Maria, Calif.
Missile City. Titusville, Fla.
Missile Land, U.S.A. Cocoa
Beach, Fla.
Missing City of Marin. San
Rafael, Calif.
Mission City. Riverside,
Calif.
Mission City. San Antonio,
Tex.
Mississippi's Best Example
of the New South. Tupelo,
Miss.
Mississippi's Finest Example
of the New South. Tupelo,
Miss.
Mississippi's Gateway to the
Sea. Gulfport, Miss.
Mississippi's Great Resort
and Historic Center.
Biloxi, Miss.
Mississippi's Industrial City.
Laurel, Miss.
Mississippi's Industrial Sea-
port. Pascagoula, Miss.
Mississippi's Largest River
Port. Greenville, Miss.
Mississippi's Thriving In-
dustrial Center. Yazoo
City, Miss.
Missouri's Finest Deer,

Squirrel, Quail and Coon
Hunting City. Ellington, Mo.
Missouri's Historic Crafts and
Entertainment Capital. Silver
Dollar City, Mo.
Missouri's Magic City. Moberly,
Mo.
Missouri's Most Industrially
Diversified Small City. Wash-
ington, Mo.
Mistake by the Lake. Buffalo,
N.Y.
Mistake on the Lake. Cleve-
land, Ohio
Mobtown. Baltimore, Md.
Model City. Anniston, Ala.
Model City. Commerce, Calif.
Model City. Quincy, Ill.
Model City of Alabama. Annis-
ton, Ala.
Model Family Resort, Summer
and Winter. Pacific Grove,
Calif.
Model Industry City. South
Gate, Calif.
Model Mining Community. Car-
bonado, Wash.
Model Municipality. Monroe,
Wash.
Model Village. Coleraine,
Minn.
Modern American Athens.
Lowell, Mass.
Modern and Progressive Town.
Springfield, Vt.
Modern Athens. Boston, Mass.
Modern Athens. Cleveland,
Ohio
Modern Baseball Park City.
Morris, Minn.
Modern Boom Town. Gillette,
Wyo.
Modern City. Commerce,
Calif.
Modern City. Lynchburg, Va.
Modern City. Marshfield, Wis.
Modern City. Portsmouth, Va.
Modern City of Great Histori-
cal Interest. Philadelphia, Pa.
Modern City on the Move. Or-
lando, Fla.
Modern City with a Colonial
Setting. Annapolis, Md.

Modern City with a Proud
Heritage. Providence, R.I.
Modern Gomorrah. New
York, N.Y.
Modern Industrial City. Tor-
rance, Calif.
Modern Little City. Belmar,
N.J.
Modern Municipality for
Modern Industry. Parsip-
pany, N.J.
Modern Phoenix. Cloquet,
Minn.
Modern Progressive City.
Lodi, Calif.
Modern Rome. Richmond, Va.
Modern Town for Modern
Living. Vidalia, Ga.
Modern Town Rich in History.
Wiscasset, Me.
Money Hole. Conconully,
Wash.
Money Town. New York,
N.Y.
Montana's Friendly Community.
Cut Bank, Mont.
Montana's Largest and
Friendliest City. Great
Falls, Mont.
Montana's Only Billion Dollar
Market. Billings, Mont.
Monte Carlo of the West.
Las Vegas, Nev.
Monument City. Richmond,
Va.
Monument to Southwestern
Economic Growth. Houston,
Tex.
Monumental City. Baltimore,
Md.
More than Just the "Sea" and
the Shore. Atlantic City,
N.J.
Mormon City. Salt Lake City,
Utah
Mormon Metropolis. Salt
Lake City, Utah
Mormon's Mecca. Salt Lake
City, Utah
Most Accessible City. Tor-
rington, Conn.
Most Accessible City on the
North American Continent.

Buffalo, N.Y.
Most Air-Minded City in the
World. Anchorage, Alaska
Most Beautiful City. Detroit,
Mich.
Most Beautiful City in America.
Washington, D.C.
Most Beautiful City in the
State. Glenwood, Minn.
Most Beautiful College Town in
America. Princeton, N.J.
Most Beautiful Little City in
America. Madison, Wis.
Most Beautiful of All Western
Cities. Quincy, Ill.
Most Beautiful Village in New
York State. Fredonia, N.Y.
Most Bridged City in the World.
Pittsburgh, Pa.
Most Colorful Country in the
West. Sedona, Ariz.
Most Colorful Exciting City in
the World. New York, N.Y.
Most Complete Year-'Round
Resort Town in the White
Mountains. North Conway,
N.H.
Most Eastern Western Metropo-
lis. Tulsa, Okla.
Most Exclusive Residential
Town in the East. New
Canaan, Conn.
Most Fashionable Winter Resort.
Thomasville, Ga.
Most Handsome, Resurgent and
Progressive Showcase City.
Spokane, Wash.
Most Historic City in America.
Fredericksburg, Va.
Most Historic City in the East.
Salem, Mass.
Most Historic City in the North-
west Territory. Marietta,
Ohio
Most Historic Community.
Salem, Mass.
Most Historic Spot in North
Dakota. Stanton, N.D.
Most Northern Southern City.
Tulsa, Okla.
Most Opportune Locality of
the Middle West. Warsaw,
Okla.

Most Popular Summer Resort
in New England. Rockport,
Mass.
Most Promising Industrial Com-
munity of the Future.
Colonial Heights, Va.
Most Scenic City on the Con-
tinent. Seattle, Wash.
Most Spectacular and Beautiful
Part of the U.S. Ouray,
Colo.
Most Typical Western City in
Wyoming. Evanston, Wyo.
Most Unique City in America.
Jerome, Ariz.
Most Versatile Port on the
West Coast. Long Beach,
Calif.
Motel City. Perry, Ga.
Motel City of the Top O'Lake
Michigan. Manistique,
Mich.
Mother City. Yankton, S.D.
Mother City of America.
Boston, Mass.
Mother City of an Empire.
San Antonio, Tex.
Mother City of Georgia.
Savannah, Ga.
Mother City of the Dakotas.
Yankton, S.D.
Mother of Counties. Fayette,
Mo.
Mother of New Orleans.
Biloxi, Miss.
Mother of Springfield. Aga-
wam, Mass.
Mother of the South. Parowan,
Utah
Mother of the West. Mar-
shall, Mo.
Mother of Towns. Farmington,
Conn.
Mother of Towns. Mexico,
N.Y.
Motion Picture Center of the
World. Los Angeles,
Calif.
Motor Capital of the World.
Detroit, Mich.
Motor City. Detroit, Mich.
Mound Builders' City. Newark,
Ohio

Mound City. St. Louis, Mo.
Mount Vernon of Texas. Hunts-
ville, Tex.
Mount Zion. Montesano, Wash.
Mountain City. Altoona, Pa.
Mountain City. Chattanooga,
Tenn.
Mountain Gateway. Cleveland,
Ga.
Mountain Lake Vacationland.
Murphy, N.C.
Mountain Pass of Health, Ac-
cessibility Beauty. Beau-
mont, Calif.
Movie City. Los Angeles,
Calif.
Movie-Making City. New York,
N.Y.
Movie Village. Hollywood,
Calif.
Movieland. Hollywood, Calif.
Mud Hen City. Toledo, Ohio
Mud Hole City. Washington,
D.C.
Mule Capital of the World.
Columbia, Tenn.
Mum City. Bristol, Conn.
Municipal Poem of Beauty, Sun-
shine, Health, Prosperity
and Happiness. Whittier,
Calif.
Murder Capital of America.
Memphis, Tenn.
Murder Capital of the World.
Birmingham, Ala.
Murder Capital of the World.
Dallas, Tex.
Murder Capital of the World.
Houston, Tex.
Murder City. Los Angeles,
Calif.
Mushroom Capital. Mesick,
Mich.
Mushroom City. San Fran-
cisco, Calif.
Mushroomopolis. Kansas City,
Mo.
Music Center of the South.
Brevard, N.C.
Music City, U.S.A. Nashville,
Tenn.
Musical Instrument Capital of
the World. Elkhart, Ind.

Muskie Capital of New York.
Bemus Point, N. Y.
Muskie Capital of the World.
Walker, Minn.
Musky Capital. Hayward,
Wis.
Must Stop on the Florida Gold
Coast. Vero Beach, Fla.

Nail City. Wheeling, W. Va.
Naples of America. Falmouth,
Mass.
Naples of America. Muni-
sing, Mich.
Nashville of the West. Bakers-
field, Calif.
Natchez of the Chattahoochee.
Eufaula, Ala.
National Anthem City. Balti-
more, Md.
National Capital. Washington,
D. C.
National Date Festival City.
Indio, Calif.
National, Industrial, Scientific,
Educational and Cultural
Center. Buffalo, N. Y.
Nationally Known Deep Sea
Salmon Fishing Center.
Westport, Wash.
Nation's Best Recreational
Area--Four Season Fun.
Biddeford, Me.
Nation's Birthplace. Phila-
delphia, Pa.
Nation's Birthplace. Plymouth,
Mass.
Nation's Busiest Inland Port.
Pittsburgh, Pa.
Nation's Capital. Washington,
D. C.
Nation's Cleanest City.
Memphis, Tenn.
Nation's Finest Winter Sports
Center. Lake Placid,
N. Y.
Nation's First Capital. York,
Pa.
Nation's First City. New
York, N. Y.

Nation's Glamor Capital. Hol-
lywood, Calif.
Nation's Great All-Year Resort.
Asbury Park, N. J.
Nation's Great All-Year Resort
City-by-the-Sea. Asbury
Park, N. J.
Nation's Great New Convention
City. Las Vegas, Nev.
Nation's Great Resort City-by-
the-Sea. Asbury Park, N. J.
Nation's Greatest City. New
York, N. Y.
Nation's Greatest Historic
Shrine. Gettysburg, Pa.
Nation's Headquarters. Wash-
ington, D. C.
Nation's Health Resort. Hot
Springs, Ark.
Nation's Hottest Town. Quartz-
site, Ariz.
Nation's Insurance Capital.
Hartford, Conn.
Nation's Largest Basque Colony.
Boise, Idaho
Nation's Largest Communica-
tions Center. New York,
N. Y.
Nation's Largest Port. New
York, N. Y.
Nation's Largest Winter Wheat
Market. Kansas City, Mo.
Nation's Most Beautiful City.
Seattle, Wash.
Nation's Most Dynamic and
Valuable Entity. Toledo,
Ohio
Nation's Most Exciting New
Convention Center. Houston,
Tex.
Nation's Most Historic Area.
Beaufort, S. C.
Nation's Most Hospitable City.
Baltimore, Md.
Nation's No. 1 Convention City.
Chicago, Ill.
Nation's No. 3 Potato Center,
Soon the First. Grafton,
S. D.
Nation's Oldest City. St.
Augustine, Fla.
Nation's Oldest Continually

Active Parish. Alamogordo,
N. M.
Nation's Oldest Seashore Re-
sort. Cape May, N. J.
Nation's Other Capital. Key
West, Fla.
Nation's Peony Capital. Fari-
bault, Minn.
Nation's Peony Center. Van
Wert, Ohio
Nation's Residential Research
Center. Monroeville, Pa.
Nation's Safest Beach. White
Lake, N. C.
Nation's Seafood Center.
Biloxi, Miss.
Nation's Second Largest Ma-
chine-Tool Center. Rock-
ford, Ill.
Nation's Sheep Capital. San
Angelo, Tex.
Nation's Smog Capital. Los
Angeles, Calif.
Nation's Southernmost City.
Key West, Fla.
Nation's State. Washington,
D. C.
Nation's Sugar Bowl. Pahokee,
Fla.
Nation's Summer Capital.
Rehoboth Beach, Del.
Nation's Thoroughfare.
Louisville, Ky.
Nation's Vacation Capital.
Rehoboth Beach, Del.
Nation's Warmest, Driest,
Sunniest Spot. Phoenix,
Ariz.
Nation's Western Capital.
San Francisco, Calif.
Nation's Winter Vegetable
Garden and Sugar Bowl.
Okeechobee, Fla.
Nation's Wood Capital. Jasper,
Ind.
Native City of Benjamin
Franklin. Philadelphia, Pa.
Natural City. Huron, S. D.
Natural Gas Capital of the
U. S. Hugoton, Kan.
Natural Gas City. Bradford,
Pa.
Natural Gas Pipeline Capital

of the Nation. Houston,
Tex.
Natural Gateway to Southern
California's Endless Charm.
Long Beach, Calif.
Natural Location for Agricul-
tural Industry. Fargo, N. D.
Natural Port City. Apalachi-
cola, Fla.
Natural Shopping Center. Green-
wood, S. C.
Natural Tourist and Convention
Center. Bethlehem, Pa.
Natural Trading Area for North
Central Florida. Gaines-
ville, Fla.
Natural Trading Center. Mer-
rill, Wis.
Nature's Air Conditioned City.
Bluefield, W. Va.
Nature's Airconditioned City.
Bluefield, Va.
Nature's Gift to Texas. Houston,
Tex.
Nature's Gift to the Gold Coast.
Pass Christian, Miss.
Nature's Greatest Boon to
Arizona. Phoenix, Ariz.
Nature's Mighty Masterpiece.
Niagara Falls, N. Y.
Nature's Own Air Conditioning.
Crossville, Tenn.
Nature's Palladium. Lyndon-
ville, Vt.
Nature's Play Ground. Libby,
Mont.
Nature's Underwater Fairyland.
Silver Springs, Fla.
Nature's Unspoiled Wonderland.
Clarksville, Va.
Nature's Wonderland. Salida,
Colo.
Naval Center. Newport, R. I.
Naval Center of the South.
Jacksonville, Fla.
Naval Stores Capital of the
World. Valdosta, Ga.
Navy Town. Vallejo, Calif.
Navy's First City of the Sea.
Portsmouth, Va.
Near to Everything Every-
where. Lebanon, Mo.
Nearby Wonder of the

World. Niagara Falls,
N. Y.
Nearest City to the Golden
Spike Site. Brigham City,
Utah
Nearest Florida Resort to
Most of the Nation.
Pensacola, Fla.
Nearest Metropolitan Center
to All Five Gateways of
Ranier National Park.
Tacoma, Wash.
Nearest Point of Land to the
Gulf Stream. Pompano
Beach, Fla.
Nebraska's Friendly City.
Plainview, Neb.
Nebraska's Game Paradise.
Norfolk, Neb.
Nebraska's Sport Center.
Ogallala, Neb.
Nebraska's Third City.
Grand Island, Neb.
Nebraskaland's Big Game
Capital. Chadron, Neb.
Neighborly Friendly Com-
munity. Fontana, Calif.
Neighborly Satisfying Com-
munity for Living. Plant
City, Fla.
Neptune Township's Ocean
Front. Ocean Grove, N. J.
Nerve Center of Alaska.
Anchorage, Alaska
Nevada's Largest City. Las
Vegas, Nev.
Nevada's Nile Valley. Love-
lock, Nev.
Never-Closed Casino City.
Las Vegas, Nev.
New American Mecca. Las
Vegas, Nev.
New Capital. Washington,
D. C.
New Car Capital of Arizona.
Glendale, Ariz.
New City for People and
Business. Columbia, Md.
New City in the Old South.
Shreveport, La.
New City of Washington.
Washington, D. C.

New Crossroads of California.
Los Banos, Calif.
New Distribution Center of the
West. Stockton, Calif.
New England Garden Spot.
Norwalk, Conn.
New England's Great Seashore
Resort. Portsmouth, N. H.
New England's Playground on
the Atlantic. Salisbury
Beach, Mass.
New England's Treasure House.
Salem, Mass.
New Gateway to World Trade.
Savannah, Ga.
New Gold Mine of the Old West.
Imperial, Calif.
New Height in American Skiing.
Jackson, Wyo.
New Helvetia. Sacramento,
Calif.
New Industrial Frontier of the
Southwest. Odessa, Tex.
New Jersey's Dynamic Location.
Woodbridge, N. J.
New Jersey's First Suburb.
Secaucus, N. J.
New Jerusalem. Salt Lake
City, Utah
New Kind of City. Atlanta, Ga.
New Market. Tumwater, Wash.
New Mexico's Capital City.
Santa Fe, N. M.
New National City. Atlanta,
Ga.
New Playground of America.
Pompano Beach, Fla.
New Pueblo. Tucson, Ariz.
New Recreational Resort Com-
munity. Silver Lakes, Calif.
New Resort Area of Florida.
Fort Myers, Fla.
New Settlement. Washington,
D. C.
New World Port. Portsmouth,
N. H.
New York of Nebraska. Omaha,
Neb.
New York of the South. At-
lanta, Ga.
New York State's Complete All-
Season Resort. Lake Placid,
N. Y.

New York State's First Capital.
Kingston, N. Y.
New York's First Capital.
Kingston, N. Y.
New York's Lake Erie Vaca-
tionland in Beautiful
Chautauqua County. Dun-
kirk, N. Y.
Newarks. Los Angeles, Calif.
Newest Most Prosperous
Fastest-Growing Urban In-
dustrial Center in America.
Houston, Tex.
Newport of Chicago Society.
Lake Geneva, Wis.
Newport of the Eastern Shore.
Easton, Md.
Newport of the Pacific. Santa
Barbara, Calif.
Newport of the South. Beau-
fort, S. C.
Newport of the West. Colorado,
Springs, Colo.
News Capital of the World.
Washington, D. C.
Next Station to Heaven. New
Canaan, Conn.
Niagara of Pennsylvania.
Bushkill, Pa.
Niagara of the South. Muscle
Shoals, Ala.
Niagara of the West. Great
Falls, Mont.
Nice Place to Live. Ashland,
N. H.
Nice Place to Live. Chow-
chilla, Calif.
Nice Place to Live and Work.
Roxbury, N. J.
Nine Hills. Richmond, Va.
1974 World's Fair City.
Spokane, Wash.
Nineteen Suburbs in Search
of a Metropolis. Los
Angeles, Calif.
No Other Place Quite Like It.
South Egremont, Mass.
Non-Stop to Everywhere.
Salina, Kan.
North Carolina's Pleasure
Island. Ocracoke, N. C.
North Central Florida's Shop-
ping Center. Gainesville,
Fla.

North Central Florida's Shop-
ping Headquarters. Gaines-
ville, Fla.
North Dakota Winter Show
Center. Valley City, N. D.
North Dakota's Favorite Con-
vention City. Minot, N. D.
North Dakota's Queen City.
Dickinson, N. D.
North Florida's Gretna Green.
Macclenny, Fla.
North Gateway to the Kaysinger
Dam and Reservoir Area.
Windsor, Mo.
North Nebraska's Largest City.
Norfolk, Neb.
North Shore Haven. Beaver
Bay, Minn.
North Star City. St. Paul,
Minn.
Northeastern Gateway to the
Grand Lake Resort Area.
Seneca, Mo.
Northeastern North Carolina
Industrial Center. Roanoke
Rapids, N. C.
Northeasternmost City in the
U. S. Caribou, Me.
Northern Entrance to the Sky-
line Drive, Shenandoah Na-
tional Park. Front Royal,
Va.
Northern Gateway to Alabama.
Decatur, Ala.
Northern Gateway to Broward
County. Deerfield Beach,
Fla.
Northern Gateway to Central
Florida. Gainesville, Fla.
Northern Gateway to Mount
Magazine and the Magazine
Recreational Area. Paris,
Mo.
Northern Gateway to the Bad-
lands National Monument.
Wall, S. D.
Northern Gateway to the Beauti-
ful Shenandoah Valley.
Winchester, Va.
Northern Gateway to the Black
Hills. Belle Fourche, S. D.
Northern Gateway to the Natural
Paradise Baxter Park. Pat-
ten, Me.

Northern Gateway to the
Shenandoah Valley. Win-
chester, Va.
Northern Michigan's Shopping
Center. Petoskey, Mich.
Northern New Mexico's Most
Unique Vacationland. Taos,
N. M.
Northern Pike Capital of the
World. Mobridge, S. D.
Northernmost Ice-Free Port.
Wrightsville Beach, N. C.
Northernmost Oasis in America.
Twenty-Nine Palms, Calif.
Northwest Arkansas' Largest
City. Fayetteville, Ark.
Northwest Gateway. Seattle,
Wash.
Northwest Montana's Business
and Shopping Center.
Kalispell, Mont.
Northwest's Custom Tailored
Convention City. Eugene,
Ore.
Now City. Irving, Tex.
Nuclear Center. Pittsburgh,
Pa.
Nugget of the Valley. Dixon,
Calif.
Number One City in the
Southwest. Houston, Tex.
Number One Host of the
Jersey Coast. Atlantic
City, N. J.

Oak City. Raleigh, N. C.
Oasis in Mountain Country.
Powell, Wyo.
Oasis in the Desert. Palm
Springs, Calif.
Oasis of Nevada. Fallon,
Nev.
Oasis of the San Joaquin
Valley. Denair, Calif.
Ocean City. Fernandina
Beach, Fla.
Ocean Paradise. Gloucester,
Mass.
Oceanographic Capital of
the World. San Diego,
Calif.

Ocosta by the Sea. Ocosta,
Wash.
Official Cowboy Capital of
Nebraska. Ogallala, Neb.
Ogunquit Is the Sea. Ogunquit,
Me.
Ohio's Beautiful Capital.
Columbus, Ohio
Ohio's City of Friends. Salem,
Ohio
Ohio's First Capital. Chilli-
cothe, Ohio
Ohio's First City. Marietta,
Ohio
Ohio's Most Progressive City.
Fairborn, Ohio
Ohio's Oldest and Most Beauti-
ful City. Marietta, Ohio
Oil and Gas Center of the Great
Anadarko Basin. Perryton,
Tex.
Oil Boom Town. Gillette, Wyo.
Oil Capital. Jackson, Miss.
Oil Capital. Joy, Okla.
Oil Capital. Mount Pleasant,
Mich.
Oil Capital. Tulsa, Okla.
Oil Capital in the Heart of the
Wheat Belt. Great Bend,
Kan.
Oil Capital of Alabama. Citro-
nelle, Ala.
Oil Capital of Alaska. Kenai,
Alaska
Oil Capital of Arkansas. El
Dorado, Ark.
Oil Capital of Florida. Jay,
Fla.
Oil Capital of Mississippi.
Yazoo City, Miss.
Oil Capital of Montana. Cut
Bank, Mont.
Oil Capital of North Dakota.
Tioga, N. D.
Oil Capital of Southwest Ne-
braska. McCook, Neb.
Oil Capital of the Rockies.
Casper, Wyo.
Oil Capital of the Southwest.
Tulsa, Okla.
Oil Capital of the United
States. Joy, Okla.

Oil Capital of the World.
Tulsa, Okla.
Oil Center. Midland, Tex.
Oil Center for Mississippi.
Jackson, Miss.
Oil Center of Illinois. Cen-
tralia, Ill.
Oil Center of the World.
Houston, Tex.
Oil City. Bayonne, N.J.
Oil City. Casper, Wyo.
Oil City. Citronelle, Ala.
Oil City. Glenrock, Wyo.
Oil City. Montpelier, Ind.
Oil City. Taft, Calif.
Oil City of the Southwest.
Odessa, Tex.
Oil, Gas, Steel, Chemical,
Clay, Lumber Center.
Marshall, Tex.
Oil Shale Capital of the World.
Rifle, Colo.
Oil Well Cementing Capital
of the World. Duncan, Tex.
O.K. City. McCook, Neb.
Old Chi. Chicago, Ill.
Old City with a New Future.
Apalachicola, Fla.
Old Dorp. Schenectady, N.Y.
Old French Town. New Or-
leans, La.
Old Garrison. San Antonio,
Tex.
Old Gold Hill. San Francisco,
Calif.
Old Island--The New Island.
Key West, Fla.
Old Lady of the Sea. Galves-
ton, Tex.
Old Maid City, Looking Under
Her Bed Every Night for
an Ocean. Duluth, Minn.
Old Mart. Clarksville, Va.
Old Pueblo. Los Angeles,
Calif.
Old Pueblo. Tucson, Ariz.
Old Roaring Capital of the
Mountainest West. Denver,
Colo.
Old Slave Market. Louis-
ville, Ga.
Old Town by the Sea. Ports-
mouth, N.H.

Old West's Newest City. New
Town, N.D.
Oldest American Town in Texas.
San Augustine, Tex.
Oldest and Largest Tobacco
Market. Douglas, Ga.
Oldest and Quaintest City in
the United States. Santa
Fe, N.M.
Oldest Chartered City in the
United States. Albany, N.Y.
Oldest City in the State. Van-
couver, Wash.
Oldest City in the United States.
St. Augustine, Fla.
Oldest City in the United States
Operating Under Its Original
Charter. Albany, N.Y.
Oldest City West of the Missis-
sippi. Ste Genevieve, Mo.
Oldest Community in Washing-
ton. Vancouver, Wash.
Oldest Continuous English-
Speaking Settlement in
America. Hampton, Va.
Oldest English Settlement in
New York State. Southamp-
ton, N.Y.
Oldest French City in the U.S.
Biloxi, Miss.
Oldest Historical City on Puget
Sound. Steilacoom, Wash.
Oldest Inland City in the United
States. Lancaster, Pa.
Oldest Newest Most Perfect
Year-Round Resort in
America. Atlantic City,
N.J.
Oldest Port in the West Gulf.
Galveston, Tex.
Oldest Settlement in Minnesota.
Grand Portage, Minn.
Oldest Sport Fishing Center in
Virginia. Wachapreague, Va.
Oldest Summer Resort in
America. Wolfeboro, N.H.
Oldest Town in Nevada. Genoa,
Nev.
Oldest Town in West Virginia.
Shepherdstown, W. Va.
Oldest White Settlement in
the State. Salina, Okla.
Oleander City. Galveston, Tex.

Oleander City by the Sea.
Galveston, Tex.
Oleman House.   Port Madison,
Wash.
Olympic Village.   Lake Placid,
N.Y.
Once Confederate Capital of
America.   Cassville, Mo.
One Hundred Square Miles of
Picturesque Pleasure.
Martha's Vineyard, Mass.
One Hundred Suburbs in Search
of a City.   Los Angeles,
Calif.
One of America's Best Planned
Cities.   Richardson, Tex.
One of America's Fastest
Growing Cities.   Las Vegas,
Nev.
One of America's Fastest
Growing Cities.   Twin Falls,
Idaho
One of America's Fifty Best
Vacation Spots.   Bemidji,
Minn.
One of America's Foremost
All-Year Resorts.   Asbury
Park, N.J.
One of America's Four Unique
Cities.   San Antonio, Tex.
One of America's Great Cities.
Toledo, Ohio
One of America's Greatest
Playgrounds.   St. Peters-
burg, Fla.
One of America's Most Im-
portant Inland Port Centers.
Buffalo, N.Y.
One of America's Most
Interesting Cities.   Chat-
tanooga, Tenn.
One of America's Most Inter-
esting Cities.   Montgomery,
Ala.
One of America's Most Unique
Cities.   Butte, Mont.
One of America's Oldest Play-
grounds.   Lake Placid,
N.Y.
One of America's Outstanding
Cities.   Newark, N.J.
One of America's Top Twenty
Tourist Attractions.   Lan-
caster, Pa.

One of California's Choicest
Communities.   Burlingame,
Calif.
One of California's Historic
Communities.   Lodi, Calif.
One of Florida's Finest Smaller
Communities.   Lake Alfred,
Fla.
One of Georgia's Golden Isles.
Jekyll Island, Ga.
One of Illinois' Top Industrial
Cities.   Joliet, Ill.
One of Mississippi's Fastest
Growing Cities.   Greenville,
Miss.
One of New England's Most
Famous Coast Resorts.
Wells, Me.
One of Pennsylvania's Fastest
Growing Communities.
Ambler, Pa.
One of the Banner Agricultural
Counties in the South.   Pop-
larville, Miss.
One of the Busiest Freshwater
Ports in the World.   Toledo,
Ohio
One of the Country's Leading
Burley Markets.   Green-
ville, Tenn.
One of the Fastest Developing
Areas in the Nation.   Clarks-
ville, Tenn.
One of the Fastest Growing Areas
in the Nation.   Lorain, Ohio
One of the Fastest Growing
Cities in the Nation.   Jack-
son, Miss.
One of the Fastest Growing
Cities in the South.   Mur-
freesboro, Tenn.
One of the Fastest Growing
Communities in the West.
Sparks, Nev.
One of the Fastest Growing
Resort Centers.   Naples,
Fla.
One of the First American
Cities of the Industrial Age.
New Haven, Conn.
One of the Great Natural
Wonders of the World.
Silver Springs, Fla.

One of the Great Scenic
Wonders of the United
States. Ausable Chasm,
N.Y.

One of the Last Pieces of
Gold on the Gold Coast.
Coral Springs, Fla.

One of the Leading Health
and Tourist Resorts of the
East. Asheville, N.C.

One of the Leading Tobacco
Markets for Bright Leaf
Tobacco. Henderson, N.C.

One of the Most Accessible
Cities in the Eastern
States. Springfield, Mass.

One of the Most Accessible
Cities on Earth. Atlanta,
Ga.

One of the Most Attractive
Communities in Southern
California. Fontana, Calif.

One of the Most Beautiful
and Popular Vermont Towns.
Woodstock, Vt.

One of the Most Beautiful
Cities in the Nation.
Pittsburgh, Pa.

One of the Most Colorful
Cities in America. Butte,
Mont.

One of the Most Fashionable
Winter Resorts of the
South. Aiken, S.C.

One of the Most Favorable
Winter Resorts of the
South. Aiken, S.C.

One of the Most Rapidly Developing Industrial Cities.
Vicksburg, Miss.

One of the Nation's Best
Locations. Houlton, Me.

One of the Nation's Largest
Spring Lamb Producing
Centers. Lexington, Ky.

One of the Oldest Cities in
Washington. Couper-
ville, Wash.

One of the South's Fastest
Growing Cities. Jack-
son, Miss.

One of the South's Foremost
Educational Centers.
Lexington, Ky.

One of the Ten Fastest Growing
Communities. Orlando, Fla.

One of the World's Great Airplane Manufacturing Centers.
Wichita, Kan.

One of the World's Greatest
Industrial Research Centers.
Pittsburgh, Pa.

One of the World's Greatest
Resort Cities. Hot Springs,
Ark.

One of the World's Largest
Long-Staple Cotton Markets.
Greenwood, Miss.

One of the World's Largest
Manufacturers of Cigarettes.
Richmond, Va.

One of the World's Largest
Markets for Dark Fired
Tobacco. Clarksville, Tenn.

One of the World's Largest
Rose Growing Centers.
Pana, Ill.

One of the World's Leading
Convention Centers. Albu-
querque, N.M.

One of Wisconsin's Fastest
Growing Cities. Beloit,
Wis.

Onion City. Naugatuck, Conn.

Only Cedartown in the U.S.A.
Cedartown, Ga.

Only Electric-Lighted Cemetery in the United States.
Butte, Mont.

Only Grand Forks in the Nation.
Grand Forks, N.D.

Only Henniker on Earth. Henniker, N.H.

Only International Streetcar
Line City. Alamogordo,
N.M.

Only Town in the United States
with an Apostrophe in Its
Name. Coeur d'Alene, Idaho

Only Twin Cities in South Carolina. Batesburg, S.C.

Only Twin Cities in South Carolina. Leesville, S.C.

Opal of America. Ouray,
Colo.

Opportunity City. Indianapolis,
Ind.

Opportunity for History.
Gonzalez, Tex.
Optimist City. Sheridan, Wyo.
Orange Capital of the World.
Eustis, Fla.
Orchard City. Burlington,
Iowa
Orchid Capital of Hawaii.
Hilo, Hawaii
Ore and Grain Port. Duluth,
Minn.
Oregon's Beautiful Capital
City. Salem, Ore.
Oregon's Own Homebase for
Fun, Culture and Scenic
Splendor. Forest Grove,
Ore.
Oregon's Second Market.
Eugene, Ore.
Organ Town. Brattleboro, Vt.
Original Site of Californication.
Los Angeles, Calif.
Original Winter Resort of the
South. Thomasville, Ga.
Other Place to Go in Florida.
Fort Lauderdale, Fla.
Our Lady of the Angels. Port
Angeles, Wash.
Outdoor Recreation City.
Spokane, Wash.
Outdoorman's Paradise.
Bristol, Tenn.
Outstanding American City.
Cambridge, Mass.
Outstanding City. Palo Alto,
Calif.
Outstanding Fast-Growing City.
Bethlehem, Pa.
Outstanding Seaside Resort of
the Pacific Coast. Cata-
lina Island, Calif.
Over a Mile High, a Mile
Long, a Mile Wide and a
Mile Deep. Lead, S. D.
Overgrown Country Town.
Cleveland, Ohio
Overgrown Cow Town. Kansas
City, Mo.
Overgrown Small Town.
Detroit, Mich.
Overgrown Village. Buffalo, N.Y.
Overlooked City. Pittsburgh,
Pa.

Oyster Capital of Florida. Apa-
lachicola, Fla.
Oyster Center of the State.
Houma, La.
Ozark Wonderland. Harrison,
Ark.
Ozark's Western Gateway.
Vinita, Okla.

Pacemaker of the Piedmont.
Gastonia, N. C.
Pacesetter of Progress. Phila-
delphia, Pa.
Pacific Northwest's Most Pro-
gressive Community. Boise,
Idaho
Packers' Town. Green Bay,
Wis.
Paddlefish Capital of the World.
Fort Thompson, S. D.
Paincourt. St. Louis, Mo.
Painters' Paradise. Copper-
hill, Tenn.
Palace of King Cotton. Waco,
Tex.
Palm City. Phoenix, Ariz.
Palmetto City. Charleston,
S. C.
Panama Port. Pensacola, Fla.
Pancake Capital of the World.
Villa Grove, Ill.
Pancake Center. Liberal, Kan.
Pancake Center of the World.
Liberal, Kan.
Panhandler's Heaven. Boston,
Mass.
Panther City. Fort Worth,
Tex.
Paper City. Holyoke, Mass.
Paper City. Johnsonburg, Pa.
Paper City. Neenah, Wis.
Paper City of the World.
Holyoke, Mass.
Paper City of the World.
Neenah, Wis.
Paper Manufacturing City.
Fitchburg, Mass.
Paradise for the Sportsman and
the Family. Walker, Minn.
Paradise in a Nut Shell. Wal-
nut Creek, Calif.

Paradise in the Pines. Crockett, Tex.

Paradise of Fishing, Hunting and Swimming. Blountstown, Fla.

Paradise of New England. Salem, Mass.

Paradise of Outdoor Recreation. Lander, Wyo.

Paradise of the South. Miami, Fla.

Paradise Sullied. Los Angeles, Calif.

Parent of the West. St. Louis, Mo.

Paris of America. Cincinnati, Ohio

Paris of America. New Orleans, La.

Paris of America. San Francisco, Calif.

Paris of the Ozarks. Springfield, Mo.

Paris of the Pacific. Sitka, Alaska

Paris of the West. San Francisco, Calif.

Parish of Unity. South Berwick, Me.

Park City. Bridgeport, Conn.

Park City. New Rochelle, N.Y.

Park Place. Monroe, Wash.

Parking Lot City. St. Louis, Mo.

Parlor City. Binghamton, N.Y.

Parlor City. Cedar Rapids, Iowa

Parrot's Paradise. Ormond Beach, Fla.

Parsippany Means Business. Parsippany, N.J.

Partially Restored Pioneer Mining Village. Winthrop, Wash.

Pathway to Progress. Buffalo, N.Y.

Paul Bunyan's Capital. Brainerd, Minn.

Paul Bunyan's Playground. Bemidji, Minn.

Payroll Town. Moss Point, Miss.

Peaceful Friendly Town. Blue Rapids, Kan.

Peaceful Valley in the Heart of the Green Mountains. Waitsfield, Vt.

Peach Bowl of the United States. Marysville, Calif.

Peach Bowl of the United States. Yuba City, Calif.

Peach Capital of Arkansas. Nashville, Ark.

Peach Capital of Texas. Stonewall, Tex.

Peach Capital of the World. Modesto, Calif.

Peach Center. Fort Valley, Ga.

Peach Center of Texas. Johnson City, Tex.

Peach City. Hughes Springs, Tex.

Peanut Capital of the World. Blakely, Ga.

Peanut Capital of the World. Enterprise, Ala.

Peanut City. Suffolk, Va.

Peanut City, U.S.A. Plains, Ga.

Pear City. Medford, Ore.

Pearl City. Muscatine, Iowa

Pearl of the Florida Panhandle. Panama City, Fla.

Pearl of the Pee Dee. Darlington, S.C.

Pearl of the South. Anniston, Ala.

Pecan Capital of the World. Chandler, Okla.

Pecan Capital of the World. San Saba, Tex.

Peerless Princess of the Plains. Wichita, Kan.

Peerless Summer, Winter and Health Resort of America. Saratoga Springs, N.Y.

Penn State City. State College, Pa.

Penn's Town. Reading, Pa.

Pennsylvania Athens. Wellsboro, Pa.

Pennsylvania's Above-Average Market of Industry and Agriculture. Lancaster, Pa.

Pennsylvania's Capital City.
Harrisburg, Pa.
Pennsylvania's Economic
Bright Spot. Lancaster,
Pa.
Pennsylvania's Highest City.
Hazleton, Pa.
Pennsylvania's New Vacation-
land. Huntingdon, Pa.
Peony Capital of the World.
Sarcoxie, Mo.
Peony Center of the Mid-
west. Rosendale, Wis.
Peony Center of the World.
Faribault, Minn.
Peony City of America.
Van Wert, Ohio
People Prefer Mesquite.
Mesquite, Tex.
Peoples' City. Demopolis,
Ala.
Pepper Sauce Capital of the
World. New Iberia, La.
Perchville, U.S.A. Tawas
City, Mich.
Perfect Central Florida Lo-
cation. Plant City, Fla.
Perfect Family Vacation
Spot. Wildwood Crest,
N.J.
Perfect Place for Growing
Up. Brookhaven, Miss.
Perfect Place to Live.
Plant City, Fla.
Perfect Playground for the
Young in Heart. Pompano
Beach, Fla.
Perfect Spot to Work, to
Play, to Enjoy Life.
Dothan, Ala.
Perfect Vacation Spot.
Rockaway Beach, Mo.
Perfect Year-Round Wonder-
land. Ocean Gate, N.J.
Permanent Home of the Pine.
Cass Lake, Minn.
Perry Davis' Pain Killer
City. Providence, R.I.
Petroleum Capital of Kansas.
Wichita, Kan.
Petroleum World Center.
Houston, Tex.
Petunia Capital. New Hampton,
Iowa

Petunia Capital of the World.
Dixon, Ill.
Petunia Capital of the World.
Webster, S.D.
Pheasant Capital of Kansas.
Norton, Kan.
Pheasant Capital of the World.
Huron, S.D.
Pheasant Capital of the World.
Sioux Falls, S.D.
Pheasant City, U.S.A. Sioux
Falls, S.D.
Pheasant Country. Denver,
Iowa
Pheasant Paradise of America.
Howard, S.D.
Phenomenal Example of Ameri-
can Growth. Aliquippa, Pa.
Philadelphia of the West.
Jefferson, Ohio
Philly. Philadelphia, Pa.
Phoenix City. Chicago, Ill.
Phoenix of the Pacific. San
Francisco, Calif.
Phone Capital of the World.
Washington, D.C.
Photo Capital of the World.
Rochester, N.Y.
Photogenic Sun Capital of the
East. Miami Beach, Fla.
Photographer's Paradise.
Valdez, Alaska
Photographic and Optical Cen-
ter of the World. Rochester,
N.Y.
Photography Capital. Rochester,
N.Y.
Piano Center of America.
Steger, Ill.
Picnic City. Mobile, Ala.
Picture Postcard Bay. Santa
Monica, Calif.
Picturesque Heart of Central
Florida. Haines City, Fla.
Picturesque Old World Village.
St. Donatus, Iowa
Picturesque, Progressive and
Prosperous. Cedar Rapids,
Iowa
Picturesque Village South of
Mount Monadnock. Fitz-
william, N.H.
Pigopolis. Chicago, Ill.

Pigopolis. Cincinnati, Ohio
Pig's Eye. St. Paul, Minn.
Pilgrim Land. Plymouth,
Mass.
Pimiento Center of the World.
Griffin, Ga.
Pine Tree Capital. Perry,
Fla.
Pine Tree Country. Swainsboro,
Ga.
Pinhook. Independence, Va.
Pioneer Log Cabin Village.
Boise, Idaho
Pioneer Mormon City. Provo,
Utah
Pioneer Resort Town.
Winslow, Ark.
Pioneering Center of Aviation.
Dayton, Ohio
Pipeline Capital of the World.
Drumright, Okla.
Pipeline Capital of America.
Shreveport, La.
Pipeline Center of the Nation.
Lima, Ohio
Pittsburgh of New Jersey.
Dover, N.J.
Pittsburgh of the Big West.
Terre Haute, Ind.
Pittsburgh of the South.
Birmingham, Ala.
Pittsburgh of the West.
Joliet, Ill.
Pivot City of the Central South.
Shreveport, La.
Pivot City of the Great Lakes.
Toledo, Ohio
Pivot City of the South.
Shreveport, La.
Pivot of the Piedmont.
Greensboro, N.C.
Place by the Winding River.
Haverhill, Mass.
Place Convenient to the Lakes
and Mountains. Center
Sandwich, N.H.
Place for All Seasons. Bolton
Landing, N.Y.
Place for Excellent Surf
Bathing. Weekapaug,
R.I.
Place for Home, Industry,
Recreation. Barton, Vt.

Place for Sun, Fun and Friend-
ship. Lehigh Acres, Fla.
Place for Those Who Want to
Get Away From It All--But
Not Too Far. Montauk, N.Y.
Place for Vacations Year 'Round
and for Year 'Round Living.
Fryeburg, Me.
Place in the Sun to Visit, to
Play, to Work, to Live.
Edgewater, Fla.
Place of Good Abode. Memphis,
Tenn.
Place of Many Waters. Walla
Walla, Wash.
Place of Personal Prestige and
Practical Advantages. Cherry
Hill, N.J.
Place that Has Everything.
Islamorada, Fla.
Place to Enjoy Yourself. Mis-
soula, Mont.
Place to Go in Florida. Fort
Lauderdale, Fla.
Place to Let Yourself Go in
Florida. Fort Lauderdale,
Fla.
Place to Live. Norwalk, Conn.
Place to Live. Washington, Mo.
Place to Live, a Place to Work.
Anderson, S.C.
Place to Live, Play and Work.
Skowhegan, Me.
Place to Live, Relax and
Play--Night and Day. Ware-
ham, Mass.
Place to Live, Relax and Play
... On Miles of Water.
Ruskin, Fla.
Place to Live, Work and Play.
Gilford, N.H.
Place to Live, Work and Play.
Mineral Wells, Tex.
Place to Live, Work or Play.
Denmark, Me.
Place to Play by Night and Day.
Seaside Heights, N.J.
Place to Watch. Skowhegan,
Me.
Place where California Began.
San Diego, Calif.
Place where Every Day's a
Holiday. Las Vegas, Nev.

Place where Friendly People
Come to Stay. Belton,
S. C.
Place where Fun Never Stops.
Los Angeles, Calif.
Place where Lake Meets
Forest. Grand Marais,
Minn.
Place where Lakes Meet
Mountains. Tamworth,
N. H.
Place where Life Is Real
Throughout the Year.
Vineyard Haven, Mass.
Place where the End Is Just
the Beginning. Montauk,
N. Y.
Place where the Sunshine
and Sea Meet. Blue Lake,
Calif.
Place where the Waters Meet.
Oconomowoc, Wisc.
Place with Excellent Hunting
in Season. Blytheville,
Ark.
Plains Empire City. Amarillo,
Tex.
Plank Island. Aberdeen, Wash.
Planned Adult Community.
Zellwood, Fla.
Planned Growing City. Garden
Grove, Calif.
Plant Capital of Central
Florida. Apopka, Fla.
Play Around the Clock Time.
Las Vegas, Nev.
Playground for Vacationers.
Gonzalez, Tex.
Playground of High Society.
Saratoga Springs, N. Y.
Playground of New Orlean's
People. Grand Isle, La.
Playground of Paul Bunyon.
Blaney Park, Mich.
Playground of Presidents.
Superior, Wis.
Playground of Southern Cali-
fornia. San Bernardino,
Calif.
Playground of the Adirondacks.
Schroon Lake, N. Y.
Playground of the Americas.
Miami, Fla.

Playground of the Americas.
Miami Beach, Fla.
Playground of the Desert. Las
Vegas, Nev.
Playground of the Dunes. Gary,
Ind.
Playground of the Northwest.
Seaside, Ore.
Playground of the "Now" Set.
Las Vegas, Nev.
Playground of the World. At-
lantic City, N. J.
Playground of the World. Las
Vegas, Nev.
Playground of Vacationland.
Old Orchard Beach, Me.
Playtown, U. S. A. Decatur, Ill.
Playtown, U. S. A. Las Vegas,
Nev.
Pleasant All Year Vacation
Center. Pensacola, Fla.
Pleasant New England Town.
Berlin, Conn.
Pleasant Place. Beaufort, S. C.
Pleasant Place to Live and
Work. Altoona, Pa.
Pleasant Place to Visit.
Mitchell, S. D.
Plough-Share City. York, Pa.
Plow City. Moline, Ill.
Plumb Line Port to Panama.
Charlestown, S. C.
Plymouth of the Pacific Coast.
San Diego, Calif.
Plymouth of the West. San
Diego, Calif.
Plymouth of the Western Re-
serve. Conneaut, Ohio
Plymouth Offers Progress.
Plymouth, Mass.
Plywood Capital of the World.
New Albany, Ind.
Plywood Center. New Albany,
Ind.
Poinsettia City. Ventura, Calif.
Point of Opportunity. West
Point, Miss.
Poker City. Gardena, Calif.
Poker-Playing Capital of the
West. Gardena, Calif.
Polish City. Hamtramck, Mich.
Polish City in Texas. Panna
Maria, Tex.

Political Front. Washington, D.C.

Polk County's Largest City. Lakeland, Fla.

Polo Capital of the Nation. Aiken, S.C.

Polo Capital of the South. Aiken, S.C.

Pony Express City. Gothenburg, Neb.

Poor Man's Paradise. San Francisco, Calif.

Popular Convention City. Asheville, N.C.

Popular Convention City. Duluth, Minn.

Popular Summer Resort. Brevard, N.C.

Popular Summer Resort on Lake Champlain. Basin Harbor, Vt.

Popular Tourist Center. Port Angeles, Wash.

Popular Vacation and Convention Spot. Coronado, Calif.

Popular Vacation Land. Jacksonville, Fla.

Population Center. Worcester, Mass.

Population Center of Texas. Temple, Tex.

Population Center, the Highway Center and the Rail Center of New England. Worcester, Mass.

Population Center, U.S.A. Centralia, Ill.

Pork City. Chicago, Ill.

Porkopolis. Chicago, Ill.

Porkopolis. Cincinnati, Ohio

Porkopolis of Iowa. Burlington, Iowa

Port and Playground of the Southwest. Galveston, Tex.

Port City. Beaumont, Tex.

Port City. Mobile, Ala.

Port City. Portsmouth, N.H.

Port City Mid-America. Muskogee, Okla.

Port City of the Corn Belt. Muscatine, Iowa

Port City of the Delta. Greenville, Miss.

Port O' Missing Men. San Francisco, Calif.

Port of Distinction. Green Bay, Wis.

Port of Entry. Port Townsend, Wash.

Port of Entry and Business Center. Vineyard Haven, Mass.

Port of Entry to the Missouri Great Lakes. Yankton, S.D.

Port of Friendliness. Avalon, Calif.

Port of Gold. San Francisco, Calif.

Port of Hospitality on the Great Father of Waters. Davenport, Iowa

Port of Last Call. Mystic, Conn.

Port of Many Ports. New York, N.Y.

Port of Opportunity. Texas City, Tex.

Port of Personal Service. Wilmington, Del.

Port of Sea Captains. Coupeville, Wash.

Port of the Pilgrims. Provincetown, Mass.

Port of the Southwest. Galveston, Tex.

Portage. Granite Falls, Wash.

Portage City. Hollidaysburg, Pa.

Portal to Palomar. Escondido, Calif.

Portal to Romance. Sitka, Alaska

Portal to the Quint States. Salida, Colo.

Postmark of Distinctive Trademarks. Hamilton, Ohio

Post City. Lawton, Okla.

Potato Capital of the West. Monte Vista, Colo.

Potato Capital of the World. East Grand Forks, Minn.

Potato Capitol. Shafter, Calif.

Pottery Center. East Liverpool, Ohio

Pottery City. Zanesville, Ohio

Poultry Capital of the World.
Gainesville, Ga.
Poultry Center. Vineland,
N. J.
Powder Snow Capital of
Colorado. Winter Park,
Colo.
Power City. American Falls,
Idaho
Power City. Fulton, N. Y.
Power City. Keokuk, Iowa
Power City. Niagara Falls,
N. Y.
Power City. Rochester,
N. Y.
Power City. Stanton, N. D.
Power City of Scenic Wonders.
Niagara Falls, N. Y.
Powerhouse of the Niagara
Frontier. Niagara Falls,
N. Y.
Prairie. Chicago, Ill.
Prairie City. Bloomington,
Ill.
Praline Capital of the World.
Bay St. Louis, Miss.
Precision City. Waltham,
Mass.
Precision Valley. Springfield,
Vt.
Preeminent Vacation Center.
Asheville, N. C.
Preferred City on the Penin-
sula. Redwood City,
Calif.
Premium Wine Capital of the
United States. St. Helena,
Calif.
Prettiest Little Town this
Side of Heaven. Winter
Haven, Fla.
Prettiest Resort in the World.
Daytona Beach, Fla.
Prettiest Small Town Between
New York and Miami.
Manning, S. C.
Prettiest Spot in Maine.
Camden, Me.
Prettiest Town in Dixie.
Cheraw, S. C.
Pretzel City. Lancaster,
Pa.
Pretzel City. Reading, Pa.

Pride of Magic Long Beach
Island. Long Beach Town-
ship, N. J.
Pride of the Mississippi Valley.
St. Louis, Mo.
Pride of the Pacific. Long
Beach, Calif.
Prime Beef Capital. Monmouth,
Ill.
Prime Beef Center of the
World. De Witt, Iowa
Prime Beef Center of the
World. Monmouth, Ill.
Prime Residential Community
in the Bay Area. El Cerrito,
Calif.
Princess City of Puget Sound.
Edmonds, Wash.
Principal Shopping Center.
Anacortes, Wash.
Printing Capital of the World.
New York, N. Y.
Prison City. Jackson, Mich.
Private Flying Capital of the
World. Lock Haven, Pa.
Problem Capitol of the World.
Washington, D. C.
Productive Agricultural Com-
munity. Weatherford, Okla.
Profit Center of the Southwest.
Phoenix, Ariz.
Progress City of the Rockies.
Casper, Wyo.
Progress Through Precision.
Springfield, Vt.
Progress Through Vision.
Hershey, Pa.
Progressive Agricultural Re-
gion. Redwood Falls, Minn.
Progressive American City.
Springfield, Ill.
Progressive Business Community.
Morris, Minn.
Progressive City. Athens, Tenn.
Progressive City. Augusta, Ga.
Progressive City. Brunswick,
Ga.
Progressive City. Eau Gallie,
Fla.
Progressive City. Grand Isle,
Neb.
Progressive City. Keokuk,
Iowa

Progressive City. Memphis, Tenn.

Progressive City. Osawatomie, Kans.

Progressive City. Peoria, Ill.

Progressive City. Plant City, Fla.

Progressive City. Sioux Falls, S. D.

Progressive City Planning Today for the Events of Tomorrow. Brunswick, Ga.

Progressive City with a Bright Future. Norwalk, Conn.

Progressive City with the Rich Heritage and Charm of the Old River Days. Davenport, Iowa

Progressive Community. Belleview, Fla.

Progressive Community. Clewiston, Fla.

Progressive Community. Hendersonville, Tenn.

Progressive Community. Milan, Tenn.

Progressive Community. Moultrie, Ga.

Progressive Community. Starke, Fla.

Progressive Community Hewn from a Wilderness. Maumee, Ohio

Progressive Community Hewn from a Wilderness. Perrysburg, Ohio

Progressive Community with a Bright Future. Belleview, Fla.

Progressive Gateway City to the Dakotas. Sioux Falls, S. D.

Progressive Metropolis. Lynchburg, Va.

Progressive, Prosperous and Peaceful Community. Lewiston, Me.

Progressively Growing Well-Seasoned City. Springfield, Ohio

Prosperous Agricultural Area. Moberly, Mo.

Prosperous Center of a Rich

Farming District. Charlotte, Tex.

Prosperous City of Beauty and Good Living. Beatrice, Neb.

Proud City. Bridgeport, Conn.

Proud City. Hutchinson, Kans.

Proud City with a Bright Future. Maiden, Mass.

Proud Port of the Pacific. Long Beach, Calif.

Proudest Small Town in America. Cadiz, Ohio

Proven Progressive City. Salina, Kan.

Pumpkin Capital of the World. Eureka, Ill.

Puritan Village. Sudbury, Mass.

Purple Martin Capital of the World. Griggsville, Ill.

Pure Bred Jersey Capital of America. Carthage, Mo.

Puritan City. Boston, Mass.

Puritan Zion. Boston, Mass.

Push Root. Lander, Wyo.

Quad Cities. East Moline, Moline, Rock Island, Ill., and Davenport, Iowa

Quail Capital of Nebraska. Auburn, Neb.

Quail Haven. Cedar Vale, Kan.

Quaint Seacoast Town at the Tip of Cape Ann. Rockport, Mass.

Quaker City. Newberg, Ore.

Quaker City. Philadelphia, Pa.

Quaker City. Salem, Ohio

Quaker City. Whittier, Calif.

Quaker City of the West. Richmond, Ind.

Quaker Town. Wilmington, Del.

Quakertown. Philadelphia, Pa.

Quality City. Fitchburg, Mass.

Quality City. Niagara Falls, N. Y.

Quality City. Rochester, N. Y.

Queen City. Allentown, Pa.

Queen City. Alma, Ga.

Queen City. Bangor, Me.

Queen City. Burlington, Vt.

Queen City. Charlotte, N. C.
Queen City. Cincinnati, Ohio
Queen City. Cumberland, Md.
Queen City. Davenport, Iowa
Queen City. Dickinson, N. D.
Queen City. Galveston, Tex.
Queen City. Hastings, Neb.
Queen City. Manchester, N. H.
Queen City. Marinette, Wis.
Queen City. San Francisco, Calif.
Queen City. Seattle, Wash.
Queen City. Sioux Falls, S. D.
Queen City. Spearfish, S. D.
Queen City. Williamsport, Pa.
Queen City in the Garden State. Plainfield, N. J.
Queen City of Alabama. Gadsden, Ala.
Queen City of Florida's Sugar Bowl. Clewiston, Fla.
Queen City of Lake Superior. Marquette, Mich.
Queen City of Maine. Manchester, Me.
Queen City of New Hampshire. Manchester, N. H.
Queen City of New Jersey. Plainfield, N. J.
Queen City of Southeast Kansas. Independence, Kan.
Queen City of the Ark-La-Tex Area. Shreveport, La.
Queen City of the Black Belt. Selma, Ala.
Queen City of the Border. Caldwell, Kan.
Queen City of the Cherokee Strip. Enid, Okla.
Queen City of the Colorado. Yuma, Ariz.
Queen City of the Coosa. Gadsden, Ala.
Queen City of the Cow Towns. Dodge City, Kan.
Queen City of the Cumberland. Clarksville, Tenn.
Queen City of the East. Bangor, Me.
Queen City of the Gas Belt. Marion, Ind.
Queen City of the Golden Valley. Clinton, Mo.

Queen City of the Great Lakes. Buffalo, N. Y.
Queen City of the Gulf. Mobile, Ala.
Queen City of the Highland Rim. Tullahoma, Tenn.
Queen City of the Hills. Spearfish, S. D.
Queen City of the Hudson. Poughkeepsie, N. Y.
Queen City of the Hudson. Yonkers, N. Y.
Queen City of the Iron Range. Virginia, Minn.
Queen City of the Lakes. Buffalo, N. Y.
Queen City of the Lehigh Valley. Allentown, Pa.
Queen City of the Merrimac Valley. Manchester, N. H.
Queen City of the Midland Empire. Billings, Mont.
Queen City of the Mississippi. St. Louis, Mo.
Queen City of the Mountains. Knoxville, Tenn.
Queen City of the Northland. Marquette, Mich.
Queen City of the Northwest. Dubuque, Iowa
Queen City of the Northwest. Seattle, Wash.
Queen City of the Ohio. Cincinnati, Ohio
Queen City of the Ohio River. Cincinnati, Ohio
Queen City of the Otter Tail Empire. Fergus Falls, Minn.
Queen City of the Ouachita. Camden, Ark.
Queen City of the Ozarks. Springfield, Mo.
Queen City of the Pacific. San Francisco, Calif.
Queen City of the Pacific. Seattle, Wash.
Queen City of the Pacific Coast. San Francisco, Calif.
Queen City of the Panhandle. Amarillo, Tex.
Queen City of the Plains. Amarillo, Tex.

Queen City of the Plains.
Denver, Colo.
Queen City of the Plains.
Fort Worth, Tex.
Queen City of the Prairies.
Dickinson, N. D.
Queen City of the Prairies.
Fort Worth, Tex.
Queen City of the Prairies.
Sedalia, Mo.
Queen City of the Range.
Virginia, Minn.
Queen City of the Rio Grande.
Del Rio, Tex.
Queen City of the Sea.
Charleston, S. C.
Queen City of the Shenandoah
Valley. Staunton, Va.
Queen City of the Sound.
New Rochelle, N. Y.
Queen City of the Sound.
Seattle, Wash.
Queen City of the South. At-
lanta, Ga.
Queen City of the South.
Brownfield, Tex.
Queen City of the South.
Charleston, S. C.
Queen City of the South.
Richmond, Va.
Queen City of the State with
All Modern Facilities.
Manchester, N. H.
Queen City of the Teche.
New Iberia, La.
Queen City of the Trails.
Independence, Mo.
Queen City of the West. Cin-
cinnati, Ohio
Queen City of the West.
Denver, Colo.
Queen City of the West. San
Francisco, Calif.
Queen City of Vermont.
Burlington, Vt.
Queen of America's Lakes.
Lake George, N. Y.
Queen of American Lakes.
Lake George, N. Y.
Queen of Beauty. Niagara
Falls, N. Y.
Queen of Cow Towns. Dodge
City, Kan.

Queen of Lake Erie. Cleveland,
Ohio
Queen of Ocean Resorts. As-
bury Park, N. J.
Queen of Resorts. Atlantic City,
N. J.
Queen of Summer Resorts. New-
port, R. I.
Queen of the American Lakes.
Lake George, N. Y.
Queen of the American Nile.
Memphis, Tenn.
Queen of the Beaches. Long
Beach, Calif.
Queen of the Brazos. Waco,
Tex.
Queen of the Comstock Lode.
Virginia City, Nev.
Queen of the Cow Countries.
Los Angeles, Calif.
Queen of the Cow Towns.
Dodge City, Kan.
Queen of the Golden Empire.
Sacramento, Calif.
Queen of the Hills. Piedmont,
Calif.
Queen of the Lakes. Buffalo,
N. Y.
Queen of the Lakes. Chicago,
Ill.
Queen of the Missions. Santa
Barbara, Calif.
Queen of the Mountains. Helena,
Mont.
Queen of the Neches. Beau-
mont, Tex.
Queen of the Ohio. Cincinnati,
Ohio
Queen of the Pacific. San
Francisco, Calif.
Queen of the Prairie. Omaha,
Neb.
Queen of the Prairies. Wagoner,
Okla.
Queen of the Resorts. Newport,
R. I.
Queen of the Rockies. Denver,
Colo.
Queen of the Silver Camps.
Tonopah, Nev.
Queen of the South. New Or-
leans, La.
Queen of the Spas. Saratoga
Springs, N. Y.

Queen of the Three Valleys.
Durant, Okla.
Queen of the Valley.   Glendale, Calif.
Queen of the West.   Cincinnati, Ohio
Queen of World Resorts.   Newport, R.I.
Queen on the James.   Richmond, Va.
Queen Shoe City of the World.
Haverhill, Mass.
Queen Village of the Adirondacks.   Warrensburg, N.Y.
Quiet Historical New England
Village.   Brandon, Vt.
Quiet New England Village.
Bethel, Me.
Quiet, Restful, Relaxing Smog-Free Community.   Denair, Calif.
Quiet Rural Town.   Glendora, Calif.
Quint City.   Aberdeen, S.D.
Quintessenial Stronghold of
the American Blueblood.
Charleston, S.C

Radiant Garden Spot of California.   Redlands, Calif.
Ragtown.   Altoona, Ga.
Rail and Harbor City.   Elizabeth, N.J.
Rail Center.   Buffalo, N.Y.
Rail Center of New England.
Worcester, Mass.
Rail Center of the Northwest.
Pierre, S.D.
Rail City.   Sparks, Nev.
Railroad Center.   Pierre, S.D.
Railroad Center Since 1850.
Crestline, Ohio
Railroad City.   Altoona, Pa.
Railroad City.   Atlanta, Ga.
Railroad City.   Indianapolis, Ind.
Railroad City.   St. Albans, Vt.
Railroad Hub of the Dakotas.
Aberdeen, S.D.
Railroad Metropolis of the

West.   Milwaukee, Wis.
Railroad Town.   Carlin, Nev.
Railroad Town.   Pierre, S.D.
Rain City.   Ketchikan, Alaska
Raisin Capital of the World.
Selma, Calif.
Raisin Center of the World.
Fresno, Calif.
Raisinland, U.S.A.   Dinuba, Calif.
Ranching Center.   Elko, Nev.
Rapid City.   Cedar Rapids, Iowa.
Razor Clam Capital of the
World.   Cordova, Alaska
Real Garden Spot.   Boca Raton, Fla.
Real Hoosier City.   New Albany, Ind.
Real Paradise for Family
Living.   Crestview, Fla.
Real Western City.   Pierre, S.D.
Rebel Capital.   Philadelphia, Pa.
Recreation and Industrial Center
of East Texas.   Marshall, Tex.
Recreation Capital of the World.
Oxford, Miss.
Recreation Center.   Anaheim, Calif.
Recreation Center.   Midland, Tex.
Recreation Center of New Hampshire.   Waterville Valley, N.H.
Recreation Center of the West.
Thermopolis, Wyo.
Recreation Convention Center
of New Hampshire.   Waterville Valley, N.H.
Recreation Crossroads of Vermont.   Waterbury, Vt.
Recreation Hub of the Historical Colorful West.   Sidney, Neb.
Recreation Paradise on Beautiful Lewis and Clark Lake.
Yankton, S.D.
Recreational Center.   Madison, Wis.
Recreational Center.   Mitchell, S.D.

Recreational Center for
Generations. Bridgeport,
Conn.
Recreational Center of Central
Maine. Belgrade, Me.
Recreational, Educational and
Cultural Center of North-
eastern Ohio. Youngstown,
Ohio
Recreational Industrial City.
Duluth, Minn.
Recreational Mecca of the
Fabulous Southeastern Coast
of Florida. Lake Worth,
Fla.
Recreational Slum. Lake
Tahoe, Calif.
Recreational Sportland of
Minnesota. Blackduck,
Minn.
Red Bud City of Oklahoma.
Shawnee, Okla.
Red Light Queen. Muskegon,
Mich.
Red Rose City. Lancaster,
Pa.
Redwood City of Illinois.
Auburn, Ill.
Refrigeration Capital of the
World. Evansville, Ind.
Refuge from Resorts. Naples,
Fla.
Region of Great Natural Won-
ders. Belleview, Fla.
Relaxing Playspot on Florida's
Semi-Tropical West Coast.
Sarasota, Fla.
Renaissance by the River.
Detroit, Mich.
Renaissance City. Detroit,
Mich.
Renaissance City of America.
Pittsburgh, Pa.
Republican Party City.
Ripon, Wis.
Resaca City. San Benito, Tex.
Research Capital of the Mid-
west. Ann Arbor, Mich.
Research Center. Pittsburgh,
Pa.
Research Center of the
Midwest. Ann Arbor,
Mich.

Research City. Stamford, Conn.
Residential Community. Bolton,
Mass.
Residential Haven. Islip, N.Y.
Residential Research Center of
the Nation. Monroeville,
Pa.
Residential Town on Long Island
Sound. Darien, Conn.
Resort and Artist's Colony.
Boothbay, Me.
Resort and Convention Play-
ground of the Alleghenies.
Bedford, Pa.
Resort Area. Daytona Beach,
Fla.
Resort Area Family Playground.
Lake George, N.Y.
Resort Area of Cape Kennedy.
Cocoa Beach, Fla.
Resort Area of the Adirondacks.
Lake George, N.Y.
Resort Center. Red Lodge,
Mont.
Resort Center. Virginia Beach,
Va.
Resort City of Blue Ridge.
Hendersonville, N.C.
Resort of Enjoyment. Asbury
Park, N.J.
Resort Town on Rhode Island.
Middletown, R.I.
Resort Town on Rhode Island.
Narragansett, R.I.
Resort Town, U.S.A. Estes
Park, Colo.
Resort Town where the Fisher-
man Is King. Marathon, Fla.
Resort Where Fun Never Sets.
Surfside, Fla.
Restaurant City. New York,
N.Y.
Resting Place of Unknown Ameri-
can Soldier. Arlington, Va.
Restored Colonial City. Wil-
liamsburg, Va.
Retail Center of Southwest
Nebraska and Northeast
Kansas. McCook, Neb.
Retail Shopping Center of the
Peninsula. San Mateo, Calif.
Retail, Wholesale, Industrial,
Medical Institution Center

of Kentucky. Lexington,
Ky.
Retire in Roswell for a Life
of Health and Happiness.
Roswell, N.M.
Retire, Relax, Relive. Or-
mand-by-the-Sea, Fla.
Retirement Center. Harlingen,
Tex.
Retirement Center of the Na-
tion. Tucson, Ariz.
Rhode Island's Most Historic
Town. Newport, R.I.
Rice and Catfish Capital of
Texas. Winnie, Tex.
Rice and Duck Capitol of the
World. Stuttgart, Ark.
Rice Capital. Hazen, Ark.
Rice Capital of Louisiana.
Lake Charles, La.
Rice Capital of the World.
Crowley, La.
Rice Center of America.
Crowley, La.
Rice Center of the U.S.A.
Hazen, Ark.
Rice City. Hazen, Ark.
Rice City of America.
Crowley, La.
Rich Agricultural and Indus-
trial Heartland of Mid-
America. Rockford, Ill.
Rich Busy Pride of Texas.
Dallas, Tex.
Rich Prosperous Market
Area. Columbus, Ohio
Richest Hill on Earth. Butte,
Mont.
Richest Square Mile on Earth.
Central City, Colo.
Richest Town in the World.
Brookline, Mass.
Richest Town in the World.
New Canaan, Conn.
Richest Village on Earth.
Hibbing, Minn.
Rifle City. Springfield,
Mass.
Right Climate for Business
and Family Living.
Bonifay, Fla.
Ringling City. Sarasota, Fla.
River City. Cairo, Ill.

Riviera of America. Miami
Beach, Fla.
Riviera of the Pacific. Laguna
Beach, Calif.
Riviera of the Pacific. Santa
Barbara, Calif.
Riviera of the Southeast U.S.A.
Cape Coral, Fla.
Robbers' Roost. Ellensburg,
Wash.
Robbers' Roost. Fruitland,
Wash.
Rock Capital of the Nation.
Dubois, Wyo.
Rock City. Batavia, Ill.
Rock City. Nashville, Tenn.
Rock City. Wabash, Ind.
Rock Fish Capital of the World.
Weldon, N.C.
Rocket Capital of the Nation.
Huntsville, Ala.
Rocket City. Alamogordo,
N.M.
Rocket City. Huntsville, Ala.
Rocket City, U.S.A. Hunts-
ville, Ala.
Rockfish Capital. Weldon,
N.C.
Rockhound's Paradise. Paris,
Maine
Rodeo City. Ellensburg, Wash.
Rodeo of the Ozarks Town.
Springdale, Ark.
Roger Williams City. Provi-
dence, R.I.
Rollicking, Hilarious Tent and
Shack City. Lawton, Okla.
Roman Goddess of Fruit Trees.
Pomona, Wash.
Roof Garden of America. Salida,
Colo.
Roof Garden of Florida. Lake
Placid, Fla.
Roof Garden of Pennsylvania.
Somerset, Pa.
Roof Garden of Texas. Alpine,
Tex.
Roof Garden Resort of Texas.
Alpine, Tex.
Roof of Eastern America.
Boone, N.C.
Rooftop of New Hampshire.
Dixville, N.H.

Rose Capital. Tyler, Tex.
Rose Capital of America.
Newark, N.Y.
Rose Capital of Texas.
Tyler, Tex.
Rose Capital of the World.
Columbus, Ohio
Rose Capital of the World.
Tyler, Tex.
Rose Center. Pana, Ill.
Rose Center of the United
States. Richmond, Ind.
Rose City. Jackson, Mich.
Rose City. Madison, N.J.
Rose City. Manheim, Pa.
Rose City. Pleasantville,
Iowa
Rose City. Portland, Ore.
Rose City. Thomasville,
Ga.
Rose of New England. Nor-
walk, Conn.
Rose of New England. Nor-
wich, Conn.
Rose Town. Lowell, Wyo.
Roundup Capital. Wicken-
burg, Ariz.
Round-Up City. Pendleton,
Ore.
Royal City. Santa Fe, N.M.
Rubber Capital of the United
States. Akron, Ohio
Rubber Capital of the World.
Akron, Ohio
Rubber City. Akron, Ohio
Rubber City. Wethersfield,
Conn.
Rubber's Home Town. Akron,
Ohio
Russian-American Capital.
Sitka, Alaska
Rye Grass Capital of the
World. Albany, Ore.

Sacto. Sacramento, Calif.
Saddle Horse Capital of the
World. Mexico, Mo.
Safe Place for Children.
Jamestown, R.I.
Safest Beach in the World.
Fort Myers Beach, Fla.

Safest Spot in the World. Fort
Collins, Colo.
Sailfish Capital of the World.
Stuart, Fla.
St. Anthony's Town. San An-
tonio, Tex.
St. Moritz of the Rockies.
Anaconda, Mont.
St. Petersburg of Tom Sawyer.
Hannibal, Mo.
Saintly City. St. Paul, Minn.
Saints Rest. Oak Park, Ill.
Salad Bowl of America. Rus-
kin, Fla.
Salad Bowl of the Nation.
Ruskin, Fla.
Salina Has More of Everything.
Salina, Kan.
Sailing Capital of the World.
Newport, R.I.
Salmon Capital of Alaska.
Ketchikan, Alaska
Salmon Capital of the World.
Ketchikan, Alaska
Salmon City. Astoria, Ore.
Saloon Queen. Muskegon,
Mich.
Salt City. Hutchinson, Kan.
Salt City. Manistee, Mich.
Salt City. Syracuse, N.Y.
Salt Water People. Quilcene,
Wash.
Salt Water Trout Capital of the
World. Cape Canaveral,
Fla.
Salt Water Trout Capital of the
World. Cocoa, Fla.
San Berdoo. San Bernardino,
Calif.
San Francisco's Bedroom. Oak-
land, Calif.
San Francisco of Tomorrow.
Atlanta, Ga.
Sand Hills of the Eastern Bar-
barians. San Francisco,
Calif.
Santa's Lookout. Middletown,
Mass.
Santa's Village. Dundee, Ill.
Santa's Village. Jefferson, N.H.
Santa's Village. Lancaster, N.H.
Santa's Workshop. North Pole,
N.Y.

Saratoga of the West. Waukesha, Wis.

Sardine Capital of the U.S. Eastport, Me.

Sardine City. Eastport, Me.

Sassy New Pittsburgh of the Southern Rim. Houston, Tex.

Satanic City. Devils Lake, N.D.

Saturday Town. Decatur, Ala.

Sawdust City. Eau Claire, Wis.

Sawdust City. Lock Haven, Pa.

Sawdust City. Minneapolis, Minn.

Sawdust City. Muskegon, Mich.

Sawdust City. Oshkosh, Wis.

Sawdust City of America. Williamsport, Pa.

Scale Manufacturing Center of the World. St. Johnsbury, Vt.

Scenic and Recreation Center of Alaska. Juneau, Alaska

Scenic California's Scenic Playground. Santa Cruz, Calif.

Scenic Capital of Central Pennsylvania. Williamsport, Pa.

Scenic Center of the South. Chattanooga, Tenn.

Scenic City. Berlin, Pa.

Scenic City. Chattanooga, Tenn.

Scenic City of Five Flags at the Top of the Gulf of Mexico. Pensacola, Fla.

Scenic City of Nightless Summer Days. Juneau, Alaska

Scenic City of Southern Minnesota. Redwood Falls, Minn.

Scenic Gateway. Laurel, Mont.

Scenic Gateway to America. Niagara Falls, N.Y.

Scenic Health Resort of California. Elsinore, Calif.

Scenic Hub of the Golden State. Fresno, Calif.

Scenic Land of the Standing Stone. Huntingdon, Pa.

Scenic Sportland. Las Vegas, Nev.

Scholarship City. Fall River, Mass.

Science City. New York, N.Y.

Scientific Center. Rolla, Mo.

Scrapple City. Allentown, Pa.

Screenland. Hollywood, Calif.

Sea and Sand Vacationland. Sea Isle City, N.J.

Sea Gate to the Southwest. Lake Charles, La.

Sea Turtle Capital of the World. Jensen Beach, Fla.

Seafood Capital of the World. Crisfield, Md.

Seamy Little Swamp Town. Houston, Tex.

Seaport City. Helena, Ark.

Seaport for the Landlocked State of Idaho. Lewiston, Idaho

Seaport of Central New York. Oswego, N.Y.

Seaport of Iowa. Los Angeles, Calif.

Seaport of the West. Galveston, Tex.

Seaport Village. Mystic, Conn.

Seashore at Its Best. Stone Harbor, N.J.

Seashore Community of Modern Summer Cottages. Ocean Beach, N.J.

Seashore with the Suburban Look. North Wildwood, N.J.

Seaside Golf Capital of the U.S.A. Myrtle Beach, S.C.

Seat of Amherst College. Amherst, Mass.

Seat Capital of the World. Yakima, Wash.

Seat of Empire. New York, N.Y.

Seaway Vacationland. Massena, N.Y.

Second City Syndrome. Chicago, Ill.

SECOND

Second Largest Aircraft Pro-
duction Center in the
Country. Fort Worth, Tex.
Second Largest Grain Shipping
Center of the Northwest.
Craigmont, Idaho
Second Largest Port on
the Great Lakes. Toledo,
Ohio
Second Largest Railroad
Center in the United States.
Buffalo, N.Y.
Second Major City on Puget
Sound. Tacoma, Wash.
Second Murder City. Los
Angeles, Calif.
Second Oldest City in the U.S.
St. Marys, Ga.
Second Oldest Settlement in
Oklahoma. Vinita, Okla.
Second Oldest Town in Ken-
tucky. Bardstown, Ky.
Second Rome. Washington,
D.C.
Sedate Capital of the Bible
Belt. Oklahoma City,
Okla.
Senior Citizens' Capital of
the World. St. Peters-
burg, Fla.
Sentinel City in the Pines.
Prescott, Ariz.
Service Center for Industrial
Agriculture. Scotts Bluff,
Neb.
Seventh Largest Seaport in
the U.S. Baton Rouge,
La.
Service Center to Mainstream
U.S.A. Greenville, Miss.
Shade Tobacco Capital.
Quincy, Fla.
Shade-Grown Tobacco Capital.
Quincy, Fla.
Shake-Rag. Mineral Point,
Wis.
Shangri-La of Alaska. Homer,
Alaska
Shangri-La of the Western
Hemisphere. Miami Beach,
Fla.
Sharpest Town in the West.
Gillette, Wyo.

Sheep Capital of the State of
California. Dixon, Calif.
Shelterbelt Capital of the World.
Larimore, N.D.
Ship Harbor. Anacortes, Wash.
Shipbuilding Capital. Bath, Me.
Ship-Building City. Chester,
Pa.
Shipbuilding City. Quincy,
Mass.
Shipping Center of the South-
west. Dodge City, Kan.
Shipping City. Bath, Me.
Shire City of Androscoggin
County. Auburn, Me.
Shire City of Waldo County.
Belfast, Me.
Shire Town and Hub of the
County. Farmington, Me.
Shoe and Slipper City. Norwalk,
Conn.
Shoe Capital of America. St.
Louis, Mo.
Shoe Capital of the World.
Lynn, Mass.
Shoe City. Auburn, Me.
Shoe City. Brockton, Mass.
Shoe City. Hanover, Pa.
Shoe City. Johnson City, N.Y.
Shoe City. Lynn, Mass.
Shoe Town. Haverhill, Mass.
Shooters' Town. Bodie, Calif.
Shopping Center for 50,000
Minnesotans. Morris, Minn.
Shopping Center of Chester
County. West Chester, Pa.
Shopping Center of Franklin
County. Farmington, Me.
Shopping Center of Northeast
Montana. Wolf Point, Mont.
Shopping Center of Northern
Maine. Houlton, Me.
Shopping Center of Southern
Berkshire Country. Great
Barrington, Mass.
Shopping Center of the Appa-
lachians. Bristol Tenn.
and Bristol, Va.
Shopping Center of the Raritan
Bay Area. Perth Amboy, N.J.
Shopping Center of Western
Virginia. Roanoke, Va.
Shore Village. Guilford, Conn.

Shovel City of the World.
Marion, Ohio
Show Country of New England.
Pittsfield, Mass.
Show Place of Southern California. Redlands, Calif.
Showboat City. St. Louis,
Mo.
Showplace of Southeast Alaska.
Sitka, Alaska
Showplace of the Lakes.
Mackinac Island, Mich.
Showplace of the Nation.
Atlantic City, N.J.
Shrimp Capital of Alaska.
Petersburg, Alaska
Shrimp Capital of the World.
Brunswick, Ga.
Shrimporee City. Aransas
Pass, Tex.
Shrine of Old Homes. Guilford, Conn.
Shrine of the South. Lexington, Va.
Shuffleboard Capital. Lake
Worth, Fla.
Sierra "Coney Island." Lake
Tahoe, Calif.
Sight-Seeing City of the Middle West. Leavenworth,
Kan.
Sightseeing Center of Florida.
Tampa, Fla.
Sightseeing Hub of the West
Coast of Central Florida.
Brandon, Fla.
Silk City. Paterson, N.J.
Silver Boom Town. Austin,
Nev.
Silver City. Meriden, Conn.
Silver City of the World.
Meriden, Conn.
Silver Dollar City. Billings,
Mont.
Silver Queen of the Rockies.
Georgetown, Colo.
Silver Town. Tonopah, Nev.
Sin Center. Terre Haute,
Ind.
Sin City. Atolia, Calif.
Sin City. Las Vegas, Nev.
Sin City. Port Chester,
N.Y.

Sinema Land. Hollywood,
Calif.
Sinful City. Las Vegas, Nev.
Sister City. Calumet City, Ill.
Sister City of the Sun. Miami
Beach, Fla.
Sister Community. Hammond,
Ind.
Site of Colby College Nestled
in Maine Countryside.
Waterville, Me.
Site of the Eastern States' Exposition. West Springfield,
Mass.
Site of the First U.S. Homestead. Beatrice, Neb.
Site of the Oahe Dam. Pierre,
S.D.
Site of the World's Championship Timber Carnival. Albany, Ore.
Site of Two of New Hampshire's Oldest Churches.
Claremont, N.H.
Ski Capital of Colorado.
Georgetown, Colo.
Ski Capital of the East. Stowe,
Vt.
Ski Capital U.S.A. Aspen,
Colo.
Ski Capitol of Michigan. Gaylord, Mich.
Ski Crossroads of the World.
St. Johnsbury, Vt.
Ski Town, U.S.A. Steamboat
Springs, Colo.
Skier's Heaven. Snow, Vt.
Skiing Center of America.
Idaho Springs, Colo.
Skinner's Mudhole. Eugene,
Ore.
Sky City. Acoma, N.M.
Skyline City. Mission, Kan.
Skyline of Romance. Atlantic
City, N.J.
Skyscraper City of the
Prairies. Bismarck, N.D.
Slash Town. Ashland, Va.
Slaughter House. Auburn,
Wash.
Sled Dog Center of the U.S.
Wonalancet, N.H.
Sleepy Town. Philadelphia, Pa.

Small Boat Capital of the World. Little Falls, Minn.

Small Enough to be Neighborly, Large Enough to Supply Your Every Need. Holly Hill, Fla.

Small Town with a Big Welcome. Saratoga, Wyo.

Small Town with the Bustling Activity of a Growing City. Maitland, Fla.

Small Village in the Berkshires. South Lee, Mass.

Smallest Capital in America. Carson City, Nev.

Smallest Capital in the World. Carson City, Nev.

Smart Shopping Center for the Central Willamette Valley. Albany, Ore.

Smartest Address on the Golden Desert. Palm Desert, Calif.

Smelter City. Anaconda, Mont.

Smile of the Great Spirit. Winnipesaukee, N.H.

Smog City. Los Angeles, Calif.

Smoke on the Water. Skamokawa, Wash.

Smokeless Coal Capital of the World. Beckley, W. Va.

Smoky City. Pittsburgh, Pa.

Smooth Water. Sequim, Wash.

Snapshot City. Rochester, N.Y.

Snow Basket of the Empire State. Buffalo, N.Y.

Snow or No, Go to Stowe, Any Season, Many Reasons. Stowe, Vt.

Snow Paradise. Stowe, Vt.

Snowmobile Capital of the Southwest. Chama, N.M.

Snowmobile Capital of the U.S. Thief River Falls, Minn.

Snowmobile Capital of the World. Rhinelander, Wis.

Snowshoe Town of America. Norway, Me.

So Near to So Much. Cleveland, Miss.

Sober-Minded. Dedham, Mass.

Socially Attractive Community. Allentown, Pa.

Sodom-by-the-Sea. Coney Island, N.Y.

Sodom of the South. Memphis, Tenn.

Soil Pipe Center of the World. Anniston, Ala.

Solano County's Twin Cities. Fairfield, Calif.

Solano County's Twin Cities. Suisan City, Calif.

Solid City. St. Louis, Mo.

Something for Everyone City. Chicago, Ill.

Something to Write Home About. North Wildwood, N.J.

Soo. Saulte Ste. Marie, Mich.

Sour Dough Flats. Waterville, Wash.

Source of the Au Sable. Grayling, Mich.

South Arkansas' Busy Port City. Camden, Ark.

South Carolina's Capital City. Columbia, S.C.

South Dakota's City of Opportunity. Mitchell, S.D.

South Dakota's Newest Convention City. Watertown, S.D.

South Dakota's Opportunity City. Mitchell, S.D.

South Dakota's Prairie Oasis. Faith, S.D.

South Florida Hub. Hialeah, Fla.

South Florida's Oldest Pioneer Village. Bradenton, Fla.

South Georgia's Market Place. Moultrie, Ga.

South Sea Isles of America. Miami, Fla.

Southeastern Entrance to the Redwood Empire. Napa, Calif.

Southeastern Gateway to Vermont. Brattleboro, Vt.

Southern California's Big "Oh". San Luis Obispo, Calif.

Southern California's Desert
Playground. Indio, Calif.
Southern California's Most
Modern Resort. Porto-
fino, Calif.
Southern Crossroads City.
Atlanta, Ga.
Southern Entry to the Cape
Kennedy Area. Melbourne,
Fla.
Southern Gateway. Moose
Lake, Minn.
Southern Gateway of New
England. Providence, R.I.
Southern Gateway to Maine.
York, Me.
Southern Gateway to the Black
Hills. Chadron, Neb.
Southern Gateway to the Black
Hills. Hot Springs, S.D.
Southern Gateway to the Lewis
and Clark Lake. Norfolk,
Neb.
Southern Gateway to the
Sequoia. Bakersfield,
Calif.
Southern Gateway to the
Smokies. Murphy, N.C.
Southern Gateway to Vermont's
Largest City. Burlington,
Vt.
Southern Gateway to Vermont's
Largest City. South
Burlington, Vt.
Southern Holiday Highland.
Blowing Rock, N.C.
Southern Kentucky's Largest
Shopping Center. Bowling
Green, Ky.
Southern Portal to the Wine
Producing Country. Peta-
luma, Calif.
Southern Sea-Air Gateway to
Alaska. Ketchikan, Alaska
Southernmost City in the
Continental United States.
Key West, Fla.
Southernmost U.S. Ski Area.
Alamogordo, N.M.
Southland at Its Best. Tal-
lahassee, Fla.
South's Fastest Growing City.
East Point, Ga.

South's Greatest City. New
Orleans, La.
South's Largest Producer of
Cotton Cloth. Spartanburg,
S.C.
South's Leading International
Cruise Port. Port Ever-
glades, Fla.
South's Most Beautiful and
Interesting City. Macon,
Ga.
South's Most Strategic and
Distribution Center. De-
catur, Ala.
South's Most Strategic Indus-
trial and Distributional
Center. Decatur, Ala.
South's No. 1 Cruise Ship Port.
Port Everglades, Fla.
South's Oldest Industrial City.
Columbus, Ga.
South's Prettiest Town. Eden-
ton, N.C.
Southwest Arkansas' Most Con-
veniently Located City.
Hope, Ark.
Southwest Metroplex. Dallas,
Tex.
Southwest Metroplex. Fort
Worth, Tex.
Southwest Sun Country. Tucson,
Ariz.
Southwest's Foremost Educa-
tional Center. Houston, Tex.
Southwest's Greatest Health
Resort. Marlin, Tex.
Southwest's Leading Financial
Manufacturing and Distribu-
tion Center. Dallas, Tex.
Southwest's Sightseeing Center.
Phoenix, Ariz.
Southwestern Factory City.
Fort Smith, Ark.
Southwestern Gateway to the
Historic Four Season Vaca-
tionland. Bennington, Vt.
Southwestern Headquarters of
American Business. Dallas,
Tex.
Southwestern Minnesota's Finest
Shopping Center. Redwood
Falls, Minn.

Soybean Capital of the World.
  Decatur, Ill.
Soybean Capital of the World.
  Taylorville, Ill.
Soybean Center. Decatur, Ill.
Spa Center of America. Hot
  Springs, Ark.
Spa City. Saratoga Springs,
  N.Y.
Space Age City. Danbury,
  Conn.
Space Age City. Muscle
  Shoals, Ala.
Space Age Community.
  Blacksburg, Va.
Space Capital of the Nation.
  Huntsville, Ala.
Space Capital of the World.
  Huntsville, Ala.
Space Center. Houston, Tex.
Space City, U.S.A. Houston,
  Tex.
Space City, U.S.A. Hunts-
  ville, Ala.
Space Headquarters, U.S.A.
  Houston, Tex.
Space Hub. Cape Canaveral,
  Fla.
Space Port USA. Galveston,
  Tex.
Spaceport, U.S.A. Cape
  Kennedy, Fla.
Spanish Peanut Center of the
  World. Dawson, Ga.
Spanish Town. Half Moon
  Bay, Calif.
Spanish Town. Tampa, Fla.
Spanish Village. San Cle-
  mente, Calif.
Sparkling City by the Sea.
  Corpus Christi, Tex.
Sparkling Sand, Golden Sun-
  shine on the Atlantic
  Shore. Pompano Beach,
  Fla.
Spawning Ground of Realtors.
  Los Angeles, Calif.
Spearhead of the New South.
  Charlotte, N.C.
Special Library Capital of
  the World. Pittsburgh, Pa.
Spectacular Convention Center.
  Las Vegas, Nev.

Speed Skating Capital of the
  World. Northbrook, Ill.
Splendid Community. Boca
  Raton, Fla.
Splendor of the West. Las
  Vegas, Nev.
Spinach Capital of the World.
  Crystal City, Tex.
Spindle City. Fall River,
  Mass.
Spindle City. Lewiston, Me.
Spindle City. Lowell, Mass.
Spinster City. Portland, Ore.
Spokane of Oregon. Eugene,
  Ore.
Sponge City. Tarpon Springs,
  Fla.
Spoonbill Capital of the World.
  Warsaw, Mo.
Sport Center of the South.
  Aiken, S.C.
Sport Parachuting Center of
  U.S.A. Orange, Mass.
Sportfishing Capital of the
  World. Islamorada, Fla.
Sportland of the Gulf. Mobile,
  Ala.
Sports Capital of the South.
  Atlanta, Ga.
Sports Capital of the West.
  Denver, Colo.
Sports Center of the Southwest.
  Dallas, Tex.
Sportsman's Paradise. Apa-
  lachicola, Fla.
Sportsman's Paradise. Cherry-
  field, Me.
Sportsman's Paradise. Chin-
  coteague, Va.
Sportsman's Paradise. Clinton,
  Mo.
Sportsman's Paradise. Green-
  wood, Miss.
Sportsman's Paradise. Laurel,
  Mont.
Sportsman's Paradise. Punta
  Gorda, Fla.
Sportsman's Paradise. Salida,
  Colo.
Sportsman's Playground. Mar-
  shall, Tex.
Sportsman's Town. Bishop,
  Calif.

Sportsman's Town. Umatilla, Fla.

Spot for a Home and a Life of Joy. Grove, Okla.

Spot Forever Texas. Kingsville, Tex.

Spring City. Waukesha, Wis.

Springboard into the Four-Season Area. Springfield, Vt.

Springs of Health and Bits of Wealth. Buhl, Minn.

Springtime City. Clearwater, Fla.

Squaw Harbor. Anacortes, Wash.

Squawkiewood. Hollywood, Calif.

Squire City. Springdale, Wash.

Stage Coach Town. Fort Worth, Tex.

Star City. Lafayette, Ind.

Star City of the South. Roanoke, Va.

Star City with a Great Future. Bethlehem, Pa.

Star of the Big Sky Country. Billings, Mont.

Star of the North. Malone, N.Y.

Star of the Southland. Long Beach, Calif.

Stardom. Hollywood, Calif.

Starland. Hollywood, Calif.

State City. Harrisburg, Pa.

State Recreation Area. Morris, Minn.

State Rice Branch Experiment Station. Stuttgart, Ark.

States Largest Oceanside Resort Town. Carolina Beach, N.C.

Steak Capital of the World. Omaha, Neb.

Steak Center of the Nation. Kansas City, Mo.

Steamtown, U.S.A. North Walpole, N.H.

Steel-Built City. Youngstown, Ohio

Steel Capital of the West. Fontana, Calif.

Steel Capital of the World. Pittsburgh, Pa.

Steel City. Bethlehem, Pa.

Steel City. Gary, Ind.

Steel City. Pittsburgh, Pa.

Steel City. Portsmouth, Ohio

Steel City. Youngstown, Ohio

Steel City of the West. Pueblo, Colo.

Steel-Making City. Gary, Ind.

Steel Town. Pittsburgh, Pa.

Still Water. Sequim, Wash.

Stone City. Bedford, Ind.

Storytown, U.S.A. Lake George, N.Y.

Stove City. Taunton, Mass.

Stowe Is the Place to Be. Stowe, Vt.

Strategic Geographical Location for Industry. Hurst, Tex.

Strawberry Capital of Alaska. Haines, Alaska

Strawberry Capital of America. Hammond, La.

Strawberry Capital of Texas. Poteet, Tex.

Strawberry Capital of the World. Watsonville, Calif.

Strawberry City. Starke, Fla.

Strawberry Festival City. Garden City, Calif.

String Town. Bremerton, Wash.

String Town. Manette, Wash.

Stringtown on the Pike, East Liberty, Pa.

Strong Water. Shelton, Wash.

Studioland. Hollywood, Calif.

Study in Contrasts. Pompano Beach, Fla.

Submarine Capital of the World. Groton, Conn.

Submarine Capital of the World. New London, Conn.

Sub-Treasury of the Pacific Northwest. Portland, Ore.

Suburb of Washington. Chevy Chase, Md.

Sugar Bowl of America. Pahokee, Fla.

Sugar Bowl of the Southeast.
Savannah, Ga.
Suicide Capital of the United
States. San Francisco,
Calif.
Summer and Health Resort.
Hendersonville, N. C.
Summer and Winter Paradise.
Somerset, Pa.
Summer and Winter Resort.
Intervale, N. H.
Summer and Winter Year
'Round Resort. St. Augu-
stine, Fla.
Summer Capital. Portland,
Ore.
Summer Capital of America.
Superior, Wis.
Summer Capital of Golf in the
U. S. Rangeley, Me.
Summer Capital of Society.
Newport, R. I.
Summer Capital of the Presi-
dents. Long Branch, N. J.
Summer City. Duluth, Minn.
Summer Fun Capital of the
South. Daytona Beach,
Fla.
Summer Resort. Newport,
R. I.
Summer Paradise. Lake
George, N. Y.
Summer Resort in the Blue
Ridge Mountains. Caesar's
Head, S. C.
Summer Resort Near Many
Scenic Points of Interest.
Woodstock, N. H.
Summer Vacationland and
Winter Wonderland. Lake
Placid, N. Y.
Summer Wonderland. Macki-
nac Island, Mich.
Summit City. Akron, Ohio
Summit City. Fort Wayne,
Ind.
Summit City. Kane, Pa.
Summit Town. Glassboro,
N. J.
Sun and Fun Capital of the
World. Miami Beach, Fla.
Sun'n Fun Land. Bradenton,
Fla.

Sun and Fun! Sand 'N Sea. Old
Orchard Beach, Me.
Sun City. Corpus Christi, Tex.
Sun City of the Big Sky Country.
Billings, Mont.
Sun, Fun and Action Town.
Las Vegas, Nev.
Sun Fun Capital. Myrtle Beach,
S. C.
Sun Fun City. Myrtle Beach,
S. C.
Sun Shines on Fun in New
Smyrna Beach. New Smyrna
Beach, Fla.
Sun Smiles Happily on Industry
in Riviera Beach where
There Is Everything to Make
You Happy. Riviera Beach,
Fla.
Sun Town. Calumet City, Ill.
Sunfish Capital of the World.
Becker, Minn.
Sunfish Capital of the World.
Detroit Lakes, Minn.
Sunniest City in California.
San Diego, Calif.
Sunny Community of Leisurely
Living and Happy Holidays.
Surfside, Fla.
Sunrise of Opportunity. Brooks-
ville, Fla.
Sunshine Capital of the South-
west. Tucson, Ariz.
Sunshine Capital of the United
States. Yuma, Ariz.
Sunshine Capital of the World.
Miami, Fla.
Sunshine City. Fort Lauderdale,
Fla.
Sunshine City. St. Petersburg,
Fla.
Sunshine City. Sarasota, Fla.
Sunshine City. Tucson, Ariz.
Sunshine Town. Newport, N. H.
Super City. New York, N. Y.
Surfing Capital of the South.
Cocoa Beach, Fla.
Surprise City. Oakland, Calif.
Sweatshirt Capital of the World.
Martinsville, Va.
Sweet Wine Capital of the
World. Fresno, Calif.

Sweetheart of South Texas.
Alice, Tex.
Sweetheart Town.   Loveland,
Colo.
Swell Place to Live.   Tempe,
Ariz.
Swimming Pool City.   Palm
Springs, Calif.
Swing Is to Palm Beach
County.   Palm Beach, Fla.
Swiss Cheese Capital of the
United States.   Monroe,
Wis.
Swiss Cheese Center of Ohio.
Sugarcreek, Ohio
Switchback City.   Mauch
Chunk, Pa.
Switzerland of Alaska.   Valdez,
Alaska
Switzerland of America.   Afton,
Wyo.
Switzerland of America.
Baker, Ore.
Switzerland of America.
Dixville Notch, N. H.
Switzerland of America.
Durango, Colo.
Switzerland of America.
Lake Placid, N. Y.
Switzerland of America.
Mauch Chunk, Pa.
Switzerland of America.
Ouray, Colo.
Switzerland of America.
Terre Haute, Ind.
Switzerland of Iowa.
Decorah, Iowa
Switzerland of Maine.
Jackman, Me.
Switzerland of Ohio.   Busi-
nessburg, Ohio
Switzerland of Texas.
Bandera, Tex.
Switzerland of the Catskills.
Hancock, N. Y.
Switzerland of the Ozarks.
Eureka Springs, Ark.
Sycamore City.   Terre
Haute, Ind.

Table-Land.   Mesa, Wash.

Table Wine Center of the World.
Napa, Calif.
Table Wine Center of the World.
St. Helena, Calif.
Tailhold.   Rogue River, Ore.
Tailholt.   Carrollton, Ind.
Talked-About City.   St. Cloud,
Minn.
Tall Tower Town.   Raymond,
Me.
Tallest Town in Oregon.   Lake-
view, Ore.
Tannery City.   Blossburg, Pa.
Tanning City.   Woburn, Mass.
Target of Opportunity.   Waco,
Tex.
Tarrara City.   Boykins, Va.
Tater Town.   Gleason, Tenn.
Taterville.   Gleason, Tenn.
Taxpayer's Haven.   Hialeah,
Fla.
Teasel Capital of the Country.
Skaneateles, N. Y.
Telegraph Hub.   Syracuse,
N. Y.
Ten Square Miles of the World's
Finest Skiing.   Vail, Colo.
Tennessee's Beauty Spot.   Nash-
ville, Tenn.
Tennis Capital of the World.
Salisbury, Md.
Tennis Town.   Newport, R. I.
Tent City.   Wildwood, N. J.
Tent Town.   Douglas, Wyo.
Terminus of the Allagash Canoe
Trip.   Fort Kent, Me.
Terrace City.   Yonkers, N. Y.
Texas' First Stop.   Denison,
Tex.
Texas' Largest Isolated Market.
Lubbock, Tex.
Texas' Only Atlas Missile
Sites.   Abilene, Tex.
Texas's Sparkling City by the
Sea.   Corpus Christi, Tex.
Textile Capital of the World.
Lawrence, Mass.
Textile Center.   Lewiston, Me.
Textile Center of the World.
Greenville, S. C.
Textile City.   Reading, Pa.
There Is Only One Stowe.
Stowe, Vt.

There's a Lot to Like About
Ocean City. Ocean City,
Md.
There's More in Milwaukee.
Milwaukee, Wis.
There's More than Coal in
Coalgate. Coalgate, Okla.
There's Something for Every-
one in Hollywood. Holly-
wood, Calif.
Thermopylae of Middle Ten-
nessee. Tullahoma, Tenn.
Third Largest City in Orange
County. Garden City,
Calif.
Third Largest City in Wash-
ington. Tacoma, Wash.
Third Largest Rail Center
in the Nation. Toledo,
Ohio
Third Largest Tobacco
Market in Virginia. South
Hill, Va.
Thirty Acre Industrial Tract.
Auburn, Neb.
This Pleasant Land Among
the Mountains. Man-
chester, Vt.
Thoroughbred Capital of
Florida. Ocala, Fla.
Thoroughbred, Standardbred
and Saddle Horse Center
of America. Lexington,
Ky.
Thread City. Willimantic,
Conn.
Three Forks. Pullman, Wash.
Three Spits. Bangor, Wash.
Threshold of Theodore Roose-
velt National Memorial
Park. Dickinson, N.D.
Thrifty New England Com-
munity Steeped in Colonial
Tradition and Democracy.
Norwalk, Conn.
Thriving and Progressive
Community. Nacogdoches,
Tex.
Thriving Capital City.
Montgomery, Ala.
Thriving City in Pennsylvania's
Dynamic Lehigh Valley.
Allentown, Pa.

Thriving Community. Aransas
Pass, Tex.
Thriving Lively Town. Camden,
Me.
Thriving Pleasant City. Peru,
Ind.
Thriving Supply Point. Camp-
bellton, Tex.
Thriving Tourist Capitol.
Biloxi, Miss.
Thriving Town where Prosperity
and Contentment Go Hand-in-
Hand. Schulenburg, Tex.
Thriving Well Balanced Indus-
trial Town. Wallingford,
Conn.
Tide-Water City. Troy, N.Y.
Timber Capital of the Nation.
Roseburg, Ore.
Timber Capital of the World.
Roseburg, Ore.
Timber Capital of the World.
Saginaw, Mich.
Time of Your Life City.
Dallas, Tex.
Timeless Wonderland. San
Francisco, Calif.
Tin Horn Village. Newton,
Mass.
Tinsel Town. Hollywood, Calif.
Tip of Cape Cod. Province-
town, Mass.
Tire Capital of the World.
Akron, Ohio
Tire City of the United States.
Akron, Ohio
Tire Cord Capital of the U.S.
Thomaston, Ga.
Titletown, U.S.A. Green Bay,
Wis.
Toast of the Coast. Rockport,
Tex.
Tobacco and Farming Center.
Clayton, N.C.
Tobacco Capital of South Caro-
lina. Mullins, S.C.
Tobacco Capital of the World.
Richmond, Va.
Tobacco Center. Lyons, Ga.
Tobacco Center. Viroqua, Wis.
Tobacco City. Danville, Va.
Tobacco City. Edgerton,
Wis.

Today's City with Tomorrow's
Vision. Ottumwa, Iowa

Tomato Capital of South Central Texas. Yoakum, Tex.

Tomato Capital of the World.
Dania, Fla.

Tomato Capital of the Ozarks.
Green Forest, Ark.

Tomato Center of the World.
Dania, Fla.

Tomato Plant Capital. Tifton,
Ga.

Tomatopolis of the World.
Crystal Springs, Miss.

Toothpick Center of Maine.
Strong, Me.

Toothpick Center of the World.
Oxford Co., Me.

Top of New England. Mount
Washington, N.H.

Top of the San Fernando
Valley. Sylmar, Calif.

Top of the World. Point
Barrow, Alaska

Tops in Sun'n Fun. St.
Petersburg, Fla.

Total Community Committed
to Building a Vital City.
Utica, N.Y.

Totem City. Ketchikan,
Alaska

Toughest Town in Texas.
Luling, Tex.

Tour Entrance to the Kennedy
Space Center. Titus-
ville, Fla.

Tourist and Convention Center.
Jacksonville, Fla.

Tourist Capital of North
Dakota. Bismarck, N.D.

Tourist City. Statesboro, Ga.

Tourist Mecca and Antiques
Center of the South.
Dania, Fla.

Tourist Mecca of East Texas.
Jacksonville, Tex.

Tourist Mecca of the South.
Allendale, S.C.

Tourist's Paradise. Index,
Wash.

Touropolis of America.
Flagstaff, Ariz.

Tower Tree City. Greensburg,
Ind.

Town Among the Willows.
Wilton, Conn.

Town at the Headwaters of
Tuttle Creek Lakes. Blue
Rapids, Kan.

Town Blessed by an Ideal Year
'Round Climate. Las Vegas,
Nev.

Town Famous for Its Great
Mansions. Newport, R.I.

Town for Those in Live with
Life. Marietta, Ohio

Town in the Beautiful North
Coup Valley. Ord, Neb.

Town in the Gateway to the
Beautiful Red Section of
Florida. Davenport, Fla.

Town in the Heart of Iowa's
Scenic Vacation Land.
Waukon, Iowa

Town in the Heart of the White
Mountains. Lincoln, N.H.

Town in the Land of the Pineys.
Houston, Mo.

Town Just Rite for Your Plant
Site. Houlton, Me.

Town of Friendly People.
Pearl River, N.J.

Town of Happy Homes. Greenwood, Ind.

Town of Homes. Westport,
Conn.

Town of Hospitality and Progress. Victoria, Va.

Town of Many Opportunities.
Uvalde, Tex.

Town of Millionaires. Brookline, Mass.

Town of Motels. Breezewood,
Pa.

Town of Progress. Lake Havasu
City, Ariz.

Town of Sandy Beaches. Sebago
Lake, Me.

Town of Schools--And a College.
Wellesley, Mass.

Town of the Fearless. Hammond, Ind.

Town of Tradition. Bards-
town, Ky.

Town of Tumbling Waters.
Shelburne Falls, Mass.
Town of "Up and Down."
Eureka Springs, Ark.
Town on the Connecticut River
in Scenic Northern New
Hampshire. Colebrook,
N. H.
Town on the Ridge in the
Heart of Orangeland.
Davenport, Fla.
Town on the Shore of Historic
Casco Bay. Yarmouth, Me.
Town Rich in Historic Beauty.
Boothbay Harbor, Me.
Town Rich in History.
Manassas, Va.
Town Rich in Year-Round
Recreational and Cultural
Diversions. Camden, Me.
Town Situated in the Beautiful
Ashuelot River Valley.
Keene, N. H.
Town that Changed America's
Viewpoint on Retirement
Living. Sun City, Ariz.
Town that Climate Built.
Miami, Fla.
Town that Friendship Built.
Hamburg, N. Y.
Town that Gave the World a
Great Idea. Nebraska
City, Neb.
Town that Has Become a
University. Winter Park,
Fla.
Town that Is Going Places.
Meredith, N. H.
Town that "Jack" Built.
Joplin, Mo.
Town that Made Garbage
Illegal. Jasper, Ind.
Town that Moved Overnight.
Hibbing, Minn.
Town that Outlives and Out-
grows the Oil Boom.
Titusville, Pa.
Town that Roses Built.
Pasadena, Calif.
Town the Atom Built. Rich-
land, Wash.
Town to Grow With. East
Windsor Hill, Conn.
Town to Live In. Darien, Conn.

Town Too Tough to Die. Tomb-
stone, Ariz.
Town Two Miles Long and Two
Yards Wide. St. Francis-
ville, La.
Town Unmatched in Growth,
Beauty, Home. Long Beach
Township, N. J.
Town where Industry's Contribu-
tion to the Community is
Appreciated. Foley, Ala.
Town where Natural Beauty and
Industry Meet to Create.
Mount Joy, Pa.
Town where Oil Derricks Loom
in Almost any Yard. Okla-
homa City, Okla.
Town where People Count Most.
La Porte, Ind.
Town where Rail Meets Water.
Kalama, Wash.
Town where the Action Is.
Custer City, S. D.
Town where the Memory Lingers
On. Smithville, N. J.
Town where the Office Ledger
Has Replaced the Horse
Pistol. Oklahoma City, Okla.
Town where Summer Is Air-
Conditioned. Chatham, Mass.
Town where the Trout Leap in
Main Street. Saratoga, Wyo.
Town where there Is Fun for
the Entire Family. Plymouth,
Mass.
Town where Your Summer Fun
Begins. Riverhead, N. Y.
Town which Held the Key.
Orondo, Wash.
Town with a Gunsmoke Flavor.
Custer City, S. D.
Town with a Future. Blue
Rapids, Kan.
Town with a Future. Stratford,
Conn.
Town with a Heart. Norwalk,
Conn.
Town with a Heart. Salida, Colo.
Town with a Split Personality.
Islip, N. Y.
Town with Grow Power. South
Windsor, Conn.
Town with Matchless Climate.
Encinitas, Calif.

Town with Old-Fashioned
Courtesy. Newport, N.C.
Town with the Most to Offer
Industry. Columbus, Miss.
Town with Traditional New
England Hospitality. Am-
herst, Mass.
Toy Town. Winchendon, Mass.
Track and Field Town, U.S.A.
Jemez Pueblo, N.M.
Trade Capital of Florida's
West Coast. Tampa, Fla.
Trade Center. Pratt, Kan.
Trade Center for Southeast
Arkansas. Pine Bluff, Ark.
Trade Center of Mid-East
Nebraska. Fremont, Neb.
Trade Center of Southwest
Georgia. Albany, Ga.
Trade Center of the Rich
Blue Grass, Tobacco and
Livestock Region. Lexing-
ton, Ky.
Trading Center. New Bedford,
Mass.
Trading Center. Raleigh,
N.C.
Trading Center. Wheeling,
W. Va.
Trading Center for the
Rangeley Lakes Chain.
Rangeley, Me.
Trading Center of East Ala-
bama. Opelika, Ala.
Trading Center of the Inland
Empire. Spokane, Wash.
Trading Post of Yesterday--
A Great Industrial Center
Today. Texas City, Tex.
Trail's End. International
Falls, Minn.
Tranquil Living in a Natural
Paradise. La Belle, Fla.
Transport Center of the Na-
tion. Buffalo, N.Y.
Transportation and Traffic
Center of New Mexico.
Albuquerque, N.M.
Transportation Center. Mid-
land, Tex.
Transportation Center of
North America. Superior,
Wis.

Transportation City. Cumber-
land, Md.
Transportation City. Easton,
Pa.
Transportation Hub of the West.
Ogden, Utah
Transportation King of the Mid-
East. Harrisburg, Pa.
Travel Center of the World Re-
nowned Shenandoah Valley.
Newmarket, Va.
Treasure City. Tampa, Fla.
Treasure Island of the South-
west. Galveston, Tex.
Tree City. Boise, Idaho
Tree City. Forsyth, Mont.
Tree City. Greensburg, Ind.
Tree City. Kent, Ohio
Tremont. Boston, Mass.
Tri-Cities. Bristol, Johnstown,
City and Kingsport, Tenn.
Tri-Cities. Draper, Leaks-
ville and Spray, N.C.
Tri-Cities. Florence, Sheffield
and Tuscumbia, Ala.
Tri-Cities. Kennewick, Pasco
and Richland, Wash.
Tri-Cities. Moline and Rock
Island, Ill., and Davenport,
Iowa
Tri-County City that Is Friendly,
Progressive, Alive. Ender-
lin, N.D.
Tri-County Trading Center.
Aurora, Mo.
Tri-State Capital. Memphis,
Tenn.
Trimountain City. Boston,
Mass.
Triple Cities. Binghamton,
N.Y.
Triple Cities. Endicott, N.Y.
Triple Cities. Johnson City,
N.Y.
Tropic Metropolis. Miami, Fla.
Tropical Florida's First Resort.
West Palm Beach, Fla.
Tropical Island Wonderland in
the Gulf of Mexico. Fort
Myers Beach, Fla.
Tropical Wonderland. Fort
Lauderdale, Fla.

True Capital of the West.
San Francisco, Calif.
True Center of the Rich Red
River Valley. Grafton,
N.D.
Truly Charming New England
Town. Lyme, N.H.
Truly Colonial Town. Clinton,
Conn.
Truly Complete Community.
Peru, Ind.
Truly International City.
Brownsville, Tex.
Truly Izaak Walton's Head-
quarters. Pompano Beach,
Fla.
Truly Year 'Round Vacation
Land. Wells, N.Y.
Try San Diego First. San
Diego, Calif.
Tube City. McKeesport, Pa.
Tufted Textile Center of the
World. Dalton, Ga.
Tulip Capital. Holland, Mich.
Tulip Center of America.
Holland, Mich.
Tulip City. Bellingham, Wash.
Tulip City. Holland, Mich.
Tuna Capital of the World.
Galilee, R.I.
Tung Oil Center of America.
Picayune, Miss.
Tung Tree Capital of the
World. Picayune, Miss.
Tunnel City. Greensburg,
Pa.
Turkey and Dairy Processing
Center. Valley City, N.D.
Turkey Capital. Aitkin, Minn.
Turkey Capital of Arkansas.
Berryville, Ark.
Turkey Capital of Minnesota.
Worthington, Minn.
Turkey Capital of the East.
Harrisonburg, Va.
Turkey Capital of the Nation.
Harrisonburg, Va.
Turkey Capital of the Ozarks.
Berryville, Ark.
Turkey Capital of the World.
Cuero, Tex.
Turkey Capital of the World.
Worthington, Minn.

Turpentine Capital of the World.
Baxley, Ga.
Turtle Center of the World.
Longville, Minn.
Tusselburgh. Alton, Ill.
Twenty-Four Hour Gambling
City. Las Vegas, Nev.
Twenty-Thousand Acre Play-
ground. Del Monte Park,
Calif.
Twin Cities. Aberdeen, Wash.,
and Hoquiam, Wash.
Twin Cities. Alcoa, Tenn. and
Maryville, Tenn.
Twin Cities. Auburn, Me., and
Lewiston, Me.
Twin Cities. Bangor, Me., and
Brewer, Me.
Twin Cities. Benton Harbor,
Mich., and St. Joseph, Mich.
Twin Cities. Biddeford, Me.,
and Saco, Me.
Twin Cities. Bluefield, Va.,
and Bluefield, W. Va.
Twin Cities. Bluefield, W. Va.,
and Bluefield, Va.
Twin Cities. Brewer, Me., and
Bangor, Me.
Twin Cities. Bristol, Tenn.,
and Bristol, Va.
Twin Cities. Bristol, Va., and
Bristol, Tenn.
Twin Cities. Central Falls,
R.I., and Pawtucket, R.I.
Twin Cities. Champaign, Ill.,
and Urbana, Ill.
Twin Cities. Fairfield, Calif.,
and Suison City, Calif.
Twin Cities. Gardnerville,
Nev., and Minden, Nev.
Twin Cities. Helena, Ark.,
and West Helena, Ark.
Twin Cities. Hoquiam, Wash.,
and Aberdeen, Wash.
Twin Cities. Lafayette, Ind.,
and West Lafayette, Ind.
Twin Cities. Lewiston, Me.,
and Auburn, Me.
Twin Cities. Maryville,
Tenn., and Alcoa, Tenn.
Twin Cities. Menasha, Wis.,
and Neenah, Wis.

Twin Cities. Miami, Fla., and Miami Beach, Fla.

Twin Cities. Miami Beach, Fla., and Miami, Fla.

Twin Cities. Minden, Nev., and Gardnerville, Nev.

Twin Cities. Minneapolis, Minn., and St. Paul, Minn.

Twin Cities. Monroe, La., and West Monroe, La.

Twin Cities. Neenah, Wis., and Menasha, Wis.

Twin Cities. Pawtucket, R.I., and Central Falls, R.I.

Twin Cities. Saco, Me., and Biddeford, Me.

Twin Cities. St. Joseph, Mich., and Benton Harbor, Mich.

Twin Cities. St. Paul, Minn., and Minneapolis, Minn.

Twin Cities. Suison City, Calif., and Fairfield, Calif.

Twin Cities. Texarkana, Ark., and Texarkana, Tex.

Twin Cities. Texarkana, Tex., and Texarkana, Ark.

Twin Cities. Urbana, Ill., and Champaign, Ill.

Twin Cities. West Helena, Ark., and Helena, Ark.

Twin Cities. West Lafayette, Ind., and Lafayette, Ind.

Twin Cities. West Monroe, La., and Monroe, La.

Twin Cities. Winston-Salem, N.C.

Twin Cities by the Truckee. Reno, Nev., and Sparks, Nev.

Twin Cities by the Truckee. Sparks, Nev., and Reno, Nev.

Twin Cities of Opportunity at the Heart of the Niagara Frontier. North Tonawanda, N.Y., and Tonawanda, N.Y.

Twin Cities of Opportunity at the Heart of the Niagara Frontier. Tonawanda, N.Y., and North Tonawanda, N.Y.

Twin Cities of the Lower Sun-Coast. Bradenton, Fla., and Sarasota, Fla.

Twin Cities of the Lower Sun-Coast. Sarasota, Fla., and Bradenton, Fla.

Twin Cities of the Northern Black Hills of South Dakota. Deadwood, S.D., and Lead, S.D.

Twin Cities of the Northern Black Hills of South Dakota. Lead, S.D., and Deadwood, S.D.

Twin Cities of the Ouachita. Monroe, La., and West Monroe, La.

Twin Cities on the Bay. Niceville, Fla., and Valparaiso, Fla.

Twin Cities on the Bay. Valparaiso, Fla., and Niceville, Fla.

Twin Cities on the Red River in the Heart of Louisiana. Alexandria, La., and Pineville, La.

Twin City. Bloomington, Ill., and Normal, Ill.

Twin City. Haines, Alaska, and Port Chilkoot, Alaska

Twin City. Minneapolis and St. Paul, Minn.

Twin City. Normal, Ill., and Bloomington, Ill.

Twin City. Norwalk, Conn., and South Norwalk, Conn.

Twin City. Port Chilkoot, Alaska, with Haines, Alaska

Twin City. St. Paul and Minneapolis, Minn.

Twin City. South Norwalk, Conn., and Norwalk, Conn.

Twin City. Sun City, Ariz., and Youngstown, Ariz.

Twin City. Winston-Salem, N.C.

Twin City. Youngstown, Ariz., and Sun City, Ariz.

Twin Lakes Capital of the Ozarks. Forsyth, Mo.

Twin Ports. Duluth, Minn.,
and Superior, Wis.
Twin Ports. Superior, Wis.,
and Duluth, Minn.
Twin Towns. Damariscotta,
Me., and Newcastle, Me.
Twin Towns. Newcastle, Me.,
and Damariscotta, Me.
Twin Towns of the New
Hampshire Lakes Region.
Northfield, N. H.
Twin Towns of the New
Hampshire Lake Regions.
Tilton, N. H.
Twin Villages. Damariscotta
and Newcastle, Me.
Twin Villages. Newcastle
and Damariscotta, Me.
Twins. Minneapolis and St.
Paul, Minn.
Twins. St. Paul and Minne-
apolis.
Two Miles High But Miles
Ahead. Leadville, Colo.
Typewriter Capital of the
World. Cortland, N. Y.
Typical American City. Mid-
dletown, Ind.
Typical American City. Mun-
cie, Ind.
Typical American City.
Owatonna, Minn.
Typical New England City.
Norton, Mass.
Typical Ozark Home Town.
Gentry, Ark.
Typical Pacific Northwest
Logging Community. Mc-
Cleary, Wash.
Typical Puritan Town.
Montague, Mass.
Typical Resort City. Pensa-
cola, Fla.

U. S. Watermelon Capital.
Hope, Ark.
Ultimate City. Litchfield,
Conn.
Ultimate City. Los Angeles,
Calif.

Ultra Modern City. Palo Alto,
Calif.
Unconventional City. San
Diego, Calif.
Underwater Motion Picture
Capital of the World. Silver
Springs, Fla.
Unexcelled Water Sport Region.
Blackduck, Minn.
Unique and Distinctive Commu-
nity. Bethlehem, Pa.
Unique Year-Round Resort.
Vail, Colo.
United Nations' Conference
Center. San Francisco,
Calif.
University Center. Pittsburgh,
Pa.
University City. Cambridge,
Mass.
University City. Gainesville,
Fla.
University City. Vermillion,
S. D.
University of Light. Cleveland,
Ohio
University of Telephony. New
York, N. Y.
"Unplanned" Planned Community.
Guerneville, Calif.
Unsainted Anthony. San An-
tonio, Tex.
Unspoiled Beauty Spot of North-
ern Maine. Patten, Me.
Up and Coming Town. Sanford,
Me.
Upper Sandusky West. Los
Angeles, Calif.
Upstate Greenwich Village.
Woodstock, N. Y.
Up-to-Date Farming Center.
Greenville, Ill.
Up-to-Date Oldest Town in
Louisiana. Natchitoches, La.
Uranium Capital of the World.
Grand Junction, Colo.
Uranium Capital of the World.
Grants, N. M.
Uranium Capital of the World.
Moab, Utah
Uranium Center of South Dakota.
Edgemont, S. D.

Utah Zion. Salt Lake City,
Utah
Utica Makes It Happen.
Utica, N.Y.
Utopia of the North Atlantic.
New London, Conn.

Vacation and Health Resort.
Waynesville, N.C.
Vacation Area. Glenwood,
Minn.
Vacation Capital of Ocean
County. Seaside Heights,
N.J.
Vacation Capital of the Appa-
lachian Highlands. Elkins,
W. Va.
Vacation Capital of the Nation.
Atlantic City, N.J.
Vacation Center. Ports-
mouth, R.I.
Vacation Center. Watkins
Glen, N.Y.
Vacation Center of a Fabu-
lous Land of Contrasts.
Grand Junction, Colo.
Vacation Center of Beautiful
Lake Winnipesaukee.
Weirs Beach, N.H.
Vacation City. Cleveland,
Ohio
Vacation City. New York,
N.Y.
Vacation City. St. Louis,
Mo.
Vacation City on Casco Bay.
Portland, Me.
Vacation City Supreme. At-
lantic City, N.J.
Vacation Crossroads of New
England. Weirs Beach,
N.H.
Vacation for a Lifetime.
Lakeland, Fla.
Vacation for Every Budget.
Bolton Landing, N.Y.
Vacation Fun Spot of Western
Maine. Bridgton, Me.
Vacation Headquarters.
Blue Rapids, Kan.

Vacation Headquarters. Neosho,
Mo.
Vacation Land. Chula Vista,
Calif.
Vacation Land. Wadena, Minn.
Vacation Land in the Center of
the Berkshires. Pittsfield,
Mass.
Vacation or Year Round Home
City. Scituate, Mass.
Vacation Paradise. San Diego,
Calif.
Vacation Paradise for the Whole
Family. Islamorada, Fla.
Vacation Paradise of the Texas
Hill Country. Kerrville,
Tex.
Vacation Region of Minnesota.
Park Rapids, Minn.
Vacation Spot from June Through
October. Belgrade, Me.
Vacation Spot in Northern Maine.
Millinocket, Me.
Vacation Wonderland. Morris-
town, Tenn.
Vacation Wonderland. Park
Falls, Wis.
Vacationer's Dreamland. Bonita
Springs, Fla.
Vacationer's Paradise. Shelter
Island, N.Y.
Vacationer's Paradise. Walker,
Minn.
Vacationist's Paradise. Virginia
Beach, Va.
Vacationland for the Whole
Family. Fort Pierce, Fla.
Vacationland of a Thousand
Pleasures. Miami Beach,
Fla.
Vacationland of Northern Wis-
consin. Park Falls, Wis.
Vacationland of the Sky. Hiwas-
see Dam, N.C.
Vacationland of Unlimited En-
joyment. Speculator, N.Y.
Vacationland, U.S.A. Eastham,
Mass.
Vacationland, U.S.A. Miami
Beach, Fla.
Vacationland, U.S.A. Nor-
folk, Va.

Vacationland, U.S.A. San Diego, Calif.

Vacationland Unlimited. Medford, Ore.

Vacationland with Complete Facilities. Michigan City, Ind.

Vacationland without Equal. Treasure Island, Fla.

Vale of Beauty. Valdosta, Ga.

Valentine Has Everything. Valentine, Neb.

Valley in the Sun. Phoenix, Ariz.

Valley of the Condominiums. Vail, Colo.

Valley of the Gardens. Santa Maria, Calif.

Valley of Vapors. Hot Springs, Ark.

Valley's College Town. Tempe, Ariz.

Vanguard of a New Era of Cities. Atlanta, Ga.

Vapor City. Hot Springs, Ark.

Variety of Recreational Opportunities. Stockton, Calif.

Variety Vacation Land. Cape Carteret, N.C.

Vatican City. St. Louis, Mo.

Vegetable Bowl. Zellwood, Fla.

Vehicle City. Flint, Mich.

Venice of America. Annapolis, Md.

Venice of America. Fort Lauderdale, Fla.

Venice of America. Houma, La.

Venice of America. Stone Harbor, N.J.

Venice of America. Syracuse, N.Y.

Venice of America. Wickford, R.I.

Venice of Puget Sound. La Conner, Wash.

Venice of the New Jersey Shore. Shore Acres, N.J.

Venice of the Northwest. Willapa, Wash.

Venice of the Pacific. Union, Wash.

Venice of the Prairie. San Antonio, Tex.

Venice of the South. Tarpon Springs, Fla.

Vermont's Largest City. Burlington, Vt.

Vermont's Most Historic Town. Bennington, Vt.

Vermont's Recreation Crossroads. Waterbury, Vt.

Vermont's Second Largest City. Rutland, Vt.

Versatile City. Rome, Ga.

Versatile City. Weatherford, Tex.

Very Center of the Sunshine State. Lake Weir, Fla.

Very Heart of Florida. Orlando, Fla.

Very Heart of the Sunshine State. Orlando, Fla.

Vetch Capital of the World. Cooper, Tex.

Vibrant and Virile American City. Bethlehem, Pa.

Village Beautiful. Kinderhook, N.Y.

Village Beautiful. Williamstown, Mass.

Village Nestled in the Storied Berkshire Hills. Stockbridge, Mass.

Village Not for Tourists, Not for Excitement But for Modest Tranquil Healthful Living. Lake Mary, Fla.

Village Ideal for Retirement for Raising a Family and for Placid Everyday Living. Lake Mary, Fla.

Village of Breath-Taking Beauty and Enchantment. North Pole, N.Y.

Village of City Charm. Manchester, Conn.

Village of Destiny. Gilbert, Minn.

Village of Enchantment. North Pole, N.Y.

Village of Friendly Folk. Plainfield, Ind.

Village of Great Museums. Cooperstown, N.Y.

Village of Lovely Homes and Friendly People. Montgomery, Ohio
Village of Museums. Cooperstown, N.Y.
Village of Skis. North Conway, N.H.
Village of the Plains. Auburn, Ala.
Village Right in the Middle of Things on Beautiful Chautauqua Lake. Bemus Point, N.Y.
Village that Has Everything. Mattituck, N.Y.
Village where Nature Smiles. Cooperstown, N.Y.
Village where the Pines Meet the Sea. Cambria Village, Calif.
Village with a Past, the City with a Future. Kenai, Alaska
Violet Town. Rhinebeck, N.Y.
Virgin Capital. Washington, D.C.
Virginia's Atlantic City. Virginia Beach, Va.
Virginia's Biggest Little City. Harrisonburg, Va.
Virginia Colony's Elegant Old Capital. Williamsburg, Va.
Virginia's Dogwood Capital. Vinton, Va.
Virginia's Fast Growing Industrial Community. Suffolk, Va.
Virginia's Fastest Growing Industrial Community. Nansemond, Va.
Virginia's Inland Port. Hopewell, Va.
Virginia's Largest Market for Bright Leaf Tobacco. Danville, Va.
Virginia's Mountain Capital. Roanoke, Va.
Virginia's Seaside Playground. Buckroe Beach, Va.
Virginia's Vacation Paradise on Beautiful Buggs Island Lake. Clarksville, Va.

Visually Exciting City. Seattle, Wash.
Vital City. Pico Rivera, Calif.
Vivid Capital of the Old South. Jackson, Miss.

Wagon Capital of the World. Abingdon, Ill.
Walking Horse Capital of the World. Shelbyville, Tenn.
Wall Street of the South. Nashville, Tenn.
Walleye Capital of the World. Fairmont, Minn.
Walleye Capital of the World. Mille Lacs, Minn.
Walnut City. McMinnville, Ore.
Washington, B.C.--Before Corn. Washington, D.C.
Washington-by-the-Sea. Rehoboth Beach, Del.
Water Capital of the Southwest. Tulsa, Okla.
Water City. Madison, S.D.
Water Polo Capital of Florida. Boca Raton, Fla.
Water-Power City. Rochester, N.Y.
Water Sports Paradise. Walker, Minn.
Water Wonderland. Orange, Tex.
Watercress Capital of the World. Huntsville, Ala.
Waterfalls. Tumwater, Wash.
Waterfront Wonderland. Cape Coral, Fla.
Watering Pot of America. Utica, N.Y.
Waterloo of the Revolution. Yorktown, Va.
Watermelon Capital. Chiefland, Fla.
Watermelon Capital. Immokalee, Fla.
Watermelon Capital of Florida. Immokalee, Fla.
Watermelon Capital of Florida. Leesburg, Fla.
Watermelon Capital of the U.S. Hope, Ark.

Watermelon Capital of the
World. Cordele, Ga.
Watermelon Capital of the
World. Weatherford, Tex.
Watermelon Center. Mineola,
Tex.
Watermelon Center Festival.
Chiefland, Fla.
Watermelon City. Hope, Ark.
Watermelon Town. Jourdan-
ton, Tex.
Waterstown. Pataha, Wash.
We Oil the World. Port
Arthur, Tex.
Weedless City. Kane, Pa.
Welcome Station City. Syl-
vania, Ga.
Welcome to the City of Lakes.
Lakeland, Fla.
Well Balanced City with Op-
portunities for All. Nor-
walk, Conn.
Well-Balanced Community.
Greenfield, Mass.
Well-Balanced Community.
Lockport, N.Y.
Well-Balanced Metropolis.
Atlanta, Ga.
Well Groomed City. Hutchin-
son, Kan.
Well Mannered City. Hutchin-
son, Kan.
Well-Planned Balanced Com-
munity. Covina, Calif.
Well Rounded Community. El
Dorado, Ark.
West at Its Best. Oakdale,
Calif.
West Coast Gateway City.
Palmetto, Fla.
West Gate to the Land-O-
Lakes. Butler, Mo.
West Point of the South.
Fort Benning, Ga.
West Side of Fresno County.
Kerman, Calif.
West Texas Industrial City.
Sweetwater, Tex.
Western Capital. Denver,
Colo.
Western City of Ships. Oak-
land, Calif.
Western Entrance to Glacier

National Park. West Glacier,
Mont.
Western Entrance to Scenic
Canyons. Carlin, Nev.
Western Gate. San Francisco,
Calif.
Western Gate to Mexico. Tuc-
son, Ariz.
Western Gateway City. Mari-
posa, Calif.
Western Gateway to Stevens
Pass. Sultan, Wash.
Western Gateway to the Chain
O'Lakes. McHenry, Ill.
Western Gateway to the Nation's
Capital. Bethesda, Md.
Western Gateway to the Skyline
Drive. New Market, Va.
Western Mecca for Enjoyment
Unlimited. Boise, Idaho
Western Metropolis. Chicago,
Ill.
Western Oregon's Leading In-
dustrial and Marketing
Center. Eugene, Ore.
Western Shangri-La. Upland,
Calif.
Western Terminus of U.S. High-
way No. 2. Everett, Wash.
Western Water Gate. Ever-
glades, Fla.
Western Water Gateway. Ever-
glades, Fla.
Westernmost Port on America's
Fourth Seacoast. Duluth,
Minn.
Westernmost Suburb of Des
Moines. Los Angeles, Calif.
West's Fastest-Growing Trans-
portation and Industrial
Center. Ogden, Utah
West's Largest Ghost Town.
Jerome, Ariz.
West's Most Western Commu-
nity. Scottsdale, Ariz.
West's Most Western Town.
Scottsdale, Ariz.
Whaling Capital of the World.
New Bedford, Mass.
Whaling City. New Bedford,
Mass.
Whaling City. New London,
Conn.

What the West Is All About.
Tucson, Ariz.
What We Make Makes Us.
Gastonia, N. C.
Wheat Capital. Onida, S. D.
Wheat Capital of America.
Colfax, Wash.
Wheat Capital of the World.
Wellington, Kan.
Wheat Heart of the Nation.
Perryton, Tex.
When You See San Antonio,
You See Texas. San
Antonio, Tex.
Whip City. Westfield, Mass.
Whiskey Town. Peoria, Ill.
White City. Chicago, Ill.
White Collar City. Denver,
Colo.
White Leghorn City of the
West. Petaluma, Calif.
White Marlin Capital of the
World. Ocean City, Md.
White Pine Producing Center
of the World. Marinette,
Wis.
White Rose City. York, Pa.
White Stallion. Touchet,
Wash.
Whole New World with Every
Sunrise. Virginia Beach,
Va.
Wickedest City in America.
Phenix City, Ala.
Wickedest Little City in
America. Dodge City,
Kan.
Widest Street in the World.
Greenwood, S. C.
Wilderness Capital of Lincoln's
Land. Vandalia, Ill.
Wilderness City. Washington,
D. C.
Wilderness Town. Bedford,
Mass.
Wildlife Refuge Center.
Lawton, Okla.
Wildwood Crest for Pleasure
and Rest. Wildwood
Crest, N. J.
Williamsburg of Texas.
Jefferson, Tex.
Williamsburg of the Mid West.
Washington, Mo.

Williamsburg of the North.
Bennington, Vt.
Williamsburg of the North.
Litchfield, Conn.
Williamsburg of the Sea.
Mystic, Conn.
Window to the Future. Water-
ford, Calif.
Windy City. Chicago, Ill.
Wine and Olive Colony. Demopo-
lis, Ala.
Winter and Summer Playground.
Steamboat Springs, Colo.
Winter and Summer Vacation
Center of Florida. Eustis,
Fla.
Winter Capital of America.
New Orleans, La.
Winter Fishing Capital. Glen-
wood, Minn.
Winter Golf Capital of the World.
Palm Springs, Calif.
Winter Golf Capital of America.
Atlanta, Ga.
Winter Golf Capital of America.
Pinehurst, N. C.
Winter Golf Capital of the World.
Augusta, Ga.
Winter Golf Capital of the World.
Palm Springs, Calif.
Winter Golf Mecca. Palm
Desert, Calif.
Winter Home of the National
League Philadelphia "Phillies."
Clearwater, Fla.
Winter Paradise. Laguna Beach,
Calif.
Winter Playground. Great Bar-
rington, Mass.
Winter Playground of America.
San Antonio, Tex.
Winter Sports Capital of the
Nation. St. Paul, Minn.
Winter Sports City. Kane, Pa.
Winter Strawberry Capital of
the World. Plant City, Fla.
Winter Vegetable Capital of
the U. S. Pahokee, Fla.
Winter Wonderland. Park
Rapids, Minn.
Wisconsin's Beautiful Capitol
City. Milwaukee, Wis.
Wisconsin's Second City. Ra-
cine, Wis.

Witch City. Salem, Mass.
Witchcraft City. Salem, Mass.
Wizard's Clip. Middleway,
W. Va.
Wonder City. Decatur, Ala.
Wonder City. Hopewell, Va.
Wonder City. New York, N.Y.
Wonder City in the Middle of
the Land of Lakes. El
Dorado Springs, Mo.
Wonder City of America.
Buffalo, N.Y.
Wonder City of the World.
Miami, Fla.
Wonder City of the World.
New York, N.Y.
Wonder Convention City.
Scranton, Pa.
Wonderful Community.
Apache Junction, Ariz.
Wonderful Place of Recrea-
tional Enjoyment. Tucum-
cari, N.M.
Wonderful Place to Live.
Augusta, Ga.
Wonderful Place to Live.
Mitchell, S.D.
Wonderful Place to Live.
Sebring, Fla.
Wonderful Place to Live.
Tyler, Tex.
Wonderful Place to Live and
Work. Garland, Tex.
Wonderful Place to Live and
Work. Richardson, Tex.
Wonderful Place to Live, to
Work, and Play. Port-
land, Me.
Wonderful Place to Live, to
Work, to Play. Augusta,
Ga.
Wonderful Place to Live,
Work, Play. New Britain,
Conn.
Wonderful Place to Live, Work,
Play. Stratford, Conn.
Wonderful Place to Play.
Provo, Utah
Wonderful Place to Rear Your
Family Beneath Wide-Open
Missouri Skies. Stock-
ton, Mo.
Wonderful Place to Visit and

A Better Place to Live.
Waynesboro, Va.
Wonderful Town. Chicago, Ill.
Wonderful Town. New York,
N.Y.
Wonderful Weather Land.
Tucson, Ariz.
Wonderland City in the North
Woods. Park Falls, Wis.
Wonderland of America.
Boulder, Colo.
Wonderland of Lakes. Bridg-
ton, Me.
Wonderland of the Ten Thousand
Islands. Everglades, Fla.
Wonderland of the 10,000 Is-
lands and Southern Collier
County. Everglades, Fla.
Wonderland on the Potomac.
Washington, D.C.
Woods. Boise, Idaho
Woods. Middletown, R.I.
Wool City. Eaton Rapids,
Mich.
Wool City. Waterville, Me.
Woolworth Town. Watertown,
N.Y.
Work Clothing Center of the
World. Winder, Ga.
Working City. Lewiston, Me.
Workshop of the World.
Pittsburgh, Pa.
World Capital of Fashion.
New York, N.Y.
World Capital of Stereograph
Production. Littleton, N.H.
World Capital of Learning to
Ski. Killington, Vt.
World Capital of the Orange-
growing Industry. Eustis,
Fla.
World Center of International
Activities. Washington, D.C.
World Center of Oceanology.
Long Beach, Calif.
World Famous Bath and Scien-
tific Massage Center.
Mineral Wells, Tex.
World Famous Manufacturing
Center. Dayton, Ohio
World Famous Resort and Con-
vention Center. Las Vegas,
Nev.

World-Famous Zoo City. San
Diego, Calif.

World Gliding Center. Bishop,
Calif.

World-Known Processing
Center for Corn and Soy-
beans. Decatur, Ill.

World of Variety. Los
Angeles, Calif.

World of Warmth. Vail, Colo.

World Port. Seattle, Wash.

World Renowned Strip. Las
Vegas, Nev.

World's Best Beach. Cocoa
Beach, Fla.

World's Best Little Town.
Bedford, Pa.

World's Best Tobacco Market.
Danville, Va.

World's Busiest Airport City.
Chicago, Ill.

World's Capital City. New
York, N.Y.

World's Celery Center.
Sanford, Fla.

World's Central Livestock
Market. Sioux City, Iowa

World's Championship Duck
Calling City. Stuttgart,
Ark.

World's Citrus Center. Lakeland, Fla.

World's Egg Basket. Petaluma,
Calif.

World's Fair City. Chicago,
Ill.

World's Fair City. New York,
N.Y.

World's Financial Capital.
New York N.Y.

World's Finest and Safest
Bathing Beach. Wildwood,
N.J.

World's Finest Beach. Jacksonville Beach, Fla.

World's Finest Natural White
Sand Beaches. Longboat
Key, Fla.

World's Finest Vacationland.
San Diego, Calif.

World's First Rodeo. Pecos, Tex.

World's Great City. Atlanta,
Ga.

World's Greatest Halibut Port.
Seattle, Wash.

World's Greatest Harbor.
Hampton Roads, Va.

World's Greatest Harbor. Newport News, Va.

World's Greatest Mining Camp.
Butte, Mont.

World's Greatest Mule Market.
Galesburg, Ill.

World's Greatest Resort.
Miami Beach, Fla.

World's Greatest Storehouse of
Raw Material. Fort Worth,
Tex.

World's Greatest Workshop.
Philadelphia, Pa.

World's Heart Transplant Capital. Houston, Tex.

World's Largest Anthracite Coal
Mining City. Scranton, Pa.

World's Largest Art Pottery
City. Macomb, Ill.

World's Largest Black Walnut
Factory. Gravette, Ark.

World's Largest Cardinal Gardens. Griggsville, Ill.

World's Largest Coal Shipper.
Toledo, Ohio

World's Largest Coal-Shipping
Port. Toledo, Ohio

World's Largest Fresh Water
Port. Philadelphia, Pa.

World's Largest Family Resort.
Daytona Beach, Fla.

World's Largest Gambling
Center. Las Vegas, Nev.

World's Largest Hardwood
Lumber Market. Memphis,
Tenn.

World's Largest Import Export
Air Cargo Terminal. Miami,
Fla.

World's Largest Lilac Center.
Rochester, N.Y.

World's Largest Livestock and
Meat Packing Center.
Omaha, Neb.

World's Largest Loose-Leaf
Tobacco Market. Lexington,
Ky.

World's Largest Lumber Shipping
Port. Coos Bay, Ore.

World's Largest Mineral Hot Springs. Thermopolis, Wyo.

World's Largest Mobile Home Manufacturing Center. Elkhart, Ind.

World's Largest Peanut Center. Suffolk, Va.

World's Largest Peanut Market. Nansemond, Va.

World's Largest Railroad Center. Chicago, Ill.

World's Largest Rattlesnake Roundup City. Sweetwater, Tex.

World's Largest Safest Bathing Beach. New Smyrna, Fla.

World's Largest Salmon Hatchery Site. Leavenworth, Wash.

World's Largest Seed and Nursery Center. Shenandoah, Iowa

World's Largest Shallow Oil Field. Nowata, Okla.

World's Largest Spanish Peanut Market. Dawson, Ga.

World's Largest Spot Cotton Market. Memphis, Tenn.

World's Largest Specialty Jewelry Manufacturing Center. Plainville, Mass.

World's Liveliest Ghost Town. Virginia City, Nev.

World's Luckiest Fishing Village. Destin, Fla.

World's Metropolis. New York, N.Y.

World's Most Beautiful City. Washington, D.C.

World's Most Beautiful Waters and the Whitest Sand Beaches. Destin, Fla.

World's Most Exciting All Year Round Vacation Center. New York, N.Y.

World's Most Famous Beach. Daytona Beach, Fla.

World's Most Famous Playground. Santa Cruz, Calif.

World's Most Richly Endowed Resort Area. Fort Lauderdale, Fla.

World's Next Great City. Atlanta, Ga.

World's Oyster Capital. Norwalk, Conn.

World's Petroleum Capital. Houston, Tex.

World's Playground. Atlantic City, N.J.

World's Premier Winter Resort. Palm Beach, Fla.

World's Railroad Capital. Chicago, Ill.

World's Railroad Mecca. Chicago, Ill.

World's Saddle Horse Capital. Mexico, Mo.

World's Safest Bathing Beach. Edgewater, Fla.

World's Salmon Capital. Ketchikan, Alaska

World's Sandstone Center. Amherst, Ohio

World's Spinach Capital. Crystal City, Tex.

World's Submarine Capital. Groton, Conn.

World's Turkey Capital. Harrisonburg, Va.

World's Winter Golf Capital. Palm Springs, Calif.

World's Workshop. Pittsburgh, Pa.

Worsted Mill Capital of the World. Lawrence, Mass.

Wurst City of the World. Sheboygan, Wis.

Wyoming's Big Little Town. Glendo, Wyo.

Wyoming's Most Progressive City. Casper, Wyo.

Wyoming's Year 'Round Health and Scenic Center. Thermopolis, Wyo.

X-Ray City. Covington, Ky.

Xanadu by the Sea. Newport, R.I.

"Y" Bridge City. Zanesville, Ohio

Yachting Capital of New
England. Boothbay Harbor,
Me.
Yachting Capital of the
World. Marblehead, Mass.
Yachting Capital of the
World. Newport, R.I.
Yachting Center of the World.
Marblehead, Mass.
Yankee Athens. New Haven,
Conn.
Yankee City. Newburyport,
Mass.
Ye Friendly Towne. Whit-
tier, Calif.
Year Around Living at Its
Best. Lake Weir, Fla.
Year Around Playground.
Rutland, Vt.
Year Around Vacationland.
Lake Luzerne, N.Y.
Year-Round Attraction City.
Chattanooga, Tenn.
Year-Round Beachfront
Condominium Resort.
Panama City, Fla.
Year Round Center for
Major Spectator Events.
Las Vegas, Nev.
Year-Round Convention and
Meeting Center. Jekyll
Island, Ga.
Year-Round Convention and
Resort Metropolis of the
Pacific. Long Beach,
Calif.
Year-Round Convention City.
Los Angeles, Calif.
Year-Round Family Beach
Resort. Jekyll Island,
Ga.
Year Round Golf Capital of
the World. Monterey,
Calif.
Year-Round Health and Rec-
reational Resort. Kane,
Pa.
Year-Round Paradise for
Sportsmen. Dinuba,
Calif.
Year Round Playground.
Duluth, Minn.
Year-Round Playground.
Kerrville, Tex.

Year Round Playground of the
Americas. Miami Beach,
Fla.
Year Round Playground of the
Pacific. Long Beach, Calif.
Year-Round Resort. Rangeley,
Maine
Year 'Round Resort and Con-
vention Center. Biloxi,
Miss.
Year-Round Resort Capital of
New England--where the Fun
Stays After the Snow Is Gone.
Stowe, Vt.
Year Round Sportsman's Para-
dise. Okeechobee, Fla.
Year-Round Sportsman's Para-
dise. Philipsburg, Mont.
Year Round Vacation Playland.
Atlantic City, N.J.
Year Round Vacation Town in
the White Mountains. North
Conway, N.H.
Year Round Vacationland.
Burlington, Vt.
Year 'Round Vacationland. Old
Forge, N.Y.
Yosemite of Arizona. Portal,
Ariz.
Yosemite of Texas. Junction,
Tex.
Yosemite of the East. Ausable
Chasm, N.Y.
You'll Like Living in Houlton.
Houlton, Me.
Young Capital. Washington,
D.C.
Young City Going Places.
Amarillo, Tex.
Young Man's Capital of the
World. Tulsa, Okla.
Young Town with a Progres-
sive Attitude. Altavista, Va.
Youngest Big City in the United
States. Phoenix, Ariz.
Youngest of the World's Great
Cities. Birmingham, Ala.
Your Cool Mountain Vacation-
land. Hendersonville, N.C.
Your Home Away from Home.
Winter Park, Fla.
Your One-Stop Sports Paradise.
Valentine, Neb.

Your Place in the Sun.
 Millbrae, Calif.
Your Site in the Sun. Santa
 Maria, Calif.
Your Tropical "Home Town."
 Englewood, Fla.
Your Vacation Center. Wat-
 kins Glen, N.Y.
Youthful Community. Pitts-
 field, Mass.

Zenith City. Duluth, Minn.
Zenith City of the Unsalted
 Seas. Duluth, Minn.
Zion. Salt Lake City,
 Mo.
Zone of Ozone. Beaumont,
 Calif.

COUNTY INDEX

by state; showing nicknames
for each county

ALABAMA

DEKALB
Alabama's Natural Wonderland
The Land of Natural Beauty
The Land of Natural Wonders

GREENE
The Focus of the Nation

ARIZONA

APACHE
The Land of Pine and Painted
Desert

COCHISE
Arizona's Wonderland of
Rocks

COCONINO
Arizona's Land of Superla-
tives
The County in Which There
Is Room to Have Fun In,
Room to Live In
The Scenic Empire

GILA
The Land of the Famed
Apaches

GRAHAM
The Land of the Storied Gila

GREENLEE
The Place Where Coronado
Walked

MARICOPA
Arizona's Valley of the Sun

MOHAVE
The Land of Blue Lakes

NAVAJO
The Land of Sand and Slick
Rock

PIMA
The County in the Heart of
the Sun Country

PINAL
The County in the Shadow of
The Superstitious

SANTA CRUZ
America's Gateway to Sonora,
Mexico

YAVAPAI
The County Where the His-
toric Verde Flows

YUMA
The County Where the Sun
Is King

371

ARKANSAS

NEVADA
The Pine Tree County

CALIFORNIA

ALPINE
The Sportsmen's Paradise

AMADOR
The County in the Heart of
the Mother Lode
The Cradle of California
The Heart of the Mother Lode

CALAVERAS
The Jumping Frog and Big
Tree County

CONTRA COSTA
The Largest Industrial County
in California

EL DORADO
The County in the Fabulous
Mother Lode of California
The Gold Discovery County

FRESNO
The Agricultural and Recrea-
tional Center of California
The Agricultural and Scientific
Hub of the Golden State
The Richest Agricultural
County in the World

GLENN
The Eden of Plenty
The Land of Fun

HUMBOLDT
California's Redwood Wonder-
land
The Heart of the Redwood
Region

INYO
The Photographers Playground

The Picture County
The Vacation and Recreation
Land

KERN
California's Golden Empire
The Land of Magic

LAKE
The Year 'round Fun County

MARIN
The Pleasure Boating Center
of the Bay Area

MARIPOSA
The Southern Gateway to the
Mother Lode

MONO
The Fisherman's Paradise

MONTEREY
The Premier Co. of California

PLACER
The Continent within a County
The Northern Gateway to the
Mother Lode

PLUMAS
California's Feather River Co.

RIVERSIDE
The County Serving the West's
Largest Market
The Key County of Southern
California
The Key to America's Largest
Market

SAN BENITO
The County with California's
Finest Year 'round Climate

SAN LUIS OBISPO
California's Newest Vacation-
land
The County Nature Preserved

SISKIYOU
California's Uncrowded
Sportsland

SONOMA
 The County of Agriculture,
 Industry and Recreation

STANISLAUS
 The Gateway County of the
 Great Joaquin Valley

TULARE
 The County in the Garden
 of the Sun
 The Place to Work and Relax

TUOLUMNE
 The Home of Columbia
 "Gem" of the Southern
 Mines

YOLO
 California's Reserve Fuel Bin

COLORADO

WELD
 The Land of Milk, Honey,
 Spuds and Sugar
 The Largest County in the
 U.S.A.

CONNECTICUT

FAIRFIELD
 The Bedroom Community for
 Manhattan Executives
 The Research County

MIDDLESEX
 The Maritime County

DELAWARE

SUSSEX
 Delaware's Walking Giant

FLORIDA

BRADFORD
 The Berry Capital of the
 World
 The County of Planned
 Progress
 Florida's "Four Season"
 County
 Florida's Winter Strawberry
 Market
 The Heart of Florida's Crown

BREVARD
 The Fastest Growing County
 in the Nation

BROWARD
 The County where It's Always
 Sun and Fun Time

CALHOUN
 The Land of Opportunity
 The Paradise for All

CHARLOTTE
 The County where Your Vaca-
 tion Land Suddenly Becomes
 Your New Home

CITRUS
 The All-In-One Vacationland
 The County with Rural Charm
 and Modern Living

CLAY
 The Invitation to Unlimited
 Potential

COLLIER
 Florida's Fifth Fastest Growing County

CUMBERLAND
 The County where Your Vacation Land Suddenly Be-
 comes Your New Home

ESSEX
 The Heart of Heritage Land,
 U.S.A.

GILCHRIST
The County Way Down Upon
the Suwannee River
Florida's Land of Oppor-
tunity
The No-Better-Place-to-
Live County
The No-Better-Place-to-
Hunt County
The Sportsman's Paradise

HAMILTON
The Florida Crown

HENDRY
America's Winter Market
Basket

HOLMES
The Hub of the Florida
Panhandle

JACKSON
North Florida's Greatest
Agricultural County

JEFFERSON
The County of Charm,
Culture, Tradition
The Crossroads of Florida

LAKE
America's Finest County
The County where the
Latchkey Is Always Out
The Natural Advantages
for Health and Recrea-
tion County

MANATEE
The Keystone of the Florida
Suncoast

MARION
The Kingdom of the Sun
Marion County Is Horse
Country

MARTIN
Martin County Has More

ORANGE
The County for Your Outdoor

Recreation and Relaxa-
tion
The Hunter's Paradise

PALM BEACH
It's Easy to Swing in Palm
Beach County
The Swing Is to Palm Beach
County for Fun

PINELLAS
Florida's Fastest Growing
Major County
The County Near the Blue
Waters of the Gulf of
Mexico

POLK
The County of Progress and
Opportunity
The Heartland of Florida
The Land of Flowers

PUTNAM
The Bass Capital of the
World

SARASOTA
The County where You Work
and Play the Very Same
Day
Florida's Distinctive Resort
Area
Sarasota County Has Every-
thing

SEMINOLE
The County that Offers a
New Adventure in Living
The Gateway to Nova
The Paradise Living for All
the Family
The Retirement Haven
The Retirement Haven, The
Retirement Heaven

SOUTH BREVARD
The Southern Entry to the
Cape Kennedy Area

SUMTER
The County where Business Is
a Pleasure and Pleasure

Is a Business
The Growing County in a
Growing State
The Place to Locate

SUWANNEE
The County in the Heart of
the Famous Suwannee
River Valley
The Home of the Florida
Sheriff's Boys Ranch
(home for boys)
Florida's Largest Tobacco
Growing Center

GEORGIA

BULLOCH
The County where Nature
Smiles and Progress Has
the Right-of-Way

COFFEE
The Heart of the South
Georgia Empire

IDAHO

ADA
The Center of Idaho's
Industry, Agriculture,
Mining, Government and
Playgrounds

BONNER
Idaho's Year 'Round Rec-
reational Wonderland

ILLINOIS

JOHNSON
The Land of George Rogers Clark

PIKE
The County Beautiful by
Nature
The County Progressive by
Choice
The County Steeped in History

SHELBY
The Heart of Illinois

INDIANA

BROWN
The County in the Hills of
Scenic Southern Indiana

KOSCIUSKO
Indiana's Favorite Vacation-
land
Indiana's Popular Lake Area

PARKE
The Covered Bridge Capital
of the World
The Covered Bridge County
of the United States of
America

SPENCER
The Scenic County

IOWA

WINNESHIEK
The Scenic Wonderland of
Iowa

KANSAS

SUMNER
The Wheat Capital of the
World

LOUISIANA (Parishes)

EAST BATON ROUGE
    The Capital Parish of the
      State Named for Louis
      and Anna
    The Prime Industrial Center

JEFFERSON
    The Industrial Giant of
      Louisiana

MADISON
    The Queen of the Delta

ST. TAMMANY
    The Ozone Belt
    The World Famous Ozone
      Belt

TENSAS
    The Cotton Bowl of the
      South

TERREBONNE
    The Gulf Coast Land of
      Terrebonne

MAINE

ANDROSCOGGIN
    The Industrial Heart of
      Maine
    The Potato Empire of the
      World

AROOSTOOK
    The Potato Empire
    The Potato Empire of the
      Nation
    The Potato Empire of the
      World
    The Second Richest Agri-
      cultural County in the
      United States

CUMBERLAND
    The Gateway to Vacationland
    The Scenic Wonderland

KENNEBEC
    The County of Vacations
    The Heart of the Nation's
      Vacationland
    The Heart of Vacationland

KNOX
    Maine's Maritime Scenic
      Wonderland

OXFORD
    The Toothpick Center of the
      World

PISCATAQUIS
    The County of Lakes
      (252,872 acres of water)

SOMERSET
    The Four Season County

WASHINGTON
    The Sunrise County of the
      U.S.A.

YORK
    Maine in a Nutshell
    The Show Window of Maine
    The Southern Gateway to
      Maine

MARYLAND

DORCHESTER
    God's Country
    The Sportsman's Paradise

GARRETT
    Western Maryland's Top
      Playground
    Western Maryland's Mountain
      Top Playground

KENT
  Maryland's Goose Capital
  Maryland's Goose Hunting
    Capital

MONTGOMERY
  The Historic County
  The Science Center, U.S.A.

ST. MARY'S
  The County where the
    Fishing Is Always Good

MASSACHUSETTS

BRISTOL
  The Bargain Hunter's
    Paradise
  The Gateway to Cape Cod
  There's Fun for the Whole
    Family in Delightful
    Colorful Bristol County

ESSEX
  The County of Presidents
  The County where Hawthorne
    and Whittier Were
    Turned On
  The County where the Focus
    Is on Fun
  The Focus on Fun and
    History
  The Heart of Heritage Land,
    U.S.A.
  The Heart of New England
  The Heartland of History
  The Jewel of New England

NORFOLK
  The County of Presidents
    (John Adams, John
    Quincy Adams and John
    Fitzgerald Kennedy
    born here)

MIDDLESEX
  The County where It All
    Began

PLYMOUTH
  The County where There Is
    Fun for the Entire Family
  The Vacationland with Liva-
    bility
  The Vacationland with Lova-
    bility

MICHIGAN

BARRY
  The Only Northern Peninsula
    County in Southern Michi-
    gan

GLADWIN
  The Year Around Vacation-
    land

KEWEENAW
  The Copper Country

MARQUETTE
  The Rockhound's Paradise

OTSEGO
  The Great Place to Live,
    Work, Play, Retire

ROSCOMMON
  The Summer Pleasure
    County

MINNESOTA

AITKIN
  Family Fun for All Seasons

BECKER
  The Sunfish Capital of the
    World

ST. LOUIS
  America's Finest Fishing
    Country

Minnesota's Arrowhead
Country
The Fisherman's Paradise
The Fishing Area in Our
Country
The Largest Concentration
of Fresh Water Lakes
in the United States
The Vacation Land Supreme
Your Target for Vacation
Pleasure

MISSISSIPPI

JACKSON
Mississippi's Number One
Fort and Industrial
County

LAFAYETTE
The Reforestation Capital
of the World (great num-
ber of individual reforestation of pine tree farms)

LEE
The Capital of the Great
Chickasaw Nation

MADISON
The Banner County

OKTIBBEHA
The Nation's Birthplace of
the Jersey Cow Industry

YAZOO
The Mecca for the Sports-
man

MISSOURI

HOWARD
The Mother of Counties (of
Missouri)

MONTANA

DEER LODGE
Magicland Headquarters

NEBRASKA

DAWSON
The County in the Heart of
the Platte Valley

NEVADA

ELKO
The Cattle County

LINCOLN
The Home of the State Parks

NYE
The County that Makes Silver
Booms to Atom Bombs

PERSHING
Nevada's Nile Valley

NEW JERSEY

ATLANTIC
The County on the Move
The Fishing Paradise of the
World

BURLINGTON
The Hub of Your Business
Wheel of Progress
The New Look for Industry

CAPE MAY
  The Heart of New Jersey's
    Vacationland
  The Ideal Place to Live,
    Work, Play

GLOUCESTER
  The Land of Life Worth
    Living

MERCER
  Heartland
  New Jersey's Heartland of
    Research and Industry
  The Heartland of Industry
    and Research
  The Heartland of New Jersey
  The Major Center of Re-
    search

MONMOUTH
  New Jersey's Front Window

MORRIS
  The County with a History
    and a Future

OCEAN
  New Jersey's Sparkling County
  The County where Parkway
    Meets Atlantic Ocean
  The County where Progress
    Is a Habit
  The County where Progress
    Is Planned for Tomorrow
  The County where the Pines
    Meet Picturesque Barne-
    gat Bay
  The County where the Tang
    of the Sea Meets the
    Scent of Pine
  The Fastest Growing County
    in the State
  The Land and Sea of Ro-
    mance, Sportsmanship
    and Opportunity
  The Sun Sea of New Jersey

SUSSEX
  The Highlands of New
    Jersey
  The Top of New Jersey

UNION
  The County with 100 Years of
    Progress

NEW YORK

CATTARAUGUS
  The All Season Vacationland.
    It's All Here, All Year

CLINTON
  New York's Loveliest Vaca-
    tion Area
  The Famous Popular Vaca-
    tion Area
  The Gateway to the Adiron-
    dack Mountains
  The Heart of the Big Lake
    Country

COLUMBIA
  The Heart of the Northeast

DELAWARE
  The Newest Four Season
    Vacationland

FRANKLIN
  Northern New York's Year-
    Around Adirondack Vaca-
    tionland

FULTON
  Leatherland, U.S.A. (leather
    apparel manufacturing)
  The County of Forty-Four
    Lakes
  The Unspoiled Adirondack
    Vacation Land
  The Unspoiled Vacationland

GENESEE
  The Mother of Counties
  The Promised Land

GREENE
  The Beautiful Land of Rip
    Van Winkle

The County for Vacation
Fun
The Heart of the Catskills
The Land of Rip Van Winkle
The Mountains Vacationland
The Place to Grow
The Romantic Land of Rip
Van Winkle
The Scenic, Healthful,
Historical County

NASSAU
The Gateway to New York
City

NIAGARA
The Hub of the World's
Richest Market

ONEIDA
The Keystone County for
Industrial Progress in
New York State

QUEENS
The Biggest Borough in the
Biggest City in the
World
The Borough of Magnificent
Opportunities
The Fastest Growing County
of New York City

SARATOGA
The County where the Past
Meets the Future
The County with a Practi-
cal Step to Profit, Health
and Fun
The Fun County, U.S.A.
The Gateway to the Adiron-
dacks

SUFFOLK
The Sunrise County

SULLIVAN
The Great Place to Live,
Work and Raise a
Family
The Playground for the
Entire Year
The Vacationland of Colorful

Concentrate ... in Season,
Scenery, Activities and
Accommodations
More to Do ... More to See
The County of Hunting,
Fishing, Touring, Golfing,
Camping, Harness-Racing
and Skiing
The Vacation Wonderland
The World's Fairest Vaca-
tionland

TOMPKINS
The Gateway to the Finger
Lakes

WARREN
New York State's "Happiest"
Vacationland
The All Season Vacation
Paradise
The Convention Center
The County Close to Home
Wherever You Live
The County of Historical
Interest and Incomparable
Beauty
The Gateway to the Adiron-
dacks
The Gateway to the Adiron-
dacks Convention Center
The Honeymoon Haven
The Perfect Place for Every
Taste and Budget
The Playground of the Adi-
rondacks
The Summer Country
The Vacation Paradise in
Any Season
The Vacation Paradise in
the Adirondacks
The Vacationist's Paradise
The Warpath of the Nations
Winter Country

WESTCHESTER
The County where Fun and
Play are Never Far Away
The County where Growing
Comes Naturally
The Nation's Corporate
Leadership County

NORTH CAROLINA

BRUNSWICK
The South Eastern North
Carolina's Land of En-
joyment

CARTERET
The Gateway to Action
The Ocean Gateway to the
Phosphate Chemicals,
Industrial Phosphate
Field, Chemical Complex

IREDELL
The Dairyland County in
North Carolina
The Dairyland of the South-
eastern United States

OHIO

CLINTON
The Garden Spot of the
U.S.

OTTAWA
The Playground of Ohio

TUSCARAWAS
The Birthplace of Ohio's
History

VINTON
The Wonderland of Ohio

WARREN
The Warpath of the Nations

OKLAHOMA

LE FLORE
The Natural Vacation Land

MAJOR
The Agricultural Leader

MURRAY
The Redbud Center of the
State of Oklahoma

OREGON

CLACKAMAS
The Cool Green Oregon Va-
cationland

CROOK
The Agate Capital of the
United States
The County where You Will Re-
lax and Play and You'll
Come Back and Stay Someday
The Feel Younger County

DOUGLAS
The County to Stay and Play

KLAMATH
The Center of the Great Western Market in Southern Oregon's Finest Recreationland

LINCOLN
America's Finest Vacationland

MULTNOMAH
The Land of Adventure and
Opportunity

TILLAMOOK
The Land of Trees, Cheese
and Ocean Breeze

PENNSYLVANIA

ADAMS
The County where the Apple
Is King

ARMSTRONG
The Sportsman's Paradise

BUCKS
The Key County of the Keystone State

DELAWARE
The County where Pennsylvania Began

INDIANA
The Christmas Tree Capital of the World
The Christmas Tree County (cutting approximately 750,000 trees annually)
The Coal Capital of Central Pennsylvania (in the heart of the bituminous coal region)

LANCASTER
The County of Contrasts
The Garden Spot of America
The Garden Spot of the World
The Heart of the Pennsylvania Dutch Country
The Home of the Pennsylvania Dutch

LEBANON
The Valley of Planned Progress

LUZERNE
Pennsylvania's Excitement County

MONROE
Pennsylvania's Picturesque Playground

MONTGOMERY
The Key to the Keystone State

NORTHAMPTON
Everybody Enjoys the Good Life in Northampton County

POTTER
The Big Game Country of Pennsylvania

SCHUYLKILL
The County Known by the Company It Acquires and Keeps

SOMERSET
The "Roof Garden" of the Keystone State

TIOGA
The Canyon Country
The Country where There Is Vacation Fun for Everyone
The Gateway to the Endless Mountains of Pennsylvania

RHODE ISLAND

NEWPORT
America's First Resort
America's First Vacationland

WASHINGTON
The South Country

SOUTH CAROLINA

CHEROKEE
The Peach of the Piedmont

SOUTH DAKOTA

FAULK
The Heart of Dakota
The Heart of Pheasant Country

GREGORY
The Mixed Bag Capital of
South Dakota

ROBERTS
The Pan Fish Capital of
the World

WALWORTH
The Community of Attrac-
tive Opportunities
The County of Attractive
Opportunities

TENNESSEE

BLOUNT
The Most Scenic Entrance
to the Great Smoky
Mountains

ROANE
The County Boosting and
Building a Better Life
for All
The County in the Heart of
the Tennessee Valley

TEXAS

BLANCO
The Heartland of a Great
American (home of Presi-
dent Lyndon Baines
Johnson)

CHAMBERS
The County Rich in the
Heritage of Historical
Events
The County with Excellent
Fishing
The County with Unexcelled
Duck and Goose Shooting

GUADALUPE
The Gateway to South Texas

HOUSTON
The Largest Cattle County
in East Texas

KERR
The Fun Country

MASON
The Recreation and Hunting
Paradise

PECOS
The Highest Cotton Producing
County in the World

WOOD
The Jewel of East Texas

UTAH

WASATCH
America's Switzerland

VERMONT

ADDISON
The Land of Milk and Honey

LAMOILLE
The Heart of Recreational
Vermont

VIRGINIA

BATH
Historic Past, Active
Present, Progressive
Future

Nature's Gift to Every-
one

The County where You
Enjoy Life as It Was
Meant to Be

The Exciting Year 'Round
Playground in the Heart
of Virginia's Alleghe-
nies

Year 'Round Playground

BOTETOURT
Beautiful Botetourt for
the Good Life
The County for the Good
Life

BUCHANAN
Nature's Wonderland
The Gateway to the
Breaks Interstate
Park
The Home of the Grand
Canyon of the South
on the Virginia and Kentucky
State Line
Through Industry We Thrive

CHARLOTTE
This Is the Place to Va-
cation

CHESTERFIELD
The Ruhr Valley of the
South

CLARKE
Virginia's Gateway to
the Shenandoah Valley

CROOK
Relax and Play, You'll
Come Back and Stay
Someday

FLUVANNA
Forward Friendly Flu-
vanna

GLOUCESTER
The County in the Heart of
Historyland
The Land of Life Worth
Living

GRAYSON
The Rooftop of Virginia

LOUDOUN
The County where the Past
and the Present Blend
Graciously
The Gateway to the World
The Good Place to Live to
Play to Work
Virginia Hunt Country
Virginia's Garden County

MATHEWS
An Abundance of Every-
thing for which One
Could Wish
The County that Captures the
Heart of the Sports-Loving
Vacationist
The Midway Garden Spot of
the Atlantic Coast

NORFOLK
The County of Presidents

ORANGE
The County with a Proud
Heritage, a Promising
Future

RUSSELL
A Proud Heritage, A Promising Future

WESTMORELAND
The Athens of Virginia (for
its many distinguished
statesmen)
The Land of Worthwhile
Living

WISCONSIN

DOOR
The Air Conditioned Play-
ground
The Cape Cod of the Mid-
west
The County where Nature
Smiles for Miles and
Miles
The Vacation Paradise
Wisconsin's Air-Conditioned
Peninsula Playground
Wisconsin's Peninsula
Playground

KEWAUNEE
The County of Opportunity

LA CROSSE
The Community of Oppor-
tunity Rich in Economic,
Social and Natural
Resources
The Gateway to the Wis-
consin Coulee Region

MILWAUKEE
The Fun Center of the
Midwest
The Great Place to Live,
to Work, to Play

ONEIDA
The County in the Heart

of Wisconsin's "Lake
Rich" Region
The County where Nature
Lingered Longer
The Four Season Vacation
Center where Nature
Lingered Longer
The Water Wonderland
of Wisconsin's North
Woods
The World's Most Concen-
trated Lake Region (over
1, 200 lakes, 10 fresh
water streams)
Wisconsin's Leisureland

SAWYER
The County in the Indian-
head Country

WAUKESHA
The Fastest Growing County
in the State

WYOMING

TETON
The Last of the Old West

UINTA
The Gateway to Wyoming's
Parks, Mountains and
Great Scenic Attractions

Abundance of Everything for
Which One Could Wish.
Mathews Co., Va.
Agate Capital of the United
States. Crook Co., Ore.
Agricultural and Recreational
Center of California. Fres-
no Co., Calif.
Agricultural and Scientific Hub
of the Golden State. Fresno
Co., Calif.
Agricultural Leader. Major
Co., Okla.
Air Conditioned Playground.
Door Co., Wis.
Alabama's Natural Wonderland.
DeKalb Co., Ala.
All-in-One Vacationland. Citrus
Co., Fla.
All Season Vacation Paradise.
Warren Co., N.Y.
All Season Vacationland; It's
All Here, All Year. Cat-
taraugus Co., N.Y.
America's Finest County.
Lake Co., Fla.
America's Finest Fishing
Country. St. Louis Co.,
Minn.
America's Finest Vacationland.
Lincoln Co., Ore.
America's First Resort. New-
port Co., R.I.
America's First Vacationland.
Newport Co., R.I.
America's Switzerland. Wa-
satch Co., Utah
America's Winter Market
Basket. Hendry Co., Fla.
Arizona's Gateway to Sonora,
Mexico. Santa Cruz Co.,
Ariz.

Arizona's Land of Superlatives.
Coconino Co., Ariz.
Arizona's Valley of the Sun.
Maricopa Co., Ariz.
Arizona's Wonderland of Rocks.
Cochise Co., Ariz.
Athens of Virginia (for its many
distinguished statesmen).
Westmoreland Co., Va.

Banner County. Madison, Miss.
Bargain Hunter's Paradise.
Bristol Co., Mass.
Bass Capital of the World.
Putnam Co., Fla.
Beautiful Botetourt for the Good
Life. Botetourt Co., Va.
Beautiful Land of Rip Van Winkle.
Greene Co., N.Y.
Bedroom Community for Man-
hattan Executives. Fairfield
Co., Conn.
Berry Capital of the World.
Bradford Co., Fla.
Big Game Country of Pennsyl-
vania. Potter Co., Pa.
Biggest Borough in the Biggest
City in the World. Queens
Co., N.Y.
Birthplace of Ohio's History.
Tuscarawas Co., Ohio
Borough of Magnificent Oppor-
tunities. Queens Co., N.Y.

California's Feather River
County. Plumas Co., Calif.
California's Golden Empire.
Kern Co., Calif.
California's Newest Vacationland.
San Luis Obispo Co., Calif.

387

California's Redwood Wonderland. Humboldt Co., Calif.

California's Reserve Fuel Bin.
Yolo Co., Calif.

California's Uncrowded Sportsland. Siskiyou Co., Calif.

Canyon Country. Tioga Co.,
Pa.

Cape Cod of the Midwest.
Door Co., Wis.

Capital of the Great Chickasaw
Nation. Lee, Miss.

Capital Parish of the State
Named for Louis and Anna.
East Baton Rouge, La.

Cattle County. Elko Co., Nev.

Center of Idaho's Industry,
Agriculture, Mining, Govern-
ment and Playgrounds. Ada
Co., Idaho

Center of the Great Western
Market in Southern Oregon's
Finest Recreationland. Kla-
math Co., Ore.

Christmas Tree Capital of the
World. Indiana, Pa.

Christmas Tree County (cutting
approximately 750,000 trees
annually). Indiana Co., Pa.

Coal Capital of Central Pennsylvania (in the heart of the
bituminous coal region).
Indiana Co., Pa.

Community of Attractive Opportunities. Walworth Co.,
So. Dak.

Community of Opportunity Rich
in Economic Social and
Natural Resources. La
Crosse, Wis.

Continent within a County.
Placer Co., Calif.

Convention Center. Warren
Co., N.Y.

Cool Green Oregon Vacationland. Clackamas Co., Ore.

Copper Country. Keweenaw
Co., Mich.

Cotton Bowl of the South.
Tensas Parish, La.

County Beautiful by Nature.
Pike Co., Ill.

County Boosting and Building

a Better Life for All. Roane
Co., Tenn.

County Close to Home Wherever
You Live. Warren Co., N.Y.

County for the Good Life.
Botetourt Co., Va.

County for Vacation Fun. Greene
Co., N.Y.

County for Your Outdoor Recreation and Relaxation. Orange,
Fla.

County in the Fabulous Mother
Lode of California. El
Dorado Co., Calif.

County in the Garden of the
Sun. Tulare, Calif.

County in the Heart of Historyland. Gloucester Co., Va.

County in the Heart of the Famous Suwannee River Valley.
Suwannee Co., Fla.

County in the Heart of the Mother Lode. Amador Co.,
Calif.

County in the Heart of the Platte
Valley. Dawson Co., Neb.

County in the Heart of the Sun
Country. Pima Co., Ariz.

County in the Heart of the Tennessee Valley. Roane Co.,
Tenn.

County in the Heart of Wisconsin's "Lake Rich" Region.
Oneida Co., Wisc.

County in the Hills of Scenic
Southern Indiana. Brown
Co., Ind.

County in the Indianhead Country. Sawyer Co., Wisc.

County in the Shadow of the
Superstitious. Pinal Co.,
Ariz.

County in which There Is Room
to Have Fun In, Room to
Live In. Coconino Co., Ariz.

County Known by the Company
It Acquires and Keeps.
Schuylkill Co., Pa.

County Nature Preserved. San
Luis Obispo Co., Calif.

County Near the Blue Waters
of the Gulf of Mexico.
Pinellas Co., Fla.

County of Agriculture, Industry and Recreation. Sonoma Co., Calif.

County of Attractive Opportunities. Walworth Co., S.D.

County of Charm, Culture, Tradition. Jefferson Co., Fla.

County of Contrasts. Lancaster Co., Pa.

County of 44 Lakes. Fulton Co., N.Y.

County of Historical Interest and Incomparable Beauty. Warren Co., N.Y.

County of Hunting, Fishing, Touring, Golfing, Camping, Harness-Racing and Skiing. Sullivan Co., N.Y.

County of Lakes. Piscataquis Co., Me.

County of Opportunity. Kewaunee Co., Wisc.

County of Planned Progress. Bradford Co., Fla.

County of Presidents. Essex Co., Mass.

County of Presidents. Norfolk Co., Va.

County of Presidents (John Adams, John Quincy Adams and John Fitzgerald Kennedy born here). Norfolk Co., Mass.

County of Progress and Opportunity. Polk Co., Fla.

County of Vacations. Kennebec Co., Me.

County on the Move. Atlantic Co., N.J.

County Progressive by Choice. Pike Co., Ill.

County Rich in the Heritage of Historical Events. Chambers Co., Tex.

County Serving the West's Largest Market. Riverside Co., Calif.

County Steeped in History. Pike Co., Ill.

County that Captures the Heart of the Sports-Loving Vacationist. Mathews Co., Va.

County that Makes Silver Booms to Atom Bombs. Nye Co., Nev.

County that Offers a New Adventure in Living. Seminole Co., Fla.

County to Stay and Play. Douglas Co., Ore.

County Way Down Upon the Suwannee River. Gilchrist Co., Fla.

County where Business Is a Pleasure and Pleasure Is a Business. Sumter Co., Fla.

County where Fun and Play Are Never Far Away. Westchester Co., N.Y.

County where Growing Comes Naturally. Westchester Co., N.Y.

County where Hawthorne and Whittier Were Turned On. Essex Co., Mass.

County where It All Began. Middlesex Co., Mass.

County where It's Always Sun and Fun Time. Broward Co., Fla.

County where Nature Lingered Longer. Oneida Co., Wis.

County where Nature Smiles and Progress Has the Right-of-Way. Bulloch Co., Ga.

County where Nature Smiles for Miles and Miles. Door Co., Wisc.

County where Parkway Meets Atlantic Ocean. Ocean Co., N.J.

County where Pennsylvania Began. Delaware Co., Pa.

County where Progress Is a Habit. Ocean Co., N.J.

County where Progress Is Planned for Tomorrow. Ocean Co., N.J.

County where the Apple Is King. Adams Co., Pa.

County where the Fishing Is Always Good. St. Mary's Co., Md.

County where the Focus Is on Fun. Essex Co., Mass.

County where the Historic
Verde Flows. Yavapai
Co., Ariz.
County where the Past and
the Present Blend Gra-
ciously. Loudoun Co., Va.
County where the Past Meets
the Future. Saratoga Co.,
N.Y.
County where the Pines Meet
Picturesque Barnegat Bay.
Ocean Co., N.J.
County where the Sun Is King.
Yuma Co., Ariz.
County where the Tang of the
Sea Meets the Scent of
Pine. Ocean Co., N.J.
County where There Is Fun
for the Entire Family.
Plymouth Co., Mass.
County where There Is Vaca-
tion Fun for Everyone.
Tioga Co., Pa.
County where You Enjoy Life
as It Was Meant to Be.
Bath Co., Va.
County where You Will Relax
and Play and You'll Come
Back and Stay Someday.
Crook Co., Ore.
County where You Work and
Play the Very Same Day.
Sarasota Co., Fla.
County where Your Vacation
Land Suddenly Becomes
Your New Home. Charlotte
Co., Fla.
County where Your Vacation
Land Suddenly Becomes
Your New Home. Cumber-
land Co., Fla.
County with a History and a
Future. Morris Co., N.J.
County with a Practical Step
to Profit, Health and Fun.
Saratoga Co., N.Y.
County with a Proud Heritage,
a Promising Future.
Orange Co, Va.
County with California's Finest
Year Round Climate.
San Benito Co., Calif.

County with Excellent Fishing.
Chambers Co., Tex.
County with 100 Years of
Progress. Union Co., N.J.
County with Unexcelled Duck
and Goose Shooting. Cham-
bers Co., Tex.
County with Rural Charm and
Modern Living. Citrus Co.,
Fla.
Covered Bridge Capital of the
World. Parke Co., Ind.
Covered Bridge County of the
United States of America.
Parke Co., Ind.
Cradle of California. Amador
Co., Calif.
Crossroads of Florida. Jeffer-
son Co., Fla.

Dairyland County in North
Carolina. Iredell Co., N.C.
Dairyland of the Southeastern
United States. Iredell Co.,
N.C.
Delaware's Waking Giant.
Sussex Co., Del.

Eden of Plenty. Glenn Co.,
Calif.
Everybody Enjoys the Good Life
in Northampton County.
Northampton Co., Pa.
Exciting Year 'Round Playground
in the Heart of Virginia's
Alleghenies. Bath Co., Va.

Famous Popular Vacation Area.
Clinton Co., N.Y.
Famous Popular Vacation Area.
Clinton Co., N.Y.
Fastest Growing County in the
Nation. Brevard Co., Fla.
Fastest Growing County in the
State. Ocean Co., N.J.
Fastest Growing County in the
State. Waukesha Co., Wisc.
Fastest Growing County of New
York City. Queens Co., N.Y.

Feel Younger County. Crook
Co., Ore.
Fisherman's Paradise. Mono
Co., Calif.
Fisherman's Paradise. St.
Louis Co., Minn.
Fishing Area in Our Country.
St. Louis Co., Minn.
Fishing Paradise of the
World. Atlantic Co., N.J.
Florida Crown. Hamilton
Co., Fla.
Florida's Distinctive Resort
Area. Sarasota Co., Fla.
Florida's Fastest Growing
Major County. Pinellas
Co., Fla.
Florida's Fifth Fastest Grow-
ing County. Collier Co.,
Fla.
Florida's "Four Season"
County. Bradford Co., Fla.
Florida's Land of Opportunity.
Gilchrist Co., Fla.
Florida's Largest Tobacco
Growing Center. Suwannee
Co., Fla.
Florida's Winter Strawberry
Market. Bradford Co., Fla.
Focus of the Nation. Greene
Co., Ala.
Focus on Fun and History.
Essex Co., Mass.
Forward Friendly Fluvanna.
Fluvanna Co., Va.
Four Season County. Somer-
set Co., Me.
Four Season Vacation Center
where Nature Lingered
Longer. Oneida Co., Wis.
Fun Center of the Midwest.
Milwaukee Co., Wis.
Fun County. Kerr Co., Tex.
Fun County, U.S.A. Sara-
toga Co., N.Y.

Garden Spot of America. Lan-
caster Co., Pa.
Garden Spot of the United
States. Clinton Co., Ohio
Garden Spot of the World.
Lancaster Co., Pa.

Gateway County of the Great
Joaquin Valley. Stanislaus
Co., Calif.
Gateway to Action. Carteret
Co., N.C.
Gateway to Cape Cod. Bristol
Co., Mass.
Gateway to New York City.
Nassau Co., N.Y.
Gateway to Nova. Seminole
Co., Fla.
Gateway to South Texas.
Guadalupe Co., Tex.
Gateway to the Adirondack
Mountains. Clinton Co.,
N.Y.
Gateway to the Adirondacks.
Saratoga Co., N.Y.
Gateway to the Adirondacks.
Warren Co., N.Y.
Gateway to the Adirondacks
Convention Center. Warren
Co., N.Y.
Gateway to the Breaks Inter-
state Park. Buchanan Co.,
Va.
Gateway to the Endless Moun-
tains of Pennsylvania.
Tioga Co., Pa.
Gateway to the Finger Lakes.
Tompkins Co., N.Y.
Gateway to the Wisconsin
Coulee Region. La Crosse
Co., Wis.
Gateway to the World. Lou-
doun Co., Va.
Gateway to Vacationland. Cum-
berland Co., Me.
Gateway to Wyoming's Parks,
Mountains and Great Scenic
Attractions. Uinta Co.,
Wyo.
God's Country. Dorchester
Co., Md.
Gold Discovery County. El
Dorado Co., Calif.
Good Place to Live to Play to
Work. Loudoun Co., Va.
Great Place to Live, to Work
and to Play. Milwaukee
Co., Wis.
Great Place to Live, Work, Play,
Retire. Otsego Co., Mich.

Great Place to Live, Work
and Raise a Family. Sul-
livan Co., N.Y.
Growing County in a Growing
State. Sumter Co., Fla.
Gulf Coast Land of Terre-
bonne. Terrebonne Parish,
La.

Heart of Dakota. Faulk Co.,
S.D.
Heart of Florida's Crown.
Bradford Co., Fla.
Heart of Heritage Land, U.S.A.
Essex Co., Fla.
Heart of Heritage Land, U.S.A.
Essex Co., Mass.
Heart of Illinois. Shelby Co.,
Ill.
Heart of New England. Essex
Co., Mass.
Heart of New Jersey's Vaca-
tionland. Cape May Co.,
N.J.
Heart of Pheasant Country.
Faulk Co., S.D.
Heart of Recreational Vermont.
Lamoille Co., Vt.
Heart of the Big Lake Country.
Clinton Co., N.Y.
Heart of the Catskills. Greene
Co., N.Y.
Heart of the Mother Lode.
Amador Co., Calif.
Heart of the Nation's Vacation-
land. Kennebec Co., Me.
Heart of the Northeast.
Columbia Co., N.Y.
Heart of the Pennsylvania
Dutch Country. Lancaster
Co., Pa.
Heart of the Redwood Region.
Humboldt Co., Calif.
Heart of the South Georgia
Empire. Coffee Co., Ga.
Heart of Vacationland. Kenne-
bec Co., Me.
Heartland. Mercer Co., N.J.
Heartland of a Great American
(home of President Lyndon
Baines Johnson). Blanco
Co., Tex.

Heartland of Florida. Polk Co.,
Fla.
Heartland of History. Essex
Co., Mass.
Heartland of Industry and Re-
search. Mercer Co., N.J.
Heartland of New Jersey.
Mercer Co., N.J.
Highest Cotton Producing County
in the World. Pecos Co.,
Tex.
Highlands of New Jersey. Sus-
sex Co., N.J.
Historic County. Montgomery
Co., Md.
Historic Mackinac. Mackinac
Co., Mich.
Historic Past, Active Present,
Progressive Future. Bath
Co., Va.
Home of Columbia "Gem" of
the Southern Mines. Tuolumne
Co., Calif.
Home of the Florida Sheriffs
Boys Ranch (home for boys).
Suwannee Co., Fla.
Home of the Grand Canyon of
the South on the Virginia and
Kentucky State Line. Bu-
chanan Co., Va.
Home of the Pennsylvania Dutch.
Lancaster Co., Pa.
Home of the State Parks.
Lincoln Co., Nev.
Honeymoon Haven. Warren Co.,
N.Y.
Hub of the Florida Panhandle.
Holmes Co., Fla.
Hub of the World's Richest
Market. Niagara Co., N.Y.
Hub of Your Business Wheel of
Progress. Burlington Co.,
N.J.
Hunter's Paradise. Orange Co.,
Fla.

Idaho's Year Round Recreational
Wonderland. Bonner Co.,
Idaho
Ideal Place to Live, Work
and Play. Cape May Co.,
N.J.

Indiana's Favorite Vacation-
land. Kosciusko Co., Ind.
Indiana's Popular Lake Area.
Kosciusko Co., Ind.
Industrial Giant of Louisiana.
Jefferson Parish, La.
Industrial Heart of Maine.
Androscoggin Co., Me.
Invitation to Unlimited Poten-
tial. Clay Co., Fla.
It's Easy to Swing in Palm
Beach County. Palm
Beach Co., Fla.

Jewel of East Texas. Wood
Co., Tex.
Jewel of New England.
Essex Co., Mass.
Jumping Frog and Big Tree
County. Calaveras Co.,
Calif.

Key County of Southern Cali-
fornia. Riverside Co., Calif.
Key County of the Keystone
State. Bucks Co., Pa.
Key to America's Largest
Market. Riverside Co.,
Calif.
Keystone County for Industrial
Progress in New York
State. Oneida Co., N.Y.
Keystone of the Florida Sun-
coast. Manatee Co., Fla.
Key to the Keystone State.
Montgomery Co., Pa.
Kingdom of the Sun. Marion
Co., Fla.

Land and Sea of Romance,
Sportsmanship and Oppor-
tunity. Ocean Co., N.J.
Land of Adventure and Oppor-
tunity. Multnomah Co.,
Ore.
Land of Blue Lakes. Mohave
Co., Ariz.
Land of Flowers. Polk Co.,
Fla.

Land of Fun. Glenn Co., Calif.
Land of George Rogers Clark.
Johnson Co., Ill.
Land of Magic. Kern Co.,
Calif.
Land of Milk and Honey. Ad-
dison Co., Vt.
Land of Milk, Honey, Spuds
and Sugar. Weld Co., Colo.
Land of Natural Beauty. De
Kalb Co., Ala.
Land of Natural Wonders.
De Kalb Co., Ala.
Land of Opportunity. Calhoun
Co., Fla.
Land of Pine and Painted
Desert. Apache Co., Ariz.
Land of Rip Van Winkle.
Greene Co., N.Y.
Land of Sand and Slick Rock.
Navajo Co., Ariz.
Land of the Famed Apaches.
Gila Co., Ariz.
Land of the Storied Gila.
Graham Co., Ariz.
Land of Trees, Cheese and
Ocean Breeze. Tillamook
Co., Ore.
Land of Worthwhile Living.
Westmoreland Co., Va.
Largest Cattle County in East
Texas. Houston Co., Tex.
Largest Concentration of Fresh
Water Lakes in the United
States. St. Louis Co.,
Minn.
Largest County in the U.S.A.
Weld Co., Colo.
Largest Industrial County in
California. Contra Costa
Co., Calif.
Last of the Old West. Teton
Co., Wyo.
Leatherland U.S.A. (leather
apparel manufacturing).
Fulton Co., N.Y.

Magicland Headquarters. Deer
Lodge Co., Mont.
Maine in a Nutshell. York
Co., Me.

Maine's Maritime Scenic
Wonderland. Knox Co.,
Me.
Major Center of Research.
Mercer Co., N.J.
Marion County Is Horse Coun-
try. Marion Co., Fla.
Maryland's Goose Capital.
Kent Co., Md.
Maryland's Goose Hunting
Capital. Kent Co., Md.
Maritime County. Middlesex
Co., Conn.
Martin County Has More.
Martin Co., Fla.
Mecca for the Sportsman.
Yazoo Co., Miss.
Midway Garden Spot of the
Atlantic Coast. Mathews
Co., Va.
Minnesota's Arrowhead
Country. St. Louis Co.,
Minn.
Mississippi's Number One
Port and Industrial County.
Jackson Co., Miss.
Mixed Bag Capital of South
Dakota. Gregory Co., S.D.
More to Do ... More to See.
Sullivan Co., N.Y.
Most Scenic Entrance to the
Great Smoky Mountains.
Blount Co., Tenn.
Mother of Counties. Genesee
Co., N.Y.
Mother of Counties (of Mis-
souri). Howard Co., Mo.
Mountains Vacationland.
Greene Co., N.Y.

Nation's Birthplace of the
Jersey Cow Industry.
Oktibbeha Co., Miss.
Nation's Corporate Leadership
County. Westchester Co.,
N.Y.
Natural Advantages for Health
and Recreation County.
Lake Co., Fla.
Natural Vacation Land.
Le Flore Co., Okla.

Nature's Gift to Everyone.
Bath Co., Va.
Nature's Wonderland. Buchanan
Co., Va.
Nevada's Nile Valley. Pershing
Co., Nev.
New Jersey's Front Window.
Monmouth Co., N.J.
New Jersey's Heartland of Re-
search and Industry. Mercer
Co., N.J.
New Jersey's Sparkling County.
Ocean Co., N.J.
New Look for Industry. Bur-
lington Co., N.J.
New York State's "Happiest"
Vacationland. Warren Co.,
N.Y.
New York's Loveliest Vacation
Area. Clinton Co., N.Y.
Newest Four Season Vacation-
land. Delaware Co., N.Y.
No-Better-Place-to-Hunt County.
Gilchrist Co., Fla.
No-Better-Place-to-Live County.
Gilchrist Co., Fla.
North Florida's Greatest Agri-
cultural County. Jackson
Co., Fla.
Northern Gateway to the Mother
Lode. Placer Co., Calif.
Northern New York's Year-
Around Adirondack Vacation-
land. Franklin Co., N.Y.

Ocean Gateway to the Phosphate
Chemicals, Industrial Phos-
phate Field, Chemical Com-
plex. Carteret Co., N.C.
Only Northern Peninsula County
in Southern Michigan. Barry
Co., Mich.
Ozone Belt. St. Tammany
Parish, La.

Pan Fish Capital of the
World. Roberts Co., S.D.
Paradise for All. Calhoun
Co., Fla.
Paradise Living for All the

Family. Seminole Co.,
Fla.
Peach of the Piedmont.
Cherokee Co., S.C.
Pennsylvania's Excitement
County. Luzerne Co., Pa.
Pennsylvania's Picturesque
Playground. Monroe Co.,
Pa.
Perfect Place for Every Taste
and Budget. Warren Co.,
N.Y.
Photographers Playground.
Inyo Co., Calif.
Picture County. Inyo Co.,
Calif.
Place to Grow. Greene Co.,
N.Y.
Place to Locate. Sumter
Co., Fla.
Place to Work and Relax.
Tulare Co., Calif.
Place where Coronado Walked.
Greenlee Co., Ariz.
Playground for the Entire
Year. Sullivan Co., N.Y.
Playground of Ohio. Ottawa
Co., Ohio
Playground of the Adirondacks.
Warren Co., N.Y.
Pleasure Boating Center of
the Bay Area. Marin Co.,
Calif.
Potato Empire. Aroostook
Co., Me.
Potato Empire of the Nation.
Aroostook Co., Me.
Premier County of California.
Monterey Co., Calif.
Prime Industrial Center.
East Baton Rouge Co., La.
Promised Land. Genesee Co.,
N.Y.
Proud Heritage, Promising
Future. Russell Co., Va.

Queen of the Delta. Madison
Parish, La.

Recreation and Hunting Paradise. Mason Co., Tex.

Redbud Center of the State of
Oklahoma. Murray Co.,
Okla.
Reforestation Capitol of the
World (great number of indi-
vidual reforestation of pine
tree farms). Lafayette Co.,
Miss.
Relax and Play, You'll Come
Back and Stay Someday.
Crook Co., Va.
Research County. Fairfield
Co., Conn.
Retirement Haven. Seminole
Co., Fla.
Retirement Haven, the Retire-
ment Heaven. Seminole Co.,
Fla.
Richest Agricultural County in
the World. Fresno Co.,
Calif.
Rockhound's Paradise. Mar-
quette Co., Mich.
Romantic Land of Rip Van
Winkle. Greene Co., N.Y.
"Roof Garden" County of the
Keystone State. Somerset
Co., Pa.
Rooftop of Virginia. Grayson
Co., Va.
Ruhr Valley of the South.
Chesterfield Co., Va.

Sarasota County Has Everything.
Sarasota Co., Fla.
Scenic County. Spencer Co.,
Ind.
Scenic Empire. Coconino Co.,
Ariz.
Scenic, Healthful, Historical
County. Greene Co., N.Y.
Scenic Wonderland. Cumber-
land Co., Me.
Scenic Wonderland of Iowa.
Winneshiek, Iowa
Science Center, U.S.A. Mont-
gomery Co., Md.
Second Richest Agricultural
County in the U.S. Aroos-
took Co., Me.
Show Window of Maine. York
Co., Me.

South County. Washington
Co., R.I.
South Eastern North Caro-
lina's Land of Enjoyment.
Brunswick Co., N.C.
Southern Entry to the Cape
Kennedy Area. South
Brevard Co., Fla.
Southern Gateway to Maine.
York Co., Me.
Southern Gateway to the
Mother Lode. Mariposa
Co., Calif.
Sportsman's Paradise. Arm-
strong Co., Pa.
Sportsman's Paradise. Dor-
chester Co., Md.
Sportsman's Paradise. Gil-
christ Co., Fla.
Sportsmen's Paradise. Al-
pine Co., Calif.
Summer Pleasure County.
Roscommon Co., Mich.
Summer Country. Warren
Co., N.Y.
Sun Sea of New Jersey.
Ocean Co., N.J.
Sunrise County. Suffolk Co.,
N.Y.
Sunrise County of the U.S.
Washington Co., Me.
Swing Is to Palm Beach
County for Fun. Palm
Beach Co., Fla.

There's Fun for the Whole
Family in Delightful
Colorful Bristol County.
Bristol Co., Mass.
This Is the Place to Vacation.
Charlotte Co., Va.
Through Industry We Thrive.
Buchanan Co., Va.
Toothpick Center of the
World. Oxford Co., Me.
Top of New Jersey. Sussex
Co., N.J.

Unspoiled Adirondack Vacation Land. Fulton Co.,
N.Y.

Unspoiled Vacationland. Fulton Co., N.Y.

Vacation and Recreation Land.
Inyo Co., Calif.
Vacation Land Supreme. St.
Louis Co., Minn.
Vacation Paradise. Door Co.,
Wis.
Vacation Paradise in Any
Season. Warren Co., N.Y.
Vacation Paradise in the Adiron-
dacks. Warren Co., N.Y.
Vacation Wonderland. Sullivan
Co., N.Y.
Vacationist's Paradise. War-
ren Co., N.Y.
Vacationland of Colorful Con-
centrate ... in Season,
Scenery, Activities and Ac-
commodations. Sullivan Co.,
N.Y.
Vacationland with Livability.
Plymouth Co., Mass.
Vacationland with Lovability.
Plymouth Co., Mass.
Valley of Planned Progress.
Lebanon Co., Pa.
Virginia Hunt Country. Loudoun
Co., Va.
Virginia's Garden County.
Loudoun Co., Va.
Virginia's Gateway to the
Shenandoah Valley. Clarke
Co., Va.

Warpath of the Nations. Warren
Co., N.Y.
Warpath of the Nations. Warren
Co., Ohio
Water Wonderland of Wisconsin's
North Woods. Oneida Co.,
Wis.
Western Maryland's Mountain
Top Playground. Garrett
Co., Md.
Western Maryland's Top Play-
ground. Garrett Co.,
Md.
Wheat Capital of the World.
Sumner Co., Kan.

Winter Country.   Warren Co.,
  N.Y.
Wisconsin's Airconditioned
  Peninsula Playground.
  Door Co., Wis.
Wisconsin's Leisureland.
  Oneida Co., Wis.
Wisconsin's Peninsula Play-
  ground.   Door Co., Wis.
Wonderland of Ohio.   Vinton
  Co., Ohio
World Famous Ozone Belt.
  St. Tammany Parish, La.
World's Fairest Vacationland.
  Sullivan Co., N.Y.

World's Most Concentrated
  Lake Region (over 1,200
  lakes, 10 fresh water
  streams)

Year Around Vacationland.
  Gladwin Co., Mich.
Year Round Fun County.
  Lake Co., Calif.
Year 'Round Playground.
  Bath Co., Va.
Your Target for Vacation
  Pleasure.   St. Louis Co.,
  Minn.

STATE INDEX

showing all nicknames
for each state

ALABAMA

The Cornucopia of the South, The Cotton State (cotton plantations), The Deep South, The Family Funland, The Heart of Dixie, The Heart of the Deep South, The Land of Flowers, The Land of Opportunity, The Lizard State (lizards), The Pioneer Space Capital of the World, The Star of the South, The State of Productive Farms, The State that Has It All, The Vacationland, The Yellowhammer State (the uniforms of the Confederate soldiers had a home-dyed yellow tinge)

ALASKA

America's Last Frontier, America's Last Great Frontier, America's Last Outpost, America's Last Primeval Wilderness, America's New Frontier of Travel, America's Newest Gayest Frontier, America's Northern Frontier, American Land of the Midnight Sun, The Arctic Land of the Eskimo, The Arctic Treasureland, The Beautiful Northland of Opportunity, The Big Land, The Big State, The Eskimoland, The Far North Frontier, The Gibraltar of the North, The Great Bear's Cub, The Great Land, Johnson's Polar Bear Garden, The Land of Adventure, The Land of Now (title of book by D. A. Noonan), The Land of Opportunity, The Land of Promise, The Land of Tomorrow, The Land of Yesterday, Today and Tomorrow, The Land of the Midnight Sun, The Land where the Summer Sun Never Sets, The Last American Frontier (the 49th state, admitted Jan. 3, 1959), The Last Frontier, The Midnight Sunland, The Nation's New Playground, The New Frontier, The Northern Wonderland, The Northernmost State, The Northland, Seward's Folly (William Henry Seward, U. S. Secretary of State, advocated and negotiated purchase from Russia for $7,200,000), Seward's Ice Box (U. S. Secretary of State arranged for Alaska's purchase from Russia), The State of Contrasts, Uncle Sam's Icebox, The Vacationland of Opportunity, The Wonderland Unsurpassed

ARIZONA

Amazing Arizona, where You Can Always Expect to Enjoy the Unexpected, See All of Arizona--It's Wonderful, The Apache State (Indian tribes), The Aztec State (Aztec names), The Baby State (48th state, admitted Feb. 14, 1912), The Canyon State, The Copper State (copper production), Friendly Arizona, The Grand Canyon State, The Healthful State, The Italy of America (scenic), The Jewel in the West, The Land of Sunshine and Scenic Grandeur, The Land where the Sun Spends the Winter, One of America's Most Popular Playgrounds, The Sand Hill State (desert), The State of Discovery in a World of Sunshine, The State where the Sun Shines Bright, The State where You Can Always Expect to Enjoy the Unexpected, The Sunset Land, The Sunset State, The Vacation State of the Nation, The Valentine State (admitted on Valentine's Day, Feb. 14), The Wonderland, The Youngest State (the 48th state, admitted Feb. 14, 1912), To Live Here Is to Enjoy Each Hour

ARKANSAS

Arkansas Is a Natural, The Bear State (bears), The Bowie State (bowie knives used), The Guinea Pig State (proving ground for experiments of Department of Agriculture), The Home of the Peach, Strawberry and Vine, The Hot Water State (numerous hot springs), The Land of Opportunity, The Land of Majestic Beauty, The Nation's Cool Green Paradise, The Place where Plant Sites and Pine Forests Grow Side By Side, The Toothpick State (bowie knives in handles), The Wonder State

CALIFORNIA

America's Number One Market, The Cornucopia of the World, The El Dorado State, The Eureka State, The Gateway to the Pacific, The Glorious Land, The Golden State (gold discovered in 1848; golden poppies each spring), The Grape State (grape production), The Land of Discoveries, The Land of Gold, The Land of Living Color, The Land of Opportunity, The Land of Promise, The Land of Sunshine and Flowers, The Nation's Leading Vacation and Recreation State, The Sunshine Empire, The Wine Land of America, The World Within a State

COLORADO

America's Vacation Paradise, Cupid's Hometown, The Buffalo Plains State, The Centennial State (admitted August 1, 1876, the hundredth anniversary of the Declaration of Independence), The Colorful Colorado, The Fastest Growing Ski Center of the U.S.A., The Gateway to the Rocky Mountain West, The Glorious Vacation Playground, The Highest State (highest mean elevation, 54 of its peaks over 14,000 feet in height), The Highest State in the Union (average

altitude 6,800 feet), The Land of Contrasts, The Lead State (lead
production), The Rocky Mountain Empire, The Silver State (silver
production), The Ski Country, U.S.A., The Sky Land of Sporting
Snows and Sunshine, The State of Magnificent Scenery, The State
Everything's In, The State on the Move, The Switzerland of
America (numerous high mountains), The Top of the Nation (mountain peaks), The Top Vacation State of the Nation, The Vacation
Country, The Valentine Capital of the World, The Winter Paradise
of America

CONNECTICUT

Connecticut Achieves, The Arsenal of the Nation, The Blue Law
State (New Haven blue laws), The Brownstone State (quarries), The
Constitution State (1639, first written constitution, the Fundamental
Orders, official nickname, enacted by Public Act 121, Jan. ses-
sion 1959), The Doorway to Nostalgic New England, The Freestone
State (freestone quarries), The Holiday State, The Insurance State,
The Land of Steady Habits, The Nutmeg State (wooden nutmegs),
The State Alive with Variety and Fun to See, The State that Has
Something for Everyone All Year 'Round, The State where the Good
Life Pays in More Corporate Dividends, The Wooden Nutmeg State

DELAWARE

See the First State First, The Blue Hen State (a fighting hen popular in the Revolutionary War for its bravery), The Blue Hen's
Chickens State (see above), The Diamond State (because it is small
in size yet important), The Economic Sunshine State, The First
State (Delaware on December 7, 1787 was the first state to ratify
the Constitution), New Sweden (name of fort built in 1638 by Peter
Minuit whose expedition was sent out by Queen Christiana), The
Peach State (used in the 1840's), The Seacoast Homeland, The State
that Started a Nation, Uncle Sam's Pocket Handkerchief

FLORIDA

Fun in the Sun for Everyone, The Airconditioned State, The Alligator
State (alligators), America's Dream Vacation State, The Everglades
State (everglades), Fabulous Florida, The Gateway to the World, The
Gulf State (on Gulf of Mexico), The Honeymoon Capital of the World,
The Land of Flowers, The Land of Fun, Sun and Sand, The Land
of Sunshine, The Land of Sunshine and Flowers, The Marina Capital
of the U.S.A., The National Country, The New American Frontier,
The Orange Land, The Orange State (orange and citrus production),
The Peninsula of Pleasant Experiences, The Peninsula State (geo-
graphical), The Place for You, The Scenic Wonderland, The Second
Fastest Growing State, The Southernmost State, The Sports Capital
of the World, The State of Excitement, The State of Festivals,
Theatre, Museums and Music, The Sunniest Winter Climate in the

Eastern United States, The Sunshine State, The U.S. Gateway to
Latin America, Winter Salad Bowl

GEORGIA

Georgia's Got It, The Adventure in Happiness, The Airlift Center of
the World, The Buzzard State, The Cracker State, The Different Vacation State, The Empire State of the South, The Goober State, The
Keystone of the Growing South, The Land of Blossoms and Relaxed
Living, The Land of Industrial Romance, The Land of Peanuts, Pecans and Peaches, The Pace Setter of the South, The Peach State,
The Quail Capital of the World, The South's Empire State, The State
of Adventure, The State of Increditable Variety, The Yankee Land of
the South, Year 'Round Vacation Wonderland

HAWAII

The All-American Playground, The Aloha State (official nickname
enacted by Joint Resolution No. 1, April 23, 1959, 30th Territorial
Legislature), The Big Island, The Convention Center of the Pacific,
The Fiftieth State of Enchantment, The Gateway to the Orient, The
Gateway to the Pacific, The Gem of the Pacific, The Island Para-
dise, The Island State, The Jewel of the Pacific, The Land of Leisure,
The Nation's Only State of Islands, The Orchid Isle, The Paradise of
the Pacific, The Pineapple State (second and most important product),
The Playground of the Pacific, The Scenic Isle, The State at the
Crossroads of the Pacific, The Tropical Paradise, The Window on
the East, The Youngest State (the 50th state, admitted Aug. 21, 1959),
Your Dreamland of Pleasure

IDAHO

The Gem of the Mountain States, The Gem of the Mountains, The
Gem State (72 kinds of precious and semi-precious stones), The
Land of Pleasure, The Place to Go, The Place to Go Is Idaho, The
State of Shining Mountains, The Vacation Land, The Vacation Land
of Your Fondest Dreams, The Vacation Wonderland, There's Fun
in Idaho

ILLINOIS

The Corn Belt State, The Corn State, The Crossroads of America,
Egypt, The Garden of the West, The Great Lakes State, The Heart
of the Nation, The Hub of the Nation, The Jubilee State for '68, The
Land of Lincoln, The Land of the Illini, The Livestock Feeding
State, The Prairie State, The Sucker State, The Vacation Target for
Millions of Americans, The Vacationland

INDIANA

The Center of the Commercial Universe, The Crossroads of America
(official nickname enacted March 2, 1937, House Joint Resolution
No. 6, chapter 312), The Hoosier State (claimed to originate from
early pioneer greeting "Who'shyer"), The State of Surprises

IOWA

A Place to Grow--A Place to Go, The Beautiful Land, The Beautiful
Land Between Two Great Rivers, The Brightest Star in the Ameri-
can Constellation, The Food Market of the World, The Greatest Food
Producing Area in the World, The Haven for the Traveler, The Hawk-
eye State (Indian Chief Hawkeye), The Land of Industrial Opportunity,
The Land of the Rolling Prairie, The Land Rich in History, Heri-
tage and Hospitality, The Last Frontier of Industrial Development,
The Leading Farm Crop, The New County where Factory and Farm
Share Prosperity, The Peerless State, The State where the West
Begins and Progress Never Ceases, The Vacation Haven in Mid-
Nation

KANSAS

Bleeding Kansas (the seven hectic years, 1854-1861, while slavery
was at stake), Fun in Every Season, The Breadbasket of the Nation,
The Central State (geographical location), The "Clean Air" Country,
The Cyclone State, The First in Clean Air, The Friendly State, The
Garden of the West, The Garden State, The Grasshopper State, The
Great State, The Jayhawk State (irregular troops and pillaging bands
in Civil War--one of several explanations, a bird), Midway U.S.A.
(center of travel and transportation, commerce and industry), The
Salt of the Earth (enough salt reserves to provide the U.S. for
375,000 years at the present rate of use), The Squatter State (squat-
ters who arrived about 1854), The Sunflower State, The Wheat State,
The Wheat State of America, The Wheatheart of the Nation (first in
wheat production and flour milling)

KENTUCKY

The Blue Grass Region, The Bluegrass State (blueish tinged grass),
The Corncracker State (corn-cracker birds), The Dark and Bloody
Ground State (battleground of Indian tribes), The Hemp State, The
Land Alive with Beauty and Good Times, The Most Northern of the
Summer States, One Hundred Vacation Lands Into One, The Pioneer
Commonwealth, The State where Big Things Are Happening, The
State within a Day of Seventy Percent of the United States Market,
The Tobacco State, The Vacation Center of America, The Vacation
Paradise

LOUISIANA

The Bayou State, The Bayou Wonderland, The Child of the Mississippi River, The Creole State (creoles of French and Spanish descent), The Fisherman's Paradise, The Holland of America (numerous canals), The Lovely Louisiana, The Metropolis of the West
Coast, The Nation's Growth Frontier, The Nation's Industrial Frontier, Nature's Cornucopia, The Pelican State (the brown pelican
native to the shore), The Picturesque Historic Land of Early America, The Right to Profit State, The Sportsman's Paradise, The State
that Has to Be Seen to Be Believed, The Sugar State, The Variety
Vacationland

MAINE

America's Top Vacation Land, The Angler's Paradise, The Border
State, The Complete Vacationland, The Convention State, The Down
East State, The Four-Season State, The Great Place to Live, Laze,
Locate, The Great Recreation Center, The Health Resort of Ameri-
ca, The Land of Remembered Vacations, Lobsterland, The Lumber
State, The Nation's Vacationland, The Old Dirigo State (state motto
"Dirigo"), The Pine Tree State (pine tree depicted on the coat-of-
arms), The Place to Live, Work and Play, The Playground of the
Nation, The Polar Star State, The Scenic Wonderland, The State
where Every Season Is Vacation Time, State where History and
Hospitality Began, The Summer Playground of the Nation, The Switzer-
land of America (scenic), The Vacationland, The World of Good that
Awaits You

MARYLAND

America in Miniature, The Cockade State (a type of hat worn by
patricians), The Delightful Land, The Delightsome Land (the description of Maryland in the log book of Captain John Smith in 1608), The
Free State, The Monumental State (because of its monuments, prin-
cipally in Baltimore), The Old Line State (the dividing line between
the crown land grants of William Penn and Lord Baltimore), The
Oyster State (oyster fisheries), The Queen State (named for Queen
Henrietta Maria), The Star-Spangled Banner State

MASSACHUSETTS

Massachusetts Means Progress, Money, Manpower, Management, Mar-
kets, Materials, The Baked Bean State, The Bay State (Massachusetts
Bay), The Bean Eating State, The Bean State, The Beautiful State of
Mind, The Bicentennial Began Here, The Birthplace of American De-
mocracy, The Birthplace of American Freedom, The Custodian of
America's Heritage, The Custodian of America's Historical Heritage,
The Custodian of the Nation's Heritage, The Four-Season Vacationland,
The Historic Vacationland, The Hub of the Universe, The Most Varied

State of the Fifty, The Old Bay State, The Old Colony State, The
Pilgrim State, The Puritan State, The Space Center of the World,
The State where History and Hospitality Began, The Vacationland of
Fun and Plenty, The Wellspring of Art and Culture, The World of
Fun and Relaxation, The Year 'Round Vacationland

MICHIGAN

Michigan Is Everything Under the Sun, The Auto State, The Automobile State, The Big Fish State, The Four Season Vacation Fun
Land, The Great Lake State, The Jewel of Many Facets, The Lady
of the Lake (Lake Michigan), The Lake State (touches Lakes Michigan, Superior, Erie, Huron and St. Clair), One of the Great Resort
States of the Middle West, The Peninsula State, The Playtime Country, The Tourist Empire of the Inland Seas, The Water Wonderland,
The Water-Winter Wonderland, The Winter Wonderland, The Wolverine State, The Wonderland of 11,000 Lakes

MINNESOTA

It's Good to Be in Minnesota, The Bread and Butter State (flour and
dairy industry), The Fresh Water Fishing Capital, The Get-Away-
From-It-All State, The Gopher State (gophers), The Lake State (14,215
lakes over 10 acres in size), The Land of 10,000 Lakes (see above),
The Nation's Vacation Land, The New England of the West, The
North Star State (the state seal has the motto L'Etoile du Nord, the
star of the north), The Playground of 10,000 Lakes, The Rich and
Varied Land, The United Nations in Miniature, The Wheat State

MISSISSIPPI

A Great Agricultural State, America's State of Opportunity, The
Bayou State (bayous, rivulets), The Border-Eagle State (eagle
depicted on the coat-of-arms), The Cotton Kingdom, The Crossroads
of the South, The Eagle State (see above), The Fastest Growing
Cattle State, The Fun and Sun Land, The Fun-Filled Vacation Land,
The Gateway to the Southland, The Groundhog State, The Heart of
the Deep South, The Hospitality State, The Magnolia State (magnolia
trees), The Mud-cat State (name for catfish), The Mud-waddler
State, The Place to Be, The State of Opportunity, The State of the
Future, The State Rich in Beauty and Abundant Resources, The
State where Cotton Is Still King, The Tadpole State (young French
settlers; "frogs" being nickname applied to their elders), Variety
Vacationland for All the Family

MISSOURI

The Bullion State (Thomas Hart Benton, known as Old Bullion), The
Cave State (26 caves open), The Family Vacationland, The Fire Clay

Capital, The Great River Road Country, The Heart of America, The
Heart of the Nation, The Heartland of Hospitality, The Iron Mountain
State (Iron Mountain), The Land of Many Faces, The Lead State
(lead production), Little Dixie, Memorable Missouri, The Mother
of the West, The National Gateway to the Frontierlands, The Num-
ber One Cave State (2,000 caves and 25 commercially operated
caves), The Ozark State (Ozark Mountain), The Pennsylvania of the
West, The Puke State, The Show Me State, The State where North,
South, East and West Meet, The Vacation Capital of the Midwest,
The World's Saddle Horse Capital

MONTANA

The Big Ski Country, The Big Sky Country, The Big Sky Vacation-
land, The Bonanza State, The Four Season Vacationland, The Impor-
tant Agricultural Production State, The Land of Enchantment, The
Land of Scenic Splendor, The Land of the Shining Mountains, The
Last of the Big Time Splendors, The Lead State (lead production),
The Singed Cat State, The State with Recreation for Everyone, The
Stub Toe State, The Treasure State, The Vacation State, The Won-
derland

NEBRASKA

The Antelope State (antelopes), The Beef State (cattle production),
The Big Country, The Birthplace of Rodeo, The Black Water State
(dark soil which makes water appear dark), The Bug-eating State
(bull bats which eat bugs), The Corn Husking State, The Cornhusker
State, the Cowboy Country, The Healthiest State in the Union, The
Land of the Good Life, The Land of the Pioneer, The Land of the
Oregon Trail and the Pony Express, The Land where the West Be-
gins, The Leisureland State, The Nation's Mixed-bag Capital
(77,227 square miles of diversified hunting), Nebraskaland, The
Sportsman's Paradise, The State on the March, The State where
the West Begins, The Tall Corn State, The Treeplanter State, The
Western Playground, The Year-'Round Playground

NEVADA

The Battle Born State (Nevada was made a territory in 1861 and
admitted as a state in 1864 during the Civil War), The Early Mormon
Ranching Community, The Entertainment Capital of the World, The
Mining State, The Nation's Fastest Growing State, One Sound State
(slogan because of good financial condition in 1929-1933 depression),
The Sage State (prevalence of wild sage), The Sage-hen State (a
common-type of fowl), The Sagebrush State (wild sage), The Silver
State (silver mines), The State where Man and Nature Gamble, The
Vacation State, Your Vacation State

NEW HAMPSHIRE

The Granite State (granite is the bedrock underlying most of the surface), The Land of Peace and Beauty, The Land of Scenic Splendor, The Mother of Rivers, The Old Man of the Mountain State (rock formation), The Scenic State, The State in the Heart of New England, The State for Vacation Pleasure at Any Season, The State of Surprise, The Switzerland of America (scenic), The White Mountain State (White Mountains), The Yankee Playground

NEW JERSEY

People, Purpose, Progress, The Adaptable State, The Camden and Amboy State (Camden and Amboy Railroad), The Center of World Transportation, and Clam State (seafood production), The Cockpit of History, The Cockpit of the Revolution (used in 1776), The Cradle of Industrial Research, The Crossroads of the East, The Crossroads State, The Energy-packed State, The Foreigner State (see New Spain State), The Garden State, The Garden State for Pleasure and Business, The Geographic Center of the World's Richest Market, History's Main Road, The Hub of Commerce, The Industrial Park State (more industrial parks per square mile than any other state), The Jersey Blue State (blue uniforms worn by Revolutionary Army troops, or blue laws), The Land of Amazing Advantages, The Land of Amazing Industrial Advantages, The Mosquito State, Nature's Showcase, The New Spain State (in 1812 Joseph Bonaparte, King of Spain, fled to Bordentown, N. J., where he bought 1, 400 acres), The Pathway of the Revolution (nearly 100 battles were fought on New Jersey soil), The Riviera of America, The Sharpbacks State, The Small State, Big in Agriculture, Big in Industry, The State of Camden and Amboy (see above), The State of Spain (see above), The State where You Come for a Visit and Come Back for a Lifetime, U.S. Gateway to the World, The Vacationland the Year 'Round

NEW MEXICO

The Cactus Land (profusion of cactus), The Colorful Past with the Thriving Present, The Colorful State, The Land of the Cactus (cactus plants), The Land of Enchantment, The Land of Hearts' Desire, The Land of Opportunity, The Land of Sunshine, The Land of the Delight-Makers (from the book "The Delight Makers" by Adolf Bandelier), The Playground of the Southwest, The Space Age Research Center for the Free World, The Spanish State, The State of Diversity, The State of Spain State, The State where Modern Cities, Picturesque Villages and Storied Ghost Towns Mix the Colorful Past with the Thriving Present, The State where the Fun Never Sets, The Sunshine State, The Unspoiled Empire, Vacation and Industrial Nucleus of the Southwest, The Vermin State

NEW YORK

All Roads Lead to Fun in New York State, America's Cultural
Capital, The Apple State, The Center of American Culture, The
Empire State, The Excelsior State (motto), The Gateway to Expo
67 (International Fair at Montreal, Canada), The Host State for the
World's Fair, The Knickerbocker State (short loose trousers worn
by the early Dutch settlers), The Land of Infinite Variety, The Nation's Showcase, The Seat of Empire, The State that Has Everything, The Vacation Empire, The Vacation Variety, The World of
Scenic Beauty, The Year-Round Vacationland

NORTH CAROLINA

First in Freedom (Mecklenburg Declaration adopted May 20, 1775),
The Dixie Dynamo, The Game Fish Junction, The Golf State U.S.A.,
The Goodliest Land Under the Cape of Heaven, The Ireland of
America, The Land of Beginnings (site of the first settlement in
America, Roanoke Island), The Land of the Sky (many mountain
peaks), Nature's Mineral Specimen Case (over 300 different minerals
found), The Old North State (north of South Carolina), The Rip Van
Winkle State (used in the 1830's when it was undeveloped and back-
ward), The Second Nazareth, The Tarheel State (a derisive name
applied by Mississippi soldiers to North Carolinians who failed to
hold their position, and did not put tar on their heels), The Turpentine State (product obtained from the pine trees), The Variety Vacationland, The Year-Round Mid-South, The Year 'Round Vacation State

NORTH DAKOTA

America's Newest Family Vacationland, The Big Country, The
Crossroads of All America, The Crossroads of the Continent, The
Fabled Land of the American Indian, The Flickertail State (the
flickertail squirrel), The Friendly State, The Gateway to the Big
Country, The Great Central State (center of the wheat belt), The
Land of the Dakotas (Dakota Indians), The Land of Fresh Horizons,
The Land of the Long North Furrow, The Land of the North Fur-
row, The Land of Theodore Roosevelt and General Custer, The Land
of Western Hospitality, The Land Rich in Heritage, The Northern
Prairie State, The Peace Garden State, Roughrider Country, The
Sioux State (Indian tribe), The State where the Old West Lives Again,
The State where the Sunshine Spends the Winter, The West of Song
and Legend, Visit North Dakota for Family Water Fun, The Wide
Horizon Country

OHIO

The Buckeye State (buckeye or horse-chestnut, buckeye resemblance
to the seed, both in color, shape and appearance to the eye of the

buck), The Gateway State (to the Northwest Territory), The Gateway
to the Northwest Territory, The Land of History, The Land of Op-
portunity, The Modern Mother of Presidents (birthplace of Grant,
Hayes, Garfield, B. Harrison, McKinley, Taft and Harding), The
Mother of Presidents, The Nation's Number One Market Area, The
Number One State, The Oldest State West of the Thirteen Original
Colonies, The State of Many Countries, The State on the Move, The
State where History and the Present Make Your Visit Delightful,
The Tomato State (first in tomato production under glass, 500 acres
of greenhouses), The Transportation Center of America, The Yankee
State (because of its free institutions), The "You-Name-It-We-Make-
It" State

OKLAHOMA

America's Newest Vacationland, America's Vacation Treasureland,
America's Year Round Adventureland, The Adventurous State, The
Boomers' Paradise (the "boomers" who opened Oklahoma, April 22,
1889), The Buckle on the Sunbelt, The Empire State Dedicated to
Progress, The Fastest Fun in the West, The Heart of the Cow
Country, The Hub of Recreational Facilities, The Land of the Red
Men, The Land of Tomorrow, The Landscape of the Future, The
Sooner State ("sooners" were those who entered Oklahoma sooner
than the designated legal time), The State of Fun, The State of
Industry, The State of Many Countries, The State Pioneering in
Progress, The State with New Ideas, The State where the Wind
Comes Sweepin' Down the Plains, The Tomorrow Country, The Va-
cation Adventureland, The Wonderous Place to Visit

OREGON

America's Finest Vacationland, America's Northwest Playland, The
Beaver State, The Cool, Green Vacationland, The End of the Trail,
The Hard-case State (rough life of the early settlers), The Land of
Exciting Contrasts, The Land of Opportunity, The Land where Dreams
Come True, Nature's Wonderland, The Pacific Wonderland, The
Scenic State, The State of Excitement, The Sunset State, The Thres-
hold of Paradise, The Web-foot State (excessive rain in winter), The
Welcome State

PENNSYLVANIA

Pennsylvania Is an Active State, The Birth State of the Nation
(Declaration of American Independence signed July 4, 1776), The
Bicentennial State, The Birthplace of a Nation, The Coal State
(coal mines), The First State in Safety, The Honeymoon Capital of
the World, The Keystone of Early America, The Keystone State
(central geographical position among the thirteen original colonies),
The Nation's Family Playground, The Nation's Ideal Family Playground, The Quaker State (founded in 1680 by William Penn),

The State First in Transportation, The State of Excitement, The
State of 1001 Vacation Pleasures, The State where American Industry Began, The Steel State (industry), The Tourist State, The Workshop of the World

RHODE ISLAND

America's First Vacationland, Rhode Island Is Oceans of Fun, The
American Venice, The Land of Roger Williams (founded Providence
1636), Little Rhody, The Nation's First Tourist Host, The Ocean
State, Our Social Capital, The Plantation State (the State of Rhode
Island and Providence Plantations), The Smallest State, The Southern
Gateway of New England, The State where History Is Around Every
Corner, The State where the Action Is

SOUTH CAROLINA

See Surprising South Carolina, The Cotton Mill State, The Iodine
State, The Keystone of the South Atlantic Seaboard (wedge shape),
The Land of Recreation and Progress, The Palmetto State (tree),
The Rice State (rice production), The Sand-lapper State (humorous,
designation of poor people who lapped up sand for subsistence), The
State that Forgot (title of book by W. Ball), The State where Re-
sources and Markets Meet, The Swamp State (rice fields), The Va-
cationland from the Mountains to the Sea, The Wonderful Iodine
State

SOUTH DAKOTA

America's Favorite Fun Country, The Artesian State (artesian wells),
The Blizzard State (gales, storms), The Coyote State (coyotes), The
Friendly Land of Infinite Variety, The Frontier of Pleasure, The
Frontier of Pleasure on the Old West Trail, The Land of Infinite
Variety, The Land of Perfect Vacation, The Land of Plenty, The
Land of Wonder, The Pheasant Capital of the World, The State
that's Geared for Profit, The State with Many Landscapes, The Sun-
shine State, The Swiagecat State

TENNESSEE

America at Its Best, America's Central Vacation Land, America's
Most Interesting State, The Big Bend State (Indian name for the
Tennessee River), The Hog and Hominy State (leader in corn and
pork products in the 1830's), The Inter-state State, The Lion's Den
State, The Mother of Southwestern Statesmen (Jackson, Polk, Andrew
Johnson), The Nation's Most Interesting State, The River with the
Big Bend (the Tennessee River), The Scenic Wonderland, The State
of Historic Sites, The State of Scenic Beauty, The State of Unparal-
leled Outdoor Recreation Facilities, The State where Everything Just

Comes Naturally, The State where Nature Put It All Together, The
State where the People Are Friendly, The State where Every Season
Is Vacation Time, The Three States in One, The Volunteer State
(on May 26, 1847 during the Mexican War, Governor Aaron Vail
Brown called for 2,800 volunteers and 30,000 responded), The
Unique State

TEXAS

America's Fun-tier, The Banner State (descriptive word, leading,
excelling, etc.), The Beef State (cattle production), The Blizzard
State (dust storms and wind storms), The Jumbo State (referring to
size, name of large elephant exhibited by P. T. Barnum), The Land
of Contrast, The Land of Opportunity, The Land of Promise (title
of book by Joseph Lynn Clark), The Lone Star State (single star in
its coat-of-arms and flag), The New World of Adventure, The Republic, The State of the Confederacy, The Total Vacation Land for
Everyone, The World Cotton Center

UTAH

The Beehive State (emblem on the coat-of-arms of Utah), The Center
of Scenic America, The Colorful Vacation Land, The Deseret State
(the name by which Utah was known in 1849-1850), The Friendly
State, The Good Highway State, The Honey State (the product found
in beehives), The Hub of the West, The Land of Blossoming Valleys,
The Land of Color, The Land of Color and Contrasts, The Land of
Contrasts, The Land of Endless Scenic Discovery, The Land of
Honey Bees, The Land of Mormons (the Book of Mormon, or Golden
Bible written by the prophet Mormon), The Land of the Saints (the
Mormons whose official church name is the Church of Jesus Christ
of the Latter-Day Saints), The Magic Land of Colorful Past and
Interesting Future, The Mormon State, Nature's Wonderland, The
Salt Lake State (the Great Salt Lake, area 1,500 square miles), The
Tourist's Delight, the Sportsman's Haven, The World of Scenic
Beauty, The Year 'Round Paradise

VERMONT

The Beauty State of New England, The Beckoning Country, The Bec-
koning State, The Country with a Heritage, Every American's Second
State, Everybody's Second State, Everything for Outdoor Living, The
Four-Season State, The Four Seasons' Recreation State, The Green
Mountain State (name of the mountain range), The Land of Marble,
Milk and Honey, The Ski State of the East, The State where Profit
and Pleasure are Part of the Economic Mix, Vermont Is Good
Business

VIRGINIA

America's Historyland, The All-American Paradise, The Ancient
Dominion, The Battlefield of the Civil War, The Beckoning Land,
The Birthplace of Eight Presidents (Washington, Jefferson, Madison,
Monroe, W. H. Harrison, Tyler, Taylor and Wilson), The Birthplace of the Nation, The Cavalier State (cavaliers settled in Virginia sided with the king against the Parliament), The Commonwealth
(term applied to Virginia in its first constitution, adopted June 29,
1776), The Land of Romance, The Mother of Presidents, The Mother
of States (the first state to be settled, the 1609 charter embraced
West Virginia, Kentucky, Ohio, Illinois, Indiana, Wisconsin and
parts of Minnesota), The Mother of States and Statesmen, The
Mother of Statesmen (Washington, Jefferson, Madison, Monroe,
Marshall, Mason, Patrick Henry, Richard Henry Lee, Payton Ran-
dolph, Jr.), The Old Dominion State (Charles II called the colony
"the old dominion" because of its loyalty to the Crown), The State
Truly on the Move, Virginia Is for Lovers

WASHINGTON

The Boating Capital of the World, The Chinook State (Chinook
division of Indians) (for its salmon industry), The Clam Grabbers,
The Evergreen State (forests of fir and pine) (green firs), The
Exciting Dynamic State, The Exciting State of Contrasts, The Fun
State, The Gateway to Alaska and the Orient, The State of Con-
trasts, The State of Exciting Contrasts, The Surprising State

WEST VIRGINIA

The Appalachian State, The Free State, The Fuel State, The Glass
Center of the World, The Land for Relaxation, The Land of Growth
and Grandeur, The Land of Resourcefulness and Relaxation, The
Little Mountain State (Allegheny Mountains), The Mountain State,
The Panhandle State (descriptive of shape), The Place to See; The
Place to Be; for Industry, for Vacations, The State of Dynamic
Industry, The Switzerland of America (scenic), The Vacationland of
the East, Wild Wonderful West Virginia

WISCONSIN

America's Dairyland, The Badger State (so-called because the early
settlers lived underground), The Cheese Capital of the Nation, The
Copper State (copper mines), The Four Season Vacationland, The
Great Place to Live, Work, Vacation, The Land Made for Family
Vacations, The Land that Was Made for Vacations, The Nation's
Finest Vacationland, The Playground of the Middle West, The Vaca-
tion Land for All, Wonderful Wisconsin

WYOMING

The Cowboy State, The Equality State (equal suffrage extended to women in 1869), The Equality Suffrage State, The Gateway to the Scenic Wonders of the Great West, The Great Land Outdoors, The Land of Cattle and Sheep, The Land of Song and Story, The Land of the Purple Sage, The Mountain Wonderland, The Sagebrush State (wild sage growing in the deserts), The Sanctuary of Peace, The Vacation Wonderland, The Wonderland of America, Wonderful Wyoming

Adaptable State. New Jersey
Adventure in Happiness.
  Georgia
Adventurous State. Oklahoma
Airconditioned State. Florida
Airlift Center of the World.
  Georgia
All-American Paradise. Vir-
  ginia
All-American Playground.
  Hawaii
All Roads Lead to Fun in
  New York State. New York
Alligator State. Florida
Aloha State. Hawaii
Amazing Arizona where You
  Can Always Expect to En-
  joy the Unexpected. Ari-
  zona
America at Its Best. Ten-
  nessee
America in Miniature. Mary-
  land
America's Central Vacation
  Land. Tennessee
America's Cultural Capital.
  New York
America's Dairyland. Wis-
  consin
America's Dream Vacation
  State. Florida
America's Favorite Fun
  Country. South Dakota
America's Finest Vacationland.
  Oregon
America's First Vacationland.
  Rhode Island
America's Fun-Tier. Texas
America's Historyland.
  Virginia

America's Last Frontier.
  Alaska
America's Last Great Frontier.
  Alaska
America's Last Outpost.
  Alaska
America's Last Primeval
  Wilderness. Alaska
America's Most Interesting
  State. Tennessee
America's New Frontier of
  Travel. Alaska
America's Newest Family Vaca-
  tionland. North Dakota
America's Newest Gayest Fron-
  tier. Alaska
America's Newest Vacationland.
  Oklahoma
America's Northern Frontier.
  Alaska
America's Northwest Playland.
  Oregon
America's Number One Market.
  California
America's State of Opportunity.
  Mississippi
America's Top Vacation Land.
  Maine
America's Vacation Paradise.
  Colorado
America's Vacation Treasure-
  land. Oklahoma
America's Year Round Adven-
  tureland. Oklahoma
American Land of the Mid-
  night Sun. Alaska
American Venice. Rhode
  Island
Ancient Dominion. Virginia
Angler's Paradise. Maine

Antelope State. Nebraska
Apache State. Arizona
Appalachian State. West
    Virginia
Apple State. New York
Arctic Land of the Eskimo.
    Alaska
Arctic Treasureland. Alaska
Arkansas Is a Natural.
    Arkansas
Arsenal of the Nation. Con-
    necticut
Artesan State. South Dakota
Auto State. Michigan
Automobile State. Michigan
Aztec State. Arizona

Baby State. Arizona
Badger State. Wisconsin
Baked Bean State. Massa-
    chusetts
Banner State. Texas
Battle-Born State. Nevada
Battlefield of the Civil War.
    Virginia
Bay State. Massachusetts
Bayou State. Louisiana
Bayou State. Mississippi
Bayou Wonderland. Louisiana
Bean Eating State. Massa-
    chusetts
Bean State. Massachusetts
Bear State. Arkansas
Beautiful Land. Iowa
Beautiful Land Between Two
    Great Rivers. Iowa
Beautiful Northland of Oppor-
    tunity. Alaska
Beautiful State of Mind.
    Massachusetts
Beauty State of New England.
    Vermont
Beaver State. Oregon
Beckoning Country. Vermont
Beckoning Land. Virginia
Beckoning State. Vermont
Beef State. Nebraska
Beef State. Texas
Beehive State. Utah
Bicentennial Began Here.
    Massachusetts

Bicentennial State. Pennsyl-
    vania
Big Bend Country. Texas
Big Bend State. Tennessee
Big Country. Nebraska
Big Country. North Dakota
Big Fish State. Michigan
Big Island. Hawaii
Big Land. Alaska
Big Ski Country. Montana
Big Sky Country. Montana
Big Sky Vacationland. Montana
Big State. Alaska
Birth State of the Nation.
    Pennsylvania
Birthplace of a Nation. Penn-
    sylvania
Birthplace of American Democ-
    racy. Massachusetts
Birthplace of American Free-
    dom. Massachusetts
Birthplace of Eight Presidents.
    Virginia
Birthplace of Rodeo. Nebraska
Birthplace of the Nation. Vir-
    ginia
Black Water State. Nebraska
Bleeding Kansas. Kansas
Blizzard State. South Dakota
Blizzard State. Texas
Blue Grass Region. Kentucky
Bluegrass State. Kentucky
Blue Hen State. Delaware
Blue Hen's Chickens State.
    Delaware
Blue Law State. Connecticut
Boating Capital of the World.
    Washington
Bonanza State. Montana
Boomers' Paradise. Oklahoma
Border-Eagle State. Missis-
    sippi
Border State. Maine
Bowie State. Arkansas
Bread and Butter State. Minne-
    sota
Breadbasket of the Nation.
    Kansas
Brightest Star in the American
    Constellation. Iowa
Brownstone State. Connecticut
Buckeye State. Ohio

Buckle on the Sunbelt. Oklahoma
Buffalo Plains State. Colorado
Bug-Eating State. Nebraska
Bullion State. Missouri
Buzzard State. Georgia

Cactus Land. New Mexico
Camden and Amboy State. New Jersey
Canyon State. Arizona
Cavalier State. Virginia
Cave State. Missouri
Centennial State. Colorado
Center of American Culture. New York
Center of Scenic America. Utah
Center of the Commercial Universe. Indiana
Center of World Transportation. New Jersey
Central State. Kansas
Cheese Capital of the Nation. Wisconsin
Child of the Mississippi River. Louisiana
Chinook State. Washington
Clam Grabbers. Washington
Clam State. New Jersey
"Clean Air" Country. Kansas
Coal State. Pennsylvania
Cockade State. Maryland
Cockpit of History. New Jersey
Cockpit of Revolution. New Jersey
Colorful Colorado. Colorado
Colorful Past with the Thriving Present. New Mexico
Colorful State. New Mexico
Colorful Vacation Land. Utah
Commonwealth. Virginia
Complete Vacationland. Maine
Connecticut Achieves. Connecticut
Constitution State. Connecticut
Convention Center of the Pacific. Hawaii
Convention State. Maine
Cool Green Vacationland. Oregon

Copper State. Arizona
Copper State. Wisconsin
Corn Belt State. Illinois
Corn State. Illinois
Corn-Cracker State. Kentucky
Cornhusker State. Nebraska
Corn Husking State. Nebraska
Cornucopia of the South. Alabama
Cornucopia of the World. California
Cotton Kingdom. Mississippi
Cotton Mill State. South Carolina
Cotton State. Alabama
Country with a Heritage. Vermont
Cowboy Country. Nebraska
Cowboy State. Wyoming
Coyote State. South Dakota
Cracker State. Georgia
Cradle of Industrial Research. New Jersey
Creole State. Louisiana
Crossroads of All America. North Dakota
Crossroads of America. Illinois
Crossroads of America. Indiana
Crossroads of the Continent. North Dakota
Crossroads of the East. New Jersey
Crossroads of the South. Mississippi
Crossroads of the World. Alaska
"Crossroads" State. New Jersey
Cupid's Hometown. Colorado
Custodian of America's Heritage. Massachusetts
Custodian of America's Historica Heritage. Massachusetts
Custodian of the Nation's Heritage. Massachusetts
Cyclone State. Kansas

Dark and Bloody Ground State. Kentucky
Deep South. Alabama
Delightful Land. Maryland
Delightsome Land. Maryland
Deseret State. Utah

Diamond State. Delaware
Different Vacation State.
Georgia
Dixie Dynamo. North Carolina
Doorway to Nostalgic New
England. Connecticut
Down East State. Maine

Eagle State. Mississippi
Early Mormon Ranching Com-
munity. Nevada
Economic Sunshine State.
Delaware
Egypt. Illinois
El Dorado State. California
Empire Dedicated to Progress.
Oklahoma
Empire State. New York
Empire State of the South.
Georgia
End of the Trail. Oregon
Energy-Packed State. New
Jersey
Entertainment Capital of the
World. Nevada
Equality State. Wyoming
Equality Suffrage Stage.
Wyoming
Eskimoland. Alaska
Eureka State. California
Everglades State. Florida
Evergreen State. Washington
Every American's Second
State. Vermont
Everybody's Second State.
Vermont
Everything for Outdoor
Living. Vermont
Excelsior State. New York
Exciting Dynamic State.
Washington
Exciting State of Contrasts.
Washington

Fabled Land of the American
Indian. North Dakota
Fabulous Florida. Florida
Family Vacation Land. Mis-
souri
Far North Frontier. Alaska

Fastest Fun in the West. Okla-
homa
Fastest Growing Cattle State.
Mississippi
Fastest Growing Ski Center of
the U.S. Colorado
Fiftieth State of Enchantment.
Hawaii
Fire Clay Capital. Missouri
First in Clean Air. Kansas
First in Freedom. North
Carolina
First State. Delaware
First State in Safety. Pennsyl-
vania
Fisherman's Paradise.
Louisiana
Flickertail State. North
Dakota
Food Market of the World.
Iowa
Foreigner State. New Jersey
Four Seasons' Recreation State.
Vermont
Four-Season State. Maine
Four Season State. Vermont
Four Season Vacation Fun Land.
Michigan
Four-Season Vacationland.
Massachusetts
Four Season Vacationland.
Montana
Four Season Vacationland.
Wisconsin
Free State. Maryland
Free State. West Virginia
Freestone State. Connecticut
Fresh Water Fishing Capital.
Minnesota
Friendly Arizona. Arizona
Friendly Land of Infinite
Variety. South Dakota
Friendly State. Kansas
Friendly State. North Dakota
Friendly State. Utah
Frontier of Pleasure. South
Dakota
Frontier of Pleasure on the Old
West Trail. South Dakota
Fuel State. West Virginia
Fun and Sun Land. Mississippi

Fun-Filled Vacation Land.
Mississippi
Fun in Every Season. Kansas
Fun in the Sun for Everyone.
Florida
Fun State. Washington

Game Fish Junction. North
Carolina
Garden of the West. Illinois
Garden of the West. Kansas
Garden State. Kansas
Garden State. New Jersey
Garden Spot for Pleasure and
Business. New Jersey
Gateway State. Ohio
Gateway to Alaska and the
Orient. Washington
Gateway to Expo 67. New
York
Gateway to the Big Country.
North Dakota
Gateway to the Northwest
Territory. Ohio
Gateway to the Orient.
Hawaii
Gateway to the Pacific. Cali-
fornia
Gateway to the Pacific.
Hawaii
Gateway to the Rocky Mountain
West. Colorado
Gateway to the Scenic Wonders
of the Great West. Wyoming
Gateway to the Southland.
Mississippi
Gateway to the World. Florida
Gateway to where the West Be-
gan. South Dakota
Gem of the Mountain States.
Idaho
Gem of the Mountains. Idaho
Gem of the Pacific. Hawaii
Gem State. Idaho
Georgia's Got It. Georgia
Geographic Center of the
World's Richest Market.
New Jersey
Get-Away-From-It-All State.
Minnesota
Gibraltar of the North. Alaska

Glass Center of the World.
West Virginia
Glorious Land. California
Glorious Vacation Playground.
Colorado
Golden State. California
Golf State U.S.A. North
Carolina
Goober State. Georgia
Good Highway State. Utah
Goodliest Land Under the Cape
of Heaven. North Carolina
Gopher State. Minnesota
Grand Canyon State. Arizona
Granite State. New Hampshire
Grape State. California
Grasshopper State. Kansas
Great Agricultural State. Mis-
sissippi
Great Bear's Cub. Alaska
Great Central State. North
Dakota
Great Lake State. Michigan
Great Lakes State. Illinois
Great Land. Alaska
Great Land Outdoors. Wyoming
Great Place to Live, Laze, Lo-
cate. Maine
Great Place to Live, Work, Va-
cation. Wisconsin
Great Recreation State. Maine
Great River Road Country.
Missouri
Great State. Kansas
Greatest Food Producing Area
in the World. Iowa
Green Mountain State. Vermont
Groundhog State. Mississippi
Guinea Pig State. Arkansas
Gulf State. Florida

Hard-Case State. Oregon
Haven for the Traveler. Iowa
Hawkeye State. Iowa
Health Resort of America.
Maine
Healthful State. Arizona
Healthiest State in the Union.
Nebraska.
Heart of America. Missouri
Heart of Dixie. Alabama

Heart of the Cow Country.
Oklahoma
Heart of the Deep South.
Alabama
Heart of the Deep South.
Mississippi
Heart of the Nation. Illinois
Heart of the Nation. Missouri
Heartland of Hospitality.
Missouri
Hemp State. Kentucky
Highest State. Colorado
Highest State in the Union.
Colorado
Historic Vacationland. Massa-
chusetts
History's Main Road. New
Jersey
Hog and Hominy State. Ten-
nessee
Holiday State. Connecticut
Holland of America. Louisiana
Home of the Peach, Strawberry
and Vine. Arkansas
Honey State. Utah
Honeymoon Capital of the
World. Florida
Honeymoon Capital of the
World. Pennsylvania
Hoosier State. Indiana
Hospitality State. Mississippi
Host State for the World's Fair.
New York
Hot-Water State. Arkansas
Hub of Commerce. New Jersey
Hub of Recreational Facilities.
Oklahoma
Hub of the Nation. Illinois
Hub of the Universe. Massa-
chusetts
Hub of the West. Utah

Idaho Is What the Rest of the
World Would Like to Be.
Idaho
Important Agricultural Produc-
tion State. Montana
Industrial Park State. New
Jersey
Insurance State. Connecticut
Interstate State. Tennessee
Iodine State. South Carolina

Ireland of America. North
Carolina
Iron Mountain State. Missouri
Island Paradise. Hawaii
Island State. Hawaii
Italy of America. Arizona
It's Good to Be in Minnesota.
Minnesota

Jayhawker State. Kansas
Jersey Blue State. New Jersey
Jewel in the West. Arizona
Jewel of Many Facets. Michi-
gan
Jewel of the Pacific. Hawaii
Johnson's Polar Bear Garden.
Alaska
Jubilee State for '68. Illinois
Jumbo State. Texas

Keystone of Early America.
Pennsylvania
Keystone of the Growing South.
Georgia
Keystone of the South Atlantic
Seaboard. South Carolina
Keystone State. Pennsylvania
Knickerbocker State. New York

Lady of the Lake. Michigan
Lake State. Michigan
Lake State. Minnesota
Land Alive with Beauty and Good
Times. Kentucky
Land for Relaxation. West
Virginia
Land Made for Family Vaca-
tions. Wisconsin
Land Made for Vacations.
Wisconsin
Land of Adventure. Alaska
Land of Amazing Advantages.
New Jersey
Land of Amazing Industrial
Advantages. New Jersey
Land of Beginnings. North
Carolina
Land of Blossoming Valleys.
Utah
Land of Blossoms and Relaxed
Living. Georgia

Land of Cattle and Sheep.
Wyoming
Land of Color. Utah
Land of Color and Contrasts.
Utah
Land of Contrast. Texas
Land of Contrasts. Colorado
Land of Contrasts. Utah
Land of Discoveries. California
Land of Enchantment. Montana
Land of Enchantment. New
Mexico
Land of Endless Scenic Discovery. Utah
Land of Exciting Contrasts.
Oregon
Land of Flowers. Alabama
Land of Flowers. Florida
Land of Fresh Horizons.
North Dakota
Land of Fun, Sun and Sand.
Florida
Land of Gold. California
Land of Growth and Grandeur.
West Virginia
Land of Hearts' Desire. New
Mexico
Land of History. Ohio
Land of Honey Bees. Utah
Land of Industrial Opportunity.
Iowa
Land of Industrial Romance.
Georgia
Land of Infinite Variety. New
York
Land of Infinite Variety.
South Dakota
Land of Lakes and Prairies.
Minnesota
Land of Leisure. Hawaii
Land of Lincoln. Illinois
Land of Living Color. California
Land of Majestic Beauty.
Arkansas
Land of Many Faces. Missouri
Land of Marble, Milk and
Honey. Vermont
Land of Now. Alaska
Land of Opportunity. Alabama

Land of Opportunity. Alaska
Land of Opportunity. Arkansas
Land of Opportunity. New
Mexico
Land of Opportunity. Ohio
Land of Opportunity. Oregon
Land of Opportunity. Texas
Land of Peace and Beauty. New
Hampshire
Land of Peanuts, Pecans and
Peaches. Georgia
Land of Perfect Vacation. South
Dakota
Land of Pleasure. Idaho
Land of Plenty. South Dakota
Land of Promise. Alaska
Land of Promise. California
Land of Promise. Texas
Land of Recreation and Progress.
South Carolina
Land of Remembered Vacations.
Maine
Land of Resourcefulness and
Relaxation. West Virginia
Land of Roger Williams. Rhode
Island
Land of Romance. Virginia
Land of Scenic Splendor. Montana
Land of Scenic Splendor. New
Hampshire
Land of Song and Story.
Wyoming
Land of Steady Habits. Connecticut
Land of Sunshine. Florida
Land of Sunshine. New Mexico
Land of Sunshine and Flowers.
California
Land of Sunshine and Flowers.
Florida
Land of Sunshine and Scenic
Grandeur. Arizona
Land of Ten Thousand (10,000)
Lakes. Minnesota
Land of the Cactus. New
Mexico
Land of the Dakotas. North
Dakota
Land of the Delight-Makers.
New Mexico
Land of the Good Life.
Nebraska

Land of the Illini. Illinois
Land of the Long North Fur-
    row. North Dakota
Land of the Midnight Sun.
    Alaska
Land of the Mormons. Utah
Land of the North Furrow.
    North Dakota
Land of the Old West. South
    Dakota
Land of the Oregon Trail and
    the Pony Express.
    Nebraska
Land of the Pioneer. Nebraska
Land of the Purple Sage.
    Wyoming
Land of the Red Men. Okla-
    homa
Land of the Rolling Prairie.
    Iowa
Land of the Saints. Utah
Land of the Shining Mountains.
    Montana
Land of the Sky. North Caro-
    lina
Land of Theodore Roosevelt
    and General Custer. North
    Dakota
Land of Tomorrow. Alaska
Land of Tomorrow. Oklahoma
Land of Tomorrow. South
    Dakota
Land of Western Hospitality.
    North Dakota
Land of Wonder. South Dakota
Land of Yesterday, Today and
    Tomorrow. Alaska
Land Rich in Heritage. North
    Dakota
Land Rich in History, Heritage
    and Hospitality. Iowa
Land that Was Made for Vaca-
    tions. Wisconsin
Land where Dreams Come
    True. Oregon
Land where the Summer Sun
    Never Sets. Alaska
Land where the Sun Spends
    the Winter. Arizona
Land where the West Begins.
    Nebraska
Landscape of the Future.
    Oklahoma

Last American Frontier. Alaska
Last Frontier. Alaska
Last Frontier of Industrial De-
    velopment. Iowa
Last of the Big Time Splendors.
    Montana
Lead State. Colorado
Lead State. Missouri
Lead State. Montana
Leading Farm Crop State.
    Iowa
Leisureland State. Nebraska
Lion's Den State. Tennessee
Little Dixie. Missouri
Little Mountain State. West
    Virginia
Little Rhody. Rhode Island
Livestock Feeding State. Illinois
Lizard State. Alabama
Lobsterland. Maine
Lone Star State. Texas
Lovely Louisiana. Louisiana
Lumber State. Maine

Magic Land of Colorful Past
    and Interesting Future. Utah
Magnolia State. Mississippi
Marina Capital of the U.S.A.
    Florida
Massachusetts Means Progress.
    Massachusetts
Memorable Missouri. Missouri
Metropolis of the West Coast.
    Louisiana
Michigan Is Everything Under
    the Sun. Michigan
Midnight Sunland. Alaska
Midway, U.S.A. Kansas
Mining State. Nevada
Modern Mother of Presidents.
    Ohio
Money, Manpower, Management,
    Markets, Material. Massa-
    chusetts
Monumental State. Maryland
Mormon State. Utah
Mosquito State. New Jersey
Most Northern of the Southern
    States. Kentucky
Most Varied State of the Fifty.
    Massachusetts
Mother of Presidents. Ohio

Mother of Presidents. Virginia
Mother of Rivers. New Hampshire
Mother of South-Western Statesmen. Tennessee
Mother of States. Virginia
Mother of States and Statesmen. Virginia
Mother of Statesmen. Virginia
Mother of the West. Missouri
Mountain State. West Virginia
Mountain Wonderland. Wyoming
Mud-Cat State. Mississippi
Mud-Waddler State. Mississippi

National Country. Florida
National Gateway to the Frontierlands. Missouri
Nation's Cool Green Paradise. Arkansas
Nation's Family Playground. Pennsylvania
Nation's Fastest Growing State. Nevada
Nation's Finest Vacationland. Wisconsin
Nation's First Tourist Host. Rhode Island
Nation's Growth Frontier. Louisiana
Nation's Ideal Family Playground. Pennsylvania
Nation's Industrial Frontier. Louisiana
Nation's Leading Vacation and Recreation State. California
Nation's Mixed-Bag Capital. Nebraska
Nation's Most Interesting State. Tennessee
Nation's New Playground. Alaska
Nation's Number One Industrial State. Connecticut
Nation's Number One Market Area. Ohio
Nation's Only State of Islands. Hawaii
Nation's Showcase. New York

Nation's Vacationland. Maine
Nation's Vacation Land. Minnesota
Nation's Wonderland. Oregon
Nature's Cornucopia. Louisiana
Nature's Mineral Specimen Case. North Carolina
Nature's Showcase. New Jersey
Nature's Wonderland. Utah
Nebraskaland. Nebraska
Nerve Center for World Trade. New Jersey
New American Frontier. Florida
New County where Factory and Farm Share Prosperity. Iowa
New England of the West. Minnesota
New Frontier. Alaska
New Spain State. New Jersey
New Sweden. Delaware
New World of Adventure. Texas
North Star State. Minnesota
Northland. Alaska
Northern Prairie State. North Dakota
Northern Wonderland. Alaska
Northernmost State. Alaska
Number One Cave State. Missouri
Number One State. Ohio
Nutmeg State. Connecticut

Ocean State. Rhode Island
Old Bay State. Massachusetts
Old Colony State. Massachusetts
Old Dirigo State. Maine
Old Dominion State. Virginia
Old Line State. Maryland
Old Man of the Mountain State. New Hampshire
Old North State. North Carolina
Oldest State West of the Thirteen Original Colonies. Ohio
One Hundred Vacation Lands Into One. Kentucky
One of America's Most Popular Playgrounds. Arizona

One of the Great Resort States
of the Middle West.   Michi-
gan
One Sound State.   Nevada
Orange Land.   Florida
Orange State.   Florida
Orchid Isle.   Hawaii
Our Social Capital.   Rhode
Island
Oyster State.   Maryland
Ozark State.   Missouri

Pace Setter of the South.
Georgia
Pacific Wonderland.   Oregon
Palmetto State.   South Caro-
lina
Panhandle State.   West Vir-
ginia
Paradise of the Pacific.
Hawaii
Pathway of the Revolution.
New Jersey
Peace Garden State.   North
Dakota
Peach State.   Delaware
Peach State.   Georgia
Peerless State.   Iowa
Pelican State.   Louisiana
Peninsula of Pleasant Ex-
periences.   Florida
Peninsula State.   Florida
Peninsula State.   Michigan
Pennsylvania Is an Active
State.   Pennsylvania
Pennsylvania of the West.
Missouri
People, Purpose, Progress.
New Jersey
Pheasant Capital of the World.
South Dakota
Picturesque Historic Land of
Early America.   Louisiana
Pilgrim State.   Massachusetts
Pine Tree State.   Maine
Pineapple State.   Hawaii
Pioneer Commonwealth.   Ken-
tucky
Pioneer Space Capital of the
World.   Alabama
Place for All Seasons.   New
York

Place For You.   Florida
Place to Be.   Mississippi
Place to Go.   Idaho
Place to Go Is Idaho.   Idaho
Place to Grow, A Place to Go.
Iowa
Place to Live Work, and Play.
Maine
Place to See; The Place to Be;
For Industry, For Vacations.
West Virginia
Place where Plant Sites and
Pine Forests Grow Side by
Side.   Arkansas
Plantation State.   Rhode Island
Playground of Ten Thousand
Lakes.   Minnesota
Playground of the Middle West.
Wisconsin
Playground of the Nation.
Maine
Playground of the Pacific.
Hawaii
Playground of the Southwest.
New Mexico
Playtime Country.   Michigan
Polar Star State.   Maine
Prairie State.   Illinois
Puke State.   Missouri
Puritan State.   Massachusetts

Quail Capital of the World.
Georgia
Quaker State.   Pennsylvania
Queen State.   Maryland

Republic.   Texas
Rhode Island Is Oceans of Fun.
Rhode Island
Rice State.   South Carolina
Rich and Varied Land.   Minne-
sota
Right to Profit State.
Louisiana
Rip Van Winkle State.   North
Carolina
River with the Big Bend.
Tennessee
Riviera of America.   New Jersey
Rocky Mountain Empire.
Colorado

Roughrider Country. North
  Dakota

Sage State. Nevada
Sagebrush State. Nevada
Sagebrush State. Wyoming
Sage-Hen State. Nevada
Salt Lake State. Utah
Salt of the Earth. Kansas
Sanctuary of Peace. Wyoming
Sand Hill State. Arizona
Sand-Lapper State. South
  Carolina
Scenic Isle. Hawaii
Scenic State. Oregon
Scenic State. New Hampshire
Scenic Wonderland. Florida
Scenic Wonderland. Maine
Scenic Wonderland. Tennessee
Seacoast Homeland. Delaware
Seat of Empire. New York
Second Fastest Growing State.
  Florida
Second Nazareth. North
  Carolina
See All of Arizona--It's
  Wonderful. Arizona
See Surprising South Carolina.
  South Carolina
See the First State First.
  Delaware
Seward's Folly. Alaska
Seward's Ice Box. Alaska
Sharpbacks State. New Jersey
Show Me State. Missouri
Silver State. Colorado
Silver State. Nevada
Singed Cat State. Montana
Sioux State. North Dakota
Ski Country, U.S.A. Colorado
Ski State of the East. Ver-
  mont
Skiingest State in the East.
  New York
Sky Land of Sporting Snows
  and Sunshine. Colorado
Small State, Big in Agriculture,
  Big in Industry. New Jersey
Smallest State. Rhode Island
Sooner State. Oklahoma
Southern Gateway of New
  England. Rhode Island

Southernmost State. Florida
South's Empire State. Georgia
Space Age Research Center for
  the Free World. New
  Mexico
Space Center of the World.
  Massachusetts
Spanish State. New Mexico
Sports Capital of the World.
  Florida
Sportsman's Paradise. Louisiana
Sportsman's Paradise. Maine
Sportsman's Paradise. Nebraska
Squatter State. Kansas
Star of the South. Alabama
Star-Spangled Banner State.
  Maryland
State Alive with Variety and
  Fun to See. Connecticut
State at the Crossroads of the
  Pacific. Hawaii
State Everything's In. Colorado
State First in Transportation.
  Pennsylvania
State for Vacation Pleasure at
  Any Season. New Hamp-
  shire
State in the Heart of New Eng-
  land, a Land of Peace and
  Beauty. New Hampshire
State of Adventure. Georgia
State of Camden and Amboy.
  New Jersey
State of Contrasts. Alaska
State of Contrasts. Washington
State of Discovery in a World
  of Sunshine. Arizona
State of Diversity. New Mexico
State of Dynamic Industry.
  West Virginia
State of Excitement. Florida
State of Excitement. Oregon
State of Excitement. Pennsyl-
  vania
State of Exciting Contrasts.
  Washington
State of Festivals, Theatre,
  Museums and Music. Florida
State of Fun. Oklahoma
State of Historic Sites. Ten-
  nessee
State of Increditable Variety.
  Georgia

State of Industry. Oklahoma
State of Magnificent Scenery.
  Colorado
State of Many Countries.
  Ohio
State of Many Countries.
  Oklahoma
State of One Thousand and One
  Vacation Pleasures. Penn-
  sylvania
State of Opportunity. Mis-
  sissippi
State of Productive Farms.
  Alabama
State of Scenic Beauty.
  Tennessee
State of Shining Mountains.
  Idaho
State of Spain. New Jersey
State of Spain State. New
  Mexico
State of Surprise. New
  Hampshire
State of Surprises. Indiana
State of the Confederacy.
  Texas
State of the Future. Missis-
  sippi
State of Unparalleled Outdoor
  Recreation Facilities.
  Tennessee
State on the March. Nebraska
State on the Move. Colorado
State on the Move. Ohio
State Pioneering in Progress.
  Oklahoma
State Rich in Beauty and
  Abundant Resources.
  Mississippi
State that Forgot. South
  Carolina
State that's Geared for Profit.
  South Dakota
State that Has Everything.
  New York
State that Has It All. Alabama
State that Has Something for
  Everyone All Year 'Round.
  Connecticut
State that Has to Be Seen to
  Be Believed. Louisiana
State that Started a Nation.
  Delaware

State Truly on the Move.
  Virginia
State where American Industry
  Began. Pennsylvania
State where Big Things Are
  Happening. Kentucky
State where Cotton Is Still
  King. Mississippi
State where Every Season Is
  Vacation Time. Maine
State where Every Season Is
  Vacation Time. Tennessee
State where Everything
  Just Comes Naturally.
  Tennessee
State where History and
  Hospitality Began. Massa-
  chusetts
State where History and the
  Present Make Your Visit
  Delightful. Ohio
State where History Is Around
  Every Corner. Rhode Island
State where Man and Nature
  Gamble. Nevada
State where Modern Cities,
  Picturesque Villages and ·
  Storied Ghost Towns Mix the
  Colorful Past with the
  Thriving Present. New
  Mexico
State where Nature Put It All
  Together. Tennessee
State where North, South, East
  and West Meet. Missouri
State where Profit and Pleasure
  Are Part of the Economic
  Mix. Vermont
State where Resources and
  Markets Meet. South
  Carolina
State where the Action Is.
  Rhode Island
State where the Fun Begins on
  the Old West Trail. South
  Dakota
State where the Fun Never Sets.
  New Mexico
State where the Good Life Pays
  in More Corporate Dividends.
  Connecticut
State where the Old West Lives
  Again. North Dakota

State where the People Are Friendly. Tennessee

State where the Sun Shines Bright. Arizona

State where the Sunshine Spends the Winter. North Dakota

State where the West Begins. Nebraska

State where the West Begins and Progress Never Ceases. Iowa

State where the Wind Comes Sweepin' Down the Plains. Oklahoma

State where You Can Always Expect to Enjoy the Unexpected. Arizona

State where You Come for a Visit and Come Back for a Lifetime. New Jersey

State with Many Landscapes. South Dakota

State with New Ideas. Oklahoma

State with Recreation for Everyone. Montana

State within a Day of Seventy Percent of the U.S. Market. Kentucky

Steel State. Pennsylvania

Stub Toe State. Montana

Sucker State. Illinois

Sugar State. Louisiana

Summer Playground of the Nation. Maine

Sunflower State. Kansas

Sunniest Winter Climate in the Eastern U.S. Florida

Sunset Land. Arizona

Sunset State. Arizona

Sunset State. Oregon

Sunshine Empire. California

Sunshine Peninsula. Florida

Sunshine State. Florida

Sunshine State. New Mexico

Sunshine State. South Dakota

Surprising State. Washington

Swamp State. South Carolina

Swiagecat State. South Dakota

Switzerland of America. Colorado

Switzerland of America. Maine

Switzerland of America. New Hampshire

Switzerland of America. West Virginia

Tadpole State. Mississippi

Tall Corn State. Nebraska

Tarheel State. North Carolina

There's Fun In Idaho. Idaho

Three States in One. Tennessee

Threshold of Paradise. Oregon

Throbbing Pulsating Major Industrial Market. South Carolina

To Live in Arizona Is to Enjoy Each Hour. Arizona

Tobacco State. Kentucky

Tomato State. Ohio

Tomorrow Country. Oklahoma

Toothpick State. Arkansas

Top of the Nation. Colorado

Top Vacation State of the Nation. Colorado

Total Vacation Land for Every Season. Texas

Tourist Empire of the Inland Seas. Michigan

Tourist State. Pennsylvania

Tourist's Delight, the Sportsman's Haven. Utah

Transportation Center of America. Ohio

Treasure State. Montana

Treeplanter State. Nebraska

Tropical Paradise. Hawaii

Turpentine State. North Carolina

Uncle Sam's Icebox. Alaska

Uncle Sam's Pocket Handkerchief. Delaware

Unique State. Tennessee

United Nations in Miniature. Minnesota

U.S. Gateway to Latin America. Florida

U.S. Gateway to the World. New Jersey

Unspoiled Empire. New Mexico

Vacation Adventureland. Okla-
homa
Vacation and Industrial Nucleus
of the South West. New
Mexico
Vacation Capital of the Mid-
west. Missouri
Vacation Center of America.
Kentucky
Vacation Country. Colorado
Vacation Empire. New York
Vacation Haven in Mid-Nation.
Iowa
Vacation Land. Idaho
Vacation Land for All. Wis-
consin
Vacation Land of Fun and
Plenty. Massachusetts
Vacation Land of Your Fondest
Dreams. Idaho
Vacation Paradise. Kentucky
Vacation State. Montana
Vacation State. Nevada
Vacation State of the Nation.
Arizona
Vacation Target for Millions
of Americans. Illinois
Vacation Variety. New York
Vacation Wonderland. Idaho
Vacation Wonderland. Wyoming
Vacationland. Alabama
Vacationland. Illinois
Vacationland. Maine
Vacationland. New York
Vacationland from the Mountains
to the Sea. South Carolina
Vacationland of Opportunity.
Alaska
Vacationland of the East.
West Virginia
Vacationland the Year 'Round.
New Jersey
Valentine Capital of the World.
Colorado
Valentine State. Arizona
Variety Vacationland. Louisiana
Variety Vacationland. North
Carolina
Variety Vacationland for All
the Family. Mississippi
Vermin State. New Mexico
Vermont Is Good Business.
Vermont
Virginia Is for Lovers. Virginia

Visit North Dakota for Family
Water Fun. North Dakota
Volunteer State. Tennessee

Water Wonderland. Michigan
Water-Winter Wonderland.
Michigan
Web-Foot State. Oregon
Welcome State. Oregon
Wellspring of Art and Culture.
Massachusetts
West of Song and Legend.
North Dakota
Western Playground. Nebraska
Wheat State. Kansas
Wheat State. Minnesota
Wheat State of America.
Kansas
Wheatheart of the Nation.
Kansas
White Mountain State. New
Hampshire
Wide Horizon Country. North
Dakota
Wide Wonderful West Virginia.
West Virginia
Window on the East. Hawaii
Wine Land of America.
California
Winter Paradise of America.
Colorado
Winter Salad Bowl. Florida
Winter Wonderland. Michigan
Wolverine State. Michigan
Wonder State. Arkansas
Wonderful Iodine State. South
Carolina
Wonderful Wisconsin. Wisconsin
Wonderful Wyoming. Wyoming
Wonderland. Arizona
Wonderland. Montana
Wonderland of America.
Wyoming
Wonderland of 11,000 Lakes.
Michigan
Wonderland Unsurpassed. Alaska
Wonderous Place to Visit. Okla-
homa
Wooden Nutmeg State. Con-
necticut
Workshop of the World. Penn-
sylvania

World Cotton Center.   Texas
World of Fun and Relaxation.
  Massachusetts
World of Good that Awaits
  You.   Maine
World of Scenic Beauty.   New
  York.
World of Scenic Beauty.   Utah
World within a State.   Cali-
  fornia
World's Saddle Horse Capital.
  Missouri

Yankee Land of the South.
  Georgia
Yankee Playland.   New
  Hampshire
Yankee State.   Ohio
Year Round Mid-South.
  North Carolina

Year 'Round Paradise.   Utah
Year 'Round Playground.
  Nebraska
Year 'Round Vacation State.
  North Carolina
Year 'Round Vacation Wonder-
  land.   Georgia
Year 'Round Vacationland.
  Massachusetts
Year-Round Vacationland.
  New York
Yellowhammer State.   Alabama
"You-Name-It-We-Make-It"
  State.   Ohio
Youngest State.   Arizona
Youngest State.   Hawaii
Your Dreamland of Pleasure.
  Hawaii
Your Four-Season Vacationland.
  Massachusetts
Your Vacation State.   Nevada